RICHARD III AND HIS RIVALS

RICHARD III AND HIS RIVALS:

MAGNATES AND THEIR MOTIVES
IN THE WAR OF THE ROSES

MICHAEL HICKS

THE HAMBLEDON PRESS
LONDON   AND   RIO GRANDE

Published by The Hambledon Press, 1991

102 Gloucester Avenue, London NW1 8HX (U.K.)

P.O. Box 162, Rio Grande, Ohio 45672 (U.S.A.)

ISBN 1 85285 053 1

British Library Cataloguing in Publication Data

Richard III and his rivals: magnates and their
    motives in the Wars of the Roses
    1. Wars of the Roses
    I. Title
    942.04

Library of Congress Cataloging-in-Publication Data

Hicks, M.A. (Michael A.)
    Richard III and his rivals: magnates and their motives in
    the Wars of the Roses/Michael Hicks
    Includes bibliographical references and index
    1. Great Britain – History – Wars of the Roses, 1455-1485
    2. Great Britain – History – Richard III, 1483-1485
    3. Richard III, King of England, 1452-1485
    I. Title
    DA250.H54   1991   91-25371
    942.04 – dc20   CIP

Printed on acid-free paper and bound in Great
Britain by Bookcraft Ltd., Midsomer Norton, Somerset

Contents

Acknowledgements

The following articles reproduced here first appeared in the following places and are reprinted here with permission.

3. *Parliamentary History* iii (1984).

4. *The Church in Pre-Reformation Society*, ed. C. Barron & C. Harper-Bill (Boydell & Brewer, Woodbridge, 1985).

5. *Journal of Ecclesiastical History* xxviii (1987).

6. *Wiltshire Archaeological Magazine* 77/78 (1984).

7. *Journal of Legal History* iv (1983).

8. *Northern History* xx (1984).

9. *Kings and Nobles in the Later Middle Ages*, ed. R.A. Griffiths & J.W. Sherborne (Alan Sutton, Gloucester, 1986).

10. *Southern History* viii (1986).

11. *Patronage, Pedigree and Power in Later Medieval England*, ed. C.D. Ross (Alan Sutton, Gloucester, 1979).

13. *Borthwick Paper* 70 (1986).

15. *The Ricardian* 95 (1986).

16. *English Historical Review* c (1988).

18. *Bulletin of the Institute of Historical Research* ii (1979).

19. *Bulletin of the Institute of Historical Research* iii (1981).

20. *Wiltshire Archaeological Magazine* 72/73 (1980).

21. *Northern History* xiv (1978).

22. *Northern History* xxii (1986).

23. *English Historical Review* xc (1978).

Introduction

This volume collects twenty-three papers on late medieval English history published during the last twelve years and researched in the last twenty. They are all products of the school of history founded by the late K.B. McFarlane. I was too young to know the Master in person, but his teachings were passed to me by his pupils C.D. Ross, T.B. Pugh and J.R.L. Highfield, and by his friend and colleague C.A.J. Armstrong.

My inchoate interests first settled on late medieval England in 1969-70, when I took the Bristol University Special Subject on Yorkist and Early Tudor England 1471-1501 conducted by Dr Ross. Then Reader and subsequently Professor of Medieval History, Charles Ross was the outstanding Yorkist historian of his generation and later the author of the (still) standard biographies *Edward IV* (1974) and *Richard III* (1981). He encouraged my natural biographical bent and focused my attention on the Yorkists. He also referred me to his co-author T.B. Pugh at Southampton, who reinforced my scholarly method and my appreciation of McFarlane's approach to the late medieval nobility. It was my Southampton University M.A. dissertation on the 4th Earl of Northumberland,[1] supervised by Pugh and examined by Ross, that awoke those interests in the North, bastard feudalism, and arbitration that have since proved so fruitful. At Oxford my D.Phil. thesis on the Yorkist prince George, Duke of Clarence, was supervised by John Armstrong, who was and is unique for his expertise both on Richard III and on continental sources.[2] The thesis was in the McFarlane tradition of extensive archival research, in the location of its subject within his estates, income, and local roots, and in the detailed political narrative from the point of view of the opposition. Clarence's career was always intended as the book duly published in 1980,[3] but I then considered it secondary to, and a vehicle for, the

---

[1] 'The career of Henry Percy, Fourth Earl of Northumberland, with special reference to his retinue' (Southampton University M.A. dissertation 1971).

[2] 'The Career of George Plantagenet, Duke of Clarence, 1449-78' (Oxford D. Phil. thesis 1975).

[3] *False, Fleeting, Perjur'd Clarence: George Duke of Clarence, 1449-78* (Alan Sutton Publishing, Gloucester, 1980).

exploration of bastard feudalism: how retinues were formed; how they died; whether the Wars of the Roses marked a stage in their death; and the role of arbitration.

Following my thesis, I worked in turn for the Victoria County History of Middlesex (1974-8) and at King Alfred's College, Winchester. These posts gave me less time for my own research, little opportunity to teach my chosen field, no opportunity to supervise theses, and no incentive to keep up-to-date with publications on medieval Europe. On a more positive note, they developed my interests in other ways: into local and regional history stretching up to the present; into the early modern economy and society; into religious history; and into historiography. These new areas of strength have shaped increasingly the articles collected here. And it was the demands of other work, the limitations of time, and the need for attainable targets that directed my publications into the case-studies that have suited me so well.

Initially the transition from full-time research into full-time employment curtailed my original work. My evenings were fully occupied in writing up my Southampton dissertation and my Oxford thesis for publication. My first published article, in fact, was a seventeenth-century Middlesex lawsuit,[4] but there followed my monograph *False, Fleeting, Perjur'd Clarence* (1980), which gave rise to an entertaining debate in *The Ricardian*;[5] an article on the 4th Earl of Northumberland (ch. 21); and three papers on the Warwick Inheritance (chs. 18 and 19). 1979-80 was a first *annus mirabilis*. My rebellious urges to do something new resulted in papers on Sir Thomas Cook (ch. 23) and on the Wydevilles (ch. 11). The latter was written for the Bristol symposium of 1978 and distracted me from bastard feudalism for a temporary period that grew to ten years. Charles Ross had encouraged me to develop my work on bastard feudalism, offering me – as he offered other members of the Bristol Connection – the advantage and support of his co-authorship of what he envisaged as a single paper on the topic and I always thought would be several. Much research and a considerable amount of writing was done before the call of the Wydevilles took precedence. At a time when I did not expect to return to the field of bastard feudalism, I revised the ten-year old section on Clarence's arbitration and good lordship from my thesis, which was published in 1983 (ch. 7). Once ahead of its time, it now coincided with three other papers on arbitration, but still contained much that is new.

[4] '*Draper* v. *Crowther*: The Prebend of Brownswood Dispute 1664-92', *Transactions of the London and Middlesex Archaeological Society* xxviii (1977).

[5] M.A. Hicks, 'The Middle Brother: "False, Fleeting, Perjur'd Clarence"', *The Ricardian* 72 (1981); I. Wigram, 'Clarence Still Perjur'd', ibid. 73 (1981); M.A. Hicks, 'Clarence's Calumniator Corrected', ibid. 74 (1981); I. Wigram, 'Clarence and Richard' and M.A. Hicks 'Richard and Clarence', ibid. 76 (1982).

The next substantial piece of work was the paper on 'Attainder, Resumption, and Coercion' (ch. 3), which again developed an important theme from my thesis, but involved much new research. It was complemented by the paper on the Duke of Somerset (ch. 8), which arose from the chance find of a lost act of parliament. The themes of treason, resumption, and attainder have recurred in subsequent work.

But when the opportunity recurred in the early 1980s for further research, the topic chosen was Richard III, Clarence's brother. It was logical to build on my knowledge of him as Duke of Gloucester: I had already discussed his relations with Clarence, with Northumberland, and the Warwick inheritance. Starting with his career as duke, I developed his relations with the de Veres and the Hungerfords in four items below (chs. 5-6, 8 and 9). The papers on Romsey, the Duke of Bedford, and MS Cotton Julius BXII were staging posts along the way (chs. 17, 15 and 14). What was most needed was the opportunity to study in the north again, which came in Lent term 1984 as Borthwick Visiting Fellow at the University of York. There I researched and prepared a new synthesis of Richard III's ducal career (ch. 13). There too, among other things, I completed my work on the Yorkshire Rebellion of 1489 begun in my Southampton dissertation, but now informed by a knowledge of early modern popular rebellions (ch. 22). More than half the papers reprinted in this book touch on Richard, mainly from the vantage of those rivals, who suffered at his hands. They culminate in the book to be published this year,[6] but even then I expect to have more to say.

It was research into Richard III that led me to the Hungerfords. It was my desire for a local topic of research that prompted me to investigate the Hungerford cartulary at Taunton. It was my Special Subject on the Secular Church in the Age of Wyclif that made me appreciate the gold represented by the chantry deeds it contained. It was a sudden, quite unexpected, revelation – perhaps the only moment of this kind that I have experienced. Quite unexpectedly, I realised how intensely personal were the church services prescribed by founders and appreciated how, set in their liturgical context, they revealed the secrets of their author's pious understanding, preferences, and even personality. They offered an insight into late medieval lay piety. This was the message of the paper on the 'Piety of Margaret Lady Hungerford' (ch. 5) and on other papers written at the same time, several of which, such as those on her father-in-law and on the Minoresses, have since been published.[7] Further research

---

[6] *Richard III: The Man Behind the Myth* (Collins and Brown, London, 1991).

[7] 'Walter Lord Hungerford (d. 1449) and his Chantry in Salisbury Cathedral', *Hatcher Review* xxviii (1989); 'The English Minoresses and their Early Benefactors, 1281-1367', *Monastic Studies: The Continuity of the Tradition*, ed. J. Loades (Headstart Publications, Bangor 1990). 'Four Studies in Conventional Piety', also first written in 1983-4, if forthcoming in *Southern History* xiii (1991).

uncovered the fragments of a truly exceptional archive: at Trowbridge
and Devizes; San Marino in California; the Public Record Office; and
Sheffield. Four other papers followed. There is scope for more.

As befits a pupil of McFarlane, my early work interpreted the actions of
the nobility in purely material terms. Self-interest, self-advantage, and
self-preservation featured largely; ideological considerations and the
principles that manifestoes appealed to were disregarded as mere
propaganda and lip-service. It was a cynical view of a cynical and self-
seeking world. By 1984 I had published papers on good lordship and
dynasticism, demonstrating how such ideals actually did influence
medieval magnates in practice, and others were in preparation on the
impact of moral obligation (honour), piety, and lineage on the politics of
the Wars of the Roses (ch. 7). Yet I did not recognize what I was doing. It
was Professor Dobson, then at York University, who revealed that I was
putting the human face back into the fifteenth century and prompted me
to make an overall assessment of the role of idealism in late medieval
English politics into a major aim. It was a big project that called for
further research and much thought. In the meantime priority had to be
given to two books: *Who's Who in Late Medieval England, 1272-1485* and to my
edition of the papers of the 1987 conference on Recent Research in
Fifteenth-Century England, both completed in 1988 and published in
1990-1.[8] Non-material or intangible motivation coloured the biographies
of the former and formed a section of the introduction of the latter. Only
my study leave in Lent term 1989 permitted a fuller exploration of
political idealism in the fifteenth century that is published below (ch. 2). It
conicides with the complementary paper of Dr Powell.[9] It treats not just
explicit ideals *per se*, but unconscious assumptions, conventions, and the
role of propaganda in exploiting shared principles and expectations. The
latter are explored at greater length in my *Richard III*.

Always in the background, but apparently unattainable, was a full
scale study of bastard feudalism. Charles Ross did not revive our project
after 1978 and Dr Harriss's proposal for a co-operative paper by myself
and Dr Carpenter foundered on our incompatible points of view. At
intervals my interest was revived: for my paper on good lordship; by
reviews of new books; by papers that ignored or contradicted my own
work; and by my own false starts, notably papers on Lord Hastings that
did not get off the ground. The field was developing apace and not in
directions of which I could approve. In the 1970s Charles Ross and myself
had four simple aims: to demonstrate that McFarlane's interpretation

[8] *Who's Who in Late Medieval England, 1272-1485* (Shepheard-Walwyn, London, 1991);
Profit, Piety, and the Professions in Later Medieval England (Alan Sutton, Gloucester, 1990).

[9] E. Powell 'McFarlane's Century and the Poverty of Patronage: A Plea for
Constitutional History', Manchester Conference Proceedings, ed. R.G. Davies (Alan
Sutton, Gloucester, forthcoming).

had superseded rather than refuted those of his predecessors, which still had much to offer; to connect the thirteenth century situation with that of the sixteenth; to reveal bastard feudalism as a social cement as well as a source of disharmony; and to refute the alleged responsibility of bastard feudalism for the breakdown of order and the Wars of the Roses associated with Professors Storey and Bellamy. There were three contradictory and incompatible schools of thought by the late '80s and all appeared to me to be wrong. All exalted material motivation to the point where ideas had no meaning, all employed evidence in an exclusive way that disregarded its limitations, and all postulated a conflict model of society that I could not recognize. They were dangerous distortions which, I recognized increasingly, needed correction before they were accepted. Their incompatibilities needed to be exposed and their more glaring errors indicated, so that future scholarship could proceed from sounder ground in more profitable directions. This was the work of three papers, two first published below (chs. 1, 12) and another on the 1468 Statute of Livery elsewhere.[10] The paper on idealism (ch. 2) is complementary and is an ingredient in future interpretations yet to be devised. *Bastard Feudalism* is to be my next book.

From simple beginnings a complex web of interests has developed. My work still features my original themes of inheritance, patronage, coercion, treason and loyalty, my earlier expertise in estate documentation and judicial records, my initial emphasis on the interconnection of national and local politics, and my reliance on the biographical mode. On to them now has been grafted an interest in piety and expertise in the liturgy, a faith in idealism and a search for explicit expressions of motivation, and a sense of a more socially diffuse political nation. Motives are more complex. Explanations are multi-thematic and are often distinctively medieval. The understanding of personal piety is a vehicle for understanding political motivation. Politics remains the objective, but it is a politics of wider significance than the mere defence of essential interests or personal self-advancement that interested me when I started. Those earlier essays listed here are not wrong. The themes they explored did matter, idealism did not always override material motives, and the sources seldom survive. But they did not consider the full range of possibilities.

This book collects my more important papers on late medieval England of the last decade. Some of purely ephemeral interest have been omitted.[11]

---

[10] 'The 1468 Statute of Livery', *Historical Research* lxiv (1991).

[11] See note 5 above; 'The Warwick Inheritance – Springboard to the Throne', *The Ricardian* 81 (1983); 'Did Edward V Outlive his Reign or did he Outreign his Life?', ibid. 108 (1990); 'Landlady Sells Up. Businessman becomes Country Gent. The Sale of the Botreaux Lands in Hampshire in the 1460s'. *Hampshire Field Club Newsletter* new series 5 (1986); 'An Intermittent Abbot of Quarr', ibid. 6 (1986).

Two have been published elsewhere.[12] Those on topics after 1500 fall outside the scope of the volume.[13] What is collected here has a natural unity. They proceed from a single mind, they are interrelated, and they often cite one another. They focus on a single period – the late fifteenth century – and a single individual, Richard III, features in most of them. Yet he is seldom the focus. This is a book about the political system and localities that he knew, the ideas that he shared, and predominantly about those he strove against. Almost all these papers focus on *Richard III and his Rivals*.

The debts accumulated over twenty years are enormous. My supervisors' assistance cannot easily be measured. I owe much to the Bristol Connection, especially Professor Ralph Griffiths, Dr Tony Pollard, Miss Margaret Condon and Dr Michael K. Jones. Professor Barrie Dobson, Dr Gerald Harriss and Dr Carole Rawcliffe have been a constant source of encouragement. A range of editors have contributed to the refinement of these papers and it is the kindness of Mr Martin Sheppard that has enabled them to be reprinted. King Alfred's College has twice allowed me study leave. My children have put up with a lot. But this book must be dedicated to my wife Cynthia who has read, heard, and proof-read successive variants of each paper and suffered all the other personal inconveniences that accompany spare-time authorship conducted in the home and from our private income. Without her tolerance and support, these papers would not exist to be collected.

Michael Hicks
April 1991

[12] See notes 7 & 10 above.
[13] For the most important, see note 4 above; 'John Nettleton, Henry Savile of Banke, and the Post-Medieval Vicissitudes of Byland Abbey Library', *Northern History* xxvi (1990); '*Lessor* v *Lessee*: Nether Wallop Rectory 1700-1870', *Proceedings of the Hampshire Field Club and Archaeological Society* xlv (1990).

1

Bastard Feudalism: Society and Politics in Fifteenth-Century England

'Modern study of England's history in the later middle ages lost its founding genius with the death of K.B. McFarlane in 1966', writes Professor R.L. Storey.[1] For Dr Richmond, 'the fifteenth century is McFarlane's century. It will be so for longer than the sixteenth century was Tawney's'.[2] Many other tributes to his influence can be collected.[3] In 1978 there was a conference of McFarlane's pupils and their pupils 'even unto the third generation' and in 1982 Dr Richmond felt obliged to include McFarlane's name in his first paragraph.[4] And when discrepancies were found between his work and that of McFarlane, a professor of late medieval history, no less, retracted his offending views.[5]

What a cosy unanimity there is about 'McFarlane's century'! Most scholars are his pupils or grand-pupils, all acknowledge his influence, and all cite his work. The master's influence over his devotees compares to that of Karl Marx or Chairman Mao. Or does it? His blessing is claimed for many different enterprises: the study of noble families, of individual kings, noblemen or gentry, of gentry societies, crime, central government, and war. His own work was just as varied and not all he wrote was right. It evolved and changed. Towards the end he was moving, we are told,

---

[1] R.L. Storey, *The End of the House of Lancaster* (2nd edn Gloucester 1986), vii. The late Professor Charles Ross suggested this project and kindly criticised my earlier drafts of what was to have been a joint article. My principal debt is to him. P.R. Coss, 'Bastard Feudalism Revised', *Past and Present* 125 (1990), 27-64, which is relevant to the 13th and 14th centuries.

[2] C. Richmond, 'After McFarlane', *History* lxviii (1983), 46.

[3] E.g. M.A. Hicks, 'Restraint, Mediation and Private Justice: George, Duke of Clarence as "Good Lord"', below, p. 133; C. Given-Wilson, *The English Nobility in the Later Middle Ages* (1987), x; M.C. Carpenter, 'Law, Justice and Landowners in Late Medieval England', *L[aw] and H[istory] [Review]* i (1983), 205n; J.G. Bellamy, *Bastard Feudalism and the Law* (1989), 1-2, E. Powell, *Kingship, Law and Society: Criminal Justice in the Reign of Henry V* (Oxford 1989), 2-4.

[4] *Patronage, Pedigree and Power in Later Medieval England*, ed C.D. Ross (Gloucester 1979), 8; *The Church, Politics, and Patronage in Later Medieval England*, ed R.B. Dobson (Gloucester 1984).

[5] Storey, loc cit, x, citing his 'Bastard Feudalism Revisited', *B[ulletin of the] M[anorial] S[ociety of Great Britain]* iii (1983), 7-15.

towards a new synthesis,[6] one decidedly different from his seminal beginnings, one inevitably rejecting some earlier conclusions. There was only one McFarlane, but his legacy reflects different stages in his work and different preoccupations. He left no definitive work, no *Das Kapital* or Little Red Book, to which we can all appeal.

Everybody does appeal, of course, but to different parts of his work, sometimes perhaps genuinely inspired, often, no doubt, to find the clincher for a case already formulated. All do not agree. Each scholar ploughs a lonely furrow, building patterns from recalcitrant evidence, citing those of like mind and McFarlane, ignoring those who disagree. Claiming McFarlane's blessing is a game all can play. Surveys of the post-McFarlane scene and manifestos for the future are contradictory,[7] but there has been no debate, for late medievalists do not wish to sour their social harmony with Early Tudor acrimony. There is, in fact, no consensus about premises, methodology, and hence conclusions, and thus the impressive corpus of publications is not altogether compatible. Differences need to be confronted, not because there is a right or a wrong answer, not to impose a new orthodoxy or a correct reading of the master, but better to appreciate the range of insights and methods and to understand more fully their implications.

McFarlane ranged widely across three centuries, England and France, politics, government, economy, society, religion, and much else besides. But his work can be narrowed down to a central core: the fifteenth century and politics and within that bastard feudalism,[8] the bond between lord and retainer, which introduces (as Dr Harriss realised) his other work and from which his most celebrated contributions sprang.[9] Certain aspects of bastard feudalism, such as its origins and demise, regulation by statute, parliamentary representation, arbitration, and recruitment for foreign war, are subsidiary to this main theme, possess their own copious literature, and have been excluded here. McFarlane's essays of 1943-5 marked a new beginning and superseded all that went before, but if McFarlane himself questioned that earlier work, so too should we. This essay looks first therefore to what went *before* McFarlane; to the work of McFarlane and others in his own lifetime; and then focuses on three approaches since his day associated with Professors Storey and Bellamy;

[6] K.B. McFarlane, *The Nobility of Later Medieval England* (Oxford 1973), xxix.

[7] M.C. Carpenter, 'The Duke of Clarence and the Midlands: A Study in the Interplay of Local and National Politics', *Midland History* xi (1986), 23-6; Given-Wilson, op cit; G.L. Harriss 'Introduction' in K.B. McFarlane, *England in the Fifteenth Century* (1981), ix-xxvii; C. Richmond, '1485 and All That, or what was going on at the Battle of Bosworth?', *Richard III: Loyalty, Lordship and Law*, ed P.W. Hammond (1986), 172-206; Richmond, *History* lxviii 46-60; Storey, *BMS* iii 7-15; Powell, *Kingship*, 4-9.

[8] Richmond, *History* lxviii 46.

[9] Harriss, op cit ix.

the county community school; and Dr Richmond. Each offers a radically different model not just of bastard feudalism, but of the social and political systems within which it operated. The intention is to distinguish their approaches and methods and to point out some pitfalls and incompatibilities. That many other scholars are omitted here, perhaps regrettably, is not to undervalue their work. Space is a factor, but their work is omitted (rather than overlooked) principally because this essay focuses on those propagating new methods and approaches or, at least, novel interpretations of McFarlane. The conclusion draws the threads together and seeks a sound basis for future advance and debate.

It is a commonplace that sixteenth-century historians deplored the civil war, noble faction, and general disorder of late medieval England and credited the Tudors with eradicating them. This perspective was retained by subsequent historians and coloured even the work of the professional academics of the 1870s and '80s:

> Another main cause of the paralysis of the government was the overgrown power and insubordination of the nobles . . . The reign of Edward III . . . saw the beginning of that bastard feudalism which, in place of the primitive relation of lord and tenants, surrounded the great man with a horde of retainers, who wore his livery and fought his battles . . . while he in turn maintained their quarrels and shielded their crimes from punishment.[10]

Thus runs Charles Plummer's celebrated denunciation of 1885. But Plummer, although the first begetter of the label bastard feudalism, did not originate the interpretation, which he shared with such other principled Victorian churchmen as J.R. Green, William Denton and William Stubbs. By offending against the Whig tradition of England's orderly progression towards parliamentary democracy and the rule of law, bastard feudalism naturally attracted their moral disapprobation, which was nevertheless soundly based on such contemporary sources as the works of Sir John Fortescue, the statutes, and, above all, the Paston Letters. James Gairdner's edition of 1872 included not just the letters and a factual commentary, suggestive in themselves, but an introduction to 'Social Aspects of the Wars of the Roses'. He did not denounce bastard feudalism nor make it responsible for the Wars of the Roses, but he did identify it as a necessary precondition:

> At no time in England's history was there a stronger feeling of the needful subordination of different parts of society to each other; but under a king incapable of governing this feeling became a curse, not a blessing . . . That civil

---

[10] J. Fortescue, *Governance of England*, ed C. Plummer (1885), 14-16.

war should have broken out in a state of society like this need occasion no surprise. The enormous retinues of feudal noblemen were in themselves sufficiently dangerous to the peace of the kingdom, and when the sense of feudal obligation to the sovereign was impaired, the issue could not be doubtful.

A magnate like Warwick, who lavishly feasted all-comers:

> had no difficulty in obtaining friends to fight for him in the day of battle. He maintained, in fact, what might be called a little standing army at all times, and if an emergency arose, doubtless many who had dined at his table would flock to his standard and take his wages.

Henry VII curbed abuse by executing rivals and prosecuting retainers.[11]

Gairdner had said enough. There followed in 1878 a brief comment by Green and a massive contribution by Stubbs drawing on a wider range of sources. If feudalism itself had died, a nobleman nevertheless maintained his lifestyle and power with cash:

> he could . . . support a vast household of men armed and liveried as servants, a retinue of pomp and splendour, but ready for any opportunity of disturbances; he could bring them to the assizes, to impress the judges, or to parliament, to overawe the king.

They backed him by force and law. Chivalry, so Stubbs thought, encouraged his pomp and display, prompted him to scatter his livery and protect recipients against violence and justice alike. Maintenance increased, for liveries gave 'effective security to the malefactor' and 'became badges of the great factions of the court, and the uniform, so to speak, in which the wars of the fifteenth century were fought'. Livery connected two evils, maintenance and dynastic faction, and was eradicated not just by legislation but by enforcement in Star Chamber.

Stubbs broke much new ground with this impressive synthesis. He recognised good lordship as 'a revival, if not a survival, of the ancient practice by which every man was to have a lord, and every lord was to represent his men or be answerable for them in the courts'. He saw that Edward III's indenture system was applied to domestic strife, that the system could promote cohesion between nobility and gentry, and that retainder could subordinate the parliamentary Commons to their Lords. He criticised households inflated beyond functional need and remarked the co-existence of indenture of retainer, of livery and household, of

---

[11] *The Paston Letters, 1422-1509*, ed J. Gairdner (3 vols 1872-5), iii lxiv-v. Gairdner says almost nothing on the subject in his *Houses of Lancaster and York* (1874).

payment for service and lordship. By coupling 'livery and maintenance', he blamed the former for the latter.[12]

Stubbs touched on almost every aspect of bastard feudalism investigated since. His contemporaries Denton and Plummer added a few refinements: the manpower of the Wars of the Roses came from disgruntled French veterans, the wars themselves arose from the escalation of private feuds among the nobility, and bastard feudalism itself developed over time.[13] For seventy years, however, most historians were content to repeat Stubbs' interpretation and saw no need for the thorough institutional study that feudalism had received or for detailed investigation of bastard feudalism's effects on domestic politics and justice. Attention moved instead to parliamentary representation and warfare abroad: areas strictly irrelevant to this essay, but which influenced the themes it treats.

Military history brought out the central importance of the indenture of retainer. Most important in the armies of the Wars of the Roses, according to Professor Oman, were those:

men gathered under the system of 'Livery and Maintenance' . . . knights and esquires of a district bound themselves, by written agreement, to some great neighbouring lord to espouse his quarrels in every place from the lawcourt to the battlefield.

Professor Prince was yet more emphatic:

the practice of Livery and Maintenance, with its uses and abuses, was based upon and derived from, the Indenture organization. It is hardly an exaggeration to aver that the indenture system was mainly responsible for the English triumphs (and defeats) in the Hundred Years' War and subsequently for the Wars of the Roses.

And in 1945 Professor Lewis's meticulous analysis of surviving indentures illuminated such contracts in detail.[14]

Miss Helen Cam switched the focus firmly back to peace-time politics

---

[12] W. Stubbs, *Constitutional History of England in the Middle Ages* (3 vols 1874-8) iii, 304-5, 573-88, 591. For the impact of the Paston Letters on Stubbs, see *Letters of William Stubbs, Bishop of Oxford, 1825-1901*, ed W.H. Hutton (1904), Stubbs to Freeman 3 January 1877. For Green's similar interpretation, see J.R. Green, *History of the English People* (4 vols 1877-80), ii 16-17.

[13] W. Denton, *England in the Fifteenth Century* (1888), 274-306; Plummer, 14-19.

[14] C. Oman, *History of the Art of War in the Middle Ages* (2 vols 2nd edn 1924), ii 407; A.E. Prince, 'The Indenture System under Edward III', *Historical Essays in Honour of James Tait*, ed J.G. Edwards, V.H. Galbraith & E.F. Jacob (1933), 283; N.B. Lewis, 'The Organisation of Indentured Retinues in Fourteenth Century England', *T[ransactions of the] R[oyal] H[istorical] S[ociety]* 4th ser xxvii (1945), 29-39.

and the control of local government and justice. For her the corruption of the late medieval legal system arose from the retainder by lords of its officers – sheriffs, judges, jurors, JPs – who manipulated it for their lords. Lords bought up retainers, who willingly perverted justice or fought for them, so that the nobility, in effect, took over royal administration and exercised authority through it.

> If this be called feudalism, it is a parasitic institution, deriving its strength from an institution hostile to itself, cut off from its natural roots in the soil, and far removed from the atmosphere of responsibility, loyalty and faith which had characterised the relationship of lord and vassal.

The parasite was scotched by the Tudors, who confiscated noble estates and prosecuted retainers in Star Chamber.[15]

Cam's paper of 1940 was thus the first major re-appraisal of Stubbs' work and tended to vindicate it. Others were actively studying aspects of the subject, H.G. Richardson and Lewis as well as the young McFarlane, and there was a not unimpressive record of publications on the subject. These have been neglected for the past forty years because outdated and superseded by McFarlane, but it is doubtful whether this is wholly justified. These early writers were considerable scholars and particularly well-versed in the literary sources we neglect today for records. McFarlane was the product of this tradition, the master of both literary *and* record sources. He drew extensively on and adapted what they had done, and subsequent writers, perhaps unconsciously, have covered much of the same ground. Moreover McFarlane did not *refute* what went before, he offered an alternative – an alternative that has been *preferred* but not *proven*. Nor was McFarlane alone in reassessing Stubbs, even if his contribution appears most enduring. His two classic papers of 1943-5 can be seen as replies to Cam, Lewis and Richardson, two of whom, incidentally, respond.[16]

When McFarlane began work, late medieval politics was seen through the eyes of the king: the barons were irritating opponents of royal policy and constitutional advance. McFarlane substituted a pluralist approach, in which the viewpoints of both parties received sympathetic treatment, and in which politics was seen not in a determinist perspective, which no contemporary could recognise, but as the debate of king and magnates

[15] H.M. Cam, 'Decline and Fall of English Feudalism', *History* xxv (1940), 223 sqq; see also 'The Relation of English Members of Parliament to their Constituencies in the Fourteenth Century', *Liberties and Communities in Medieval England* (1944), 223-35.

[16] See H.G. Richardson, 'The Commons and Medieval Politics', *TRHS* 4th ser xxviii (1945), 21-45; H.M. Cam, 'The Quality of English Feudalism', *Law-Finders and Law-Makers* (1962), 44-58.

found in the chronicles. The new approach called for a fuller understanding of the noble's outlook, which was not necessarily primarily
political, and hence led McFarlane into a massive assault on surviving
noble records and their multi-dimensional study. His Ford lectures of
1953 treated not just noble politics, but the education, finances, family
strategies, and other influences conditioning their whole outlook and
hence their politics.

This was the vantage point from which McFarlane re-appraised
bastard feudalism, which he saw as quite different from the classic
feudalism it superficially resembled. The payment by lords for services
hitherto exacted from feudal tenants arose from the substitution by the
crown of paid service for unpaid feudal service. Royal contracts for troops
for particular campaigns prompted captains to subcontract with their
inferiors on a more permanent basis. Royal indentures survived from the
late thirteenth century and subcontracts are common from the mid
fourteenth century. While insufficient for a whole retinue of war,
subcontracts provided the nucleus of retainers on each occasion. The
indenture of retainer, which usually traded service *for life in peace and war*
for an annuity, was the most normal arrangement. Just as characteristic,
so McFarlane argued, was the fragility of the contractual bond: it lacked
the stability of a tenurial tie; gentry often served several lords, offering
neither exclusive nor overriding obedience; retainer for life could be
broken and often was. Within certain constraints, lords and men had
freedom of choice, in which their mutual advantage was the main
consideration. This theme was expanded in a second, contemporary,
article, which challenged the idea that the parliamentary commons were
pawns of the lords. Their experience of affairs and their wealth barely
distinguished them from their lords and suggested that they would have
been relatively independent, an argument he substantiated by a careful
analysis of the county elections in the Paston Letters. In East Anglia, at
least, lordship conferred little authority over dependants, who endured it
only so long as it was good and abandoned it when it ceased to be
advantageous:

> And so around a hard core of household and estate officials there accumulated
> a vast but indefinite mass of councillors, retainers and servants, tailing off into
> those who were believed to be well-wishers.[17]

Politics was about power, self-interest, and personalities, not ideals or
principles, still less the Lancastrian Constitutional Experiment.

---

[17] K.B. McFarlane, 'Bastard Feudalism', *B[ulletin of the] I[nstitute of] H[istorical]
R[esearch]* xx (1945), 161-80; 'Parliament and "Bastard Feudalism"', *TRHS* 4th ser xxvi
(1944), 53-79; reprinted as chs 1 & 2 of idem, *England*.

McFarlane had eclipsed Cam, Richardson, and even Lewis. His many research students preached his new orthodoxy in the expanding universities. For thirty years the mainstream represented in a host of theses (including my own) was the noble family or individual nobleman. Research students took records from many repositories, national and local, bearing on many topics, usually starting with the noble estate and finances and working outwards. The localities were studied as part of a wider canvas covering the whole range of the nobles' interests and activities and concentrating on what seemed most important, which was often not local at all. Some noblemen were indeed backwoodsmen, others courtiers, diplomats, or warriors; some estates and localities were central to them, others were not. One chapter – and usually no more – considered the retinue. There were never enough indentures of retainer, so students relied more on office-holding, annuities, and other evidence of service, stopping short of feoffees and witnesses to deeds. Whilst aware that many gentry were multiply retained, a rule of thumb and *feel* for locality and retinue was employed to identify their priorities. Multiple retaining need not entail rivalry between lords and often a second fee was evidence that the second lord wished for influence through the retainer with the first. Such analyses treated the whole affinity, focusing on those areas seen as most important. Riots were attributed to particular lords by checking rioters against retainers and attendance of retainers at battles was interpreted as service to their lords. To measure the local importance of the retainers and the magnate's local influence, the personnel of county administration and elections to parliament were analysed. Whilst magnates may not always have determined such matters, they sometimes did, and the negative argument – that men with such ties could not act against their lord's influence – was sometimes employed.[18] The strengths of such an approach were that it was selective in coverage, for only areas *adequately documented* were treated, that it ordered a lord's priorities – local and national, political and military, dynastic and cultural – and that it was not restricted to one line of motivation, although this was perhaps more often deduced than stated by contemporaries. Its most obvious weakness was that it rested on a series of generally unstated assumptions, that were not confronted at the time and have been challenged in recent work. It also diluted the classical purity of McFarlane's arguments.

Most of these theses added data consistent with McFarlane's stance, rather than developing or correcting it, and contributed rather to our knowledge than our understanding. They did, however, push the origins of bastard feudalism back into the thirteenth century, before J.O.

---

[18] M.A. Hicks, *False Fleeting Perjur'd Clarence: George Duke of Clarence 1449-78* (1980), 73, 186-9. This para is based on personal experience and observations. The underlying assumptions were openly discussed, but seldom if ever stated in the theses themselves.

Prestwich demonstrated it co-existed with, rather than succeeded, feudalism, and forward into the sixteenth century, where Tudor historians had (and still have) perforce to seek a new chronology and explanation of demise.[19]

For bastard feudalism itself a chronology of evolution was offered by the American Professor W.H. Dunham. Relying solely on the sixty-seven indentures surviving in California from the retinue of William Lord Hastings (d. 1483), Dunham argued for a movement from military to civil retaining and from payment to good lordship. Instead of a debasement of feudalism, he postulated a progressive refinement, payment being easier than subinfeudation and 'the final substitution of good lordship . . . for the fee created a more refined, certainly a more subtle, relationship'. It was by retaining those running local government and sitting in parliament that noblemen now exerted their power. Dunham argued that this could benefit not just lords but the king. The risk of abuse diminished as retaining became less military and was confined progressively to the most trusted of the social and political élite.[20] Narrowly based though they are, Dunham's views recur in textbooks, stimulated Mr Morgan's claim that Edward IV used bastard feudalism to control the localities, and help explain Professor Lander's declaration that:

> The noble retinue, the affinity, in other words the 'bastard feudalism' which has been so often condemned as an unmitigated evil, was an essential part of Yorkist and Tudor government.

Dunham's view of bastard feudalism was particularly rosy; others still saw it as a curse. McFarlane was cautiously optimistic. Like Dunham and perhaps partly because of Dunham's work, McFarlane increasingly adopted a civil rather than military justification for retaining. Where he had seen the origins in payment for military service and 1400 as dividing the age of the indenture from the more casual and less stable relationships

[19] E.g. G.A. Holmes, *The Estates of the Higher Nobility in Fourteenth Century England* (Cambridge 1957), 58-74; J.R. Maddicott, *Thomas of Lancaster, 1307-22* (1970), 40-66; M. Prestwich, *War, Politics and Finance under Edward I* (1972), 61-2; J.O. Prestwich, 'The Military Household of the Norman Kings', *E[nglish] H[istorical] R[eview]* xcvi (1981), 1-35; C.S.L. Davies, *Peace, Print and Protestantism 1450-1558* (1977), 54-5; A. Cameron, 'The Giving of Livery and Retaining in Henry VII's Reign', *Renaissance and Modern Studies* xviii (1974), 19-37.

[20] W.H. Dunham, *Lord Hastings' Indentured Retainers, 1461-83* (Transactions of the Connecticut Academy of Arts and Sciences xxxix, 1955). The Hastings affinity has been repeatedly misunderstood: see below ch. 12. For what follows, see E.F. Jacob, *The Fifteenth Century, 1399-1485* (1961), 337 sqq; B. Wilkinson, *Constitutional History of England in the Fifteenth Century, 1399-1485* (1964), 337 sqq; D.A.L. Morgan, 'The King's Affinity in the Polity of Yorkist England', *TRHS* 5th ser xxiii (1973), 17 sqq; J.R. Lander, *Crown and Nobility 1450-1509* (1976), 69.

of the Paston Letters, later he gave higher priority throughout to good lordship and peacetime service and even speculated whether it was the fourteenth century that was 'the century of unbridled livery'. Undoubtedly bastard feudalism could subvert justice and fuel civil strife, but it had caused neither the breakdown of order nor the outbreak of civil war. Enforcement of the law and royal control over lords were adequate safeguards, which failed not because bastard feudalism was uncontrollable, but because kings were weak. As good lords of all good lords, kings should have settled disputes and kept order. Where Henry VI failed, Henry V and Henry VII triumphantly succeeded. Abuses existed before bastard feudalism and the chorus of complaints and even legislation indicate rising expectations rather than escalating problems or moral degeneration.[21] Substantiating this case, unfortunately, was never a priority of his research and he never tackled the three interrelated fields that are now generally regarded as containing the answers: the operation of the law; the gentry; and provincial (or county) society. Work on the first already threatened his interpretation at his death; since then, work on the latter two, often ostensibly inspired by him, has replaced the nobility in the mainstream and has offered perspectives contradicting his own.

Traditional hostility to bastard feudalism proved perfectly compatible with McFarlane's mechanics and was even stimulated by it. Miss Cam returned to the fray. Accepting Dunham's argument that livery 'was again a perfectly legitimate practice in its proper place' did not justify it when 'worn by men not of the household and supplemented by badges . . . serving . . . as rallying points for gangs of men'. Retainer 'by indenture extended far beyond the bona fide members of a noble household or active officials of a great estate'. Lords could maintain retainers in legitimate ways, but bastard feudalism was associated with illegitimate maintenance. Local government was endangered by the suborning of its officials and domestic peace because unlike feudalism, with its hereditary tenurial stability and raison d'être of fighting for the king, 'in these contracts the military service is to a subject'. Bonds of service were too easily broken or multiplied. Bastard feudalism remained, despite McFarlane:

> a pest that riddled the countryside . . . making law and justice a dead letter there. From the reign of Edward II onwards this complex of private loyalties threatened revolt and civil war. Bastard feudalism was indeed a disease of the body politic, a disease which had to be mitigated, if not eradicated, by the Tudors.[22]

---

[21] McFarlane, *Nobility*, 107n, 114-19; idem, *England*, 40-1, 238-40, 247-8.
[22] Cam, *Law-Finders and Law-Makers*, 44-58.

Cam's arguments could be dismissed as a last Stubbsian relic if not supported from an impressively up-to-date quarter. A newly sorted source, the ancient indictments of the court of King's Bench, offered copious evidence of aristocratic crime and disorder. From them Professor Storey argued in 1966 that the courts' inability to settle noble feuds enabled them to esculate into private and then civil war. Bastard feudalism gave lords the manpower to corrupt justice and practise violence. He too blamed it for a degeneration from the (idealised) legal and constitutional achievements of earlier centuries, when there was an orderly system of royal justice, a military system based on contracts between the king and those who served, a government that increasingly involved all landed classes, and a local administration run by gentry freed from meaningful ties and thus politically independent. The growth of retaining drove gentry into affinities and those retained needed noble protection to secure favourable treatment before the law. Should their interests clash, lords could call out those wholly dependent on their good lordship. No social stability could be founded on so slight a basis as mutual satisfaction.[23]

Storey's book clashed with McFarlane's Raleigh Lecture, which may have caused him to modify some opinions. Like Cam, he came to accept some positive aspects of bastard feudalism, as in arbitration, though even these called for royal supervision. He pushed its growth back to the ineffective kingship of Henry VI and used this expansion to explain later legislation to curb it and eliminate abuse. His basic hypothesis, however, was unchanged and in 1971 he carried it back to the ineffective rule of Richard II. Bastard feudalism facilitated Richard's deposition and was already a source of corruption and disorder. Two strands of contemporary thought mirrored modern historical debate: while the Lords asserted their *privilege* and capacity to control their retainers, the Commons trusted in the commissions of the peace and restrictions in retaining. Short-term royal preoccupations alone explain why legislation was so circumscribed and the county commissions were left to the mercy of the lords. Public order *demanded* a ban on extraordinary retaining. Local disturbances prompted him to assert in 1973 that 'bastard feudalism was inherently incompatible with the rule of law':[24] as extreme a position as any observed so far.

Storey's opinions were the current orthodoxy for his pupil Professor J.G. Bellamy. Right at the start of his book on late medieval crime Bellamy remarked that:

---

[23] Storey, *Lancaster* (1966), esp 6-17.

[24] R.L. Storey, *The Reign of Henry VII* (1968), 35-40, 151-6; 'Liveries and Commissions of the Peace 1388-90', *The Reign of Richard II*, ed F.R.H. Du Boulay and C.M. Barron (1971), 133; 'The North of England', *Fifteenth-century England, 1399-1509: Studies in Politics and Society*, ed S.B. Chrimes, C.D. Ross and R.A. Griffiths (Manchester 1972), 133.

It was the large followings of the magnates which made the task of local law enforcement so difficult since the enforcers were often attached to one of the great lords, as were a considerable number of those they brought into court.

Judicial corruption and bastard feudalism were already entwined in 1300. Their prevalence and persistence stemmed from:

the increasing local influence of those who were already powerful and the way the law was corrupted by this influence. What historians have not yet established is whether influence increased because of the lowering of the quality of public order or public order deteriorated because of the magnates' desire and ability to attract supporters. The more common view is that the known partiality of justice compelled men with complaints . . . to resort to dishonest means. This meant ultimately seeking the good offices of a lord who was so powerful in the region that none would readily wish to offend him . . .

Here again are the growing power of the nobility, the simultaneous and dependent decline in public order, and the centrality in recruitment of good lordship. In some places a lord's authority was 'quite stifling' and made redress of grievances impossible. Because lords were indiscriminate, they retained professional criminals, who set bad examples to fellow retainers engaged in local government. The latter 'must also have been corrupted' as 'constant witnesses to the misapplication of the law and misuse of office' by their lords. Lords wanted retainers at least partly to dominate the king and good order suffered whenever king and magnates clashed. As cure Bellamy saw the release of the gentry from their indentures and longer terms of local office, but no king acted appropriately until the sixteenth century.[25]

Bellamy remains convinced of the causal connection between bastard feudalism and corruption of the law and just as hostile to them both. In 1984 he identified maintenance and riot as characteristic and endemic crimes of the aristocracy. It was to combat them that much new legislation bypassed those procedures most liable to corruption by substituting informers, examination and summary judgement. So successful were these that they were transferred to other areas of law, yet procedures had to be repeatedly strengthened as aristocratic crime nevertheless increased. Yet if much of Bellamy's interpretation remains unchanged, the emphasis had altered substantially, bastard feudalism with all its evils appearing now less as an end than a means.

Although historians have talked a great deal about the abuses of livery giving . . . at the heart of the disruption of public order in fourteenth- and fifteenth-century England, a very good case can be made for forcible entry and riot

[25] J.G. Bellamy, *Crime and Public Order in England in the Later Middle Ages* (1973), esp 1-24.

being the prime causes, with the other evils springing from them. Because this was where their wealth was centred, the upper classes thought first and foremost about their property in land and ways of extending and defending it, as the Plumpton, Stonor, and Paston correspondence clearly shows.[26]

This argument was substantiated in 1989 in the first full-scale book on bastard feudalism, which is profoundly hostile to McFarlane and his school and dismissive of their perfunctory treatment of its social effects.

Having accepted as 'incontrovertible fact that so many aspects of late-medieval English life were intertwined with bastard feudalism', Bellamy set out to devise a 'model' that identified the central and subsidiary features of the relationship. Only thus, he argues:

is it possible to reach a conclusion on whether the evils which have at various times been attributed to bastard feudalism were created, fuelled, or even perhaps kept within reasonable limits by the administrators and the administration of the law; and whether this dark side, was, as has sometimes been implied, the result of an ill-conceived, malfunctioning, or corrupt legal system.

Pride of place goes to the 'land wars' or 'gentlemen's wars', concepts devised by himself in 1978 and employed (but not explained) in 1984. Land was the essential foundation of aristocratic estates, wealth, and lifestyle and its defence or acquisition were vital preoccupations of nobility and gentry alike. Contemporary land-law gave no security of tenure and fomented disputes, in which every gentleman participated and in which no opportunity was missed in bending the law to his will, as Bellamy illustrates copiously from contemporary correspondence. Hence the mass of litigation, forcible entries, feuds, violence and other consequent 'evils', which were, he argues, widely recognised and attacked repeatedly in legislation:

Kings, ministers, and parliaments worked repeatedly, if not persistently, towards the eradication of the evils attendant on bastard feudalism but, because these were an integral part of the very structure of society, progress was necessarily slow . . . This amounted to taking advantage of almost every procedural device possible under the criminal law to ensure accusations were forthcoming and also loading, although legitimately, the method of trial to make conviction much more likely than acquittal.

Actually the situation was much improved even by the fifteenth century, when feuds were almost 'bloodless', serious crime by the aristocracy –

---

[26] J.G. Bellamy, *Criminal Law and Society in Late Medieval and Tudor England* (Gloucester 1984), esp 70. This is one of a number of works that has rehabilitated the late medieval legal system.

felonies rather than trespass – decidedly unusual, felony itself had become less common, and there were no more Folville and Coterel gangs. Although vestiges survived into the seventeenth century, bastard feudalism was repeatedly restricted and was undermined by developments in land-law that gave greater security and certainty and thus obviated the need for chicanery, violence, and retaining alike.[27]

Storey's early work undoubtedly idealised earlier centuries, when the virtues of royal justice and local government now look less obvious and for which abuse may be less well-documented but certainly occurred. He underplayed the growing influence of fifteenth-century gentry. Bastard feudalism and judicial abuse did not begin suddenly, but evolved gradually in the twelfth to thirteenth centuries. Similarly Bellamy originally relied on causes célèbres – crimes recognised as exceptional even by contemporaries – which tells us little of the mundane and sordid crime of every day. It is as though we judged our public order by the Hungerford Massacre and the Yorkshire Ripper. Strangely in his second book Bellamy relied wholly on the statutes, not apparently even searching for evidence of offences and enforcement in the records of the courts, and deduced the problem *and* the effectiveness of counter-remedies from the statutes. Few cases of riot and forcible entry are recorded for the early fifteenth century, yet they must have existed, because 'If they were not, then there would have been lacking a basic reason for the frequent promulgation of statutes not only against riot, but illicit retaining, livery giving, and maintenance in the crucial period 1380-1430'. The new procedures, he writes, 'demonstrate how serious a problem riots were becoming'. Yet 'no examples of these examinations . . . survive today, but then no others from the fourteenth or early fifteenth centuries for common law purposes do either', an admission that does not prevent him from asserting, firstly, that they were effective, and, secondly, that the crimes attacked nevertheless increased. Thirdly, he speculates why they were disobeyed. From this short summary it is surely obvious that by applying a pre-existing interpretation to the statutes, Bellamy forces them to carry too many mutually-contradictory elements of his argument. It *could* all be explained by 'rising standards of order rather than a rising tide of crime',[28] as indeed he has now implicitly recognised.[29] The same circular arguments about the causes and results of legislation occur also in his latest book.[30] Substantiation of either hypothesis depends on the

---

[27] J.G. Bellamy, *Bastard Feudalism and the Law* (1989), esp 4-6, 8n (p. 146), 9, 12-15, 84, 98-101, 123 sqq; for the term 'gentlemen's wars' see Bellamy, *Criminal Law*, 65, 70, 84.

[28] Bellamy, *Criminal Law*, esp 64-5, 67; see my review in *Parliamentary History* vii (1987), 168-70; Powell, *Kingship*, 112.

[29] Bellamy, *Bastard Feudalism*, 100.

[30] E.g. ibid 83-6.

correlation of legislation with the records of enforcement, which even his latest book does not attempt.

Moreover there is no easy equation between crime and the ancient indictments, which require handling as careful as any other source. The records of many courts, such as commissions of the peace and gaol delivery, are lost and we can only guess at their contents.[31] Indictments are charges, not convictions, contain errors and are not proven; they are the products of that same legal system whose probity is in dispute, as indeed are convictions; as few ever came to trial, we know nothing of the case for the defence and have few convictions; and events are expressed in legal formulae and categories and not necessarily as they actually happened.[32] Moreover they need to be seen not in isolation, but in several contexts. More cases came before royal courts as rival jurisdictions declined. New laws may indicate rising expectations and changing standards of what was tolerable, not changed conduct, or may instead reflect the sectional interests of pressure groups rather than public demand.[33] They may not even have created new crimes, as when new legislation substituted statutes of forcible entry for the assize of novel disseisin and redefined much violence as the new offence of riot.[34] They may *merely* introduce new procedures for handling old offences. More laws inevitably mean more offences and more prosecutions, whether or not conduct has deteriorated or changed. The accessible and surviving court records treat only formal litigation, not the complementary conciliar or private resolution of disputes by mediation or arbitration, which *may* have been as or more extensive, but for which the records were private, unsystematic, and are largely lost.[35] Many suits never reached court and many, perhaps most, that did were settled out of court. If recorded crime increased in the later middle ages, this does not necessarily mean that public order declined and indeed it is more likely to have improved. Bellamy now admits that aristocratic gangs and felonies were more common in the early fourteenth than in the fifteenth century. Perhaps respect for human life increased? More recorded crime certainly indicates more resort to the royal courts and *perhaps* therefore a growing respect for royal justice and the law.

Professor Storey, in fact, claims to have recanted his earlier views. What he now believes is not easy to distinguish from those he cites and, indeed, he appears now to see more in the work of McFarlane and others that agrees with his older work. He rejects binding ties of lordship, accepts

---

[31] Ibid 4-5. For the rest of this paragraph, see Carpenter, *L & HR* i 207-9.

[32] E.g. T.B. Pugh, *Henry V and the Southampton Plot of 1415* (Gloucester 1988), 130-1.

[33] See Carpenter, *L & HR* i 231.

[34] E.g. Bellamy, *Criminal Law*, 54, 65.

[35] Hicks, below, 145-6.

McFarlane's claims that maintenance could be legitimate, and that 'the English aristocracy of the later middle ages was, on the whole, a highly responsible body, with a vested interest in public order and good governance'. Bastard feudalism could be controlled and it was because of his 'inanity' that Henry VI's 'personal authority was non-existent' and disorder escalated. This retraction, less than complete though it is, is concealed in a particularly obscure periodical and is therefore less influential than his original use and interpretation of the ancient indictments.[36]

They are a standard source for today's historians. A host of historians have analysed particular disputes and feuds in print.[37] The best show a proper discrimination in their employment, but this is a time-consuming process liable to produce only tentative results. To confine oneself to convictions, for example, would deny oneself the bulk of the evidence. Often their use is less scrupulous. Whilst admitting the difficulties in interpreting legal evidence and that 'the impartiality of the commission [of oyer and terminer for Herefordshire in 1457] had been challenged in a court of law', Ailsa Herbert nevertheless treats its unsubstantiated proceedings as fact and draws conclusions about the strength of local government and the shape of local politics. By deducing from the low level of convictions and high rate of acquittals that king's bench 'had little success in punishing crime' and was unable 'to complete cases' she assumes even those acquitted were guilty,[38] a decidedly dangerous presumption shared by Dr Powell and Dr Carpenter, who also presumes charges of judicial chicanery to be true! Although innocent of the methodological implications of 'social crime', applied to the later middle ages only by Dr Hanawalt,[39] Dr Carpenter is not alone in seeing forcible entry and riot as crimes characteristic of the late medieval nobility and gentry.[40] Even the scrupulous Professor Griffiths encourages Bellamy's picture of endemic aristocratic crime by itemising major cases (and assuming their accuracy) in chapters on 'Lawlessness and (Aristocratic) Violence' in his monolithic *Reign of King Henry VI*; and a similar chapter by

---

[36] Storey, *Lancaster* (2nd edn Gloucester 1986), x; 'Bastard Feudalism Revisited', *BMS* iii 7-15.

[37] Many references to studies by Cherry, Griffiths, Jeffs, Virgoe and others are collected in the bibliography of R.A. Griffiths, *The Reign of King Henry VI, 1422-61* (1981).

[38] A. Herbert, 'Herefordshire, 1413-61: Some Aspects of Society and Public Order', *Patronage, The Crown and the Provinces in Later Medieval England*, ed R.A. Griffiths (Gloucester 1981), 103-22, esp 112, 115-17. For the next phrases, see M.C. Carpenter, 'The Beauchamp Affinity: A Study of Bastard Feudalism at Work', *EHR* xcv (1980), 525; Powell, *Kingship*, 234.

[39] B.A. Hanawalt, 'Fur-collar Crime: The Pattern of Crime among the Fourteenth-Century English Nobility', *Journal of Social History* viii (1974), 1-17.

[40] For Bellamy, see above.

Dr Powell appears in a recent volume on Henry V.[41] In short, there is a danger, despite Professor Storey's recantation, that bastard feudalism may nevertheless become entrenched as the commonplace instrument of everyday aristocratic disorder.

Why does it matter? After making due allowance for deficiencies in the sources, there surely remains overwhelming evidence that aristocrats did commit such crimes and that bastard feudalism was their instrument. A majority of gentry engaged in litigation, Professor Bellamy *and* Dr Carpenter tell us,[42] and the preservation of order was and is a vital function of government. Quite. The principal problem with all this, however, is that over-reliance on legal records generates a conflict model of society. So too does Bellamy's latest reliance on correspondence about legal disputes.[43] Both suggest a society in perpetual friction and turmoil. But one must have a sense of proportion. Court records and correspondence about lawsuits *can* only reveal crime and conflict. We have nothing of comparable consistency or quantity to illustrate concord and co-operation. Correspondence tells us about much other than lawsuits.[44] Litigation and much maintenance were not only legal, but normal and integral features of society. Not all litigation was contentious, not all brought recourse to maintenance and violence, and much ended in compromise. Compulsive litigants, large-scale confrontations, and long and bloody disputes occurred everywhere, but they were not normal, continuous, or all-embracing. Even the Great Berkeley Lawsuit, the Paston-Fastolf dispute, or the Bonville-Courtenay feud did not flare up every day, week, month or even year, did not embroil all the aristocracy of the affected areas, and produced surprisingly little bloodshed. The Fight at Clyst (1455) must of course be deplored, but that only twelve deaths created such a furore reminds us how exceptional such a level of violence was considered.[45] Although employing a ritualised violence and described in such terms in legal records, most disputes were, as Bellamy admits, bloodless. How appropriate, then, are the terms 'land wars' and 'gentlemen's wars', which have connotations of brute-force, violence, and bloodshed that are completely lacking here? Bellamy and Carpenter alike stress the *quantity* of litigation and litigants, but a single lawsuit per gentleman per lifetime is unimpressive and does not add up to a litigious

---

[41] Griffiths, *Henry VI* (1981); E. Powell, 'The Restoration of Law and Order', *Henry V: The Practice of Kingship*, ed G.L. Harriss (Oxford 1985), ch 3.

[42] Bellamy, *Bastard Feudalism*, 34; Carpenter, *L & HR* i 524.

[43] Bellamy, *Bastard Feudalism*, 6 & passim; see also the apposite comment of McFarlane, *Nobility*, 115.

[44] Cf. H.S. Bennett, *The Pastons and their England* (2nd edn 1932) passim.

[45] M. Cherry, 'The Struggle for Power in Mid-Fifteenth-Century Devonshire', *Patronage, The Crown and the Provinces*, ed Griffiths, 137. Cf. A. Macfarlane, *The Justice and the Mare's Ale: Law and Disorder in Seventeenth Century England* (Oxford 1981).

society. Conflict was the exception rather than the rule and the conflict model is wrong. Surely a relatively law-abiding and orderly society is an essential backcloth for a breakdown of order in the 1450s that nevertheless never approached social or political anarchy? Far from condoning violence and political corruption, subjects looked for remedies to king, parliament, and the courts, and were not disappointed, as Bellamy himself argues. Progressively stricter legislation against bastard feudalism may reflect progressively stricter standards of tolerance. The medieval past cannot be judged by the civilised standards attained today.

The gentry are the focus of the county community school of historians. The county community is a concept first applied to the early modern period and justified theoretically by Professor Everitt. Shires were not merely administrative, but social, political, and cultural units. County gentry focused politically on county government, concentrated social life on fellow gentry within county boundaries, and saw themselves as distinct from and sharing different interests from central government and neighbouring counties alike. Everitt's 'federation of county communities' succeeded Given-Wilson's 'federation of lordly spheres of influence'.[46]

Everitt's late medieval counterparts treat peace, rather than war. Most play down the peerage and play up the gentry. None focus on the nobility, the great estate, or the great connection. For some the late medieval county/region was *the* valid social, political, and cultural unit. All concentrate on the many gentry who collectively held most manors and crop up most in records rather than the few nobles and their few documents (though more per head). Dr Wright is typical in that her 'overriding concern is the reconstruction of gentry attitudes and the complexities of gentry society'; Dr Bennett, yet more ambitiously, aims at 'a more "rounded" picture of English society' through the examination of 'individuals, groups and communities . . . interacting in the widest possible range of capacities'. Much of the time and for many activities the gentry were operating independently: managing their estates, administering the county, intermarrying, conveyancing, and litigating. Noblemen feature relatively seldom, in clearly-restricted areas, and thus appear either as mere *members* of the community much like other gentry, or as *outsiders* intermittently intruding on a self-sufficient society that did not need them to 'work'. They exploited pre-existing societies for their own ends and thus appear unnecessary. To be retained created one extra tie

---

[46] A. Everitt, 'Local Society and the Great Rebellion' (Historical Association, 1969); A. Everitt, *The County of Kent and the Great Rebellion 1640-60* (Leicester 1966); Given-Wilson, *English Nobility*, 1. For what follows, see M. Bennett, *Community, Class and Careerism: Lancashire and Cheshire Society in the Age of Sir Gawain and the Green Knight* (Cambridge 1983); S.M. Wright, *The Derbyshire Gentry in the Fifteenth Century* (Derbyshire Record Society viii, 1983); and papers cited subsequently by Carpenter and Rowney.

among many and not necessarily the most important. Since society came first and lordship afterwards, lordship had to conform to social realities and did not shape them. In lieu of an ordered hierarchy subject to a lord, there is a 'richness of texture' arising from the interplay of multiple influences on hundreds of gentry in constant demographic flux.[47]

Dr Bennett's Northwest England comprises Lancashire and Cheshire *c*. 1370-1425. The gentry of each county formed a genuine community. They intermarried, turned out in force to settle property or elect MPs, and ran county administration. In 1400 and 1403 the Cheshiremen rebelled and Lancastrians rallied for the king, manifesting 'the existence of a framework of trust, consensus, and co-operation' in each county. Such events, the differing national policies of their lords, and indeed county boundaries could not impede a natural regional solidarity born of physical proximity, a common dialect and ecclesiastical government, economic and social similarities, and commercial interdependence. This 'regional solidarity . . . was most strikingly demonstrated' by the 200 local gentry who supported Sir Robert Grosvenor in the Scrope and Grosvenor controversy, but it emerged also in shared administrative responsibilities, private co-operation, intermarriage, and the burgeoning regional sentiment in literature of the later fourteenth century. There were lords, of course, and indeed many north-westerners were recruited in war and political crises by kings and great magnates. Soldiers not only enhanced their wealth and rank, they also established connections 'readily transposed to a civilian setting' which brought 'material assistance through "livery and maintenance"' and access to 'pardons, protections, aid in dealing with bureaucracies, and other indulgences from the authorities'. Quite apart from grants of office both Richard II and the Lancastrian kings distributed fees of up to half their annual revenues in the region. So one-sided was the balance of advantage that:

> it is tempting to conclude that . . . the earls of Chester and the dukes of Lancaster were administering their estates in the Northwest mainly for the benefit of the local gentry . . .

During the fourteenth century great landlords were losing ground to the gentry. Before 1425, with 'no great aristocratic lineage' to settle disputes informally, 'the system was one of mutual credit and collective security' in which leading gentry exercised a social control 'perhaps as typical a feature of English society at this time as the more notorious system of "bastard feudalism"'. The county community itself linked king and subjects, 'royal household and the lesser gentry', but already Sir John Stanley was emerging as leader of regional society, anticipating the family

---

[47] The phrase is Dr Richmond's, *History* lxviii 58.

hegemony later to replace the community as broker with the crown and submerge it 'in the swelling tide of aristocratic challenge'.[48]

Several historians give detailed narratives of county politics subdivided mainly by the careers of particular magnates and characterised by rapid change. In Dr Rowney's Staffordshire, for example, lords constantly competed to control county administration and the gentry that ran it. Fees mattered, but only:

> by protecting and furthering the interests of his supporters could a lord achieve the same for himself. Similarly, it was by obtaining 'good lordship' that a gentleman was best able to preserve and enhance his position and possessions.

The intervention in the county of Humphrey Stafford (later Duke of Buckingham) in the late 1430s was resisted by Lord Ferrers of Chartley, many of whose men deserted to the duke even before his own death in 1450 prompted Buckingham and Warwick to recruit those who remained. Buckingham won. In the 1460s Warwick and Clarence had a free hand, for Lord Hastings did not extend his interests into the county:

> Indeed, why should they have done, given that this would have brought him into rivalry with other loyal intimates of Edward IV, namely, Warwick and the king's brother George, duke of Clarence?

Hastings did take over in 1474. Buckingham in the 1450s and Hastings in the 1470s controlled the county. That there were nevertheless unaligned sheriffs in the 1450s was due to reluctance to serve and the reality that 'a sheriff who had made an enemy out of . . . Buckingham, would find it difficult, if not impossible, to act effectively'. There were also JPs unretained by Hastings, but:

> Surely we are not to believe that Edward IV's right hand man would suffer this region of special interest to him, to be governed by men hostile to him?

So too with shire elections. Buckingham could not force his man on the gentry, for that 'would have produced massive gentry resentment', but could rest assured 'that no-one unacceptable . . . might reasonably hope to be elected'. 'Blatant partisanship' occurred only during national crises, when retainder proved a fragile tie. Lords could not always – or even often – commit their men to battle. Buckingham's feed men would not support him in battle:

> They were unprepared to fight in their own county and certainly had no intention of going elsewhere to do so . . . Gentry immobility was due less to

---

[48] Bennett, *Community*, esp 33, 39-40, 73, 84-5.

cowardice or apathy than to a confident assumption of immunity from reprisal. Bastard feudalism was above all a voluntary business relationship with patronage and service as unenforceable contractual obligations.

So Buckingham was killed. And when their next lord Clarence 'marched throughout the heartland of the honour in March 1470', he overlooked 'the latent apostasy of the gentry', who declined to follow him. Clarence, indeed:

> only ever won over men's heads not their hearts; and it was their hearts he needed to mould an affinity into a retinue. There is no evidence that John [Curzon] III ever followed Clarence into revolt or battle. However, the ties between them grew closer with time . . . Yet Curzon was wise enough to avoid becoming so closely involved . . . that he fell from grace with his patron.[49]

There are parallels here with Dr Cherry's analysis of the 210 and 351 men indicted for the Earl of Devon's risings in 1451 and 1455, which demonstrate the falling participation of the gentry and thus how such irresponsible violence could alienate retainers and lead to the disintegration of the Courtenay affinity.[50] Noblemen could only solicit their retainers, not command them.

A third example is Dr Carpenter's Warwickshire, where bastard feudalism was such a 'part of the normal fabric of society' that:

> all the more prominent Warwickshire gentry can be shown to have been of the affinity of at least one lord. In view of the social and political significance of bastard feudalism this was to be expected: only the unimportant would be without a lord.[51]

The retinue existed to protect a lord's lands against rival claimants. To achieve this, he needed to dominate county government – the key to criminal and civil justice – and that in turn called for control of as much of the county and as many gentry as possible. Only by thus 'dominating the local administration' could he 'really help his men and secure their

---

[49] I. Rowney, 'Government and Patronage in Staffordshire, 1439-1459', *Midland History* viii (1983), 49-69, esp 51, 54-5, 58, 65-6; 'The Hastings Affinity in Staffordshire and the Honour of Tutbury', *BIHR* lvii (1984), 35-45, esp 45; 'Resources and Retaining in Yorkist England: William, Lord Hastings and the Honour of Tutbury', *Property and Politics: Essays in Later Medieval English History*, ed A.J. Pollard (Gloucester 1984), 139-55, esp 140, 150; I. Rowney, 'The Curzons of Fifteenth-Century Derbyshire', *Derbyshire Archaeological Journal* ciii (1983), 111.

[50] Cherry, 123-44, esp 137n (p. 143).

[51] Carpenter, *EHR* xcv 514-32. For what follows, see ibid esp 517, 523; M.C. Carpenter, 'Sir Thomas Malory and Fifteenth-Century Local Politics', *BIHR* liii (1980), 29-43, esp 33; idem, *Midland History* xi 22-48, esp 23-8.

support'. It was the duty of any gentleman like Sir Thomas Malory:

> to protect his landed inheritance for both himself and his posterity and to
> pursue all claims to land that lay with the Malory family. This obligation – one
> that was rendered exceedingly difficult by the complexities and delays of the
> legal system – was the overriding preoccupation of the gentry and one that
> necessitated the most careful choice of protectors and friends. It was in aiding
> such families in the preservation and improvement of their landed and social
> status that the nobility could establish their 'worship' and hence their support
> amongst the gentry . . . [For Malory] like all the gentry . . . the game of local
> politics [was] a game where the stakes were high, for they were no less than the
> lands without which a gentry family could have no existence.

Dr Carpenter begins with Richard Beauchamp, Earl of Warwick
(1401-39), certainly the greatest lay landholder and dominant lord in the
county. His affinity and those of his allies, with which it intermingled,
'provided the major unifying force amongst the Warwickshire gentry'. It
enabled him to control county administration and gave him the clout
necessary for a good lord, even by chicanery and violence. His rule
contented the majority and meant the areas 'of his hegemony could be left
in great part to run themselves' without royal interference. Even
Beauchamp had few lands in parts of the county, where he could not
attract retainers. No magnate could:

> maintain an affinity unless he held land in demesne nearby. Without the threat
> of military force, that could be raised from the land, retainers could not be
> brought to heel, nor mastery over rival affinities demonstrated.

Here he allied with local notables. Whenever such lands changed hands,
potential rivals undermined his local authority, indirectly threatened
control of the whole county, and thus forced him to reassert himself
vigorously in the affected areas. On Beauchamp's death in 1439, leaving a
minor, Buckingham became 'the focal point of an alliance system',
attracting former Beauchamp retainers into his affinity. Others opposed
him, dividing county society and the Beauchamp affinity alike. Duke
Henry Beauchamp briefly ousted Buckingham in 1445-6, when he died
leaving an heiress, and not until 1449 could Earl Richard Neville begin
'recreating the splintered Warwick affinity'. He was probably behind
Malory's attacks on Buckingham and his men. Their 'struggle for mastery
. . . eventually became enmeshed with the national political crisis' and it
was the Yorkist victory in 1461 that saved him. His conduct in 1469-71
again split the affinity and his son-in-law Clarence 'was not the man to
restore the balance'. Seriously weakened to his east and north and by
consequent competitive recruiting, Clarence's failure to keep order led
King Edward to intervene and begin 'enlarging his own authority at the
expense of Clarence'. Needing to prove himself not to be trifled with,

Clarence murdered Ankarette Twynho and backed Thomas Burdet –
actions that led directly to his execution.

Such precision is achieved in spite of gaps in the evidence, as Dr
Carpenter admits:

> Tracing changes in power in the late medieval localities is by no means easy.
> The evidence at the historian's disposal is problematic, lacking as it does direct
> avowals of motive, and consisting principally of indications of friendship
> (indenture, service, witnesses, feoffees, beneficiaries of wills and so on) and of
> conflict (primarily the judicial records).

The personnel of local government can also be analysed. Whereas for Dr
Rowney proof of retainer is *supplemented* by evidence of service 'as tenants,
estate officials, feoffees or witnesses to deeds',[52] Dr Carpenter reverses the
priority. Since a lord's prime objective was to protect his land and
transmit it to his heirs, he would take especial care to choose trustworthy
feoffees, witnesses, and executors for such conveyances.

> From this two conclusions follow: firstly that, within reasonable limits, such
> evidence must take precedence over evidence of retainder and service; and
> secondly that the real strength of a lord's affinity may be judged by the extent
> to which the common factor linking groups of associates within his
> geographical sphere of influence is a connection with that lord. Given these
> premises it is evident that, within the parameters imposed by the availability of
> local lordship, each gentry family would have a shifting pattern of allegiances,
> responsive to formal links with magnates, to relations with friends and
> neighbours, and to the broader pattern of local and national politics. Changes
> in the balance of power in the localities have to be traced from the functioning
> of these complex networks.

Her 'second main assumption' is that, since 'political power' depended
on 'local military might', which 'was determined primarily by its tenurial
structure' and modified by changes in it, the 'utmost attention' must be
given 'to geographical factors'. So important was county government
that:

> no magnate . . . could afford to ignore the politics of each of the counties where
> his lands lay . . . [and] had to acquire enough followers in each of the counties
> where he had a concentration of estates to give him significant authority over
> the local officers and a large body of military support if litigation developed
> into violence.

If not, not. So lords and gentry alike were committed to a constant policy
of aggressive retaining and local politicking to remain where they were

[52] Rowney, *Midland History* viii 52.

and this in turn shaped national politics.

Here we have a new methodology and two new interpretations of bastard feudalism, society and politics. But are they soundly based? Several areas need reviewing now: the treatment of the county community; the place of lordship; the nature and use of evidence; the objectives of local politics; and the character and operation of local political society. Other broader areas raised, such as the nature and activities of the nobility and the purpose of their retinues, will be discussed later in this essay.

Let us begin with the concept of the county community. There is no doubt that medieval people lived in communities and were capable of a sense of community, even a county or regional one: thus the Paston circle often meant their county when referring to their country and northerner was more than a label of abuse for others.[53] It does not follow, however, that the aristocracy necessarily, universally, or exclusively saw themselves in terms of the county, for their horizons may have been larger or smaller. County institutions were the only organs through which much local financial, judicial, electoral, feudal and other business was *expressed*: their use does not prove county-mindedness. The existence or evolution of the county community is not, however, the issue here, nor indeed the validity (and very considerable value) of its study for economic, social, religious, and even political history of this period, but the way these *particular* studies apply it to politics.

There are a number of related problems, not all shared by them all. Firstly, counties are not necessarily natural geographical entities and Carpenter, Rowney and Wright sometimes treat only part of a regional phenomenon, for example only the Warwickshire, Staffordshire or Derbyshire section of Lord Hastings' indentured retinue. Secondly, the county community appears as an alternative to lordship, whereas it was not or was not necessarily so. The Paston circle's county-mindedness co-existed with noble dominance of local politics. Thirdly, the community is given priority in time, lordship coming after, whereas the community itself depends on patterns of land tenure based on feudal lordship which evolved, without a break, into the late medieval situation. There can never have been a time when there were no lords and lordship was not a formative influence. As the gentry were also lords – the distinction between the two branches of the aristocracy being somewhat semantic – lordship existed everywhere, even where there were no titled peers.

<hr/>

[53] R. Virgoe, 'Aspects of the County Community in the Fifteenth Century', *Profit, Piety and the Professions in Later Medieval England*, ed M.A. Hicks (Gloucester 1990), 5-6; 'John Benet's Chronicle, 1400-62', ed G.L. and M.A. Harriss, *Camden Miscellany* xxiv (1972), 187-8.

[54] M. Clanchy, *From Memory to Written Record: England 1066-1307* (1979), 2 sqq.

Lordship coloured the lives of those who were not retained just as literacy affected the illiterate.[54] Fourthly, the lords are presented as *intruders* who must take account of social realities and take over the pre-existing network of gentry: the possibility is ignored that such relationships might have been *shaped* by membership of the great's lord's affinity, as in Dr Pollard's Richmondshire and Dr Carpenter's Warwickshire.[55] And finally from this stems a belief that lordship is relatively weak, an assumption epitomised by Dr Bennett's decision to relegate it to chapter 10 of his book and Dr Wright to chapters 6 on. To keep an open mind is admirable; but it can shape the results obtained.

Dr Bennett's book claims to treat independent county and regional communities that managed affairs for themselves without dominance of a single lord. This strains credibility, for it was the king who was Earl and Prince of Chester; John of Gaunt and the Lancastrian kings were Dukes of Lancaster. Such lords needed no intermediaries. Their palatine counties were marked off by privilege from neighbouring shires and possessed central institutions that prevented recourse to Westminster. Naturally inhabitants looked inward; naturally they attended assemblies when summoned.[56] It was their lords' privilege and government, exercising exceptional authority from close at hand, that recruited the gentry on a large-scale, and used them to overawe parliament, for civil and foreign warfare. The Cheshire revolts and Lancastrian resistance demonstrate organisation and commitment to respective lords that carried them into battle. Those retained gained both good lordship and fees, which were not meant to and did not only benefit themselves. Military support from these Lancastrians justified their fees. Such lords had no need or desire for a broker, who would erode their own authority. It was only gradually that the Lancastrian kings, notably Henry VI, became absentees,[57] that the palatinates became like other shires, and that scope for an intermediary developed.

Let us move on to Staffordshire and Warwickshire, where precise narratives give magnate connections a central place in spite of the inadequate evidence of retainer. There are, for example, no receiver-general's accounts, valors, household accounts, comprehensive sets of ministers' accounts, or other archives of any part of the Warwick estate for the thirty years after 1449. The Stafford archive has survived better, but those of the Earl of Wiltshire and Lord Ferrers of Chartley have not. These gaps are filled by evidence of co-operation in land transactions and

[55] A.J. Pollard, 'The Richmondshire Community of Gentry during the Wars of the Roses', *Patronage, Pedigree and Power*, ed Ross, 37-56, esp 52; see above p. 22.

[56] In the Scrope and Grosvenor controversy, witnesses testified at formal sessions at Warrington and Lancaster, Bennett, *Community*, 16.

[57] Cf. C.D. Ross, 'The Yorkshire Baronage, *c*. 1399-1436' (Oxford D.Phil. thesis 1952).

litigation, which justify Dr Carpenter's claim that everyone belonged not just to *a* connection but to *successive* connections at different dates. But feoffees were often chosen for reasons of prestige, to deter opponents, and links need not be close; witness lists are evidence only of *association*. Given that feoffees frequently denied knowledge of the purpose of their enfeoffment and that deeds – including enfeoffments – were not necessarily signed by all those present in company on the day stated, the argument from association to political commitment is thin. At best, it suggests amicable terms, not necessarily an alliance. As for crimes, leaving aside Dr Carpenter's unduly literal interpretation of indictments, they disclose a difference, not necessarily a decisive one; so too does litigation. A great magnate like Clarence was engaged in many lawsuits at any one time, some initiated by himself, some by his council, some trivial, others fundamental. Not all could be allowed to be decisive. 'Because the Duke of Somerset and the Earl of Warwick disputed the lordship of Glamorgan, did the latter kill the former at the first battle of St Albans?' parodies Dr Richmond.[58] We need a sense of proportion and priorities.

These items become important because of the assumptions that go with them and are so clearly stated by Dr Carpenter. She is not alone in stressing the importance of land-disputes: the present author indicated that magnates' lands were essential interests,[59] and Professor Bellamy sees them as root-cause of bastard feudal corruption and violence.[60] There were certainly many of them. But again a sense of proportion is needed. Given that many estates were disputed and every lord had a stack of claims to make good in favourable circumstances, it does not follow that this was true of every estate, that all claims were pursued aggressively, that the struggle was continuous, or that control of county administration was decisive. The Great Berkeley Lawsuit and the Talbot-Lisle dispute flared up at irregular intervals over many years. Such feuds were decided, if at all, at the centre, not in the localities. That properties had to be defended need not mean aggressive self-aggrandisement, though some particularly favoured magnates, such as Suffolk in the 1440s and Gloucester in the 1470s, do seem to have pursued every vestigial claim. Similarly with great magnates, all of whom had isolated manors in counties far from their seats of power: it does not follow that Clarence's manors in Surrey or Norfolk were under constant threat. It was not necessary for him to build up an affinity in these counties to control county government and he did not try. Most magnates spent most of their time

---

[58] Richmond, *History* lxvii 59 (though this is a less absurd example than Dr Richmond intended).

[59] M.A. Hicks, 'Descent, Partition and Extinction: The "Warwick Inheritance"', below, 333.

[60] For Bellamy, see above.

away from most of their estates, yet did not lose them. Indeed, did any fifteenth-century nobleman or gentry *permanently* lose their lands because of purely *local* violence and chicanery? The *regional* hegemony of the Earl of Warwick extended beyond the bounds of his estates, included that majority of lands he did not hold, and was not threatened by the geographical fine-tuning on which Dr Carpenter places such store. Reliance on records of title and litigation about land has been allowed to unduly colour her interpretation.

Similarly, knowledge of the personnel of county administration and our capacity to analyse them has evidently prompted us all to exaggerate their political significance. What did they actually *do*? The day of the sheriff was past and JPs were not yet the omnicompetent body of a century later. The sheriff's servicing of the central courts and the JPs judicial proceedings were largely routine. Neither surviving sessions rolls nor indictments returned to king's bench suggest much business of political significance, nor indeed does the low attendance of justices – usually only three to five, mainly professional experts – who actually attended.[61] *Pace* Dr Maddicott, the routine of the county court is unlikely to have attracted more and even shire elections were normally uncontested.[62] The puzzle of the uncommitted Staffordshire JPs, sheriffs and MPs is perhaps more easily explained by accepting that these offices were *not* always the focus of factional competition. Historians of the nobility and county community are equally wrong.

Their evidence prompted Dr Carpenter, Dr Rowney, Dr Wright and indeed Professor Bellamy to postulate a conflict model of society. To *defend* their lands, magnates *must* control county administration. Since only one of them can do it, they are engaged in *aggressive* competition. For a gentleman to be retained committed him politically; to be retained again indicates a change of loyalty, the subsequent tie taking priority, and rivalry between lords. Fluctuations in witness lists indicate the ebb and flow of loyalties. If you are not for me, you are against me. It is such *presumptions* that determine much of the interpretation. Witnessing deeds was part of normal social intercourse. To witness a deed was not to make a political commitment. To be retained more than once occurred because loyalties were generally compatible. It may well be, as Professor Bean suggests, that different contracts carried different obligations, and/or that duties were highly specific and thus did not clash, as Dr Horrox argues.[63] Lords were not necessarily constantly feuding: they could coexist

[61] Based on PRO Ancient Indictments, 1461-85.

[62] J.R. Maddicott, 'The County Community in Fourteenth Century England', *TRHS* 5th ser xxviii (1978), 29-30.

[63] R.E. Horrox, *Richard III: A Study of Service* (Cambridge 1989), 18-19; J.M.W. Bean, *From Lord to Patron: Lordship in Late Medieval England* (Manchester 1989), 186.

peacefully, retain one another, agree about parliamentary elections,[64] litigate without feuding, and even compromise about land disputes.[65] Good lordship could involve following a retainer into conflict with a rival's lord; it could also involve joint arbitration by the two lords, just as each lord settled disputes within his own affinity.[66] Lords saw local politics in a wider context of other estates, localities, and activities and did not necessarily wish to feud with their kinsmen, friends, and colleagues. Sometimes, of course, they did and we know about many such feuds, but not everywhere or all the time. Stresses and strains exist in any relationship, but they do not invariably or even usually result in breakdown, which is often worse than the problem.

The conflict model is again inappropriate. So, too, therefore must be many (but not all) the deductions and studies based upon it. The most likely reason for the non-aligned gentry in high office in Staffordshire 'at the time of the power struggle between Buckingham and Warwick' in the 1450s was because, as in the 1470s, there was no power struggle. If Lord Hastings did not intervene in Staffordshire in 1462, it was not because he feared clashing with Warwick, his brother-in-law and patron. Earl Richard Beauchamp did indeed 'control' Warwickshire, but is there any evidence worth considering that there were subsequently power struggles between Buckingham and Ferrers in the 1440s, Buckingham and Earl Richard Neville in the 1450s, or Clarence and Edward IV in the 1470s? They *could* have happened, but we have no real evidence for them. That local politics was as volatile as this is surely contradicted by the long-term stability of ties between lords and retainer over many generations and their survival of disasters. If the Courtenays' affinity disintegrated in the 1450s and Clarence's in the 1470s, how can we account for the formers' successful recruitment for the Tewkesbury campaign in 1471 and the pro-Warwick rebellion in the West Midlands in 1486? How was the newly restored Northumberland able to play such a decisive role in 1471? If Richard III's northern retainers deserted him in 1485, why did some rebel again in 1486-7 and again in 1535? Clearly there is more to connections and local politics than kaleidoscopic change and self-interest. If a century is a short time in economic and social history, what about the history of political structures? How different was the Gloucestershire political *system* in 1500 from 1400 and 1300? Bennett's Northwest England suggests that there was no direct transition from magnate's spheres of influence to county communities and that new lords could still rise from the gentry to

---

[64] M.A. Hicks, 'Dynastic Change and Northern Society: The Fourth Earl of Northumberland 1470-89', below, 370-5; McFarlane, *England*, 10.

[65] See e.g. Lord Neville's quitclaim to the Duke of Gloucester in 1478, below, 331.

[66] E.g. below, 140-5.

take over from old ones. The county community can be a successful approach to politics provided inappropriate assumptions and methodologies are avoided, but the geographical and chronological fine-tuning of some recent studies is probably always impossible and of doubtful validity. The studies of Dr Saul and Dr Virgoe are effective precisely because they confine themselves to what is adequately documented and they do not find it necessary to write continuous detailed narratives of what is not. Theirs are the examples to follow. Counties vary: the next study should perhaps focus on a shire in which the *peerage* actually were weak. But there will still be lords and lordship.

McFarlane cited many instances of the bonds of retainer being broken, of the gentry's capacity for independence, and of the careful management required of lords to carry their retainers with them. These formed the starting point for the work of his pupil Dr Richmond, who has approached the subject not from the nobility, but from the study of the gentry and local society. His work is highly critical of both the nobility and county community schools of historians, whose careful filing of retainers from archives is an outside job that misses the 'richness of texture' of relationships.[67] A changed angle of approach has brought new perspectives to the subject. Beginning merely by asserting the importance of the gentry, Dr Richmond now attaches little political significance either to the nobility or bastard feudalism.

For Richmond the 'political importance and independence' of the Commons is axiomatic. It was substantial gentry like the knights of the shire who ran local government, managed their own extensive affairs, and engaged in litigation. Already they (and their immediate inferiors) 'were effectively in politics in the fifteenth century',[68] by the 1550s they were active opponents of government in and out of parliament, and their role was even more crucial a century later. They could make their own independent decisions on matters of political significance, for example whether to rebel with the Bastard of Fauconberg in Kent in 1471 or whether to attaint the king's brother seven years later. They could even choose not to engage in politics or local government, like the Suffolk squire John Hopton, and were not driven by external pressures into doing so or being retained by a lord. Hopton's neutrality may even have been more typical than the notorious partisanship of the Pastons.

[67] Richmond, *History* lxviii 58, 60. For the next four paras see ibid 46-60, esp 58-9; idem, 'Fauconberg's Kentish Rebellion of 1471', *EHR* lxxxv (1971), 673-92, esp 689, 691; idem, 'The Nobility and the Wars of the Roses, 1459-61', *Nottingham Medieval Studies* xxi (1977), 71-85, esp 83-5; *John Hopton: A Fifteenth-Century Suffolk Gentleman* (Cambridge 1981); '1485 and All That', loc cit 173-206, esp 179-80, 196 (n50), 197-8 (n59).

[68] So too were those of East Anglia, see R. Virgoe, 'Aspects of the County Community in the Fifteenth Century', *Profit, Piety, and the Professions*, ed Hicks, 10-11.

Fauconberg's Kentish gentry had no lord to make up their minds for them and perforce had to decide for themselves. But even when there were lords, they could not *command* compliance with their wishes. Noble power:

> depended on the co-operation of the gentry to exercise it on their behalf. . . . It was not William Lord Hastings who 'ran' the honour of Tutbury; the local gentry did – that is why he made them his retainers. He needed them more than they wanted him. So it was everywhere . . .

Lords took advantage of pre-existing communities of gentry: Lord Hastings '"bought" a clan rather than constructed an affinity',[69] and the clan continued to run local government thereafter. Retainer did not change this. How could it? By the mid-fifteenth century it was neither firm nor exclusive. Instead, it was too indiscriminate to be effective, many gentry were retained by several lords, and thus an indenture of retainer need have determined no-one's loyalties.

> Discover one and you have discovered an obligation, but it is only one of many . . . it may not have been the most important . . . A lord could never be sure of his retainers in the fifteenth century, no lord could ever have been . . . Fifteenth-century England is not like some twentieth-century mechanical toy called perhaps 'Connection': press a button marked William Lord Hastings . . . and you have won the central Midlands . . . For the point about the ties between lords and men is that they were not binding . . .

Contracts were based on mutual advantage, which constantly shifted. They varied in intensity and from time to time and by themselves cannot reveal 'how the political society of a region "works"'. Gentry made their own decisions, lordship being merely one factor taken into consideration, and often not the decisive one. Were loyalties 'ever simple or straightforward enough to *pre*determine their behaviour?'

Of course they were not, as Richmond strove to demonstrate by analysing participation in battles. Most peers and many gentry fought in 1461, carrying Edward IV to the throne, but in 1485 noblemen and gentry alike avoided committing themselves at Bosworth:

> A bare handful of peers fought for their King on that occasion, even fewer fought against him, and it is after all an encounter notorious for the fact that two noblemen, who were in a position to engage in the fighting, did not do so . . . Nearly four-fifths of them, by simply staying away, avoided the issue that was decided there that day.

And so too did the gentry. Richard's northerners suffered few casualties

---

[69] This is actually Rowney's phrase, *Property & Politics*, 145.

because they were not there,[70] unless perhaps in Northumberland's division and thus prevented from fighting:

> Yet need we accept an explanation which involves Richard's retainers being there with Northumberland? Can we not simply take it that they were not there at all? And if they were not, ask why not?

Might they not have decided not to back him, in their own self-interest or even the public interest? If so:

> If the Cumbrian gentry failed him . . . then the whole structure of authority as represented by lord and retainer is called into question. Richard in Cumbria was . . . the most over-mighty subject of them all: that was as Duke of Gloucester in 1483.[71] Can two years of kingship have undermined such authority? The Cumbrians had gained as much from Richard's royal patronage as had his other northern retainers: good lordship is not what is at issue here. So, if where he was apparently strong – at his strongest on most readings of the way in which power 'worked' in the fifteenth century – he was weak, we have surely to look again at Richard's kingship as well as at where power lay (and how it worked) in the fifteenth century.

Even those at Bosworth may have come to prosecute private quarrels of purely local origin from purely local issues rather than from loyalty to their lords. Was loyalty chiefly a 'literary device', asks Dr Richmond, 'that operated only when a lord's success made his retainer's self-interest coincide?'

Influenced perhaps by the ambiguous balance of advantage of lord and retainer remarked by his pupil Dr Rowney[72] and by his own observation that gentry ran lords' estates for them, Dr Richmond identifies the key retainers as the lawyers, who:

> were the councillors of many masters. It is these men who managed things, who were at the heart of political life, whether of town, shire, or kingdom. Their loyalties were never predetermined, because they owed them everywhere; they were their own men because they were everyone else's. If power has to be located in one place then it should be here with these gentlemen.

---

[70] Professor Ross preferred the testimony of the near-contemporary 'Ballad of Bosworth Field' that they were present, *Richard III* (1981), 212-25, 235-7, but Richmond rejects this evidence and takes *no* account of it in his calculations.

[71] This is based on a misunderstanding. Cumberland was not Richard's strongest area before its elevation to a palatinate only in 1483, an elevation that did not take effect, see M.A. Hicks, *Richard III as Duke of Gloucester: A Study in Character*, below, 268-9; see also below, 372.

[72] Rowney, *Property & Politics*, 149-51.

They had turned their employers into their dependants:

> noble lords had become by the mid-fifteenth century no more than socially
> prestigious puppets, whose strings were worked by knights, esquires and
> gentlemen. This is incontrovertibly revealed when the military aspect of
> retaining is considered. In spring 1471 Edward IV's return depended not on
> William lord Hastings but on William lord Hastings' retainers; they got both
> lord and king back into power.

Similarly Richard III's retainers let him go in 1485. It was the retainers
who chose, their freedom that made politics so unpredictable, and
hundreds of them, not a few noblemen, who determined the results, and
whom historians should be studying.

Starting from a cautious scepticism, Dr Richmond has thus reduced
late medieval politics to meaningless anarchy and, in McFarlane's name,
has rejected the work not only of McFarlane, but of everyone else who has
ever addressed the topic. Fortunately such a radical reassessment is not
required. His preliminary premise that retainer was not binding and his
claim that lords were tools of their retainers will be discussed later in this
essay. What must be reconsidered here is the supposed independence of
the gentry; their capacity for independent decision-making; the
unimportance of lordship; and the inability of magnates to carry their
retainers into battle.

The claim to independence for the gentry is debatable rather than
objectionable and not inherently improbable. The number of
extraordinary retainers is known to be surprisingly small and there were
surely too many gentry for all to be feed by the nobility. But the evidence
is deficient: invariably for the composition of noble households, which
were supposedly growing; merely normally for the payment of fees. Is it
ever sufficiently comprehensive for us to be *certain* any individual was not
retained? Dr Saul also has gentry 'outside the embrace of "bastard
feudalism"', but the 'trouble with 'independent gentry', as Dr Carpenter
pointed out, 'is that they only remain independent until evidence turns up
to link them with a magnate affinity', as two of Saul's have since been.[73] So
too with Dr Richmond's Kentishmen, whose *apparent* independence
overlooks affiliations with Warwick the Kingmaker during his ten-year
term as warden of the Cinque Ports and his fifteen-years as the captain of
Calais.[74] John Hopton, too, is an improbable candidate for such a role.
Assuming that his blindness set in late and did not force his withdrawal
from public life,[75] he and his son were nevertheless connected over fifty

---

[73] Carpenter, *L & HR* i 206n. This depends, however, whether one accepts Dr
Carpenter's methodology.

[74] *CPR, 1452-61*, 300; *1461-7*, 45.

[75] C. Richmond, 'When did John Hopton become blind?', *Historical Research* lx (1987),
103-6. See the scepticism of Prof Storey, *Lancaster* (1986), ix.

years with the Earl of Salisbury (d. 1460), Duke of Gloucester (d. 1485), and two Dukes of Suffolk (d. 1450 & 1491): two families linked by Alice Chaucer (d. 1475), Countess of Salisbury and Duchess of Suffolk. John's presence in Henry VI's household would normally be regarded as conclusive not of neutrality and detachment, but of dependence and service. Wholly independent gentry there may have been, but they are not easy to find. Perhaps they did decide for themselves, but where, apart from the Paston Letters, is the evidence? Are not our explanations for their actions pure supposition, since direct evidence of motivation is almost invariably lacking?

Dr Richmond and Dr Rowney come very close to saying that lordship is without meaning. The gentry contracted themselves and took their fees, but did not commit themselves – indeed never intended to – because their contracts were unenforceable. To accept this is to deny the fundamental point accepted by contemporary legislators, law-enforcers, Fortescue and the Pastons, that retaining influenced how people behaved towards the law and in battle. However exaggerated and however misguided contemporaries may have been, they thought lordship *did* determine action. That perspective cannot be omitted from our interpretation, however many exceptions we can find to the rule. To be retained was normally voluntary, not compulsory. To be retained by indenture was not an essential part of the process, even to secure a fee: many, probably most, were not. Indentures of retainer were not static, fossilised, or archaic, but evolved with changing needs and therefore reflected contemporary reality. By signing and sealing an indenture, the retainer solemnly and deliberately pledged his faith to serve his lord in peace and war and risked dishonouring himself if he broke faith. Nobody could have made such a contract if, as Richmond and Rowney suggest, they had no intention of keeping it. And if none of them turned out, where did the manpower come for those armies, thousands and tens of thousands strong, accepted to have fought the major battles?

How, then, can one explain their absence from the battlefield? First of all, one must remember that service in battle was different in kind as well as degree from other sorts of service. By the fifteenth century retainers specifically excluded service against the king and often his heir, and kings expected this provision to be observed.[76] In dynastic strife, many retainers had a perfectly reasonable (if unpalatable) justification for deserting their lords – *and*, of course, serving the de facto king. But that is not to say that they did.

Richmond and indeed Rowney and Cherry rely heavily on *absence* from

---

[76] E.g. Dunham, *Hastings*, 123-4; 'Chronicle of the Rebellion in Lincolnshire', ed. J.G. Nichols (Camden Miscellany i, 1847), 13-15. *Pace* Horrox, *Richard III*, 19, there was a difference between allegiance and loyalty to a lord, which contemporaries understood very well.

the battle, not attendance. If an individual is not mentioned as present, they deduce his absence. One would suppose from this that comprehensive muster rolls or lists of combatants survive, but this is not the case. Out of thousands of combatants at each battle, we never possess more than a couple of hundred names and often much less. For 1459-61 Dr Richmond is on safer ground, for with six battles to treat he has two acts of attainder, numerous chronicle accounts, several lists of casualties and knights dubbed on the field, and many grants recording the gratitude of the successful king. But the nobility are much better recorded than their inferiors. The vanquished had no interest in advertising their presence, for they wished to avoid attainder, and those who compounded to avoid this fate are normally unrecorded.[77] Cherry's indictments are unlikely to be comprehensive: if his Courtenay gentry were indeed absent, we do not *know* why, only that there were enough to achieve their lord's objective. Only chance evidence of short-term custody of the Tower kept the Earl of Kent from the Lincolnshire campaign; only isolated survivals reveal the Pastons' presence at and Henry Vernon's absence from Barnet, where there died retainers of Gloucester not otherwise known to have attended.[78] Even for these relatively well-recorded campaigns, therefore, one cannot safely assume absence without confirmatory evidence. In 1485, as Richmond admits, 'Bosworth is badly documented'.[79] It was a single battle, not the six of 1459-61, and many present did not fight. There is only one act of attainder, no contemporary narrative, no casualty list, King Richard made no knights, and Henry VII's patents are much less circumstantial. We cannot deduce who was absent and it is better to admit to ignorance than overstrain the evidence. There are, after all, many things that our sources will not permit us to undertake. As we do not know where the Staffordshire men were in 1459 and 1470, the Devonians in 1455, or the northerners in 1485, we cannot tell whether or why they deserted their lords. Even for 1471, the comments of *The Arrivall* about the Percy retinue are highly ambiguous,[80] and Lord Hastings had not yet taken over at Tutbury or created his indentured retinue.

All this publication has revealed much that is new, but little of it can command general agreement. Hitherto there has been little of that historical debate that advances understanding. If not worthless, the new material is of decidedly limited value. Some accepted criteria are needed if

[77] E.g. Sir William Plumpton, *The Plumpton Correspondence*, ed T. Stapleton (Camden Soc iv, 1839), lxvi-ix.

[78] Hicks, *Clarence*, 73-184; C.D. Ross, 'Some Servants and "Lovers" of Richard III in his Youth', *Richard III: Crown and People*, ed J. Petre (1985); *Paston Letters and Papers in the Fifteenth Century*, ed N. Davis (2 vols Oxford 1971-6), i 437-8.

[79] Richmond, *Nottingham Medieval Studies* xxi 84n.

[80] *Historie of the Arrivall of Edward IV*, ed J. Bruce (Camden Soc i, 1836), 6.

more work is not to be misdirected, particularly at a time when resources, monetary and human, are so relatively restricted. An essay that has criticised everyone, including its author, cannot hope to create a consensus out of such discord, nor does it offer a blueprint for the future, but in these last pages it seeks to clear up some remaining confusions and identify some of these criteria. Topics treated are the nature of the nobility, the bastard feudal bond, and the nature of motivation.

There is much confusion about the nature and role of the nobility. This is surprising in view of the work of McFarlane, Rosenthal, Given-Wilson and so many others.[81] It arises perhaps from the narrow angles of viewpoint of these studies, which McFarlane's Ford lectures seem scarcely to have touched. He devoted chapters to foreign war, the family, income and expenditure. The nobility were an international class, often engaged in fighting or negotiation abroad; they were a national élite, knew the king and one another personally, attended court and parliament, engaged in government and politics; they had local roots, often in several or many localities; and they were an affluent leisured aristocracy, living a 'noble life' in large households stocked with servants and hung with tapestries, eating and dressing splendidly, and amusing themselves hunting, jousting, dicing, reading and so on. Their perspectives were much wider than earlier sections of this essay would suggest. Civil war was intermittent. Normally noblemen did not litigate, assault, or corrupt in person: they had servants to do these things. They did not even often sit on the commissions to which they were appointed unless they were unusually important. They stood above local politics and routine. That does not mean that they were uninterested, that they did not mix with the gentry or intervene decisively on occasions, but that their outlook was wider and that such local matters did not preoccupy them. Staffordshire or Warwickshire was not their whole world.

Richmond suggests magnates were puppets of their retainers, just as Professor Galbraith suggested some fifty years ago. McFarlane's reply to Galbraith remains valid today.[82] Of course, some were mere puppets, the classic instance being the last Mowbray Duke of Norfolk,[83] but such occasional instances do not make a generalisation. Since lords and retainers shared the same educational background and ethos, why should the former be helpless puppets of the latter? Most noblemen participated in government, some becoming ministers, many commanded in the field, or engaged in diplomatic missions, hardly the marks of the incompetent or effete. Some have left detailed evidence of their application to business:

---

[81] McFarlane, *Nobility*; J. Rosenthal, *Nobles and the Noble Life 1295-1500* (1976); Given-Wilson, *English Nobility*.
[82] McFarlane, *England*, 19.
[83] *Paston L & P* i 544.

Henry Bourchier Earl of Essex; John Duke of Norfolk; Anthony Earl
Rivers; and Edward Duke of Buckingham.[84] They were exceptional, of
course, but probably because their records survive rather than because of
their activities and competence. Admittedly peers lacked the professional
expertise of lawyers and men of business, but these did not handle
everything: litigation, conveyancing, London debts and purchases, and
detailed negotiations. Not even (or not by themselves) collection of
revenues, estate management, expenditure, and audit, which were
handled by others. These estate managers supervised rigorously the
gently born estate officers, who, in the last resort, could be sacked and
sued for debt or illegal hunting, as Clarence indeed did.[85] Moreover a lord
had so many other activities, delegated to other servants, which he co-
ordinated and for which he determined the priorities. Medieval
nobleman, like medieval bishops, were good delegaters and had reliable
administrations, but they were not out of touch.

They also had retinues. Most of the debate here has been about the role
of the gentry – the 'extraordinary retainers' – but they were not the only
element, nor indeed perhaps the most important. The others were the
household and tenants. Central to any affinity, surely, was the nobleman's
household, probably never less than thirty strong, often much larger and
apparently growing.[86] This gave him a military nucleus, should he need it,
not just of gentry upstairs but also menials downstairs, who were selected
partly on physical grounds and were also expected to fight.[87] Lords could
control them closely: hence their exclusion from the livery laws. They
were agents always to hand and in whom, as members of his *family*, a lord
could repose much trust. Loyalty was obligatory and could be pleaded in
mitigation of treason. Betrayal carried the same penalties as treason.[88]
Here, surely, was the mobile force necessary to discipline Dr Carpenter's
recalcitrant retainers.

Second come the lord's tenants. It was these who made up the rank and
file – the sheer numbers – when a retinue turned out in force, for example

[84] McFarlane, *Nobility*, 50-2; L. Clark, 'The Benefits and Burdens of Office: Henry
Bourgchier (1408-83), Viscount Bourgchier and Earl of Essex and the Treasurership of the
Exchequer', *Profit, Piety and the Professions*, 119-36; E.W. Ives, 'Andrew Dymmock and the
Papers of Antony Earl Rivers, 1982-3', *BIHR* xli (1968), 220-5; A. Crawford, 'The Private
Life of John Howard: A Study of a Yorkist Lord, his Family and Household', *Richard III* ed
Hammond, 6-24.
[85] Hicks, *Clarence*, 176, 184.
[86] K. Mertes, *The English Noble Household 1250-1600: Good Governance and Politic Rule*
(Oxford 1988), 15, 141, 186-8.
[87] See e.g. Hicks, *Clarence*, 183; *Paston L & P* i 318-9; T. More, *Utopia*, tsl & ed P. Turner
(1965), 45.
[88] Morgan, *TRHS* 5th ser xxiii 7; J.G. Bellamy, *The Law of Treason in England in the Later
Middle Ages* (Cambridge 1970), 225-31. By 1260 domestic servants were already treated as
children at law, A. Macfarlane, *Origins of English Individualism* (Oxford 1978), 150n.

in civil war. They can seldom have known the lord in person and we cannot be sure why they turned out: on command and on penalties, perhaps, for instructions to estate officers to bring them survive;[89] but the survival of sentiment for particular families suggests more than that and points to a less commercial relationship than ministers' accounts. Here, perhaps, was where lords were at the mercy of retainers: when Henry Vernon failed Clarence in 1471, presumably his tenants remained unarrayed.[90] Though to retain them was illegal, they could be suborned by rival lords, which the crown at least tried to stop. The tenants of a great estate also constituted a military resource greater than that of any gentry. The tenants, if anyone, were blindly loyal – or, more probably, blindly obedient.

And so to the extraordinary retainers: the gentry. These were generally of three types: the lawyers, the estate officers, and the annuitants. The lawyers had many clients, like modern solicitors, and no overriding loyalty could be expected of them. So, too, perhaps the estate officers, whose duties however were surprisingly varied and enforced. Even if exercised by deputy, these were not sinecures. The annuitants were independent gentry, who were paid retaining fees. In civil war, they could bring significant accretions of strength from themselves, their households, and tenants;[91] a separate contract was needed for foreign war. In peacetime they came with their men to augment the lord's escorts, e.g. to the royal council,[92] ran his errands, back him in local politics and in traditional bastard feudal abuses. Perhaps these were their functions; perhaps rather they were decorative adornments to the household, which was the lord's home and his power-house about which so little is known.[93] Before 1400 extraordinary retainers were numerous, substantially afforcing noble retinues; in the fifteenth century, outside the north, they were not numerous,[94] though there is some evidence for competitive recruiting towards 1461.[95] Certainly extraordinary retainers enjoyed good lordship, not necessarily to their taste, for lords could impose settlements on their quarrels, but they also enjoyed fees, small sums in relation to their total incomes, but *extra* and hence effective inducements.[96] Modern academics receive the vast bulk of their income

---

[89] E.g. Hicks, *Clarence*, 183; Cameron, *Renaissance & Modern Studies* xviii 21-2; *pace* Bellamy, *Bastard Feudalism*, 92-3.

[90] Hicks, *Clarence*, 184; cf Bean, *Lord and Patron*, 174.

[91] E.g. *Paston L & P* ii 458; *Plumpton Correspondence*, 42; Sheffield Pub Libr MS WWM/ D98.

[92] Sheffield MS WWM/D98.

[93] Given-Wilson, *English Nobility*, 25.

[94] T.B. Pugh, 'The magnates, knights and gentry', *Fifteenth-century England*, ed Chrimes, Ross and Griffiths, 101-3; Bean, *Lord and Patron*, 174.

[95] McFarlane, *England*, 236n.

[96] A point made by Given-Wilson, *English Nobility*, 156.

from their employment, only pittances from publishers, speaking engagements, and A Level marking, yet give a high priority to the latter. The parallel is exact. It was marginal funding.

Were extraordinary retainers loyal? Is this the right question? What is the evidence that they were not? Our starting point, let us remember, is the indenture of retainer, a formal contract entered into voluntarily, *in the light of existing obligations*, setting out reciprocal duties that were regularly updated, pledging the retainer's faith and sealed with his seal. Did gentry ever attest more formal documents? Our presumption, like Professor Lewis's and Professor Bean's,[97] must surely be that they meant what they said. McFarlane relied heavily on the omission of living former retainers from John of Gaunt's list and assumed, perhaps mistakenly, that service had ended; if Gaunt were still alive, he ought to be surprised that more weight is attached to the minority missing from the second list rather than the majority who stayed. McFarlane emphasised multiple retaining, which was not necessarily incompatible or where a retainer (e.g. Hungerford or Bagot) was retained *precisely* because of his commitment to *and hence influence with* his main lord. And he drew on East Anglian politics,[98] much of it perhaps involving non-retainers. Some contracts specifically reserve prior ties,[99] and very few annuities are known to have been cancelled for non-performance.[100] *Perhaps* lords could not force even Staffordshire gentry to follow them into battle, but that there were no penalties for default seems unlikely. Given the existence of such indentures, our proper presumption, it seems to me, is that those contracting gave them priority over other ties and kept them *unless* they can be shown otherwise. If they did not, why did Buckingham have to wait until Hastings' death before retaining his men? If not, why were people shocked that Northumberland's feed men left him alone with an angry mob?[101] Even if evidence of attendance was adequate, participation in civil war is not a fair test, given that allegiance was reserved and that kings expected overriding loyalty from all their subjects. There are besides ample examples of commanders leading retainers into battle on different sides than those for which they were recruited.[102] The prime measure is surely those peacetime duties at which we can only guess. It is improbable that such contracts were not binding and therefore did not mean what they said. Even if they were, it hardly determines one's understanding of

[97] Lewis, loc cit; Bean, *Lord and Patron*.

[98] McFarlane, *England*, 31-2, 36-9.

[99] E.g. ibid 250; Dunham, *Hastings*, 124.

[100] Bean, *Lord and Patron*, 14-15.

[101] *Stonor Letters and Papers of the Fifteenth Century, 1290-1483*, ed C.L. Kingsford (2 vols Camden 3rd ser xxix-xxx, 1919), ii 161; M.E. James, 'The Murder at Cocklodge', *Durham University Journal* lvii (1964-5), 80-7.

[102] E.g. Henry IV in 1399; Lord Grey of Ruthin at Northampton in 1460; Warwick and Clarence in 1470; Edward IV in 1471; Clarence in 1471; Richard III in 1483.

contemporary politics, given that they were so few and becoming fewer.[103]

Indentures pledged a retainer's honour, scarcely mentioned by any recent late medievalist, yet given a high priority in the motivation of Elizabethan aristocrats by Mr James.[104] Indeed, one impression of the recent scholarship reviewed here is the poverty of motivation.[105] To deduce from events, especially ones requiring so much interpretation, is to rely on material motivation and to oversimplify. Self-interest, self-preservation, and self-advancement are carefully calculated and condition a chilly friendship, a dutiful dynasticism, a superficial loyalty, and a mechanical good lordship. Other obligations are mentioned, other motives – e.g. 'altruism', the 'honourable' nature of service, the 'public interest', the sacred nature of inheritance – are acknowledged, and Dr Richmond even allows for his Kentishmen to have made up their minds, presumably on the issues. McFarlane's emphasised naked self-interest, but expressed this in other ways. Even the crudest motives depend on a scale of values specific to each society: self-interest may promote avarice or display, land purchases or sales, accumulation of wealth or its dispersal in works or charity, piety, or the purchase of titles; self-preservation may apply to self (cowardice), family and estates (dynasticism), or salvation (religion); and self-advancement may depend (Dr Bennett's careerism) on notions of status, the nobility or demeaning character of particular careers, and career structures. That these leave little impact on the records of politics or those we use to study politics, merely exposes the poverty of records. Language is full of ideas. So is literature, but Dr Bennett looked at Northwestern alliterative poetry only for regional solidarity and did not test the relevance of its other ideas against the society that generated it. From parliamentary records emerge views of society – conventions of dress and status, for example – and the doctrines of necessity, attainder, and allegiance. Proclamations and manifestos appealed to principles, which Stubbs and his fellows took seriously and more modern historians reject as propaganda. So it is, but it was designed to evoke a favourable response from its audience, to appeal to their own principles. Sometimes ideas and idealism can be shown to have motivated political behaviour, not merely among the unrealistic.[106] There was more

---

[103] Apart from Hastings's contracts, there are few outside the north for the Yorkist period and almost none thereafter, Cameron, *Renaissance and Modern Studies* xviii 20.

[104] M.E. James, 'English Politics and the Concept of Honour', *Society, Politics and Culture: Studies in Early Modern England* (Cambridge 1986), 308-415.

[105] Powell, *Kingship*, 5-6. Dr Carpenter warns against oversimplifying motives, *L & HR* i 207, yet does so herself.

[106] M.A. Hicks, 'Edward IV, the Duke of Somerset, and Lancastrian Loyalism in the North', below, 149-64; 'Piety and Lineage in the Wars of the Roses: The Hungerford Experience', *Kings and Nobles in Later Medieval England: A Tribute to Charles Ross*, ed R.A. Griffiths and J.W. Sherborne (Gloucester 1986), also below 165-84; below, 133-48.

to politics than political manoeuvring and ideas must be one ingredient.[107] And these will include constitutional ideas and the work of those constitutional historians whom McFarlane superseded, but did not refute.

This discussion has revealed many-sided disagreement not just about bastard feudalism, but the society and political system of which it formed a part. In most cases the approaches should bear useful dividends, but too many of them have rested on unsound methodologies and on unrecognised biases in the evidence. Given the generally accepted deficiencies of the source material, too many historians, especially of the county community, have made much out of nothing and have burdened what there is with a weight of interpretation it cannot stand. It is better to write about what we know than what we do not. Bold though his syntheses were, McFarlane always worked from the best evidence, wherever he found it. Perhaps we should all do the same.

---

[107] *Pace* Lander, 'Family, "Friends", and Politics in Fifteenth-century England', *Kings and Nobles*, 37.

Idealism in Late Medieval English Politics

Late medieval literature allegedly has little relationship to late medieval realities. Its chivalry, religious quests, and courtly love merely offered an escape from a harsh and brutal world. 'Was chivalry ever more than a polite veneer?' asks Dr Keen.[1] One model of chivalry, the Black Prince, is remembered most for the sack of Limoges; another, Chaucer's Knight, has become a 'medieval mercenary'.[2] 'Is not loyalty of man to lord chiefly a literary device', asks Dr Richmond, 'only active in reality when the lord is successful, that is when self-interest (or mutual interest) binds man and lord together?'[3] People were out for what they could get:

> In this loosely knit and shamelessly competitive society, it was the ambition of every thrusting gentleman . . . to attach himself for as long as it suited him to such as were in a position to further his interests. It was a partnership to their mutual advantage, a contract from which both sides expected to benefit. . .[4]

Whilst historians sometimes mention ideas and ideals, such as justice, good lordship, 'bone governance' or good government, peace, prosperity, and even altruism,[5] they ignore them when explaining what actually happened, which stemmed instead from self-interest, self-preservation, and self-advancement. The 'security of their estates' was 'a compelling and potentially all-embracing necessity even in times of peace', writes Dr

---

[1] King Alfred's College kindly awarded me study leave in Lent term 1989, when this essay was written. For the first para, see W. Stubbs, *Constitutional History of England* (3 vols Oxford 1875-8), ii, iii, passim; *Select Charters*, ed W. Stubbs. Dr E. Powell's '"After McFarlane" – The Poverty of Patronage. A Plea for Constitutional History' was delivered after this essay was written. For his preview, see E. Powell, *Kingship, Law and Society: Criminal Justice in the Reign of Henry V* (Oxford 1989), 4-6.

[2] S.B. Chrimes *English Constitutional Ideas in the Fifteenth Century* (Cambridge 1934), 1.

[3] K.B. McFarlane, *England in the Fifteenth Century* (1981), chs 1 and 2.

[4] He thought that it was, M. Keen, *Chivalry* (New Haven, Conn 1984), 1. For what follows, see T. Jones, *Chaucer's Knight: Portrait of a Medieval Mercenary?* (1980).

[5] C. Richmond, '1485 And All That, or What Happened at the Battle of Bosworth?', *Richard III: Loyalty, Lordship and Law*, ed P.W. Hammond (1986), 196; K.B. McFarlane, *England in the Fifteenth Century* (1981), 18.

Carpenter[6] to a chorus of applause. In crises the men of Staffordshire habitually deserted their lords, writes Dr Rowney: 'Bastard feudalism was above all a voluntary business relationship with patronage and service as unenforceable contractual obligations.'[7] Richard III was deserted by his northerners. And why not, given that 'the ties between lord and retainer, patron and client, in the fifteenth century were so patently ones of self-interest?'[8] At Bosworth Field allegiance, loyalty, gratitude, and duty all gave way to self-interest and self-preservation. And kinship bound even less than lordship, especially in crises, when Professor Lander concludes that:

> such loyalties as there were were often cancelled by self-interest. Fundamentally based as it was on property and personalities, political life was even more a jungle than it is today, when it is at least to some extent tempered by principle.[9]

Material motivation was everything, idealism figured not at all. Politics was about patronage and faction. Had terms like allegiance, loyalty, faith and honour any meaning?

Medievalists accept that the Reformation injected principles into politics, generating alternative dynastic and foreign policies and causing Englishmen to rebel and die for their faith. But not all Tudor issues arose from the Reformation. The religion that bolstered the hierarchy and the crown was non-denominational and could have operated before the Reformation.[10] Perhaps it did.[11] Professor Tawney traced the Church's

---

[6] For justice, see M.C. Carpenter, 'Law, Justice, and Landowners in Late Medieval England', *Law and History Review* i (1983), 205-37, esp 237; for good lordship, my 'Restraint, Mediation and Private Justice: George Duke of Clarence as "Good Lord"', below, 133-48; for good government and 'bone governance', see C. Richmond, 'Fauconberg's Kentish Rising of May 1471', *E[nglish] H[istorical] R[eview]* lxxv (1970), 673; Powell, *Kingship*, 119 sqq; for peace, prosperity, and altruism, see I. Rowney, 'Arbitration in Gentry Disputes in the Later Middle Ages', *History*, lxvii (1982), 374.

[7] M.C. Carpenter, 'The Duke of Clarence and the Midlands: A Study in the Interplay of Local and National Politics', *Midland History*, xi (1986), 24; for what follows, see e.g. M.A. Hicks, 'Descent, Partition and Extinction: The "Warwick Inheritance"', below, 333; C. Given-Wilson, *The English Nobility in the Late Middle Ages* (1987), 141; J.G. Bellamy, *Bastard Feudalism and the Law* (1989), 35.

[8] I. Rowney, 'Government and Patronage in Staffordshire, 1439-1459', *Midland History*, viii (1983), 49-66, esp 66; C. Richmond, '1485 And All That', 173-9.

[9] J.R. Lander, 'Family, "Friends", and Politics in Fifteenth-century England', *Kings and Nobles in the Late Middle Ages*, ed R.A. Griffiths and J.W. Sherborne (Gloucester 1986), 27-40, esp 37.

[10] A. Fletcher, *Tudor Rebellions* (2nd edn 1973), 3-7; P. Laslett, *The World We Have Lost Further Explored* (Cambridge 1983), 216-19, 222; E.M.W. Tillyard, *The Elizabethan World Picture* (2nd edn 1963), 18-28, 37-50.

[11] E.g. Tillyard, 41.

restrictions on usury far back into the middle ages.[12] That concept of honour invoked by M.E. James to explain 'the pervasive violence of the Tudor social world' emerged 'out of a long-established military and chivalric tradition',[13] which late medievalists deny existed in practice. The 'good lordship and faithfulness' and 'kinship, lineage, and ancestral connection' so powerful in James's Tudor North were *survivals* from a past,[14] when medievalists deny they worked at all.

Mr James has substantiated his case. The problem for medievalists is one of evidence. Without statements of motive, they deduce motives from events with predictably crude and materialistic results: self-interest, self-preservation, and self-advancement. That aristocrats depend on land may make its defence an essential interest *provided their priorities were the same as our own*, which is improbable. Defence of land may sometimes suffice as motivation, but so too can allegiance, loyalty to a lord, good lordship, dynasticism, lineage, honour, or the salvation of the soul.[15] Occasionally a source states an ideal; sometimes it is the only explanation for actions otherwise inexplicable. That known examples are few arises most probably from gaps in our evidence and because it is harder to *deduce* idealism. It would be wrong to invoke contemporary ideas only to explain the inexplicable or eccentric and to leave the rest to material motivation. Even material motives evolve with time and circumstances, both physical and ideological, and are shaped by contemporary conventions, values, and expectations, which have not always carried the same priority, meaning, and weight as in our cynical late twentieth century.

No doubt many late medieval people were as materialistic as Chaucer presents them.[16] This essay seeks to restore idealism as an *ingredient* in explanations of contemporary politics. It does not distinguish between ideals strictly defined, principles, and ideas, since all were intangible, or non-material factors shaping political action. It cannot be comprehensive

[12] R.H. Tawney, *Religion and the Rise of Capitalism* (1926).

[13] M.E. James, *Society, Politics and Culture: Studies in Early Modern England* (Cambridge 1986), 308-9.

[14] Ibid 2.

[15] For allegiance, see below; for loyalty, see W.H. Dunham, *Lord Hastings' Indentured Retainers, 1461-83* (Transactions of the Connecticut Academy of Arts and Sciences, xxxix, 1955), 13-26; for dynasticism, see M.A. Hicks, 'Edward IV, the Duke of Somerset, and Lancastrian Loyalism in the North', below, ch. 8; for honour or moral obligation, see M.A. Hicks, 'Counting the Cost of War: The Moleyns Ransom and the Hungerford Land-Sales, 1453-87', below, ch. 10; for lineage, see 'Piety and Lineage in the Wars of the Roses: The Hungerford Experience', below, ch. 9; for salvation, see ibid; Hicks, 'Counting the Cost of War', below, ch. 10; 'Chantries, Obits and Hospitals: The Hungerford Foundations 1325-1478', *The Church in Pre-Reformation Society*, ed C. Barron and C. Harper-Bill (Woodbridge 1985), below, 91-4.

[16] G. Chaucer, *Complete Works*, ed F.N. Robinson (1966), esp 18-19, 21-2, which relate to churchmen who professionally propagated ideals.

either in subject matter or chronology and will focus attention on particular cases taken principally from the landed aristocracy of the fifteenth century. First, it will consider the intellectual constraints on all motivation: those conventions, standards, values, expectations and connotations discussed above. Secondly, it will use honour to illustrate an ideal not strictly political, but with direct repercussions on politics. Thirdly, it will show that principles did influence politics in practice.

That self-interest and self-preservation have been frequently cited as explanations for political conduct is hardly surprising, for they are obvious motives of universal applicability. This section demonstrates that even they have changed over time.

At its simplest self-interest comprises the defence and pursuit of material advantage. It is modified by the particular character of each society. Late medieval society was based on tenure of land and its politics dominated by leading landholders, who exercised authority primarily through paid retainers. Retainers dominated local and national government and manipulated justice for them and fought their battles. Landholders' essential interests were to defend their lands against rivals and extend them if they could. Consequently they needed to dominate local government and tap royal patronage, since only thus could they maximise their rents and retainers and offer the good lordship necessary to attract men and keep them satisfied. Failure lost them retainers and authority and exposed them dangerously to rivals. It is often assumed that they were pursuing this obviously appropriate course.

Yet is the self-interest even of the aristocracy so easily defined? They held their land not freely, but as tenants, in return for the performance of services. Most services, no doubt, were obsolete and meaningless (even the King's Champion rebelled in 1470!)[17]; but wardship and marriage remained. Land law restricted alienation, conferred dower on widows, regulated inheritance by heirs, and thus limited each tenant's freedom. Some such restrictions each accepted, willingly or unwillingly, whilst others were evaded or modified. Whenever a trust was created to evade feudal incidents, the tenant was admitting a commitment to his heirs and seeking to protect their interests from depredations after his death. Whenever land was entailed, he commited himself to a particular type of inheritance, generally favouring issue before collaterals and sons before daughters. Providing jointures for wives or dowries for daughters marks a particular conception and valuation of marriage, a commitment to matches between social equals, and a responsibility to support after death both daughters and widows. By remarrying late in life 'that God would

---

[17] J. Warkworth, *Chronicle of the First Thirteen Years of Edward IV*, ed J.O. Halliwell (Camden Soc vi, 1839), 8.

sende him Eyres male', magnates preserved the lineage at the cost of existing daughters,[18] and saddled heirs with longlived dowagers. The descent of land was modified by conceptions of inheritance, lineage, marriage and parenthood, which changed over time and shaped the law in turn.[19]

Landholders were theoretically free to spend their revenues as they chose, but in practice were obliged to support the whole family – wife, children, brothers, sisters – and to meet such family commitments as marriage portions and ransoms. Land bestowed status and landholders were expected to live in the style appropriate to it. The nobility were expected to live noble lives : their clothes and jewels, houses and furnishings, households and retinues, even their hospitality and alms, were expected to conform to particular standards. Inability or unwillingness to comply could result in demotion in rank,[20] and anyway detracted from their *worship*, their reputation or estimation. *Largesse* or generosity, which we deem extravagance, was a chivalric virtue.[21] Conspicuous consumption, which we condemn, was an aristocratic duty, whereas thrift and investment, which we admire, were condemned as avarice. Spending was admired, mere solvency was not.

Before lands are identified as an essential interest, account must be taken of the conventions governing their tenure, the obligations attached to them, and the uses to which they were put. To preserve the integrity of the estate and transmit it intact was *not* always the top priority.[22] Not all aristocrats resolutely defended their lands and many sold them, usually because the absence or distance of heirs released them from normal conventions. Not all were as aggressive as the younger Despenser and Sir John Moleyns, who combined favourable opportunites with the absence of conventional restraints of family and inheritance.[23] Richard Duke of Gloucester, probably the most aggressive claimant of the 1470s, was a younger son who had inherited nothing and was thus free to acquire and

[18] E.g. Richard Beauchamp, Earl of Warwick (d. 1439) and William Lord Botreaux (d. 1462), M.A. Hicks, 'The Beauchamp Trust, 1439-87', below, 339-40; Hicks, 'Piety and Lineage', below, 171.

[19] As shown e.g. by K.B. McFarlane, 'The English Nobility in the Later Middle Ages', *The Nobility of Later Medieval England* (Oxford 1973), 269-78.

[20] E.g. the Dukes of Suffolk and Bedford, 'John Benet's Chronicle, 1400-62', ed G.L. and M.A. Harriss, *Camden Miscellany* xxiv (1972), 224; J.E. Powell and K. Wallis, *History of the House of Lords in the Middle Ages* (London 1968), 522, 535.

[21] Keen, *Chivalry*, 2.

[22] See Dr Carpenter's comments in 'The Beauchamp Affinity: A Study of Bastard Feudalism at Work', *E[nglish] H[istorical] R[eview]*, xcv (1980), 521; 'Duke of Clarence and the Midlands', 25.

[23] N.M. Fryde, *The Tyranny and Fall of Edward II 1321-26* (Cambridge 1979), passim; N.M. Fryde, 'A Medieval Robber Baron: Sir John Moleyns of Stoke Poges, Buckinghamshire', *Medieval Legal Records*, ed R.F. Hunnisett and J. Post (1978), 198-207.

alienate without considering his heirs.[24] Not all who failed to pursue
claims, who conceded them, compromised, or alienated lands had such
excuses. Material motives cannot explain why Earl Thomas Beauchamp
(d. 1369) and his grandson deprived their heirs of so many manors in the
West Midlands for 114 years between 1369 and 1487 and thus gravely
weakened their authority. In Thomas's case it was to provide for a
younger son, in Richard's to provide for his soul, and in both instances
these motives took priority over the rights of those sons they had preferred
over their female descendants.[25] The childless Lord Berkeley repeatedly
disinherited his brother for promotion in turn as viscount, earl, and finally
marquis.[26] After saving her inheritance for her heirs, Lady Hungerford
sold lands when she need not, gave others to the Church, and indeed
surrendered some for licence to give others to the Church. Her daughter-
in-law gave lands to the king in return for settling some on her children
and others to her chantry. Also her husband was pardoned,[27] like the
spouse of Maud Lady Willoughby, who disinherited her heirs so that he
should live. Walter Hungerford spoilt his chances of recovering his
inheritance by going on pilgrimage in 1485;[28] many others spent careers in
war or government rather than in preserving or extending their estates.
Far from being foolish or irrational, these decisions show there is no easy
equation between lands and interests. Sometimes, indeed often,
aristocrats acted as we would expect, less certainly for the reasons we
expect, but lands were for use. What use was made of them depended not
just on such material circumstances as the existence or absence of heirs or
rivals, but on a variety of familial obligations, social, political or military
ambitions, and pious aspirations which could – and often did – take
precedence. And if land proves so complex, how can we safely assume that
self-interest *required* lords to seek local or national prominence, to compete
for retainers, or to prove themselves good lords?

   What of self-preservation? There were certainly those who gave their
lives a high priority. Foreign war could be avoided by the cowardly, but
private and civil war were more difficult. Many fled from battlefields,
James Earl of Wiltshire repeatedly;[29] others confessed under
examination,[30] presumably in return for similar immunity; yet others

---

[24] M.A. Hicks, *Richard III as Duke of Gloucester: A Study in Character* (Borthwick Paper 70, 1986), below, 250, 275-6, 278.

[25] G.A. Holmes, *The Estates of the Higher Nobility in Fourteenth-Century England* (Cambridge 1957), 49; Hicks, 'Beauchamp Trust', below, 339-40.

[26] Powell, *House of Lords*, 523, 527, 534.

[27] Hicks, 'Piety and Lineage', below, 174.

[28] Ibid 98.

[29] G.E.C. *Complete Peerage of England etc.*, ed H.V. Gibbs et al (13 vols 1910-59), x 127-8.

[30] *The Plumpton Correspondence*, ed T. Stapleton (Camden Soc iv, 1839), 19-20.

avoided battle;[31] and the nobility as a whole were cowed and craven by the battle of Bosworth.[32] That those who fought for a de facto king were guaranteed immunity from forfeiture at the hands of his conqueror by parliament in 1489 suggests that Henry VII's attainder of Richard III's adherents had made men reluctant to support him.[33] Here, as in some of the other cases, it was not perhaps fear of death that was decisive, but fear of forfeiture. Not only might the individual die, but the blood of himself and his heirs was corrupted and dishonoured, his property was forfeit, his wife and children impoverished, their future blighted, and nothing could be done for his soul.[34] From 1415 on it was common for those fighting abroad to make wills and to secure licences to resettle their lands, sometimes secured by act of parliament, thus averting wardship for their heirs and making provision for their souls.[35] Self-preservation could indeed be purely personal, although cowardice brought dishonour and to flout loyalties could have serious repercussions. Some certainly gave priority to honour and worship rather than their personal survival. When attainders were reversed, they restored the honour of the victims;[36] some heirs sought reversals even when no lands were involved merely to remove the shame and corruption of blood of their kinsmen and themselves. Self-preservation could also involve the survival of the whole family. By accepting Henry VI's cause to be hopeless in 1461, Lord Rivers saved his family from forfeiture,[37] whereas those who fought hopelessly on exposed their women and children to destitution and molestation.[38] When the redoubtable Lady Hungerford saved the Hungerford estates, notions of justice, lineage, and inheritance overcame physical discomfort, imprisonment, and threats.[39] Yet self-preservation for her and others also meant the salvation of the soul and mitigation of the pains of purgatory. Purgatorial sufferings could be reduced by good works on earth and Margaret was conventional in founding a chantry, which took precedence

[31] E.g. Henry Vernon, M.A. Hicks, *False, Fleeting, Perjur'd Clarence: George Duke of Clarence, 1449-1478* (Gloucester 1980), 183-4.

[32] McFarlane, *England*, 260-1.

[33] For the facts, see R.L. Storey, *The Reign of Henry VII* (London 1968), 579, 583. The interpretation is my own. See also D.A.L. Morgan, 'The King's Affinity in the Polity of Yorkist England', *T[ransactions of the] R[oyal] H[istorical] S[ociety]* 5th ser xxiii (1973), 8.

[34] E.g. the Hungerfords, see Hicks, 'Counting the Cost of War', below, 199.

[35] E.g. *C[alendar of] P[atent] R[olls], 1467-77*, 531, 538, 539; *Statute Rolls*, ii 550-1; W. Dugdale, *History and Antiquities of Warwickshire*, ed W. Thomas (2 vols London 1730), i 232.

[36] E.g. Hicks, 'Edward IV and the Duke of Somerset', below, 162.

[37] J.R. Lander, *Crown and Nobility, 1450-1509* (London 1976), 105-6.

[38] M.A. Hicks, 'The Last Days of Elizabeth Countess of Oxford', below, chapter 16; 'Counting the Cost of War', below, chapter 10; J.T. Rosenthal, 'Other Victims: Peeresses as War Widows, 1450-1500', *History*, lxxii (1987), 213-30.

[39] Hicks, 'Piety and Lineage', below, chapter 9.

over the rights of her heirs that she had tried so hard to preserve.[40] Forty
years before, her father-in-law exploited his position as Lord Treasurer
also to found a chantry.[41] Elaborate and valuable bequests show how
strong were aristocrats' fears for the next world. Self-preservation has
several meanings and was conditioned by ideas of chivalry, honour,
lineage, inheritance, familial affection, salvation and purgatory. These
ideas were interrelated, priorities varied, and we cannot safely equate
contemporary reactions with our own, for none of these ideals is potent
today.

One ideal that did determine political action is exemplified in an exchange
of challenges. On 22 November 1455 William Lord Bonville (d. 1461)
wrote to Thomas Courtenay, Earl of Devon (d. 1458):[42]

> All due salutacions of frendlihode laide aparte. Forasmuche that it is openly
> knowen vnto god and alle the worlde and namely to the kynges highnesse his
> lordis and communes of this his lande that thow by diuers tymes and often
> falsly cowardly and traitorously haste arraied & laide in awaite to myscheue
> and murdre me & my servaunts being the kynges trew liegemen had not be the
> greate & especiall grace & rightwisnesse of god and by colour of the same
> aswele ayenste the lawe of god and of man as that shulde perteigne to thine
> estate in trowthe has made diuers and many assemblees of suche as shulde be
> the kynges trew liege people beyng arrant theves housbrenners & murderers
> be thyne abettement procuryng receyuyng & mayntenaunce. And theruppon
> taken robbid murdered and also beseged assauted & put at Raunsom the
> kynges true liege people by the same entendyng the destruccion of the
> commune wele. Like as I shal my selfe in propre person vpon thi body in that
> quarell fight & make it good. Requiring that vppon suche worship as can be
> thought in the that thou in saluacion not all oonly of the kinges Citee & his
> trewe liege people within the same dwelling but also of alle suche as bene
> faithfully & trewly disposed vnto the and me belonging be to morrow at viij of
> the clokke in the felde & envaunce thi selfe to bide & fighte in thi proper
> personne in opteignyng of suche worship as thou holdist thi self of. Promittyng
> the as I am the kinges trewe liegeman & knighte that I shall in my diffence
> vppon the premisses as for the commune wele of all the kynges trew liege
> people and namely for the dwelleres of this shire ful redy to rencontre the &
> topteyne or dye. Therefore yif god will yif thou be oon tyme of the day
> apperalle and vppon this request & present writyng sende me answer. Leting
> the wete yif thou do not I shal put me in goddes rightfulnesse in this trewe &
> Juste querrell tassayle the & all suche as be of thy fals oppynyon and assent
> ther as I may haue knowlege whersoever that you bee. Wreten at Bisshoppis
> Cliffe.
>   William lord of Bonville

[40] Hicks, 'Chantries, Obits and Hospitals', below, 88-9.
[41] See below, 84-5.
[42] British Library Additional MS 48031 f 185; another, damaged, version is in
Huntington Library Battle Abbey MS 937.

Next day, presumably *after* 8 a.m., the earl took up the challenge:

> All frendly greting stonde for nought. And where as thou in thy writyng falsely pretendest that I by diuers tymes & ofte falsly cowardly & traitorously haue arraied & laide in awaite to mischiue & to murthre the & thi seruauntes ayenst the lawes of god & of man & by diuers & mani assembliesse of suche as shuld be the kinges liege people being as thou rehersest arrant thefes howsbrenners & murderers be abettment procuring resceytting and mayntenaunce taken brenned robbed murdered & also beseged assawted & put at raunsom the kynges trewe liege people and bi the same entending the destruccion of the commune wele. I saye that thou in thi sayng in all such premisses arte fals and vntrew & all othere of thy oppynyon being in thy companye. And that wol I in my propre person as a trewe knight and the kynges trewe liegeman vpon thy fals body proue at tyme & place by me and the appoynted, the kinges highnesse not displeased, in avoiding of sheding of blode of all other the kinges trewe liege people. Wretin vnder my signet at the citie of Excestre.
>
> Thomas Erle of Deuonshire

They fought on 15 December at Clyst, where Bonville and his men were put to flight.[43]

Dr Cherry observed that:

> The 'battle' itself had been heralded some weeks before be a formal declaration of hostilities thinly disguised in the chivalric mode of a challenge to a duel. The opening sentence of these documents neatly parodied the customary form of greeting of contemporary letters.

But evidently he finds the letters superfluous and 'The Struggle for Power in Mid-Fifteenth Century Devonshire' self-explanatory without them.[44] Yet the endemic violence that preceded the 'Fight at Clyst' could have continued. That it did not was because matters came to a head in battle as both principals decided it should. Bonville's letter provoked the battle not just because it was offensive, not just because it condemned the earl by divine and human law, not just because it charged him with acting against the public interest but because it declared him false, treacherous, and cowardly and Bonville to be 'the kynges true liegeman and knyght'. Whatever his previous intentions, the earl could not ignore such a slur on his honour, and promised *immediately* to vindicate himself personally 'as a true knyght and the kynges true liegeman . . . vppon thi fals body.' Each may have hoped to win, but each risked his life, which had been carefully avoided hitherto. The earl won the battle and vindicated his honour, whereas Bonville – a knight of the Garter – was dishonoured by his flight.

---

[43] R.L. Storey, *The End of the House of Lancaster* (2nd edn Gloucester 1986), 171-2.

[44] M. Cherry, 'The Struggle for Power in Mid-Fifteenth Century Devonshire', *Patronage, The Crown and the Provinces in Later Medieval England*, ed R.A. Griffiths (Gloucester 1981), 123.

The 'chivalric mode' was therefore more than Dr Cherry's thin disguise, but it was certainly conventional. The Berkeley-Lisle dispute culminated in a similar exchange of letters in 1469, when Viscount Lisle denounced Lord Berkeley, denied charges of recruiting Welshmen 'to destroy and hurt my one nation and Cuntry', and 'to the proof hereof' required him:

> of knighthood and of manhood to appoint a day to meet me half way, there to try between God and our two hands, all our quarrell and title of right, for to eschew the shedding of Christian menns bloud . . . An answere of this by writing, as ye will abide by, according to the honor and order of knighthood.

The quarrel concerned an inheritance and could not be determined legally in battle, as Berkeley pointed out, though if it were possible he would gladly vindicate his true title against Lisle's false one. Why, then, did Berkeley take up Lisle's challenge and meet him next day in battle at Nibley Green?

> That I trust to God it shall be shewed on thee and thine to thy great shame and disworship . . . And therefore I vouch God to record and all the company of heaven, That this fact and the scheddinge of Christen mens bloud which shall be atwixt us two and our fellowshipps, if any hap to bee, doth grow of thy quaryll, and not of mee, but in my defence, and in eschewing of reproche, and onely through thy malitious and mischevouse pourpose and of thy false Counselle and of thy own simple discretion. And keepe thy day, And the trouth shall be shewed by the Mercy of God.

It was the reproach to his honour that forced him to hazard his life and Lisle's faith that forced him to meet his rival without due preparation and for which Lisle died. Moreover, their dispute was for the title and lands of Lord Berkeley: hence Lisle called his rival 'William called lord Berkeley' and the latter referred disparagingly to Lisle's viscountcy, a title first introduced in 1444, as 'a new found thyng brough out of Strange Contryes'.[45] Berkeley would have lost his name, coat of arms, lineage, and whole identity, hardly a trivial matter. Both could have lived, but their honour took precedence over life itself.

Nor were these four noblemen alone. It was probably to purge the slur on his honour that Richard Duke of York strove to destroy his rival, the Duke of Somerset. What was fought out at first St Albans in 1455 was a personal quarrel: 'And when the seyde duke Edmonde and the lordes were slayne', writes the Yorkist chronicler, 'the batayle was ceased'.[46] So too in

---

[45] J. Smyth, *The Lives of the Berkeleys*, ed J. Maclean (3 vols 1883-9), i 109-11.
[46] M.K. Jones, 'Somerset, York and the Wars of the Roses' *EHR* civ (1989), 285-307; *An English Chronicle of the Reigns of Richard II, Henry IV, Henry V, and Henry VI*, ed J.S. Davies (Camden Soc lxxiv, 1856), 72.

1399 Lord Morley declared the Earl of Salisbury to be 'false and traytour to the king and that shall I prove with my body and proferred his wedde and manhoode on the ground'.[47] Others challenged one another to purge their honour in battle, as the Dukes of Hereford and Norfolk had sought to do the previous year, and risked their lives *unnecessarily* to vindicate their good names. The well-known challenges before tournaments were not the source of the formal conventions of the letters.[48] Trials by battle occasionally occurred,[49] the 1399 challenges were part of the official published account of the usurpation copied into many chronicles, and the Bonville-Courtenay challenges were evidently circulated.[50] The criminal indictments arising from the fight at Clyst do not refer to the letters. How many other recorded murders, assaults, and private battles were also initiated by the formal exchange of challenges?

As their letters indicate, all four lords were self-consciously *conventional* insofar as they were conforming to chivalric convention. The chivalric code set standards of conduct, commending such qualities as prowess, loyalty, franchise and trouth, the direct opposites of the cowardice, falsehood, and treachery with which Bonville had charged Devon. Breach of faith was no light matter. Berkeley taunted Lisle with his false councillors Mulle, who was 'attaynt of falsenes and rasynge of the kings records', and Holt, who had broken an oath, 'sworne on a masse booke', both of whom 'every worshipfull man should refuse to have them in his fellowship'.[51] 'Hold thy peace, Michael,' a former Lord Chancellor was told in 1387, 'it becometh thee right evil to say such words, thou that art damned for thy falsehood both by the lords and by parliament'.[52] All were discredited by their bad faith. It was the promise of security 'on the faith and fealty by which I am bound to God and as I am a gentleman and a faithful knight' that prompted the lawyer Nicholas Radford to place himself in the power of Devon's son. His subsequent murder, in defiance of convention, was a cause célèbre immensely damaging to his murderer.[53] So too was the Duke of Clarence's rapprochement with Edward IV in 1471:

[47] *The Great Chronicle of London*, ed A.H. Thomas and I.D. Thornley (London 1938), 79-80; for what follows, see ibid 77, 81-2; A. Steel, *Richard II* (Cambridge 1941), 245, 247-8.

[48] E.g. C.L. Scofield, *The Life and Reign of Edward IV* (2 vols 1923), i 374.

[49] J.G. Bellamy, *The Law of Treason in England in the Later Middle Ages* (Cambridge 1970), 109-10.

[50] For the 1399 account, see *Great Chronicle*, 51-81. Both (significantly different) versions of the 1455 letters survive in copies, see above n. 42.

[51] Smyth, *Lives*, i 110.

[52] *DNB* under Pole.

[53] G.L. Harriss, *Cardinal Beaufort: A Study of Lancastrian Ascendancy and Decline* (Oxford 1988), 236; Storey, *Lancaster*, 168-9; Cherry, loc cit 123, 136.

and so alle covandes of fydelite . . . were clerly brokene and fosakene of the
seide Duke of Clarence; whiche, in conclusione, was distruccion both to hym
and them; for perjury schall nevere have better ende, witheoute grete grace of
God . . .[54]

Warwick, in contrast, held to his promises and died for them.[55] It is
difficult to believe that the pledges of fidelity in indentures of retainers
were taken any more lightly.

It was not enforcement but good fame that prompted people to keep
faith, for bad faith tarnished honour and reputation alike. A moral rather
than a legal obligation prompted Lady Hungerford to pay off the ransom
of her dead son.[56] Dishonour compelled Sir John Fastolf to exculpate
himself from the charge of cowardice.[57] Parts of the code however were
strictly regulated and enforced. The law of arms comprised
internationally accepted regulations administered by officers of arms and
could be sued before the Parlement of Paris in France or the court of
chivalry in England. Cases handled by the English court included
conflicting claims to ransom, coats of arms – the visible marks of rank,
lineage, and renown – and honourable duties at coronations. Those who
did not fulfil honourable obligations, such as payment of a ransom, might
be made to pay *and* shamed in public, for example by having their arms
reversed or being expelled from noble orders of chivalry.

Loyalty to one's king was an essential chivalric virtue and treason was
dishonourable. In 1418 Henry V executed as an offender against the code
a French knight, traitor not against himself but against the King of
France.[58] In 1323 the Earl of Carlisle was deprived of both earldom and
knighthood, his sword was broken and spurs hacked off, he was drawn,
hanged, beheaded and quartered, his heart and bowels were burned.[59] Sir
Ralph Grey's surrender of Bamburgh Castle to the king's enemies was not
mere treason, but unknightly and a breach of trust:

Sir Rauf Grey, thou hast take the ordir of Knyghthode of the Batthe, and any
soe taking that ordir ought to kepe his faithe the whiche he makes . . . thou hast
drawen the with force of armes unto the Kyng oure most natural soverain
Lorde, the whiche tho wotest wele yave unto the suche trust, and in suche wise
mynystred his grace unto the, that thou haddist his castels in the Northe partie
to kepe; thou hast betraied Sir John Asteley Knyght, and brother of the gartier
. . .

54 *Warkworth's Chronicle*, 15.
55 *Historie of the Arrival of Edward in England*, ed J. Bruce (Camden Soc i, 1836), 12.
56 Hicks, 'Counting the Cost of War', below, chapter 10.
57 He was suspended from the order of the Garter, Keen, *Chivalry*, 175.
58 James, *Society, Politics & Culture*, 319.
59 Bellamy, *Treason*, 52.

He was condemned not just to death and forfeiture, but to have his spurs struck off by a cook, his coat of arms ripped off and reversed, and he was to be 'disgraded of thy worshipp, noblesse, and armes, as of the order of Knyghthode'.[60] Faced by yet more abominable treason in 1470, Edward IV refused requests for safe-conducts, charging the rebels 'upon the feithe and trouthe that ye naturelly owe' to come humbly before him to answer the charges against them and declaring 'that he wolde use and entreate theym as a souveragne lord owethe to use and entreate his subgettes'.[61] Since they were still free and in force, pure pragmatism might have dictated a more conciliatory response.

The chivalric code dictated actions in warfare that otherwise seem irrational. At Bannockburn in 1314 the third best knight in Christendom guided King Edward II to safety and then returned to die fighting, so that his honour should not be besmirched by flight. When the battle of Poitiers was already decided in 1356, an Englishman sought renown in single combat against a knight, whom he taunted with cowardice and was defeated, captured, and ransomed. Sir William Marmion, who had vowed to wear a golden helmet until he had performed some glorious feat of war, sallied alone from Norham Castle against the Scots and was fortunate to survive.[62] Such knight errantry is rarer for the fifteenth century. Perhaps the headlong charges of Somerset at Tewkesbury in 1471 and Richard III at Bosworth fall into this category and there is a case for equating the hopeless resistance of Lancastrians after 1464 and Yorkists after 1487 to such considerations.

Perhaps chivalry was indeed becoming more a matter of forms than an impulse to action, but it still provided standards against which individuals were measured and could still prompt idealistic behaviour not strictly rational in purely material terms. The concept of honour itself has a long history ahead and has been blamed for many problems in sixteenth-century England:

People carried weapons; there was a latent irascibility in the air. Men were prone to brawl and take offence. Silly quarrels escalated into battles in the street. Conflicts were rapidly translated into the language of the sword . . . [The] root of the matter lies in the mentality defined by the concept of honour . . . [and] is characterised above all by a stress on competitive assertiveness; it assumes a state of affairs in which resort to violence is natural and justifiable;

---

[60] *Warkworth's Chronicle*, 38-9.

[61] 'Chronicle of the Rebellion in Lincolnshire 1470', ed J.G. Nichols, *Camden Miscellany*, i (1847), 13-15.

[62] Keen, *Chivalry*, 117; N. Denholm-Young, *The Country Gentry in the Fourteenth Century* (Oxford 1969), 154-5; J. Froissart, *Chroniques*, ed S. Luce, vi (Société de l'histoire de France, Paris 1874), 50-2.

the recurrence of personal and political situations in which conflict cannot be
otherwise than resolved violently.[63]

Honour may have been important in late medieval quarrels too, but far
from being silly or frivolous these commonly had serious origins in
disputed inheritances.[64] Arbitration, which Lisle declined, was an
effective alternative to violence even where blood was shed and the crown
commonly imposed order.[65] It is no accident that there was no effective
monarch at the times of Clyst and Nibley Green and that following the
former both lords were indicted and Devon was imprisoned. There was
little bloodshed and what there was often included that of the principal
protagonists. In the late middle ages the concept of honour was more than
an unthinking propensity to violence. It provided both an additional
motive for political action and a series of conventions channelling its
expression.

'The history of England in the fifteenth century', observed Professor Ross,
'is marked by a vastly increased use of propaganda'. There were songs,
ballads, rhymes, broadsheets, manifestos, sermons, proclamations,
genealogies, newsletters and official chronicles. 'The use of propaganda
was largely a response by governments to the circulation of seditious
rumours.' Absurd though many of these were – for the gullibility and
credulity of late medieval Englishmen knew few bounds – it was
imperative for government to correct wrong impressions. 'Both rumour
and propaganda reflect also a growing awareness . . . of the importance of
influencing popular opinion within the realm.'[66] Why? Firstly, because it
could be influenced; secondly, and equally obviously, because it affected
popular actions. Governments can only have cared about the *practical
effects* of what people thought. Accurate information, as well as
disinformation, had its place. By the fifteenth century, we are told, not just
the nobility and gentry, but the urban artisans and rural yeomen were in
politics and could make up their own minds.[67] *Warkworth's Chronicle*
records avowedly popular responses to many political events – fear,
sorrow, displeasure, hatred, and moral disapproval.[68] Much propaganda
was aimed at the aristocratic or parliamentary élite and/or the literate,

[63] James, *Society, Politics & Culture*, 308-9.

[64] Bellamy, *Bastard Feudalism*, 34-5.

[65] Smyth, *Lives*, i 111. For what follows, see the 'blood money' provided in some awards,
e.g. Storey, *Lancaster*, 155; Powell, *Kingship*, 103 states such settlements 'were
commonplace in the fifteenth century'.

[66] C.D. Ross, 'Rumour, Propaganda and Popular Opinion during the Wars of the
Roses', *Patronage, Crown & Provinces*, 15.

[67] Richmond, 'Fauconberg's Rebellion', 689-92.

[68] *Warkworth's Chronicle*, 4, 5, 8-9, 15.

but much also was aimed at those present in market-places and churchyards, when proclamations were read or sermons preached. Some was tailored to particular audiences.

Since the aim was to influence people, such propaganda reveals what the authors thought would appeal to or frighten the intended audience. If Sir Robert Welles' claim that Edward IV was coming to 'destroie the comons' of Lincolnshire was absurd, it was nevertheless effective in winning him a following calculated to be 30,000 strong.[69] The proclamation of 1462 that made a 'blatant appeal to English nationalism' indicates that such nationalism was potent enough to be worth invoking.[70] If the miracle at Daventry in 1471 was indeed 'a play upon both the religiosity and credulity of the medieval populace, with the added element of emphasising the personal piety of Edward IV',[71] it was recounted because such factors influenced political behaviour. In 1469 favourable political results were expected from accusing the queen's mother of sorcery and from the absurd claim that the king's taxation of the clergy threatened the country with an interdict![72] The king's commitments in 1467-8 to 'live of his own' and to justice certainly excited the popular imagination.[73] When the king made peace at Picquigny in 1475, the conciliar minute named all participants and was exemplified, Lord Hastings kept his French pension secret, and the king remitted uncollected taxes,[74] all self-evidently to dispel principled criticism. Even Richard III's notorious attacks on the illegitimate antecedents of Henry Tudor may be evidence less of his own hypocritical prurience than an appeal to the moral standards of his subjects.[75] Richard was a considerable propagandist in his own right, who rewrote much of his earlier career once he was king and made the most of his English birth.[76] Nothing was more damaging to him, however, than the charge of infanticide, albeit unsubstantiated, which flouted the most fundamental religious beliefs and moral standards.[77]

That such appeals were pointless if misdirected does not prove that they were successful. In 1470, however, the king issued an official account of Warwick and Clarence's rebellion in Lincolnshire, much of which can be substantiated independently and much of which conforms precisely to

[69] Ross, 'Rumour', 19; Nichols, 'Lincolnshire Rebellion', 6, 10.
[70] Ross 'Rumour', 18.
[71] Ibid 24.
[72] Hicks, *Clarence*, 50; *Warkworth's Chronicle*, 49.
[73] *RP* v 572, 622; see below p.
[74] *CPR 1467-77*, 583; C.D. Ross, *Edward IV* (London 1974), 234, 236.
[75] Ross, 'Rumour', 27-28.
[76] C.D. Ross, *Richard III* (London 1981), 90. Richard's propaganda is more fully explored in my *Richard III: The Making of the Myth* (1991).
[77] L. Attreed, 'From *Pearl* Maiden to Tower Princes: Towards a New History of Medieval Childhood', *Journal of Medieval History*, ix (1983), 43-55, esp 53-5.

the proclamation he issued at the time. The image presented and that he *wished to present* was of 'a prince enclyned to shew his mercy and pite to his subgettes, raither then rigure and straitenesse of his lawez', who had pardoned those offending against him, had been betrayed, and yet was willing to forgive again provided they returned unreservedly to his allegiance. Allegiance to the sovereign was fundamental, a duty not a virtue, overrode all other loyalties and could not be compromised. Instead, however, Warwick and Clarence summoned their Yorkshire supporters, 'noo mencion made of us', just as eight years later Clarence was apparently sealing indentures of retainer that did not reserve allegiance to the king. For Warwick's Yorkshire retainers, however, allegiance took precedence over loyalty to him:

> thinkyng by the maner of the saide erle of Warrewike writing sent thidre in his own name oonly, to arreise the people, that theire stirring shuld be ayenst the king, and feryng his speedy comyng into theiz parties with his oost, left theire gadering, and satt still.

Warwick's earlier efforts to recruit in his West Midlands heartland backed by a royal commission of array had failed to raise 'no suche nowmbre of people as thay loked aftre',[78] no doubt for the same reason. Next year, when the deposed Edward IV landed at Ravenspur, Yorkshiremen were unwilling to upset their new-found allegiance to Henry VI or to entertain Edward's dynastic claim to the crown, but they agreed that he should have the duchy of York, 'the whiche was his inherytance of ryght'.[79] In between, when Warwick was reconciled with the Lancastrians, it was doubtless for his retainers' consumption that he claimed more credit than his due for the agreement with the Lancastrians. Later it was these same retainers, whose distinction between their loyalty to Richard III's Neville wife and their allegiance to him as king forced him to renounce his proposed marriage to Elizabeth of York.[80] On this evidence, provincial notables at least were capable not only of acting on principle, but of making fine distinctions between the principles that activated them.

Much of the propaganda takes the form of manifestos couched in the language of constitutional idealism that criticised existing regimes and proposed remedies in the interests of good government. Political historians of the forty years from 1447 have generally not explained events by constitutional idealism. As Dr Richmond says:

---

[78] Nichols, 'Lincolnshire Rebellion', 1, 11-13; *Warkworth's Chronicle*, 54.

[79] *Warkworth's Chronicle*, 13-14; *The Arrivall*, 3-6.

[80] Hicks, *Clarence*, 80-1; *Crowland Chronicle Continuations, 1459-86*, ed N. Pronay and J. Cox (1986), 176.

It is not easy to know now whether the demand for good government in the second half of the fifteenth century was a real issue to all or some politicians or merely part and parcel of the political jargon of the age. The manifesto put out by Warwick and Clarence in July 1469 might consist of time-honoured catch phrases, the usual recriminations and denunciations of opposition, but who can say that they did not express genuinely-held beliefs or touch such beliefs in others?

If Richmond is correct, they certainly touched a responsive chord in the people of Kent in 1470.[81] Two learned academics also thought such ideals had a wide appeal. Henry VI's second accession in 1470, so pleasing to 'the more parte of peple' as well as his partisans, contrasted sharply with the situation in 1461, when 'alle Englonde for the more partye hatyd hym, and were full gladde to haue a chounge', caused Warkworth to reflect on the politics of the previous twenty years. King Henry's death next year prompted John Veysy to chronicle events since his coronation in Paris in 1431. Veysy recalled a glorious prosperity up until King Henry was:

> gouerned & reuled by diuers of his counsele suche as were not be comen of the blood Roiall but they that were broughte up of noughte throughe whos sinister counselle envye and prepensed malice not aloonly caused the subuercion & falle most dolorouse of the said king Henry from his mooste Roiall and excellent dignite and astate but also caused execrabley many & diuers grete mischefes lossis insurreccions & ciuile battaylis to the extreme pouite and the utmoste destruccion & depoulacion of subgiettes and people.

The first crime attributed to these 'insaciable coueitous persones and diabolic counseillours' was the murder in 1447 of the king's uncle Humphrey, Duke of Gloucester; the surrender of Anjou and Maine, Jack Cade's rebellion, and a whole series of murders and battles were laid at their door. Warkworth too explains Henry's unpopularity in these ways:

> the good Duke of Gloucester was put to dethe, and Jhon Holonde, Duke of Excetre, poysond, and that the Duke of Suffolke, the Lorde Say, Danyelle Trevyliane, and other myscheves peple that were aboute the Kynge, were so covetouse towarde them selff, and dyde no force of the Kynges honour, ne of his wele, ne of the comone wele of the londe, where Kynge Herry trusted to them that thei schuld do, and labour in tyme of innocence evere for the commone wele, whiche thei dyde contrary to his wille; and also Fraunce, Normandy, Gascogne, and Guyane was lost in his tyme. And these were the causes, withe other, that made the peple to gruge ageyns hym, and alle bycause of his fals lordes, and nevere of hym; and the comon peple seyde, yf thei myghte have another Kynge, he schulde gett alle ageyne and amende all manere of thynges that was amysse, and brynge the reame of Englond in grete prosperite and reste.

[81] Richmond, 'Fauconberg's Rebellion', 673, 692.

It is a great credit to Yorkist propaganda that two chroniclers no longer
Yorkists should accept that Gloucester was murdered and still attribute
foreign and domestic disasters of the late 1440s and 1450s to the king's
favourites. Both chroniclers – and, on Warkworth's testimony, the
common people too – could distinguish between the innocent king and his
evil councillors, as indeed Jack Cade's rebels did. As Yorkist propaganda
dictated, Veysy disliked them as upstarts and both men criticised their
exploitation of patronage at the public cost. Peace and prosperity, the
king's honour and the common weal, were what was expected of
government. But the hopes of 1461 'came not', Warkworth recording
mounting disillusion with the 1460s and Veysy listing one misfortune after
another. Battle succeeded battle, bringing 'moche troble and grete losse of
goodes amonge the commone peple', who were repeatedly taxed and
arrayed for military service away from home at their own expense. Trade
suffered and English goods were not so respected either at home or
abroad.[82]

How well Warwick and Clarence's manifestos of 1469-70 were
designed to appeal to these prejudices and aspirations! Like Veysy and
Warkworth, their 1469 manifesto attributed the 'grete inconveniencis and
mischeves' of Henry VI's reign to his exclusion from the council of 'the
gret lordis' of the blood royal and to his reliance instead on lesser men who
cared not for 'the wele of the seid princes, ne to the comonwele of this lord,
but only to theire singular lucour and enrichyng of themself and theire
bloode'. Hence the impoverishment of the crown, the taxation of the
people, and the breakdown of law and order, evils that were then located
in Edward IV's England, thanks to such new upstart favourites as the
earls Rivers, Pembroke and Devon, appealing to 'the wele and surete of
the Kyng oure sovereigne lord, And the common-wele of this lond', which
all desired, the 'treue and feythefulle subjettes and commons of this lond'
petitioned humbly for the removal of Edward's evil councillors; for the
assignment of revenues to meet his ordinary peacetime expenses, 'So that
he nor noon of his heires, hereafter, of necessite, nede to charge and ley
uppon his true Commons and subjettes suche gret imposicions', as he
himself had promised at the last parliament; for patronage to be
restrained, always a popular request; for customs to be applied to the
defence of the seas; and for the laws to be enforced. The prayers of the
'trewe commons' to the 'trew lords spirituelle and temporelle' was
answered by Warwick, Clarence, and Archbishop Neville, who found
them 'reasonabyll and profitable for the honoure and profite of oure seid
sovereyn Lord and the commune welle of all this his realme' – again, the
right note is struck – and summoned the Kentishmen to Canterbury

[82] *Warkworth's Chronicle*, 11-12; BL Add MS 48031 f 120.

'defensabyly arrayede' next Sunday.[83] A Kentish force was indeed raised. There followed victory at Edgecote, the execution of the three upstart earls, Edward IV's imprisonment, and the rule of Warwick, Clarence, and the archbishop in his name. Their propaganda worked.

Whether or not the propagandists were sincere or believed their own propaganda, it is abundantly clear even from these snapshots that the ideals they propagated could indeed impel recipients into political action. Many ideals, no doubt, are mundane, but others are sophisticated: the commonwealth ideal and the obligation of allegiance rested on an elaborate structure of theory and religious sanctions. Besides such overtly political ideals, politics was shaped by a world picture fundamentally different from our own that gave alternative meanings to material concepts familiar to ourselves. There were also many ideals that impinged on politics that were not strictly political. We should not suppose, however, that these are a *substitute* for political principles in our modern sense, for these existed too: it was differences on foreign policy, for example, that set Humphrey Duke of Gloucester against Cardinal Beaufort and the Suffolk faction in the 1440s and Warwick against the Wydevilles in the 1460s. Patronage versus solvency was a fundamental issue under Henry IV and Henry VI; and patronage versus reconciliation an explosive issue in the 1460s.[84] There were many ideals impinging on politics, which sometimes conflicted with one another or with more material motives. Conflict and tension, however, were not essential: often God's will and self-interest must have coincided. It may well be that more research will reveal a hierarchy of ideals, just as allegiance commonly prevailed over loyalty to a lord and salvation over inheritance. What can no longer be doubted, however, is that there was idealism in late medieval English politics and that late medieval historians must find a place for it in their interpretations. Literary ideals and conventions were not irrelevant to the real world.

---

[83] *Warkworth's Chronicle*, 46-51.

[84] R.A. Griffiths, *Reign of King Henry VI 1422-61* (1981), ch 17; *Crowland Continuations*, 115; Lander, *Crown and Nobility*, 133-6; Hicks, 'Edward IV and Somerset', below, 150-1, 155-7; B.P. Wolffe, 'Acts of Resumption in Lancastrian Parliaments, 1399-1456', *Historical Studies of the English Parliament*, ed E.B. Fryde and E. Miller (Cambridge 1970), 61-91.

3

Attainder, Resumption and Coercion, 1461-1529

Late medieval and early modern England was a mixed monarchy, in which power was shared.[1] English kings could not rule arbitrarily, but had to co-operate with their greater subjects and with Parliament when making war, when levying taxes, and even for the everyday government of the localities. The primacy of an English monarch derived less from his overriding sovereignty than from his role as suzerain, as pinnacle of both an increasingly obsolete feudal system and an archaic jumble of overlapping jurisdictions. Within this framework the initiative of kings and subjects ebbed and flowed, but the essentially miscellaneous basis of royal power remained. In 1509, during that upswing of kingly fortunes that threatened to become a Tudor despotism, Henry VII was accused of abuse of powers arising from the livery of lands and temporalities, disputed inheritances, the marriage and ravishing of wards and widows, negligence and corruption in office, breach of the peace, and lawsuits in various courts. The 84 heads demonstrate the potential value to a determined monarch of 'light matters onely upon surmyse', but do not disguise their traditional and occasional nature, dependent on opportunity, dependent on the chance to exploit a wardship or punish an offence, and dependent ultimately upon the resolution to carry them through.[2] Against a nobleman of full age, guilty of no offence but nevertheless unco-operative or even obstructive, there was no way of enforcing compliance. Hence the importance of patronage, a lure attractive to all, for no magnate could dispense wholly with royal favour, if he hoped to act as 'good lord' in his own locality.[3]

Failing the big stick, the Crown had many carrots as inducements for service and obedience. There was something on offer for everyone, ranging from grants of land in perpetuity to annuities, leases, and such windfalls as wardships and the custody of idiots. Candidates for such enticing titbits began by petitioning the King: indeed, all royal grants probably originated in supplications, and the royal clerks were constantly recasting such bills

[1] G.L. Harriss, 'Medieval Doctrines in the Debates on Supply 1610–29', *Faction and Parliament: Essays on Early Stuart History*, ed. K. Sharpe (Oxford, 1978), pp. 73–4.
[2] C.J. Harrison, 'The Petition of Edmund Dudley', *E.H.R.*, LXXXVII (1972), 87–90. See also P. Williams, *The Tudor Regime* (Oxford, 1979), p. 397.
[3] E.g. M.E. James, *A Tudor Magnate and the Tudor State: Henry, Fifth Earl of Northumberland* (Borthwick Institute of Historical Research, University of York, Borthwick Papers, No. 30, 1966).

into the correct epistolary form.[4] Decisions were made by the reigning
monarch, who ideally weighed the grant against the suitor and aimed at a
fair but sparing distribution of largesse. The ideal was seldom attained
because of the sheer volume of royal bounty and the numbers of competing
suitors able successfully to penetrate those departments of the Household
that interposed like a costly filter between the King and the world outside.
If James I's subjects were 'most importune and unmannerly of asking', and
Henry VI was plagued by 'importunite of suytours', the young Henry VIII
– so it was alleged – found it easier to sign papers than read them.[5] Even
Henry VII found 16 bills a day too many for each to receive the attention it
truly deserved. To monitor royal patronage properly was really beyond the
capacity of one man, but no king would delegate more than peripheral areas
to others.[6] To do so was to shrug off the panoply with the burden of
kingship and leave all to the unrestrained interplay of faction.

The weakest kings could not parry suitors, and extravagantly alienated
what they themselves required. Henry VI was already financially and
politically bankrupt, yet he became ever more dependent on patronage and
thus found it impossible to escape a descending spiral of lost income,
prestige and power. It was this glaring insolvency that prompted Fortescue
to advocate the resumption of royal grants, so that enough could be
appropriated to the King's use and the remainder employed as required.
Ideally patronage would be confined to such offices and other favours
which could be awarded without disinheriting the Crown.[7] Such a programme was vigorously opposed by Henry VI, who fully appreciated that
the cancellation of his letters patent undermined his good lordship and with
it the quality of service that he might expect. In time, however, royal
priorities changed, greater emphasis was placed on solvency *vis-à-vis*
patronage, and eventually Henry VII approached Fortescue's ideal. By then
fears of self-seeking courtiers exploiting royal generosity had given way to
Dudley's alarm at 'covetous counsell' urging kings to amass treasure. A
king's true profit, as Henry VIII might have agreed, 'dependith in the grace
of god which is won by marcie and liberalytie'.[8]

As early as 1449, when it was employed to divest unpopular courtiers of
their ill-gotten gains, resumption was seen to possess political as well as
financial potential. It was, however, only gradually after the accession in
1461 of Edward IV, the first king wholeheartedly to embrace resumption,

[4] J.A. Tuck, 'Richard II's System of Patronage', *The Reign of Richard II: Essays in Honour of May McKisack*, eds. F.R.H. Du Boulay and Caroline M. Barron (1971), pp. 4–19; *British Library Harleian Manuscript 433*, eds. Rosemary Horrox and P.W. Hammond (Richard III Soc., 2 vols., Upminster, 1979–80), I, pp. xiv–xv; *Letters and Accounts of William Brereton of Malpas*, ed. E.W. Ives (Lancashire and Cheshire Record Soc., CXIV, 1976), pp. 23–4.
[5] Harriss, 'Medieval Doctrines', p. 85; Sir John Fortescue, *The Governance of England . . .*, ed. C. Plummer (1885), p. 144; *Letters and Papers . . . Henry VIII*, II (1), pp. 71–2. For the next sentence see W.C. Richardson, *Tudor Chamber Administration* (Baton Rouge, 1952), p. 12; *Rotuli Parliamentorum*, VI, 403.
[6] As Fortescue evidently perceived: *Governance*, p. 143 *et seq.*
[7] *Ibid.*, pp. 137, 142–3, 151. For the next sentence see R.A. Griffiths, *The Reign of King Henry VI: The Exercise of Royal Authority 1422–1461* (1981), pp. 319, 388.
[8] E. Dudley, *The Tree of Commonwealth . . .*, ed. D.M. Brodie (Cambridge, 1948), p. 28.

that its full implications were recognized. It was Edward too who extravagantly dispersed the vast estates forfeited by the Lancastrians, thus rendering them eligible for resumption and greatly extending the scope of such acts. Separately and in combination attainder and resumption made frequent revisions of patronage both practicable and relatively painless. It is the contention of this paper that these two weapons facilitated the growth of coercion by the Crown and contributed to a shift in political initiative in the King's favour in the 70 years before the assembly of the Reformation Parliament.

Since the themes discussed span the whole period, they are here treated thematically rather than chronologically. A year by year, king by king approach, involving exhaustive analysis of each of the six reigns in question, is not at present possible and must await further research. A purely chronological approach would in any case obscure both the elements of unity and of change in the period under discussion, and would in particular reinforce the traditional but often artificial barrier of 1485. This paper will explore in turn attainder, resumption and the interaction of the two, and finally examine the defensive apprehensiveness of the potential victims.

2

What was different about the forfeitures of the Wars of the Roses was their frequency, their relative permanence and their completeness, since they affected chattels and lands held not only in fee simple but also in trust and tail. Splendid analyses of parliamentary attainder by Professors Lander and Lehmberg have supplied concrete answers to most of the questions that one would wish to ask.[9] Both authors approached their subject from the angle of their victims and charted their success in securing restoration. Edward IV revoked no less than 42 of his 140 attainders, and Henry VII 46 of his 138; but the ultimate proportion was much higher constituting 64 per cent of all those attainted between 1453 and 1504, and no less than 84 per cent of those who belonged to the nobility. For long periods the tide apparently ran strongly in favour of restoration: 36 sentences were reversed during Edward's second reign, when there were only 13 new ones; and in 1509–29 three new forfeitures were easily outweighed by 15 reversals. Moreover, these figures may be underestimates, as some acts and pardons may be lost.[10] Together, Lander and Lehmberg have proved that most attainders were annulled, but what neither investigated was the implications for recipients of royal patronage and the consequent scope for coercion by the monarch.

What we are concerned with here is not the total number of those attainted,

[9] J.R. Lander, *Crown and Nobility 1450–1509* (1976), pp. 127–58, 307–8; S.E. Lehmberg, 'Parliamentary Attainder in the Reign of Henry VIII', *Historical Journal*, XVIII (1975), 675–702. These sources are the basis of this paragraph, which is restricted to parliamentary attainder, and employs Professor Lander's figures wherever possible.

[10] For acts see R.A. Griffiths, 'The Hazards of Civil War: The Mountford Family in the Wars of the Roses', *Midland History*, V (1979–80), 8–9, 17–19; for pardons see Lander, *Crown and Nobility*, pp. 131–2.

nor even their goods and chattels, but only those holding landed estates. These are most easily identified for the reign of Edward IV, when they represent only 63 per cent of those attainted.[11] Most lands were confiscated in 1461, when they fuelled a display of royal munificence that cast the petty extravagances of Henry VI in the shade. Edward IV was, after all, an impetuous young usurper, with a host of expectant supporters to reward. So far did alienation progress that in 1464 he had to dip deeply into the Crown lands and duchy of Lancaster to endow his queen and next brother. By 1463 sufficient had been granted away to patronize 96 recipients (that is nine peers, 77 gentry and ten others). Most are readily recognizable as members of the King's family, his immediate entourage, and the faction that made him king. Thus the peers included the Earl of Warwick, the Chamberlain and Controller of the Household, and four barons – Ferrers, Herbert, Ogle and Wenlock – who had fought on his side in 1461. Hardly an attainder had been annulled by 1463, but reversals became common thereafter. At least during the 1460s new attainders outweighed restorations, so that the number of recipients swelled to 133 in 1470, before falling somewhat to 124 in 1472, 93 in 1478 and 94 in 1483. By Edward's death less land was spread more widely, with significantly more peers and fewer gentry among the beneficiaries and a smaller average holding allocated to each.[12] This development mirrors the broadening support of the new dynasty from the narrow faction of 1461 to include the Wydevilles by the late 1460s and former Lancastrians after the Readeption. In the process more of the political nation were exposed to loss from the restoration of forfeitures and hence to coercion by the Crown.

TABLE 1: FORFEITURE OF LAND UNDER EDWARD IV

| | Parliaments | | | |
	1461	1465	1475	1478
Number attainted	114	8	13	1
Number attainted with land	65	7	11	1
Reversals of landholders	59	5	13	
Landholders unrestored	6	3		1

This table concerns parliamentary attainders and excludes provisional attainders. It is based on *Rot. Parl.* V–VII; printed Chancery rolls; and Chancery (C.140) and Exchequer (E.149, 152, 153) inquisitions post mortem.

TABLE 2: RECIPIENTS OF FORFEITURES UNDER EDWARD IV

	29 Apr. 1463	3 Jun. 1467	15 Oct. 1470	6 Oct. 1472	15 Jan. 1478	17 Jan. 1483
Queens			1	1	1	1
Dukes	2	2	2	2	2	1

[11] See Table 1.
[12] See Table 2.

Marquesses			1			1
Earls	1	2	4	4	3	3
Viscounts						
Barons	6	7	12	11	9	9
All peers	9	11	20	18	15	15
Knights	13	20	21	20	18	16
Other gentry	64	81	71	68	49	50
Others	10	15	21	18	11	13
Total	96	127	133	124	93	94

This table is based on Table 1 and sources there cited. The successive dates are for the opening of Parliaments and the beginning of the Readeption of Henry VI.

Grants of forfeitures were an alluring element in Edward's patronage, since such alienations could be permanently added to family estates for the benefit of generations yet to come. The size of the grants leaves little question of their importance to recipients. How can one dispute the value to Warwick the Kingmaker of those lands in Craven and the West March, late of his Percy and Clifford rivals, which enabled him to sustain the Lieutenancy of the North sought – but never achieved – by his Neville forbears?[13] Can one exaggerate the significance to the Duke of Clarence of those forfeitures that supplied half his income, still less those grants made to Kent, Northumberland, Pembroke and Devon to support their new comital dignities? William Neville, Earl of Kent received 58 manors in a single patent, his nephew the Earl of Northumberland was awarded £700–worth of Percy lands; and of the 29 manors held by the first Lord Mountjoy at his death, nine were forfeitures.[14] The £666-worth of lands given by Richard III to Sir Richard Ratcliffe is no less striking. The value of such grants to lesser men emerges in the willingness with which Richard's northern gentry took on property and attendant responsibilities far from home, no less than in the warm memories of him that lingered on in the Tudor North.[15] In proportion to the wealth and size of their own estates the grants made to those of lower rank were as important, if not more so, to the recipients than the awards bestowed upon the nobility. What weight did Sir Thomas Montgomery attach to his four Whittingham manors in Buckinghamshire, or the cadet William Hugford to his Northamptonshire manor of Braunston, or even Richard Jones, a humble yeoman trayer of the

---

[13] *Calendar of Patent Rolls*, 1461–7, pp. 186, 189; E.315/49/157. For what follows see T.B. Pugh, 'The Magnates, Knights and Gentry', *Fifteenth-Century England*, eds. S.B. Chrimes, C.D. Ross and R.A. Griffiths (Manchester, 1972), pp. 91–3, 116–17; M.A. Hicks, *False, Fleeting, Perjur'd Clarence* (Gloucester, 1980), p. 180.

[14] *Cal. Pat. Rolls*, 1461–7, p. 225; 1467–77, pp. 24–5, 27; J.M.W. Bean, *The Estates of the Percy Family 1416–1537* (Oxford, 1958), pp. 80, 89–90; *Calendarium Inquisitionum Post Mortem Sive Escaetarum* (4 vols., 1806–28), IV, 367.

[15] J.H. Ramsay, *Lancaster and York* (2 vols., Oxford, 1892), II, 534; A.J. Pollard, 'The Tyranny of Richard III', *Journal of Medieval History*, III (1977), 147–65; idem, 'North, South and Richard III', *The Ricardian*, LXXIV (1981), 387–9.

cellar, to that tenement of Groves in South Ockendon (Essex) that brought him £4 a year?[16] The attractiveness to patentees is illustrated by efforts which they subsequently made to convert life-estates into perpetuities, and render lands heritable in the female line by those without sons; in the ceaseless competition for concealments and reversions, and in the attempt by the King's own brother-in-law to realize a reversion without awaiting the decease of the incumbent dowager.[17] Few seem to have alienated their forfeitures in mortmain or for cash, choosing in preference to transmit them to their heirs. Such was the course pursued by Lord Hastings, whose massive Roos, Butler and Beaumont holdings had transformed his modest inheritance. Edward's distribution of forfeitures thus created a vast vested interest in his regime, a lesson taken to heart by his brother Richard, as he bound his supporters more permanently to himself by appealing ever more cynically to their sense of greed.

The hundred or so Yorkist aristocrats imperilled by reversals of attainders predictably clung to what they had. Knowing that most forfeitures were repealed, it is easy to argue that they were mistaken and should have come to terms with the victims, but this was not necessarily apparent at the time. Progress towards restoration was neither continuous nor without setbacks. Reversals mounted less from an irresistible long-term trend than from the changed political circumstances of two dynastic revolutions. Probably no more than seven reversals (six lasting) during the 1460s restored landed property,[18] and even during Edward's second reign 30 of the 36 reversals had occurred by 1475. This was not the start but the end of a trend, as hitherto irreconcilable Lancastrians submitted. Most were gentry, and the majority of the losers were also of modest estate, although inevitably the great lost something.[19] It was no doubt the influence of the royal Dukes of Gloucester and Clarence, their sister of Exeter, and the Lords Essex, Hastings and Mountjoy, that prevented the recovery of the Hollands, Courtenays, Cliffords, Rooses and Beaumonts, and confined the Earl of Ormond to his Irish holdings. That only six attainders were reversed in Edward's last two Parliaments made it seem less, not more, likely that patentees would be dispossessed of grants of 20 years standing. The wholesale reversals after Bosworth were eased by the absence of Gloucester and Clarence, both attainted; of Essex, Hastings and Mountjoy, all minors; and by the confusion generated by Richard's proscription of so

[16] *Cal. Pat. Rolls*, 1461–7, pp. 121–2, 367–8, 520; D.L.37/36/10.
[17] M.A. Hicks, 'The Changing Role of the Wydevilles in Yorkist Politics to 1483', *Patronage, Pedigree and Power in Late Medieval England*, ed. C.D. Ross (1979), below, ch. 11, 221. For what follows see *Testamenta Vetusta . . .* , ed. N.H. Nicolas (2 vols., 1826), I, 372–4; Horrox and Hammond, *B.L. Harl. MS. 433*, II, 4–5.
[18] Only one magnate estate was involved and at least two losers were bought out: Lander, *Crown and Nobility*, pp. 134–6, 148–50; *Rot. Parl.*, V, 548, 616–18; VI, 230–1; *Cal. Pat. Rolls*, 1461–7, p. 267. For grants of forfeitures see *ibid., passim*. Twelve patentees lost property other than Beaufort lands.
[19] E.g. the Duke of Clarence lost his Tailbois lands: Hicks, *Clarence*, Appendix II. For what follows see Lander, *Crown and Nobility*, pp. 138–41; S.C.8/29/1432. Clifford was resident in England from 1472 until the reversal of his attainder in 1485: Lander, *Crown and Nobility*, p. 141.

many Yorkist patentees and his redistribution of their property. When Richard's victims were restored in 1485, they were understandably glad to recover their inheritances and were ill-prepared to thwart the similar claims of their new-found Lancastrian companions-in-arms. This first Tudor Parliament alone restored 38 landholders attainted under Edward IV and at most seven such sentences ultimately remained in force.[20]

Henry VII's attainders were as numerous as those of Edward IV, but they were less lucrative and a smaller proportion of forfeited property was alienated, more being kept in hand. Certainly the number and size of grants were reduced – there were no parallels to the huge alienations of the Yorkist kings – although Lord Delawarr and Sir William Willoughby, Sir David Owen and Sir Edward Poynings were individuals with solid grounds for satisfaction.[21] Nevertheless, forfeited property remained a major field of patronage and the only one where estates were likely to be obtained in perpetuity. In 1509, however, parsimony gave way to liberality, accumulated forfeitures were dispersed, and new ones were dissipated in a flood of grants, until in 1515 Henry VIII had little left to give.

Although Henry VIII was lavish in reversing attainders, thereby depleting his revenues by £2,535 by 1515,[22] yet only 39 per cent – 54 out of 141 – of early Tudor forfeitures were ever repealed. This much reduced proportion owed most perhaps to the unusual obscurity of the victims. No more dynastic revolutions intervened to save such irreconcilables as the De La Poles. A third factor was certainly the increasing rigour of Henry Tudor himself: having revoked 20 attainders from his first Parliament by 1495, 12 apparently without conditions,[23] from 1504 he withdrew such matters from the public of Parliament into private, where he could more easily drive hard bargains. Some, indeed, proved too tough to stomach, which was all to the good for his patentees, who also benefited from his reluctance to permit their eviction. His patronage was carefully tailored to the recipient, so he too had a vested interest in permanence.[24] The longer the time since the original attainder, the more alienated land was excluded from any reversal, until eventually it became debatable whether restoration was worth seeking. When Sir Robert Chamberlain's 1492 attainder was annulled in 1531, no land changed hands,[25] and only one manor was recovered in 1534 on repeal of the 1495 sentence against Sir Simon Mountford. No wonder that only one attainder was annulled under the 1523 act entitling Henry VIII to revoke attainders by letters patent.

Barring changes of dynasty, the initiative rested with those in possession,

---

[20] Based on Table 1; *Rot. Parl.*, VI, *passim*; 'Rotuli Parliamentorum' [Vol. VII], *L.J.*, I [hereafter *Rot. Parl.*, VII], pp. i–ccl.
[21] *Cal. Pat. Rolls*, 1485–94, pp. 127–8, 250, 275.
[22] *L.P. Hen. VIII*, II (1), p. 369.
[23] Lander, *Crown and Nobility*, p. 142; *Rot. Parl.*, VI, *passim*. For what follows see *Rot. Parl.*, VI, 526. He could henceforth offer more than mere future reversal: see *Cal. Pat. Rolls*, 1494–1509, pp. 238–9.
[24] As he commanded his son: *L.P. Hen. VIII*, I (1), pp. 1–3. See also *Rot. Parl.*, VI, 339.
[25] Lander, *Crown and Nobility*, p. 308. For what follows see *ibid.*, p. 144, n.; *L.P. Hen. VIII*, VII, 174–5; Victoria County History, *Warwickshire*, IV, 53.

but they could not afford to be complacent. Attainders did not cover the rights of dowagers, jointures of wives, estates of younger children, or inheritances descending *via* other routes, so powerful victims remained a constant threat. A flood of one-time rebels quickly made their submissions, secured pardons and began scheming for recovery of their lands. Those with influential allies at court fared best, and unscrupulous royal favourites, like the first Herbert Earl of Pembroke, soon realized that there was more advantage in reversing attainders than in competition on an otherwise congested patronage market.[26]

Attainders were generally repealed without reservations, to the total loss of grantees, up to 1485 and to some extent afterwards. In 1506, when Thomas Polgreve's sentence was reversed by letter patent, the event was recorded laconically in the King's account book: 'Item delivered for the restitution of Thomas Polgreve is landes latelie geven to Sr John Pecche xl li'.[27] Similar entries record the dispossession of the second Earl of Essex and Matthew Baker. Given that restoration could not be averted, the next best thing for patentees was to secure their exemption from the act of reversal, but even so the limitations of such an alternative emerges from the two Yorkist examples. A clause saving Sir James Blount's grant of Apedale (Chester) in the act reversing the attainder of Sir John Delves obviously resulted from prior agreement, yet once the act was passed Blount needed all his influence at court to avoid being ousted.[28] When Thomas Ormond's attainder was reversed in 1472, the property of his brother of Wiltshire was specifically excluded; yet one patentee, the Earl of Essex,

> consideryng that it is thought by the Councell of the kyng oure soueraigne lorde and the Councell of the same Erle lerned in the lawe that the said Atteynder by Right and lawe of this lande in no wise may ne owe extende vnto the said Thomas Ormond Squier ne to [the] forfaiture of his lyuelode possessionns or Enheritaunces . . .

found his position untenable and surrendered his rights to Ormond.[29] While his action appears somewhat precipitate in retrospect, it reminds us that provisos of exemption could confer only limited rights of ownership. Once an heir was restored in blood, the value of possession was much reduced for any grantee, since he could not convey an estate free of encumbrances: any purchaser would be foolish to accept the land even at a discount without a release from the former holder as security against litigation. The second Berkeley reversal of 1515 safeguarded Lord Dudley's tenure of Northfield and Weoley (Worcestershire), yet he still had a separate proviso appended to the act.[30] He was thus exempted from the effects of the act; but could

[26] E.g. Hicks, *Clarence*, pp. 38–9.
[27] B.L., Lansdowne MS. 127, f.34v. For the next sentence see *ibid.*; E.36/214, p. 434. None of these grants appear on the patent roll.
[28] *Rot. Parl.*, VI, 218; *Cal. Pat. Rolls*, 1467–77, p. 536; *Calendar of Close Rolls*, 1476–85, pp. 364–5, 384–5, 421–2, 431–2; Horrox and Hammond, *B.L. Harl. MS. 433*, II, 40. The manor was eventually recovered by the Delves family.
[29] *Rot. Parl.*, VI, 26; S.C.8/29/1432; C.146/7039.
[30] House of Lords R.O., original act, 3 Hen. VIII, no. 38.

otherwise have sold out only to the Berkeley family. Thus an act of reversal qualified by provisos created an equity of redemption, which did not grow stale but could be exerted at any time.

This uncertainty emerges also in other ways, for example in the frequent preference among patentees for compromise with the former traitor. Some, like Sir John Howard, sold up for the highest attainable price; others, like Sir Reginald Bray in 1495, promoted restoration in return for a good title to those lands still held of royal grant.[31] The rights of proscribed landowners were always marketable commodities, notably as suitable security for loans to buy back their estates. After reversal they were placed in a still more favourable position, since their reversionary interest in any outstanding royal grants made it virtually impossible for the patentees to sell out to anybody else. This explains how Roger Wake, whose 1487 reversal was qualified by seven provisos, could nevertheless have recovered almost everything by his death in 1503, when he left instructions for the recovery of a final quarter-manor and for the foundation of a chantry.[32] Such men could drive hard bargains with the occupants of their lands, especially when backed by the sovereign: Lord Delawarr and John Winslow had little choice but to compromise in 1495 'at the request of the said lord king', even though they received only three years' purchase price in compensation,[33] which was much less than the going market rate. Even so, such payments mounted up: it may have been sensible economy, rather than inability to agree, that delayed the recovery of some forfeitures until the deaths of childless patentees like Sir James Blount (*d.* 1493), Viscount Welles (*d.* 1499), Sir John Risley (*d.* 1512) and Sir Edward Poynings (*d.* 1521).

Much property was recovered long after the original act of attainder or even sometimes its reversal, and in consequence patentees were alive to their rather precarious position. The act of 1504, authorizing Henry VII to reverse attainders by letters patent, further undermined the title of patentees, particularly those holding lands formerly owned by the nine individuals specifically named in the act: nor was this uncertainty dispelled by Henry's failure to compound with six of those previously attainted.[34] Contrary to the interpretation of Professor Lander, a similar act of 1523 can likewise be seen as evidence of alarm and insecurity in the ranks of patentees. Whereas the professor interprets the provisos to this act as evidence of the patentees' success in retaining forfeitures long after the relevant attainders, the fact that six of these men sought confirmation of

[31] Lander, *Crown and Nobility*, p. 149; *Cal. Close Rolls*, 1485–1500, p. 270; V.C.H., *Bedfordshire*, III, 371, 391.

[32] *Rot. Parl.*, VI, 393–4; *Calendar of Inquisitions Post Mortem . . . Henry VII*, II, 543–6; J. Bridges, *History and Antiquities of the County of Northampton* (2 vols., Northampton, 1791), I, 350, 352; V.C.H., *Northamptonshire*, IV, 225; *Buckinghamshire*, IV, 333.

[33] R. Virgoe, 'The Recovery of the Howards in East Anglia 1485–1529', *Wealth and Power in Tudor England: Essays Presented to S.T. Bindoff*, eds. E.W. Ives, R.J. Knecht and J.J. Scarisbrick (1978), esp. pp. 12–14; *Cal. Close Rolls*, 1485–1500, pp. 243, 276; E.159/274, *commissiones*, Easter, 13 Hen. VII. In 1468 Sir Edward Grey was awarded only six years' purchase for Loxton (Somerset): Northamptonshire R.O., Stopford-Sackville MS. 6113 (transcript kindly supplied by Dr Carole Rawcliffe).

[34] *Rot. Parl.*, VI, 526. Only the Baynton, Tyrell and Ratcliffe attainders were thus reversed.

titles which dated back to attainders of the 1480s and requested not only provisos against the claims of families subsequently restored but also against those of Bodrugan, Charlton, Lovell and De La Pole, who never actually recovered their lands, is surely a sign of serious disquiet on the part of certain, if not all, patentees. This impression is further reinforced when one considers that the act affected only lands still in royal hands, not those granted out to others, and clearly excluded the De La Poles from restoration.[35] This apprehension was more than justified, as no less than 15 attainders were reversed between 1509 and 1529, and *all* the lands alienated between 1488 and 1495 were restored by 1523.[36] One can hardly doubt the effectiveness of this form of political control even at such a late date, when one finds that four earls, five barons and seven gentry thought it worth being exempted from the 1523 act, and that a marquess, four earls, five barons, 14 knights and 13 other gentry secured provisos at the same Parliament to the attainder – not even the reversal of the attainder – of the third Duke of Buckingham.[37]

Professor Lander has shown how Henry VII employed restorations as a system of probation, which allowed former traitors to show their *bona fides* and win back their possessions through good service,[38] and the same applies to patentees. Indeed, the politics of attainder may be described as a rather complex game in which the King wrote the rules *and* cast the dice. For the recipient of forfeitures the struggle had only just commenced when he had his patent authenticated by the great seal. Not only had he to ensure a favourable verdict from any inquisitions, but he had often to seek new patents describing the premises more accurately, to remove any defects of the original grant, or otherwise to regularize his title. In his dispute with Sir Thomas Fulford, John Staplehill was not helped by the invalidity of his first patent, although a replacement was sanctioned by the King.[39] Such co-operation on the part of the monarch could not, however, always be guaranteed. When the shamefaced Sir John Bourchier asked that the name 'Kenforth' be amended to 'Kenne', Edward IV agreed, but directed that the manor of Fretheby be struck out of the patent, 'Charging that ye elles in noo Wise amende the said word Kenforth'.[40] The patentee could also contest the traitor's suit for a pardon, for restoration of his lands, or for a licence to buy them back, and failing these could even have such favours misinterpreted.[41] Alternatively he might find himself pressurized into concessions by the King. Agreement with even a few patentees would immeasurably strengthen a petition for reversal in Parliament,[42] but even after the passage of a bill the King could be induced to reject it or qualify it

[35] *Rot. Parl.*, VII, pp. cxxi–cxxxi.
[36] *L.P. Hen. VIII*, III (2), p. 863; Lehmberg, 'Parliamentary Attainder', p. 699; V.C.H., *Bucks.*, IV, 403; *Warwicks.*, VI, 151.
[37] *Rot. Parl.*, VII, pp. cxxi–cxxxi.
[38] Lander, *Crown and Nobility*, pp. 154–6.
[39] C.81/1491/35.
[40] P.S.O.1/30/1554.
[41] E.g. Lander, *Crown and Nobility*, pp. 144–5, 148–9.
[42] *Rot. Parl.*, VI, 230.

with exemptions. The personal approval of the King and, indeed, his signature was required at every stage, offering him repeated opportunities to weigh the respective merits of both parties and to transfer his patronage if he wished. An incumbent had to be eternally vigilant, devoted in service, and secure of royal favour. He was made acutely conscious of his dependence on royal grace by repeated recourse to it and learnt to regard mere permission to retain what he already had as a most valuable expression of royal patronage.

3

Royal manipulation of attainder bears a remarkable resemblance to royal management of resumption. A parliamentary act of resumption revoked letters patent, thereby dispossessing the patentees and placing the premises at royal disposal, but its effects were modified by whatever exemptions might be approved by the King. Most of these exemptions benefited private individuals. This procedure emerges most clearly in 1467, when decisions were summarized on the surviving provisos as well as in the lost signet archives.[43] Once the act was passed, patentees sought access to the King to reveal what they held of royal grant and to learn what they might keep. Some retained everything, others made sacrifices, still others lost out altogether. Having made their 'apoyntement' with the King, the lucky ones drafted provisos in correct petitionary form for the royal sign manual. Before signing, Edward freely amended the grammar and terminology, compared the scope with his records, and often modified his decision, striking out particular items or rejecting whole provisos. Once signed, the proviso was passed to the clerk of Parliament, who enrolled it and notified the Chancellor and other interested parties of the contents. Their provisos enrolled, the patentees then petitioned for letters of *mittimus* – again requiring the royal signature – to the appropriate officers, to ensure that their fees were paid and lands and offices not resumed. Those without exemptions, often through oversight, petitioned for new patents in direct competition with those seeking some of what had been resumed. The system offered great scope for the monarch to assess patronage and reallocate it according to present needs, but it called for an encyclopaedic knowledge of personalities and the capacity to rebuff suitors in person – both of which Edward possessed[44] – as well as a sustained effort that kings could seldom maintain.

Lancastrian resumptions are well documented and described in the

---

[43] This paragraph is based on original provisos in C.49/36, 54, 59–60, 62–5; S.C.8/141/7008; S.C. 8/107/5322; writs of *mittimus* in C.81/1380; D.L. 37/30. Records of the subsequent Exchequer processes are of little value.

[44] *Ingulph's Chronicle of the Abbey of Croyland* . . ., ed. H.T. Riley (1854), pp. 480, 484.

seminal article and subsequent books of Dr Wolffe,[45] but Yorkist acts have been treated only cursorily and early Tudor ones scarcely at all, so their importance and number is quite unappreciated. Edward's four major acts – 1461, 1465, 1467 and 1473 – all resumed the possessions of Crown and duchy of Lancaster; the first three covered the duchy of Cornwall, the principality of Wales and the earldom of Chester; and the final pair embraced forfeitures as well. Everything except Henry VII's own aliena-tions were resumed in 1486, but the 1487 act affected only accounting offices and that of 1515 little but offices and increases in fees. Besides these major acts there were a host of more limited ones, such as the appropria-tions of 1483, 1485 and 1510 and the resumptions of the Queens' lands (1467, 1487, 1510), of the appanage of the Princes of Wales (1472, 1495) and of the duchy of York, Woodstock and Calais (all 1495). Nor had resump-tion ceased by the Reformation Parliament, when it features in another act of appropriation and in acts relating to the earldom of March, the Queen's and Duke of Richmond's lands.[46] The most innocuous acts could clearly be used for this purpose; and other resumptions doubtless lurk unrecognized among enactments assuring Henry VIII of particular estates. By varying their scope, time limit, and exemptions, resumptions could be made highly specific and flexible instruments of coercion.

Most broad, general acts were concerned mainly with offices. From the date of their respective coronations both Edward IV and Henry VII (who were kings by conquest) regarded all offices as in their gift. This applied even to posts which had been bought by their current occupants, such as the constellation in Wales for which Sir Walter Scull had paid 600 marks.[47] Henry VII gave away the offices of subjects both living and loyal, such as some previously held by John Luthington, who was confirmed in his other posts. The auditors in the west parts were told to make no further payments of Ricardian annuities.[48] From the start, Henry VII strove to regulate his patronage, denying the paradise beneath the receipt to his new ushers of the Exchequer, and converting many bailiwicks and receiverships from tenure for life to less secure occupancy at royal pleasure.[49] Yet with approximately 1,050 offices and 789 grantees handled during his first five months, Henry could not be too selective; and he subsequently resumed all those offices granted by the Yorkists *and* himself before 20 January 1486. In practice he was less drastic than some feared, and 'many of his houshold' had less cause

[45] B.P. Wolffe, 'Acts of Resumption in the Lancastrian Parliaments 1399–1456', *Historical Studies of the English Parliament*, eds. E.B. Fryde and E. Miller (2 vols., Cambridge, 1970), II, 61–91; *idem, The Crown Lands 1461–1509* (1970); *idem, The Royal Demesne in English History* (1971). For the rest of the paragraph see *Rot. Parl.*, V, 462–75, 514–48, 572–613, 624–8; VI, 9–16, 71–98, 198–202, 299–304, 336–84, 386–7, 403–8, 459–62, 465–8; *Statutes of the Realm*, II, 580–1; III, 14–15, 66–7, 153–6.

[46] *Statutes of the Realm*, III, 338–48, 479–81, 525–7, 697–8.

[47] C.81/1489/25.

[48] *Materials for a History of the Reign of Henry VII*, ed. W. Campbell (2 vols., 1873–7), I, 18, 44; D.L.41/11/23 (7 Sept. 1486).

[49] C.82/2/120. What follows is based on an analysis of *Rot. Parl.*, VI, 336–84; Campbell, *Materials*, I, *passim; Cal. Pat. Rolls*, 1485–94, *passim.*

than they had anticipated to be 'plesyd with yt'.[50] In fact, 52 of Edward's patentees secured favourable provisos, the Chancellor was instructed to confirm any other of Edward's patents tendered to him,[51] and relatively few individuals had their offices resumed and regranted. As if vetting provisos for 482 beneficiaries was not enough, the resumption of all offices substantially swelled the flow of suitors. Next year a further act sensibly confined itself to accounting offices, not actually revoking them but allowing their review by a committee, which made appointments at leisure and granted new leases, using the Treasurer's bills to move the great seal. Henceforth entries on the patent as well as the more usual fine roll were warranted in this way and the Chancery files contain bills signed not just by the Treasurer but by the other commissioners too.[52] The committee ceased work in about 1492, and only selective resumption was felt necessary thereafter.

By 1515 Henry VIII had given away revenues worth £21,222, including alienations of £3,457 conferred on five peers and peeresses (including two dukes), 16 knights and 12 others.[53] The exceptional strains of continental war then forced him to undertake a resumption and to revive the General Surveyors to administer it. In North Wales, for example, they halved the fees of the new Duke of Suffolk, Sir Roland Vielville, John Pilston and John Salisbury; at Restormell they stopped the fee of the constable as a sinecure; and at Middleham £70 due to Lord Conyers was respited as being unreasonable. Although they were primarily financial officers, the commissioners understood the political realities of life: they freely denied fees to the humble, but only respited £116 1s. 4d. due to the Earl of Worcester pending a warrant from the King.[54] That only 10 individual provisos were added to the act testifies to Henry's original determination to retrench, even though subsequently warrants were forthcoming for such as Sir Henry Marney and new patents for others.[55] Despite such limitations, the act caused some alarm, notably to members of the Tournai garrison, whose fees were resumed.

These resumptions thoroughly reviewed royal patronage and reinforced the demand for royal grace, even on the part of those with an apparent freehold in their offices, an aspect also well represented in Yorkist resumptions. The 1467 act was immediately preceded by a declaration of Edward's intention to live of his own and he cut back rigorously at the expense of 53 identified individuals.[56] Even the great lost something – Warwick his leases, his brother Northumberland £100 a year – and many

[50] *The Plumpton Correspondence,*, ed. T. Stapleton (Camden Soc., IV, 1839), 49–50.
[51] Only grants to London were excluded: C.82/14/21.
[52] *Rot. Parl.*, VI, 403–8; F.C. Dietz, *English Government Finance 1485–1558* (Urbana, 1921), p. 26; Richardson, *Tudor Chamber Administration*, p. 66; *Cal. Pat. Rolls*, 1485–94, p. 219 *et seq.*; *Calendar of Fine Rolls*, 1485–1500, *passim*; C.82/38–41 *et seq.*
[53] S.P.1/12, ff.45–6v.
[54] *Statutes of the Realm*, III, 145–56; S.C.11/837; S.C.6/Hen. VIII/345, mm. 2d, 45, 83–4, 104d.
[55] *Statutes of the Realm*, III, 153–6; S.C.6/Hen. VIII/345, mm. 3–d; *L.P. Hen. VIII*, II (1), pp. 178, 207, 252. For what follows see *ibid.*, p. 531.
[56] *Rot. Parl.*, V, 572–613. The next two paragraphs are based on *ibid.*; VI, 71–98; on analysis of the sources in n.43 above; and on Tables 1 and 2.

prominent courtiers like Sir John Scott and Avery Cornburgh made considerable sacrifices. Lord Hastings, the King's chamberlain, Lady Beaumont and Sir Thomas Burgh all suffered resumption in order that a thorough readjustment might be made of their shares in the forfeited Beaumont estates.[57] Some, however, lost nothing, notably the King's Herbert and Wydeville favourites, and Lord Audley, the Bourchiers and Blounts featured largely in the grants that followed.[58] This political element was recognized by the chronicler pseudo-Worcester, who noted, with evident surprise: 'The lords of Clarence and Warwick and many others were provided for *nevertheless.*'[59] Whatever Edward's original intentions, the effects proved purely political, as the spoils were rapidly dispensed in patronage in the crisis that immediately ensued.

If the prime object of the 1473 act was to bring his brother, the Duke of Clarence, to heel, Edward did not miss the chance to revise his patronage. His lower estimation of the second Earl of Pembroke and Sir Thomas Vaughan compared with their fathers emerges from the resumption of inherited grants.[60] His growing dissatisfaction with Sir Henry Pierpoint and William Hugford, already indicated by the reduction of their entailed estates to grants merely for life in 1467, was emphasized by further resumptions this time round. Hugford had given concrete grounds for displeasure, as a Warwick retainer who fought at Tewkesbury and recalled long after the battle: 'it liked your grace to comaunde him that he shuld not attende in service upon any persone but onely upon your highnes. . .' Likewise, the signet clerk Nicholas Harpsfield was in 'the moost sorowful cas . . . enstraunged from your moost noble service', faced with 'extreme perdicion', unable despite 'divers billes for the Releef and reconfort of him his Wyf' and children to 'obteyne your Royall favoure ne grace as yet in noo manere wise', and hence took service abroad and had no proviso to the act.[61] Edward evidently felt his generosity would be wasted on such as widow Gyrlington, young Richard Wrottesley, or the executors of dead favourites. He was highly discriminating, and started from the premise that past rewards were justified only by continued service, a viewpoint poles apart from his servants' desire to pass on their gains to their heirs. Similarly, Henry VII freely added obligations, notably unpaid military service and benevolences, as the price for continued tenure of past grants.[62] Promises in perpetuity secured more committed service, but in the harsh light of

---

[57] *Rot. Parl.*, V, 581, 601; C.49/54/4; *Cal. Pat. Rolls, 1467–77*, pp. 26–7, 34.

[58] *Cal. Pat. Rolls, 1467–77*, pp. 22, 24–5, 27, 38, 47, 51.

[59] *Letters and Papers Illustrative of the Wars of the English in France . . .* , ed. J. Stevenson (Rolls Series, No. 22, 2 vols., 1861–4), II (2), p. [787].

[60] Sir Robert Somerville, *History of the Duchy of Lancaster* (2 vols., 1953–66), I, 242.

[61] C.81/1521/41; E.28/90/58. For what follows see also *Cal. Pat. Rolls, 1461–7*, pp. 215, 381, 457, 516. For the Earl of Kent's executors see *ibid.*, p. 225; *ibid., 1467–77*, p. 458; *Rot. Parl.*, V, 604.

[62] *Statutes of the Realm*, II, 582, 648–9; *Rot. Parl.*, VI, 525; *Letters and Papers Illustrative of the Reigns of Richard III and Henry VII*, ed. J. Gairdner (Rolls Ser., No. 24, 2 vols., 1861–3), II, 86. See also G.R. Elton, *Studies in Tudor and Stuart Politics and Government* (2 vols., Cambridge, 1974), I, 47: 'any grant which did not specify the kind of service upon which it rested was construed to imply military tenure.'

realpolitik did not have to be respected indefinitely.

Both these acts and that of 1486 also covered forfeitures, which greatly extended their scope and the potential risk to royal patentees. All Yorkist holders of forfeited lands – a quarter of the peerage and between 66 and 101 prominent gentry – were liable to loss from both resumption and reversals; and their heirs faced the same risks. The changing emphasis of patronage and the enlarged Crown estate resulted in the exclusion from later acts of forfeited lands, but not of the offices on them, which were also at risk from restorations of returning traitors. If resumption by itself stretched widely and cut deeply, when combined with reversals it permitted regular coercion of the most powerful, and operated with such subtle flexibility that its full force was seldom required. Such factors were made even more telling by ease of management, as penalties followed from the mere denial of further favours – a proviso – or even of access to the King.

With such awesome and irresistible powers to hand, what need was there for actual acts to seize what was required? There was always an arbitrary element in English kingship, but for exercise it required the kind of self-confidence which Henry VI conspicuously lacked. Royal assertiveness was, however, encouraged by these new coercive powers, which emboldened kings to demand the surrender of patents in advance of reversals or resumptions. The new strength of the monarchy is evident also in the resettlement of hereditary estates: arrangements were, for example, made to divert (and sometimes redirect) the Dacre (1461–72), Welles (1475–83), Exeter (1461–83), Warwick (1474–87), Norfolk (1478–83) and Courtenay (1485–1510) inheritances, to the loss of the rightful heirs;[63] and, moreover, exchanges of property were successfully demanded by Edward IV, Henry VII and Henry VIII. With the initiative so firmly with the King, none but a fool would deny him and thus imperil his chance of compensation.[64]

4

Coercion of this kind inevitably inspired wariness and defensive reflexes on the part of those oppressed. It is insecurity, perhaps, that explains the decay into which Belvoir and Weoley castles were allowed to lapse, and which caused the Earl of Northumberland in 1484 to divert grants away from the main Percy line to a younger son.[65] In 1466 a lease of forfeited property allowed for recovery within the term; and specific provisions for resumption and reversal appear in grants made between 1485 and 1486. Some patentees sought guarantees of compensation, such as Richard

---

[63] *Rot. Parl.*, VI, 43–5, 144–8, 286–7, 298–9; *Cal. Pat. Rolls*, 1461–7, pp. 40, 534; 1485–94, pp. 28–9; Pugh, 'Magnates, Knights and Gentry', pp. 110–12; *L.P. Hen. VIII*, I (1), no. 749 (23); M.A. Hicks, 'Descent, Partition and Extinction: The "Warwick Inheritance"', *B.I.H.R.*, LII (1979), below, 329-32.

[64] E.g. John Neville, even though he regarded his compensation as derisory: J. Warkworth, *Chronicle of the First Thirteen Years of the Reign of King Edward the Fourth*, ed. J.O. Halliwell (Camden Soc., X, 1839), p. 10. Cf. Ives, *Brereton Letters and Accts.*, p. 23.

[65] Lander, *Crown and Nobility*, p. 151, n.; *V.C.H., Worcestershire*, III, 195; *Cal. Pat. Rolls*, 1476–85, p. 409.

Quatermains in 1467, Clarence in 1472, and the Dukes of Norfolk and Suffolk in 1514; others inserted clauses declaring their patents immune from resumption.[66] None of these measures were effective, however, since resumptions revoked *all* patents and no king would honour outdated promises. The only remedy was confirmation by Parliament, secured by the Dukes of Norfolk and Suffolk (1515) for royal grants; by Lord Stanley (1472) and others as security against resumption; and by Lord Dudley and Simon Digby (1495) as protection against reversals.[67] Such acts could themselves be reversed and sometimes were, but nothing more could be done. A similar unease explains the proliferation of provisos: individual ones duplicated general savings, others were appended to acts that did not otherwise cover them,[68] and there was near panic in 1523. Arbitrary and tyrannical oppression had its attractions to the ruling monarch, but such powers required sparing use if patronage was not to be devalued, and, more important, if faithful subjects were not to grow restless or even rebel.[69] There was always the risk that the nobility would lapse into apprehensive inactivity[70] or even fall victim to the dangerous paranoia of Clarence's last years, when he imagined that 'the Kyng entended to consume hym in lyke wyse as a Candell consumeth in brennyng, whereof he wold in brief tyme quyte him'. Just as Henry VII felt it necessary to give statutory assurance that adherents rendering military support would not be attainted by an incoming usurper, so he and his son came to patronize their patentees more consistently at the expense of returning traitors, whose loyalty was, after all, a variable commodity.

5

The powers described above were not, of course, employed continuously or systematically as part of a relentless coercion of the political nation by fifteenth- and early sixteenth-century monarchs, still less by each individual king. Such an approach, involving an attack on all the most important of their subjects, could only have resulted in rebellion. The wide potential of attainder and resumption did, however, offer opportunities for coercion, which successive kings employed as desired against patentees who had offended them or whose service was no longer valued. Other instruments of coercion were open to the New Monarchy, but these two weapons were of exceptional importance in their drastic effects, broad sweep and ease of operation. They had priority of time in the assertion of royal authority and went far towards creating that regal ascendancy and

---

[66] Campbell, *Materials*, I, 190, 251; *Cal. Pat. Rolls*, 1467–77, p. 40 ; *Cal. Fine Rolls*, 1461–71, p. 183; *Rot. Parl.*, VII, pp. xlv–xlvii; Hicks, *Clarence*, p. 115.

[67] *Rot. Parl.*, VI, 46–7, 483–4, 492; VII, pp. xlv–xlvii. For the next sentence see e.g. Hicks, '"Warwick Inheritance"', below, 332-3.

[68] See e.g. Roger Ree's proviso in the 1465 Act of Resumption and the addition of three further provisos in 1472 (*Rot. Parl.*, V, 516–17, 535).

[69] E.g. Montagu: Warkworth, *Chronicle*, pp. 10–11.

[70] E.g. K.B. McFarlane, 'The Wars of the Roses', *Proceedings of the British Academy*, L (1964), 119. For what follows see *Rot. Parl.*, VI, 194.

atmosphere of fear that was exploited first by Henry VII in his use of bonds, fiscal feudalism, and much abused traditional powers, and then by Henry VIII when he came to impose authoritarian reforms and eliminate his opponents. By 1529 the balance of power had shifted far indeed, largely through the development of an offensive royal armoury that traced its origins back to the fortuitous coincidence of attainder and resumption.

Yet patronage could be revised without going to such extremes. Attainder had been perfected through a process of trial and error dating back at least to the reign of King Stephen: a whole series of monarchs had proscribed their domestic foes and redistributed the forfeited estates among their adherents, and the same was to be done by the parliamentary side in the English Civil War. Some disasters, such as those of 1397 in 1399, were rapidly reversed, but others were more lasting, and some even permanent. John Ferrers's failure to recover his earldom in 1307 owed much to undue haste, to his impatient refusal to await the death of Edward I,[71] but others bided their time to better effect. It was only in 1367 that the second Earl of March secured Denbigh, forfeited in 1330, and not until 1397 that the Earl of Nottingham recovered Gower, lost in 1354, but both were ultimately recovered. Each owed his good fortune to the cancellation by the ruling monarch of grants made earlier to fathers of the incumbent earls.[72] Each phase of civil strife generated new claims, far outweighing the lands available, to be nourished in hope by watchful heirs, and every king exploited these ambitions to create new obligations. Almost any royal alienation might some day be revoked or might itself result from some earlier resumption. The revision of patronage, like the well attested outbursts of royal munificence, is a recurring theme in English history, as relevant for the study of the 'anarchy of Stephen's reign' and of the Disinherited, Contrariants, Appellants and Delinquents as it is for the New Monarchy itself.

[71] K.B. McFarlane, *The Nobility of Later Medieval England* (Oxford, 1973), p. 256.
[72] G.A. Holmes, *The Estates of the Higher Nobility in Fourteenth-Century England* (Cambridge, 1957), p. 16; *Glamorgan County History*, III, 253.

4

Chantries, Obits and Almshouses: The Hungerford Foundations, 1325-1478[1]

The new foundations of late medieval England are a neglected field of study. This is understandable, since the largest and best documented institutions were already ancient. The few later foundations of comparable size have not been overlooked. Large and imposing as university colleges and Henry V's abbeys were, however, they were not representative of late medieval benefactions, which were typified instead by almshouses, by schools and above all by chantries. Pioneering surveys of such categories have not been adequately followed up and the direction of much recent research has been away, towards specific status groups and classes of record. Both approaches are valuable and indeed complementary: without some understanding of the institutions themselves, breakdowns of benefactors and types of benefaction are little use. Nevertheless there are methodological drawbacks to each method: concentration on the fullest records or those most susceptible to quantitative analysis involves a loss of context and hence of relevant source material. The study of foundations in the round, using all the available evidence, offers a chance of fuller knowledge and understanding. This is the justification of the case study of restricted scope, which treats foundations within a natural geographical, institutional or intellectual framework – such as the city or county of York. Strangely there is still no case study of the most natural group of all – the foundations of a particular family – even though the family is accepted as an appropriate unit for economic, political and social history.

This paper fills the gap by studying the new foundations of the Hungerford family in the later middle ages. Emerging from obscurity only in the early

[1] Unless otherwise stated, all places are in Wiltshire and all documents cited are in the PRO.

fourteenth century, the Hungerfords reached the peerage in 1426 and weathered with difficulty the Wars of the Roses. Professor Rosenthal has identified them as notable benefactors of the Church and twelve chantries, seven obits, and two almshouses feature in this account.[2] The Hungerfords were lavish benefactors of the most conventional type.

TABLE I: The Hungerfords.

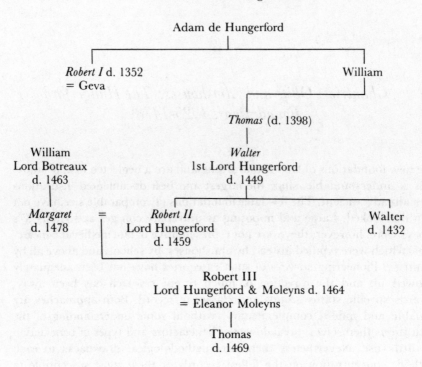

Dr Raban has shown that information on foundations derives mainly from two sources, the records of the crown and those of the Church.[3] This article has relied equally on the records of the patrons, comprising the Hungerford cartularies, estate accounts, deeds and wills. This third source not only yields more accurate evidence of particular foundations, but it facilitates interpretation by supplying the context specifically relevant in each case. A fresh approach can cast new light on familiar topics of broader significance, such as attitudes to inherited obligations, the financing of foundations, and alienation in mortmain. This study therefore amplifies and occasionally corrects the more wide-ranging surveys of other historians.

[2] J. T. Rosenthal, *Purchase of Paradise: Gift Giving and the Aristocracy*, 1972, 50–51.
[3] S. Raban, *Mortmain Legislation and the English Church 1279–1500*, Cambridge 1982, 10.

While ranging over the whole period, this study concentrates on the fifteenth-century foundations of Walter, Lord Hungerford (d. 1449) and his daughter-in-law Margaret (d. 1478). The first part is a chronological account of the individual foundations and contains the raw material for two substantial sections of conclusions.

TABLE II: Hungerford Foundations and Bequests.

		Robert d. 1352	Thomas d. 1398	Joan d. 1412	Walter d. 1449	Robert d. 1459	Margaret d. 1478
Religious houses:							
Benedictines	Bath (Soms.)				F		x
	Canterbury (Kent)				f		
Benedictine nuns	Amesbury (Wilts.)				x	x	
Cistercians	Stanley (Wilts.)	F					
Augustinian	Bruton (Soms.)				x		
	Edington (Wilts.)		F		x	x	x
	Ivychurch (Wilts.)	F					
	Launceston (Corn.)						x
	Lesnes (Kent)		F				
	Llanthony (Gloucs.)	f					
	Longleat (Wilts.)		F	x	x		
	Maiden Bradley (Wilts.)				x	x	x
Augustinian nuns	Lacock (Wilts.)				x		
Carthusians	Henton (Soms.)				x	x	
	Sheen (Surr.)				x		
	Witham (Soms.)					x	
Bridgettines	Syon (Middx.)						x
Trinitarians	Easton (Wilts.)	F					
	Hounslow (Middx.)						x
Dominicans	Bodmin (Corn.)				x		f
	Exeter (Devon)				x		
	Ilchester (Soms.)				x		x
	Salisbury (Wilts.)				x	x	x
Franciscans	Bridgwater (Soms.)				x		x
	Salisbury (Wilts.)					x	
Carmelites	Marlborough (Wilts.)				x		x
All friars	Bristol (Gloucs.)				x		
	Cambridge (Cam.)						x
	Exeter (Devon)				x		
	London				x		
	Oxford (Oxon.)				x		
Secular churches:							
Cathedrals	Salisbury (Wilts.)	F		x	fF	x	F
	Wells (Soms.)			x	x		
Colleges	Heytesbury (Wilts.)			x	x		
	Merton (Oxon.)				x		
	Salisbury, St Edmund (Wilts.)				x		
	Westminster (Middx.)				F		
Hospitals	Bedlam (Lond.)					x	
	Bradford (Soms.)					x	
	Calne (Wilts.)	F					
	Heytesbury (Wilts.)				F	x	x

Parish churches				
Chippenham (Wilts.)			F	F
Farleigh (Soms.)	x	x	2F	x
Hungerford (Berks.)	F			
Salisbury (Wilts.):				
St Clement			x	x
St Martin			x	x
St Thomas		x	x	x
Teffont Evias (Wilts.)		x	x	
Wellow (Soms.)			x	x	x

Road: Standerwick causeway (Soms.).

Sources: foundations and wills.

Key: F = foundation; x denotes bequest; f = confraternity.

Walter (d. 1449) made bequests to a further 18 churches, Margaret to St Martin's Ludgate, the anchorite of London wall, and prisoners in two Salisbury gaols.

Sir Robert de Hungerford (Robert I, d. 1352) founded four chantries: at Holy Trinity chapel in Hungerford church (1326), where he was buried; at Salisbury cathedral (1334), where a capitular nominee celebrated for the souls of him and Archdeacon Walter de Hervy; at St Edmund's chapel in Calne church (1336), where the cantarist was nominated by (or perhaps was) the warden of the nearby hospital of St John and St Anthony; and at the Trinitarian friary at Easton, where Robert gave only £1 0s 4d income to endow an extra brother. Although a fifth chantry at the Augustinian priory of Ivychurch (1321) was stillborn, an obit was founded there in 1336 and the priory paid the pension that supported the cathedral cantarist. There was a second obit at the Cistercian abbey of Stanley.

A man of limited means, Robert put off alienating his endowments and some never reached the intended recipients. A royal licence to alienate a Salisbury messuage to Stanley Abbey was secured in 1331, but it had not been conveyed at Robert's death and could not then be completed, as no licence was forthcoming: this may indicate refusal by the immediate overlord, the bishop of Salisbury, or the expiry on Robert's death of the royal licence. Instead the property was sold and the abbey accepted the proceeds as endowment for the obit. In two cases, at Easton and Calne, the income was too small to support a priest and Easton in particular had a bad bargain, since it presumably paid Robert's £3 life annuity for sixteen years. The penalties imposed for non-performance were severe, in two cases tantamount to disendowment, which actually befell at Calne a century later.[4]

Robert's nephew Thomas bestowed his favours elsewhere. In 1365 he founded an obit for himself, his first wife, parents and uncle at the priory of Bonshommes at Edington. In 1377 a chantry at the Austin abbey of Lesnes (Kent) was his price for the quitclaim of the manor of Northwood in Lesnes. Thirdly, his will ordained a chantry at Longleat priory, near his residence at

[4] *VCH Wilts* iii, 291n, 325, 334; *CPR 1324–27*, 191; SRO, DD/SAS H348 (hereafter Hungerford cartulary), fos. 259v–60, 262.

Heytesbury.[5] He was actually buried at Farleigh Hungerford (Soms.) in the north chapel of St Anne, which he added in the 1380s to the parish church he had earlier rebuilt. His widow Joan provided in her will for the foundation of a chantry there for their souls and those of her ancestors.[6]

Thomas did not manage to complete his foundations in his own lifetime. It was to support two further canons that he had enfeoffed North Tidworth manor to the use of Longleat priory. By 1401 the priory had sold it for £106 13s 4d, which it lent to Walter for his pilgrimage to Jerusalem. In 1407 Walter was licensed to appropriate Rushall church to Longleat and in 1410 conveyed it the advowson and prescribed the ordinances of the chantry. Yet in spite of episcopal approval, no appropriation occurred. Walter later blamed his failure on an entail, not new but old and hence unbreakable, which certainly did exist.[7] His failure was surely fortunate for Longleat, since the endowment was inadequate for the commitments. Rushall church, taxed at only £10 before the establishment of a vicarage, was sufficient endowment only for one chaplain and North Tidworth was worth even less. Probably no chantry was established, since it passed unnoticed among Joan's bequests to Longleat in 1411 and £106 13s 4d remained due in 1449, when Walter ordered its repayment – without interest – subject to the return of the relevant deeds, the advice of Salisbury cathedral chapter, but apparently not to the establishment of his father's chantry.

In her will Joan required Walter to found a chantry at Farleigh with two hundred marks (£133 6s 8d) already in his hands. Although nothing permanent was done until 1426, Thomas's obit was scrupulously kept meanwhile.[8] By 1429 a daily mass was said by John the chaplain, perhaps John Gody, first perpetual chaplain, who was paid £2 salary and one shilling a week board, total £4 12s. Joan's scanty endowment and Walter's public commitments may have contributed to the delay, but another factor was probably the difficulty and/or cost of securing a royal licence to alienate in mortmain. Such licences almost dried up in Henry V's last years and Henry VI's minority council was anxious to keep the young king's rights

[5] J. S. Roskell, *Parliament and Politics in Late Medieval England*, 1981, ii, 37; Hungerford cartulary, fos. 261v–3; see below. Northwood had belonged to Thomas's parents, *HMCR* lxxviii, *Hastings* i, 215–16.
[6] R. Wilcox, 'Excavations at Farleigh Hungerford Castle, Somerset, 1973–6', *Somerset Archaeology and Natural History* cxxiv, 1981, 87–94; *Farleigh Hungerford Castle* (DOE Guide, 1979), 4; N. Pevsner, *North Somerset and Bristol*, Harmondsworth 1958, 191–2.
[7] Lambeth P(alace) L(ibrary), Reg. of Archbishop Stafford fo. 115; *CCR 1399–1402*, 325; *CPR 1405–8*, 384; *Reg. Hallum* nos. 1071–2; Salisbury C(athedral) M(uniments), Reg. Viringe p. 30; Devizes Museum (Canon Jackson's) Hungerford (Family) Collections, Places iii, fos. 57–8. For what follows, see K. L. Wood-Legh, *Perpetual Chantries in Britain*, Cambridge 1965, *passim*; J. I. Kermode, 'The Merchants of three northern towns', *Profession, Vocation and Culture in Later Medieval England*, ed. C. H. Clough, Liverpool 1982, 25.
[8] *Test. Vet.* i, 181; PRO, SC 6/970/29 m.3; /971/2 m.3d. In 1429 93 priests and 363 paupers attended and in 1430, 43 priests and 572 paupers (PRO SC 6/1119/9 m.2; Devizes Museum, Hungerford Colls., Personal i, 126). For what follows, see Hungerford Colls., Personal i, 133.

intact until he came of age, so the number of such licences dwindled.[9] Soon after becoming a councillor, Walter agreed to serve abroad at a council meeting on 18 February 1423, which was dominated by the concessions that he extracted for going. Among these the council agreed to his performance of a vow on his return.[10] While the vow is unspecified, surely only a licence to alienate would have required conciliar approval for its fulfilment? If so, it was not redeemed until 14 June 1426, when Walter had just become a baron and as treasurer of England was particularly influential.

By advice and assent of the great council the licence allowed alienation of £10 revenue for a chantry at the altar of St Mary, not St Anne, Farleigh Hungerford for the benefit of the souls of the king, Walter and his wife, his parents, their ancestors and all the faithful dead.[11] In 1431 the foundation deed ordained services for the souls of Walter, his wife, his parents, ancestors and all the faithful departed, but not for the king. The endowment comprised a house and £8 income, from which was to be paid the cantarist's salary, essential expenses and repairs, and the cost of Thomas's obit. Each 2 December the chaplain and seven other priests were to repeat matins and evensong of the dead and on 3 December, the anniversary proper, each was to say mass separately. For this the cantarist was to provide dinner and pay each priest 4*d*; thirteen paupers were to receive 1*d* each to pray for Thomas's soul and four others 1*d* each to remember him.

From 1428 the rector of Farleigh was also obliged to celebrate Thomas's obit at his own expense: he and seven other priests were to say the services of the dead the night before and a mass each on 3 December, each priest receiving dinner and 4*d*; another thirteen paupers were to receive 1*d* each; and two 1 lb tapers were supplied. This stemmed from the union of Farleigh with the adjoining parish of Rowley, across the boundary with Wiltshire and the diocese of Salisbury. Rowley was a deserted village with a rectory worth only 15*s*, too little for any rector to reside. Immediately after acquiring the advowson, Walter applied for the union of Rowley with Farleigh. The parishioners of Rowley agreed on conditions, which included the preservation of their church and the upkeep of the chancel by the rector of the combined living. As justification the bishop of Bath and Wells cited the pastoral needs of the people of Rowley and the poverty of the rector of Farleigh – a somewhat hollow claim in view of the extra burdens imposed. Over a third of the rector's extra income was appropriated to particular expenses and he and his successors were henceforth bound by oath on institution to observe the new arrangements on pain of a fine to the Wells cathedral fabric.[12] The real

[9] Griffiths, *Henry VI*, 88.
[10] Roskell ii, 113; *PPC* iii, 37–8.
[11] *CPR 1422–29*, 347. For what follows, see J. E. Jackson, *Guide to Farleigh Hungerford*, Chippenham 1879, 110–34.
[12] J. E. Jackson, 'Rowley *alias* Wittenham', *WAM* xiii (1872), 230–31, 235, 238–48; Salisbury CM, Reg. Harding fo. 92v.

beneficiary was Walter himself, who secured a splendid obit for his father at no cost to himself.

In 1426 Walter intended endowing his Farleigh chantry himself, but actually provided only a house, the balance being a pension of £8 from Bath cathedral priory, which also agreed to celebrate the obits of Walter, his wife and parents at an annual cost of £1.[13] This was not just another pension financed by alienations to a religious house, for it emanated from Olveston church (Gloucs.), part of the priory's preconquest estate. The exceptionally full documentation does not mention any consideration paid by Walter to justify acceptance by the monastery of perpetual commitments of £9 a year, a life pension of £32 above £20 stipend for the vicar, and the heavy cost of appropriation from a living worth only £21 4s 8d to it at the dissolution. It already enjoyed a pension of three and a half marks (£2 6s 8d) from the living and had fought off a challenge to its patronage in 1352.[14] Probably Bath priory already wished to appropriate the church, but could not because a royal licence was refused or was too expensive. Walter, however, already had a licence and as royal councillor and treasurer could have it adjusted to permit the appropriation. The council's warrant to the chancellor prescribed a reasonable fine, but in spite of the earlier licence, £40 was charged – four years' income: what would a wholly new licence have cost?[15] If this interpretation is correct, Walter paid for his chantry and obit by exercising his influence in council.[16]

At that same 1423 council meeting Salisbury cathedral chapter was licensed to acquire £50 income for the repair of the spire and for the increase of divine worship for the soul of the king and the donors of such new endowment. Walter was present and, as a member of the cathedral confraternity, presumably supported the application.[17] Perhaps he hoped to benefit from it and had already reached an understanding with the chapter. However that may be, it was under this blanket authority that in 1427 he was licensed to alienate to the cathedral land and the advowson of St Sampson's church, Cricklade and to appropriate the church. The gift was worth £16 13s 8d and the fine was £33 6s 8d, two years' purchase. In 1429 the property was conveyed, St Sampson's church was appropriated, and the chapter were bound to maintain a chantry of two priests, Walter's obit, and to mention him and his wife in their Sunday litanies. The chapter supplied a house in the close, subject to rent for earlier obits, and Walter erected a chantry chapel in the north nave arcade. Those commemorated were Henry V and Henry VI, Walter and his spouse, their heirs, his parents and grandparents, and his

[13] Jackson, *Farleigh Hungerford*, 112–17, 129–30, 133–4.
[14] Jackson, *Farleigh Hungerford*, 133–4; *VCH Somerset* ii, 78; *Monasticon* ii, 273; BL MS Egerton 3316 fos. 79v, 93v.
[15] PRO, C 81/690/2006–7; *CPR 1422–9*, 541–2.
[16] This point is expanded below, pp. 139–40.
[17] Salisbury CM, Reg. Pountney p. 1; *CPR 1422–9*, 70; *PPC* iii, 37–8.

great-uncle Robert I and great-aunt Geva. Of the actual income of £30 9s 2d,
£16 was to be paid to the chaplains, £1 6s 8d was for essential expenses, £4 4s
at least was for Walter's obit, and only £2 specifically for the spire. Should
the endowment prove too little, it was the money for the belltower, doles and
repairs that was to be withdrawn first.[18]

Heytesbury church housed an ancient secular college and lay within the
peculiar of the dean of Salisbury, who was also dean of Heytesbury. There
were two chantries dedicated to St Mary and St Katherine, of which the
former was in Hungerford patronage by 1408. It was presumably with the
dean's approval that Walter used an embassy to the Council of Constance to
secure a bull transferring the chantry to his oratory at Heytesbury, which he
proposed developing into a chantry college with more chaplains and clerks.
This was justified, quite untruthfully, by poverty so grave 'that for a long
time no priest has celebrated in it'. The prior of Bath, nominated to
investigate, duly appeared at Heytesbury in 1415–16, but the scheme was
stillborn.

In 1438 Walter proposed the union of the two Heytesbury chantries with
another at Upton Scudamore, Robert I's at Calne, and the free chapel of
Corston in Hillmarton, the latter three of Walter's patronage and all said to
be too poor to support chaplains. Inquiries revealed all to be impoverished,
with incomes ranging from 8s to £3 10s, but some did have incumbents. If
amalgamated, they would provide a comfortable income of £8 1s 4d and a
house for a single chaplain.

By contemporary standards the Hungerfords were a charitable family.
Thomas supported ten paupers at Farleigh in 1377–78 and he, his wife and
son all left money for their poor tenants. All Walter's foundations provided
for charitable distributions and by 1428 he was pensioning thirteen paupers
on his estates at 4d a week each, 17s 4d a year. It was logical to bring these
pensioners together in a hospital, which he built at Heytesbury by 1442.
Only on 19 July 1442 did Bishop Aiscough annex Corston chapel, Calne and
Upton chantries to St Mary's chantry, Heytesbury, whose chaplain was
henceforth to commemorate all the founders. Four days later Walter declared
his trust, instructing his feoffees to hold two manors until they were licensed
to amortise them to Heytesbury hospital. Meanwhile they were to pay
£23 6s 8d annually to support twelve almsmen and two almswomen in his
new hospital and to perform other almsdeeds on particular days for the soul
of Walter and others specified. To this combined almshouse and chantry
Walter had added a school by his death in 1449. One of a group of five such
foundations established in 1422–42 by Walter and his associates in govern-

---

[18] *CPR 1422–9*, 390; H. de S. Shortt, *Hungerford and Beauchamp Chantry Chapels*, Salisbury 1970,
2–4; Salisbury CM, Reg. Harding fo. 43; Hungerford cartulary fos. 250–5v. For the next three
paragraphs, see M. A. Hicks, 'St. Katherine's Hospital, Heytesbury: Prehistory, Foundation
and Re-foundation 1408–72', below, 120-6.

ment, Heytesbury was undoubtedly influenced by Henry VI's college at Eton.

Heytesbury hospital was one of Walter's three later foundations. In 1441 a second chantry at St Mary's altar, Farleigh Hungerford was licensed to acquire £10 income. Those commemorated were King Henry V, King Henry VI, Walter and his first wife, his parents and ancestors. No fine was charged for the first licence, but fines were levied in ancillary licences and one alienation was rated higher than the inquisition valuation. Walter soon appreciated that his two chantry chaplains sufficed to staff the tiny church of Farleigh Hungerford if it was relieved of its parochial responsibilities. These were no doubt inconvenient, since it now lay within Walter's new outer ward of the castle. By 1443 he had rebuilt the parish church at a distance and had taken over the old church at his chapel. Apparently the second chaplain was transferred from St Mary's altar to the high or St Leonard's altar.[19]

St Mary's chantry in the south chapel of Chippenham church was founded jointly by Walter and his son Robert II. In 1442 they were licensed to alienate £10 income to a priest to sing for the souls of Henry V, Henry VI, Walter and his first wife Katherine, Robert II, Walter's other children and ancestors. Already complete in 1442, the chapel was endowed in 1447. £11 11s fine was charged.

Walter's standard endowment of a house and £8 stipend was unusually generous. His Salisbury chantry stands apart, since the chapter took on the selection and oversight of chaplains, which Walter therefore did not need to regulate. Two candidates were nominated by the chapter at each vacancy for Walter to select from. His other chantries were free-standing corporations, fully constituted benefices requiring episcopal institution, and were in his gift. In general his statutes made commonplace provision for visitations, preservation of property, and for the prevention of pluralism and exchanges. They were not particularly stringent, the chaplains being allowed to hold compatible offices of the Hungerford family and to have female visitors to stay. In Walter's lavish and wide-ranging will, his chantries took pride of place. He ordered his executors to remedy any deficiencies in statutes, endowments or equipment, and he assigned to his foundations first claim on his residuary estate.[20]

The principal obligation Walter left was the endowment of Heytesbury hospital, which eventually devolved on his daughter-in-law Margaret. The chantry, almshouse and school were united by 1454 in a single person, the *Magister Scolarum*, who maintained both paupers and chantry. Robert II had asked, so Margaret also claimed, that the endowment be completed and in

[19] *CPR 1441–6*, 94–5, 269, 327; *Reg. Bekynton* i, 3; *Survey and Rentals of Chantries, Colleges and Free Chapels*, ed. E. Green (SRS, ii), 1888, no. 119; *Reg. Stillington*, 2, 30, 33. For the next paragraph, see *CPR 1441–6*, 151; PRO, C 143/450/27.

[20] Jackson, *Farleigh Hungerford*, 118–27; *Reg. King*, 158; Hungerford cartulary, fos. 252–5v. For the next paragraph, see below 126-7.

1469 she secured the consent of the Duke of Gloucester, holder of the reversion of her estates, who promised

> to be mediator and meanes to the kinges highnes and his effectual labour and diligence to get the kynges licence thereof in due fourme to be made within the space of xij monthes next folowyng or rather if he godely can or may at the costes of the said Margaret.

Edward IV signed the agreement, but it was not until 1472 that the licence was secured, endowment conveyed, and statutes compiled. The foundation now consisted of twelve poor men and only one woman, perhaps from economy, more probably because thirteen was the number commonly favoured in imitation of Christ and the Apostles.

Although not executrix to her father Lord Botreaux, Margaret inherited obligations on his death. In 1449 Lord Botreaux, his heirs and assigns were licensed to alienate 100 marks (£66 13s 4d) revenue to any religious house of his choice and in 1459 he initiated a series of inquisitions *ad quod dampnum* into his proposals to alienate lands in Somerset and Hampshire to Bath cathedral priory. In 1458–59 he ordained a chantry there and evidently also erected an almshouse for thirteen poor men.[21] Some properties may have been formerly alienated at his death, since they were held by the priory's feoffees in 1481, but others were recovered by his daughter and sold. It is not known what befell the chantry, but the almshouse was disendowed. Margaret had already decided not to complete it in 1469 and probably earlier, since the thirteen paupers of the first half of 1464–65 dwindled to twelve in the third quarter, eleven in the final quarter and, on average, only ten in 1468–69. In 1477 Margaret ordered

> þat my Fathers poremen at Bath be paide yerely every oon jd a day according to my saide lordes ordynaunce yerely duryng þe lyff of þe personys þat now remayneth þer and afterward to cesse.[22]

The almshouse does not recur.

By will of 1459 Robert II asked for burial before the altar of the newly canonised St Osmund in Salisbury cathedral. His wish was performed: in 1464–65 and 1468–69 a chaplain was celebrating there.[23] From 1469 on Margaret claimed that Robert had asked in his will for the foundation of a chantry of two priests there. No such provision appears in his will, otherwise lavish in pious bequests, and the proximity in date of his death renders such a change of plan unlikely. Certainly the form of the chantry was determined by Margaret. Dedicated to Jesus and the Virgin, it was housed in a new chapel abutting on the north side of the Lady Chapel in mirror image of the

---

[21] W. Dugdale, *Baronage of England*, 1675, i, 630; *CPR 1446–52*, 230; PRO, C 143/452/20, /30. For the next sentence, see *Anc. Deeds* iii, A5499; *CCR 1461–8*, 334–5.
[22] BL MS Cotton Julius BXII fo. 123; PRO, SC 6/1061/21 m.2; SC 6/1119/15 m.4; Devizes Museum, Hungerford Colls., Personal i, fo. 270v.
[23] *Som. Med. Wills, 1383–1500*, 186; PRO, SC 6/1119/14 m.4, /15 m.4.

Beauchamp Chapel of 1461 to the south. Chapel, altar and tomb were consecrated in 1471 by Bishop Beauchamp himself. Robert II's effigy was placed in an arch in the south wall overlooking both the new altar and, presumably, that of St Osmund. In 1472 Margaret was licensed to alienate forty marks (£26 13s 4d) revenue to Salisbury cathedral and conveyed to it the manors of Folke (Dors.), Imber and Winterbourne Homington and her two free chapels of Imber and Folke. She declared her statutes in the cathedral chapter house. Imber chapel was appropriated in 1474. Altogether the Hungerford chapel cost £823 to build and equip. The foundation deed named as beneficiaries Margaret and Robert II, their parents, John Cheyne and John Mervyn co-feoffees and co-founders, the king, Bishop Beauchamp and Dean Goldwell, but the prescribed prayers commemorated only Margaret and Robert II, their parents and children, and all those for whom they were bound to pray.[24]

Margaret's other benefaction was at Syon Abbey, where she was confined in 1470. She left her heart for burial there and paid £100 '*et vltra*' for the insertion in the Syon martyrology of herself, Robert II, Walter, Robert III and her grandson, all Lords Hungerford.[25]

The twenty-one statutes of Margaret's chantry at Salisbury are more detailed and exacting than those of Walter's comparable foundation and forty-eight provided for Heytesbury hospital. They share a common core of twelve. Margaret relied for continuity after death on Salisbury cathedral chapter rather than her heirs, who were not to be patrons. The chapter would collate to the chantry and the hospital was in the gift of the cathedral chancellor if resident, of the chapter if not. The chapter could remove cantarists and the hospital keeper not just for notorious crime, but for waste and immoral conduct. Supervision of the chantry was easy, but at Heytesbury Margaret offered financial inducements for annual visitations by the dean's official. Although a remarkably rigorous *code*, the individual regulations against waste and for management of the poor are commonplace.

Whereas the Salisbury cantarists had purely liturgical functions, the Heytesbury keeper was expected to say mass daily, to teach daily except on Sundays and feast days when he joined in matins, high mass and evensong in the church, and to manage the almshouse. Outside vacation, his freedom was extremely restricted. For these reasons the post was difficult to fill, even though the salary – £16 8s 8d with house and £1 for a servant – was double that of the Salisbury cantarists. Those commemorated were Robert II and Margaret, their parents, their ancestors, descendants and 'all the soulis thei

---

[24] C. Wordsworth, *Ceremonies and Processions of the Cathedral Church of Salisbury*, Cambridge 1901, 286; BL MS Cotton Julius BXII fo. 123; W(iltshire) RO, 490/1465d; WRO Registrum Rubrum, fos. 140–42; Hungerford cartulary, fos. 317v–27, 345–62; *CCR 1468–76*, no. 1122; see also R. C. Hoare, *History of Modern Wiltshire*, 6 vols. 1822–40, i (2), 128, 130.

[25] BL MS Add. 22285, fos. 49v, 71. The next three paragraphs are based on J. E. Jackson, 'Ancient Statutes of Heytesbury Almshouse', *WAM* xi, 1869, 289–308; Hungerford cartulary, fos. 322a–24; *VCH Wilts* iii, 337–8; Wordsworth, *Ceremonies*, 285–6.

be bounde to pray for', and Margaret's co-feoffees Cheyne and Mervyn.

Several statutes reflect Margaret's modification of Walter's intentions. Apart from Walter and his wife, those commemorated cannot be those whom Walter had in mind and the beneficiaries of the dissolved former chantries were omitted. Margaret's stress on the Virgin's chastity recurs in the statutes and her cult of Jesus no doubt explains her insistence on unmarried almsmen, on the restriction of numbers to thirteen, insisted on in her statutes, and in the emblazoning on their gowns of JHU.XRT. (Jesus Christ). St Katherine is not mentioned.[26]

This study illuminates the Hungerfords as religious patrons. They held many advowsons of parish churches, chantries and monasteries and acquired others deliberately, rather than as mere appendages to particular manors. Presentations advanced clients ranging from household chaplains to future bishops and a few were promoted from living to living. Naturally such dependants looked for patronage to the Hungerfords, who accepted their responsibilities and acted on them. Their arms on churches of their patronage, as at St Sampson, Cricklade, imply contributions to the fabric like those known elsewhere from their wills and accounts. They wholly rebuilt Farleigh church at least once and probably twice. Their bequests of vestments and ornaments, like Robert II's provision of a chalice for St Anne's, Teffont, often reveal first-hand knowledge of particular local needs. Over three generations they relieved their poorer tenants through bequests, through pensions and ultimately through collecting them in Heytesbury hospital. Only Margaret, however, seems to have patronised churches primarily because they were in her patronage and even her will benefited other institutions. The Hungerford arms feature on the Lacock Abbey cloisters, on the tower of St Andrew, Chippenham and at Mickle Hall, Oxford, none of which were of Hungerford foundation.[27] Some family livings were hardly patronised at all: in particular the chantries of their predecessors were generally neglected.

Neglect, however, was preferable to being sacrificed to higher priorities. Like other patrons, the Hungerfords often presented to their livings those who were certain to be absentees. They did not hesitate to employ parochial incumbents as household chaplains, receivers-general and in other posts necessitating non-residence.[28] Indeed many of their churches were scheduled

---

[26] See below, chap. 6, 127–32. Unless otherwise stated, the rest of this article is based on the preceding sections and wills in Lambeth PL, Reg. Stafford fos. 115–16v; Reg. Arundel, ii, fo. 152; *Som. Med. Wills, 1383–1500*, 186–93; Hoare, *Wiltshire*, i (2), 95–100; Devizes Museum, Hungerford Colls., Personal i, fos. 271v–6; table II.

[27] J. E. Jackson, 'On the History of Chippenham', *WAM* iii, 1857, 43; J. M. Fletcher, 'The Tomb of Lord Walter Hungerford K.G. in Salisbury Cathedral', *WAM* xlvii, 1935–37, 448; Roskell, *Parliament and Politics* ii, 99.

[28] E.g. John Pratt, rector of Winterbourne Homington and household chaplain of Joan Hungerford, and John Carter, rector of Camerleton and receiver-general to Walter.

for appropriation, notably parish churches at Blunsdon St Andrew, Rushall, Cricklade and Rowley and free chapels at Corston in Hillmarton, Imber and Folke (Dors.), with potentially adverse effects on the ministry to the laity. They also suppressed chantries at Heytesbury, Upton Scudamore and Calne, diverting the endowments to other purposes. The standard justification for this, that the livings could not be filled and that divine service was thereby increased, is sometimes demonstrably untrue. The Hungerfords had to submit to local inquiries, where their arguments could be refuted and local opposition expressed. Where this happened, however, the bishops over-looked it in their eagerness to satisfy such great people, who as patrons were supposed to have the best interests of their foundations at heart. Bishops, of course, were quite accustomed to diverting parochial revenue into higher education and diocesan administration, to which they accorded a higher priority. Walter and Margaret thus acted within their rights and indeed in accordance with accepted contemporary standards, but they were not observing the spirit of the original founders' wishes.

Such transactions imperilled a founder's soul. Given the belief that every mass alleviated the founder's sufferings in purgatory, how could Walter justify stoking the flames by suppressing an existing chantry or by diluting its efficacy through annexation to another? In 1442, when refounding St Mary's chantry, Heytesbury, Bishop Aiscough had ordered commemoration of all the founders, which Margaret conveniently forgot. No doubt the claims of unknown and unrelated founders could be rejected painlessly, but how did Walter justify to himself the suppression of the Calne chantry of his great-uncle Robert I, whom he had himself commemorated elsewhere? It was accepted that references in another's masses were no substitute for masses of one's own, yet this fault was not uncommon.[29] Indeed it has often been observed that strange moral standards, even fraud, were perfectly compatible with genuine piety.

Each generation inherited obligations from its parents – wills to perform, foundations to complete, and vows to fulfil. Preoccupied with the future of his own soul and encouraged by the belief that the pains of purgatory could be alleviated after his death, the medieval testator devised a range of tasks, often numerous, strenuous, expensive and tedious, for his executors to perform. The burden (and indeed expense) often fell most heavily on the heirs. Walter's pious instincts were not those of his parents, yet he was absorbed by their foundations until 1429, when he was about fifty years of age. He himself left unfinished business that was not completed until twenty-three years after his death. As each defunct testator receded into the past and most bequests were executed, the living became increasingly concerned with their own interests. If Margaret can be believed, most of Robert II's legacies had been

---

[29] Wood-Legh, *Chantries*, 308; for what follows, see e.g. M. A. Hicks, 'The Neville earldom of Salisbury 1429–71', below **359, 361**.

largely fulfilled by *c.* 1472, when she admitted to only £35 6*s* 8*d* still outstanding, which she enjoined her executors to carry out. She listed them again in 1476, again leaving them to her executors.[30] Whether her instructions were observed we cannot know, but Margaret's conscience was thereby salved. Likewise founders' heirs remembered the failed foundations at Longleat and Bath: Walter's qualms were assuaged by repayment of his debt and Margaret's by provision of life-pensions to the remaining almsfolk, not by execution of their fathers' wishes. These were conscience payments like the often derisory bequests for forgotten tithes. Heirs could close their eyes to sufferings in purgatory prolonged by their delay and neglect, yet – perhaps because of this – were only too aware that their wishes might be ignored and their foundations allowed to fail. Walter and Margaret were far from unique in menacing their feoffees and executors with the 'day of doom' or 'dredfull day of Jugement', but threats alone would have little effect until those at risk composed themselves for death. Such clauses and rigorous statutes were no substitute for trust, for reliable executors, and it was on 'the grete love and trust that hath long bene betwene theym and me' that Margaret really relied. The trustworthy heirs and executors were constrained for much of their lives by the dead hand of the past. In all fairness, they faithfully performed most of the burdensome obligations that their parents had heaped onto them.

Heirs moulded their parents' foundations to suit themselves. All Walter's chantries were dedicated to the Virgin or the Annunciation, even that which his mother wanted for St Anne, and Margaret's personal preferences took priority both at Heytesbury hospital and her husband's burial place. Individual taste coloured bequests and foundations and long-term changes are discernible, although the progression is not continuous or direct. Thomas patronised only Austin canons, principally the Arrouasians and Bonshommes, whereas his uncle Robert had patronised them together with other regular orders and had endowed three secular chantries in sharply contrasting locations. Apart from the obits at Bath and Syon abbeys, all later foundations were secular. The hospitals, Walter's school at Heytesbury, and the Syon obit can all be classed as 'forward–looking' benefactions. They can be supplemented by Walter's munificence to Merton College, Oxford and by the bequests of himself and Robert II to the Carthusians. But this neat progression is denied by the wills, where the bequests span almost the whole spectrum. Austin canons, miscellaneous nunneries and Dominican friaries far outnumber Carthusian and Bridgettine houses. Religious houses eclipse in numbers and size of bequest the few hospitals mentioned. Parish churches are also prominent. In short, the range of religious interests remained unchanged, but new foundations – infinitely more expensive than mere legacies – were confined to secular chantries and hospitals. Foundations and bequests alike were concentrated in the Hungerford heartland of north-east

[30] WRO, 490/1465d; Devizes Museum, Hungerford Colls., Personal i, fos. 271v, 276.

Somerset and west Wiltshire, but the wills reveal more peripheral interests in Oxford, London, Middlesex and the far west among different testators.

As Professor Rosenthal also found, those commemorated in foundations were normally in the direct line of the founder, especially the male line.[31] Ancestors took precedence over descendants and chantries were smothered with ancestral shields. Apart from Robert I and Geva, whose repeated commemoration testifies to their importance for a parvenu family, later Hungerfords did not normally remember collaterals, even siblings or children. Walter remembered none of his brothers and merely commemorated his children in general terms. Living offspring received education, marriages, estates and bequests, once dead their obits were entered in family service books, but they were not specific beneficiaries from family foundations. The obit of Walter's son Walter (d. 1432) was entered in his father's missal, but he was remembered neither in his father's later foundations nor in his will.[32] Margaret did not remember her three dead sons, nor (except at Syon) her grandson Thomas, nor indeed her own siblings. While men understandably commemorated the male line, ignoring – except heraldically – their maternal ancestors, the women recalled their female progenitors. Thus Joan asked for *her* ancestors to be prayed for, a wish overlooked by her son. Margaret specifically remembered only her father among her Botreaux ancestors, although others unnamed were known to lie at Little Cheverell chantry and Launceston priory (Corn.), but she commemorated not only her mother at Bridgewater (Som.), but her maternal grandparents and uncle. She provided no prayers for her stepmother, nor her father-in-law's second wife, whose own will of 1455 betrays mistrust of both Margaret and her husband.[33] As Walter commemorated only his mother, not his father's first wife, the step was apparently a genuine barrier to family feeling.

The principal beneficiaries were the founders, whose tastes took precedence over all other considerations and even militated against consistency in family piety and benefactions. Hence the multiplication of foundations. Walter could have augmented Robert I's chantries and been commemorated with him, but this cheap alternative was rejected in favour of new foundations. The overlap from generation to generation was remarkably small, even though territorial continuity compelled regular contact with earlier foundations. Just as devoted to the Austin canons as his uncle and in-laws, Thomas patronised Edington, Longleat and Lesnes, not Ivychurch nor Maiden Bradley. None of Robert I's or Thomas's foundations were supplemented by their heirs. The search for personal benefits resulted not just in the prolifera-

---

[31] Rosenthal, *Purchase of Paradise*, 14–20; compare P. W. Fleming, 'Charity, Faith and the Gentry of Kent 1422–1529', *Property and Politics: Essays in Later Medieval English History*, ed. A. J. Pollard, Gloucester 1984, 51.

[32] V. Leroquais, *Les Sacrementaires et les Missels Manuscrits des Bibliothèques Publiques de France*, Paris 1924, iii, 24.

[33] PRO, PROB 11/4 (PCC 3 Stokton, will of Eleanor, countess of Arundel).

tion of foundations, but also in their duplication, so that there came to be three Hungerford foundations in Salisbury cathedral and two in Farleigh chapel. Robert I lay at Hungerford, sixteenth-century relatives at Heytesbury. Without a single, imposing mausoleum, such as Bisham Abbey (Montagu), Warwick College (Beauchamp) or Tewkesbury Abbey (Despenser), the Hungerfords were commemorated in paltry chantries, where at the dissolution half-forgotten chaplains celebrated daily in tattered vestments from antique mass-books.[34] This striking individuality emerges yet more clearly from the liturgical provisions of these foundations, not discussed here.

Few non-relatives were commemorated at these chantries, but every licence names the monarch of the day. This was an essential inducement for him to permit its endowment.[35] Similarly the commemoration of Dean Goldwell and Bishop Beauchamp at Salisbury and Heytesbury was probably the price Margaret paid for their support. However that may be, neither the reigning monarch nor these ecclesiastics are mentioned in her statutes: privileges granted to smoothe the course of foundation could be conveniently forgotten later.

The principal obstacle to the would-be founder was the necessity for a royal licence to alienate in mortmain. Securing a licence was never a formality. Mortmain has generally been discussed by reference to licences on the patent roll, but such enrolments both overestimate and underestimate the numbers: many enrolments never took effect, many licences went unenrolled, and illegal alienation without licences was common. Thus mortmain cannot be studied purely from the licences, which represent the result of intrigue uncertain of success. Problems in securing licences or the high fines charged forced monasteries to sell donations for ready cash. Licences were not always forthcoming even at a prohibitive price.

In contrast Dr Raban writes:[36]

> Mortmain legislation involved the church in expense and effort. It did not greatly inhibit its freedom of action. There was little to prevent acquisition if the extra cost was judged worthwhile . . . there is no convincing evidence that it had anything other than superficial effect on ecclesiastical participation in the land market.

Dr Raban sets licences to alienate in context, but her context and hence her study is biased in several different ways. It is biased towards the recipients of amortised land; towards ancient Benedictine houses in eastern England before 1400; towards purchases of land by recipients, not gifts by patrons; and towards the success stories recorded in licences and cartularies, rather

---

[34] J. E. Jackson, 'Wiltshire Chantry Furniture', *WAM* xxii, 1885, 322–3.

[35] Wood-Legh, *Chantries*, 311.

[36] S. Raban, 'Mortmain in Medieval England', *P & P* lxii, 1974, 1–26. The next five paragraphs are based on this article and Raban, *Mortmain Legislation, passim*.

than the failures.[37] To Raban a licence is a mark of success, however long it took to secure, despite her evidence of the protracted nature of the licensing process and of intermediate tenure by nominees and feoffees pending the issue of a licence. These devices permitted greater freedom on the land market and enabled licences to be put off until piecemeal acquisitions justified the expense. While these are valid considerations, it is equally likely, indeed more likely, that approval of the desired licences was neither easy nor automatic. To secure any favour, including a licence, a suitor needed access to a monarch and a favourable response to his petition. Hard work and expense, not always successful, was required in the parallel suits for exemption from acts of resumption.[38] Evasion of the licensing regulations became more common in the fifteenth century, but it is not known whether this is due to the crown's growing leniency, as suggested by Dr Raban, or the increasing royal rigour identified by Dr Kreider.[39]

The most striking evidence for royal control of alienation in the fifteenth century is Dr Raban's own graph of licences to alienate in mortmain. Within a long-term decline there are short-term fluctuations corresponding to political changes. The end to the fourteenth-century flood of licences under Henry IV was followed by a trough during Henry V's campaigns abroad. The fifteenth-century peak coincided with Henry VI's majority to 1450. Thereafter licences declined progressively to a low point under Henry VII. It has been shown that Henry VII rigorously restricted the number of licences. Similarly the peak of 1437–50 coincided with lavish and extravagant patronage of all kinds. At this time the proportion of fines charged fell below the levels current immediately before and afterwards. When Henry VI's patronage was curbed in 1450, the number of licences also fell and the proportion of fines increased. Since, however, the actual number of fines was unchanged while the number of licences diminished, there may also have been real restrictions in the issue of licences. We know this to be true of Henry VI's minority, when almost all licences were subject to reasonable fines and the number of new licences reached the lowest level to date. Anxious to preserve the young king's rights intact, the minority council issued licences only in exceptional circumstances despite protests in parliament. After 1470 when the level of fines rose, the number of licences fell, yet the number of foundations increased: evidence not just of resistance to financial penalties, but also of limits to the number of fines available. It is striking that even Edward IV's brother only secured licences as the reward for political

[37] E.g. in Raban, *P & P* lxii, 23, when Dr Raban writes that licences to alienate 'indicate the number of churchmen who wished to receive property'. Of course many licences concern donations for which there was no single identified clerical recipient.

[38] B. P. Wolffe, *Royal Demesne in English History*, 1973, 156–7; *Rot. Parl.* vi, 389–90, 430, for All Souls College, Oxford and Monkbretton Priory.

[39] A. Kreider, *English Chantries: The Road to Dissolution*, Cambridge, Mass. 1979, 84. For the rest of the article, see ibid. 71–92; *Raban, Mortmain Legislation*, graphs 4–6.

support.[40] By the turn of the century founders could apparently not obtain licences at any price.

This impression is supported earlier in the century by the Hungerford foundations. They represent a small sample just as biased as that of Dr Raban, but biased towards the patron rather than the recipient, towards donations rather than purchases, and towards the mainstream of late medieval benefactions. Walter was particularly well-placed to secure a licence, yet he waited fourteen years before obtaining one for the Farleigh chantry – a delay hardly to be ascribed to financial motives, since he was already supporting the chaplain. Similarly he found it convenient to establish his Salisbury chantry under the chapter's general licence, but even then had to await an appropriate moment and paid a substantial fine. At Chippenham his chapel was built before he obtained a licence. At Heytesbury the hospital was already operating in 1442, when Walter envisaged an enfeoffment to use until a licence was obtained. Although the feoffees were actually financing the almspeople and this was the time of Henry VI's greatest extravagance, even Walter could not secure a licence before his death in 1449, nor was one obtained for a further twenty-three years. As part of a much wider agreement, Edward IV's brother agreed in 1469 to secure licences for the hospital and Salisbury chantry. As Margaret was prepared to pay the fines, the problem cannot have been financial. The king signed the agreement, yet Gloucester could not meet the twelve-month deadline and Margaret had to wait until 1472. Similarly in another reciprocal indenture of 1470, the king agreed to license Lady Hungerford and Moleyns to amortise land to any religious house of her choice.[41] Such cumulative evidence appears conclusive.

Assuming Walter's influence to be finite and to be deployed sparingly, it is remarkable that he squandered it on licences rather than more tangible assets. The exercise of such influence on behalf of religious corporations represented some sacrifice, for which he was rewarded by Bath priory and Salisbury cathedral with a cut of the proceeds. This price was paid willingly and indeed Salisbury's spire appears a mere pretext for extra payments to the canons residentiary. Other foundations, at Easton, Calne and Longleat, also represented exploitation, since the extra income was not commensurate with the additional burdens imposed. It was hardly in the Church's true interests to plunder the parishes to finance private masses for individual laymen.

Such arrangements suggest that Dr Raban underestimated the importance of delay even to undying religious corporations. They undoubtedly concerned laymen, for whom long delays rendered completion of foundations less likely. Too many heirs refused to complete or even overthrew their parents'

---

[40] M. A. Hicks, *False, Fleeting Perjur'd Clarence*, Gloucester 1980, 150–51. See also the comments by Mr Fleming in Pollard, *Property and Politics*, 39.

[41] Huntington Library MS HAP Box 3, indenture of Edward IV and Sir Oliver Manningham, 13 March 1470. I am indebted to the trustees of the H. E. Huntington Library, San Marino, California for permission to cite this document and for supplying a photocopy of it.

foundations. Surely it was desperation that caused donors, otherwise so careful to ensure the survival of foundations, to resort to impermanent, insecure and illegal enfeoffment of endowments? Licences were a genuine limitation to those making new foundations. No longer exercised through the bureaucratic formalities of inquisitions *ad quod dampnum* and escheators, royal control relied instead on the perusal of applications by kings as capable of assiduous attention to detail as Edward IV and Henry VII. Fifteenth-century kings may have been less concerned about alienations to the Church, but they were acutely interested in patronage and its counterpart in fines or service. Mortmain licences became another form of patronage until the level of alienations again caused concern, perhaps not until the reign of Henry VIII.

TABLE III: Rate of Attrition of Hungerford Foundations.

		Foundation Type	Date	to 1535	Dissolution 1536–39	1546–48
Religious houses:						
Benedictines	Bath	obit	1429		x	
Bridgettine	Syon	obit	1470		x	
Cistercians	Stanley	obit	1331		x	
Augustinians	Edington	obit	1365		x	
	Ivychurch	obit	1336		x	
	Ivychurch	chantry	1321	x		
	Lesnes	chantry	1377	x		
	Longleat	chantry	1408	x		
Trinitarian	Easton	chantry	1336		x	
Secular churches:						
Cathedrals	Salisbury	chantry	1334	?		
	Salisbury	chantry	1429			x
	Salisbury	chantry	1472			x
College	Westminster	obit	1427			x
Hospitals	Calne	chantry	1336	x		
	Heytesbury	almshouse	1442			
Parish churches	Chippenham	chantry	c. 1442			x
	Farleigh	chantry	1429			x
	Farleigh	obit	1428			x
	Farleigh	chantry	c. 1442			x
	Hungerford	chantry	1326			x

Sources: text and chantry certificates.

Many chantries had disappeared by the Reformation. So great was the attrition that three-fifths of the early fourteenth-century chantries had disappeared by the 1540s, when the chantry certificates recorded predominantly recent foundations.[42] Dr Kreider reaches this important conclusion by comparing licences to alienate with the chantry certificates of four counties, including Wiltshire. As he appreciates, this technique involves distortion. Taking the Hungerford foundations as an example, the licences are inflated by the inclusion of chantries at Ivychurch and Longleat, which were not

[42] Kreider, 71–86, tables 3.3, 3.4.

founded, and by the use of five licences for two chantries at Farleigh; they are depressed, since obits licensed at Bath and Westminster are not recorded on the patent roll and since foundations at Heytesbury, Farleigh, Syon, Canterbury and Lesnes required no licences.[43] Heytesbury hospital, licensed in 1472 and recorded in the chantry certificates, actually represents five licensed foundations, four of them fourteenth-century chantries. Taking the twenty foundations in table III, two failed at once and another two – Calne and Lesnes – were dissolved respectively in 1442 and 1525. There should thus have remained sixteen (80 per cent) at the Reformation, of which six (30 per cent) were in monastic houses dissolved in 1536–39. Only purely secular chantries survive in the chantry certificates, the eight Hungerford examples representing 40 per cent of the original total, a figure close to the 45.7 per cent surviving from the early fourteenth century found by Kreider.[44] This low proportion results almost wholly from the dissolution of the monasteries. By omitting the dissolution from his calculations, Kreider seriously depressed the number of intercessory institutions active in early Tudor England. He particularly depressed the number of older foundations, since late in the middle ages there was a marked shift from the early fourteenth-century pattern of chantries in monasteries to purely secular foundations. Of the nine monastic foundations of the Hungerfords, two-thirds were of fourteenth-century date. It is no wonder that the chantries were dissolved in 1548, when hundreds or even thousands were abolished a decade earlier. The absence of opposition then is hardly surprising, since most were two centuries old and, as we have seen with the Hungerfords, later generations were preoccupied with their own souls and unconcerned about those of their ancestors. Family tradition played little part in shaping the piety of the individual Hungerford or the distinctive form in which it was expressed.

[43] BL MS Faustina BVIII fo. 12. For what follows, see table III.
[44] This includes the first Salisbury chantry, which may have disappeared much earlier, Salisbury CM, Reg. Hutchins fo. 52.

5

The Piety of Margaret, Lady Hungerford (d. 1478)

It is notoriously difficult for biographers of late-medieval people to recapture the personalities of their subjects, and consequently motives often have to be deduced from actions. This fundamental difficulty prompted the great Professor Jacob Burckhardt to date the emergence of the individual from the Renaissance and to assert that, rulers apart, there were few developed personalities in the Middle Ages. Medieval people saw their world through a sort of 'religious mist', perceiving things distorted rather than as they really were.[1] In spite of some recent support, Burckhardt's theory is not really tenable, but historians still find the prevalent religious aura difficult to penetrate. We may know the official doctrine and moral teaching of the Church, but we cannot safely assume that they were understood by the laity, when both contemporary sermons and literature proclaim the contrary. Even were the Church's teaching understood, historians would still not know in what ways and to what extent religion influenced other fields of individual activity – economic, social or political. Burckhardt's problem remains of more than purely religious importance.

For this reason, those not primarily historians of religion are now studying the piety of the late medieval laity, hoping thereby to 'relate their attitudes to faith and charity to some of their other pre-occupations'.[2] The usual approach is through analysis of wills, normally of a specific social

BL = British Library; EETS = Early English Text Society; PRO = Public Record Office; SRO = Somerset Record Office; *WAM = Wiltshire Archaeology and Natural History Magazine*; WRO = Wiltshire Record Office. All documents are cited by their repository call-numbers. Financial support for the preparation of this article has been provided by King Alfred's College, Winchester.

[1] J. Burckhardt, *Civilisation of the Renaissance in Italy*, ed. S. G. C. Middlemore and I. Gordon, London 1960, 121.

[2] P. W. Fleming, 'Charity, faith and the gentry of Kent 1422–1529', in *Property and Politics: essays in later medieval English history*, ed. A. J. Pollard, Gloucester 1984, 37. The following two paragraphs are based on ibid. 36–58; J. T. Rosenthal, *Purchase of Paradise*, London 1972; M. G. A. Vale, *Piety, Charity and Literacy among the Yorkshire Gentry 1370–1480*, (Borthwick Paper l, 1976); *Church, Politics and Patronage in the Fifteenth Century*,

group or locality. Wills are at once the most personal and most numerous records of late medieval piety and are therefore those most susceptible of statistical analysis and generalisation. This is now an accepted approach to the relative popularity of Catholicism and Protestantism after the Reformation and of Catholicism and Lollardy before it. It is less fruitful when applied to the orthodox. So far, such studies have confirmed the prevalence of fear of death and of belief in purgatory and the efficacy of good works. They have tabulated the popularity of different types of bequest and have tentatively identified some developments over time. They have not, however, penetrated deeply into the minds of testators, nor established the degree of understanding or fervour underlying their bequests. They have not substantiated the superstitions or excesses denounced by contemporaries: if such beliefs were confined to those socially inferior to testators, it would invalidate Mr Peter Heath's claim that the 'self-revelations' of Hull's 'governing elite...provide limits within which to locate the sentiments and priorities of the community at large'. The emergence of varying patterns of bequests between social groups and regions also casts doubt on the value of such studies for generalisation. It is on such frail foundations that Mr Heath concludes that

their faith was remarkably insular, inert and shallow, untouched by new devotions, perfunctory almost in the old ones, uninterested in and showing no deep acquaintance with doctrine...The assumption that most medieval people were anguished by the prospect of the horrors awaiting them in the next world rests particularly upon the frequent and vivid portrayals of purgatory and hell in literature, sermons, paintings and stained glass of the period; yet may not their frequency and intensity (as with all those statutes against livery and maintenance) simply testify to their futility and neglect?

Such qualitative conclusions, perhaps valid for Hull, are flatly contradicted by P. W. Fleming for Kent, who finds both 'a more personal, less institutionalised form of worship' and that 'religion pervaded daily life'.

There are even fewer studies of everyday religion, those of Professor J. T. Rosenthal and Dr Colin Richmond reaching diametrically opposite conclusions. More promising are the studies of particular individuals – the first duke of Lancaster, Margery Kempe, Henry VI and Cecily, duchess

ed. R. B. Dobson, Gloucester 1984, ch. ix (by C. F. Richmond) and ch. x (by P. Heath); J. T. Rosenthal, 'Richard, duke of York: a fifteenth-century layman and the Church', *Catholic Historical Review* l (1964), 171–87; K. Fowler, *Henry of Grosmont, Duke of Lancaster*, London 1961, ch. xv; C. A. J. Armstrong, 'The piety of Cecily, duchess of York: a study in late medieval culture', in *England, France and Burgundy in the Fifteenth Century*, London 1983, 135–56; R. Lovatt, 'John Blacman: biographer of Henry VI', in *The Writing of History in the Middle Ages*, ed. R. H. C. Davis and J. M. Wallace-Hadrill, Oxford 1981, 415–44; J. A. F. Thomson, 'Piety and charity in late medieval London', this JOURNAL xvi (1965), 178–95; A. Goodman, 'The piety of John Brunham's daughter of Lynn', in *Medieval Women*, Studies in Church History, Subsidia i (1978), 347–58.

of York – which throw a flood of light on their subjects. The fervour of these individuals contrasts sharply with the shallow conformity of the burgesses of Hull. Such studies, unfortunately, are based on unique sources, which exist only because of the exceptional qualities of those depicted. They do not therefore illuminate the conventional phrases of the wills.

At present there is no historical consensus on the theological beliefs or moral principles of the late medieval laity. If one could explore such aspects of medieval piety, it would be easier to penetrate the 'religious mist' and recapture medieval personalities, to chart the scope and extent of individualism, and to discuss motivation in other fields of history with greater confidence. Moreover, one could measure by results the pastoral success of the much maligned medieval parish clergy and assess the preparedness of the laity for the challenges of Lollardy and Lutheranism. Such questions cannot now be answered for the bulk of the population and perhaps never will be, but it is the contention of this article that they can be answered for many individuals. From such concrete results it may become possible to generalise for the whole rural elite and urban patriciate. As a first stage, this article aims to provide answers for one individual whose piety can be reconstituted – Margaret, Lady Hungerford and Botreaux, who died in 1478.

Margaret, Lady Hungerford, was one of those formidable dowagers, who played such a prominent role in late medieval England. The daughter and eventually sole heiress of William, Lord Botreaux (d. 1462), Margaret married the eldest son of the parvenu Sir Walter Hungerford, Speaker of the House of Commons, royal councillor and Treasurer of England, Knight of the Garter, and ultimately first Lord Hungerford. At Walter's death in 1449 his income of over a thousand pounds a year was more than the qualifying level for an earl and placed him well above the poorest baron, but far below the greatest contemporary magnates. Margaret herself only emerged from the shadows on the death of her husband Robert, Lord Hungerford in 1459. On his deathbed Robert confided to her his lands and the responsibility for paying the huge ransom of their eldest son Robert, Lord Moleyns. Her problems were enormously exacerbated by the political miscalculations of her descendants in the Wars of the Roses. Moleyns was attainted in 1461 and executed in 1464, and his eldest son was executed in 1469. Margaret herself was arrested three times. For almost twenty years she battled to save the family inheritance against almost overwhelming odds, discovering a talent for politics and turning her obstinacy, single-mindedness and stamina into political assets. She had to become devious and cunning, had to distort the truth when arguing her case and had to make unpalatable decisions about priorities. She could not have clean hands, but in 1476 she claimed to have saved most of the inheritance for her heirs, her grandson Walter

Hungerford and her great-granddaughter Mary Hastings. Passing on less than she started with, she nevertheless felt the need to justify to her heirs their attenuated heritage.[3]

Margaret also had to justify herself to God, an alarming prospect. Impending death and her hope of salvation concerned her increasingly from 1469, just as acutely as her younger and more leisured counterparts Cecily, duchess of York and Margaret Beaufort. By 1476 Margaret had completed her mortuary chapel at Salisbury and the chantry within it, had established her obit at Syon Abbey and had permanently endowed the almshouse at Heytesbury originally established by her father-in-law.

During these years Margaret's religious activities created a wealth of source material which, this article contends, illuminates the quality of her personal religion. Pride of place must go to the splendid series of foundation deeds and statutes of Heytesbury hospital and her Salisbury chantry preserved in the Hungerford cartulary at Taunton, which also contains an inventory of the furnishings of the chantry chapel. Secondly, there are three wills of her lands of 1471, c. 1473 and 1476 and a single will of her moveables of 1477.[4] Thirdly, there are the descriptions and illustrations of the chapel itself made by the eighteenth-century antiquarians. Finally, all these can be supplemented by her estate records and the records of the recipient institutions. What is conspicuously lacking is anything relating to her religion before 1469 and evidence casting light on her everyday routine. Despite such omissions, however, the evidence gives a remarkably vivid impression of Margaret Hungerford and her piety.

Obviously there was much involved in her foundations that Margaret could not perform herself, notably the casting of her statutes into Latin, for which she had expert – no doubt ecclesiastical – help. About 1473 she wrote:

all the wich my wille and declaracion of the same, I have perfitely comend and shewed unto the right reverend Fader in God my Lord the Bishop of Salisbury, as to my Diocisan and Fader, beryng the cure of my soule for the discharge of my consciens. And forasmuch as my seall and subscripcion is not to meny men knowen, to my saide speciall Lorde and Fader I haue made requeste and humble besechyng in witnesses of the premisses to put his grete sealle. And I, the saide Bisshop at the requeste of the saide Lady Margaret, to this presente writynge have putte my seale, and signed it with myne hande. And for the more evydent

---

[3] R. C. Hoare, *History of Modern Wiltshire*, 6 vols., London 1822–40, i. (2). 100–2; *Somerset Medieval Wills 1383–1500*, ed. E. Weever (Somerset Record Society xvi, 1901), 191–2.

[4] These wills are: PRO, C 54/312 rot.8d (lands, 1471); H. A. Huntington Library, California, HAP Box 3 (lands, c. 1473); Hoare, i (2). 95–100 (lands, 1476); WRO, 490/1544 (chattels, 1477), now largely illegible but transcribed in Devizes Museum, Canon Jackson's Hungerford Family Collections, Personal i, fos. 269–78v. I am indebted to the Trustees of the H. A. Huntington Library for permission to cite the will quoted above.

knowlege to witnesse the same, at my speciall requeste and praier, aswel my maister the Dene and Chapitre of Salisbury have putte their comen sealis.[5]

The same words, signature and seal of the bishop and chapter seal appear in her 1476 will. The foundation of her chantry was sealed in the Salisbury chapter house by the founders, Bishop Beauchamp and the cathedral chapter. It was to future deans, chancellors and the chapter that she confided the direction of both foundations after her death. Both required the licence of the bishop and Dean Goldwell, who were therefore included among the founders. Two other canons were executors. They were not, however, the executors in whom she reposed most trust, nor were there any churchmen among the overseers made privy to her will. Her self-criticism points to the activities of a confessor, but she mentions none in her will, except perhaps Dominican friars at Fisherton, far from her principal seat. Her final will was made 'by good avisement', but was also her personal composition. We know of no other mind responsible for the iconography or vestments of her chapel, themselves consistent with the prayers in her statutes. All combine elements of the Sarum primer and the Syon use. What bishop, dean or canon of Salisbury could employ in Salisbury cathedral anything other than the use of Sarum? How Margaret saw herself, from at least 1465 until death, appears on her seal, which depicts her kneeling at prayer with an open book upon her lap. The consistency of wills, buildings, furnishings, statutes and seal is convincing evidence that the plans were devised by Margaret and merely approved by the bishop.[6]

Margaret's father was a generous benefactor of the Church, the founder of St Michael's College, North Cadbury and of an almshouse and chantry at Bath. The education provided for his daughter taught her to read both English and French and to write in a large, sprawling hand. She habitually signed her wills and other formal documents, and in her final year, in her mid-seventies, she added a codicil of thirty lines to her will in her own hand. Apart from a French *Golden Legend*, the standard collection of saints' lives and Old Testament stories bound up with her psalter, Margaret is recorded as owner only of service books, including three for her personal use. One was her primer, that 'matyns boke covered with blew velvet and clapsed with silver and gilt with my worde "Myne Assured Trouth"'. Another was her psalter, illuminated throughout, and a third was her book of the use of the Brigettines of Syon.[7] This was

[5] Huntington Library, HAP Box 3; Hoare, i (2). 100. For what follows, see Hoare, i (2). 124–33; Devizes Museum, Personal i, fos. 269–70, 278; SRO, DDX/SAS H348 fo. 320–v (Hungerford cartulary); J. E. Jackson, 'Ancient statutes of Heytesbury almshouse', *WAM* xi (1869), 291–6; Winchester College MSS 10157–8, 10160a–b, 10162 (seals).

[6] W. Dugdale, *Baronage of England*, London 1679, i. 630; for what follows, see Huntington Library HAD 2314, 2210; WRO, 490/1544; WRO, 251/53.

[7] Lambeth Palace Library, Register of Archbishop Stafford, fo. 117a; Devizes Museum, Personal i, fos. 269, 275; WRO, 490/1544.

presumably the English *Myroure of oure Ladye* used by the nuns rather
than the Latin breviary of the brothers. Use of such works need not imply a
knowledge of Latin: psalters were often bilingual and many primers – like
the *Myroure* – were in English. Even if her primer was in Latin, this need
imply only a capacity to read Latin, not to understand it. Medieval
children often learned to read from Latin service books, yet as the
anonymous author of the *Myroure* told the sisters of Syon, 'forasmoche as
many of you, though ye can synge and rede, yet ye can not se what the
meanynge therof ys... I haue drawen youre legende and all youre seruyce
in to Englyshe... '

If the Syon nuns could read and sing a Latin service and if even literate
paupers could read the psalms without comprehending Latin,[8] so, too,
could Margaret Hungerford. English remained the mother tongue of her
wills, formal indentures and even of the inventory of her chantry
furnishings.

The Hungerford men were literate also in Latin. Margaret's father-
in-law read both poetry and theology and was charitable and pious: even
before founding Heytesbury hospital, he habitually supported a dozen
paupers. Although he failed to elevate his oratory at Heytesbury into a
college, his household chapel there was staffed in 1436 by Master John
Russell, 'rector capelle domini mei Hungerford', other priests, a cleric
awaiting ordination as a priest, boys and clerks. He founded four chantries
dedicated to St Mary or her Annunciation, which Margaret must have
known well.[9] His son Robert probably visited the Holy Land, shared in his
father's foundation of St Mary's chantry, Chippenham and possessed a
silver gilt statuette of the Blessed Virgin. He helped Salisbury Cathedral
secure the canonisation of St Osmund, before whose altar he asked to be
buried. At death he owned missals, a breviary and gradual, six altarcloths,
two complete sets of vestments for priest, deacon and subdeacon, six spare
copes, a chalice, sacring bell, pyx, two cruets, a holy water dish with
aspersorium and an almsdish shaped like a hand.

Margaret, 'my most dear consort', received some of these items,[10] and
in 1477 her chapel at Heytesbury, staffed by at least two priests, was hung
with 'rede tapestry worke with lyons and Aungells hedys' and equipped
with at least two altarcloths, chasuble, alb, stole, phane and periers. The
stock was presumably reduced *c.* 1463, when she lost £1,000-worth of
moveables in a fire at Amesbury and had to replace the destroyed
building, an unfortunate experience that perhaps explains the absence of

[8] *Myroure of oure Ladye*, ed. J. H. Blunt (EETS, extra series xix, 1873), 2; N. Orme,
English Schools in the Middle Ages, London 1973, 63; Jackson, 'Ancient Statutes', 300.
[9] M. A. Hicks, 'St Katherine's Hospital, Heytesbury: prehistory, foundation and
refoundation',   below, chapter 6, 123-4;   N. Orme, *Education in the West of England*, Exeter
1976, 142; M. A. Hicks, 'Chantries, obits and hospitals: the Hungerford foundations
1325-1478', in *The Church in Pre-Reformation Society*, ed. C. Barron and C. Harper-Bill,
Woodbridge 1985, below 83-8.
[10] *Catalogue des rolles gascons, normands et françois*, ed. T. Carte, London 1743, ii. 255;
Somerset Medieval Wills, 186–88; *Calendar of Patent Rolls 1441-6*, 151.

any legacy to Amesbury Abbey![11] She could probably have escaped liability in the 1460s for her son's debts, but considering herself 'bonden only at the speciall instaunce & praier of her said housband... to the vttermost of her power' regarded payment of outstanding creditors as a pious duty essential for the salvation of his soul and indeed her own.[12] The binding obligations laid on her as trustee before her son's forfeiture proved useful in her battle with the grantees of the family lands who were thereby compelled to permit expenditure and even alienation of property. Probably this is why, repeatedly from 1471, she stated that Robert had ordered the establishment of the Salisbury chantry in his last will, a claim that cannot be accepted.[13] The will written less than a month before his death requested no permanent chantry and asked for burial before St Osmund's altar in the cathedral Lady chapel, where in 1464–9 Margaret endowed a daily mass for his soul. The new chantry and chapel were her idea: doubtless she thought them so beneficial for his soul that they outweighed his choice of burial place and believed her patrons to be more effective intercessors than St Osmund, who features nowhere in the foundation. Likewise her Heytesbury statutes ignore the dedication to St Katherine, but refer repeatedly to Jesus and the Virgin.

If in 1469 she intended to found a permanent chantry at St Osmund's altar or adjoining it, this was a plan modified by her sojourn in Syon Abbey. Following the Lincolnshire Rebellion of March/May 1470, Edward IV arrested Margaret and permitted her, for a payment of £200, to withdraw to Syon.[14] There she was evidently admitted as a sister, 'partener of al spiritual subsidies... in lyfe and in dethe' and was promised that

whan any knowlage of zour decese comethe to us, or to our successours, the same suffrages schal be done for zowe... wonte to be done for brethren and sustres of our chapitre... And yf they of ther own mocion and fre wyl do any benefete of notable substaunce to the monastery, this owethe to be wryten withe ther names, and they schal be rekened amonge to the benefactours.

The martyrology was read daily at a special service unique to Syon, when the sisters visited a grave 'kept constantly open, into which the abbess cast some earth, saying the Psalm *De profundis*'. Like the earth-stained coffin placed by the church door for those entering to see, the service was meant to put

a remembrance of death in their mind, & consider in their hearts that they are earth, and unto earth they will return... to beholde also the shortnes and vnstablenes of this lyf, the hastynes of dethe, the ferefulnes of dome, the bytternes of paynes, and the swete and ioyful rewardes of blysse... [And] to arme you in

[11] Hoare i (2). 125–34; Devizes Museum, Personal i, fos. 270r–v, 274r–v.

[12] PRO, C 1/28/111D.

[13] PRO, C 54/312 rot. 8d; WRO, 490/1465. For what follows, see *Somerset Medieval Wills*, 186–93, esp. p. 186; PRO, S.C.6/1119/14 m.4,/15 m.4; C. Wordsworth, *Ceremonies and Processions of the Cathedral Church of Salisbury*, Cambridge 1901, 228.

[14] BL, Cott. MS Jul. BXII, fo. 124; Hoare, i (2). 102.

the name of the blessed trinyte with mynde of your dethe and of your dome ageynst all temptacyons in youre dayly dedes.

In a second service unique to Syon, *Indulgete*, the sisters forgave one another's faults in preparation for death.[15] Impressed, Margaret took up the proffered prayers, ordered her heart to be despatched to Syon immediately after her death, paid £100 and more for the insertion of herself and her relatives in the martyrology and adopted elements of the Syon office of compline in her own mortuary chapel.[16]

Margaret later displayed considerable knowledge of the Syon use, drawing on items from different services and days. The English translations in the *Myroure* cannot have been her sole source for these items, as they do not represent accurately the tonal qualities of the Latin original, whose importance to Margaret is indicated by the predominance of versicles, hymns and anthems among her selected texts. That Margaret was musical is suggested not just by commonplace requests for sung masses before her funeral and for participation by her cantarists on Sundays and festivals in sung services and processions in the cathedral choir, but also in her provision for them of an antiphoner, a psalter and two processionals even though only low mass would be said – not sung – in their chapel.[17] After leaving Syon, Margaret could not have used the *Myroure* as a source for the Latin texts, but must have relied either on subsequent communication or memory. Her knowledge is most obviously explained by her own experience of the sisters' services at Syon – in short, by full participation in their observances during her stay.

The Syon use provided for 'constant praise of God by women with and through the Virgin Mother'. It gave extended consideration to St Mary in the context of Christian history from the creation to the Assumption. The *Myroure* helped the sisters appreciate 'how worthy and holy praysynge of oure gloryous Lady is contente therein, & the more deuoutly and knowyngly synge yt & rede yt and say yt to her worshyp...'. It translates each prayer and expounds its meaning and the liturgical significance of each prayer, service and day, but does so only once, where each item first occurs.[18] In cases of doubt it has been assumed that the first occurrence in the *Myroure* is Margaret's source and the explanation there has been employed to interpret her use of particular elements.

Margaret left Syon after King Edward's deposition in October 1470 and by 12 January 1471 had drafted ordinances for her chapel; the altar

[15] G. J. Aungier, *History and Antiquities of Syon Monastery*, London 1840, 271, 245; *Myroure*, xxvii–ix, 166.

[16] Devizes Museum, Personal i, fo. 269; BL, Add. MS 22285 fo. 71 (martyrology of Syon); see below, 33.

[17] J. E. Jackson, 'Inventory of chantry furniture AD 1472, Hungerford Chapel, Salisbury Cathedral', *WAM* xi (1869), 338; SRO, DDX/SAS H348 fo. 324v; Devizes Museum, Personal i, fos. 269r–70v.

[18] *Myroure*, 3–5; *Bridgettine Breviary of Syon Abbey*, ed. A. J. Collins (Henry Bradshaw Society xcvi, 1969), ix.

was consecrated on 14 October by Bishop Beauchamp himself, Margaret kneeling devoutly throughout.[19] There were alternative dedications to Jesus and the Virgin or the Trinity and the Virgin, whose significance for Margaret emerges in such invocations as 'the high and individual Trinity and especially of Jesus Christ our redeemer and the Blessed Virgin his mother' and her bequest of her soul to them, God and all saints. Christ's membership of the Trinity and Mary's closeness to it are recurrent themes in Margaret's thoughts that were appropriately symbolised by her chapel's proximity to the Trinity or Lady Chapel next door.

The Hungerford chapel abutted on the north of the Lady chapel in mirror image of the slightly earlier Beauchamp chapel on the south.[20] A plain stone structure much lower and somewhat shorter than the Lady chapel, it was divided internally into two compartments by a central surbased arch. The altar against the east wall was flanked by niches, presumably containing the figures of Christ and the Virgin mentioned in the statutes: the foundress gave two linen cloths 3 × 9 ft to 'cover ye ymages with in the Lente'.[21] To the right of the altar an arch in the Lady chapel wall contained the table tomb of Robert, Lord Hungerford, whose alabaster effigy faced the altars both of the chantry and of St Osmund next door. Left of the altar was ample space for Margaret's tomb, but instead her tall marble monument in imitation of a pall lay beneath the central arch in the very heart of the chapel. There was no permanent furniture in the western compartment, but on the west wall were murals of St Christopher and the Annunciation. Over the south entrance the figure of a man in parliamentary robes or academic dress, perhaps Robert Hungerford himself, held an inscription. On either side of the door were panels of Death addressing men in contemporary dress before open coffins depicting two scenes from the Legend of the Three Living and the Three Dead.[22] Limited space and the absence of other panels suggest that there

[19] PRO, C 54/312 rot. 8d; Wordsworth, *Ceremonies*, 285n, citing Salisbury Cathedral Muniments, Chapter Act Book Machon, p. 72. For what follows, see SRO, DDX/SAS H348 fo. 319v; Jackson, 'Inventory', 334; Devizes Museum, Personal i, fos. 269, 277v-8.

[20] The description of chapels and decorations is based on *History and Antiquities of the Cathedral-Church of Salisbury and the Abbey Church of Bath*, London 1719, 128–32; R. Symonds, *Diary of the Marches of the Royal Army during the Great Civil War*, ed. C. G. Long (Camden Society lxxiv, 1859), 130–2; J. Hutchins, *History and Antiquities of the County of Dorset*, ed. W. Shipp and J. W. Hodson, London 1870, iv. 176–8; R. Gough, *Ancient Sepulchral Monuments in Great Britain*, London 1796, ii (2). 186–91 and plates 70–2; Bodleian, Oxford, Gough Map 32 fos. 43–v, 51, 53–v; H. de S. Shortt, *Hungerford and Beauchamp Chantry Chapels*, Salisbury 1970.

[21] Jackson, 'Inventory', 339; Wordsworth, *Ceremonies*, 286.

[22] The figures used to be considered fragments of a Dance of Death: Gough, *Sepulchral Monuments*, ii (2), 187–8; J. M. Clark, *Dance of Death in the Middle Ages and the Renaissance*, Glasgow 1950, 10–11. However, this view is untenable. For the new interpretation, see P. Tristram, *Figures of Life and Death in Medieval English Literature*, London 1976, 162–9, esp. p. 168. Although no verses come from Lydgate's *Dance of Death*, his poem also features a 'Gallant Squire', *Dance of Death*, ed. F. Warren (EETS, original series lxxxi, 1931), p. xxvi. Two ages of man and two stages of decomposition – a corpse and a skeleton – were depicted.

never was a third scene. Inside and out the chapel was adorned with armorial bearings. Of the original decorations, only the glass is irretrievably forgotten.

Medieval visitors first glimpsed the chapel through the arch over Robert's tomb. Upon entering, they would be reassured by the figure of St Christopher, protector against sudden death, and then appalled, as at Syon, by what at first sight appeared a coffined corpse on a bier awaiting burial. Further progress into the inner compartment was barred by Margaret's monument. There visitors paused to pray as the memorial plate requested. Passing on to the altar and images, visitors were lent Margaret's own illuminated psalter for 'þeir deuocions' if a 'man or woman of worship' or 'suche as be right worshipfull and of grete estate'.[23] Any who were dazzled by the chapel's splendour – like the chapter clerk at Robert's obit in 1472 – were reminded of the vanity of worldly pomp by the versicle on either side of the central arch, 'Not for us, not for us, O lord, but only to thee be the glory'. Praying before Robert's tomb, they would see in gold on the wall: 'O quyene of heuens enclyne thyn ere to vs. To whome the lorde of lordes enclyned hymselfe for vs.' Such sentiments befitted the chapel of Jesus and Mary and were also versicle and response from Sunday matins at Syon marking 'a lytel torning' from psalmody to lessons, from praise to seriousness, from negligence to doing God's will.[24]

Turning to leave, the repeated warning on the central arch against vanity was surely reinforced by the juxtaposition, as with a cadaver, of Robert's lifelike effigy and Margaret's pall. On passing her monument, the by-now chastened visitor was confronted on either side by the horrifying panels of the Living and Dead, linked somewhat unusually, as at Syon, by yawning, open coffins. On one panel of *Death and the Galant*, a young man dressed in the height of fashion *c.* 1470 lamented:

> Alasse, Dethe, alasse a blessful thyng yo were
> Yf thow wolldyst spare us in our lustynesse
> And cum to wretches yt bethe of hevy chere
> When they ye clepe to slake there dystresse...

Unfortunately, 'owte alasse thyne owne sely selfwyldnesse', Death would not stick to those ready to die. Nobody, he sternly warned, could be sure of the hour of death:

> Grasless galante in all thy luste and pryde
> Remembre that thou ones schalte dye
> Deth shold fro thy body thy sowle devyde
> Thou mayst him not ascape certaynly.

---

[23] Devizes Museum, Personal i, fo. 274. For what follows, see Salisbury Cathedral Muniments, Chapter Act Book Machon, 89. The text 'Non nobis, domine, non nobis sed nomini tuo da gloriam' comes from the thanksgiving after mass, J. Wickham-Legg, *Missale*, 217. In what follows, the Latin text is identified from the Syon breviary and quoted from the English translation in the *Myroure*.   [24] *Myroure*, 99–100; *Syon Breviary*, 15.

To ye dedd boddys cast downe thyne ye
Biholde thayme well, consydere and see,
For such as thay ar, such schalt thou be.

The panel was not meant just to horrify but, as at Syon, to force the visitor to face death and damnation and to bring home the message of the transience of human life and worldly pleasures. The 'grasless galante' had committed the deadly sins of lechery and pride, and others were no doubt denounced in the panel for which the inscription is lost. The panels had a didactic, admonitory purpose: called to repent, the visitor was assured of sufficient time by the presence of St Christopher nearby.

St Christopher carried the Christ Child and the sins of the whole world across the river of death: this mural also signifies Christ's conquest of death and his resurrection, symbolised as well on the panels of the *Legend* and throughout the chapel by the symbols Ihs Xpt and thorns. Over the door an inscription recorded the 'Passion that Christe Jesus sufferyd for redempcion' and instructed worshippers to say two Hail Marys (Ave Maria) for Robert who 'lyeth here and dyed'. Repeating the angel's salutation before the painting of the Annunciation, the visitor was reminded of the Virgin's influence with her son and the Trinity. Sobered by the inevitability of death, alerted to the necessity for repentance, reassured by Christ's redeeming passion and by the intercession of the Virgin, nearest to the Trinity, he passed between the two panels of death through the door to the Trinity chapel.[25]

The furnishings conform to the same scheme, while also meeting the requirements of the liturgical year and the service of Jesus and Mary. Margaret supplied nothing second-hand to the chapel, spending £250 on the moveable furnishings, and even such items as corporas cases were embroidered with Ihs, Maria or both. Most impressive were the nine sets of altarcloths – two to a set – frontals and vestments suitable for the whole liturgical year. For everyday use there was a set of red and green baldechin and for Sunday crimson sarsenet embroidered 'Jesus Maria' with her motto. For Lent, besides the curtains to cover images and murals, there was a set of linen cloths with a black frontal appropriately embroidered 'Who knoweth the secret things of our heart, spare our sins'. Of three black or purple-and-black outfits suitable for Good Friday, two bore the Virgin and St John at the foot of the cross and the third the invocation 'Jesus have mercy, Christ have mercy'. Two white sets, probably for Easter and the feasts of the Virgin, had no embroidery associated with the resurrection, but bore respectively an image of Our Lady and a Syon versicle calling on her to intercede with the Son.

Most interesting is the blue damask set provided for Christmas. Embellished with branches of roses and lilies (symbols of the Virgin), all carried Latin texts from Syon. One cloth 'to hang above the Auter', depicting the Virgin and Child standing in a sun upon a moon, bore the

[25] Hoare, i (2). 102; Jackson, 'Inventory', 334–9. For what follows, see ibid. 334–6.

opening of the anthem from Wednesday compline: 'O florysshynge rose, fayre mother of god, O mylde vyrgyn, O moste plenteous vyne, thou that arte brighter then the morow tyde, pray besyly for vs.' Another depicting the Annunciation bore the start to the hymn from Thursday lauds: 'The thynges that ysaye prophesyed. are fulfylled in the vyrgyn. the aungell hath done his mesage. and the holy goste hathe fulfylled.' A third, 'to hang be nethe', had the blessing from Thursday matins: 'The vyrgyn that was gryete of an aungel. vouche safe to do awaye oure synnes. Amen.' On the frontal and chasuble was the beginning of the hymn from Sunday lauds: 'Holy father that madest thyne onely begotten sonne to be borne for vs wretches of the womb of the chaste vyrgyn.' Thus Mary is treated as the fulfilment of Old Testament prophecy, conceiving the Son by the Holy Ghost for redemption, ideal intercessor with the Trinity.[26]

The Syon use also features in the statutes which prescribe specific observances for the chaplains. On first entering the cathedral the chaplains were to say before the sacrament (Corpus Christi) reserved at the high altar a Latin prayer from Sarum primers normally intended for the elevation of the host. Moving on to their own chapel, each was to say mass, matins, evensong, the office of the dead and then a special evening service. Kneeling to Christ before his image, they besought the founders' inclusion among his saints and elect with a prayer from compline of the feast of the Name of Jesus. Then, kneeling before the Virgin's image, they asked for her prayers in an anthem from Friday compline at Syon. Third, standing between the two tombs, they prayed:

Almighty endeless God, that hast vouched safe to be borne fo vs of the most chaste virgyn, we pray the make vs to serue the with chast body. & to plese the with meke harte...And we pray the moste mercyfull vyrgyn mary. quene of the worlde & of aungels, that thow gette refresshyng to them whome the fyre of purgatory purgyth, to synners forgiuenesse. to rightewyse people. perseuerance in good. and defende vs frayle presente pareyles, that is to say from pareyles that contynewally falle vnto vs. By the same our lorde Iesu cryste, Amen.

Common to both Syon and the Sarum use, where it was the final collect for chastity and meekness, this prayer was followed by the commemoration of benefactors, *De profundis* and a collect from the office of the dead.[27]

Combining diverse elements, the service formed a natural completion to the day. Father, Mother and Son were praised in turn, their intercession was sought for salvation and mitigation of purgatorial pains, and the

---

[26] Ibid. 335; *Syon Breviary*, 21, 73, 77n, 113; *Myroure*, 129–30, 220, 225, 232.

[27] SRO, DDX/SAS H348 fos. 323–v, partly quoted in Wordsworth, *Ceremonies*, 285–6; *Myroure*, 137–8, 257; *Missale ad usum insignis et praeclarae ecclesiae Sarum*, ed. F. H. Dickinson, Burntisland 1861–3, ii. 874*; E. Hoskins, *Horae Beatae Mariae Virginis or Sarum and York Primers with Kindred Books*, London 1901, 111–12; *Breviarium ad vsum insignis ecclesiae Sarum*, ed. F. Procter and C. Wordsworth, Cambridge 1886, iii. 619. The prayer 'O glorious king' also occurs in the Sarum compline on Passion Sunday, *Sarum Breviary*, i. dccxv, ii. 231, where it immediately follows the Nunc dimittis – itself a feature of compline at Syon, *Myroure*, 171.

inspiration of the Holy Ghost was requested so that, in the words of the hymn from Sunday lauds cited above, 'ye shulde be the better dysposed and the more able to receyue the graces that ye aske'.[28] From the vestments, texts and these prayers, it appears that Margaret only preferred the Syon use to the Hours of the Virgin, retaining the Sarum use for other purposes. In her will she was actually not particularly generous to Syon and remembered no sister individually.

Margaret valued the prayers by rote of almsmen, the orisons of lay visitors to her chantry, of unordained clerics and of her chaplains at the canonical hours, but for her – as in all chantries – the liturgy centred on the mass, the observance most 'pleasing to the Divine Majesty...whereby not only is merit imputed unto living men, but...relief is obtained after death unto the dead'.[29] Whereas the Sarum use generally conformed to the Christian year, votive masses had a weekly cycle – the Trinity on Sunday, the Angels on Monday, the 'Salvation of the people' ('Salus populi') on Tuesday, the Holy Ghost on Wednesday, Corpus Christi on Thursday, the Holy Cross on Friday and the Virgin ('Salve sacre parens') on Saturday. While variations could be introduced to taste, this authoritative sequence was widely observed. Late in the Middle Ages, new cults generated new votive masses, among them the 'Name of Jesus' and the 'Five Wounds of Christ' as alternatives to the Holy Cross on Friday. The 'Name of Jesus', supposedly originating with Robert Hallum, bishop of Salisbury (d. 1413), was not officially recognised until 1488 and does not feature in the printed breviaries of the 1480s. Although apparently later in origin, the 'Five Wounds' was well known at Syon[30] – featuring in the abbey badge – and occurs in the earliest printed Sarum missal of 1484. That both were prescribed by Margaret for her chantry is another sign of her awareness of the newest liturgical developments.[31] Presumably she encountered the 'Name of Jesus' at Salisbury and the 'Five Wounds' at Syon. Forty days' indulgence attached to celebration in each case was an added attraction,[32] but both new votives, of course, were devotions especially fitting for this chapel.

The second chaplain was to say the Sarum mass of the day except on Monday, when he was to celebrate the mass of the Virgin ('Rorate coeli desuper') associated with the Annunciation by the Angel Gabriel to Mary – a fitting choice, since the normal votive mass for Mondays was of the Angels. The first chaplain was to say a different mass daily in

[28] *Myroure*, 129.

[29] Taken from Walter, Lord Hungerford's foundation deed for his Farleigh Hungerford chantry, printed from the Hungerford cartulary in J. E. Jackson, *Guide to Farleigh Hungerford*, Chippenham 1879.

[30] Dickinson, *Sarum Missal*, 735* ff.; K. L. Wood-Legh, *Perpetual Chantries in Britain*, Cambridge 1965, 288; Lovatt, 'John Blacman', 444.

[31] R. W. Pfaff, *New Liturgical Feasts in Later Medieval England*, Oxford 1970, 62–91. For what follows, see Wordsworth, *Ceremonies*, 286.

[32] Dickinson, *Sarum Missal*, 750*; Pfaff, loc. cit.

unconventional order – Holy Trinity on Sunday, 'Name of Jesus' on Monday, Holy Ghost (Tuesday), requiem (Wednesday), Corpus Christi (Thursday), 'Five Wounds' (Friday) and St Mary ('Salve sacre parens') on Saturday. As only one new votive could be celebrated on the proper day, Friday, the other – the 'Name of Jesus' – had to be located elsewhere. Margaret's addition of a Wednesday requiem mass also displaced the Holy Ghost to Tuesday. This left Monday vacant for the 'Name of Jesus', particularly suitable as the day of the second chaplain's Annunciation mass and of the chapel's original consecration. On Monday there were masses in honour of both patrons of the chapel.

Yet the daily sequence was not determined purely by the need to accommodate new votive and requiem masses, entailing displacement of the Angels and 'Salvation of the People', repositioning the Holy Ghost and leaving only the Trinity, Corpus Christi and the Virgin undisturbed.[33] Margaret was just as devoted to the Trinity, Holy Ghost and Our Lady, for it was these masses that she wanted sung while awaiting burial, and she also revered the sacrament itself. In place of the traditional votive cycle, Margaret had amplified the emphasis on the Trinity and Virgin with new masses on the name and passion of Jesus.

The original Sarum cycle had entailed focusing daily on different aspects of the Trinity and the Virgin, whose votive mass on Saturday symbolised *inter alia* her role as gateway to Sunday, the Trinity and eternal life.[34] As elaborated by St Bridget, all Brigettine worship focused on the Virgin in a similar weekly cycle. On Sunday, day of the Sarum mass of the Trinity, the sisters of Syon considered how the Trinity 'ioyed euer from wythout begynnynge of the gloryous vyrgyn Mary, hauynge her endelesly as presente in the syght of hys Godly forknowynge'. On Monday they considered the angels' joy in her 'that was then vnmade', on Tuesday the creation, fall and Old Testament prophecies of Our Lady, on Wednesday 'her meruelous clene concepcion', on Thursday 'the maruyllous incarnacyon of oure lorde Iesu Criste in her', on Friday her sorrows especially during Christ's passion, and on Saturday her holy life and glorious assumption.

This Virgin-orientated week underlay all the Bridgettine services. Margaret, it seems, had no interest in their observances on Monday (angels) or Tuesday (creation and fall), and her veneration of the Virgin derived not at all from their Saturday story. Similarly selective as regards offices, she took nothing from prime, terce, sext, none, with their marginal relevance to the Virgin, and nothing even from evensong, borrowing only from compline on Wednesday and Friday and the Sunday and Thursday offices of matins and lauds.

The *Myroure* explains that St Mary should be served at matins as 'that ster that socoureth mankynde in the troubelous se of this worlde, &

---

[33] Wordsworth, *Ceremonies*, 286; for what follows, see above, 27; Devizes Museum, Personal i, fos. 269–70v.

[34] Dickinson, *Sarum Missal*, 760*; for what follows, see *Myroure*, 4–5.

bringeth her louers to the hauen of helth'. Appropriately, therefore, Margaret used only two brief requests for Mary's intercession. Lauds symbolises the resurrection and praise: Margaret again selects items bearing on the annunciation and incarnation, in particular a Thursday prayer and Sunday hymn dwelling on Mary's unique proximity to the Trinity as a Virgin conceiving by the Holy Ghost (Monday) and the mother of God (Thursday), the theme justifying her intercessory role at matins.[35]

Three texts derive from compline, two from the Bridgettine and one from the Sarum use.[36] Compline meant for Margaret the same as for the *Myroure*, which states:

Complin is thende of the day, & in thende of our lyfe...For complyn betokeneth the ende of mannes lyfe. or the ende of the worlde. when the chosen of oure lorde shall be delyuered from all trauayle and wo. and be broughte to endelesse quiete. and reste. And therfore eche persone oughte to dyspose hym to bedde warde. as yf hys bedde were hys graue.

The *Myroure* reminded the sisters of their daily visit to the grave and *Indulgete*, of their preparation for death.[37] That Margaret took all this to heart is shown by her evening service at Heytesbury Hospital, where the almsfolk daily

after Soper come to gedere unto ye Chapel of ye said Almeshous, and sey togeders they that canne...ye Psalme of 'De profundis' with ye versicles and Orisons accustomed to be saide for dede men; and they that cannot, sey devoutly for ye same soules three paternosters with as many aves and a crede of the faith.

The service ended with the commemoration of benefactors.[38] Margaret's evening office at Salisbury also ended with a bidding prayer, psalm and collect, sought repentance for sinners and perseverance in good for the righteous very much in the compline tradition at Syon.

As at Syon, Margaret's evening offices indicate a patient acceptance and preparedness for death, present also in her last will of 1477. When dictating it, feeling near to death, she invoked the aid of 'my lorde of mercy', and at the end she thanked him for enabling her to complete her task.[39] Margaret faced up to the possibility that she might lose her wits and to the inevitable decomposition of her body, instructing that

assone as hit is possible after the departyng of my soule oute of my body and my body throughout colde I wull that myne harte be take oute of my body cered and enclosed in lede...And also that my body to be bowelled and chested...for ye drede of ennoyng or effectyng the people there.

This is not the contemptuous loathing for the flesh of Lollards and some

[35] *Myroure*, 14, 99–100, 122–3, 129–30, 225, 232; *Syon Breviary*, 15, 21, 24, 73, 77.
[36] *Myroure*, 220, 257; *Syon Breviary*, 113–14; *Sarum Breviary*, iii. 619.
[37] *Myroure*, 151, 164–7.   [38] Jackson, 'Ancient statutes', 300.
[39] Devizes Museum, Personal i, fos. 269, 278. The next four paragraphs are based on ibid. fos. 269–78.

others, for she planned seemly and lavish funeral arrangements, but is rather a realistic recognition that her body would become an inanimate, decaying corpse. Alluding frequently and casually to when 'God call me owte of this lyfe' or 'visiteth me with bodely deth', she could even write: 'and if our lorde *of his grete goodness* visiteth me with bodely deth at Salisbury'. She wanted to complete her will

to thentent that when eny bodely sikenesse or dethe comyth unto me of our lordes ende that I may take hit in patiens and not to be trobled, ne vexed in this worldell in no thyng but onnly attendyng the wille of our lorde criste Jesu and saluacion for my soule.

Not just resigned to death, she even welcomes it as 'bodely deth' to be followed by eternal life. Fearful that something has been left out, she appeals to God and Christ 'to put in myne mynde what that ought to be done' for the honour and glory of them, all the company of heaven, and all christian souls. 'And if they so do I schall...': Margaret was utterly responsive to the voice of God expressed through her conscience.

To ensure salvation, Margaret wanted her will to be exemplary in its settling of accounts on earth and was therefore glad of the opportunity to write: 'by good avisement hoole without sikenesse and with all my right mynde not vexed ne troubled in fortune the present tyme with no thyng that schulde lette me in mynde in this occupacion...'. But she was nevertheless beset with nagging fears. What if she were subsequently to give in to 'myne obstynacy that I wuld not be corrected nor avised but my selfe' and were thus to mar her present will and imperil her soul? Why then, her executors must 'take the avise of those...surveyours of my testament whom I haue made prevy to all the same as they wull aunswere bifore god at the dredfull day of jugement' and 'do the contrary of that I have ordained' after this will. 'And if god visite me with such bodely sikenesse afore my deth that my mynde and my wittes be no verry parfite to remember any thing that me ought to do...' then whatever in the present will accorded with her outstanding obligations should be performed.

And yet Margaret still had no certainty of salvation. In her lifetime, she had established obits, the chantry and the almshouse to assure masses and prayers for her soul. Her will ordered despatch of her heart for an impressive funeral at Syon and a lying-in-state at Fisherton Dominican friary or Heytesbury, where three masses would be celebrated daily and the psalter chanted continually. For her burial 100 marks ($£66$ 13*s.* 4*d.*), not including doles for the poor, was to be spent on 'blak cloth for my servauntes, wax and other necessary thynges'. The almsfolk and other paupers were decked out in black. Other legacies, sometimes large sums, sometimes payable in instalments, were left to Salisbury Cathedral, Syon Abbey, Maiden Bradley and Launceston priories, four Dominican friaries, to houses of Franciscans, Trinitarians and Carmelites, to six parish churches including three at Salisbury, to the poor prisoners of Salisbury and Fisherton and to the anchorite at London wall. Some legacies were for specific purposes, indicating a knowledge of particular needs. Careful thought also went into the choice of recipients for the prayers she endowed. Besides all this, Margaret ordered the return of any loans to the owners on 'dew provis'. Surely nothing was left to chance. Yet in 1456 Margaret and her husband had secured a papal indult for plenary remission of all their sins at death.[40] *Pace* the satirists, this indulgence did not cause Margaret to forget her fear of sin, the need for contrition or the terrors of the Last Judgement, which her chapel decorations conveyed to others.

If this paper appears to have concentrated unduly on death, surely Christianity is a faith supremely concerned with death and what lies beyond. That death was not the end was fortified in the Middle Ages by belief in the Last Judgement, with which Margaret threatened her executors, feoffees and heirs and to which she herself looked with apprehension. Since the judgement was predetermined by conduct while alive, fear of damnation inevitably coloured the way life was lived on earth. As the pains of purgatory were mitigated by meritorious deeds after death, this too was reflected in religious foundations and pious bequests. In all these ways, therefore, Margaret was utterly conventional. Moreover, death was of overwhelming significance to Margaret herself, to whom in 1471 the chantry and almshouse were those 'thyngis I most charge and desyre of thyngis erthly'.[41] And in 1477, the foundations complete, nothing remained but a patient wait for death.

Was Margaret herself a reformed and penitent 'grasless galante'? Had she a pre-1471 past to live down? And what was it of which she needed to repent? Her orientation towards Jesus and Mary focused on those two scenes that stressed the virginal chastity of the 'pure chaste chosen virgin' of her will. Her cantarists and keeper, conventionally enough, were required to be celibate, but so too were her almspeople: 'alwais provyded that there be no man taken into the saide hous, neither servaunte nor tennante, ne other, that hath a wiff: for hit was ye wille of hym that furste ordeyned ye said hous, that no maner man that was maried shulde be admytted into the saide hous'.[42] As the paupers patronised by Walter, Lord Hungerford, who formed the nucleus of the original almsfolk included married couples and another couple was resident in 1472, this statement is almost certainly untrue and therefore revealing about Margaret. Her prayer at compline asked God to 'make vs serue the with chaste body, and to plese the with meke harte'. At first sight there is not much in common between the chastity of a professed nun and a widowed septuagenarian mother, surely past the sins of the flesh, but it is hardly a coincidence that the panel of *Death and the Galant* warned against the

---

[40] *Calendar of Papal Letters 1455-64*, 297.   [41] PRO, C 54/312 rot. 8d.
[42] Jackson, 'Ancient statutes', 299; for what follows, see Hicks, 'St Katherine's Hospital', below 131.

deadly sins of lechery and pride, the exact opposite to the virtues of chastity and meekness. In its gloss on the Sarum collect for chastity and meekness, which Margaret directed her chaplains to use daily and which was also used at Syon, the *Myroure* stresses meekness: 'a fayre knyttynge to gyther, a chaste body. & a meke soulle. for a chaste body may serue god, but yt can not plese god. without a meke harte'.[43] Likewise the Heytesbury almsfolk were to be 'meke in spirite, chaste of body and of good conversacion', qualities certainly required to fulfill the onerous duties Margaret laid on them. She concluded by requiring

ye saide keper poremen and women that bith nowe and shalbe in tyme to come, to haue togeder contynuell cherite to our Lorde God, Christe Jhu., and ye soulis aforesaide after this present ordynaunce laudably serve, and so lyve and be conversaunte togeder in ye foresaide hous, that they may after this lyff transsetory come to ye hous of ye kingdome of heven. The wich our Lorde God by his mouthe to poremen hath promysed.[44]

'Blessed are the poor in spirit: for theirs is the kingdom of heaven.' In this momentary glimpse of the equality of all before God, we surely have the key to Margaret's problems. Her statutes are thorough, conscientious and rigorous, but they lack charity. In politics she was resolute and singleminded, but she was neither meek nor poor in spirit. Indeed, she was proud. Witness her pride 'in the saluacion of the Hungerfordis landes',[45] in the magnificence of her chapel and its fittings and in her lineage demonstrated in the arms, crests and badges on its fabric, vestments, and those vestments bequeathed for use elsewhere. Witness, too, her repeated complaint that, despite her considerable material wealth, she made her will 'not accordyng to the degre and condicion that almighty god hath called me unto...'.[46] She had cause to remind herself, in chapel and will, that the glory was not due to her but to God. She could not overlook the tension between her wealth and salvation, as her counterpart Margaret Beaufort is alleged to have done.[47] Yet hard though she tried, Margaret certainly failed to escape the sin of Lucifer with which Wyclif denounced founders of chantries.[48] If her besetting sins were obstinacy and wilfulness, one can well appreciate what an effort was required to subject herself to her reverend father in God or even the will of God himself.

If Margaret's chapel, with its call for repentance and compline prayer, had a special relevance to her, what of the second panel of the *Legend* for which the message is lost? What sins did it denounce? Perhaps avarice. Perhaps also envy, for she was jealous of her stepmother. Perhaps also anger, since Margaret quarrelled with her stepmother, second mother-in-law, daughter-in-law and the young duchess of Norfolk.[49] If she tried to guard against these sins, her wills and writing annexed show that she

---

[43] *Myroure*, 137–8.
[44] Jackson, 'Ancient statutes', 298, 308.
[45] PRO, C 1/28/111.
[46] Devizes Museum, Personal i, fo. 276.
[47] J. R. Lander, *Government and Community 1450–1509*, London 1980, 113–14.
[48] Wood-Legh, 305n.
[49] PRO, C 1/28/111; Hoare, *Modern Wiltshire*, i (2). 102.

failed. Harbouring resentment over many years, it is no wonder that she had no use for the Syon service of *Indulgete* and feared that blindness regarding unconfessed sins that the *Myroure* warned against at compline. But sloth and gluttony were not among her vices, so there was no need for a third panel.

Thus it was not resemblances that drew Margaret to the Virgin, but rather the differences between them: that meekness, mildness and natural goodness so prominent in the Syon use and expected of the Syon sisters, which Margaret could only strive to imitate. Unlike the Bridgettines, Margaret was devoted only to certain manifestations of the Virgin: not her nativity; not – except in passing – her conception; not the visitation – a new devotion encountered at Syon; not her purification or presentation; and scarcely to her assumption – the dedication of Salisbury Cathedral – to which she required her almsmen to say a third psalter of Our Lady 'in ye worship of hir glorious Assumpcion'. Contrast this with Margaret's greater enthusiasm for the other two psalters:

the furste sawter, in ye worship of ye grete joye that our Lady had when she was greted by ye Aungell Gabriell, and immediattly conceyved with ye Sone of God. The seconde sawter in ye worship of ye grete joye that she hadd when she bare Criste Jhu., and she a pure chaste virgyne.[50]

Note again the familiar focus on annunciation and incarnation, relationship of mother and Son.

Margaret dwelt also on other aspects of Christ. She had evidently thought hard on his passion, deciding to substitute the 'Five Wounds of Christ' for the traditional votive of holy Cross, and on his resurrection, symbolised by St Christopher. She wrote of his suffering for her redemption and trusted in him for her salvation. She invoked his name in her will, in a votive mass, in her compline service and in her chapel decorations. At Heytesbury the almsfolk, reduced by her from 14 to 13, (the number of the Apostles), wore a badge saying Ihs Xpt in black letters on their white gowns and in white letters on their black gowns for her funeral.[51] And she also revered Corpus Christi, the sacrament itself.

Margaret expected her almspeople to live in the charity of Jesus Christ, reminding them of God's promise in the beatitudes, but she was no democrat. She saw Christ as her redeemer, rather than the saviour of all, showing much less interest in 'pore creatures' than her father or father-in-law, concentrating in her Heytesbury statutes on the duties of paupers to the exclusion of their welfare. It is no accident that she rejected the votive mass 'Salvation of the people', which asked for the gift of charity, talked of brethren and sisters, and for which the Gospel lesson was St Mark's account of the widow's mite.[52] She invoked all Christian souls in her will, but except for an extra daily psalter of Our Lady at Heytesbury

[50] Jackson, 'Ancient statutes', 299–300.
[51] See below 131.
[52] Dickinson, *Sarum Missal*, 742*.

seldom remembered them, concentrating instead on named relatives, ancestors, children and 'all the soules that God knogh I am bounde in consciens to pray for and that I euer had any goode of in this worlde'.[53] She was concerned with recompensing specific obligations, not with all Christians. The call for repentance in her Salisbury chapel was addressed to the literate and only those of rank might use her psalter.

If lacking somewhat in Christian charity and love for her neighbours, Margaret tried to trust in God, tried to live a Christian life, sought to control her character defects and genuinely repented of those sins of which she was aware. She showed as full an appreciation of the essentials of salvation as did Chaucer in his *Canterbury Tales*. She displayed none of the popular misconceptions and crudities deplored by contemporary satirists and modern historians. She possessed a far-reaching knowledge of the liturgy and was in tune with the latest developments, was discriminating in her selections from different uses and blended her borrowings in a coherent, sophisticated and distinctive pattern appropriate to her own tastes. In the process she took account of liturgical colours, religious symbolism, musical considerations and, beyond the scope of this article, heraldry as well. Such self-confidence and independence appear remarkable in a man, still more a woman, and testify to the success of the medieval Church in imparting Christ's teaching to aristocrats less sophisticated intellectually than Chaucer and Gower and without the mystical interests of the sedentary Cecily, duchess of York. Margaret illustrates the scope for fervour and dynamism in the faith of the literate laity at a time of intellectual stagnation in the official Church. It was not necessary to abandon conventional orthodoxy to express personal convictions and to develop a piety relevant to individual needs. And finally, in R. W. Pfaff's words, Margaret's example demonstrates how 'the complexities of liturgical development provide valuable illumination for the spiritual history of a period'.[54] The copious liturgical evidence of late medieval foundations offers the best source material for further studies of this sort. It only remains to demonstrate how religious considerations affected behaviour in other areas of everyday life.[55]

[53] Devizes Museum, Personal i, fo. 270.
[54] Pfaff, *New Liturgical Feasts*, 133.
[55] See below, chapters 9-10.

6

St Katherine's Hospital, Heytesbury:
Prehistory, Foundation, and Re-foundation, 1408-1472

Heytesbury hospital is a medieval almshouse that still performs its original function and has an assured future in the modern world. One of the better-known Wiltshire almshouses, it has twice received full-length treatment.[1] Its recorded history nevertheless contains significant gaps, none more important than its origins and early years. Modern historians have relied principally on the statutes of the co-founder Margaret, Lady Hungerford (d. 1478), even though these were compiled thirty years after the establishment of the hospital and depart in many particulars from the wishes of the first founder Walter, Lord Hungerford (d. 1449). Moreover such histories dwell on limited aspects of the foundation rather than seeing it in the round. They ignore the essential context of other Hungerford foundations and similar institutions elsewhere. It is no wonder that they have failed to bring out the full importance of Heytesbury hospital.

The hospital's origins are irrevocably entwined with the fortunes of the Hungerford family, which arose from obscurity early in the fourteenth century to national prominence a hundred years later. Sir Thomas Hungerford, speaker of the House of Commons, first established the family's prosperity, acquiring the two country seats at Farleigh Hungerford (Somerset) and Heytesbury (Wilts.). On his death in 1397, he was succeeded first by his widow Joan, so that only in 1412 did Heytesbury pass to their son Walter, a statesman of the first rank, also speaker of the Commons, royal councillor, treasurer of England, knight of the Garter, and baron. On his death in 1449 Heytesbury was held briefly by his widow Eleanor, dowager-countess of Arundel (d. 1455), his son Robert (d. 1459), and then Robert's widow Margaret. Her tenure was clouded by the political misfortunes of her son and grandson in the Wars

---

[1] J.E. Jackson, 'Ancient statutes of Heytesbury almshouse', *W[iltshire] A[rchaeological] M[agazine]* vol 11 (1869), 289-308; *VCH Wiltshire*, vol 3, 337-8; *Hospital of St John, Heytesbury* (commemorative booklet, Salisbury, 1972). Unless otherwise stated, all places in this essay are in Wiltshire. Manuscripts in the Public Record Office (PRO) are cited by their call-numbers, as are those in Wiltshire Record Office (WRO), and Somerset Record Office (SRO).

of the Roses, yet she clung on to Heytesbury and ensured its inheritance by the male line of the family.

The Hungerfords were outstanding benefactors of the church, founding between 1325 and 1472 eleven chantries, eight obits, and two hospitals. These were scattered throughout Wiltshire, Somerset, Gloucestershire and London, but were concentrated in Salisbury cathedral, where there were three Hungerford chantries, and at Farleigh, where there were two. Sir Thomas had ordered the foundation of a chantry in Longleat priory, near Heytesbury, but it failed, in the last resort because his son Walter was more interested in other foundations. Apart from Heytesbury hospital, Walter established four chantries and three obits.[2] Heytesbury is the odd one out – at once the most elaborate and the most charitable, the fruit of his declining years, and the end result of thirty years' experience. This essay traces the hospital's prehistory, its foundation by Walter and its re-foundation by Margaret up to the issue of her statutes.

Heytesbury lay within the peculiar of the dean of Salisbury, the area over which the dean exercised the authority of a bishop, and was served from the ancient collegiate church of St Peter and St Paul with its chapter of four canons and a dean, who was also dean of Salisbury. In practice the chapter were never resident, the church being served by stipendiary priests. To laymen they were the parish priests of their parish church. About 1472 it was served by two priests, two deacons, and the chaplain of the confraternity of St Mary. In 1409 there were only five chaplains, one serving the outlying chapel of Knook and two others the chantries at the altars of St Katherine and St Mary.

Both chantries were in the south part of the church, presumably – in the absence of other evidence – in the south choir aisle and south transept.[3] By at least 1436 the north transept was dedicated to St Michael: it acquired its Perpendicular stone screen adorned with Hungerford sickels in the early sixteenth century, when it was the chosen sepulchre of Sir Walter (d. 1516) and Sir Edward Hungerford (d. 1521).[4]

St Katherine's chantry was founded by William Mount of Heytesbury for the souls of himself, his ancestors and all Christians in about 1317, when he was licensed to alienate a message and curtilage, two cottages with curtilages, 30 acres of arable and a parcel of meadow, all at Heytesbury. By the early fifteenth century the Leigh family were patrons. St Mary's chantry, founded before 1339 by Lucy Clifton, was endowed

[2] For the Hungerford foundations, see Chapter 4.
[3] Jackson (note 1), 307; *VCH Wiltshire*, vol 3, 390-1 (to be used with caution); WRO, Register of Deans Chandler and Sydenham, part 1, fos 118-19.
[4] PRO PROB 11/3 (PCC 21 Luffenam, will of William Sergeant); PRO PROB 11/8 (PCC 21 Holder).

with a messuage, curtilage, three virgates of land and 10s rent for masses for the souls of herself, her late husband Gaudinus de Albo Monasterio, her ancestors, and her heirs. Seven successive chaplains were said to have served the chantry up to 1409, when it was in the gift of Lucy's heirs, the Hungerfords. Both chantries were fully constituted ecclesiastical benefices, being subject to institution by the dean on presentation by the patron.[5]

The Hungerford involvement is first recorded in 1408, when Joan presented John Wademan. Her right was questioned, so on 11 September Bishop Hallum ordered an inquiry. Wademan was nevertheless instituted on 22 September, before the inquiry on 10 February 1409, which found the chantry to be in the gift of the founder's heirs, but failed to identify them. A search of the cathedral registers uncovered Lucy's charter to Heytesbury prebendal church (9 January 1411) and confirmed the Hungerfords as patrons.

On Joan's death in 1412, her son Walter proposed changes so radical that Dean Chandler, fearing for his deanery, consulted with the cathedral chapter. His colleagues authorised him to conclude his negotiations at his discretion to the best interests of himself and his successors. Whatever was envisaged, Walter was admitted to the cathedral confraternity on 8 December 1413 and enjoyed good relations with the chapter thereafter.

Probably it was with Chandler's consent that Walter used his embassy to the General Council of the Church at Constance to secure, on 18 March 1415, a papal bull transferring St Mary's chantry to his household oratory at Heytesbury, which he proposed developing with more chaplains and clerks. This proposal was justified, quite untruthfully, by its poverty, so great 'that for a long time no priest has celebrated divine office in it'. The privilege depended on a favourable report from the papal commissioner, the prior of Bath, who duly appeared at Heytesbury in 1415-16 'for executing of a certain bull of the lord pope there', consuming victuals to the value of 12s 3d. Whatever the reason, the proposed transfer never took place, and in 1421 Walter presented another chaplain to the chantry.[8]

The most likely reason for an unfavourable report was that the chantry was not vacant nor normally so. Moreover the scheme was designed to part-finance Walter's own household chapel from Lucy Clifton's

[5] WRO Chandler (note 3), part 1, fo 119-v; *Calendar of Patent Rolls, 1313-17*, 610; E.C. Stokes (ed), *Abstracts of Wiltshire Inquisitions Post Mortem, Edward III* (London: British Record Society no. 48, 1914), 134; see also SRO DD/SAS H348, fos 114-v, 116v (Hungerford Cartulary).

[6] WRO Chandler (note 3), part 1, fos 118-19v; part 2, fo 29; Salisbury Cathedral Muniments, Register Viringe, 58.

[7] Salisbury Cathedral Muniments, Register Viringe, 92; Register Pountney, 1.

[8] *Calendar of Papal Letters, 1404-15*, 490-1; *VCH Wiltshire*, vol 3, 391; PRO SC 6/1153/14 m 4.

endowment in defiance of her original wishes. That Walter was finding the chapel costly and wanted some financial assistance is suggested by the scale of its staff in 1436, when it included Master John Russell 'rector of the chapel of my lord Hungerford', other chaplains, a cleric yet to be ordained priest, other clerks and boys, presumably choristers.[9] By 1443 he had enclosed Farleigh parish church within the castle walls and had taken it over, establishing chantries of two priests in it, yet in 1450 his son maintained two other stipendiary chaplains there. The pomp of the Hungerfords' domestic chapel emerged from the lavish fittings in their wills: Margaret kept at least two priests, had her chapel hung with red tapestries, and possessed a wealth of vestments and assorted paraphernalia.

Thwarted in one direction, Walter did not abandon hope of developing his Heytesbury chantry. Perhaps it was on it that he expended £80 3s 4d on building at Heytesbury church in 1428-31.[10] By 1438 he had reached an agreement with Elizabeth Leigh, patron of St Katherine's chantry, which was far too poor to support a chaplain. On 1 April 1438, the selfsame day that the incumbent of St Mary's chantry died, both patrons secured from Bishop Neville a commission of inquiry into a proposed union of their chantries, two others at Upton Scudamore and Calne, and the free chapel of Corston in Hillmarton, all of Walter's patronage, all (so it was alleged) too poor to support an incumbent, and all, therefore, long desolate and neglected. Inquiries were held at Heytesbury, Warminster, Calne and the manor of Compton Burnell on 7-8 April, the haste probably being occasioned by the need to complete the union before the presentation to St Mary's chantry devolved by lapse on the dean of Salisbury rather than Walter himself. It was found that St Mary's chantry was now worth only £2 a year, St Katherine's chantry only 8s, the Scudamore chantry at Upton Scudamore only £3 10s, that of Sir Robert de Hungerford (d. 1352) at Calne only £1 10s, and Corston chapel only £1 3s 4d. United they would provide an income of £8 11s 4d and a tied house, comparable with the generous endowment provided by Walter elsewhere. All four chantries and the free chapel were poor, but not too impoverished to attract incumbents: St Mary's chantry, Heytesbury was regularly filled; that at Upton Scudamore was not vacant, although

[9] PRO PROB 11/3 (PCC 21 Luffenam). For what follows, see J.E. Jackson, *Guide to Farleigh Hungerford* (Chippenham: 1879), 48-50; H.C. Maxwell-Lyte and M.C.B. Dawes (ed), *Register of Thomas Bekynton, Bishop of Bath and Wells, 1443-65*, vol 1 (Somerset Record Society no. 49, 1934), 3, 135; F.W. Weaver (ed), *Somerset Medieval Wills, 1383-1500* (Somerset Record Society no. 16, 1901), 187-9; Devizes Museum, [Canon Jackson's] Hungerford [Family] Collections, Personal, vol 1, fos 270, 274v.

[10] PRO SC 6/1119/9 m 3; Hungerford Collections (note 9), vol 1, fo 37.

[11] WRO D1/2/9, part 2, fos 55-56v (Register Neville).

admittedly the chaplain had been absent at Abingdon Abbey for thirty years; and the Calne chantry had been served by the warden of the hospital there, for whom it represented a valued supplementary income.[11]

In spite of the favourable report of the commissioners, the bishop did not act at once, perhaps because not all the livings were vacant. There was nothing, however, to prevent amalgamation of the Heytesbury chantries, which may indeed have been united at this stage. There is no record of any such transaction, but it would have been registered not in the extant register of the bishop but that of the dean, now lost. Certainly St Katherine's chantry does not occur again. The union was never implemented in the form originally envisaged.

'At the basis of all medieval pious foundations there lies the idea of continuous intercession for the living and the departed.'[12] Clearly true of monasteries and even more obviously so of chantries, which existed solely for the soul of the departed, this dictum applies also to hospitals. Charity was a department of piety: it was a Christian duty to relieve the sick and indigent. They, in turn, reciprocated by praying for benefactors, a duty given institutional expression in the hospital. 'The newer foundations, even more explicitly than the older, were "bede-houses" or houses of prayer', in which the inmates prayed continuously for their founders. Founders were not much concerned with the problem of poverty, seeing its relief 'only as a means to an end'. The medieval hospital was decidedly not a 'medical institution. It was for care rather than for cure: for the relief of the body, when possible, but preeminently for the refreshment of the soul'. Founders did not want sick people in their hospitals, who were unable to carry out the arduous observances required of them. Most hospitals were mere almshouses, sources of shelter and keep for the indigent, who lived out their days in strict discipline.

By such late medieval standards, the Hungerfords were a charitable family. In 1386-7 Thomas was supporting ten paupers at Farleigh Hungerford on pensions of ¾d a day. Perhaps they lived in the unendowed almshouse mentioned in 1465-6. His will and that of his widow provided for works of charity. All Walter's foundations included doles for the poor, he left money for the relief of poor tenants on twenty-two manors, and he possessed a best almsdish of silver shaped like a hand. In 1428-31 he was supporting thirteen paupers on his estates: two at Down Ampney (Gloucs) and South Cadbury (Soms), four (counted as

[12] A.H. Thompson, *English Clergy and their Organisation in the Later Middle Ages* (Oxford: 1947), 132. For the rest of paragraph, see R.M. Clay, *Medieval Hospitals of England* (London: 1909), especially xvii-xviii, 29; M.A. Seymour, 'Organisation, Personnel and Function of the Medieval Hospital in the Later Middle Ages' (London MA thesis, 1946), especially 24.

one) at Rushall (Wilts), and one each at Farleigh, Saltford, Mapperton, Wootton Courtenay, Sutton Lucy, Backwell (Soms), Teffont and Cheverell Hales (Wilts). Including a married couple, each was paid 4d a week, 17s 4d a year. It was a logical step to bring them together into an almshouse at Heytesbury.[13] In 1444-5, after the foundation of Heytesbury hospital, Walter's receiver-general was pensioning only three paupers, none the same: two at Hungerford (Berks), one dead by 1448, and a hermit at South Cadbury, all at the old 17s 4d annual rate.

Walter had erected the hospital buildings at Heytesbury and had installed the almspeople by 19 July 1442, when Bishop Aiscough at last annexed Corston chapel and the Upton and Calne chantries to St Mary's chantry, Heytesbury, whose chaplains were henceforth to commemorate all the founders:[14] Lucy Clifton, her husband, ancestors and heirs; Sir Walter Scudamore, his wife, ancestors and heirs; Sir Robert de Hungerford and Geva his wife, their ancestors and heirs; and perhaps also William Mount and his ancestors, although St Katherine's chantry is not mentioned. Four days after the episcopal decree, Walter announced that the trustees of his manors of Cheverell Burnell and Cheverell Hales were to hold them until a royal licence for their alienation in mortmain to the hospital had been secured. Meantime they were to pay £33 6s 8d annually to William Cook, cantarist at St Mary's altar in Heytesbury church:

> and to his successors there priests for evermore by the said Walter, Lord Hungerford ordained . . . to the use, exhibition, sustentation and relieving of twelve poor men and two women for to keep the said twelve poor men in an hospital there, by the said Walter, Lord Hungerford made, named Saint Katherine's Hospital and . . . to do other almsdeeds and works of pity upon Good Friday, and other certain days of the year . . . for the said Walter, Lord Hungerford, and for all them that he hath ordained there to be prayed for in the said chantry.

The trustees had sworn 'as they shall answer before God to keep it, and by their assigns, and by the assigns of their assigns'. This declaration is what Margaret, Lady Hungerford meant, when she said that Walter had founded the hospital in his last will.

What Walter did was to combine the almshouse and the chantry: while managing the chantry as before, the cantarist would direct the hospital as well, disbursing money as required; the paupers would also pray for the

---

[13] Lambeth Palace Library, Register Arundel ii, fo 152; Register Stafford fos 115-16v; PRO SC 6/970/22 m 2; SC 6/971/14 m 3; SC 6/1119/9 m 2; Hungerford Collections (note 9), vol 1, fo 132. For what follows, see PRO SC 6/1119/11 m 2, /12 m 2.

[14] WRO D1/2/10, part 2, fo 48-v (Register Aiscough); SRO DD/SAS H348 fo 27-v. For what follows, see J.S. Davies (ed) *The Troponell Cartulary*, vol 2 (Devizes: 1908), 265-6; WRO 490/1469, 14-15.

founders. The declaration of 1442 makes no mention of a school, but by 1449 Walter had built a house for the schoolmaster, who had taught many times at Heytesbury. The schoolmaster was also left a share of Walter's residuary estate.[15] The most likely explanation for the dedication is derivation from the other Heytesbury chantry, although St Katherine is a common patron for medieval hospitals.

Late medieval hospital resembled chantries and foundations combining chantries and schools were not unusual. Founders never set up schools by themselves. Only five late-medieval foundations, however, combined almshouse, school and chantry, of which Heytesbury was one. The others were established at Higham Ferrers (Northants) by Archbishop Chichele, at Ewelme (Oxon) by the Duke of Suffolk, at Tattershall (Lincs) by Lord Cromwell, and at Eton (Bucks) by King Henry VI. Long close colleagues in government, the founders undoubtedly influenced one another, although the direction of such influence is far from clear. Higham Ferrers, founded in 1422, is the earliest of the five and the accepted dates of Ewelme (1437), Tattershall (1439), and Eton (1440) all precede that – 1442 – when Heytesbury hospital can first be proved to exist.[16]

There are grounds, however, for suggesting Heytesbury hospital was founded or at least conceived before 1442. Since the act of union of the chantries does not refer to the simultaneous establishment of the hospital, it may be that this was already envisaged at the inquiry in 1438 and passed unmentioned because it did not require episcopal consent. The dedication to St Katherine may commemorate Walter's first wife Katherine Peverell, who died about 1436 and for whose soul Walter performed other pious works, notably the construction of Standerwick causeway (Soms).[17] And .if St Katherine's chantry was included, a date near 1438 is likely. Commemoration in the prayers of the almspeople may have compensated the Leigh family for the loss of the patronage of their moribund chantry.

However early the hospital, the school – as at Ewelme and Tattershall – was an afterthought, inspired by the example of Eton College, where it was intended from the start as part of Henry VI's twin foundations of Eton and King's College, Cambridge. Walter himself was educated and cultured, read both poetry and theology, and was a benefactor of Merton College, Oxford. He probably expected more than one person to fill the roles of warden, cantarist and schoolmaster at Heytesbury, since we know that he added a house for the schoolmaster, although there was already one for the cantarist. His will speaks of his chantries at Farleigh,

[15] Lambeth Palace Library, Register Stafford, fo 118; R. Colt Hoare (ed), *Modern Wiltshire* (London 1822-40), vol 1, part 2, 102.

[16] N. Orme, *Education in the West of England* (Exeter: 1976), 143.

[17] Weaver (note 9), 189.

Heytesbury, and Chippenham quite apart from the school, a separation
pointing to a clear distinction in his own mind. The terms used, 'for the
augmentation of the master of the scholars who many times lives and
works there',[18] point both to different endowments and to the possibility
that Walter may have been endowing an existing school. At Eton,
Tattershall and Ewelme, admittedly larger establishments, the three
functions were undertaken by more than one man. Combination of all
duties in one man could have been an economy in salaries, if it were not
that the stipend for the cantarist alone was more than for most
schoolmasters and that the income of the combined official about 1472
was more than that of the master at Winchester College, Eton College or
even John Colet's St Paul's school. School and almshouse were certainly
combined in a single individual in 1454, but we have only the testimony of
Margaret Hungerford – not a reliable witness – that the arrangement
originated with Walter himself.

Walter died without securing the licence necessary for the permanent
endowment of the hospital, which was obtained neither by his widow, nor
his son, nor until 1472 by his daughter-in-law Margaret. Either they
lacked sufficient influence at court or the fine demanded was too high.
During the thirty years 1442-72 the combined foundation is sporadically
illuminated by odd references in wills and Hungerford estate accounts. In
1454-5 the Heytesbury ministers paid the schoolmaster (*Magister
Scolarum*) subsistence for fourteen paupers, £2 for his chantry and a further
£1 for his servant, total £22 15s 0½d. In 1461 10s 4d was spent on repairs
to the almshouse and £1 5s 6d for the support of the almsfolk. In 1464-5
the rent collector at Upton Scudamore paid £5 3s 5d to the schoolmaster
as ordered by Margaret, Lady Hungerford.[19] Without accounts for the
Cheverell manors one cannot be sure of the normal arrangement, but
payments appear to have been *ad hoc* from the family purse rather than
from strict application of the terms of the 1442 declaration of trust.
Meanwhile the trustees were reduced by death to two in 1472, when both
last survivors, John Cheyne and John Mervyn, joined in the re-
foundation.

Unlike her father and father-in-law, Margaret was not particularly
charitable. She was not involved in Walter's project either as an executor
or trustee and had pressing problems of her own that took priority for a
decade over the hospital. There was a parallel situation at Bath, where her
father Lord Botreaux had left his almshouse with the formalities of
endowment incomplete. In that instance Margaret sold the endowment,

    [18] Lambeth Palace Library, Register Stafford, fos 115, 118. For what follows, see below;
Orme (note 16), 143.
    [19] PRO SC 6/971/12; SC 6/1054/7 mm 3, 4; SC 6/1061/21 m 2.

merely pensioning the inmates until death, thus ensuring eventual closure of the hospital.[20] Fortunately she took a different view at Heytesbury. In her agreement in 1469 with the future Richard III, she secured his assurance of a royal licence within a year 'if he goodly may'. Richard failed to keep his promise, so in her 1471 will Margaret required her executors to obtain the licence and to found also a new chantry at Salisbury, which together 'I most charge and desire of things earthly'. Actually Margaret survived to achieve both herself, securing a licence to alienate the two Cheverell manors on 20 February 1472 and conveying them to the hospital in her foundation deed of 4 April following.[21]

There is nothing to confirm Margaret's claim in 1476 that she acted 'at the request of the said Robert, late Lord Hungerford, my husband, son and heir to the said Walter'.[22] Certainly she took the obligations laid on her by Robert seriously, but there is no other evidence that this was one of them. The paltry £1 left by Robert to the hospital does not indicate much interest and Margaret left even this unpaid until 1474. We know to be untrue her similar claim that Robert wanted a chantry chapel at Salisbury cathedral.[23] If Margaret preferred to endow Heytesbury rather than Bath, its convenient proximity to her home may have been a factor. Another probable influence was the opportunity to benefit the souls of her husband and herself, a takeover reflected in the new seal of 'Custos, Poormen and Women of the Hospital of Walter and Robert, late Lords of Hungerford and Heytesbury'. This process had begun by 1471, when the number of women had been reduced from two to one,[24] and was carried further in her statutes.

Margaret regulated the hospital both in her foundation deed and her statutes. The deed named Robert Stephens as custos or keeper, twelve men as almsmen, and Alice Sawter – perhaps wife of the almsman John Sawter – as almswoman. All vacancies would be filled by Margaret for life. Thereafter the keeper was to be appointed by the chancellor of Salisbury cathedral and her veteran retainer John Mervyn for life, by her grandson Walter for life, and then by successive lords of Heytesbury. On admission both keeper and almsfolk would swear obedience to these and to any other statutes by the founders.

The surviving copy of the Heytesbury statutes lacks the dating clause,

[20] W. Dugdale, *Baronage of England* (London, 1675), vol 1, 630; SC 6/1061/21 m 2; SC 6/1119/15 m 4; Hungerford Collections (note 9), vol 1, fo 270v.
[21] British Library MS Cotton Julius BXII fo 123; PRO C54/312 rot 8d; *Calendar of Patent Rolls, 1467-77*, p. 306; Hoare (note 15), vol 1, part 2, 128-31.
[22] Hoare (note 15), vol 1, part 2, 102. For what follows, see Weaver (note 9), 187; WRO 490/1465.
[23] See above, 88-9.
[24] PRO C54/312 rot 8d. For the next paragraph, see Hoare (note 15), vol 1, part 2, pp. 102, 125.

but they probably belong to 1472-4. Obviously they postdate the deed of 4 April and they are also later than the statutes of Margaret's Salisbury chantry, which they amplify by providing a £1 annual pension from the hospital towards the repair of chantry ornaments. The dating of the Salisbury statutes is also missing, but they are certainly subsequent to the chantry's foundation deed of 1 May 1472. Both sets of statutes survive as copies in the Hungerford cartulary at Taunton where they are grouped with related deeds of 1473-4, but unfortunately internal evidence does not help in dating them. Clearly both sets of statutes must precede Margaret's death in 1478. Just as the final version of the Salisbury statutes precedes the Heytesbury ones, so the first draft is also earlier. There was a draft of the Salisbury statutes by 14 January 1471, when the Heytesbury ones remained to be written.[25] Such considerations are relevant to the hospital because its ordinances are based on those of the chantry, twelve being little more than translations of the Latin originals.

Chantry statutes resemble one another, reflecting the same preoccupations; the precise regulation of services, especially the weekly cycle; the desire for permanence, involving precautions against embezzlement and waste, and the wish for regular services, involving a ban on absenteeism, other forms of neglect, and delays in new appointments. Some common solutions feature in Walter's statutes of 1429 for two other chantries, which are Margaret's most likely source. While thorough, these are not especially rigorous and unusually allow his chaplains to hold office of the family compatible with their daily duties and even to entertain female relatives. Margaret arranged and amplified these into a longer, more comprehensive and tougher code. She tried to legislate for every eventuality and to exclude offences by shutting off loopholes and by a system of checks and balances. An authoritarian woman, only too aware of human frailty and intolerant of it in others, she tried to regulate it out. It is symptomatic that her Heytesbury statutes commence with the procedure and justification for depriving the keeper. Canon Jackson justifiably considered her code 'could hardly have been more minute and elaborate had it been prepared for the establishments of Greenwich and Chelsea'.

As Margaret's first love was her chantry, the heart of her twenty-one Salisbury statutes are liturgical and without parallel at Heytesbury. At both she relied on the cathedral chapter not just for appointments but for dismissals. Holidays were limited to a month and carefully defined. No exceptions were permitted to chaplains and keeper regarding the

---

[25] SRO DD/SAS H348 fos 317-end; C 54/312 rot 8d. The next four paragraphs are based on J.E. Jackson, *Farleigh Hungerford*, 118-27; Jackson, 'Statutes' (note 1), 289-308; C. Wordsworth, *Ceremonies and Processions of the Cathedral Church of Salisbury*, (Cambridge: 1901), 285-6; SRO DD/SAS H348 fos 322a-4v, 255.

prohibition on exchanges and pluralism. On admittance inventories were compiled. There was an annual audit, at Heytesbury before the estates steward, and annual inventories were authenticated by witnesses. At each foundation there were chests with multiple locks. At Salisbury there was a three-lock chest beneath the altar for valuables and an aumbry with two locks for everyday vestments and ornaments. At Heytesbury the three-lock chest was in the almshouse, where it remains, and contained the common seal and the common fund. It was accessible only by co-operation between the keeper, the dean's official, and an honest parishioner nominated annually by the latter; the vestment and ornament coffer in the church had two keys, one kept by the keeper and another by an almsman. There were financial inducements for annual inspections by the dean's official and for annual public readings of the statutes by the parish clerk.

Whereas the Salisbury cantarists had purely liturgical functions, the Heytesbury keeper was busier and more versatile. He could not be spared even briefly without nominating a deputy, and outside vacations might only 'walk a mile or two for his recreation at certain times, not absenting himself from his place by night time'. Although the keeper was appointed by the chancellor, the cathedral dignitary in charge of education, his re-designation from schoolmaster to keeper indicates a lower educational priority and, indeed, only one statute dealt wholly with the school. Unlike Walter, Margaret was no Latinist or university patron. As in 1471, she foresaw difficulties in finding an adequate teacher and allowed for temporary appointments to chantry and almshouse pending discovery of the right man. This was in spite of the high pay, £16 8s plus £1 for his servant, twice as much as Margaret's Salisbury chaplains, besides the tied house. The keeper had 'the rule and governance' of the hospital and the 'administration of the same'. As cantarist he celebrated mass daily, once or twice a week in the almshouse and otherwise in the church. Those commemorated were Margaret, her husband, her parents, his parents, John Cheyne, John Mervyn, 'and all the souls that the said Walter and Katherine, Robert and Margaret be come of and all the souls that be come of them, and all the souls that be bound to pray for'. Apart from directing the almshouse and celebrating mass daily, the keeper taught all levels at school every day except Sundays and feastdays, when he was released to share in matins, high mass and evensong at the church. Only Sunday prayers and the annual obit were left to the parish priests.

The seventeen statutes regarding the poor are independent of the Salisbury chantry, but are commonplace for medieval almshouses. The paupers received shelter, food and clothing, but little care, for Margaret had cut the sisters from two to one. Lepers were excluded and any with lingering or noxious illnesses were isolated. Detailed statutes regulated their possessions, alms, income and wills. To be of good character, they were selected from servants and tenants of the Hungerfords, swore obedience on admission and could be expelled if not. They were expected to 'study and intend to execute and fulfil the charges in the foundation and statutes aforesaid with all his power as poor men should do'. All had to learn the Lord's Prayer, Hail Mary and Creed, and were examined on them quarterly. On getting up, all said three Lords Prayers, three Hail Marys, and a Creed 'in confirmation of the faith'. At leisure, the illiterate said four psalters of Our Lady, each of fifteen Hail Marys, five Lords Prayers and a Creed, while the literate said matins of Our Lady, twenty-one psalms and the associated lessons before lunch and the office of the deed afterwards. After supper, while the literate said the psalm *De Profundis* (Psalm 130) with the accustomed versicles and prayers, the illiterate muttered a further three Lords Prayers, three Hail Marys and a Creed. It was a taxing programme of unbelievable boredom, involving endless repetition of Latin prayers, especially for the illiterate with their sixty-six Hail Marys, twenty-six Lords Prayers, and six Creeds, but it was in no way unusual.

In these statutes Margaret did her meticulous best to provide for every eventuality and planned to give freely of her time until death. But what need was there for her labour? In 1442 Walter had dedicated the hospital, fixed the complement of paupers, settled the almsdeeds to be done, and ordained those to be commemorated in prayers. The terms of his instruction in his will to his executors to remedy any deficiencies in statutes, endowments or ornaments at his three later foundations do not suggest that he foresaw much need for them to intervene and certainly they indicate some existing provision. Indeed at Farleigh Hungerford we know that no amendments to the statutes were required. This is hardly surprising, since statutes preceded settlement of the endowment in his first three chantries. Whatever statutes Walter had ordained were sufficient to guide the hospital safely through its first thirty years. They may not have been comprehensive and some extra regulations may have been needed. They may have been unsatisfactory in detail, but there is little sign that Margaret's code was a response to specific defect. Certainly the twelve statutes borrowed from her Salisbury chantry can hardly be in response to local conditions at Heytesbury. Margaret seems to have started from scratch, not by recasting existing statutes, and in the process departed from Walter's wishes in many particulars.

Take the chantry. The 1442 union had provided for daily masses at St Mary's altar in Heytesbury church and nowhere else – not, however convenient, in the hospital chapel. Masses were for the souls of those named in the original chantries plus Walter's additions, which would certainly have included his parents and not Margaret. Margaret, however, omitted all beneficiaries of the original chantries, went no further back in the Hungerford line than Walter and Katherine, and brought in her own parents and maternal relatives. Bishop Aiscough had assigned the endowment of all chantries, which Margaret confirmed only after including them in her provisions.[26] The only exception, incidentally, is Corston chapel, which somehow escaped annexation in 1442.

Margaret's innovations owe much to her cult of Jesus and Mary, the patrons of her Salisbury chantry. She reduced the number of paupers to thirteen – the magic number of Christ and the Apostles – insisting that sick paupers in isolation must 'always be taken and called of the number of the said twelve poor men and woman during her life, so the number of poor men in Heytesbury be not augmented'. Similarly she ordained doles for thirteen other paupers of Heytesbury on Friday before Whitsun – not on Good Friday, as Walter had wanted. The almsfolk were to wear white gowns with badges bearing the initials JHU.XRT (Jesus Christ) in black letters; for her obsequies they and thirteen other paupers wore black gowns with similar lettering in white. The same point emerges in the final statute, that keeper and paupers should:

> have together continual charity to our Lord God Christ Jesu, and the souls aforesaid after this present ordinance laudably serve, and so live and be conversant together in the foresaid house, that they may after this life transitory come to the houses of the kingdom of heaven. The which our Lord God by his mouth to poor men hath promised.[27]

If these poor were really to be saved, as the beatitudes said, it would please Him to model the almshouse on Him and his apostles.

Margaret, conventionally enough, wanted her almsfolk to eschew illicit sex, but, more than that, she wanted them to be as celibate as monks:

> Always provided that there be no man taken into the said house, neither servant, nor tenant, nor other, that hath a wife: for it was the will of him that first ordained the said house, that no manner of man that was married should be admitted to the said house.[28]

Nothing about Walter suggests that he would have taken such a line. The pensioners, who probably formed the nucleus of the original almsfolk, included at least one married couple; another may have been resident in 1472. It is more likely that this clause is further evidence of Margaret's devotion to the chastity of the Virgin, perhaps dating from her sojourn in Syon Abbey in 1470. Similarly, what Margaret expected of the inmates was prayers in honour of St Mary, not St Katherine, their patron saint. St Katherine features neither in her deed or statutes. Margaret called the

---

[26] Jackson, 'Statutes' (note 1), p. 304; WRO D1/2/10, part 2, fo 48. For what follows, see Jackson (note 1), 304; J.E. Jackson, 'Ancient chapels', *WAM*, vol 10 (1867), 274.

[27] Jackson, 'Statutes' (note 1), 302, 305, 307-8; Hungerford Collections (note 9), vol 1, fo 275v.

[28] Jackson, 'Statutes' (note 1), 299.

hospital by the names of her husband and her father-in-law.[29] Any confusion about the dedication, such as the modern stress on St John the Baptist, is excusable.

Some of Margaret's changes may have improved the hospital's organisation. It made better sense to hold the masses sometimes in the hospital chapel and to limit full participation in the canonical hours to days when the school was closed. It was vital that such a pivotal figure as the keeper should be restricted in his movements. In all these ways Margaret achieved the best possible compromise, but it was still a compromise. But was it really Walter's intention to overburden one man with three functions or had he intended two – a keeper/cantarist and a schoolmaster? If the latter, the compromise would have been unnecessary. If this was Walter's intention, it was changed early on – not by Margaret, but by Walter's widow – and the price paid was a high one. The cantarist could not perform all his functions, and surely both almshouse and school must have suffered from divided attention. Ultimately the school lost out. As Margaret foresaw, it proved hard to find ordained priests competent as schoolmasters, willing to work so hard for even a princely salary, so the teaching was often in the hands of an usher. Even at the end of the middle ages, the well-qualified gave priority to quality of life.

Heytesbury hospital was the result of evolution: a fourteenth-century prehistory, foundation in the currently fashionable form, and re-foundation on more conservative lines. Later generations re-worked the provisions of their ancestors. Had Margaret failed to endow it properly, Heytesbury hospital might have faded away like the Botreaux foundation at Bath or lingered on obscurely like the unendowed Farleigh almshouse. Most of the forty-one hospitals and *maisons dieu* at late-medieval York, Beverley and Hull were unendowed,[30] and the unendowed poor-house is a familiar post-Reformation phenomenon. Even before the Reformation, endowment did not equal existence: almshouses and schools are not to be numbered merely by counting endowments. But Heytesbury hospital could not have survived until the present day without its endowment, which it owed in the last analysis to its location at the centre of Hungerford power. Closure of the hospital would have been a blow to family prestige. It was self-esteem and family pride, not filial piety, that caused Margaret to complete Walter's foundation.

[29] Ibid, *passim*; Hoare (note 15), vol 1, part 2, p. 125.
[30] J.I. Kermode, 'The Merchants of Three Northern English Towns', in C.H. Clough (ed), *Profession, Vocation and Culture in Later Medieval England* (Liverpool 1982), 30.

7

Restraint, Mediation and Private Justice:
George, Duke of Clarence as 'Good Lord'[1]

It is just over a century since the late medieval English nobility first
acquired their present unsavoury reputation.[2] Since then almost every
vice has been attributed to the magnates and they have been customarily
portrayed as factious, unjust, self-interested and grasping, hell-bent on
selfish advantage in violent disregard of the rule of law. They were
originally exposed by reference to little more than the records of parliament and new editions of the *Paston Letters* and Chief Justice Fortescue's
Governance of England, but the more extensive research of recent years
has not rehabilitated them. From 1885 until 1940 an unbroken chain of
historians not only condemned the nobility as a class, but denounced also
the social system to which they belonged as 'bastard feudalism', a degeneration from the classic feudalism of an idealised past. Detailed studies of
particular localities have often revealed individual magnates in tenacious
pursuit of unworthy ends, apparently epitomising the vices characteristic
of their class.

This dismal picture has been changed surprisingly little by the studies of
the last thirty years associated with the late K. B. McFarlane,[3] his pupils
and disciples. It is largely thanks to McFarlane that there is now more
understanding of the bastard feudal tie, the contractual relationship
between lord and retainers, which is now recognised as 'the natural heir to
feudalism ... not an illegitimate offspring'. This bond is now less often
seen as a cover for crime and resort of criminals, but rather as an

---

1. I am indebted to Mr. C. A. J. Armstrong, Dr. C. Rawcliffe and Professor A. Rogers for
   advice and criticism of this paper, which does not necessarily reflect their views. Unless
   otherwise stated all manuscripts cited are in the Public Record Office and are referred
   to by their P. R. O. call numbers.
2. In 1878, see J. R. Green, *History of the English People*, London, 1878, vol. 2, 16-17; W.
   Stubbs, *Constitutional History of England*, London, 1878, vol. 3, 573-88. For what
   follows, see esp. Sir John Fortescue, *Governance of England*, ed. C. Plummer, Oxford,
   1885, 14-19; H. M. Cam, 'Decline and Fall of English Feudalism', *History*, 25(1940),
   216sqq.
3. For McFarlane's contribution, see esp. his 'Bastard Feudalism', *B[ulletin of the]
   I[nstitute of] H[istorical] R[esearch]*, 20 (1943-5), 161-80; 'Parliament and "Bastard
   Feudalism"', *Transactions of the Royal Historical Society*, 4th series, 26 (1944), 53-79;
   'The Wars of the Roses', *Proceedings of the British Academy*, 50 (1965), 87-119.

honourable tie sought by respectable gentry everywhere.[4] Bastard feudalism was not merely inseparable from society, it was a force holding society together, and it could only be eradicated by changing the whole character of late medieval English society. McFarlane himself, however, was careful to stress the personal nature of the tie, its fragility and instability rather than its permanence. To him the system was not itself corrupt, but there was great potential for abuse.

Since historians have seen bastard feudalism as essentially a legal problem it is hardly surprising that they should have turned for information on its actual operation to records of the royal courts, particularly the Ancient Indictments of the court of King's Bench. Since these comprise prosecutions, research of this kind has predictably produced findings remarkably like the contemporary criticisms culled from literature. Numerous instances are now known of retainers, who employed force or perverted justice in the interests of their lords. Others dared to commit crimes, secure in the protection of lords able to manipulate the machinery of justice, sometimes apparently with the wholehearted support of the king's own judges. Indeed bastard feudalism has been condemned as 'inherently incompatible with the rule of law' by the most eminent of those professional historians, who find the old hostile interpretation easy to reconcile with the results of modern research.[5] This approach has coloured the work even of historians of the nobility, supposedly approaching the subject from within, who often seem to start from a presumption of guilt or are prepared to assume guilt in the absence of concrete proof.

The present writer believes this interpretation to be fundamentally misconceived, but intends in this article to demonstrate only that it is based on too restricted a range of evidence and too narrow a view of baronial activity. This result will be achieved by examining a neglected aspect of bastard feudalism in the light of the relations of one great magnate with his retinue. The nobleman in question is George Plantagenet, Duke of Clarence (1449–1478), brother of Edward IV and in his day the equal of any other English magnate. He has been reviled as much as any other late medieval nobleman, even including the repulsive Thomas of Lancaster, and was forever branded by Shakespeare as 'false, fleeting, perjur'd Clarence'. While generally preferring litigation to the use of force, the Duke of Clarence certainly employed his retainers in his

4. M. C. Carpenter, 'The Beauchamp affinity: a study of bastard feudalism at work', *E[nglish] H[istorical] R[eview]*, 95 (1980), 531. Contrast the conflict postulated in J. R. Maddicott, *Law and Lordship: Royal Justices as Retainers in Thirteenth- and Fourteenth-Century England*, Past and Present Supplement, 4, 1978, 85.
5. R. L. Storey, 'The north of England', *Fifteenth-Century England, 1399–1509: Studies in politics and society*, ed. S. B. Chrimes, C. D. Ross and R. A. Griffiths, Manchester, 1972, 133. For what follows, see Carpenter, *EHR* 95 (1980), 525; Maddicott, *Law and Lordship*, 82.

quarrels when desired: violence and maintenance featured largely in his judicial murder of Ankarette Twynho, one of the most flagrant abuses of noble power in late medieval England. However, there were two sides to the bastard feudal contract: on the one hand the lord received service from his retainers; on the other he paid for it in monetary rewards and in 'good lordship'. 'Good lordship' has been largely ignored by modern historians. It is the purpose of this article to examine Clarence's activities as 'good lord', first with regard to his patronage, then with reference to mediation and arbitration.

*   *   *   *

No noble retinue of the late middle ages is as well documented as modern historians would like, and certainly Clarence's connection falls far short of the ideal. Yet enough material does survive to establish the identity, if not always the functions, of his principal retainers. Clarence's affinity does not appear exceptional in any respect, other than the great size and broad geographical spread, which directly reflected the exalted rank, vast income and far flung estates of its head. Like all other magnates Clarence enjoyed the support of a council: while relatively little is *known* about its composition, it is easy to single out certain lawyers, administrators and confidants, who must surely have belonged. The other central institution, the household, was again of exceptional size and was staffed by gentry drawn from the whole range of the duke's estates. The lands themselves supported thousands of tenants, who were supervised in peace and marshalled in war by gentry officials appointed by the duke. Similar in proximity to Clarence, though quite different in character, were the religious houses of which he was patron – Tewkesbury Abbey, for example – and towns like Warwick where he was seigneur. Beyond these the duke enjoyed relations with other gentry: some were retained for life, so their servants became his own; for others the relationship with Clarence was as peripheral to their essential interests as it doubtless was to him.[6] Each component of his affinity had its own interests, pulling in many different directions, most of which were compatible, but some of them conflicting. All that united them was subordination to a single lord, from whom all hoped to benefit, some financially, others by ecclesiastical preferment, but all from the exercise of 'good lordship'. Thus Clarence was obliged to support and further their particular interests.

At the simplest level 'good lordship' meant favour or patronage. A household clerk served in the expectation of eventual promotion to a benefice, a gentleman yearned for a fee or office. For more valued

6. M. A. Hicks, *False, Fleeting, Perjur'd Clarence: George, Duke of Clarence 1449-78*, Gloucester, 1980, 182-9.

servants Clarence could offer more valuable rewards. As the strictly
contemporary Black Book of Edward IV's household put it,

> These lordes rewarde theire knyzts, capeleyns, esquiers, yomen,
> and other of theyre seruauntes, after theyre desertes. Some of his
> chapleyns with officyashippes, deanriez, prebendez, fre chapels,
> personages, pensions, or suche other; and for the secular men,
> stewardshippes, receuours, counstables, portershippes, baylẙ-
> wikes, wardenshippes, foresters, raungers, verders, vergers,
> shreues, eschetours, corouners, custumers, countrollers, serchers,
> surueours, beryngis of veres giftes, wardes, mariages, corrodiez,
> perkers, and wareners.[7]

Certainly most of these rewards were in Clarence's gift. Similarly religious houses of which he was patron wanted confirmation of their charters, grants of property in mortmain, and expenditure on improvements
to the conventual church; Warwick borough benefited, or hoped to
benefit, from improvements projected by the duke.[8] We know from other
sources that such magnates were not limited in their generosity to their
own patronage, but could often persuade others to advance a protégé. In
1466, for instance, Clarence wrote to the dean and chapter of Salisbury on
behalf of his 'welbeloued seruaunt William Whateley'. He wanted confirmation to Whateley of the office of parker of Sherborne conferred on
him by Bishop Beauchamp. In 1471 the duke was instrumental in the
pardon of and restitution of charters to the city of Bristol by Edward IV. It
is difficult to detect his part in royal decisions, largely because Yorkist
letters patent seldom record at whose instance they were issued. Certainly his influence explains the promotion of his servants John Delves and
Piers Courtenay as treasurer of the king's household and king's secretary
respectively.[9] These appointments were made in 1470–1, when Clarence
was at the height of his power; later, when his influence at court was much
reduced, success on this scale could not be expected.

It was a lord's recognised duty to assist his servants in their just causes.
This is commonly taken to mean physical protection against their enemies
or support in lawsuits. In Clarence's case there is little sign of either. So
far as is known, he never maintained a retainer in a lawsuit, still less
suborned or intimidated a sheriff, justice or jury on a retainer's behalf.
Only once did he offer protection, on behalf of John Glyn against Thomas
Trethewy: these were two Cornishmen whose quarrel was notorious, but

7. *Household of Edward IV*, ed. A. R. Myers, Manchester, 1959, 98.
8. R. Dodsworth and W. Dugdale, *Monasticon Anglicanum*, London, 1846, vol. 4, 356;
   Hicks, 'The Beauchamp Trust 1439–87', *BIHR* 54 (1981), 141; Hicks, *Clarence*, 196.
9. Salisbury D[iocesan] R[ecord] O[ffice], Chapter Act Book 12 (Newton), 116; *Great
   Red Book of Bristol*, ed. E. W. W. Veale, Bristol Record Society, vol. 16, 1950, 95;
   Hicks, *Clarence*, 91.

Clarence's protection seems to have been carried no further than the court of King's Bench.[10] The absence of such evidence suggests that historians have taken too combative a view of baronial careers, treating occasional feuds in court records as representative of 'good lordship' rather than highly exceptional.

Clarence's support of his retainers' just causes more commonly took the form of oversight of a will or service as a trustee. Thus he was feoffee of Richard Nanfan, whose family had served his wife's ancestors for several generations, and was overseer of the will of the Lincolnshire knight Arthur Ormeshy, who had sat for his pocket borough of Ludgershall in 1467.[11] This was a peaceful and usually a nominal form of support, since the great tended to accumulate trusteeships as some modern businessmen collect directorships and were generally not required to act. This was not always so, however, as involvement in trusts could draw magnates into litigation over disputed titles and there can be little doubt that landholders with shaky titles often chose powerful feoffees with this in mind. Clarence was twice drawn into such disputes, which offered him ample opportunity to show himself a 'good lord' and a man worth serving.

The first such case relates to Buckenham Castle and several associated manors in Norfolk, which had been bought by the naturalised Danish war veteran Sir Andrew Ogard of the childless Sir John Clifton. Sir Andrew settled them on trustees to his own use, who conveyed them on his death to his widow Alice. On her death in 1460 their heir was their nine-year-old son Henry Ogard, whose minority was the opportunity for Clifton's nephew John Knyvet to seize the lands. Henry VI and Edward IV in turn ordered him out, but he was able to persuade Edward that his title was good. Titles deriving from purchase were notoriously vulnerable to claimants by inheritance. Knyvet was pardoned, permitted to take possession, and licensed to convey the estates to feoffees. Among these he wisely included the Duke of Clarence, still a minor, but heir to the throne and a formidable figure for the future. Moreover, Clarence's interests coincided with that of the Knyvets, since he had been granted the Rye House (Herts.) and Hakebech (Norf.) on the grounds that Henry Ogard had forfeited them. Henry Ogard had taken refuge with the Lancastrians in Scotland, but he was never attainted, so Clarence's title was at least as slender as that of the Knyvets. Though still a minor, Ogard was pardoned in 1466, and on coming of age in 1472 he forcibly entered the Buckenham lands, but was sued by the feoffees and forced to pay damages. The dispute was far from over in 1478, when the estates were conveyed to a new set of feoffees of the Knyvets: this signalled the replacement of the late Duke of Clarence as patron by the Duke of Buckingham, one of the new feoffees, whose aunt William Knyvet had recently married. Clarence's personal interest may well have ended earlier, since he lost his share of the inheritance to Sir Henry Ogard, but in return for his patronage he had enjoyed consistent military support from the Knyvets in

1469-71.[12]

The other case relates to the forfeited Luttrell of Dunster inheritance. In 1461 the important Somerset knight Sir James Luttrell was among those Lancastrians who suffered attainder and in 1465 Dunster was granted to William, Lord Herbert of Raglan (later first Earl of Pembroke), whose eldest son and heir was created Lord Dunster. Pembroke died in 1469, when his son was still a minor and custody of all his lands except Dunster was granted to his countess.[13] Luttrell's widow belonged to the branch of the Courtenay family from Powderham in Devon. No fewer than seven of her brothers served Clarence in important capacities and she herself was to act as godmother to his son in 1476. It was probably through Clarence's influence at court that in 1472 the custody of Dunster was granted to him and several Courtenays. This was on behalf of Lady Luttrell, who again took up residence in Dunster Castle. It may have been intended as the first stage in the restoration of the Luttrells, but the Countess of Pembroke recovered possession shortly after, no doubt with the backing of her powerful Wydeville relatives.

A magnate was expected to restrict his support to his retainer's just cause. It is doubtful whether either case falls into this category. In the Knyvet dispute it is apparent that at the very least the rights and wrongs were far from obvious. As for the Luttrell case, speculation on reversals of attainder was an unsavoury business: it was, however, commonly done, notably by the Herberts themselves, and contemporary prejudice strongly favoured the heir by inheritance against the grantee. Reversals in fact were normal. Both examples illustrate Clarence's readiness when necessary to back his retainers against formidable opponents: the Herberts could count on aid from their in-laws, the Wydevilles, the family of the queen; Ogard was backed by John Bourchier, Lord Berners,[14] brother of the Earl of Essex and uncle by marriage of the king and indeed Clarence himself. In 1468, in yet another dispute, Clarence backed his retainers, the Vernons of Netherhaddon against Lord Grey of Codnor in a feud that might have drawn him into conflict with Grey's lord, Lord

12. This summary is based on W. Worcestre, *Itineraries*, ed. J. H. Harvey, Oxford, 1969, 48; C[alendar of] P[atent] R[olls], *1461–7*, 67, 135, 226, 323; *1467–77*, 218; *Calendar of Documents relating to Scotland*, ed. J. Bain, Edinburgh, 1888, vol. 4, 268; C.81/1488/27; C.67/45, m.21; E.159/238, Rec.Trin.1 Edw.IV, rot.2 (1-2d); P.S.O.1/44/2287; K. B.27/821, placita, rot.25d; K.B.27/843, placita, rot.1d; K.B.27/848, rex, rot. 8d; K. B.27/849, placita, rot.28d; K.B.27/850, placita, rot.35.

13. *CPR 1467–77*, 366-7; *Letters and Papers Illustrative of the Wars of the English in France*, ed. J. Stevenson, London, 1864, vol. 2(2), 786. For the rest of the paragraph, see Bodleian Library, MS. Top. Glouc.d.2, f.39 (Tewkesbury chronicle); J. A. F. Thomson, 'The Courtenay Family in the Yorkist Period', *BIHR* 45(1972), 230-46; M. A. Hicks, 'The Career of George Plantagenet, Duke of Clarence (1449–1478)', Oxford Univ. D. Phil. thesis, 1974, 373-5; *CPR 1467–77*, 330, 364.

14. Bain, op. cit., vol. 4, 268. For what follows, see Stevenson, *Wars*, vol. 2 (2), 788-9; C[alendar of] C[lose] R[olls], *1468–76*, nos. 93-5; K.B.9/13; Hicks, thesis, 348-60.

Hastings. Might not each lord have done better to restrain his retainers rather than oppose their rival? This was the practice of certain other magnates – notably the Duke of Gloucester and Earl of Northumberland in the 1470s[15] – but there is no sign of it in this case. Instead the two lords exchanged words at court and the king swiftly quelled further disturbances.

There was a real risk that the quarrels of retainers would generate friction among lords, but actually the scope of disputes was successfully limited. King Edward lived up to his duty, intervening when disputes threatened to escalate, and it appears that Clarence – like Richard Beauchamp, Earl of Warwick[16] – generally kept conflict within bounds. Magnates understandably preferred amicable co-operation with one another rather than unnecessary conflict on issues peripheral to their own interests. It is worth noting that neither the Knyvet nor Vernon cases developed into feuds between lords or, indeed, precluded amicable relations between Clarence and Lords Berners and Hastings, then or in the future. Similarly, Clarence's lawsuits seem to have had little impact on politics. Magnates could not permit minor local differences about arrears of rent, poaching or the rights of retainers to determine their national political alignment. On this evidence a mere handful of cases brought 'good lords' into conflict and even fewer had wider repercussions. There are strong grounds for suggesting that the attention given by modern historians to minor litigation among magnates is out of proportion to its real importance. 'Good lordship' did not have to mean violent support of retainers against all-comers, as historians have too readily supposed. Clarence's activity as 'good lord' shows him to have been primarily a pacific patron and trustee, who avoided undue friction with other lords.

*   *   *   *

The successful 'good lord' had to be more than merely a generous patron, who gave what his retainers asked. He had to distribute his patronage evenly, so as to satisfy as many dependants as possible, and he had to balance his own requirement of efficient management of estates and household against the demands of patronage. He had to exercise discipline among his retainers and employ a series of penalties, ranging from exclusion from favour, dismissal from office or even from his service altogether; Clarence sued several defaulting ministers and poachers in the ranks of his own retainers. In short, a lord's advantage could not always be that of his servants and conflicts of interest sometimes arose among members of the same retinue.

15. M. A. Hicks, 'Dynastic Change and Northern Society: The Career of the Fourth Earl of Northumberland 1470–89' , below, 375.
16. Carpenter. *EHR* 95(1980), 530-1.

Some such differences were readily settled by the lord alone. When complaints reached Clarence of the misdemeanours of James Norreys, his governor of the Channel Isles, the duke replaced him in that office. In other respects he remained his good lord.[17] On another occasion the duke's tenants at Ashbourne in Derbyshire complained that they were constantly vexed by Lawrence Lowe, a local gentleman. Clarence ordered him to desist and to explain his conduct before the ducal council, but Lowe declined to attend and persisted in his misconduct. On 10 April 1468 Clarence wrote to him, marvelling at his temerity, and informed him that the treasurer of his own household would 'declare vnto you in that behalue our entent'. This particular dispute probably arose from Lowe's quarrel with John Cockayne of Ashbourne, whom he had sued at the exchequer of pleas for breaking down his enclosures. Cockayne had long enjoyed an evil reputation, so Lowe may well have been justified. Neither his aggression nor his disobedience could be tolerated by the duke, although he took no sides and offered Lowe a hearing. The result would probably have been the imposition of a settlement, but regrettably we do not know the sequel.

The court of Chancery offered an equitable jurisdiction in matters for which the common law offered no remedy, for example in cases of misbehaviour by feoffees to uses. In Chancery, and later in other prerogative courts, defendants consistently claimed that jurisdiction belonged to the courts of common law. However, litigation in King's Bench and Common Pleas was expensive and time-consuming, even when the complex technicalities of pleading were not abused, and cases were frequently lost on procedural points rather than merit. There was therefore an incentive to settle by arbitration. As there was no provision for this at common law, advance agreement was necessary from both parties. It was essential to determine beforehand the scope of the inquiry, the date before which the award had to be made, the personnel of the panel of arbitration, and the means by which it was enforced.

The main difficulty concerned the composition of the panel of arbiters, as each side sought a favourable settlement. Frequently each party selected an equal number of arbiters, who acted as a committee. Many disputes were settled amicably in this way. Even so deadlock among the arbiters often resulted, for which alternative procedures were frequently prescribed. A common variation was for each party to choose his lord as arbiter: several times the Duke of Gloucester and Earl of Northumber-

17. T. W. M. De Guerin, 'Notes on some old documents', *Transactions of the Guernsey Society of Natural Sciences and Local Research*, 7(1914), 166-8; E.159/255, Brevia Hil.18 Edw.IV, rot.8d; C.47/10/29. For what follows, see the letter in Hicks, *Clarence*, 181; E.13/151, rot. 12-d,13; *R[otuli] P[arliamentorum]*, London, 1777, vol. 6, 368; R. L. Storey, *End of the House of Lancaster*, London, 1966, 157-8.

land co-operated in this way.[18] In such cases arbitration might result less from mutual desire for a settlement than from co-operation among the lords. They might interpret their obligation of 'good lordship' as the arrangement of an equitable solution, not in the maintenance of their retainers' quarrel, and they had the power to enforce their award. Such an approach accords with Clarence's letter to Lawrence Lowe.

The trust of both parties in the good faith and impartiality of their lord was a prerequisite to arbitration by him alone. When settling the differences between Worcester cathedral chapter and his college at Warwick, Clarence protested his affection for each and his earnest desire for a just solution. Certainly neither corporation had any reason for dissatisfaction with the settlement.[19] In 1471, when he offered his services to the city and cathedral chapter of Salisbury in their long-running struggle, he was prompted as much by his distress at the imprisonment of certain burgesses in London as by his love of the cathedral itself. The chapter declined his offer, but did not doubt his impartiality. Indeed, when reporting the incident to Bishop Beauchamp, they wrote enthusiastically: 'Thanks be to God, who has given such a benevolent and devout prince into the tutelage of the Church'.[20] This kind of confidence was essential on both sides before arbitration could take place. One safeguard against a biased judgement was the certainty that it would cause the aggrieved party to withdraw from the lord's service: a lord would go to considerable lengths to avoid such an eventuality, such a blow to his reputation as a lord worth serving.

The procedure was swift and flexible, but the legal rules were those of the common law. In his offer to the Salisbury chapter the award was to follow investigation by the justices and others learned in the law.[21] In other cases the facts and legal issues were examined informally by trained lawyers in Clarence's service. Since the decisions had to be enforceable at law, it was normal for the parties to bind themselves beforehand by recognisances to abide the award. If they failed to obey it, the sums named in the bonds were forfeited and actions of debt could follow in the court of Common Pleas. Often the award provided for action in the royal courts, either for the termination of existing litigation or for the conveyance of the disputed land in Common Pleas. An element of equity was implied in the contemporary term *compromisum*.

The college of St. Mary, Warwick was in the duke's patronage and benefited directly from his interest. Sir Richard Verney of Compton Murdock was probably Clarence's retainer. His son Edmund Verney certainly was. Father and son were bound in £100

18. E.g. *CCR 1468–76*, no. 1317.
19. Worcestershire Records Office, Reg. Carpenter II, BA 2648/6(iii), pp. 138-41.
20. Salisbury DRO, Chapter Act Book 13 (Machon), p. 214 (my trans.).
21. Ibid.

> to stonde to the awarde of certeyne arbitoures by vs for thaime
> endeferently named and chosen to awarde ordeine and deme be-
> twixe thaime of and Vppon all acciones trespasses causes and
> stryves wronges harmes and other matiers quarels and demaundes
> hadde moved and done by thaim or eny of thaime.

The arbiters had to reach a decision by Lady Day 1475. If they could not
agree, the parties were to accept the 'dome of vs the said Duke Umpere'.
Any award was to be made before midsummer. As the arbiters failed to
make an award, Clarence

> caused diuerse trustie and wel disposed persons as well of the
> councelle of both the said parties as oure concell to examyne and
> vnderstonde the trouth of the matiers of variance betwixe thaime
> and to certayue vs thereof to thentente that we might truely and
> honorably proced to awarde ordinance and judgemente in the
> same.

Twenty-three years earlier the college had farmed the site, oblations,
tithes and glebe of Compton Murdock rectory to Sir Richard Verney for
the annual rent of £2 13s. 4d. Over the intervening years the sum due had
risen to £61, none of which had ever been paid. This claim is confirmed by
ministers' accounts of the collegiate estates for 1465–6 and 1474–5.[22]
Verney could not show that he had paid. Accordingly Clarence ordered
that Verney should renounce his stewardship of the college's lands and
should pay £20 by fixed instalments. He was to find sureties for £40 to the
college. The college was to take possession of part of the rectory and lease
the remainder to Sir Richard and Edmund Verney at the old rent, with
the option of renewal at the going rate. The resultant lease was sealed six
days before the date stipulated in the original recognisances.[23] As far as is
known, the settlement was permanent and both sides obeyed it.

On 16 June 1468 Clarence arbitrated another dispute, this time between the prioress of Amesbury, Thomas Delamare and Stephen Shad-
well on one side and John Hall, his sons and daughters on the other.
Clarence was chosen as arbiter by both parties. To ensure that he obeyed
the award, Hall found four sureties for £500. Each of these was an
esquire, for Hall was a man of means and a former mayor of Salisbury.
This may have been why the prioress claimed him as her serf and imprisoned him, hoping thereby to acquire his wealth: this was not unprecedented conduct, as Professor Hilton has shown.[24] Hall reacted vigorously by suing her in the royal courts. Clarence and his council had heard

22. *Ministers' Accounts of the Collegiate Church of St. Mary, Warwick, 1432–85*, ed. D.
    Styles, Dugdale Society, vol. 26, 1969, 93-4, 135-6.
23. Birmingham Reference Library, MSS. 437204-5.
24. R. H. Hilton, *Decline of Serfdom in Medieval England*, London, 1969, 52-5.

the case of each side, examined the case of each side, examined the 'fair and notable evidence and proves' of both, but could not establish what was the truth. Modern historians have also failed to unravel Hall's origins. This was apparently a genuine case of doubt, not merely a frivolous suit by the prioress. Accordingly Clarence sought in his award to protect her from the consequences of her action. Existing lawsuits were to be released by both sides and Hall, his sons and daughters were not to sue the prioress or her agents for the injuries which they had suffered. The prioress and convent were to recognise the free status of Hall and his children in open court at Hall's expense.[25] Two years later, as one of the burgesses imprisoned by the Salisbury cathedral chapter, Hall was again to benefit from Clarence's intervention.

Three days after the Amesbury award Clarence settled a dispute between Sir Nicholas Latimer and Sir Edward Grey of Groby (later Viscount Lisle) over the Somerset manor of Loxton. The surviving award tells nothing of the points at issue,[26] but fortunately these can be reconstructed from other sources. Latimer was one of the Lancastrians attainted in 1461 for supporting Henry VI and had forfeited his estates. Some had been retained by the king, but most was granted to Sir John Howard, treasurer of the royal household and soon to be ennobled; Loxton was given to Sir Edward Grey, another royal servant, in consideration of his faithful service. Latimer, however, quickly reconciled himself to the new regime, securing a pardon in 1463 and the grant of some of his former lands in 1466, and entered Clarence's service. With this concrete evidence of royal favour and such a powerful patron it could only be a matter of time before his attainder was reversed. This was foreseen by Howard, who sold his share of the lands back to Latimer and withdrew his opposition to the latter's restoration. That left only Loxton to be recovered: by himself Grey evidently lacked sufficient political weight either to thwart Latimer's restoration or to secure acceptable terms in return for his title. His (and Howard's) rights were safeguarded by provisoes to the 1467 act of resumption, but they were annulled by 3 June 1468, when Latimer's act of reversal was exemplified in Chancery. Grey, however, continued to make trouble, perhaps refusing to surrender Loxton, and Latimer appealed to Clarence as good lord. Both men took out bonds of £200 to abide his award and on 19 June 1468, having 'herde the allegeans, titles and replicacions of the said partyes of and in

---

25. Wiltshire Record Office, MS.214/8 (arbitration award). For Hall's career, see J.C. Wedgwood, *History of Parliament, 1439–1509*, London, 1936, vol. 1, 407.
26. Northamptonshire Record Office, Stopford Sackville MS.4113. I am indebted to Dr. C. Rawcliffe for drawing my attention to this document and supplying a transcript. For the rest of this paragraph, see ibid.; J. R. Lander, *Crown and Nobility 1450–1509*, London, 1976, 148-9; *RP* v. 582, 583, 585; *CPR 1461-7*, 111, 178, 200, 269, 525, 537; Hicks, *Clarence*, 48, 217.

the premisses and by goode deliberacion thaim understanden', Clarence had no difficulty in reaching a decision. Loxton obviously belonged to Latimer and was duly awarded to him. It seemed unreasonable, however, that Grey should go wholly uncompensated and so Clarence provided that he should be paid £100 in seven yearly instalments by Latimer or his executors. In case Latimer declined to pay, taking a stand on his unquestionable right to the property, he was to take out a bond of statute staple of £100 forfeitable in the event of default. Both parties had good reason to be satisfied with the verdict. Latimer was able to liquidate the last remaining claim to his property: his appreciation is suggested by his political support for Clarence's Lincolnshire rising in 1470. For Grey the mere offer of arbitration ensured some compensation for a claim that could not be legally enforced: furthermore he had every reason to expect favourable treatment from the chosen arbiter.

Another award related to the disputed manors of Knights Washbourne and Stanford-on-Teme in Worcestershire, the patrimony of the Washbourne family.[27] By his first wife John Washbourne had a daughter Isolda, who married and bore a son, Humphrey Salwey. By his second marriage John Washbourne had a son, Norman Washbourne. On John's death it was Norman who took possession of both manors on the basis of an entail in his favour. His right was disputed by Humphrey Salwey, who claimed that Knights Washbourne had been settled on the issue of John Washbourne's first marriage. The result was protracted litigation in the court of Common Pleas. Eventually, 'willynge unyte and peas to be hadd herafter' and considering 'the nyghnes of bloode that ys betwixt the seid p(ar)ties', they agreed to abide the award of the Duke of Clarence. Both were probably his retainers: Salwey's son was to serve him and both families had a tradition of service to the Duchess of Clarence's family.[28] The award provided for the division of the lands. Salwey was to have Stanford with an annuity of eight marks (£5 6s. 8d.) from Knights Washbourne, while Norman Washbourne was to have Knights Washbourne itself. To secure their titles a strict timetable was prescribed for complicated transactions in the court of Common Pleas. The settlement was delayed by the deaths of both Clarence and Norman Washbourne, but was ultimately carried out. Evidently Clarence had established the justice of Salwey's case, but his award nevertheless recognised the desire of the Washbourne family to retain the manor that bore their name. Instead Salwey was compensated with Stanford and the annuity.

The common factor in all these cases is that the arbiter first established the facts on the basis of evidence submitted by the contestants, to which each had a right of reply, and then reached his decision. An award was a

27. This paragraph is based on J. Davenport, *Washbourne Family of Little Washbourne and Wichenford in the County of Worcester*, London, 1907, 8-17.
28. *List of Sheriffs*, London, 1898, 157-8.

compromise. The prioress, Verney, Grey and Washbourne all failed to substantiate their claims, but their losses were less than they might have been in a court of common law. They were not charged damages and they were protected against future litigation. The proposed settlements were final, or were at least expected to be final. The desire of both parties to avoid fines, amercements and damages clearly emerges from the legal provisions of these awards. Clarence had many lawyers on his payroll and readily drew on the expertise of the king's justices, several of whom may have been among his retainers. The judges clearly accepted that arbitration performed a useful function. Not only did it save the parties expense and provide a speedy solution to knotty legal problems, but it prevented self-help. In one instance the duke explained that he acted

> entending to sette quiete and reste betwixe the said parties in the said matiers both for their wele and for the rest of that contrey.[29]

A measure of his achievement is that none of these thorny disputes resulted in violence.

* * * *

Obviously such material does not provide a complete picture of Clarence as arbiter, still less does it portray arbitration in general, but it does collect together all that survives of Clarence's arbitration. Evidently he did not support his retainers' just causes without discrimination and his own declared motives appear exemplary. While one cannot demonstrate that the surviving evidence reflects all that once existed, the material from eight cases suggests that arbitration was a significant function of the ducal council. Four of Clarence's awards (one a copy) survive unaccompanied by recognisances, one recognisance exists without an award; in addition there are two offers of arbitration and a settlement which may have resulted from arbitration.[30] Obviously much has been lost, certainly much more than survives. There are no registers of magnate councils[31] to provide records comparable in completeness with, for example, the rolls of the central courts of common law, and no baronial archive remains in even the state of incompleteness of the fifteenth-century court of Chan-

29. Birmingham Reference Library MS.437204.
30. These are the seven cases discussed above, plus the recognisance of 27 January 1467 in Sir John Gresley v. Burton Abbey, *Descriptive Catalogue of Charters and Muniments belonging to the Marquis of Anglesey*, ed. I. H. Jeayes, Collections for the History of Staffordshire, 1937, no. 719.
31. See C. Rawcliffe, 'Baronial Councils in Fifteenth-Century England', *Patronage, Pedigree and Power in Late Medieval England*, ed. C. D. Ross (Gloucester, 1979). Dr. Rawcliffe kindly permitted me to consult in typescript her paper 'The Great Lord as Peacemaker: Arbitration by English Noblemen and their Councils in the Later Middle Ages', forthcoming.

cery. Awards were handed to the warring parties and were not title deeds to be cherished. They were less important than the documents which fulfilled their terms, which might not mention arbitration at all. Even such title deeds have not survived well: what proportion of final concords are known only from the feet of fines at the Public Record Office? They were also less important than any releases in the central courts, like those prescribed in the Amesbury-Hall and Salwey-Washbourne suits, which would certainly not mention any award. How many actions of debt against men defaulting on recognisances stemmed from unfulfilled awards? At present one can only say that some did.[32] Many plaintiffs in Chancery were seeking enforcement of awards rather than exacting the penalty stipulated in the recognisance. Usually the records of such cases survive in part and cannot readily be connected with existing awards, let alone be verified. The fact that none apparently relate to Clarence need not mean that he was seldom asked to act: perhaps it was because his awards successfully ended disputes, as the four discussed above did.

The magnate's role as arbiter has long been recognised, most recently by Dr. Griffiths,[33] but scarcely investigated. Professor Storey, for example, admits that it had a part to play, but thinks that close supervision by the crown was essential to prevent abuse by the lords.[34] He seems here to be exaggerating the virtues of royal justice and the common law courts: the historian of King's Bench recorded her 'strong impression of a court more ineffective than any such body could afford to be if it were to survive'.[35] Professor Storey was also underestimating the degree of contact already existing between royal justice and private arbitration. Certainly private arbiters sometimes pressurised parties into accepting mediation, but the crown also found coercion necessary – to persuade defendants to attend, for example. Determined litigants, who could already exploit the technicalities of the common law, rapidly learnt to play off the conciliar courts. Indeed, by accepting indiscriminate complaints from individuals and compelling their opponents to attend, the prerogative courts actually encouraged malicious and frivolous suits. A measure of discipline was found to be essential.[36]

Private arbitration, however, was essentially voluntary, because it depended on the prior consent of the parties, who could easily refuse, as Clarence found at Salisbury. It could only be enforced, in the last resort, by the royal courts of Chancery and Common Pleas. Should an award be resisted, the royal judges were already in a position to supervise its

32. C. Rawcliffe, *The Staffords, Earl of Stafford and Dukes of Buckingham 1394–1521*, Cambridge, 1978, 165.
33. R.A. Griffiths, *Reign of King Henry VI*, London, 1981, 596.
34. R.L. Storey, *Reign of Henry VII*, London, 1968, 38.
35. M. Blatcher, *Court of King's Bench 1450–1550: A Study in Self-Help*, London, 1978, vii.
36. J. Guy, *Cardinal's Court*, Hassocks, 1977, passim.

enforcement or review its terms. Perhaps they often did so, but they did not object to private arbitration in principle. There was no clear distinction between the two systems, no need for conflict, for many of the personnel involved and the law administered were the same.[37] Magnates drew on the same judges, who presided in the common law and conciliar courts, and often paid them annuities.[38] No doubt these judges found it a pleasant change to apply their expertise unhampered by procedural technicalities and with a better chance of reaching a lasting verdict. Did these judges distinguish between the justice they administered on Clarence's council and, for example, in the Council of Wales? Henry VI's chancellor and council sometimes referred matters to private arbitration and private arbiters sometimes provided that, failing a settlement within a specified time, the case would go to Chancery as last resort.[39] Even after the emergence of Star Chamber, cases were frequently delegated for settlement to local worthies, who may well have been arbitrating others privately. Yet lords may have been able to abuse the system, as Professor Storey feared, but it was hardly in their interests to do so: any lord, whose lordship was bad, could expect only bad or indifferent service. This, perhaps, explains why great magnates like Clarence and his father[40] thought it worth taking such pains over knotty disputes among their retainers. A clear sign that such efforts were appreciated is the persistence of private arbitration long after improvements in judicial procedure and the establishment of prerogative courts.

*   *   *   *

Clarence's experience indicates that 'good lordship' was more complex than has generally been supposed. Even this discredited magnate was able to patronise his retainers peacefully, without being drawn willy-nilly into his retainers' more dangerous quarrels. Even then, such disputes were limited by the good sense of magnates, who understandably wished to avoid divisive feuds and sought to settle differences without resort to arms or the law. Public order, from which the great had so much to gain,

---

37. This facet of the subject, completely ignored by Dr. Maddicott, casts considerable doubt on his assertion that 'the alliances between magnates and the king's judges' meant that the 'interests of the crown itself were at stake', *Law and Lordship*, 83.
38. E.g. Chief Justice Fairfax and Chief Baron Andrews, J. M. W. Bean, *Estates of the Percy Family 1416–1537*, Oxford, 1958, 92n; *Testamenta Eboracensia*, ed. J. Raine, Surtees Society, vol. 45, 1864, 306; Rawcliffe, *Staffords*, 219. At least some fifteenth-century lawyers retained by towns lost their fees on promotion to the bench, R. E. Horrox, 'Urban Patronage and Patrons in the Fifteenth Century', *Patronage, the Crown and the Provinces in Later Medieval England*, ed. R. A. Griffiths, Gloucester, 1981, 150-1.
39. Griffiths, *Henry VI*, 609n. For the next sentence, see Guy, op. cit., 46-7, 97sqq.
40. J. T. Rosenthal, 'Feuds and Private Peace-Making: A Fifteenth-Century Example', *Nottingham Medieval Studies*, 14(1970), 84-90.

was an important consideration to Clarence at least, who wanted to preserve peace, which was the normal condition: feuds, even in the 1450s, were exceptional and far from continuous, and Clarence avoided involvement in anything comparable. Seen in this light, 'good lordship' contributed to the social cohesion promoted by bastard feudalism in particular localities. Just as patronage, however undesirable nowadays, is now recognised as a positive element in medieval politics and society, so too must 'good lordship' be approached with an eye to its constructive role.

Professor Bellamy has depicted a late medieval England dominated by criminal gangs directed by magnates, who unscrupulously manipulated the law and corrupted their retainers to do likewise. Only three pages are devoted to arbitrations and other settlements out of court.[41] Similarly a recent examination of the working of an affinity in practice, while admitting that peace was normal, concentrated on feuds and only referred to the existence of two arbitration awards. This imbalance is understandable, since it is very much easier and more obviously rewarding to rely on the records of the central courts, which survive in such overwhelming bulk and which historians have scarcely begun to exploit. Such advantages largely compensate for the infrequency of verdicts, the problem of substantiating what is said, and the probablility that many indictments are propaganda. Arbitrations are less deceptively straightforward to employ and their references to 'justice' and 'equity' can be easily dismissed as mere common form or lip-service. Yet the central courts and arbitration were different facets of a single system of justice concerned with administering the same law with overlapping personnel. To achieve a balanced picture all the evidence must be taken into account. This means that more attention must be given to this positive side of bastard feudalism than the weight of extant documentation would otherwise suggest. It has been the contention of this article that not only was there a positive side to bastard feudalism, but that it was expected by retainers of even the most disparaged of late medieval magnates.

41. J.G. Bellamy, *Crime and Public Order in England in the Later Middle Ages*, London, 1973, esp. 117-20. For the next sentence, see Carpenter, *EHR* 95(1980), 530.

8

Edward IV, the Duke of Somerset and Lancastrian Loyalism in the North[1]

ON 29 MARCH 1461 EDWARD IV, the first Yorkist king, defeated his Lancastrian counterpart Henry VI at Towton near York. Although King Henry, Queen Margaret and their son escaped, most of their principal adherents were killed or executed. Towton was regarded as decisive over most of the kingdom and resistance continued only in remote parts of Wales and on the northern borders. Too weak to confront the Yorkists on equal terms, the Lancastrians were ousted from the three Northumbrian castles of Alnwick, Bamburgh, and Dunstanburgh on three separate occasions — c. September 1461, in July 1462, and in December 1462/January 1463. That they recovered the castles each time resulted from the treachery of the custodians and the military assistance of the French and Scots. Defeat at Hexham on 15 May 1464, however, was conclusive: the castles fell for a fourth and final time; Henry VI himself was recaptured; and Harlech castle remained the sole Lancastrian possession on the British mainland. Still at liberty, Queen Margaret and her son held court in Bar, intriguing ineffectively with supporters in England even after Harlech fell in 1468. It was only Yorkist dissidents, however, who made possible the shortlived restoration of Henry VI in 1470–71.

As conspicuous Lancastrians Henry Beaufort, Duke of Somerset, his brother-in-law Sir Henry Lewis, and Sir Nicholas Latimer were attainted by Edward IV's first parliament in 1461. All three remained at arms and were among the garrison of Dunstanburgh castle on its capitulation on 27 December 1462. They, together with Sir Ralph Percy, were then

---

[1] Unless otherwise stated, this article is based on: G. E. C[okayne], *Complete Peerage of England, Ireland, Scotland and the United Kingdom*, ed. H. V. Gibbs and others (12 vols, 1910–59), XII (1), 54–56; C. L. Scofield, 'Henry, Duke of Somerset and Edward IV', *English Historical Review*, XXI (1906), 300–02; idem, *Life and Reign of Edward the Fourth* (1923), I, 265, 273–74, 292–93, 312–13; J. Gillingham, *Wars of the Roses* (1981), pp. 136–55; J. R. Lander, *Crown and Nobility 1450–1509* (1976), ch. 5, esp. pp. 134–35; C. D. Ross, *Edward IV* (1974), pp. 51–52, 58; M. K. Jones, 'Edward IV and the Beaufort Family: Conciliation in Early Yorkist Politics', *The Ricardian*, 83 (1983), 258–65; R(otuli) P(arliamentorum), ed. J. Strachey and others (Record Commission, 1767–77), V, 476–83, 511–14; and the document printed below. All manuscripts are cited by their Public Record Office call numbers. I am indebted to Dr M. K. Jones for his advice and criticism regarding this article.

granted their lands and lives,[2] swore allegiance to King Edward, and were trusted with office forthwith. To Percy was confided the command of the captured castles of Dunstanburgh and Bamburgh; and on 17 March he was even commissioned to receive the submission and oaths of allegiance of other repentant rebels.[3] Somerset participated with some distinction in the siege of the third Lancastrian castle in Northumberland, Alnwick. He was assiduously courted by the King, hunting and even sleeping with him. He received gifts of money, a tournament was arranged in his honour, and he was appointed commander of King Edward's personal bodyguard. Somerset, Lewis, and Latimer were pardoned their offences, including their attainders and consequent forfeitures, Somerset as early as 10 March 1463, Lewis on 7 May[4] and Latimer on 30 June following. However, in spite of all these favours, Somerset deserted to the Lancastrians at the first opportunity, rejoining the rebellious Percy by 1 December 1463,[5] and commanded their forces at the battle of Hexham. Captured, he was executed forthwith and his attainder was renewed in 1465.

At least some contemporaries were amazed by King Edward's willingness to trust such committed enemies of his dynasty so completely. The inhabitants of Northampton strongly resented the favour shown to Somerset, just as somewhat later the Neville faction, with rather less justification, opposed the elevation of those other former Lancastrians, the Wydevilles. Certainly contemporaries were shocked by Somerset's treachery, which appeared all the worse not just because of Edward's favour, but because Somerset had freely accepted his new allegiance. He was reported to have made overtures to the Earl of Warwick earlier in 1462.[6] By contrast other members of the Dunstanburgh garrison had taken passports to Scotland and continued their resistance to Edward IV.

Modern historians have also stressed the importance of these events. When discussing Edward's attempts at reconciliation and the opportunities offered for erstwhile Lancastrians to make their peace, Professor Lander described 'Somerset's case' as 'the most significant' of all those

[2] 'Annales Rerum Anglicarum', *Letters and Papers Illustrative of the Wars of the English in France*, ed. J. Stevenson, II (2), Rolls Series (1864), 780; J. de Waurin, *Recueil des Croniques et Anchiennes Istories de la Grant Bretaigne*, ed. W. and E. L. C. P. Hardy, v, Rolls Series (1891), 432; but see R. Davies, *Extracts from the Municipal Records of the City of York* (1843), p. 33.

[3] C(alendar of) P(atent) R(olls), 1461–67, p. 262.

[4] Ibid., pp. 261, 267, 269; C 81/1492/21, /39.

[5] C81/796/1301. I am indebted to Dr M. K. Jones for this reference.

[6] *Paston Letters and Papers of the Fifteenth Century*, ed. N. Davis (2 vols, 1971–76), I, 286.

remarkable 'examples of political amnesty and political treachery'. Somerset and Percy were not the only failures of Edward's policy. Both Lewis and Latimer rebelled again in 1469–71, together with Richard, Lord Welles and Willoughby, Sir Thomas Tresham and Sir Thomas Fulford. Other pardoned Lancastrians who defected during the fourteen-sixties were Sir Henry Bellingham and Humphrey Neville of Brancepeth in County Durham. In all seven individuals had their attainders reversed in parliament during the fourteen-sixties, but only one remained loyal. In his magisterial biography of Edward IV, Professor Ross was terse and downright in his condemnation of royal policy:

There now followed one of those political blunders which mars Edward's record as a statesman . . . nothing in the record of either Somerset or Percy seems to justify Edward in placing such trust in them; and events now proved how serious had been his miscalculation.[7]

Such in brief is the course of events and the interpretation supported by all three outstanding historians of the Yorkist period, Miss Scofield as well as Professors Ross and Lander. The great merit of this assessment is that it is based directly on contemporary opinion. What has not been fully appreciated until now, however, is how limited such evidence is and how much the relevant sources are coloured by awareness of what was to follow. The purpose of this article is to question the current orthodoxy with reference to some new evidence and to suggest an alternative interpretation, in which the episode is presented less as a bizarre incident than as an intelligible part of Lancastrian resistance in the fourteen-sixties. Such resistance itself emerges not as an obstinate refusal to accept the inevitable, but rather as a commitment to principle. The episode thus acquires a more profound significance for our understanding of the politics of the Wars of the Roses.

Edward's generosity and Somerset's ingratitude were, if anything, yet more remarkable when it is considered that the Duke's attainder was reversed within six months of his submission at the opening session of King Edward's second parliament, which met at Westminster from 29 April to 17 June 1463. The existence of such an act was recorded in Somerset's second attainder, but the original act does not survive. The text, however, has now been recovered and is printed below. The act reversed the attainder not just of Somerset but of Lewis as well, who was not attainted again in 1465 because he had remained loyal. Nevertheless

[7] Ross, *Edward IV*, pp. 51–52.

the royal Exchequer understood the second attainder as invalidating the reversal, so on 16 January 1467 Lewis secured a writ under the great seal to the Exchequer barons stating that the reversal still applied to him and enclosing a copy of the original act, then still preserved in the Chancery files. The record of the process, writ and act were recorded by them in the King's Remembrancer's Memoranda Roll.[8] Many other original acts annulling attainders are also lost and are known only through enrolments, most commonly through exemplifications on the patent roll. Others, which once existed, are certainly missing: lost originals may explain how, for example, the fourth Earl of Northumberland felt able to employ long-established Percy retainers like Gawen Lampleugh and Robert Thomlinson, whose attainders are not known to have been annulled.[9]

The revocation of the attainders of Somerset and Lewis in 1463 was presumably effected between 7 May, the date of Lewis's pardon, and 17 June, when parliament was prorogued. It is not known to which house of parliament the bill was introduced and nothing is known of its passage, except that the form of royal assent — 'Le Roy le voet' — was that normally reserved for public bills. The usual response to bills benefiting individuals was 'Soit fait come il est desire', as in the reversal of Philip Wentworth's attainder at the same session[10] and in all similar restorations in 1467–68 and 1472–75. The late Professor Gray argued for a blurred line between public and private acts, citing in support one favouring an individual — Edward IV's elder sister Anne, Duchess of Exeter — which was phrased as a public bill and was approved by 'Le Roy le voet'.[11] As this act recites the King's grants and then confirms them, it does not appear relevant to a bill without such phraseology and cast as a petition. Although benefiting an individual, it may well have been presented officially: if so, it would tend to discount — not confirm — Gray's hypothesis of a hybrid category and would itself be a public bill employing the customary formula of assent. Similarly this formula may have been used in Somerset and Lewis's reversal because the bill was sponsored by the King, in spite of its supplicatory form. Edward might reasonably have felt that he was honour bound to support a bill that merely confirmed what he had already granted by his letters patent. Unless the hostility of

[8] E 159/243, recorda Hillary 6 Edward IV m.6d.

[9] M. A. Hicks, 'Dynastic Change and Northern Society: The Career of the Fourth Earl of Northumberland 1470–89' , below, 369.

[10] There are close verbal similarities between this and the Wentworth act, *RP*, v, 548.

[11] H. L. Gray, *Influence of the Commons on Early Legislation* (Cambridge, Mass., 1932), pp. 58–59.

the chronicler Gregory to Somerset's rehabilitation was distorted by hindsight, a possibility to be considered below, parliament's approval of the bill is remarkable and requires an explanation. Unwillingness to offend the King, who was giving it overt support, is one such reason. An alternative is considered below.

The emphasis in the act on the restoration of 'name and fame', 'worship, good name and fame' points to a high valuation placed by the petitioners on their reputation. Perhaps they were thought to be bound to their new allegiance, not just by material advantage and Edward's favour, but also by their honour. There was apparently no provision for compensating those granted parts of the forfeited Beaufort and Lewis estates — John Rede, James Hyett, and the king's carver Roger Ree — and their rights were not safeguarded in the act. The only proviso of exemption for an individual was on behalf of Sir Geoffrey Gate, the Earl of Warwick's councillor, who had been granted the lieutenancy of the Isle of Wight, which Somerset had held during pleasure, and the receivership of the royal lands there, of which Somerset had been lessee.[12] It seems that the patentees lost their grants and that Somerset and Lewis were restored under act to all their lands. Moreover Edward's reported promise to the Duke of 1,000 marks (£666 13s. 4d.) a year was largely honoured, since an annuity of £222 was restored to him and a further £227 13s. 4d. was paid over in cash. Nothing was withheld that would justify the Duke's subsequent betrayal.

It would be useful to know how closely the original bill resembled the eventual act. Were the provisoes of exemption added during passage through parliament or were they integral parts of the original bill? Were they the product of opposition in parliament or of fumbling experimentation with a new form of act? Certainly the text provides further evidence of uncertainty how to reverse the attainders of individuals, whilst maintaining in force the act in which they featured. We have already seen an instance of this in the unfortunate later experience of Lewis himself. This particular act favours two people, whereas almost all other reversals of attainder benefit only single individuals or — during dynastic revolutions like 1461 and 1485 — provide blanket restorations for whole categories of people, who may not even have been alive. Apart from Gate's personal proviso of exemption, itself a feature with few parallels before 1485, there are three general saving clauses in the act. One safeguarding the rights of rival claimants to property antedating the original attainder became standard in later acts; but the others were superogatory and were omitted

[12] *CPR*, 1452–61, pp. 390–91; 1461–67, pp. 37–38, 98, 117, 220, 239.

from subsequent reversals. One covered the rights of occupants of the lands before the date of restoration, so that they would not be liable for the issues or the husbandry before 29 April 1463, 'the first day of this present parliament'. The other protected all those who had received Somerset's or Lewis's chattels, not just as far back as the act of attainder itself but for the year preceding, even though this was effectively covered by the backdating included in the attainder itself. It is also noteworthy that, on Somerset's second attainder, those with previous grants retained them. Hyett had no new patent until 1465;[13] and Rede never obtained another — or at least another was never enrolled — yet he secured a proviso of exemption for his Beaufort holdings in the 1467 act of resumption.[14]

This particular act provides further proof that acts of attainder and reversal were not passed by parliament without due consideration. Nobody subject to an existing attainder was attainted a second time, so a second attainder should be taken as evidence of a preceding reversal. Similarly, nobody secured a second reversal for the same attainder, unless the first restoration had been qualified by provisoes of exemption. An example of this is the two reversals of Sir Edmund Mountford's attainder of 1461.[15] Such restorations, even if partial, came to be seen as essential security: it became less and less common for pardoned rebels to be content with restorations by patent alone.

The wisdom of having both a royal pardon and an unambiguous act of reversal emerges clearly from the contrary experience of Sir Nicholas Latimer. At his surrender he was, according to the chronicler pseudo-Worcester, promised his life and lands on the same terms as Somerset and Lewis, yet his pardon was granted only on 30 June 1463, too late to permit a confirmatory act in the same session of parliament. Although this pardon was also drawn in precisely the same form as those of Somerset and Lewis and annulled both Latimer's attainder and consequent forefeiture, it was interpreted by royal servants merely as having 'habled [Latimer] unto your Lawes, but restored unto his lyflode'. Only in 1467 did he secure an act of reversal, for which he had to buy out the titles of Edward's grantees, Sir John Howard and Edward Grey of Groby.[16] Similarly Sir Thomas Tresham, whose attainder was reversed at the same

[13] Ibid., 1461–67, p. 434.
[14] *RP*, v, 593.
[15] R. A. Griffiths, 'The Hazards of Civil War: The Mountford Family and the "Wars of the Roses"', *Midland History*, v (1979–80), 8–9, 18.
[16] Lander, pp. 148–49; M. A. Hicks, 'Attainder, Resumption and Coercion 1461–1529', above, 68 & n.

parliament, was obliged to compensate those granted his estates. Latimer and Tresham, like Edmund Cornwall, Everard Digby and Robert Bolling in 1472, had to include elaborate justifications for their conduct in their bills of reversal.[17] In 1472 ten bills of reversal contained, or were edited to include, admissions of guilt and expressions of remorse.[18] No such requirements had been made of Somerset, Lewis or Sir Henry Wentworth, so Edward evidently adopted a stronger attitude towards those seeking restoration later, probably in the light of his unfortunate experiences with Somerset and Percy. Percy's defection did not stop Somerset's reversal, but Somerset's betrayal may have held up the completion of Latimer's restoration to his lands and cost him a good deal of money. Edward had made it too easy to secure restitution, so that it was not really valued: Sir Thomas Fulford, for example, evidently saw no need for discretion when harrying John Staplehill, grantee of the forfeited lands of Fulford's father. Edward had aggrieved his committed supporters to no advantage, taking back the rewards of their loyal service without securing the fidelity of their dispossessors. Forfeiture was diminished as a deterrent for treason and grants of land as an incentive for loyal service. In future Edward struck a different balance, demanding more from those seeking restoration from his grantees, but he never became as stringent as Henry VII. The new approach, like the old, left ample scope for discriminating in his treatment of individuals, preferring some to others, striking bargains that distinguished between the importance of grantee and attaintee.

In its denunciations of Somerset, 'ayenst nature of gentilnes and all humanitie remaynyng secretly and fraudulently in his old infaciate and cruell malice', the Duke's second attainder of 1465 discloses how generous King Edward thought he had been and how pained and angered he was at being betrayed. Similarly Gregory's chronicle emphasizes the unusual favour shown to the Duke, the hostility of the men of Northampton, and the treachery of the betrayal.[19] The other narrative sources are more laconic. It is the 1465 act and Gregory's chronicle that have prompted modern historians to regard Edward's actions with amazement and as undertaken in the teeth of the opposition of his partisans. But how

---

[17] *RP*, v, 616–17; vi, 20, 21, 230–31.

[18] Those of Thomas Maydenwell, Everard Digby, William Joseph, Sir William Stok, Sir Henry Roos, Dr Ralph Makerell, Dr John Morton, Robert Mirfyn, and Ralph, Lord Neville, *RP*, vi, 17, 21, 22, 24–28, 31–32; Griffiths, *Midland History*, v, 8–9, 18.

[19] *Historical Collections of a Citizen of London*, ed. J. Gairdner, Camden Society, new series, xvii (1876), 219–23.

much can we rely on such evidence? Only the men of Northampton are *known* to have objected and we do not really know why: Gregory's chronicle depicts them objecting to the preferment of the 'fals' Duke, but they cannot have known that he was false at the time. Their hostility may stem from earlier events irrelevant to the particular circumstances of 1463, such as the battle of Northampton (1460). Anyone writing after Somerset's defection was likely to stress how remarkable were the favours received and how unworthy of them he had proved to be. Thus Gregory's chronicle interprets the initial reconciliation in the light of the later betrayal: 'The kyng lovyd hym welle, but the duke thought treson undyr fayre chere and wordys, *as hyt apperyd*'.[20] We do not know when Somerset decided to desert, but it is extremely unlikely that he always intended to do so, even when first making his submission. Gregory cannot have known his intentions at the time and we do not know his initial reactions to the Duke's submission. Similarly Edward had not always regarded Somerset in the same light as the 1465 attainder. He personally had taken the lead in courting Somerset, but he had not acted without advice and support. It was the King and Council, not the King alone, who authorized Percy's commission to receive submissions from northern rebels;[21] parliament itself, as we have seen, duly revoked the attainders of Somerset and Lewis. In his negotiations for the surrender of the Northumbrian castles at mid-winter 1462 Edward did not act without advice.

The King's treatment of Somerset and the others was not out of line with existing practice. Having been made a king by a faction, Edward urgently needed to broaden his support. On his northern campaigns he employed many gentry who had not helped to make him king. The winning over of former Lancastrians was an essential part of this policy. Many, such as Lord Rivers and Sir William Plumpton, made their peace between Edward's victory at Towton and his first parliament,[22] thereby avoiding attainder; some attainted conditionally duly submitted; yet others, attainted or not, were pardoned later. Edward trusted and employed many of the defectors, principally on his northern campaigns, and even admitted Lord Rivers to his Council. Many were backed by his own supporters: the terms that Lord Herbert offered Sir John Scudamore for his surrender were more generous than Edward's own[23] and the

[20] Ibid., pp. 219, 221.
[21] *CPR*, 1461–67, p. 262.
[22] Lander, p. 105; *Plumpton Correspondence*, ed. T. Stapleton, Camden Society, IV (1839), lxvii–ix.
[23] *RP*, VI, 29.

restoration of the Earl of Oxford was probably due to the influence of Warwick himself, whose sister he married.[24] It became commonplace for Yorkist partisans to arrange the restoration of favoured Lancastrians. In the longer term the sanctity of the hereditary principle prevailed over the corruption of blood to secure the reversal of most attainders. While Somerset was merely the most prominent of those who submitted, his defection was a real coup for the Yorkists, as continental observers made clear.[25] It was worth treating him kindly to secure his devotion as well as his allegiance. In the words of the official record, Edward showed

unto hym bounteously and largely the pleintith of his good Lordship . . . to th'entent that therby, of verray gentilnes and the noble honour that oweth to be grounded in every Gentilman, he shuld have been stablisshed in ferme feith and trouth unto his Highnes, accordyng to his seid duete of Ligeaunce . . .[26]

Employment for him and the others was consistent with earlier precedent and made good sense given that Lancastrian resistance in Northumberland was finally being extinguished, as Edward presumably believed at Christmas 1462. Certainly Somerset's defection demoralized other Lancastrians.

Besides, what were the alternatives? It is all too easy, if true, to observe that Somerset, Percy, and Neville did not stop causing trouble for the Yorkist regime until they were dead. In fact trouble with the Lancastrians did not end with their defeat and the death of these particular leaders at Hexham, any more than it had with the apparently decisive battle of Towton in 1461, but persisted for the rest of the decade and indeed for so long as there was a Lancastrian claimant living. Was it a serious option for Edward to decline the rebels' terms in order to ensure their utter destruction? Such a course would have infringed the law of arms, prolonged the winter campaign, and might even have failed to achieve the desired effect of recovering the beleaguered castles. Alternatively, Edward could have accepted the surrender only of the castles and required the garrisons to leave the country, but this course would have guaranteed further resistance born of desperation. By suborning Somerset, Percy, Lewis, and Latimer Edward might have weakened the northern Lancastrians sufficiently to render them powerless in the future. Such an assessment would explain why he offered the rest of the Lancastrian leaders less favourable terms, as the chronicler pseudo-Worcester said, and why in March 1463 he authorised forgiveness only of those not

---

[24] M. A. Hicks, *False, Fleeting, Perjur'd Clarence* (Gloucester, 1980), pp. 40–41.
[25] Jones, *Ricardian*, p. 260. For what follows, see *RP*, v, 511.
[26] *RP*, v, 511.

attainted,[27] forcing those, who had offended him most, into exile abroad. Such a calculation may indeed have been correct: the three Northumbrian castles were subsequently betrayed to the Lancastrians rather than recaptured by them. Again, in retrospect, restoration of the other Lancastrians would appear a small price for genuine pacification, since surely neither Percy nor Neville nor Sir Ralph Grey would have rebelled again without some prospect of outside help.

The obvious risks in receiving the allegiance of former rebels needs to be set against the opportunity for a speedy end to the northern war and the possibility that reconciliation would prevent further conflict. Gregory's chronicle lays stress on the magnitude of the risk that Edward was running: 'the savynge of hys [Somerset's] lyffe at that tyme causyd mony mannys dethys son aftyr, as ye shalle heyre'. However, it is not at all clear that this is correct: even if Somerset did indeed plan to seize Newcastle upon Tyne 'with a privy mayny', he failed by a wide margin and the only extra lives lost as a result were surely his own and those of his immediate servants.[28] Somerset's power-base was in the far south, so the only direct contribution he had to make was the involvement of himself and his immediate entourage. Sir Ralph Percy's defection was militarily much more significant, since he was well-placed to commit the family retinue in his own Northumbrian homeland and seems to have done so. In any case, Edward did not take unnecessary risks. Somerset was required to demonstrate his good faith by participating in the Yorkist siege of Alnwick and his restoration progressed by stages, with submission, pardon, and reversal each separated by several months. Even then Edward appears at first to have retained in custody both Somerset's brother, although pardoned, and Percy's nephew, the young Earl of Northumberland. A further stage in Somerset's rehabilitation was marked by the release of his brother Edmund from the Tower in or soon after July 1463.[29] This policy of gradual, cautious restoration had worked well in the past and was to do so again after 1471, when Edward reversed the forfeiture of many former Lancastrians, employed them in his service, and was not betrayed. In between he distrusted them, rounding up former Lancastrians en masse in 1468 shortly after the exposure of Cook's conspiracy.[30] Once a Lancastrian, it appeared, always a Lancastrian, until after 1471 no credible Lancastrian claimant remained.

[27] Stevenson, *Wars*, II (2), 786; *CPR*, 1461–67, p. 262.
[28] *Gregory's Chronicle*, pp. 221, 223.
[29] Jones, *Ricardian*, p. 260.
[30] *Plumpton Correspondence*, pp. 19–20.

Why was it that the Lancastrians proved so untrustworthy? Why was it that resistance did not end with the battle of Hexham in 1464? Why did not the garrison of Harlech make their submissions to the royal commissioners empowered to receive them?[31] And why were new groups of Lancastrians and new plots uncovered at intervals throughout the fourteen-sixties? Historians, after all, have portrayed the battle of Towton (1461) as a decisive victory and Hexham (1464) even more so. There were plenty of contemporaries of Lord Rivers, who also saw their cause as irrevocably lost even in 1461.[32] It is easy to presume that the irreconcilables fought on because the terms offered were too harsh and they hoped to do better through force of arms, but we must not suppose that they were all fools. They must at least have appreciated that victory was no simple matter and that better terms might not be forthcoming. Several Lancastrian leaders obtained complete restoration and Somerset established an intimate personal relationship with the Yorkist King. Favourable though his position was, he broke faith, just as Lewis was to do at the Readeption. Others were apparently offered their lives but opted to continue fighting with the probability that violent death would be the outcome.

Self-interest, not principle, is usually used by historians to explain late medieval political alignments. One chronicler thought that Somerset deserted because Edward failed to honour his pledge of 1,000 marks, but this, as we have seen, was not true. Somerset may have felt politically insecure, but a large household was surely sufficient protection against the common people of Northampton and the King's favour against aristocratic envy. As Somerset's reversal and Latimer's pardon followed Percy's rebellion, it seems that Edward's favour did not falter. The recapture of the Northumbrian castles offered the Duke the opportunity for further resistance, but not the motive: the prospect was not the reconquest of England and complete vengeance on his enemies, but rather discomfort, ruin, and death. Surely no realistic assessment of personal advantage could have prompted Somerset to give up what he possessed in favour of future resistance.[33]

What motive then remains? Surely the only possibility is loyalty to the Lancastrian monarch, faith in the legitimacy of the Lancastrian title to the Crown, which was sufficient to outweigh such other considerations as life,

---

[31] *CPR*, 1461–67, pp. 355, 457.

[32] Lander, p. 105.

[33] Dr Gillingham points out that 'On the international stage Henry VI's cause was now at its lowest point', *Wars of the Roses*, p. 150.

liberty, honour, and family. Dynasticism in fifteenth-century England has recently been seen as a motive for self-interested claimants for the Crown[34] rather than as objective political principle. In theory every subject owed an overriding loyalty to his sovereign, which was expressed in the treason laws and most typically in the exclusion clauses of indentures of retainer. In the past such clauses have been regarded as common form or as re-insurance clauses enabling the retainer to evade his engagements. Little attention has been paid to them except when deliberately omitted, by Richard, Duke of York in 1460 for example.[35] That the principle of legitimacy was widely understood was shown in 1471 by those Yorkshiremen who rejected Edward IV as king, preferring Henry VI, but upheld his right to be Duke of York.[36] The dynasty, not the individual, mattered: Henry VI's Readeption advisers were loyal to the dynasty, even while restricting the power of an inadequate king.[37] After 1471, the dynasty wiped out, nothing prevented reliable service to Edward IV.

Loyalty to the dynasty explains why Lancastrians remained in arms for so long, or even in impotent exile abroad, rather than accept Edward's amnesties, however imperfect the terms. It explains why new clutches of conspirators, hitherto uncompromised, were uncovered at frequent intervals. It explains why, even after submitting and swearing new oaths of allegiance, Lancastrian aristocrats could not be relied upon to keep faith. Certainly some had personal ties with the old king like Sir Thomas Tresham, who excused his resistance to Edward by reference to his lifelong household service to Henry VI, which had forged an absolute claim on his loyalty which he 'durst not disobey'.[38] A binding prior commitment to Henry VI, which was not superseded by other oaths made under duress to Edward IV, certainly better explains their conduct than their portrayal by the Yorkists as faithless perjurers. With hindsight Somerset, Percy, Neville, Lewis, and Tresham were consistently Lancastrian and their submissions were temporary compromises with the *de facto* king, which were essential for survival. Edward himself was to act

---

[34] E.g. R. A. Griffiths, 'Sense of Dynasty in the Reign of Henry VI', *Patronage, Pedigree and Power in Later Medieval England*, ed. C. D. Ross (Gloucester, 1979), pp. 13–31; Hicks, *Clarence*, pp. 60–61, 99, 101.
[35] K. B. McFarlane, *England in the Fifteenth Century*, ed. G. L. Harriss (1981), pp. 236–37.
[36] *Historie of the Arrivall of Edward IV in England*, ed. J. Bruce, Camden Society, I (1836), 3–6.
[37] Hicks, *Clarence*, pp. 91–95.
[38] *RP*, v, 617; D. A. L. Morgan, 'The King's Affinity in the Polity of Yorkist England', *Transactions of the Royal Historical Society*, 5th series, XXIII (1973), 7.

like this in 1471, when he used his right to the duchy of York to further his claim for the Crown. These Lancastrians cannot have seen themselves as forfeiting by their actions their honour, reputation, and worship as gentlemen, in the way the 1465 attainder asserted. Surely they felt that they were vindicating these attributes by remaining faithful to their prior allegiance.

Personal ties with Henry VI were common among the Lancastrian conspirators, but what really distinguished them in the late fourteen-sixties was the tight web of kinship ties and long association built up decades before.[39] After most Lancastrians had made their peace, there remained an irreducible rump of committed loyalists, whose fidelity and numbers were not seriously diminished by setbacks and an unpromising future. Few former Lancastrians outside this group shared in the Readeption regime, although the plotters undoubtedly hoped for and even expected widespread support from former companions in arms. At each crisis of the Wars of the Roses most of the active nobility rallied behind the King *de facto*, regarding him as God's lieutenant rather than the claimant *de iure*. But there was always a minority of individuals more strongly committed to a particular claim, who were prepared to fight and die for it in apparent disregard of their own interests. For men like these all the coercive methods of kings — Edward IV's use of execution, imprisonment, forfeiture, and hostages and Henry VII's system of financial penalties — were no restraint, merely forcing conspiracy underground.

It thus appears that in the closing months of 1462 both Edward and Somerset saw as inevitable the reduction of the remaining Northumbrian castles. When Somerset made the first overtures, Edward offered terms, which Somerset accepted. Having pacified the North, Edward set about winning Somerset's devotion and the Duke tried to win his favour. Had there been no recurrence of rebellion in the North, Edward's policy might have succeeded and Somerset's change of side might have been permanent, but it was not to be. Modern historians have relied unduly on Yorkist versions of events, which understandably portray Somerset as a traitor. The Lancastrians did not pass their self-justifications down to posterity. If Somerset broke faith to Edward, he did so not in the expectation of personal reward, but in support of a dynastic principle that he shared with other committed Lancastrians. This was something that

[39] M. A. Hicks, 'The case of Sir Thomas Cook, 1468', *English Historical Review*, XCIII below, 424-5, 430;   P. J. C. Field, 'The Last Years of Sir Thomas Malory', *Bulletin of the John Rylands Library*, LXIV (1982), 445-54. I hope to discuss this more fully elsewhere.

the Lancastrians understood: how else could they have accepted him back as their commander in the field? It is time that historians did the same.

APPENDIX

Act of Reversal of Attainders of Henry Beaufort, Duke of Somerset and Sir Henry Lewis[40]

To the kyng our liege lord Mekely beseche vnto your highnesse youre humble and true liegemen Henry Beauford late Duke of Somerset and Sir Henry Lowes knyght That where they amonge other persones the fourth day of Nouembre the furst yere of your gracious reigne in youre high courte of parlement holdyn at Westminster were atteynted of high treason by which they stonde vnabled and disherited by the lawe of this land And also where the said late Duke and Henry Lowes and their heyres by auctorite of the same last parlement afore this your present parlement forfaited and were vnabled to clayme or haue all Castelles Maners landes lordshippes tenementes rentes seruices fees aduousons heredi-tamentes and possessions with their appurtenaunces which they or eyther of theym had of a state of enheritaunce or eny other to their or eyther of their vse as in the saide actes of atteindres more pleynly is conteigned Please it your highnesse by thaduise and assent of your lordes spirituelx and temporelx and your Comons in this your present parlement assembled and by auctorite of the same that the said Henry Beauford late Duke and Henry Lowes or either of theym be declared reputen and holden your feithfull liegemen and subiettes. And that the said Henry late Duke be restored to hym and his heires to all astates honours dignitees stiles and titles his name and fame which he shuld haue had yf the said actes of atteindres had neuer be ordeigned made nor had ayenst hym And that the said Duke be hable and inhabled to enherit after the decesse of any of his auncestres as he shuld haue doon yf the saide actes had neuer bene made ayenst hym. And also that the forsaid Henry Lowes knyght be restored to his worship good name and fame in as large wyse and forme as he shuld haue be yf the said actes of atteindrees had neuer be ordeigned made nor had ayenst hym And that the said Henry Lowes be habled and inhabled to enherite after the decesse of any of the auncestres as he shuld haue doon yf the said actes had neuer be made ayenst hym the same acte notwithstondyng And also that the said late Duke and Henry Lowes and their heyres and the heyres of eythir of theym be restored inheritable and able to enherite and may entre be the said auctorite into all such Castelles lordshippes Manoirs Townes Towneshippes fees hundredes aduousons annuitees libertees Frauchises landes tenementes offices rentes seruices reuersions and all maner

---

[40] E 159/243, recorda Hillary 6 Edward IV m.6–d. Unpublished Crown copyright material reproduced by permission of the Controller of H.M. Stationery Office.

rightes custumes leetes Courtes inheritementes interestes and possessions with their appurtenaunces which they or eyther of hem shuld or ought to haue had to their vse or to the vse of eyther of theym yf the said actes of atteindres had neuer be ordeyned made nor had ayenst theym or eyther of theym Sauyng to euery of youre liege people and their heires and euery of theym such right title interesse and laufull possession as they or eny of theym had in eny of the said Castelles lordshippes maners and other the premisses or any parcell therof afore the forsaid atteindres Sauyng also that by this acte Syr Geffrey Gate knyght be in nowyse hurte in or of or for eny graunte or grauntees made to hym by you liege lorde of eny thyng concernyng the same by what soeuer name the same Gefferey be named in eny of the saide grante or grauntes. And that it be ordeyned that noo persone nor persones be preiudiced troubled or vexed by the said late Duke or Henry Lowes or eyther of them or by eny other the Executours or Admynystratours of eyther of theym or by eny other persone or persones hauyng interesse to their vse or of the other of theym for eny goodes or catellys which were the said Dukes or Henry Lowes or eyther of theym the tyme of the said atteindres or eny tyme withyn the yere then next afore. And that noo persone nor persones be preiudiced troubled and vexed by the sayd late Duke or Henry Lowes or eyther of theym for eny occupacioun or manuryng of the premisses or eny parcell therof afore the furst day of this present parlement. Le Roy le voet.

9

Piety and Lineage in the Wars of the Roses: The Hungerford Experience[1]

It is notoriously difficult to gauge the motives of late medieval people. So little guidance is provided by contemporaries that historians habitually deduce intentions from actions and confine their attention to considerations of material advantage. They rarely allow for intangible motives – emotional, intellectual or spiritual – even though it is these that most divide medieval people from ourselves and bar the way to fuller understanding. The importance of religion is undeniable – undoubtedly 'attitudes to faith and charity' did shape other preoccupations[2] – but nobody has yet examined the influence of such motives on the politics of any individual in fifteenth-century England.

Sufficient evidence exists for such a study of the Hungerford family in the Wars of the Roses. Having attained the peerage in 1426, the Hungerfords were apparently destined for higher rank in 1461. Five successive marriages to heiresses culminated in those of Robert II (d.1459), the second baron, to Margaret, heiress of Lord Botreaux, and their son Robert III (d.1464), the third baron, to Eleanor Moleyns, in whose right he became Lord Moleyns from 1444. Such good fortune financed buildings, ransoms and dowries and endowed cadets and chantries in each generation.

To Professor Stone, the late medieval nobility were characterised by the Open Lineage Family. The unit was not the nuclear family – husband, wife and children – but the whole kinship network, which was united by

[1] This paper was prepared with financial assistance from King Alfred's College, Winchester. I am grateful to the Trustees of H.E. Huntington Library, San Marino, California, for supplying photocopies of documents and for permission to cite them here. Genealogical details are taken from CP.

[2] P.W. Fleming, 'Charity, Faith and the Gentry of Kent, 1422-1529', in *Property and Politics: Essays in Later Medieval English History*, ed. A.J. Pollard (Gloucester, 1984), p. 37. Other recent publications concerned with the practical effects of intangible motivation are M. Keen, *Chivalry* (1984); M.A. Hicks, 'Restraint, Mediation and Private Justice: George, Duke of Clarence as "Good Lord"', Chapter 7 above; idem, 'Edward IV, the Duke of Somerset, and Lancastrian Loyalism in the North', below, Chapter 8.

loyalty to dead ancestors and by the need to preserve and augment the family estates and to transmit them to future generations. The current head of the family was merely the trustee of the family estates, the prisoner as well as the beneficiary of the system of primogeniture. He could not disinherit his heirs or sell the family lands.[3] In contrast, Dr Houlbrooke has argued for the universality of the nuclear family and for the autonomy of the individual. Obligations towards collaterals were only moral, not legally binding, and tenants for life often did disinherit their heirs and acted with considerable freedom on their hereditary estates. Indeed, Houlbrooke argues:

> There was widespread individual desire for freedom in disposal of possessions. Men wanted such freedom, not because they wanted to leave their families unprovided for, or because they wished to depart radically from customary norms, but because they wanted more scope in choosing how to meet their familial and extra-familial obligations, and on what scale. They wanted to secure their parental authority, and, we may suspect, to be in a position to reward aptitude, application and loyalty among their children.

Religious evidence demonstrates conclusively that the nuclear family was normal. From mortmain licences, Professor Rosenthal concluded of the nobility that

> Spiritually, if not politically, the family was a nucleated one ... In some important respects these larger blocks counted for little and the real ties of affection and sympathy were confined to much closer relationships ... concern for those already dead was much greater than that for those yet to come.[4]

From wills, Dr Fleming found that the gentry of Kent had

> a predominantly patrilineal family feeling. According to this evidence, bonds of familial sentiment ran from parent to child and between husband and wife, and generally did not extend to siblings or other collateral relatives.[5]

Similarly, Hungerford testators and founders recognized a narrow nuclear family, with especially strong ties between father and son and married couples. They did not normally commemorate collaterals, not even siblings, and their sense of lineage embraced ancestors rather than

---

[3] L. Stone, *Family, Sex and Marriage in England, 1500-1800* (1977), pp. 4, 29, 85-87. For what follows, see R.A. Houlbrooke, *The English Family, 1450-1700* (1984), pp. 15, 40, 42, 231.

[4] J.T. Rosenthal, *Purchase of Paradise: Gift Giving and the Aristocracy, 1307-1485* (1972), pp. 17-18.

[5] Fleming, 'Charity, Faith and the Gentry of Kent', p. 51.

offspring, even dead ones. Men prayed for the male line, women for maternal ancestors,[6] thus substantiating Houlbrooke's claim that everyone possessed his own kinship network, distinguished by a unique set of relationships with himself, within which his own interests were paramount.

Relationships with the family were not purely selfish. Tenants for life recognized obligations to relatives and even felt obliged to account to their heirs for their guardianship of the family estates. Yet it was the salvation of the individual rather than of the lineage that prompted the endowment of chantries at the expense of future generations. The church taught that the sufferings of sinners in purgatory could be mitigated by good works, especially masses, even if performed after death. While the Hungerford foundations were exceptionally numerous, the piety they reflected was of the most conventional type. This stemmed not from ignorance or official direction, but from personal knowledge of the essentials of Christianity. Well-acquainted with church services and the most up-to-date developments, the Hungerfords had clear-cut individual preferences, which they expressed in coherent liturgical forms, generally highly personal and owing nothing to dynastic, parental or marital example. Rather than share in existing foundations, each generation established its own at much higher costs.[7] The heraldry of their chantries and vestments reveals a pride of lineage that was subjected to their wish for intercession for themselves as individual souls. Their sense of piety, like their sense of dynasty, was not a passive sentiment, but a frequently expressed impulse to vigorous and self-confident action. It is the interplay of these emotions that this essay will trace.

Robert, Lord Moleyns was captured at Castillon in 1453 and was ransomed for £6,000, a sum apparently swollen by extras to £9,961. His family accepted responsibility for paying this ransom. The widow of his grandfather left 100 marks towards his ransom in 1455.[8] In 1459 his father paid his first instalment, borrowing £2,000 on the security of Archbishop Bourgchier, other bishops and magnates. To save the sureties harmless, Lord Hungerford mortgaged all his estates, charging his feoffees in his will to

suffer my said wife and such a persone or persones as she will depute and assigne to take and Receiue all the issues profittis and Revenues commyng or

---

[6] M.A. Hicks, 'Chantries, Obits and Hospitals: The Hungerford Foundations, 1325-1478', *The Church in Pre-Reformation Society*, ed. C. Barron and C. Harper-Bill (Woodbridge, 1985), above, 93. For what follows, see Houlbrooke, *English Family*, p. 40.

[7] M.A. Hicks, 'The Piety of Margaret, Lady Hungerford (d.1478)', above, Chapter 9; idem, 'Chantries, Obits and Hospitals', above, Chapter 4.

[8] R.C. Hoare, *A History of Modern Wiltshire* (6 vols., 1822-40), I (2), 100-1; will of Eleanor, countess of Arundel, PRO, PROB 11/4 (PCC 3 Stokton).

growyng of all my forsaid londes till suche tyme as myne other dettes be paid, my Childeryn and my seruauntes Rewardid, and this my present testament in euery Article fully performed.

To facilitate the mortgage, Moleyns's mother Margaret waived her dower and jointure, accepting a smaller income in lieu. His father refused payment to younger sons of legacies made to them in 1449 by their grandfather on the grounds that he had already made adequate provision for them. Lord Hungerford himself made pious bequests of only £150 in his will, a paltry sum by family precedent, and accepted heavy debts as a burden on his soul.[9] On release, Moleyns mortgaged all his wife's inheritance as security for the second instalment, obviously reducing provision for his wife and children. The outstanding balance was to be raised *inter alia* by wasting capital assets – by felling timber on his wife's estates[10] – and from the portion paid for the marriage of Moleyns's son, Thomas. Although Lord Hungerford wanted all his dependants provided for, their interests were sacrificed for the foreseeable future for the release of his heir and the discharge of his honour.

Moleyns also suffered personally. Instead of entering his inheritance on his father's death in 1459, he succeeded only to a few advowsons and certain Wiltshire properties. Aware that the mortgages had temporarily disinherited his son, Lord Hungerford had urged Moleyns to accept them and not to 'grugge'. So Moleyns did, renouncing the *whole* Hungerford inheritance to his mother on behalf of himself and his heirs and also granting her his moveables.[11] He thus surrendered those reversionary rights that threatened the security of his creditors, although obviously he expected the feoffees to restore the lands when the trust was discharged. As the Moleyns estates were also mortgaged, he was probably dependent on the pensions from his mother, though she also paid certain extraordinary expenses.[12]

Once back in England, Moleyns committed himself politically to Henry VI's favourites and was among the Lancastrian lords who held the Tower of London against the Yorkist earls in June 1460. Following the battle of Northampton, which gave the Yorkists control of both king and government, Moleyns secured a pardon for his life and, probably at his mother's prompting, a licence to go abroad out of harm's way. He embarked for Florence on 25 August, but unfortunately returned to share

[9] *Somerset Medieval Wills, 1383-1500*, ed. F.W. Weaver (Soms. RS, XVI, 1901), pp. 186-93.

[10] *CPR, 1452-61*, p. 631; *CCR, 1454-61* pp. 451-52; PRO, CP25(1)/293/73/451.

[11] *Somerset Med. Wills*, p. 193, PRO, C139/172/1/1-3; *CCR, 1454-61*, pp. 439-41.

[12] Hoare, *Modern Wiltshire*, I (2), 100-1.

in the Lancastrian defeat at Towton on 29 March 1461.[13] His continued hostility to Edward IV ensured his attainder in November 1461 and led to his execution in 1464. His remaining brother, Sir Arnold Hungerford, also a Lancastrian, was killed in battle, but was not attainted, his two manors passing by entail to Moleyns's son, Thomas.[14]

Meantime, Moleyns's mother, wife and children stayed at home and accepted the new Yorkist régime. Moleyns's attainder did not threaten destitution, for it could not affect his wife's inheritance, nor the prior settlement by the Hungerford feoffees of eleven manors on his mother and thirteen manors in jointure on his son Thomas.[15] Thomas remained the Moleyns heir. In exactly parallel circumstances, the two Percy dowagers contented themselves with dower, jointures and inheritance. In this instance, however, united action was taken to avert forfeiture, perhaps with the long term aim of saving the inheritance for the family, but certainly to satisfy the creditors, safeguard the sureties, and thus unburden Lord Hungerford's soul.

Forfeiture applied only to lands held by the traitor in fee simple, fee tail, or to his use. Moleyns held no such estates at his attainder. Rival claims antedating the treason were specifically excluded from forfeiture in acts of attainder. This clause covered the mortgages of 1459, which the surviving sureties had an interest in preserving if they were to avoid liability for the Hungerford debts. As these sureties included such influential Yorkists as the king's uncles, Archbishop Bourgchier and the earl of Essex, and his cousin, the earl of Warwick, it may be that their support accounts for the initial success of a proviso to the act of attainder which was designed to exempt the Hungerford and Moleyns inheritances from forfeiture pending repayment of the debts in full. As the 'ffynaunce droytes and expensis' were now calculated at £8,624 3s. 9½d. and Lord Hungerford's own debts at £358 16s. 3½d., this proviso would have postponed the forfeiture indefinitely. It apparently passed the lords, but was later struck out, being replaced by a much shorter proviso assuring repayment to the feoffees only of such debts that 'can be proved due'.[16] While it was difficult to prove their title and the accuracy of the sum claimed, the principle of exemption for mortgages had been accepted and was to be exploited later.

After Moleyns's attainder, his relatives courted their Yorkist foes and sought their approval by good service. Probably they exploited their common interests with the powerful earl of Warwick, a surety in 1459, whose influence was certainly invoked. Thomas Hungerford served under

---

[13]   Ibid., I (2) 101; PRO, C76/142 rot.2.

[14]   PRO, C145/320/1/30; CP40/816 rot.2.

[15]   PRO, C145/320/1/30, 38; Wilts. RO, 490/1469 pp. 1, 5-6, 9-10; Huntington MS. HAP 3465; *HMC, 78 Hastings* I, 237, 241, 253-54, 257.

[16]   *Rot. Parl.*, V, 482; PRO, C49/52, original act of attainder, 1461.

his command against the northern rebels[17] and from 1463 Margaret's feoffees included Warwick's brother George, bishop of Exeter and chancellor of England. Another new and prominent feoffee was Margaret's diocesan, Richard Beauchamp, bishop of Salisbury, whose kinsman, Sir Roger Tocotes, another feoffee, was close to Warwick's ally, the king's elder brother, the duke of Clarence. Direct contacts with Clarence were certainly weaker than those the duke made with the Hungerfords' cousins, the Courtenays of Powderham (Devon) and the Hungerfords of Down Ampney (Gloucs.), who rebelled with him in 1470.[18] Unfortunately, Warwick and Clarence gradually lost influence at court. They failed to prevent Thomas Hungerford's execution in 1469 and it was their Lincolnshire rebellion that prompted Margaret's arrest in 1470. In the early 1460s, however, the connection may have been vital in securing a hearing for the Hungerfords at court.

It took three years for the family to secure their title to the Hungerford estates. As early as 1 April 1462 John, Lord Stourton, a feoffee, received custody of all those properties enfeoffed for repayment of the ransom and in royal hands.[19] This open-handed grant was qualified by others assuming that Moleyns *had* held certain lands and assigning these to royal patentees. Custody of all Moleyns's lands was granted to two courtiers on 30 May 1462, and on 9 September 1462 the same were granted in tail to Edward's younger brother, Richard, duke of Gloucester. This placed the onus on the Hungerfords to prove that nothing had been held by Moleyns in person or to his use, a task facilitated by the absence of inquisitions, which made King Edward dependant on the family for precise information. This enabled Margaret to suppress inconvenient material, such as the declaration of trust in her husband's will, and to confuse the various enfeoffments. Pleading that the mortgages were designed to save Bourgchier, Warwick and other magnates harmless. Margaret stated that her husband had enfeoffed all his lands to 'thentente that the same Margarete ... shuld receyue' the issues for repayment of his debts, especially those arising from the ransom, and to fulfil his last will. She specifically listed ten manors, actually from six different enfeoffments, and she asked that three enfeoffments should be recognized, that she might have dower, and that lands worth £200 might be sold. Evidently convinced that all the family estates had been mortgaged and that none had been forfeited by Moleyns, Edward approved her petition and on the same day (30 March 1463) revoked Gloucester's patent by word of

---

[17] Probably in 1463, Hoare, *Modern Wiltshire* I (2), 101. He was pardoned in November 1462 and knighted soon after; Charles Ross, *Edward IV* (1974), p. 66; for the feoffees, see *CCR, 1461-68*, pp. 271, 272.

[18] Above, 138; *CPR, 1467-77*, p. 218.

[19] *CPR, 1461-67*, p. 182. For what follows, see ibid., pp. 190, 228.

mouth.[20] Also convinced of victory, Margaret began resettling the estates in September 1463.

In this Margaret was too sanguine, as writs of 12 August 1463 initiated inquisitions in March/August 1464 which found that eleven enfeoffed manors in Devon, Somerset and Oxfordshire had been to Moleyns's use and were thus forfeited. Behind this measure may have been John Dynham, later Lord Dynham, who had received some issues since 1461 and who secured a grant of all eleven manors in tail on 31 May 1464.[21] In response, Margaret orchestrated seven petitions for new inquisitions from herself, her grandson Thomas, and her servant John Mervyn, who actually held the disputed properties. Commissions issued on 13 December 1464 resulted in inquisitions vindicating their claims.[22] To assuage royal displeasure and to prevent Dynham from causing trouble at court and in the west country, Margaret granted him 100 marks (£66 13s. 4d.) as an annuity. Both her dower lands and enfeoffed estates feature in the account of her receiver in 1464-65.

To meet the considerable cost of such intrigue, estimated at £2,155, Margaret drew on her own Botreaux inheritance from her father's death on 16 May 1462. Their relations had been clouded latterly by Lord Bortreaux's concern for his soul, involving the foundation of an almshouse at Bath,[23] and his desire for a son to carry on his name (which was reflected in his second marriage *c.* 1458). Both projects threatened what Margaret had come to regard, over the previous forty years, as her *rightful* inheritance. Although the second marriage proved childless, the new Lady Botreaux was entitled to jointure in the main Somerset estates, extended in 1462 as £236, or half the value of the whole inheritance (*c.*£460), and dower in the remainder. The latter was commuted to 100 marks, a third of the extended value, an exchange probably in Margaret's favour, but part of a royally imposed resettlement of the jointure on the lives of Lady Botreaux *and* her new husband, the Lincolnshire-based courtier, Sir Thomas Burgh.[24] A second family was thus endowed by deferring Margaret's inheritance. Her understandable resentment perhaps explains why no use was apparently made of Burgh's potentially valuable influence at court. Nothing could be done about the jointure, but

---

[20] Ibid., pp. 228, 283-84; PRO, C81/1492/28-29.

[21] *CPR, 1461-67*, pp. 301, 333, 359-60; PRO, C145/320/1/1-4, 14, 25.

[22] PRO, C145/320/1/5-13, 15, 17, 26-28; *CPR, 1461-67*, pp. 363-66, 368. For what follows see Hoare, *Modern Wiltshire*, I (2), 102.

[23] M.A. Hicks, 'St. Katherine's Hospital, Heytesbury: Prehistory, Foundation and Re-foundation, 1408-72', above, 126-7.

[24] Hoare, *Modern Wiltshire*, I (2), 102 (which gives a higher valuation than the extents); *CIPM, Henry VII*, I nos. 462, 1198; *Pedes Finium*, ed. E. Green (Soms. RS, XXII, 1906), pp. 126-27; *CCR, 1461-68*, pp. 116-17; PRO, E357/115 m.69. Margaret was already dealing in the reversion in 1455; *Pedes Finium*, p. 203.

Margaret was able to thwart the alienation of endowments to Bath cathedral priory, pensioning off the existing almsfolk. Her father's soul evidently took second place to her own obligations, here defined as the need to raise money 'for the ransom of Robert Hungerford knight her son, lately captured in the duchy of Acquitaine'.[25]

Meantime, some instalments of the mortgages became overdue and the creditors pressed for payment, threatening – or even initiating? – lawsuits against the sureties on their bonds. Maybe the sureties themselves – including prominent Yorkists whose support was so vital at court – also pressed to be saved harmless according to the original trust and Margaret's petitions to the king. Probably one such pressure group prompted the cancellation of a patent of 24 March 1463 permitting the leasing of lands in favour of another of 30 March allowing for land sales. With sound political reasons to satisfy her creditors, Margaret contracted new loans at interest, sold plate at a loss, and sold lands.[26]

In selling land, Margaret went far beyond her legal obligations. The creditors apparently had no action against her personally and her husband's will authorised only mortgages, not sales. Her own inheritance was not security for any of their debts. Margaret did not cite political pressure as her explanation then or later. She consistently pleaded a special obligation to those sureties, who 'were bounde and had leyde their seelys at the requeste and praier of me'. As two intimate servants said at the time, Margaret acted thus

> consideryng thei were bonden only at the speciall instaunce & praier of her said hosband & her to the vttermost of her power [and] . . . they were diuers tymes sued & vexed & yet nowe diuers of hem ben sued to exigentes in gret yopardie and daunger to be vtlawed.[27]

To relieve them was a pious duty, imposed on her personally by her husband in his will. The good of both their souls depended on it. This personal obligation explains both the involvement of her own estates and why she sold those Hungerford lands that he was fighting to save. She elevated her moral obligations above the hereditary expectations of her heirs.

Margaret nevertheless planned to transmit her remaining estates to her heirs. She could freely dispose of her own Botreaux inheritance during her life, but on her death it would revert to the crown under Moleyns's attainder. To avert this and to control its subsequent devolution, she

---

[25] Above, 126-7; , *HMC, 12, MSS of the Dean & Chapter of Wells*, I, 499.

[26] *CPR, 1461-67*, pp. 283-84; Hoare, *Modern Wiltshire*, I (2), 101-2.

[27] PRO, C1/28/111D; Hoare, *Modern Wiltshire*, 1 (2), 101.

enfeoffed the entire inheritance to two panels of feoffees on 4 September 1463. One panel of neighbours and dependants held lands mainly destined for sale. The other group, which also held six Hungerford manors including Heytesbury, comprised nineteen men of relative eminence headed by Bishops Beauchamp and Neville.[28] The size of the group suggests that a long period of tenure was intended. Its prestige gave added security against rivals. Apparently Margaret had already decided what to keep and what to transmit to her heirs. After Moleyns's death, the intended beneficiary was probably his eldest son Thomas, who features in Margaret's alienations and other land transactions from the summer of 1465. After her own death, Margaret probably planned (as in her later wills) that on payment of the debts her feoffees would then convey their estates to Thomas, bypassing Moleyns and thus avoiding forfeiture. Similarly, on 25 November 1466 Thomas enfeoffed his own property, to ensure that his own will was performed before his heirs entered their inheritance.[29]

Thus far the Hungerfords had displayed remarkable solidarity. Margaret and Eleanor must have co-operated at the 1461 parliament, and Margaret and Thomas collaborated over the 1465 inquisitions. Thomas sold his own lands, released his title to some of Margaret's purchasers, and shared in other conveyances. From early 1468 he enjoyed the support of his next brother Walter. Family unity, however, gradually broke down, as individuals developed different perceptions of themselves and their interests.

Eleanor, Lady Moleyns was the first to break ranks. To prevent her husband from enjoying any income from her lands, Edward IV placed Eleanor, her inheritance and her children in the custody of Lord Wenlock, who was to reduce her household and impose financial strategy. In practice, the feoffees retained Eleanor's estates, paying some issues to Margaret toward the debts and the balance to Eleanor.[30] With Moleyns's death, Wenlock's custody became unnecessary, but Eleanor's control was still impeded by the mortgage. She determined to resume control and to shrug off any further responsibility for the debts. Far from accepting liability for the whole ransom, she argued that her lands were security only for £3,000 and claimed – obviously untruthfully – that the feoffees had received more than this. When the feoffees refused to release their lands to her, she petitioned chancery, perhaps prompting thereby writs of 23 September 1464 for inquisitions into her husband's lands. These

28 *CCR, 1461-68*, pp. 271-72.
29 Wilts, RO, 490/1470 f. 267*v*.
30 *CPR, 1461-67*, p. 181; PRO, C1/28/111D. For parallels to Wenlock's custody, see e.g. *CPR, 1461-67*, pp. 87, 181.

revealed that her lands were mortgaged for £3,000, which was still unpaid, but nevertheless most feoffees released their rights to her on 11 March 1465.[31] Presumably she was the 'Lady Hungerford' who was refusing in 1468 to pay Simone Nori, her husband's principal creditor.[32] Eleanor rejected any moral obligations to her sureties and for her husband's soul and paid only lip service to legal obligations, which were no longer necessary to secure her estate from forfeiture.

Sir Thomas Hungerford was executed for treason at Salisbury on 18 January 1469. He had been heir presumptive of the Hungerford, Moleyns and Botreaux inheritances. As far as the Botreaux and Heytesbury estates were concerned, the position had not apparently changed, as Margaret could still bestow them by will on other descendants. As for the Moleyns lands, the reversion now passed to the king, who could challenge any attempts by Eleanor to dispose of it by will, as she evidently wished to do. A further probable complication was that Eleanor's second husband, Sir Oliver Manningham, was implicated in treason in 1468 and was thus compelled to compound with the king for his forfeiture.[33] This combination of pressures resulted in a complicated agreement between Eleanor and Edward IV on 13 March 1469. The whole Moleyns estate was enfeoffed to use and divided into eight parts, most of which were ultimately to pass to Eleanor's granddaughter, Mary. Two manors were to be detached for her sons Walter and Leonard and a further two would be alienated 'to suche house or place of religion & to their successours as the seyd Elianor shall lymytt and appoynt'. Before reverting to the designated heirs, two other parcels were to be used after Eleanor's death to pay her debts and raise £200 as marriage portion for her daughter Frideswide. In return for Edward's consent to these arrangements, Eleanor would receive the issues of only three parcels during her lifetime. The others were to be conveyed to her (or, in one case, to herself and Manningham jointly) 'immedyatly after they [the feoffees] by our seyde sovereygn lord . . . be requyred'. A final parcel, the manors of Ditton and Stoke Poges (Bucks.), were to be held by Edward for life, then by Eleanor for life, and then by her heirs. Oliver Manningham was pardoned on 24 March 1469.

[31] PRO, C1/28/111; C1/38/252-53; C145/320/1/35, 40, 42. She had probably married Oliver Manningham by 24 September 1465, when (as Oliver Manningham of Stoke Poges gent.) he was using force against the feoffees: see PRO, CP40/818 rot.120d. 129d. Mervyn was still acting as feoffee on 13 November 1472, *CAD*, I, A670, and litigation continued until at least 1474; Hoare, *Modern Wiltshire*, II (1), 14-15.

[32] R.de Roover, *The Rise and Decline of the Medici Bank 1397-1494* (Cambridge, Mass., 1963), p. 473; A. Grundzweig, *Correspondance de la filiale de Bruges des Medici* (Brussels, 1931), pp. 115, 121, 132.

[33] He was pardoned on 24 March 1469, *CPR, 1467-77*, p. 152; PRO, C81/825/2771. For what follows, see Huntington MS.HAP Box 3.

Edward thus surrendered his speculative reversionary rights in return for the grant of two manors for life, the issues of most of the remainder for life, and security for the good behaviour of Eleanor and Oliver. Eleanor was able to provide for her whole family, including her second husband, and for the good of her soul. Even when confronted by an infant granddaughter and adult sons, primogeniture prevailed, only minor – but significant – alienations being made to the sons. Other small alienations were made for the good of her soul and her husband benefited at the expense of future generations and the integrity of her inheritance. Unusually these concessions were bought at the price of her own comfort during her lifetime, which she had earlier declined to sacrifice for a *dead* husband's soul.

Thomas's execution posed an immediate threat to the somewhat precarious security of the Hungerford inheritance. It caused near panic among those holding alienated properties, whose quitclaims from Thomas no longer offered any security. His sister Frideswide made twenty releases to such people between 4 February and 8 April 1469. Among the recipients were Sir Thomas Burgh and Lady Botreaux, who also obtained a release from Eleanor Moleyns and her husband, whose claims were even more vestigial than those of Frideswide herself.[34] That Frideswide's deeds were enrolled in chancery and none is recorded for her brothers suggest that Walter and Leonard were already refusing to confirm sales or approve new alienations of what they now regarded as *their* inheritance.

Thomas's forfeiture exposed the Hungerford inheritance to the determined assault of the king's brother, Richard, duke of Gloucester, the former grantee and now old enough to take the lead in person. Gloucester's aspirations may indeed be behind Thomas's execution. In 1468-69, when most Lancastrian plotters were allowed to make fines with the king, only Sir Thomas Hungerford and Henry Courtenay, brother of the last earl of Devon, were executed and suffered forfeiture. Following Courtenay's death, most of his lands were granted to Humphrey, Lord Stafford of Southwick, now created earl of Devon, of whom the chronicler Warkworth reported: 'menne seyde the Lorde Stafforde of Southwyke was cause of the seyde Herry Curtenayes dethe, for he wolde be the Erle of Devynschyre'.[35] May not Gloucester's intentions explain Thomas's death sentence and the forfeiture of his inheritance? Stafford was not created earl of Devon until 17 May 1469, five months after Courtenay's execution, but Gloucester was granted the Hungerford inheritance on 23 October 1468,

[34] *CCR, 1468-76*, nos. 221-40; PRO, C140/29/9/2, 4; C140/32/9/1; *CAD*, II, C2506; see also *Pedes Finium*, p. 137.

[35] *Chronicle of the First Thirteen Years of the Reign of Edward IV*, ed. J.O. Halliwell (Camden Soc., VI, 1839), p. 6.

three months *before* Thomas's death.[36]

The patent gave him in tail male Teffont, Heytesbury (Wilts.), Farleigh Hungerford (Soms.) and all other lands held by Moleyns or held to his use. The imprecision of the patent demonstrates that it merely licensed Gloucester to secure what he could. He duly intervened, disturbing Margaret's tenure and rendering impracticable any surreptitious attempt to convey the estates to any other member of the family. Now well into her sixties, Margaret could not afford to wait for more propitious circumstances, but had instead to compromise. Their agreement of 14 May 1469 was sealed during the duke's progress through East Anglia with his royal brother, who confirmed it.

Instead of dispossessing Margaret, Gloucester concerned himself with the devolution of the estates after her death and the fulfilment of the trust. She had no right of disposal under her husband's will, which envisaged the reversion of the trust lands to Moleyns, whose rights Gloucester now held. In return for the immediate grant of Farleigh Hungerford, guaranteed succession to most of the other lands, and compensation for any waste, Gloucester agreed to leave Margaret in otherwise undisturbed possession, to let her dispose of the Heytesbury lands, and to promote her alienation of other properties in mortmain for the souls of her father-in-law and husband. Margaret promised also to discharge the lands of the mortgages; Gloucester agreed to continue the fees of any old Hungerford dependants.[37] He thus made a reality of his speculative patent, forcing Margaret to abandon hope of keeping most of the lands. A few were saved; others were kept for life to meet her debts, family obligations, and to satisfy her spiritual ambitions.

Gloucester accepted that he had no right to the proposed endowment of Heytesbury hospital, designated by Walter, Lord Hungerford in 1442. He also accepted that Lord Hungerford had ordained a chantry in Salisbury cathedral to be endowed with specified manors, even though Robert made no such provision in his will and the manors were included by him in three separate enfeoffments. Certainly the Salisbury chantry was Margaret's idea and reflected her personal brand of piety. Her reason for founding the chantry and hospital was not the overriding obligations imposed on her – surely they were no stronger than her father's wishes? – but her own spiritual fulfilment, which in 1471 made these foundations what she 'desired above all thyngis erthly'.[38]

For the permanent good of her soul, Margaret vested patronage of both

---

[36] *CPR, 1467-77*, pp. 139, 156; PRO, PS01/32/1674.

[37] Huntington MS.HAP 3466; summarised in *HMC, 78, Hastings*, I, 290-91; BL, Cotton, Julius BXII ff. 123-25; Hoare, *Modern Wiltshire*, I (2), 108-9.

[38] Hicks, 'Chantries, Obits and Hospitals', above, 88-9; above, Chapter 5 .

foundations in Salisbury cathedral chapter, an undying corporation, not in her heirs. The priority of her spiritual over dynastic considerations emerges also in her will of 14 January 1471, in which she proposed to finance her foundations by borrowing £1,333 13s. 4d. above £2,666 13s 4d. still outstanding on the security of her estates, which were to be held by her feoffees for ten years after her death or for however long was necessary. This disregard for her heirs was accompanied by apparent unconcern about the eventual devolution of her lands. Her will merely provides, somewhat ambiguously, that on fulfilment of the trust the lands should never revert 'to hym or theim that god shall then dispose to be myn heir accordyng to the law of this londe and as it ought of right to be done by cours of enheritance'. Heirs feature otherwise only as potential assistance or troublemakers for the feoffees. Their succession should take effect only if they left the feoffees undisturbed, permitted the performance of Margaret's will, and released on request any lands sold by her husband, herself or her feoffees. Failing this, the lands were to be sold for the good of the souls of Margaret, her husband and her ancestors.[39] For religious considerations, Margaret would disinherit her heirs of the lands she had fought so hard to retain.

By saving the Moleyns, Botreaux and Heytesbury estates from forfeiture, the agreements of 1469-70 raise the question of who would ultimately benefit. The male line was represented by Thomas's brother Walter, but Thomas's daughter Mary was heir presumptive to Margaret and Eleanor. Such a marital catch attracted William, Lord Hastings, who secured the grant of Mary's wardship and marriage by 1472 and resolved to marry her to his eldest son.[40] To ensure that Mary's hereditary expectations duly materialised, Hastings persuaded both Hungerford dowagers to curb their independence.

Hastings intervened to revise the 1469 Moleyns agreement in Mary's favour. He may well have threatened to disturb the tenure of Eleanor's feoffees. He certainly offered Eleanor immediate possession of those lands withheld in 1469 during royal pleasure. As the king's chamberlain, he could influence the king and was probably behind the grant of 23 October 1472, which restored all these properties, except Datchet and Ditton (Bucks.), which Edward subsequently gave to St. George's chapel, Windsor. This patent included a pardon for Sir Oliver Manningham, who

---

[39] PRO, C54/312 m.8d. summarised in *CCR, 1468-76*, no. 657.
[40] Huntington MS.HAP Box 3; *Paston Letters and Papers of the Fifteenth Century*, ed. N. Davis (2 vols., Oxford, 1971-76), I, 460-61. Mary's mother Anne Percy and stepfather (Sir Lawrence Reynford) released their rights to Hastings on 2 August 1474; Huntington MS.HAP Box 3.

also escaped attainder.[41] It needs to be considered along with the release to the king of Datchet and Ditton on 13 November by the feoffee John Mervyn and with Hastings's indenture of 6 November with Eleanor and Manningham. This agreement restricted the estates of Eleanor's younger children and gave Mary the contingent remainders. Eleanor's feoffees were restricted to two manors for only seven years and nothing was to be alienated in mortmain. Eleanor's spiritual and maternal feelings remained, but Hastings induced her to control them for more immediate temporal advantages. The principal loser may have been Frideswide, whose marriage portion had been secured on Datchet, which was now released to the king; and she became a nun instead.[42]

Hastings's agreement with Margaret was less favourable to himself. Mary was specifically excluded from the Heytesbury estates. She would succeed to the Botreaux inheritance and no more would be sold, but no attempt would be made to recover any of those alienated. Even these properties were subject to a ten-year trust to perform Margaret's will, during which Mary was to receive only 40 marks (£26 13s. 4d.). A hereditary annuity of £40 from Mary's portion was reserved to Leonard Hungerford and his brother Walter was to hold Kilmersdon, Babington and Babington hundred (Soms.) for life. Lord Hastings would secure the necessary dispensation, provide a jointure of 100 marks, assist Margaret and her feoffees, sanction the creation of estates for Walter and Leonard, act as good lord to them and Margaret's servants, and respect her annuities, which were, however, limited in number.

This indenture, dated 10 February 1474, confirmed the terms of Margaret's latest will.[43] Evidently she regarded Mary as appropriate heir to her Botreaux inheritance but a male Hungerford more suitable for Heytesbury. Like Mary, Walter was also required to co-operate with Margaret's feoffees, to confirm any alienated estates to the purchasers, and also to maintain his allegiance to the king. No doubt in response to representations from her heirs, the penalty for refusal to quitclaim was no longer sale of the lands but merely delayed entry to them. Margaret was as anxious for releases as ever, stressing their importance three times in her will, the third time as part of an elaborate justification of her land sales, which had been forced upon her by political adversity. Therefore, so that

[41] *CPR, 1467-77*, p. 368; PRO, PSO1/36/1885; *Manuscripts of St. George's Chapel, Windsor Castle*. ed. J.N. Dalton (Windsor, 1957), p. 137; *CAD*, I, A670; *Warwickshire Feet of Fines*, III, ed. L. Drucker (Dugdale Society, XVIII, 1943), no. 2700. For what follows, see Huntington MS.HAP Box 3, summarised in BL, Harley MS 3881 f.18; *HMC, 78, Hastings*, I, 303-4.

[42] *The Tropenell Cartulary*, ed. J.S. Davies (2 vols., Devizes, 1908), III, 217.

[43] Huntington MS.HAP Box 3; Wilts. RO, 490/1465. For what follows, see the will on the dorse of Huntington MS.HAP Box 3; Hoare, *Modern Wiltshire*, I (2), 95-102.

myne heires haue none occasion to grugge, for that I leve not to theyme so grete an enheritaunce as I myght . . . and that by this consideracion myne heires have the more cause to streyngthe and enforce th'astatis of all such persones as I have aliened eny of my lyvelode unto,

she set out all the exceptional expenses required of her in an annex. Probably the same as that appended to her 1476 will, this writing contained an exaggerated account of Margaret's expenses, which were presented as inescapable obligations. Her Salisbury chantry, ordained by her husband, and the relief of sureties feature as moral obligations justifying sales of land. The sales themselves imposed on her a moral obligation to maintain her side of the bargain. Her soul would suffer if her heirs dishonoured the contracts, disinherited the purchasers, and thus left her burdened with debt. Therefore, she appealed over the heads of her existing heirs to the next generation.

There was one other clause in Margaret's agreement with Lord Hastings:

And ouer this wheras the said Robard and Thomas sone to her said Robard sone to the saide lady Hungerford stonde atteynte that if the same attaynders to be adnulled and defeted than all the maners landis and tenementis the wich the said ladye Hungerford hath of the Hungerford landis in dower or Joyunctor for terme of lif wich is founden by Inquisicion of recorde after the discesse of the same lady comen to the saide Marie and the heires of hir body begoten.[44]

Most attainders were eventually reversed. Hastings wisely opted to back the heir, who could confer a safer title than a royal grant. Ultimately, in 1485, Mary did benefit from such a reversal. Many attainders were reversed in 1472, but not that of Moleyns. The influence of Hastings and Walter Hungerford, now a royal officer,[45] could not prevail against a royal patentee who was the king's own brother Gloucester, who was determined not only to maintain but to extend his hold over the Hungerford inheritance. Indeed, Gloucester regarded the 1469 indenture as an interim settlement, a basis for further gains, and he was impatient to secure possession of those properties of which he held the reversion. There is no evidence that the inheritance ever became a source of enmity between Gloucester and Hastings.

On 5 August 1474 Gloucester was granted in tail male twelve Hungerford manors, three hundreds, and the reversion of thirteen manors on Margaret's death. The patent was based on the inquisitions of 1470

[44] *HMC, 78, Hastings*, I, 304.

[45] J.C. Wedgwood, *History of Parliament, 1439-1509: Biographies of Members of the Commons House* (1936), p. 486.

and 1473, which reflect investigations into the title for the period before the 1458-59 enfeoffments.[46] There can be little doubt that Gloucester himself promoted both the historical research and the inquisitions. Obviously Lord Hungerford could only confer on his feoffees the title that he himself possessed. Ten Cornish manors, recognized as Margaret's in 1469, were found to have been settled correctly on her husband, with remainder to Moleyns. As Lord Hungerford alone had conveyed them to uses, Margaret possessed only a life estate, with remainder to Gloucester. Two other inquisitions found that twelve manors and three hundreds, recognized as Margaret's jointure or as indefinitely held to use in 1469, were either held by her and her husband jointly or by Lord Hungerford alone, and were thus covered by Moleyns's attainder. This later conclusion was quite wrong and even the former allowed Margaret a life interest that was ignored in Gloucester's patent. In possession in 1474-75, Margaret was apparently left only three manors held for life: Teffont – granted to her in 1437 – and five Heytesbury manors destined for Walter. Her inquisitions were copied into Gloucester's commonplace book, suggesting that he coveted even these.[46] At death, therefore, Margaret was able to transmit to her heirs only Heytesbury and the attenuated remnants of her Botreaux inheritance.

Such misfortune did not cause Margaret to revise her will. Her last will of 8 August 1476 was still primarily concerned with the payment of debts arising from the ransom, her husband's will, and her religious foundations apparently totalling only £1,333 6s. 8d. in 1474. Much was presumably paid off by the time of her death and in 1477, secure in the tenure by her feoffees for a further ten years, she ordered a lavish funeral and expensive bequests to the church. While certain heirlooms were reserved for Walter, Margaret was primarily concerned to die an exemplary death and to ensure that her executors discharged meticulously any remaining obligations. The familiar instruction to disinherit any troublesome descendant shows piety prevalent over lineage to the very end.[46]

Meantime, Lord Hastings secured a release of Mary's wardship and marriage from her mother (1474), a royal patent to the same effect (1478), and papal dispensations for the espousal (1475) and marriage of Mary to his son (1479). The 1478 patent recognized Mary as the heiress of certain Botreaux lands under an old entail, in defiance of Margaret's will and the 1474 indenture with Lord Hastings, and in 1481 she was granted livery of it and presumably also of the inheritance of Eleanor Moleyns, who died *c*.

[46] *CPR, 1467-77*, pp. 466-67; BL, Cotton, Julius BXII ff.294, 298-*v*; PRO, E153/1696/1.

[47] PRO, SC6/119/16; C140/67/3/2. 4, 6; E149/238/9/1, 2; BL Cotton, Julius BXII f. 298-ᵛ; Hoare, *Modern Wiltshire* I (2), 95; Wilts. RO, 490/1469 no. 20, 1502/1503a-b.

[48] Hoare, *Modern Wiltshire* I, (2), 95-100; Devizes Museum, Canon Jackson's Collections, Personal I, ff.269*v*-75*v*.

1476.[49] While Walter waited for the expiry of Margaret's trust of the Hungerford estates, Gloucester usurped the throne as Richard III, executed Mary's father-in-law, and drove Walter – an attainted traitor – into exile. His return in 1485 with the victorious Henry VII resulted in the reversal of the attainders of himself and his father Moleyns, thus extending the dispute of heirs male and heirs general to the forfeited Hungerford inheritance. Even as this litigation began, Walter conveyed his lands to feoffees for the discharge

> of and for all such sommes of money in the which the seid feoffees or any of theym be bounden for me the said Walter Hungerford to any persone or persones which I haue chevisshed for my journey to the court of Rome . . . and alle my dettes . . . and also for such other detts [£160] which I in conscience owe to content by reason of the will of my lady Dame Margaret lady Hungerford and Botreaux my grauntdame,

and for performance of his will. Prominent here was the establishment of a ten-year chantry of two priests. But dynastic considerations featured not just in the remainders from his land but also in the requirement that the feoffees pay 'in especiall . . . for the affermyng of my titill vnto all such manors, londes and tenementes nowe restyng in variaunce between Edward lord Hastyngys and Mary his wyff and me'.[50]

The same themes recur in changed circumstances.

The Hungerfords were not politically united or consistent. Moleyns placed loyalty to Henry VI above his own life, the welfare of his dependants, and the preservation of the family inheritance. His mother, wife and son temporised with the new régime, accepting Moleyns's attainder as a fact, but enlisting allies among the victors to mitigate its effects and preserve intact the family inheritance. Although Sir Thomas Hungerford ostentatiously cemented his allegiance to King Edward by serving against his own father in the north, he was actually devoted to Henry VI. Margaret's political stance is as ambiguous to us as it was to the Yorkists, who apparently arrested her *c.* 1463 for communicating with her Lancastrian son, and again in 1470 because of the involvement of the cadet line in Warwick's and Clarence's Lincolnshire rebellion. It is revealing that her Syon obit commemorates Thomas as Lord Hungerford

[49] Huntington MS.HAP Box 4; *HMC, 78, Hastings*, I, 290; *CPR, 1476-85*, pp. 101, 129, 233; C. *Pap. L.* XIII (I), 220; XIII (2), 687-93; E.W. Ives, *The Common Lawyers of Pre-Reformation England. Thomas Kebell: A Case Study* (Cambridge, 1983), pp. 94-96.
[50] *Materials for a History of the Reign of Henry VII*, ed. W. Campbell (RS, 2 vols., 1873-77), II, 123-25.
[51] Cf. K.B. McFarlane, *England in the Fifteenth Century*, ed. G.L. Harriss (1981), pp. 260-61.

despite his father's attainder, but Margaret consistently placed the survival of the family and its inheritance ahead of dynastic loyalties. Her removal of Moleyns from the political arena in 1460 was echoed by her repeated injunctions to Walter never to depart from his allegiance.[51] That Walter, like his father and brother, suffered forfeiture for his part in the Wydeville rebellion of 1483, indicates the varying perceptions of priorities within the family circle. Self-preservation and the integrity of the family inheritance repeatedly took second place to political alignments and allegiance.[52]

The Hungerfords' consciousness of a shared ancestry and lineage was a source of solidarity against external threats in times of crisis, as in 1461 and 1464. At other times the family was divided into separate nuclear families and autonomous individuals with their own interests and aspirations. In stressing the solidarity of the Hungerfords in their troubles, McFarlane relied unduly on Margaret's autobiography, which nevertheless documents Margaret's disagreements with all other members of the lineage. Margaret made little use of her wider kin, her brother-in-law and her husband's cousins, preferring to rely on the ties of neighbourhood, friendship and service.

From this evidence, it appears that the current lord saw his tenure as the result of descent from his ancestors, not as a temporary stage in a process continuing in the future. He behaved less as a life-tenant or trustee of corporate property than as an owner, free to use the inheritance as he chose during his life, and, within certain limits, to dispose of it for the good of his dependants after death. Most commonly, of course, lords entailed their lands on their heirs male, sometimes excluding specific females. Personality and individual preference influenced the settlement of lands on the issue of a second marriage or on younger sons. Apparently no lord felt qualms about settling jointure on subsequent wives or indeed in delaying the tenure of the heir by enfeoffments to the use of his last will. Perhaps dowagers showed most independence: originating from other families and thus able to stand apart, they exercised control over their jointure, inheritance and dower without feeling responsibilities to the rest of the family.[53] Just as lords alienated their own acquisitions more often than their inherited estates, so Margaret felt freer to sell or entail her Botreaux lands – her own property – than those Hungerford properties she held in trust. She fought to save these last and permitted them to descend to the right heirs, to whom she felt obliged to account for her trust.

Heirs, however, traced their pedigrees beyond the current holders to themselves and expected in due course to succeed to the family estates.

---

[52] See above, 159-61.

[53] R. Archer, 'Rich Old Ladies: The Problem of Late Medieval Dowagers' in *Property and Politics*, p. 19.

Only too well-acquainted with their inheritance, they often regarded their expectations as rights, dealing – like Margaret – in reversions due on the death of the current holder, and resenting any alienation – even the jointure of the second Lady Botreaux – as disinheritance. The entails that restricted the current tenant protected the rights of heirs, who could refuse to release their rights or help break entails, preferring to maintain the option of redemption, which they frequently made good. While unable actually to prevent sales, their non-co-operation weakened the title for sale and thus reduced the sale price, perhaps ironically forcing more to be sold for the same sum. Not surprisingly, prospective fathers-in-law of heirs or heiresses often preferred to act before the event, securing guaranteed jointures for their daughters or guarantees of succcession for their sons from the current holders. Such transactions, a feature of the Hungerford-Botreaux agreement of about 1420,[54] were revived by Lord Hastings for his dealings with the three Hungerford dowagers. Their concessions may indeed have merely involved promises not to do what they had no intention of doing.

Dynastic attitudes changed on inheritance. Margaret resented her stepmother, whose dower and jointure were carved out of *her* inheritance, yet she herself dispossessed her heirs, delayed their succession, and made their entry conditional. She corresponds to Houlbrooke's pattern of the current holder seeking freedom of disposition, in her case with the ultimate penalty of disinheritance to enforce obedience on her heirs. The main victims, her grandsons Thomas and Walter, both deferred the succession of their heirs in their wills.[55]

In agreement on the mortgages of 1459-60, the resident family adopted a common strategy to save its estates in 1460-64, which certainly conformed both with the honour and self-interest of Thomas and Margaret and with Margaret's moral obligation to her husband. The advantages were less for Eleanor, who gave priority to herself, her soul and her children over Moleyns's debts and soul once he was dead. Like Lady Botreaux and Anne Percy, whose new husbands could have been useful in the struggle for survival, Eleanor transferred her loyalty to her new husband and even surrendered her inheritance a second time on his behalf. Thomas's death, leaving an infant heir and enhancing Walter's importance, increased Margaret's isolation and made her grateful for Hastings's support. The projected division of the family possesions in 1471-76 ultimately precipitated the quarrel of heirs male and general after 1485.

Margaret's conception of family interest and honour was strongly tinged with the essentially religious obligations imposed on her by her

---

[54] Huntington MS.HAP Box 2; *HMC 78, Hastings*, I, 287-88.
[55] Cf. Chapter 4, passim.

husband for the good of his soul. Eleanor rejected a similar responsibility to her husband and the next generation understandably viewed Margaret's sentiments with disfavour. Religious issues were broadly defined and touched such everyday aspects of life as politics and the integrity of the family estates, not just at death but in life. Both Margaret and Eleanor bargained away concrete assets for spiritual gains, the tangible for the intangible. Both they and Thomas, even – or especially? – at moments of crisis, worried about the performance of their wills. While struggling to retain their estates, they planned to give them to the church. Pilgrimages were not deferred until convenient, for the business of this world mattered less than salvation. Piety was integrated with political and economic activity.

Twice a choice was made between piety and lineage. On one occasion Eleanor abandoned her chantry to augment her granddaughter's inheritance. Pride of lineage prevailed. In another, Margaret put religion first, instructing the disinheritance of her heirs if they did not release their rights as required. Instead of being 'counselled and avisid', as Lord Hungerford wished, Margaret preferred the good of their soul above the future of the family.[56] While her last will recognizes her sin of obstinacy and she abased herseslf to her spiritual directors, she could not humble herself to her heirs, appealing instead to generations yet unborn. The diminution in the family inheritance resulted not so much from wars as from Margaret's fulfilment of her husband's wishes beyond her legal obligations.

[56] *Somerset Med. Wills.* p. 192.

10

Counting the Cost of War: The Moleyns Ransom and the Hungerford Land-Sales, 1453-87

It was the late K.B. McFarlane who first tried to strike a balance of profit and loss for late medieval warfare. For 'the dogmatic belief, inherited from the nineteenth century, that wars can never be anything but damaging', he substituted more precise accounting, concluding for the Hundred Years War that 'while "England" was beaten the English were enriched' and that no generalisation about the Wars of the Roses 'is more demonstrably false' than that they resulted in 'the extermination of most of the old nobility'.

In his 1953 Ford Lectures McFarlane tabulated the opportunities during the Hundred Years War for profit from wages, booty, ransoms, grants of conquered lands, and illicit activities of all kinds. While admitting to some English ransoms, he argued that the English ended in credit and that the English nobility were thus enabled 'to achieve a standard of living, indeed of luxury' otherwise beyond them. In 1961 the winnings formed only part of a wider study of the social and economic consequences of the war, but again he found that such profits permitted upward mobility, if at all, 'within the class traditionally associated with martial prowess', enhancing its economic stability and encouraging conspicuous consumption.[1]

For Professor Postan, in contrast, no profit could make up for the waste of manpower and resources involved. 'However generous we may be in our estimates of net gains . . . we should still find it very difficult to make them equal the five millions *plus* spent on national and private accounts,' particularly as any profits were spent

---

[1] K.B. McFarlane, *Nobility of Later Medieval England* (Oxford, 1973), 19–40; *England in the Fifteenth Century*, ed. G.L. Harriss (1981), 139–49, 257. This paper was prepared with financial assistance from King Alfred's College, Winchester. Documents in the Public Record Office, London are cited by their PRO call-numbers. I am grateful to the Trustees of the Huntington Library, California for supplying photocopies of documents and for permission to cite them here. Dr M.K. Jones kindly advised and criticised this article. Genealogical details are taken from GEC *Complete Peerage of England, Scotland, Ireland and the United Kingdom*, ed. H.V. Gibbs and others (13 vols. 1910–59), ii. 282; vi. 613–23.

unproductively. For Dr Bridbury, finally, the whole debate was misconceived. War was an integral part of medieval life, the late medieval nobility were a military caste, and it is surely

> 'a very whimsical conception of national wealth that sees an enhancement of the productive powers of the community in the store of plate and jewellery and other baubles that the English brought back from France.'[2]

The main economic debate is now surely dead, but McFarlane's starting point – the significance of profits and losses of war for the nobility – retains considerable military, social and political import-ance and continues to be studied.

In much the same way, gloomy interpretations of the Wars of the Roses have been progressively dispelled by evidence that the duration of conflict, the loss of life, and physical damage have been exaggerated.[3] In 1964 McFarlane dealt briefly and conclusively with the 'myth' of the destruction of the nobility. The rate of attrition of noble houses during the Wars of the Roses was scarcely different from normal. Few families were totally destroyed that were not already at risk through lack of heirs. Similarly Professor Lander has shown that those attainted generally secured restoration and most of the rest could have done so.[4] On the other hand, the Wars of the Roses certainly caused some families to disappear that would have otherwise survived. Some sold property, which – as in 1660 – was not recovered on their restoration. Yet others lost possession to rivals, sometimes for twenty years and more, or were subjected to ransoms, made to pay fines for life and liberty, or even had to buy back their own estates. Such measures enriched the winners at the expense of the losers, permitted conspicuous consumption otherwise beyond their means, and involved transfers of wealth often of equal duration and of at least equivalent value to those of the Hundred Years War.

---

[2] M.M. Postan, *Essays on Medieval Agriculture and General Problems of the Medieval Economy* (Cambridge, 1973), 63–80; A.R. Bridbury, 'The Hundred Years War: Costs and Profits', *Trade, Government and Economy in Pre-Industrial England*, ed. D.C. Coleman and A.H. John (1976), 80–95, esp. p. 93. For what follows, see e.g. A.J. Pollard, *John Talbot and the War in France 1427–1453* (1983), 102–21; S. Walker, 'Profit and loss in the Hundred Years War: the subcontracts of Sir John Strother, 1374', *B(ulletin of the) I(nstitute of) H(istorical) R(esearch)* lviii (1985), 100–6.

[3] For some correctives, see A. Goodman, *The Wars of the Roses: Military Organisation* (1980).

[4] McFarlane, *England*, 257–9; J.R. Lander, *Crown and Nobility 1450–1509* (1976), ch. 5. For what follows, see M.A. Hicks, 'Descent; Partition and Extinction: The "Warwick Inheritance"', see below, chapter 18; 'Attainder, Resumption and Coercion 1461–1529', above, chapter 3.

The patchy source material militates against precise accounting. To amplify his well-documented cases, McFarlane deployed a wealth of illustrations from contemporary chronicles and Tudor antiquaries, many of them open to dispute. Some ransoms were never paid in full and others were subject to deductions. McFarlane and Postan swapped examples in a manner reminiscent of the early stages of the *Gentry Controversy*, before specialised local studies provided concrete evidence for evaluation. McFarlane was only too well-aware of this – hence his detailed articles on particular cases[5] – but he never undertook a thorough analysis of the operation of the ransom system. Studies of specific examples still have much to contribute to our understanding.

Both McFarlane and Postan cited the Hungerford family in support of their arguments. In 1953 McFarlane quoted the Tudor antiquary Leland for 'a commune saying that one of the Hungrefords buildid this part of the castelle (of Farleigh in Somerset) by the praye (i.e. the ransom) of the duke of Orleaunce, taken with his peers at Agincourt'. To illustrate 'the workings of this somewhat complicated system', he quoted the expenditure of Margaret Lady Hungerford on behalf of her son Robert, Lord Moleyns, captured at Castillon in 1453. Although Moleyns' ransom necessitated mortgaging the family estate, payment was still incomplete in 1476, largely because of Moleyns' attainder in 1461. Not surprisingly Postan also seized on this example, adding that Moleyns' uncle had also been ransomed in 1425. In 1965, after further research, McFarlane emphasised that Margaret had even been forced to sell her land.

'Had Robert Moleyns taken reasonable care or had reasonable luck, the mortgages would have been paid off without recourse to that last desperate remedy of the embarrassed landowner: the sale of some part of his estates. Margaret Hungerford's plan involved no raid on capital; only a temporary loss of income . . . The financial burden of her son's ransom could be carried, heavy though it was. The attainders . . . were by comparison shattering. Yet even there the effects were only temporary . . . In Henry VII's reign the attainders were reversed and her descendants were to recover everything except the manors she had been forced to sell. The loss of those manors was the permanent scar consequent upon Robert's capture at Castillon; and even that scar would have been invisible but for his adhesion to the wrong side – for the time being – in the Wars of the Roses.'

---

[5] McFarlane, *England*, chs. 8–9.

McFarlane thus played down the Hundred Years War and enhanced the Wars of the Roses. Moreover, he continued, the losses of war, obviously severe for Moleyns, need to be set in the context of the family's gains. Only one other Hungerford was ransomed and then for only £3000. Yet in 1415 eight prisoners were taken, in 1433 the vidame of Chartres was being ransomed, several French lordships were acquired, and Farleigh Hungerford castle was rebuilt. 'On balance, therefore, the family would seem to have profited greatly from the war. And few English families were as unlucky as it with two oldest sons captured in two generations'.[6]

While agreeing on the importance of the Hungerford experience, neither McFarlane nor Postan investigated it fully. It is not my intention here to examine the early gains, although it is worth observing that Walter, Lord Hungerford's expenditure on Farleigh Hungerford castle, his religious foundations, his land purchases, and the ransom of his *second* son conform better to the chronology of his royal service in England, notably as Lord Treasurer 1426–33, than to his military involvement abroad. The Moleyns ransom and Margaret Lady Hungerford's expenditure deserve more attention and are the focus of this article, which uses them to investigate the short and long-term consequences of war, foreign and domestic. The first section will assess the financial evidence, the second will analyse how the family obligations were paid, and the third will draw some general conclusions.

—*****—

Apparently originating from Hungerford (Berks.) *c.* 1300, the Hungerford family established itself at Heytesbury (Wilts.) and Farleigh Hungerford (Soms.) in the late 14th century and attained the peerage in 1426. At his death in 1449 Walter, 1st Lord, possessed substantial estates in Somerset, Wiltshire and Berkshire and outlying properties in Devon, Cornwall, Dorset, Hampshire, Middlesex and Oxfordshire; a cadet line was established in Gloucestershire. Walter's income was assessed at £911 in 1436 and in 1450–1 and 1453–4, when Walter's widow had separate dower, his son's receiver-general had liveries of £1187 9s.10d. and £900 respectively,[7] which placed the family in the middle ranks of the peerage, well above the £666 13s.4d. qualifying income for an earl. Moreover, this was not destined to be

[6] McFarlane, *Nobility*, 23, 28–30, 126–8; Postan, 77.

[7] *C(alendarium) I(nquisitionum) p(ost) m(ortem sive Escaetarum)*, Record Commission (1828) iv. 238; H.L. Gray, 'Incomes from land in 1436', *English Historical Review* xlix (1934), 615; SC 6/1119/12–13.

the limit of the family's rise. Robert, 2nd Lord Hungerford (d.1459) had married Margaret, daughter and ultimately sole heiress of William, 3rd Lord Botreaux (d.1462), whose lands were extended at £460 at his death in 1462, when they were concentrated in Somerset, Cornwall, Devon, and Hampshire.[8] Finally Robert and Margaret's son Robert, Lord Moleyns married Eleanor Moleyns, being created Lord Moleyns in her right and thus acquired her inheritance in Oxfordshire, Cornwall, Wiltshire, Buckinghamshire and other counties extended at £462 in 1464.[9] As Moleyns had three sons, it was expected that the Hungerfords would ultimately have estates of £2000 in central and southern England and become the greatest magnates in the region. In fact, as we shall see, this was prevented by the Hundred Years War and the Wars of the Roses.

The central figure in the family disasters was Margaret, Lady Hungerford (d.1478), wife of the 2nd Lord and mother of Lord Moleyns. The fundamental source is her statement of expenditure in the appendix or *writing annexed* to her will of 8 August 1476. Running to 2½ pages of print, it lists expenditure under 26 heads amounting to the phenomenal sum of 26,194½ marks (£17463) and income of 1250 marks (£833 13s.4d.) a year.[10]

Nine items totalling £9,961 relate to the repatriation of Lord Moleyns. He was wounded and captured at the decisive battle of Castillon on 17 July 1453. His initial captor, 'the master in the felde', may have been Jean du Bueil, admiral of France, who appropriated Moleyns' missal for his own use and recorded his family's obits in it.[11] Lord Moleyns was subsequently transferred to King Charles VII, who accompanied him to his embarkation at Rouen and whose mistress, called by Margaret the 'Graunte Maistresse', was among those paid £720 6s.8d. to spare his life (?) and put him to ransom. Chester Herald's negotiations cost £140 and the ransom itself was £6,000. Apparel, a horse and medicine were supplied at a cost of £176 and £760 was spent on his keep, making a total of £7796 6s.8d. According to Margaret, £7690 was shipped abroad, the Medici agent Simone d'Antonio Nori charging 10 per cent (£769) to change it into foreign currency. A further £290 6s.8d. was spent on 'dyuers gestis geuen at his departyng oute of pryson' and for his journey home. Interest payments cost £945 6s.8d. and £160 was lost in the sale of

---

[8] *CIPM* iv. 318; C 140/7/15/1–15.

[9] *CIPM* iv. 190, 199; C 145/320/1.

[10] R.C. Hoare, *History of Modern Wiltshire* (6 vols. London 1822–40), i (2). 100–2. Unless otherwise stated, this is the source of the rest of the article.

[11] V. Leroquais, *Les Sacrementaires et les Missels Manuscrits des Bibliothèques Publiques de France* (Paris 1924), iii. 23–4.

plate to raise money.[12]

Meantime, so Margaret claimed, she was supporting Lady Moleyns and her children during her husband's absence at a cost of £800; she claimed also to have supported Moleyns on his return (£186 13s.4d.). Hardly was he back, when Moleyns embroiled himself in politics, defending the Tower of London against the Yorkist earls. It cost Margaret £768 8s.4d. to secure their favour and a licence for Moleyns to go to Florence, safely out of harm's way. The sea-passage by Florentine galley[13] and spending money totalled a further £255, but Moleyns evidently disembarked en route, returning for the decisive Lancastrian defeat at Towton on 29 March 1461, attainder later the same year, and execution in 1464. Apart from paying her husband's debts (£358), Moleyns' debts (£400) and equipping Sir Thomas Hungerford for military service in the north, to save the mortgaged Hungerford lands from forfeiture Margaret paid

'to grete Lordis and with other with whom I compounded and accorded, and with some of theyme pleted, and over that made grete sutes, as well to the Kyng hym self, as in his parlements, wich sutes, composicions and accordes, and hauyng the same lyuelode oute of the Kyngis handis, and makyng of fynes for the same cause, I spended MMclv li (£2155)'.

An annuity of £100 was granted to Lord Dynham to renounce his claims. Moreover, Margaret herself was arrested on three occasions: once by the sheriff of Wiltshire, evidently in her son's lifetime – it cost her £400 to be released; once at Amesbury Abbey, probably in 1463, a stay that cost her £1000 in moveables destroyed in a fire and £200 in rebuilding the nunnery lodgings; and thirdly in 1470, at the time of the Lincolnshire rebellion, when she paid £200 to be transferred from the custody of the Duchess of Norfolk to Syon Abbey.[14]

Other inescapable expenses were pious bequests of her father-in-law Walter (d.1449) and her husband Robert (d.1459), Lords Hungerford, comprising the construction (£497) and equipping (£250) of Robert's chantry at Salisbury cathedral, the completion of her

---

[12] Margaret claimed to have paid £1,100 at 'iii yeres payment', but Lord Cromwell's executors' accounts show £639 1s. 5d. due on 'certen obligacions' in 1466. Evidently Margaret sold the plate before paying for it after 1469, Magdalen College Oxford Misc. MSS. 355, 361.

[13] C 76/142 rot. 2; M.E. Mallett, *The Florentine Galleys* (London 1966), 93–4.

[14] For her sojourn at Syon, see M.A. Hicks, 'Piety of Margaret, Lady Hungerford (d. 1478)', *Journal of Ecclesiastical History*, ch. 5 above. She sealed a deed at Amesbury on 20 Nov. 1463 (Huntington MS. HAD 2210); she was pardoned on 12 May 1462, C 67/45 m.20.

father-in-law's foundation at Heytesbury hospital (£200), and the price of licences to alienate (£167 13s.4d.).

Finally, Margaret recorded that only 700 marks had been paid of the 3500-mark marriage portion of Anne Percy to her grandson Thomas. To Margaret this represented a loss of 2800 marks (£1866 13s.4d.),[15] besides the jointure of £200 she had to provide and which Anne Percy carried to her next husband. A further 800 marks a year was assigned to her stepmother Margaret Botreaux from Margaret's inheritance.

The precise figures and circumstantial detail are surely derived from itemised accounts and indeed Margaret refers to 'dew examinacion . . . by an auditour' at one point. The seals of bishop, chapter and mayor of Salisbury add weight to the *writing annexed*, as Margaret intended that they should. But why was the *writing* compiled at all? It claims to itemise expenses 'this season of the grete troblous and adversitees wich late have be fallen on thes lande' and other inescapable costs, not to explain why they are listed. This emerges in the will itself, where Margaret recalls that she sold moveables and incurred debts,

'wich I have not done by foly, nor by cause of any excesse or undiscrete liberalitie, but oonly I haue been arted and caused by necessite of fortune and mysaventure that hath happend in this season of trobill tyme late paste'.

Therefore she compiled the *writing annexed*:

'to this ende, that my kynne and frendis, and namely, such as God wull dispose to be myne heire, shall neither haue mervaille apon my poverte, nother apon th'alienacions that I have made of parte my lyvelode . . .'

So that her heirs will not resent her losses, but will see that she had no choice but to do as she did

'and that by this consideracion myne heires have the more cause to streyngthe and enforce th'astatis of all such persones as I haue aliened eny of my lyvelode unto. Wheryn I pray theyme, and also reqyyre theyme to be benyvolente, and to do as shalbe beste to the suertee and profite of all tho to whome I haue

---

[15] Bonds totalling £2,166 13s. 4d. survive in the Hungerford archive at the Huntington Library, Huntington MS. HAF Box 2, bonds of 13 Aug. & 12 Nov. 1460.

aliened eny of my lande.'[16]

So Margaret prepared the *writing* for fear that her heirs would resent their diminished inheritance and would refuse to release their residual rights to those to whom she had sold lands. Margaret could not convey a completely secure title to purchasers even of her own inheritance without securing releases from her heirs. Such rights were sometimes used to recover wrongly alienated properties. The implication, that some such releases had been withheld, was probably true. Some were made by Thomas, Margaret's eldest grandson, by his brother Walter and by his sister Frideswide. In 1474 Lord Hastings promised that Mary Hungerford, his projected daughter-in-law, would make such releases when of age.[17] But almost no quitclaims, apparently, were made by Thomas's two adult brothers, Walter and Leonard, almost certainly because they refused. Indeed the will says that if they or Mary refused such releases,

> 'that then he that so doth agenste my wille or refusith thus to do as he shalbe thus requyred, to have no parte of the said maners, hundredis, ne annuyte, nor noon other goode heryn by me ordeyned, disposed, and dyvised unto hym'.[18]

Margaret could hardly have valued Frideswide's quitclaim ahead of her brothers and it is striking how few quitclaims by them can be set against the multiple copies surviving for Frideswide. Perhaps Margaret was appealing from unsympathetic adult heirs to others yet immature or unborn to urge them to release their rights.

Why was Margaret so anxious that her alienations, which disinherited her heirs, should be permanent? That is obvious. If her heirs abrogated sales that she had freely made, both her honour and the good of her soul would be imperilled. Far from leaving all worldly business settled, as she wished to do, she would die in debt. As Dr Fleming says,

> 'the thought of dying with debts unpaid was particularly abhorrent to the propertied classes, especially since at that period the debtor's liability died with him. Dying without

[16] Hoare, i(2).99.
[17] W(iltshire) R(ecord) O(ffice) 490/1465; *C(alendar of) C(lose) R(olls) 1461–8*, 465; *1468–76*, nos. 221–40, 1139.
[18] Hoare, i(2). 98.

providing for the payment of debts was therefore tantamount to theft, and would not go unpunished in the life to come'.[19]

Moreover, it was not just Margaret's soul that was at risk. She repaid Moleyns' debts not because she was obliged to – she was not – but for the good of her soul. Her expenditure on the Salisbury chantry and Heytesbury hospital were justified by the last wills of the two Lords Hungerford. Religion dictated the repayment of debts, which prompted her to sell lands. Her heirs disapproved, so she prepared the *writing annexed* to win them over.

The *writing annexed* is not therefore a factual statement of account, nor an objective work of history. It is deliberately slanted to present the past in a particular light, in a biased and contentious way, for an ulterior motive. It is a selective, rationalised, prejudiced narrative of Margaret's troubles seen through her own eyes. It possesses all the weaknesses as well as the strengths of an autobiography, which is what it is. Margaret needed to convince her heirs that her losses were unbearable and inescapable. She needed to maximise her expenditure by inflating the figures or including items that should not be there. She was encouraged to suppress or misrepresent items of which her heirs would disapprove.

She justified religious expenditure by the binding ordinances of her father-in-law and husband. Although the endowment of Heytesbury hospital had been ordered in 1442, Walter's wishes had been neglected for thirty years before being fulfilled by Margaret, who was neither his executor nor feoffee. Robert, Lord Hungerford asked to be buried before St Osmund's altar, Salisbury cathedral. The chantry was Margaret's idea and conformed to her religious taste.[20] Thus Margaret was able to justify expenditure that her grandchildren disliked. She does not mention that she alienated 80 marks of income to her foundations, nor that £100 was paid to Syon Abbey for her obit there.[21]

On Margaret's own figures, she did not *lose* 2,800 marks from the marriage of her grandson Thomas and Anne Percy, she gained by 700 marks. The balance was an unpaid debt, not an expense. Thomas'

[19] P.W. Fleming, 'Charity, Faith and the Gentry of Kent 1422–1529', *Property and Politics: Essays in Later Medieval English History*, ed. A.J. Pollard (Gloucester 1984), 37.

[20] M.A. Hicks, 'St Katherine's Hospital, Heytesbury: Prehistory, Foundation and Re-foundation 1408–72', *Wiltshire Archaeological Magazine* above, ch. 6, 122-7; above chapter 5 .

[21] M.A. Hicks, 'Chantries, Obits and Almshouses: The Hungerford Foundations 1325–1478', *Church in Pre-Reformation Society*, ed. C. Barron and C. Harper-Bill (Woodbridge, 1985) , above 88-9.

jointure was not an expense for Margaret: it was covered by her husband's will, Thomas would have to be supported anyway, and it was normal to settle lands jointly on the bridal couple for life, regardless of the subsequent death of the husband. Moreover the 800 marks surrendered to Lady Botreaux represented her jointure and a 100-mark annuity in lieu of dower, an arrangement much to Margaret's advantage. Understandably Margaret lamented the failure of an anticipated cash windfall to materialise, the loss of income to Anne Percy's second husband, and the prior claims of her young stepmother, but none of these was properly an expense. Neither, indeed, was the £1000 of goods lost in the Amesbury fire, except insofar as it was replaced. Even the £200 cost of rebuilding was hardly a cost of war.

Deduction of these items totalling £4115 6s.8d. in cash and 1,100 marks in income reduces the expenditure total to the still formidable sum of £13334 13s.4d. and Lord Dynham's £100 annuity. This represents Margaret's total losses of war and deserves equally close scrutiny.

—*****—

The *writing annexed* has been most valued for its unique insight into backstairs intrigue and 'extras' of the ransom system. While costs cannot now be verified, there is no reason to doubt any of them except the entry for keep. This is based on weekly payments of £2 and covers a period of at least 40 weeks – or £80 – too long for the maximum possible duration of captivity from 17 July 1453 to 31 March 1460. More seriously, all expenses up to 18 May 1459 must have been met, if at all, by Margaret's husband Robert. At this point Margaret had entered neither her inheritance, jointure, nor dower and had no resources of her own with which to make such payments. It was actually Lord Hungerford who raised the first instalment of the ransom. Surely at least some of the items of expenditure on negotiations, on bribes at the French court, for Moleyns' clothes, horse and medicine, were met by Lord Hungerford at the time, though perhaps with borrowed money. Similarly Lady Moleyns was well-able to support herself from her estates. Only after her husband's death was Margaret in full possession of the enfeoffed Hungerford lands.

The ransom was paid in two instalments. The second, paid by Moleyns himself, consisted of £3000 borrowed from the Medici agent Simone d'Antonio Nori, from John Forster skinner of London (at least £760), and from John Plummer, grocer of London, later knight and alderman. This was secured by recognizances for debt from John Eastmond, James Touker of Bradford-on-Avon (Wilts.), William

Stowford, John Tughill, John Reynold and William Somer, and was to be repaid from his wife's Moleyns inheritance to save the sureties harmless.[22] This was the second instalment of the *ransom*. Most likely, therefore, it was the first half of the ransom proper – £3000 – that was paid by Lord Hungerford in 1459. £2000 of this was borrowed from Richard Quatermains esquire, Simone Nori and others on the security of bonds of the archbishop of Canterbury and fifteen other bishops and magnates, who were to be saved harmless by the mortgage of the whole Hungerford inheritance.[23] This implies that only £1000 was paid in cash – only one year's income from the family estates, although six years had passed since Moleyns' capture and 100 marks had been left for this purpose in 1455.[24] At most £5000 was *borrowed* towards the ransom itself.

Lord Hungerford surely paid some extras from his own resources, some others with borrowed money – the involvement of Francesco Nori suggests this – and yet others may have been unpaid at death. By November 1461 all sums due to the French had been paid. Margaret reports that £7690 was shipped abroad by the Medici and charged for exchange. The similarity to the 12000 marks (£8000) of the 'ouerchargefull excessyue fynaunce and expenses' claimed by Moleyns to be due in 1459–60 should not be exaggerated:[25] Margaret's total was achieved by adding together all expenses abroad, whenever paid; her figure for exchange is probably calculated at 8d. per noble from the £7690, rather than derived from an independent source; and the £8000 is obviously a round figure. Assuming that nothing at all was paid from income, the maximum possible debt at Moleyns' release was *only* £7855. The £5000 was secured by mortgages of land worth £1500 a year and represented less than four years' income, not an unbearable burden of debt. The balance of £2855 was unsecured, but was covered by Anne Percy's marriage portion (£2366 13s.4d.), a royal grant of £1000 from the exchequer, a licence to ship 1500 woolfells free of custom, and sale of woods licensed by the king (£180).[26] Clearly McFarlane was right that the ransom itself was well-within the family's means.

This remained true even after Moleyns' return had brought further expenditure calculated at £1200 1s.8d. This included £186 13s.4d. for

---

[22] C 145/320/1/35, /40, /42; B(ritish) L(ibrary) Harley Charter 52A/27; C 1/28/111.

[23] *Somerset Medieval Wills 1383–1500*, ed. F.W. Weaver (Somerset Record Society xvi, 1901), 191; *C.C.R. 1454–61*, 439–40.

[24] PROB 11/4 (PCC 3 Stokton, will of Eleanor, Countess of Arundel). At this stage the family bought plate worth £639, Magdalen Coll. Misc. MS. 355.

[25] E 28/88/48.

[26] E 28/88/48; C(alendar of) P(atent) R(olls) 1452–61, 631; C 76/142 rot. 6; *C.C.R. 1454–61*, 411.

his keep, calculated at 6s.8d. daily for 80 weeks, a rate compatible with Lord Hungerford's instructions of £120–£180 a year, but exaggerating the duration of his sojourn in England fourfold. Also included were his political expenses (£786 8s.4d.) and his passage to Florence. Some of these, however, should have been paid from income and at least some repayments were surely paid by November 1461, when the family's indebtedness was calculated at £8624 3s.9d. for the ransom and extras and £358 16s.3d. for Lord Hungerford's debts, making a total of almost £9000.[27] This figure was not accepted without question and we do not know whether it included Moleyns' expenses cited above, which Edward IV's government would not have approved. On this reckoning, the family's total debts amounted to six years income. Allowing for the support of Ladies Hungerford and Moleyns, it might have taken a decade to pay off.[28]

All this was changed by the dynastic revolution and Moleyns' forfeiture. Nothing more could be made from Henry VI's exchequer grant or his licence to export wool fells. The attainder of the third Earl of Northumberland meant that his mother's tenure of her dower was disturbed and that she could not keep up the payments on her daughter's marriage portion. Extra expense was incurred in saving the liberty of both Margaret and her daughter-in-law Lady Moleyns, thus further increasing the family's debts. Finally, the family's tenure of its estates was upset, perhaps for several years, and payments to creditors was interrupted.

Some creditors sought to recover their money by suing – or threatening to sue – the sureties for the sums in their bonds. Although no litigation is recorded until Hilary term 1465, when Richard Quatermains sued for £416 3s.4d. in three actions in common pleas,[29] the problem was already acute in May 1462 and was explicitly stated in March 1463. As it was 'at the requeste and praier of me, the saide Margarete' that the original bonds were sealed, her honour was engaged and drastic action was required to save the sureties harmless. Moveables were sold, including Lord Cromwell's plate at a loss. New loans, carrying interest charges of £945 6s.8d., were contracted to repay the creditors. Above all lands were sold. As a result creditors were repaid, most notably Agnes Forster, who received £300 of £760 due in 1464.[30]

---

[27] C 49/52, original act of attainder 1461.

[28] But only £120 a year was allegedly due from the Moleyns lands (C 1/28/111D), implying repayment over 25 years, and in 1469 only part of the enfeoffed Hungerford lands was considered to be mortgaged, Huntington MS. HAP 3466.

[29] CP 40/814 rot. 79. For what follows, see Historic Manuscripts Commission, 12 *MSS of the Dean & Chapter of Wells* i. 498–9; *CPR 1461–7*, 284; C 81/1492/28–9.

[30] *CPR 1461–7*, 284.

It was to speed up repayments that Margaret obtained a royal licence to sell £200-worth of lands a year in 1463[31] and between 1462 and 1471 she and her grandson Thomas alienated land in altogether thirty transactions. The lands sold were not in fact those that were mortgaged, probably because of uncertainties about the title she had to sell, but consisted mainly of Margaret's own Botreaux lands and certain Hungerford lands acquired by the first two Lords Hungerford and never enfeoffed. No major estates were alienated – none were extended at more than 10 marks in 1462 and on average they were valued at only £4. In the two cases where the purchase price is known, Flexland in Soberton (Hants.) and Cheddar and Shipham (Soms.), it amounts to the surprisingly high rates of 25 and 28 years purchase. While this suggests that prices were not depressed by Moleyns' attainder, the rate is probably inflated by the undervaluations customary in inquisitions: ministers' accounts of Flexland show the extended value to be only two-thirds of the clear annual value and therefore that the purchase price was a more realistic 17 years purchase. If the extents all undervalued to the same degree, which is improbable, the purchase price for the 17 properties in 15 transactions extended at £67 would be £2100 at 25 years purchase. Assuming, which is also unlikely, that the other 16 transactions affected property of equal value to those for which we have extents, the total capital sum received would be £4000. Apart from the suspect calculations, this sum may not have been realised because land may have been alienated in return for other services or in lieu of repayment of debts. Certainly the bulk of the creditors were well-known to Margaret, since they included her brother-in-law Sir Edmund Hungerford, her feoffee Sir Richard Chok, her creditors Richard Quatermains, Robert White and John Tughill, and her servants John Mervyn, Gregory Westby, Thomas Troponell and Nicholas Lower, several of whom based their own landed estates on her sales.[32] Unfortunately we do not know the terms by which any of these bought their lands: certainly Margaret was happy with the terms of sale, as she remained grateful to the purchasers until death. It is a striking testimony to the capital resources of the Hungerfords that £4000-worth of land could be sold without including any key estates.

Assuming that only £9000 was due in 1461 and accepting Margaret's figures for interest charges and political expenses thereafter, the total level of debt and extraordinary expenditure rose to about £13000 by 1471. On 14 January 1471 Margaret described her

---

[31] B.L. Harley Charter 52A/27.
[32] See appendix and sources there cited.

liabilities as £2000 'and more' for the 'salvacion of the Hungerfordis landis' and 4000 marks (£2666 13s.4d.) for the debts of herself and her husband.[33] These round figures imply that extraordinary charges of £8000 had been settled in 1461–71, a remarkable rate of repayment. This would not be met from income, for in 1464–5 and 1468–9 – two years when Margaret was in control – her receiver-general recorded liveries of only £736 16s. and £770 19s.3½d.[34] Sales of land, large though they were, are unlikely to have covered more than half the balance. Possibly one element of the debts, the money due to the Medici, went unpaid. As an alien, Simone Nori was ill-placed to litigate: in 1464 'Lady Hungerford' declined to pay him a penny and failure to repay him was probably a major cause for his insolvency. Margaret's otherwise moral disapproval to unpaid debts, however, suggests an alternative. Nori's principal was secured on the estates of Lady Moleyns,[35] who certainly objected to further payments and wrested her lands from the feoffees. Although Margaret claimed to have paid all such liabilities, she may have regarded Nori's loan as primarily her daughter-in-law's responsibility: her will of 14 January 1471 referred to the debts of herself and her husband, *not* her son.

The will also proposed to borrow a further £1333 13s.4d. to finance her religious foundations, bringing total indebtedness up to £6000 again. This was to be secured on her enfeoffed estates, which were to be held by her feoffees for ten years after her death, a provision repeated in subsequent wills.[36] These later wills cast no light on the actual debt. Since Margaret and her feoffees held the estates for a further fourteen years – until 1485 – all debts were eventually paid. Indeed, in his will in 1487, Sir Walter Hungerford provided for repayment of £160 debts still outstanding, which he was morally bound to pay[37] and which he probably ultimately did pay.

Margaret Hungerford states the costs of Moleyns' capture to the Hungerfords as £10000, more or less. Such ransoms were carefully calculated to the family's means, one-third of its capital assets, and were paid by instalments. Substantial help was received from the crown and from the realisation of capital assets. Even allowing for these, the ransom compelled a complete change in lifestyle for the

[33] C 54/312 m.8d.

[34] SC 6/1119/14–15.

[35] R. De Roover, *The Rise and Decline of the Medici Bank 1397–1494* (Cambridge, Mass. 1963), 473; A. Grundzweig, *Correspondance de la filiale de Bruges des Medici* (Brussels, 1931), 142; C 1/28/111.

[36] C 54/312 m.8d.

[37] *Materials for a History of Henry VII*, ed. W. Campbell (2 vols. Rolls Series 1873–7), ii.123–5.

family. Lords Hungerford and Moleyns, like most magnates, lived up
to their incomes and a little beyond, drawing to a limited extent on
credit. They were unaccustomed to budgeting and major expenditure
was funded by instalments. Lord Moleyns' ransom compelled his
father to cut back his pious bequests to £150[38] – judiciously spread
but nevertheless paltry besides those of the 1st Lord in 1449. Lord
Hungerford mortgaged *all* his estates, his wife Margaret waived her
jointure and dower, and his daughter-in-law Lady Moleyns
surrendered her inheritance and jointure. The lion's share of all
income went to service the debt, curtailing household expenditure for
the two ladies and reducing Moleyns to a pension one-tenth of his
hereditary rights. All extraordinary expenditure was shelved. The
family retained its capital assets undiminished at the price of financial
and political eclipse for many years. No conceivable profits could
obviate such a disaster. The gains of war were unpredictable, the
losses certain and the two seldom balanced for any individual.

The Moleyns ransom could have been borne, but for the disasters
of domestic politics. The worst that could befall, death and attainder,
involved more than the individual. Debts might be unpaid, wills
unperformed, heirs disinherited, dependants unsupported, children
unpreferred, and dowagers confined to their jointures and
inheritances. Even such rights, as the two Percy dowagers found,
were subject to encroachment. The Hungerfords were thus uniquely
fortunate: because of the mortgages, Moleyns had nothing to forfeit,
his relatives retained control of the family estates, and some of the
worst consequences of the attainder were averted.

Attainders generally covered the lands of the offender, whether in
fee simple, tail or to his use, his hereditary expectations, and the
dower of his wife; it did not affect wives' jointures and inheritances or
lands in trust for others. Many heiresses did hold onto their jointure
and inheritances and some trusts did survive the forfeiture of ultimate
heirs.[39] As moveables were also forfeited by attainder, creditors lost
their loans, unless these were secured by mortgages from land. In the
case of the Percies, the crown recognized the prior rights of the
creditors, conceding for repayment not the land themselves – as with
the Hungerfords – but a fixed sum.[40] Had this method been adopted
in the Hungerford case, only the secured debts would have been paid
and the family would have lost control of its lands. Why did the
Hungerford and Percy experiences differ? Part of the answer is that
only certain Percy lands were mortgaged and the two Percy dowagers

---

[38] *Somerset Med. Wills*, 186–92.
[39] M.A. Hicks, 'The Beauchamp Trust 1439–87', below chapter 19.
[40] E 159/241, brevia Hill. 4 Edw. IV m.17.

were assured of dower/jointure and jointure/inheritance respectively, whereas Margaret Hungerford had no such protection and was dependent on what she could save from her late husband's estates. The Percy inheritance was strategically important and sought by the great – by Warwick the kingmaker and his brother; not only were the Hungerford estates less vital and less sought after, but the politically important as sureties were concerned to maintain Hungerford control. A third factor was the character of Margaret Hungerford. While the Percy dowagers certainly took an interest in the family, paying a marriage portion and debts properly the responsibility of the head of the family,[41] Margaret took the lead in saving the Hungerford estates, displaying a remarkable capacity for business in the process.

The remaining lands were won only by adding new liabilities to those already existing, now to be met from reduced resources. Most of the income was assigned to service the debt, capital assets were realised, and the family's standard of living was reduced. By Margaret's will Moleyns' younger sons were to receive only annuities until 1488;[42] their sister Frideswide never married, but took the veil. Margaret accepted crushing liabilities and temporarily reduced the family to political impotence. The vicissitudes and psychological stress for those left at home, to judge from this example, were surely no less than those borne by irreconcilable Lancastrians in the field. While only the Hungerfords clung on to their estates after an attainder, several wives surrendered estates to save their husbands and others paid fines to avoid attainder. Such people incurred severe financial and political penalties, which may well have been more common – though less well documented – than attainders themselves: the Hungerford *writing annexed* speaks for them all.

The principal asset of such indebted families was land, which yielded only a low income – about 5 per cent of its capital value – and was sold only as a last resort. Debts were chargeable at death only on moveable estates, not lands, so that the borrowing capacity of late medieval aristocrats was limited to the value of their chattels. Consequently much expenditure, such as marriage portions and purchases of lands, was made by instalments and much else was financed after death from lands enfeoffed to use.[43] Jewellery or other security was needed for substantial loans and debts were also run up with tradesmen. Perhaps short-term credit was regularly used to

---

[41] *Collectanea Genealogica and Topographica* iii. 168–9; see above.

[42] Hoare, i(2).98.

[43] E.g. P. Jefferies, 'The Medieval Use as Family Law and Custom: The Berkshire Gentry in the fourteenth and fifteenth centuries', *Southern History* i(1979), 54; Hicks, *BIHR* liv. 139–41.

anticipate landed income, but the overall level of unsecured debt does not appear high: in 1478 George, Duke of Clarence owed £325 19s.3d. to his officers; Lord Hungerford owed £358 at death and Lord Moleyns only £400 in 1453.[44] The late middle ages was not a period of high aristocratic indebtedness like the 16th century. Those with substantial debts were obliged, like the Percies, to fund repayments by enfeoffing their estates to the use of their creditors,[45] but this type of mortgage was apparently an innovation unpopular with borrowers and was to be relatively shortlived.

If the credit-ratings of English magnates were low, how could they pay such large ransoms? To agree a ransom was no guarantee to pay. The Hungerfords' chattels were quite inadequate to meet the cost, but Moleyns' obligation of honour was accepted by his family, by the crown, and perhaps also by those bishops and magnates who acted as sureties. It was their bonds – their credit – that gave added security to the creditors, who advanced the money with which the ransom was paid and vindicated Moleyns' honour. To discharge their creditors and save their sureties harmless, the Hungerfords mortgaged all their lands. There was no trust deed, the trust being declared in Lord Hungerford's will, which specifies neither the rate nor order of repayment. Such bonds presumably provided for staggered instalment payments to creditors.

Fifteenth-century England possessed an underdeveloped money market. It is surprising and important that large loans could be raised by individual noblemen. The most important creditor was apparently Simone Nori, whose firm paid Moleyns' French captors. How important were Italian banking services in transmitting, recycling and perhaps ultimately balancing out the profits and losses of war?[46] Although the Hungerfords were Nori's principal English clients – nobody else borrowed on such a scale – he did not meet all their requirements and they had to turn to others as well. Most of the family's other creditors were friends, neighbours and merchants of London and Margaret's own 'country'. Not all can be identified with certainty and some are quite obscure. The Londoners were Geoffrey Boleyn, mercer and alderman, John Plummer, grocer and future alderman, John Forster skinner, John Crook and William Chester.

---

[44] M.A. Hicks, *False, Fleeting, Perjur'd Clarence* (Gloucester, 1980), 142; see above.

[45] See Bean, *Percies*, 99–103. Mortgages were not (yet) among expedients adopted by Richard, Duke of York to deal with his substantial unsecured debts, J.M.W. Bean, 'The Financial Position of Richard, Duke of York', *War and Government in the Later Middle Ages*, ed. J. Gillingham and J.C. Holt (Cambridge, 1984), 191–7.

[46] Sir John Fastolf relied on the services of the Spinola of Genoa, McFarlane, *England in the Fifteenth Century*, 179, 180n, 184.

Provincial creditors included the merchants Robert White of Farnham (Surr.), John Reynold of Leicester (Leic.), James Touker of Bradford-on-Avon (Wilts.), John Tughill of Hungerford (Berks.), the clothier William Stowford of Stowford in Wingfield (Wilts.), and Richard Quatermains, an Oxfordshire esquire. Some may already have been family acquaintances – Touker and Quatermains, for example, had other dealings with Margaret – but probably more important was the fact that most dealt in wool or cloth: Boleyn was a mercer, Crook, Chester, White, Reynold and Tughill were merchants of the staple, Plummer had large stocks of wool in 1468, and Stowford was a clothier.[47] Did the Hungerfords draw on an existing stapler syndicate to supplement the large loans provided by Nori and Forster? It is unclear whether interest was charged for the initial loans, though Nori certainly charged for exchanging English coin into foreign currency. Were creditors also influenced by considerations of patriotic honour? Those contracted in the mid 1460s were certainly at high rates of interest. It is surprising that such risky loans were contracted or that more could be borrowed when mortgages were still outstanding. The Hungerford's debts were unusually large for their date, but there had been more English ransoms before 1453, thus more to be raised from the home money market, and presumably therefore more stringent terms for debtors.

Between 1453 and 1471 surprisingly large sums were available for loan on good security. For a brief period enfeoffment to use was as safe a way to borrow as the long-term mortgage after 1660. Large sums could be repaid over many years, seventeen years in one instance,[48] and increased borrowing may well have resulted. For creditors, this was a profitable and secure means of lending, but as the interest due was fixed regardless of the period of the loan, there seems to have been no incentive to lend for long terms. The mortgage was non-negotiable, the capital could not be realised until repayment, and lenders had no direct control over the rate of payments. Feoffees were chosen by the borrower and enfeoffed to his use. The estates were subject to charges other than the mortgage – e.g. support of the family – and the declaration of trust could be revised or rescinded so long as the feoffor lived. As the common law courts did not recognize trusts, the only (somewhat uncertain) remedies against the feoffees were in chancery. Alternatively sureties could be sued for debt, although in the Hungerford case several mainpernors had died or been attainted and one creditor, Nori, was unable to obtain favourable judgements. Much depended on the

---

[47] E153/520/20; *CPR 1461–7*, 487, 351.
[48] *Collectanea Genealogica and Topographica* iii. 168.

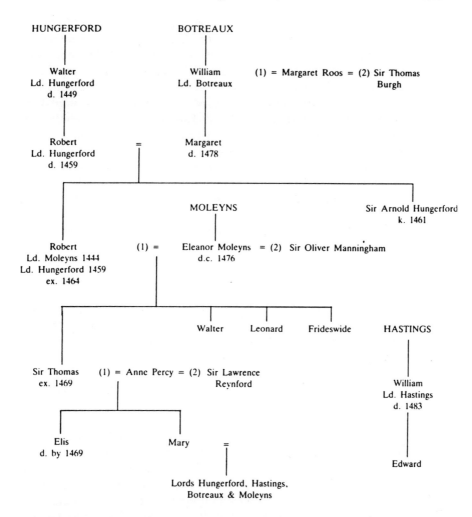

The Hungerford, Botreaux and Moleyns Inheritances

good faith of the borrower, who sometimes – like Lady Moleyns – refused further payments. Fear of damnation for unpaid debts, however, was surprisingly potent: Margaret and Thomas Hungerford, as we have seen, exceeded their legal obligations by raising new loans and selling land to save the sureties; the younger Countess of Northumberland mortgaged her estates to pay the unsecured debts of her attainted, intestate husband; Edward IV spent twenty years settling the debts left by his father Richard, Duke of York; and most of the debts due to Lord Cromwell (d.1455) and his executors were eventually paid.[49] Moral obligation was thus additional security for the lender, but this type of mortgage was decidedly less advantageous and secure for creditors than the post-Restoration variety. In the 16th century, when the common recovery made possible the alienation of entailed lands at a good price, lenders understandably insisted on land sales to meet their debts on time. Tudor debtors like Richard Grey, Earl of Kent, the 6th Earl of Northumberland, and Edward Stafford, Duke of Buckingham all faced short-term loans, penalties for non-payment, and the common recovery: all had to sell.[50] Had the Hungerfords or Percies lived under such a regime, they must have sold much of their estate. The costs of the Hundred Years War to English captives would have been reflected not in temporary loss of income but substantial sales of land.

The Hungerfords, of course, did sell lands, but that was the result of civil not foreign war. They alone avoided the forfeiture that went with political defeat, but not financial and political eclipse, which blighted the family's lives for a generation. After the Wars of the Roses, far from possessing (as expected in 1460) £2000-worth of lands and being the leading magnates in southern England, the Hungerfords' lands were attenuated and divided. While some of the lands alienated were on the periphery of the estate, many others were located on the Wiltshire/Somerset border – the original Hungerford heartland – and had been bought to complement the family's principal estates. The scar was substantial: about £200-worth of lands were alienated, in mortmain and otherwise. What remained was divided, the bulk being carried by Mary Hungerford to her absentee husband in the Midlands and only a few devolving on Walter. For

[49] Ibid. iii. 168–9; Magdalen Coll. Misc. MSS. 355, 361; Bean, 'Richard, Duke of York', 197.

[50] G.W. Bernard, 'The Fortunes of the Greys, Earls of Kent in the early 16th century', *Historical Journal* xxv (1982), 62–80; Bean, *Estates*, 148sqq; C. Rawcliffe, *The Staffords, Earls of Stafford and Dukes of Buckingham 1394–1521* (Cambridge, 1978), 139–42. As Mr Simon Payling in an unpublished paper has now shown that the common recovery existed in the 1450s, why did creditors postpone using it to pressurise lenders? 'Law and Arbitration in Nottinghamshire 1399–1461'.

McFarlane this was natural attrition, the result of Thomas Hungerford's failure to leave more than a daughter. But Thomas died prematurely, executed in 1469. He and his wife were both young and fertile – Mary was a baby – and had previously had a son, Elis, who had predeceased his father.[51] In 1469 there was every likelihood that they would have other children to succeed them. Had Thomas lived longer and left a son, the family and its estates would have been undivided. Had he left daughters, the result would have been different. It was not *natural* wastage that caused the Hungerfords to lose their inheritance. Only in 1536, again by his own efforts, did another Walter Hungerford of Heytesbury again reach the peerage. The effects of war on the Hungerfords were not, as McFarlane thought, 'purely temporary', nor were the alienated lands the only 'permanent scar', nor indeed can the costs be counted in purely monetary terms.

Appendix

Alienations of Land 1462–7

This appendix is a provisional record of alienations between 1462–78. Although most properties listed were sold, direct evidence of sale rarely survives, and it is possible that some alienations, particularly minor ones, have been missed.

Members of Margaret's family are identified by their Christian names: William was William, Lord Botreaux (d. 1462); Margaret was Margaret, Lady Hungerford and Botreaux (d. 1478); Thomas was Sir Thomas Hungerford (d. 1469) and Anne was his wife; Walter was Thomas' brother Sir Walter Hungerford (d. 1516) and Frideswide his sister. (B) signifies Botreaux and (H) denotes Hungerford lands. Valuations are taken from extents: figures for 1462 are from Lord Botreaux's inquisition post mortem. (C 140/7/15).

Berkshire
Upton Moyles (B): 1463 Margaret, Thomas & Anne to Hugh atte Fenne and others feoffees of Geoffrey Kidwelly. Value: £3/6/8d 1484. Price: at least £200. *CCR 1461–8* 190; CP 25(1)/13/87/8; C 141/5/5/2.

---

[51] C 1/28/111B.

Buckingham

Hardwick (B): 1468 Margaret to Archbishop Neville and others, perhaps feoffees of Sir Thomas Bryan, CJ. *CCR 1461–8* no. 112; *VCH Bucks*. iii.364.

Cornwall

Botreaux Molland & Knowlston (B): 1472 Margaret to Sir Philip Courtenay. Value: £10 1462; £26 1487. *CCR 1468–76* no. 1078; *Calendar of Inquisitions post mortem Henry VII*, i, no. 461.

Lananta & lands Boswythgy & Tyrwarnaill (B): By 1470. Margaret, Thomas & Anne to feoffees & to other feoffees 1466. *CCR 1461–8*, 386; CP 25(1)/34/44/12; WRO Acc 490/1510.

Trefrys (B): 1470 Margaret to John Glyn. Release: Walter 1470. Value: £5 1462. CP 40/833 rot. 128d; *CCR 1468–76*, no. 552.

Trenuddres: 1466. Margaret to Martin Hopkin. Huntington Library MS. HAD 2207.

Devon

St Winnow (B), reversion on death of Sir Thomas and Margaret Burgh: 1469 Margaret to Nicholas Lower. Value: £6/13/4d 1462. CP 25(1)/34/44/16.

Wolmerston capital messuage: 1463 Margaret to William & Joan Estcote. HMC 78 *Hastings* i.256.

Dorset

Folke chapel (H): 1472 Margaret to Salisbury cathedral chapter, above, 89.

Gloucestershire

Clifton by Bristol (B): 1463 Margaret to Henry Sampson and others feoffees for John Carpenter, Bishop of Worcester for Westbury College, *CCR 1461–8*, 174; *VCH Gloucs*. ii.108.

Hampshire

Bodenham by Fareham & Rockford Moyles (B): 1465 Margaret to Robert White merchant of Farnham. Values: £6/13/4d 1462, £6 1469. CP 40/814 rot. 303d; C 140/32/5/6.

Binstead Wyke and Binstead St. Clair (B). By 1467. Margaret to Robert White & his son John White. Values: £5 1462 & 5 marks 1469. C 140/32/5/6.

Flexland in Soberton (B): 1465 Margaret, Thomas & Anne to Winchester College. Values: £2 1462; c. £3/2s. 1460s. CP 25(1)/207/34/4; CP 40/816 rot. 155; Winchester College Muniments 10157–62, 10185–93.

Pennington by Lymington (B): 1465. Margaret to Robert White and feoffees. Values: £2 1462, £3 6s. 8d. 1469. C 140/32/5/6; CP 40/814 attornies rot. 1; C 140/32/5/6.

Somerset

Cadbury Castle & Stokeley English: 1465 Margaret, Thomas & Anne to Gregory Westby. CP 40/816 rot. 80d; CP 25(1)/46/91/10.

Cheddar & Shipham (B): 1463 Margaret to Bishop Beckington. Value: £10 1462. Price: £280. HMC 12 *Wells* i.498–99.

Cricket St. Thomas (B): 1466 Margaret to Stephen Preston. Releases: Thomas & Anne 1466; Walter 1472. Value: £6/13/4d 1470. *CCR 1461–8*, 394–5; *1468–76*, no. 1139; *Pedes Finium*, ed. E. Green (SRS xxii, 1906), 132; C 140/49/12/2.

Feltham in Frome (H): 1465. Thomas to Thomas & Cecily Rogers. Releases: Margaret 1465, Frideswide 1469. BL Add. Charters 40056–8, 40062–3; CP 40/816 rot. 2; *CCR 1468–76* no. 228.

Flintford (H): 1465 Thomas to John son of Sir Richard Chok. Releases: Thomas, Margaret & Anne 1465; Frideswide 1469. CP 40/816 rott. 2–3; SRO DD/SAS FR 56–8; *CCR 1468–76*, no. 231.

Lockington (B): By 1468. Margaret to feoffees of Sir Edmund Hungerford. Releases: Frideswide 1469; Margaret 1471; Sir Edmund Hungerford 1471; Walter 1470. Values: £3/10/4d 1462; CP 40/838 rott. 1–2; *CCR 1468–76*, no. 239; Magdalen College Oxford MS Corton 94.

Lands in Poblow & Pensford (B): 1463 Margaret to Sir Richard & William Chok. Releases: Lady Moleyns & Frideswide 1469. CP 40/816 rott. 2, 80d; CP 25(1)/46/91/10.

Raddon by Frome & Standerwick (B): 1462 Lord Botreaux to Sir Richard Chok. Releases: Margaret 1462; Lady Moleyns 1469; Frideswide 1469. *CCR 1461–8* 143–4; *Pedes Finium*, ed. E. Green (SRS xxii 1906), 137; *CCR 1468–76*, no. 230.

Lands in Stockwood by Keynsham & Cameley (B): 1465 Margaret to John Chok, Sir Richard Chok, and others. Releases: Lady Moleyns & Frideswide 1469. CP 40/816 *carte* rot. 2; *CCR 1468–76* no. 230; *Pedes Finium*, 137.

Wiltshire

Colmans tenement in Bishops Knoyle: 1474–5 Margaret, Walter & Leonard to Roger & Agnes Norman. SRO DD/SAS H348 ff. 341–4.

Charlton *alias* Hopgras: 1465 Margaret, Thomas & Anne to John Tughill. CP 40/816 rot. 80d.

Cheverell Burnell & Cheverell Hales & advowson of Great Cheverell (B): 1472 Margaret to Heytesbury hospital. Hicks, *WAM* lxxviii.67.

Great Cheverell advowson.: 1470 Margaret to Thomas Troponell.

Also other lands, 1464. *VCH Wilts.* x.43; *CCR 1468–76*, no. 245.

Corton (H): 1466 Margaret to Richard Quatermains. C 140/62/7/6; Magdalen College, Oxford MS Corton 94.

Fisherton de la Mare: By 1464 Margaret to John Mervyn. *VCH Wilts.* viii.39.

Farnhill in Fonthill & Fonthill Gifford (H): 1472 Margaret to John Mervyn. W.R. Drake, *Fasciculus Mervinensis* (1873), 56; Hoare iii, Dunworth hundred, 15.

Hardenhuish: 1468 Margaret to John Mervyn. Release. Frideswide 1469. *CCR 1461–8,* 251; *1468–76*, no. 222.

Lands in Heytesbury & elsewhere (H): 1464/66 Margaret & Thomas to John Mervyn, Releases: Thomas 1465; Frideswide 1469. WRO Acc 490/1496; CP 40/816 carte rot. 1; *CCR 1461–8,* 272; *1468–76* no. 223–5(3).

Imber chapel (H). 1472 Margaret to Salisbury cathedral chapter. Above, 89.

Tenements in Norton Bavant & Warminster: 1464 Margaret to John Mervyn, *CCR 1461–8,* 272.

Ogbourne Maizey (B): 1465 Margaret to Nicholas Hall. Release: Frideswide 1469. Value: £6/13/4d 1478. CP 40/816 rot. 123d; *CCR 1468–76* no. 229; C 140/66/9/4; *VCH Wilts.* xii.143.

Winterbourne Homington (H): 1472 Margaret to Salisbury cathedral chapter. Above, 89.

11

The Changing Role of the Wydevilles
in Yorkist Politics to 1483

The Wydevilles are one of the most unpopular families in English history: even their biographers have hardly concealed their dislike and have accepted improbable charges made against them.[1] Yet contemporary witnesses were not unanimous in condemnation and at least one hostile chronicler was biased, as Professor Lander has shown.[2] Lander did not re-evaluate the political role of the Wydevilles in the light of his discovery, which is the purpose of this paper. It will concentrate on the benefit which the Wydevilles received from the crown, rather than on their services. The name Wydeville will cover not only the queen, her parents, brothers and sisters, but also her elder sons Thomas and Richard Grey.

All previous historians have begun by asking: who were the Wydevilles in 1464? Their family tree has been traced in the *Complete Peerage* and glossed by Lander, who observes:

> Quite apart from the high birth of Jacquetta of Luxembourg, the social status of the Wydevilles . . . was not as lowly as many historians have assumed.

They were, in short, 'a decent county family' with lands in five counties, who had filled local offices since the mid-14th century, had served with distinction in France, and had started to marry into the peerage in the 1450s. While all this is true, it does not tell the whole story.

In the first place Richard Wydeville, the future Earl Rivers, was not heir of the prominent family of Northamptonshire gentry; he was son of another Richard, younger brother of the Thomas Wydeville who died about 1434. The male line of the senior branch died with Thomas, whose heirs were his sisters of the whole blood. Richard received one entailed

---

Except where otherwise indicated, all references to MSS. sources in these notes refer to documents in the Public Records Office, London: e.g. C139/77, *n.* 5, *n.* 7, *n.* 10.

[1] E.g. their alleged responsibility for the death of the Earl of Desmond, D. MacGibbon, *Elizabeth Woodville 1437-92* (1938), pp. 42-3.

[2] J.R. Lander, *Crown and Nobility 1450-1509* (1976), 110n. The next eleven paragraphs are based on *ibid.* pp. 104-25; *C.P.* xi. pp. 15-21.

manor and Grafton itself, which Thomas left him in his will,[3] but he can never have expected to inherit much. The heiress whom he is supposed to have married has not been satisfactorily identified, nor is it known what she inherited. Richard had to build his fortune more or less from scratch.

His life was spent in the service of the Lancastrian kings and royal dukes. At one time he was councillor, chamberlain, seneschal of Normandy and treasurer of finances to the Regent Bedford. A successful military career while the English were winning should have enriched him, but apparently it did not. Like Fastolf he bought manors, but at most two, one of which he wanted to be sold to pay his debts.[4] His son, the future Earl Rivers, thus inherited only four manors in three shires; sufficient only to support a minor role among the local gentry to which he properly belonged.

The elder Richard's career explains how the younger Richard had access to the widowed Duchess of Bedford, whom he married, thereby transforming his prospects. She was Jacquetta of Luxemberg, member of a great European family, endowed with wealth and powerful connections, yet still aged no more than twenty. Although initially annoyed, Henry VI's government acknowledged the marriage and assigned Jacquetta her dower.

Bedford had an income of over £4,000 in England alone, of which Jacquetta was assigned a third. He had also bought land in England and held extensive estates in France, most of which he settled on her for life.[5] Jacquetta's income was twice the qualifying level for an earldom and she and her husband seem to have been without financial problems until the mid-1450s.[6] By then their French income had been cut off and Henry VI's poverty was delaying payment of the annuities of which Jacquetta's dower largely consisted.

In 1414-15 Bedford had been granted £4,000 a year in annuities, to be exchanged for lands of equal value as these became available. Relatively little had been redeemed at his death, when annuities exceeded £3,000. Jacquetta's dower consisted mainly of annuities from the exchequer and duchy of Cornwall and of third shares rather than the whole manors.[7]

On her death her dower would revert to the crown and her husband and

[3] G. Baker, *History and Antiquities of the County of Northampton* (2 vols. 1822-30), ii. pp. 162, 252-3.

[4] Certainly 'Shalford' (Beds.) (*Register of Henry Chichele, Archbishop of Canterbury, 1414-43*, ed. E.F. Jacob, ii (Cant. & York Soc. xlii), 608) and probably the Mote, Maidstone (Kent).

[5] C 139/77; *C.P.R. 1461-7*, pp. 169-70; E.C. Williams, *My Lord of Bedford 1389-1435* (1963), p. 247.

[6] A £60-annuity was twice left uncollected for five years before 1454; afterwards it was collected promptly, E 101/143/13/1-6.

[7] *C.P.R. 1413-16*, pp. 259, 370; C 139/77.

children would be left with only his inheritance. It was therefore sensible to make the most of her dower by using the income to buy land or by converting her life estate into something more permanent. As she held only third shares, Jacquetta had not only to improve her title to any estate but also to secure possession of the other two-thirds, which were generally granted to others. Evidently this called for expenditure or a display of royal favour which was not forthcoming. Indeed, some lands had to be exchanged for annuities, and many grants made to others from the Bedford estates included the reversion of Jacquetta's share.[8] Altogether she secured only one manor and annuities of £139 10s. 7d. a year for their children; in 1455 most of this was again restricted to Jacquetta's lifetime by act of resumption.[9] In 1461 their eight scattered manors were surely inadequate endowment for a baron.

Jacquetta and Richard needed success on the marriage market, if they were to provide for all their thirteen children. By 1461 they had concluded three marriages: Jacquetta Wydeville had married Lord Strange of Knockin by 1450; Elizabeth Wydeville married John Grey, son and heir of Lord and Lady Ferrers of Groby *c.*1452; and in 1460 Anthony Wydeville married Elizabeth, in her own right Lady Scales. As these baronies were older than that of Rivers, the Wydevilles were certainly marrying above themselves. They were connecting themselves with families like the Greys of Ruthin, Bourchiers, Arundels and even the House of York. But their new in-laws did not belong to the higher nobility in rank, wealth or importance. Assessed for income tax at £666 in 1436, the Ferrers of Groby barony was the richest of the three, but it was divided beween the heirs male and heirs general in 1449: Elizabeth, Lady Ferrers inherited only the title and the less important estates.[10] Even allowing for her husband's Astley inheritance, she was poorer than her predecessors. Early in 1460 Rivers had provided for only two children; even after Anthony's marriage nine remained single.

Jacquetta's kinship to the king and queen could account for Richard's elevation to the Garter, to the peerage, and to the royal council. This is also suggested by his promotion in rank before becoming a councillor, but there is little other evidence that he carried weight at court. Those with undoubted influence over Henry VI secured grants from Bedford's estates which Rivers wanted himself.[11] His inability to compete for favour at a

---

[8] *Ibid. 1436-41*, pp. 133, 260.

[9] *Ibid. 1436-41*, pp. 438, 479, 523; *1441-6*, p. 453; *1446-52*, pp. 185, 205; *Rot. Parl.* v. pp. 310-11. For the next paragraph, see *C.P.* v. pp. 356-61; xi. p. 507; xii. i. p. 356.

[10] C 139/119/10/2; H.L. Gray, 'Incomes from land in England in 1436', *E.H.R.* xlix (1934), p. 617.

[11] E.g. Cardinal Beaufort, the Dukes of Suffolk and Warwick, Lords Cromwell, Beauchamp of Powicke and Sudeley, *C.P.R. 1436-41*, pp. 133, 260, 384, 407; *1441-6*, pp. 400-1; *1446-52*, p. 174.

time of exceptional royal prodigality shows how modest his influence really was. He seems to have avoided committing himself politically to either Suffolk or Somerset, perhaps because his primary interests were military. He served repeatedly in France, rising to be seneschal of Gascony and (like his father) lieutenant of Calais. His useful military talents may have contributed to his pardon in 1461 and his re-appearance in the council by 1463, as he certainly had little influence with Edward IV.[12]

The Wydevilles clearly had too few lands to qualify as leaders of county society, let alone maintain a peerage, for which martial talents were not enough. A lucky marriage gave Rivers wealth, connections and opportunities, enabling him to rise from the lesser gentry to become a potentially impoverished peer. Everything depended on Jacquetta's dower and her life, so he remained an upstart, in spite of attempts to construct a noble past. Such a background hardly fitted his daughter as queen and, as Professor Ross has shown,[13] Jacquetta's lineage was not enough either.

Nevertheless Elizabeth Wydeville did marry Edward IV as her second husband. Professor Lander has refuted the assertion of earlier historians that Edward was so blindly enamoured that he allowed the Wydevilles 'unbridled licence' in pursuit of their desires. Elizabeth, he pointed out, received a smaller dower than her predecessor. Lord Rivers became an earl, treasurer and constable of England, but otherwise received only minor rewards. His son Anthony received only four grants before 1469. None of Elizabeth's other brothers or sons received anything during Edward's first reign. These grants were relatively small, 'especially when compared with those made to . . . Lord Hastings and Lord Herbert' or the Nevilles, who certainly 'took more from the royal bounty in titles, lands, offices and money grants than did the Wydevilles'. Lander's interpretation rests explicitly on the comparison of grants to the Wydevilles with those made to other royal favourites. The contrast is telling, but it begs two questions: what provision was appropriate for the Wydevilles and what had Edward to give?

In 1461 Edward enjoyed all the crown lands plus those forfeited by a third of the nobility and many gentry. Such vast resources gave great scope for patronage, permitting him to raise obscure protégés to the high nobility. Usually a king's capacity to give was severely limited, for the only lands normally in his hands were escheats. His everyday patronage consisted of favours of relatively short duration. When endowing a duke or earl, kings seldom had enough lands and made up the requisite income with annuities instead. There was thus a natural check on royal

---

[12] Historical Manuscripts Commission, *78 Hastings*, i. pp. 301-2.
[13] C.D. Ross, *Edward IV* (1974), pp. 89-90.

generosity. To endow his Tudor half-brothers with the minimum income appropriate for an earl, Henry VI had to recover property formerly given to others.[14] If 1,000 marks was all a king's half-brother was worth, what was suitable for a father-in-law or brother-in-law?

By 1464 most forfeitures had been given away, together with the county of Chester and much of the duchies of Lancaster and Cornwall. Edward could not endow the Wydevilles on the scale of the early 1460s; comparisons with Herbert, Hastings and the Nevilles are therefore inapplicable. They could only be so endowed by permanently disinheriting the crown or by recovering property formerly given to others. Lands could be resumed by persuading grantees to surrender them, which meant buying them out at full valuation, or by forcing grantees to give them up. Edward could either incur great expenditure or make enemies of committed supporters. The principal beneficiaries of his patronage had been those to whom he owed most, who had influence with him, and whom he was least willing to offend. He understandably declined to redistribute patronage in the Wydevilles's favour.

What did Edward regard as appropriate provision for the Wydevilles? One pointer is Lord Rivers's earldom, which morally obliged Edward to make his hereditary income up to 1,000 marks. Edward did not do this, making only two grants in tail, but he did give Rivers two great offices and an additional income of £1,586 as councillor, treasurer and earl.[15] Rivers's income was certainly doubled to over three thousand pounds, more than that of any immediate contemporary other than Warwick and Clarence. On his death, his heir Anthony was to keep the constableship, which would suffice with his Wydeville and Scales possessions to sustain the estate of earl. Moreover, Anthony received several minor grants, together with the Isle of Wight and Carisbrooke castle. These had been given to Sir Geoffrey Gate, who exchanged them with Anthony in return for four manors elsewhere, two from Jacquetta's dower: the king merely renouncd his reversionary right and confirmed the arrangement.[16] When the Earl of Worcester went to Ireland as deputy in 1467, he sold his offices in England: Anthony secured the constableship of Portchester castle and Rivers the constableship of England, probably at Edward's expense. Another manor obtained by Rivers was surrendered by the queen for compensation elsewhere[17] and Lord Mountjoy gave up the treasureship of

---

[14] B.P. Wolffe, *Royal Demesne in English History* (1971), pp. 137, 250sqq; *Rot. Parl.* v. pp. 251-2.

[15] *C.P.R. 1461-7*, p. 516; *1467-77*, p. 19; C.L. Scofield, *Life and Reign of Edward the Fourth* (1923), i. p. 398. Rivers received £200 a year as councillor, not 200 marks, E 404/73/1/17.

[16] *C.P.R. 1461-7*, p. 535; *C.C.R. 1461-8*, p. 380; *1468-76*, no. 595; *Feet of Fines for Essex*, iv, ed. P.H. Reaney and M. Fitch (1964), p. 61; E 159/243, Rec. Mich. 6 Edw. IV m.2; Hill. 6 Edw. IV m.5.

[17] Passenham (Northants.) DL 37/37/8,/13.

England for a barony, a small annuity in tail, and 1,000 marks in cash.[18] Edward's patronage was more substantial than Lander allowed.

The other way in which the Wydevilles were advanced was by marriage. By the end of 1466 five of Elizabeth's sisters had married the Duke of Buckingham, and the heirs of the Earls of Kent, Essex, Arundel and of Lord Herbert; her elder son had married the Duke of Exeter's heiress; and a brother had married the Dowager-Duchess of Norfolk. Generally regarded as of the king's making, these matches have commonly been condemned as offensive to the magnates, especially the Nevilles. Professor Lander, however, traced this interpretation back to the *Annales* of the pseudo-William Worcestre, a Neville partisan whose hostility was due to bias. Even this chronicler made no comment about three of the marriages and objected to the others with varying intensity. In only one instance, so Lander argued, had anyone outside Warwick's immediate circle grounds for offence, and in this one case – the Herbert match – it was not the marriage itself which was condemned, but the bridegroom's creation as Lord Dunster.[19] There was little reason to suppose that the marriages gave much offence. Again Lander's remarks are persuasive and were followed by Professor Ross in his *Edward IV*, in which he pointed out that 'other Yorkist noblemen had no scruple about allowing their sons and daughters to marry the queen's kinsfolk', even when they 'had a free choice in their . . . marriages'.[20] Grounds exist, however, for doubting whether Edward was as passive and the Wydevilles as innocent as Lander would have us believe.

Let us begin by looking once more at the only marriage for which the contract survives, that with the Herberts. As Mr. Pugh pointed out, Herbert sought the freehold of two lordships held at farm and for a term and also Jacquetta's third share of St. Briavels and the forest of Dean. Herbert believed that Edward's consent could be secured by the Wydevilles, who agreed to do their 'effectual part and devoir and cause our Souerayn Lord the King' to comply. The resultant patent was based on a petition by Rivers, which recited Jacquetta's surrender of St. Briavels specifically for the benefit of Herbert. Rivers's success is hardly surprising, since the contract was made 'at the instance of our Souereyn Lord the King and his pleasure'. Evidently Edward was willing to make concessions and raised no difficulties about granting the reversion of lands already held by the two parties. Since one lordship was farmed at 100

---

[18] 'Annales rerum anglicarum', *Letters and Papers illustrative of the Wars of the English in France*, ed. J. Stevenson (Rolls series, 1864), ii.ii. p. 788; Scofield, *Edward IV*, i. pp. 397-8; *C.P.R. 1461-7*, p. 444; *1467-77*, pp. 19, 41. Mountjoy was satisfied, later remembering Rivers in his will, but Warwick was displeased, Worcestre, *Annales*, p. 785; *Tesamenta Vetusta*, ed. N.H. Nicolas (1826), i. p. 334.

[19] Lander, *Crown and Nobility*, pp. 110n, 114.

[20] Ross, *Edward IV*, p. 94.

marks,[21] Herbert's inducement beyond the marriage portion was substantial.

The same pattern emerges in other cases. When William Bourchier married Anne Wydeville, Edward verbally promised lands worth £100 a year and a lump sum of unknown size. In payment he granted forfeited land in East Anglia and a licence to ship 1,000 woollen cloths.[22] It was presumably the contract for the Arundel marriage which is behind a grant in 1467 to the earl for life, with remainder to his son Thomas and the latter's heirs male by Margaret Wydeville, who was described in the patent as daughter of Earl Rivers and the Duchess of Bedford, mother of the queen. Apparently this was what Arundel wanted: before making the grant, Edward had to obtain the surrender of Lord Say, to whom he had previously given it.[23] The marriage of the Duke of Buckingham was in the king's gift and it was again the king who 'made the marriage' between Thomas Grey and Anne Holland, the Exeter heiress.[24] One wonders what inducement was offered to Lord Grey of Ruthin to marry his heir to a Wydeville. A few suggestions may be made. First of all, Grey became Earl of Kent a few months after his sons's marriage. Secondly, Edward pandered to his dislike for Herbert's advancement in North Wales, near his lordship of Ruthin, by substituting Grey for Herbert as chief justice of Merioneth and constable of Harlech castle. Finally, Anthony Grey received a substantial grant of forfeited lands.[25]

The other marriages were more complicated. That between Thomas Grey and Anne Holland was arranged at Edward's behest, on payment of 4,000 marks by the queen, and in place of an existing understanding with the Nevilles. The Duke of Exeter was an unreconciled Lancastrian, whose lands were forfeit, but his duchess was the king's elder sister. She was granted the whole inheritance for life, together with some forfeited manors. In 1466 she settled her jointure and five other manors on Elizabeth's feoffees, probably in trust for the marriage. She was allowed to convert her life estate into tail and in 1469 the ultimate remainder was reserved to the queen, her heirs and assigns.[26] Evidently, come what may, Elizabeth wanted the Holland inheritance.

Lander says that the 'diabolical marriage' of Katherine, Duchess of Norfolk and Sir John Wydeville – a sexagenarian and a teenager – was not

---

[21] T.B. Pugh, 'The magnates, knights and gentry', *Fifteenth-century England, 1399-1509*, ed. S.B. Chrimes, C.D. Ross and R.A. Griffiths (1972), pp. 92-3; Cardiff Cent. Libr. MS. 5. 7, ff. 52-4, 57; *C.P.R. 1461-7*, p. 119; C81/809/1960.

[22] *C.P.R. 1467-77*, p. 25; *1476-85*, p. 179; C81/806/1814.

[23] *C.P.R. 1461-7*, pp. 125, 547.

[24] Worcestre, *Annales*, p. 786.

[25] *C.P.R. 1461-7*, pp. 271, 352, 355, 457, 467; *1467-77*, p. 485; *C.C.R. 1461-8*, p. 283; *C.P.* vii. p. 164.

[26] *C.P.R. 1461-7*, pp. 7, 104-5, 533; *1467-77*, pp. 32-3, 37-8. For her jointure, see DL 41/2/8.

unusual. Her career was certainly nightmarish for the Mowbrays, as she retained most of the family estate for half a century and her fourth marriage threatened their reversionary rights. The Wydevilles, however, were interested primarily in her dower and jointure from her third husband, Viscount Beaumont, as their son had been attainted and the reversion belonged to the crown. In 1467, following their marriage, the reversion of six Lincolnshire manors was granted to Sir John, with remainder to his heirs male. He later had seisin of these and certain other manors in her right.[27] On her death, which might well have been soon, he would have a substantial estate with which to endow a second marriage and family. One wonders whether Katherine married him to protect herself against powerful reversionary interests, such as the Duke of Clarence and Lord Hastings, or because the Wydevilles themselves threatened her security of tenure. Had Sir John been satisfied with the reversion on her death, there could be no objection, but it was surely improper to secure immediate possession by marrying the old lady.

Evidently strong inducements beyond the portion were needed for magnates to marry their offspring to the Wydevilles: on the open market Herbert's heir could hardly have commanded a larger portion. Incentives were even needed for those already related to the Wydevilles. Edward was willing to commit resources to alliances from which he had nothing to gain, as the Wydevilles's partners were steadfastly loyal. Probably he provided £100-worth of land to four couples and at least one portion. He was offering patronage that would otherwise have been withheld: if the recipients could have obtained it some other way, they would have had no incentive for a Wydeville marriage. Edward enabled the Wydevilles to outbid all other competitors on the marriage market, probably aggrieving others apart from the Nevilles. Without Edward's support the marriages would not have occurred.

The Norfolk marriage illustrates how royal favour could be used to wring concessions from others. Edward might intervene directly on the Wydevilles's behalf: for example, he tried to foist Sir Richard Wydeville on the Order of St. John as prior. Likewise, when Maud, Lady Willoughby was induced in 1465 to convey sixteen manors of her Cromwell inheritance to Anthony Wydeville, probably for fear for her Lancastrian husband, Sir Gervase Clifton, royal pressure was employed.[28] More frequently, with or without Edward's knowledge, the Wydevilles exploited his power to extort concessions or to render rival claims inoperable. Realising by 1466 that his wife would bear him no children, Anthony persuaded her to re-settle her inheritance on him jointly, with remainder to his feoffees rather than her heirs. Again it was

[27] *C.P.R. 1467-77*, p. 19; C 140/31/12/2.
[28] Scofield, *Edward IV*, i. p. 499n; *C.C.R. 1461-8*, p. 330.

Anthony who seized Caister castle on the pretext that John Paston was a royal serf. It was he who bought lands at North Mymms (Herts.) and then denied that it was copyhold or owed any service. His mother – or was it his father? – bought an invalid claim to a manor they coveted.[29] They were apparently ready to pursue any avenue of gain, however trifling and unworthy of their attention.

The Wydevilles could reasonably expect dower for the queen and some provision for their main line, but they should surely have supported other relatives themselves. Edward, however, felt obliged to provide for them all. Each sister-in-law was to be at least a countess and his stepson was to be a duke. What else, one wonders, did he plan for Sir John and Sir Richard Wydeville? Some grants to the Herberts, Bourchiers and Arundels were effectively patronage to the Wydevilles, who might conceivably have secured them for the main line, had they not placed their daughters first.[30] Moreover, Elizabeth received not only her dower, which was several times adjusted in her favour, but her Ferrers jointure and at least £866. 13s. 4d. to support the Stafford boys and her elder daughters.[31]

The family did not depend wholly on royal favour, as Elizabeth and Rivers could attract and reward dependants. As early as October 1464 Elizabeth was making appointments under her great seal.[32] Her officers were not chosen for her, though key figures must have required Edward's approval: this was assured for her chamberlain, their mutual kinsman Lord Berners. Kinship, neighbourhood and service account for her choice of Sir Humphrey Bourchier and Jacques Haute as her carvers and John Dyve and Robert Isham as her attorney- and solicitor-generals.[33] Even had she wished, she could hardly have staffed her household exclusively from Wydeville dependants. Some were certainly king's servants and Elizabeth wisely engaged Edward's law officers as counsel. Unlike her household, her estates were already staffed and her nominees took over only gradually. Besides, her exercise of patronage had to be reconciled with her financial needs, just as the exchequer was primarily an organ of royal finance rather than of patronage for her father. Rivers as treasurer distributed most offices, leases and custodies to people unconnected with his family, but some went to his son, to dependants or to political allies.[34]

---

[29] E 149/226/6; CP 25(1)/294/74/37; *Essex Feet of Fines*, iv. p. 62; *Paston Letters and Papers of the Fifteenth Century*, ed. N. Davis (2 vols. 1971-6), ii. p. 374; William Worcestre, *Itineraries*, ed. J.H. Harvey (1969), pp. 188-9; Baker, *Northants.* i. pp. 353-4; Westminster Abbey MS. 4784.

[30] E.g. when Jacquetta's dower was surrendered, see above p. 63.

[31] *C.P.R. 1461-7*, pp. 463-4; *1467-77*, p. 110.

[32] A.R. Myers, 'The Household of Queen Elizabeth Woodville, 1466-7', *Bulletin of the John Rylands Library*, 1 (1967-8), p. 455. This paragraph is based on *ibid.* 1. pp. 207-35, 443-81.

[33] Bourchier, Haute and Dyve were relatives; for Isham, see *C.C.R. 1447-54*, p. 257.

[34] E.g. C 81/1633/22,/27,/36.

The hub of the connection was Elizabeth's household, where she was surrounded by her sisters and sister-in-law, her sons and daughters, and by more distant relatives like the Hautes, Fogges, Hastings and Donnes. Her brothers committed themselves politically to a prospective kinsman,[35] but Rivers was more cautious. Probably it was he and Jacquetta who resolved to advance their younger children, even at the expense of the main line: Jacquetta was to provide for all her offspring in her will.[36] Presumably Rivers decided family policy, just as he directed Elizabeth's affairs without formal authority.[37] His elder sons had access to the king but Rivers's own influence seems more important, chary though he was of exercising it. He used Elizabeth as intermediary: she could secure new grants, convert feefarms from estates into outright grants, and could pass them on by surrendering them.[38] Presumably she adopted this technique because Edward would not make an outright grant. He was not subservient to the Wydevilles, but had other advisers and recipients of his bounty.

Among those with access to his ear in 1465 were twenty councillors, the chief officers of state and household, and assorted nobles.[39] Some, already related to the queen, hastily strengthened their ties, while others forged new ones, so the Wydevilles gained that acceptance among the nobility and politically influential which emerged in the pageantry of Elizabeth's coronation, the tournament with the Bastard of Burgundy, and the marriage of Margaret of York. Impressive though their rise was, they were never the sole source of patronage and power: 'the Ryvers been [never] soo hie that I coude hardly scape thorw theym'.[40] Others retained or even increased their influence. Notable among these were the Bourchiers, several of whom served Elizabeth, but who retained their own independent influence with Edward. A closer alliance was forged with another favourite, Lord Herbert. Their marriage alliance was fortified by favours secured for him by Rivers and the queen.[41] The advance of the Wydevilles and Herberts at the expense of the Nevilles was marked by Edward's increasingly anti-French foreign policy, which the former actively promoted. The Wydeville marriage gave the Nevilles several grounds for offence and the plans of Herbert, already at odds with

[35] Davis, *Paston Letters*, i. p. 540; ii. pp. 571-2.

[36] Baker, *Northants*. i. p. 354.

[37] E.g. B.L. Additional MS. 48031 f. 42v.

[38] E.g. to her father and Herbert, see notes 17 and 41.

[39] C 49/59-65; E 28/89/21,/23,/24,/37,/40,/41. For what follows, see G. Smith, *Coronation of Elizabeth Wydeville* (1975 edn.); *Excerpta Historica*, ed. S. Bentley (1840), pp. 176-212, 227-39.

[40] *Great Chronicle of London*, ed. A.H. Thomas and I.D. Thornley (1938), p. 208.

[41] C 81/1633/36. Elizabeth surrendered Crendon (Bucks.), Haseley and Pyrton (Oxon.) in his favour, DL 37/37/20,/22; R. Somerville, *History of the Duchy of Lancaster* (1953), i. p. 138n.

Warwick, threatened him and Clarence. The violence of Warwick's enmity forced the king's favourites to make common cause against a common foe. As members of the extreme anti-Neville faction, however, the Wydevilles could not command support from all their relatives against Warwick: some could work with him or even maintain friendly relations.

We are now in a position to consider the charges of Warwick's 1469 manifesto,[42] which claimed that Edward's favourites had insinuated themselves into his counsels to the exclusion of the lords of his blood and had then given him bad advice to their own profit, securing grants beyond their deserts, and denying or perverting justice. The manifesto is propaganda, but should not be wholly dismissed, as it depended for its effect on its relevance and topicality. Moreover Warwick practised what he preached, objecting neither to the influence of his own nor the king's kin, but to that of the upstarts – Rivers, his wife and sons, Herbert and others. These were indeed those with most influence on Edward, the principal channel of his patronage and the beneficiaries from it to an almost unprecedented degree, and hence beyond their deserts. They did use their power to extort and to pervert justice. Their elevation had not been designed to counter-balance the Nevilles, for Edward did not share their deep hatred for his Neville relatives. Nor was this achieved: the favourites were defeated in 1469, when the Wydevilles proved of no military use. Their influence and gains were excessive, yielded no corresponding advantage, and were therefore politically indefensible, as Edward himself came to realise.

Past experience may explain why Edward was less generous after 1471. True, he made no major grants during his second reign, but there were some spoils of victory in the great offices distributed in 1471. None fell to the Wydevilles, who even failed to secure those earmarked for them. Perhaps this reflects Edward's offence at Anthony's projected pilgrimage, possibly the slight weight that he attributed to Wydeville support, but it certainly marked a less generous attitude to his in-laws. Instead of elevating every member of the family, he did little for Anthony and his own stepsons, virtually nothing for Sir Richard and Sir Edward Wydeville. For what remained of their influence Elizabeth was even more important, yet in spite of her mediation there were painful moments when Edward preferred other claims to their own.[43] Yet, as we shall see, they established their power on a more solid base.

Elizabeth was more concerned about her sons than her brothers. Her

---

[42] This paragraph is based on *Chronicle of the first thirteen years of the reign of Edward IV*, ed. J.O. Halliwell (Camden Soc. x, 1839), pp. 46-9.

[43] E.g. Rivers's hopes of the captaincy of Calais were rapidly quashed, *C.P.R. 1467-77*, p. 450. Rivers used Elizabeth as intermediary with the king against Hastings, T. More, *History of King Richard III*, ed. R.S. Sylvester (Complete Works, ii, 1963), p. 225.

two eldest sons Thomas and Richard Grey were frequently with her, the king and their royal stepbrothers,[44] and indeed they became Edward's intimates. Thomas did not inherit the Ferrers and Astley estates until 1483, but his marriage was effected, he was created Earl of Huntingdon, and in 1473 he and his wife were conveyed lands jointly, which he kept after her premature death.[45] In 1474 the queen concluded another marriage between him and Cecily Bonville, the Bonville and Harrington heiress and a stepdaughter of Lord Hastings. Elizabeth was to keep the inheritance until Cecily was sixteen, perhaps to cover the £2,500 paid for the marriage, but in fact these revenues were pure profit as Edward credited the cost against Hastings's debts to him.[46] Now Marquis of Dorset, Thomas steadily built up his power in the West Country, where he was a royal commissioner and administrator of the lands of his mother and the duchy of Cornwall. After Clarence's fall he secured the wardship and marriage of the young Earl of Warwick and the custody of nine manors. Finally, in 1483, his infant heir was betrothed to the daughter of the late Duchess of Exeter by her second husband. She, of course, had no title to the Exeter estates to which Elizabeth held revisionary rights, so they were settled by act of parliament on her and her fiancé. A substantial estate was allocated to Dorset's younger brother Richard Grey,[47] hitherto unendowed.

The interests of Anthony, now 2nd Earl Rivers, were more diffuse. He had missed out on patronage in 1471, had lost his hold on Calais and the constableship, but had been compensated with a £200 annuity.[48] Without the treasury and his mother's dower, with only his own lands and those of Scales and Wydeville, he should have been a poor earl, but was apparently cushioned by a foreign pension and the profits of trade.[49] His own scanty estates were scattered, but they would ultimately have been doubled by grants made after his return to favour in 1473.[50] Strangely Anthony waited eight years from the death of his first wife until his second marriage to Mary Lewis, a teenager with modest estates in Essex. Stranger yet, after painfully accumulating estates, Anthony planned to divide them between his brothers,[51] neither of whom was married. The three brothers' apparent unconcern about the future prosperity of their

[44] E.g. B.L. Harleian MSS. 48 f. 80; 158 ff. 119v, 120v. For the next phrase, see D. Mancini, *Usurpation of Richard III*, ed. C.A.J. Armstrong (1969), pp. 66-7.

[45] *C.P.R. 1467-77*, pp. 373-4; *1476-85*, p. 336.

[46] *Ibid. 1467-77*, pp. 456-7, 514; *1476-85*, p. 36.

[47] *Ibid. 1476-85*, pp. 139, 174, 212, 263, 283-4; *Rot. Parl.* vi. pp. 215-18.

[48] *C.P.* vi. p. 372; *C.P.R. 1467-77*, pp. 178, 206.

[49] See Scofield, *Edward IV*, ii. p. 7; E.W. Ives, 'Andrew Dymmock and the Papers of Antony, Earl Rivers, 1482-3', *B.I.H.R.* xli (1968), p. 219n.

[50] *C.P.R. 1467-77*, pp. 421, 423; *1476-85*, p. 261.

[51] *Excerpta Historica*, p. 246.

family, or even its continuance, contrasts with their personal greed. One wonders what was the point.

They were just as grasping after 1471 as before. Anthony recovered the manors lost to Sir Geoffrey Gate without relinquishing the Isle of Wight and retained his wife's inheritance after her death in 1473, to the loss of her heirs.[52] In 1474 he was granted the reversion of nine manors on the death of Philippa, Lady Roos, widow of the attainted Lord Roos, of which she had been granted the use in 1461. She was still living in 1482, when Anthony was impatient and anxious to make good his estate. He speculated how two manors had passed to others. If their title was bad, he wrote, he would enter the manors: Lady Roos would forfeit them if she had suffered a fraudulent recovery. He wanted her husband's inquisition post mortem and her patent inspected, to see if her grant was made according to statute, or whether there were any other weaknesses of which he could take advantage. Had she committed any waste whereby she could forfeit her estate? What knights fees and woods were there? Were any lands in the accounts not properly part of her lordship? But no loopholes were exposed.[53] Simultaneously he was scrutinising the accounts of the Warwick feoffees, whose trust was certainly open to attack, but was already under assault from heirs more legitimate than he.[54] He inquired, in passing, about the lands of the late Sir Henry Lewis, his father-in-law. Lewis held little at his death, but in marrying his daughter Rivers may have hoped to recover lands lost by Lewis's attainder and to obtain a share of the possessions of Edmund Beaufort, Duke of Somerset, Mary Lewis's grandfather.[55] When drafting his will, Anthony had pangs of guilt: he ordered the righting of any wrongs regarding the Scales inheritance, moveables seized from Lady Willoughby, differences with Sir John Guildford, and enclosures at Roche Fen in Middleton (Norf.). Anthony's memory was adjustable: he could have mentioned other shady dealings, and his conscience nevertheless let him leave the Scales inheritance to his brother Edward, whose title was even worse than his own.[56] Like Anthony, his brothers would pursue any course of advancement: each sought manors on inadequate titles, one wholly false and the other based on non-observance of a trust a century old.[57] The brothers' limited success shows how restricted their influence was outside Wales.

By 1483 Prince Edward's council was the principal organ of government and justice throughout Wales and was dominated by the

[52] *C.P.R. 1476-85*, p. 365; C 149/226/6; see also *C.C.R. 1468-76*, nos. 1550-1, 1567.

[53] *C.P.R. 1461-7*, p. 87; *1467-77*, p. 423; E 315/486/2,/4,/29.

[54] E 315/486/29; for the background, see M.A. Hicks, 'Career of George Plantagenet, Duke of Clarence, 1449-78' (unpub. Oxford D.Phil.thesis 1974), pp. 317-24.

[55] For her potential title, see *Rot. Parl.* vi. p. 454.

[56] *Excerpta Historica*, pp. 246-8.

[57] Baker, *Northants.* i. pp. 352-4; ii. p. 152; DL 42/19 ff.22v-23.

Wydevilles. These results were achieved by degrees, not all at once. In 1471 Edward created his son Prince of Wales, Duke of Cornwall and Earl of Chester, granted him the appropriate estates, and set up a council and household for him. Nevertheless Edward retained the income from the estates and delegated only estate administration and temporary appointments to the council: hence the membership of Alcock and other pure administrators.[58] The other councillors were Edward's kinsmen and ministers and the prince's councillor, chamberlain and steward. The latter were Edward's choice: Thomas Milling, the prince's chancellor, had received the queen in sanctuary during the Readeption and had earned the gratitude of her, her husband and son; Sir Thomas Vaughan, the chamberlain, was treasurer of Edward's chamber; and Lord Dacre of the South, the steward, had long been a royal favourite. All were already royal councillors, so the prince's council was little more than a committee of the royal one to which minor functions had been delegated. His household was also small and unimportant. Vaughan's and Milling's new responsibilities had to be reconciled with other duties: in 1472 Vaughan carried the prince at a ceremony at Westminster,[59] where Milling normally resided with the prince's great seal. The prince, like his sisters, may have stayed in the queen's household, but at this stage there is no evidence of undue influence by her or her blood.

There was a radical change in 1472-3. A much larger expenditure was envisaged in November 1472, when the prince was granted the issues of his estates, all alienations and appointments were revoked, and he was authorised to recruit retainers.[60] Next year he moved to Ludlow with an enlarged household and council. Councillors were appointed to the border commissions of the peace and marcher lords agreed individually with the king about peace-keeping in their Welsh lordships. Together these measures constituted a coherent plan for Welsh government. In the principality, Chester, Flint and the border shires the council would have direct authority, in the lordships of the duchy of Lancaster and earldom of March indirect authority through their chancellors as councillors, and in independent lordships it would co-operate with the lords. This change from a private and administrative status is reflected in the prince's move to Ludlow, outside his estates but centrally placed, and in the addition of lawyers and marcher lords to the council.[61]

---

[58] *C.P.R. 1467-77*, p. 283; *Rot. Parl.* vi. pp. 9-15. The following five paragraphs are based on R.A. Griffiths, 'Wales and the Marches' in *Fifteenth-century England*, pp. 159-62; D.E. Lowe, 'The Council of the Prince of Wales and the Decline of the Herbert Family during the Second Reign of Edward IV (1471-83)', *Bulletin of the Board of Celtic Studies* xxvii(2) (1977), pp. 278-97. For what follows, see *C.P.R. 1467-77*, p. 283; Scofield, *Edward IV*, i. p. 546; A.R. Myers, *Household of Edward IV* (1959), p. 22; Davis, *Paston Letters*, i. p. 524.

[59] C.L. Kingsford, *English Historical Literature in the Fifteenth Century* (1913), pp. 383, 386.

[60] *Rot. Parl.* vi. p. 15; *C.P.R. 1467-77*, pp. 361, 365, 449.

[61] *C.P.R. 1467-77*, p. 366.

The council was intended to remedy defects in Welsh justice, perhaps in response to petitions in parliament. One wonders, however, if this particular remedy was promoted by the Wydevilles because it was advantageous to them. The first council, as chosen by the king, included few of them, but by the end of 1472 they dominated it. The more eminent councillors – royal dukes, ministers and bishops – probably left everyday affairs to the officials, who lacked the stature to gainsay Elizabeth and Rivers, even had they wished. In practice, they do not seem to have so wished. Milling was Elizabeth's protégé, Fogge her kinsman, and Dacre, Vaughan and Alcock were all to enjoy the friendship and favour of her and Rivers. The Wydevilles had strong motives to control the prince, for their future would depend on him after Edward's death. Meanwhile control of his administration and patronage was desirable, and in the future – certainly when he was fourteen years of age – more could be expected. Actually, as we have already seen, wider powers were conferred in 1472.

Edward aimed at effective rule in Wales, not the creation of a power base for the Wydevilles, and carefully divided and limited authority. Power rested not with the prince's officers, but with his council, which operated his signet, which in turn moved his great seal and the seals of his principality, palatinates and lordships. Control in finance did not rest with the treasurer and controller of his household, but with the queen, Alcock and Rivers, who had keys to his coffers.[62] Rivers's official powers were slender. Probably he was expected to spend little time at Ludlow. It was not he nor Milling who presided over the council, but Alcock, a former master of the rolls and chancellor of England, who was continually with the prince.[63] He should have directed matters, but More testifies to Wydeville dominance,[64] which emerges clearly from the records: payments were made on warrants under Rivers's seal; his order sufficed to present a priest to a chantry and to move the chancery seal of Carmarthen; another time, when ordering repayment of a bond, he personally changed the phrase 'I will' to 'my lord wills', but the arrangement was his and his seal sufficient warrant.[65] Power rested not with the judicial council in London, but with the council in the Marches, to which bishops, magnates and lawyers seldom came, and which must often have consisted solely of Alcock and household officials.

At first Edward planned moderate reform in Wales: most appointments were confirmed and personnel changed only gradually. Co-operation was intended with marcher lords, four of whom were councillors: most important was Lord Ferrers of Chartley, uncle of the young Herbert Earl

[62] J.O. Halliwell, *Letters of the Kings and Queens of England* (1848), ii. p. 143.
[63] E.g. SC 6/1210/6 mm.3d, 6;/1225/3 m.9.
[64] More, *Richard III*, p. 14.
[65] SC 6/1210/6 m.5 (attached bill);/1225/7 m.5.

of Pembroke. Pembroke had a Wydeville wife. So too had the Duke of Buckingham. It may have been Wydeville influence that gave Buckingham livery of his estates long before he came of age.[66] He entered an indenture of the marches, employed Wydeville protégés in key administrative positions,[67] and sat on border commissions with his brothers-in-law Rivers, Maltravers and Strange and the councillors Shrewsbury and Ferrers.[68] Evidently Rivers, Alcock and the council did co-operate with those about them.

Since Prince Edward's household grew under Wydeville direction, one might expect it to consist of their clients, but apparently it did not. Some members had neither Wydeville nor royal antecedents. Relatively few estate officers were imported, particularly in Wales, where local ministers were generally natives and their superiors were absentees. All automatically became servants of the prince, to whom they could henceforth look for local patronage, access to royal bounty, and ultimately for advancement on his accession. Ambitions and loyalties focused on the prince rather than the king, forming an affinity like that around other heirs to the throne. In his entourage one can distinguish menials and administrators without previous ties, numerous but without stature as individuals, and a few royal servants, whose interests were increasingly identified with those of the prince. Examples of the latter are Vaughan, who resided with the prince rather than the king by 1475,[69] and Sir Richard Croft, a Yorkist retainer holding office in Wales, who became an active partisan of the prince. Most important were the Stanleys, whose stranglehold on Cheshire was initially threatened by the prince's council,[70] but who later entered his service. George Stanley received preferment and his uncle Sir William had become steward of the prince's household by 1483.[71] Once Stanley predominance in Cheshire was recognised, as it was by 1482,[72] they had more to gain from the prince than the king. In the late 1470s the prince was replacing absentee officials with his own men. By 1482-3, when Rivers could raise several thousand men from Wales and Stanley another 4,000 from Lancashire and Cheshire, a major connection had been constructed.[73]

In 1478 Prince Richard married the Mowbray heiress. Like his elder brother he had a chancellor, seal, household and council to manage his

---

[66] C. Rawcliffe, *The Staffords, Earls of Stafford and Dukes of Buckingham 1394-1521* (1978), p. 125.

[67] E.g. Richard Isham, *ibid.* p. 198.

[68] KB 9/334/85,/87.

[69] He receives money for the prince, e.g. SC 6/781/6 m.7d.

[70] *Rot. Parl.* vi. p. 46; SC 6/781/2 mm.3-5.

[71] SC 6/782/5 m.5; B.L. Sloane MS. 3479 ff. 53v, 55.

[72] *Hall's Chronicle*, ed. H. Ellis (1809), p. 331.

[73] *Ibid.*

estates. His council, like that of Prince Edward, comprised the queen and a group of magnates and bishops, few of whom were Wydeville supporters. Some appointments were made by the council, others by it with the assent of the queen, a formula also found on Prince Edward's estates. It was Elizabeth who mattered, for Richard resided with her and Rivers treated his affairs as their own. The king retained a residual interest,[74] but the marriage gave the Wydevilles control of the important Mowbray estates, retinue and patronage, which they were understandably reluctant to relinquish.

The affairs of Dorset, Rivers, Elizabeth and the princes were five distinct spheres of Wydeville influence, but in practice they scarcely differentiated between them. Rivers used Prince Richard's treasurer and Prince Edward's cofferer as his own agents, paid Prince Edward's bills with his own money, appointed two of his councillors as deputy-butlers, employed their parliamentary patronage for his own nominees, and exploited offices by Prince Edward to strengthen his grip on King's Lynn.[75] There was some interchange of personnel at the top, where Lord Dacre of the South, steward of Prince Edward, became queen's chamberlain,[76] and Sir William Allington, attorney-general of Prince Edward, was deputy to Rivers and chancellor of each prince in turn.[77] There can be little doubt that the princes' households – and the princes too – identified themselves with the Wydevilles. By this I don't mean that their loyalty to the king was in question – of course it was not – or that their prime loyalty in any way lessened their allegiance to the king. Instead, under the umbrella label of loyal Yorkists and even king's men, they belonged to the faction of the prince, which was directed by the Wydevilles. In the same way Lord Hastings, whose loyalty to the king was equally committed, belonged to the faction opposed to the queen. This connection of Prince Edward was stronger than those of Rivers and Dorset, and more enduring than that of the queen. On Prince Edward's accession his connection would become a specially favoured group of the king's affinity; the queen's following would die with her. In 1483 Gloucester and Buckingham had to execute some and dismiss others in Edward V's household.[78]

In 1478, directed by the Wydevilles, all the king's relatives and servants combined to destroy their common enemy, Clarence. His destruction was

[74] DL 29/454/7312 mm.4-5; see below.
[75] *Excerpta Historica*, pp. 247-8; Ives, *B.I.H.R.* xli. pp. 222-3; E 315/486/8; *C.P.R. 1467-77*, pp. 366, 410. He was steward, constable, ranger, farmer of the demesne and warren of Castle Rising (Norf.), SC 6/933/8-d; C 1/46/25. The next three paragraphs are based on Lowe, *art. cit.*; Griffiths, *art. cit.*
[76] *C.P.R. 1467-77*, p. 283; B.L. Additional MS. 6113 f. 97v.
[77] *C.P.R. 1467-77*, p. 410; SC 8/344/1281; DL 29/454/7312 m.4.
[78] More, *Richard III*, pp. 19-20; Mancini, *Richard III*, pp. 78-9.

the fruit of the Wydeville marriages of the 1460s, for at least four of the bridegrooms were actively involved.[79] By Edward V's accession four of the marriages had ended by death, none producing an adult heir, and family ties had slackened. Elizabeth still supported her brothers and was surrounded by her sisters, but male Wydevilles had a narrower outlook. Anthony's will ignored female relatives and remembered only his brothers and his nephew Richard Grey.[80] His next brother was to leave all he could to Dorset rather than to his sisters and their issue, his coheirs.[81] If this reveals close ties between Elizabeth's brothers and sons, it shows those with their in-laws to be weak. They no longer agreed on priority of aims, each pursuing his own interests, and in Wales Elizabeth, Rivers and Grey preferred their own advantage to that of their marcher kinsfolk.

The principal development was the break of the Wydevilles with the Herberts. The creation of prince and council of Wales had always been at the expense of the young Earl of Pembroke, whose father had dominated all Wales in the 1460s. In 1471 Haverfordwest was transferred to Prince Edward[82] and by 1473 Pembroke's entail as chief justice of South Wales was annulled. This did not mark a rupture with the Wydevilles, for he was appointed steward and constable of Haverfordwest, chamberlain and chief justice of South Wales, and steward of Carmarthen for life, and was granted 340 marks a year in annuities and regards, 80 of them entailed on his issue by Mary Wydeville, the prince's aunt; his uncle Ferrers was a councillor and constable of Aberystwyth; and his mother received Wydeville support in a struggle with Clarence over Dunster.[83] The decisive break occurred in mid-1478 and the crucial factor may have been the death of his Wydeville wife:[84] the Wydevilles felt no qualm about disinheriting her daughter. The earl lost the lordship and earldom of Pembroke to Prince Edward, receiving instead lands elsewhere and the earldom of Huntingdon, and was deprived of all his offices, regards and annuities in South Wales; his uncle Ferrers was replaced as constable of Aberystwyth and one William Herbert – perhaps an illegitimate kinsman – as receiver of Haverfordwest. The result was achieved by coercion, in which king, queen and royal council combined.[85] At a stroke Herbert influence in the principality and Pembrokeshire was supplanted by that of the Wydevilles.

This illustrates the Wydevilles's steady advance in Wales, which

[79] Buckingham, Maltravers, Bourchier, Strange and Grey: Hicks, 'Clarence', pp. 169-72, 177, table VII (ii).

[80] *Excerpta Historica*, p. 248.

[81] PROB 11/8(P.C.C.44 Milles).

[82] *Rot. Parl.* vi. p. 10.

[83] *C.P.R. 1467-77*, pp. 204, 330, 364; SC 6/1225/3 mm.3, 5, 8; /1207/14 m. 4-d.

[84] She was dead by 1479, Baker, *Northants.* i. p. 354.

[85] SC 6/1225/7 mm.4-6; Lander, *Crown and Nobility*, pp. 183-4.

Edward formally recognised in 1483. He nominated Milling, Alcock and Martin to local bishoprics and gradually relinquished lordships of the duchy of Lancaster and earldom of March. Increasingly they intervened outside Wales and entertained petitions from other lordships. Such infringement of franchises had been envisaged by neither king nor marcher lords, who were now virtually unrepresented on the council. Border lords who were Wydeville kinsmen – Buckingham, Maltravers, Strange and Grey of Ruthin – might reasonably have been added, but never were; nor did they share the prince's patronage. The Wydevilles's advance at the expense of established lords may well have alienated them. This could explain the hostility of Buckingham, whose ambitions in Wales are beyond question.

Wydeville aggrandisement at this time was at the expense of others, who were given vested interests in change. The principal instances are the seizure of Pembroke and the re-settlement of the Holland and Mowbray inheritances: Prince Richard had retained the Mowbray estates after his wife's death, to the disinheritance of the heirs.[86] Nor are these the only examples, as they threatened Gloucester's tenure of the Beaufort inheritance and Hastings's hostility is well attested. The Wydevilles remained unpopular. Such factors may explain the support for Gloucester of Northumberland, Neville and Howard, but did any play a part before the decisive arrest of Rivers? Animosity for the Wydevilles should have prevented their dominance of Edward V's early councils, presumably attended by all the magnates at Edward IV's funeral, but it did not. Bereft of the king and their military power by Anthony's capture, the Wydevilles were defeated long before the usurpation.

Rivers could be seized because of divisions within his family. Doubtless he, like his sister and nephew, wanted their influence perpetuated and favoured an early coronation rather than a protectorate, but he did not regard Gloucester as an enemy. He went out of his way to meet him and unnecessarily placed himself in the duke's power; following a convivial evening, his arrest was a surprise.[87] If he saw Gloucester as a friend and had no grounds for enmity, one wonders whether More was right in charging the queen with unthinking hostility to the king's kindred?[88]

Until 1464 the Wydevilles were least among nobles, nursing tenuous ties with the great, poorly endowed and politically impotent. Afterwards they exploited Edward's sense of obligation to integrate themselves among the higher nobility. Their new patronage was still distributed among existing kinsmen and dependants; their military might, on the evidence of 1469-

[86] Pugh, *Fifteenth-century England*, p. 111.
[87] Mancini, *Richard III*, pp. 74-5; More, *Richard III*, pp. 17-18.
[88] More, *Richard III*, p. 7.

71, was nil. Later, appropriating the power of the princes, they established a regional hegemony and a powerful and committed retinue, thus becoming more than a court party.

Since there were so many of them, patronage was spread thinly, but they did much better than Lander thought. Throughout they exploited their influence to extort concessions, an activity for which they had an inordinate appetite; at least that other grasping family, the Nevilles, normally had some basis for their claims. Worst of them all, on the evidence, was Anthony; far from doing harm to no-one, as Mancini would have us believe,[89] there was nobody he hesitated to harm. None of them, in pursuit of advantage, worried much about repercussions or feared to make foes.

It is a severe criticism that Edward left them unchecked and sanctioned their shady dealings, especially as he was dominated by nobody and quite capable of refusing their blandishments. He helped them if it was not at his expense or to his disadvantage; hence the alienation and transfer of reversions, which enabled them to build on what they had. This attitude also coloured his regional policy, for he had no desire in the early 1470s to revive the Welsh and northern lieutenantcies of the previous decade. But once the Wydevilles and Gloucester had re-established them, Edward concurred and gradually conceded other estates and powers. The Wydevilles's growing power at the expense of others again generated factions within the political consensus that ultimately undermined the crown. As only they benefited, not Edward or his sons, their influence, as Professor Ross observed, was malign.

[89] Mancini, *Richard III*, pp. 66-9.

12

Lord Hastings' Indentured Retainers?[1]

William Lord Hastings (*c.* 1431-83) has acquired a prominent place in fifteenth-century history. A flurry of recent publications have confirmed the highly favourable view of him presented by St Thomas More and subsequent Tudor historians. His elimination was indeed an essential prerequisite to Richard III's usurpation of the throne. Hastings' unshakeable loyalty to Edward V arose from lifelong service (like his father before him) to the House of York. Retained initially by Richard Duke of York (d. 1460), he helped his son Edward IV seize the throne in 1461, served him throughout his reign as chamberlain of the household, and became his most devoted friend.[2] These strands were brought together in 1955 by Professor Dunham, who shifted the focus to Hastings' retinue. His ninety indentured retainers were the largest number recorded for any lord except John of Gaunt and constituted the most numerous retinue in his own day. Taking the sixty-nine surviving indentures as a base, Dunham devised a new chronology for the development of bastard feudalism and its regulation that has influenced many subsequent historians. By demonstrating Hastings' men to be substantial gentry of the type who ran local government and sat in parliament, he identified the local roots of Hastings' power in 1483.[3] He thus explained how Hastings brought 3,000 retainers to Edward IV's banner for his successful Barnet and Tewkesbury campaign in 1471. In 1483 it was to prevent Hastings mobilising them again that he was struck down.[4] Since Dunham wrote a whole series of writers have tackled the local significance of Hastings' retinue and it has entered historical orthodoxy as a rare example of one

---

[1] King Alfred's College, Winchester kindly allowed me study leave in Lent term 1989, when this essay was written. I acknowledge the helpful comments of Dr R. Cust. The principal references for the first three sentences are collected in the bibliography of C.D. Ross, *Richard III* (1981).

[2] W.H. Dunham, *Lord Hastings' Indentured Retainers 1461-83: The Lawfulness of Livery and Retaining under the Yorkists and Early Tudors* (Transactions of the Connecticut Academy of Arts and Sciences xxxix, 1955), 13-26.

[3] Ibid 27-89.

[4] Ibid 25-6.

that could be relied upon in times of crisis. The archetypal loyal servant and model retainer, Hastings is also one of the most skilful and successful lords of the fifteenth century.[5]

Hastings was thus a complex and many-sided individual, whose life was pursued as much at court, in Calais, and in the West Country as in the midlands and whose total career has yet to be fully studied. This paper does not attempt such an ambitious task. It focuses instead on the role of Lord Hastings' indentured retainers in the North Midlands. It examines the recent (and mutually incompatible) historiography on the topic, identifies misunderstandings, and clears the ground for future study.

Professor Dunham started from a late-16th-century list of ninety aristocrats said to have been retained by William Lord Hastings and from sixty-nine surviving indentures of retainer for sixty-seven of them preserved in Hastings' own archive at the Huntington Library, California. He deduced, no doubt correctly, that all ninety-two had been retained in this way. Six indentures dated from the 1460s and the remainder from 1474-83. Two recipients were barons and the remainder gentry: knights, esquires, and gentlemen. There are twenty-six different types but the differences between them are small indeed, mainly verbal, and they share a common core. All promised:

> to aid and assist . . . Hastings and his part to take against all persons within this realm of England during their lives as well in peace as war, their allegiance to the king's majesty, his heirs and successors only reserved and excepted, with so many able persons as every of them might well make to be furnished and arrayed at the cost and charges of the said lord, for the which the said lord promised them to be their good and true lord in all things reasonable, and them to aid and succour in their rightful causes so far forth as law, equity, and conscience requires.

As this brief summary indicates, Hastings offered them good lordship, not the fees commonly granted by most other lords, which were conceded in only two of these cases.[6] Yet, as we have seen, Dunham considered the contracts did indeed bind the retainer to his lord and secured the latter the service he required.

Since Hastings' indentures were far more numerous than any other lord, differed fundamentally from others that were known, and were mostly contracted *after* the 1468 statute that prohibited retaining by indenture, Dunham found it necessary to explain their existence and to postulate a chronology for the development of bastard feudalism itself.

---

[5] Ibid 13-25; C. Richmond, 'Fauconberg's Kentish Rising of May 1471', *E[nglish] H[istorical] R[eview]* lxxxv (1970), 692.

[6] Dunham, *Hastings*, 47-66, 116-34.

Noting that each indenture carefully reserved allegiance to the king and that Hastings promised only support that was compatible to the law, he argued that these indentures fell within the meaning of the 'lawful service' that the 1468 statute allowed to continue.[7] Whilst accepting that the mere promise of good lordship appeared a smaller inducement for retainers than the more normal fee or indeed the grant of land central to feudalism itself, Dunham argued for a progressive development from a crude tenurial bond to a cash fee *c.* 1300 to a promise of good lordship and from an essentially military to a civilian function for retaining. Bastard feudalism, in Dunham's eyes, was:

> a refinement, and not a degeneration, of an earlier feudal custom . . . The final substitution of what medieval men called good lordship – aid, favor, support and preferment – for the fee created a more refined, certainly a more subtle, relationship, one that could be advantageous and effectual only in a more sophisticated society . . . Did not the so-called 'pseudo-chivalry' of Edward IV's reign produce, in fact, more sophisticated arrangements for war and politics than had the socially primitive tenurial feudalism of Norman England?[8]

Although Dunham pointed out the military value of the retinue to Hastings in time of crisis, he did not consider this was its prime purpose. His indentures differ greatly from the more precise and elaborate ones of the fourteenth century and indeed those indentures of war contracted by several of his men with the king for the 1475 invasion of France. He suggested a series of civil and ceremonial uses for which Hastings might want such aristocrats and their entourages from time to time. He demonstrated that they dominated local government in Staffordshire, Derbyshire, and adjoining counties as sheriffs, justices of the peace, and escheators. They also sat in parliament, no less than twelve of them in 1478 when the nobility maximised their representation for the trial of the Duke of Clarence, which at the time when he wrote was the largest such affinity known to have sat in parliament together in the later middle ages. Hastings' influence in securing their promotion – and indeed their representation of his interests in office – was however difficult to prove, for many of them held office before the date of their indentures and were in any case the type of county gentry who normally held office anyway. This suggested to Dunham a more subtle relationship. Perhaps Hastings recruited them because of the obvious importance demonstrated by their office-holding. Alternatively they may already have been Hastings' retainers before the date of their indentures, which either formalised

---

[7] Ibid 73-88, esp. 74-7.
[8] Ibid 7-10.

existing ties or modified earlier contracts that do not survive. Two successive indentures survive for two retainers. Just because surviving indentures are concentrated in the later period does not mean that such relationships did not exist earlier.[9]

Dunham's interpretation has influenced many historians, including even the great K.B. McFarlane, and largely explains the emphasis of much modern work on good lordship rather than payment for service. Thirty years were to pass, however, before Lord Hastings' indentures were re-examined. Noting their narrow chronological range, the bulk falling in 1472-83, Professor Bean observed that this was the period when Lord Hastings was Edward IV's right-hand man and when his proximity to the king might well have tempted potential retainers into his service without fees. If indeed no fee was paid, for he points out that this characteristic gap in Hastings' indentures may not be what it seems. Two fees are mentioned, 64 indentures provide expenses, and no great innovation was needed to confine all references to the fee to the letter patent that normally accompanied each indenture. The fees apart, 65 of the 69 indentures closely tally with those of York, the Nevilles, and even John of Gaunt, and seem to fall within the broad parameters of indentures in general throughout the fourteenth and fifteenth centuries. One other striking provision, the contract for wartime service in England alone, suggests that Hastings contracted them with a view to renewed civil war after 1471.

> In the second place, Hastings wanted to bolster his own power in time of peace: he needed in the shires where he had his estates a following that was commensurate with his territorial power there and with his position at Westminster. A great courtier needed the opportunity to display his power of patronage as much as lesser men hungered for its benefits.

Starting off by emphasising that Hastings' retinue was 'a special case', Bean ends by minimising the differences and assimilating Hastings' indentures into the mainstream of retaining.[10]

Though written as recently as 1989, Bean's analysis takes up where Dunham left off and contrasts sharply from other, essentially geographical studies, of which he is clearly ignorant. Dunham's work has also shaped subsequent analyses of the distribution of power in the North Midlands in the 1470s and 1480s. Thus in 1973 Mr Morgan identified the North Midlands as Hastings' sphere of influence when outlining the territorial re-ordering undertaken by Edward IV in 1473-4. Next year

---

[9] Ibid 27-40.
[10] J.M.W. Bean, *From Lord to Patron: Lordship in Late Medieval England* (Manchester 1989), 106-9.

Mr Cameron declared Hastings' retinue to be

> very far from typical . . . One significant feature of Lord Hastings' retinue was that it was largely composed of men who had been retained by others at an earlier date, notably Warwick and Clarence, and must therefore be seen as an attempt at political control of an area which might be reluctant to support Edward IV.[11]

Also in 1974 the present author identified the territorial basis of Hastings' power as the duchy of Lancaster honours of Tutbury and Duffield and lordships of High Peak and Castle Donington in Staffordshire, Derbyshire and Leicestershire. Collectively called Tutbury honour, they were resumed by Edward IV from his brother Clarence in 1474 and managed thereafter by Hastings as steward, an office to which Clarence first appointed him in 1472. The first big group of contracts were made in 1474 with Edward's approval;[12] subsequent contracts related mainly to 'the gentlemen of the honour of Tutbury', who have been investigated in greater detail by Dr Rowney for Staffordshire, Dr Wright for Derbyshire, and Dr Carpenter for Warwickshire.[13] They reach conclusions conflicting with one another and with their predecessors.

Dr Rowney seeks to demonstrate how the retinue operated in Staffordshire in practice. There it was closely identified with the honour of Tutbury:

> The heart of the affinity lay in the honour, and the leading officials of the honour were the first to be retained . . . Given the wide spread of Hastings's estates and responsibilities . . . the prominence of the honour of Tutbury and its environs in the composition of the affinity is striking.

He too dates its arrival in Staffordshire in 1474, when there was a considerable turnover of estate officers, notably seven of ten parkers and two keepers of wards in Needwood Forest. That most came from the royal household, where Hastings was chamberlain, may indicate his influence

[11] D.A.L. Morgan, 'The King's Affinity in the Polity of Yorkist England', T[ransactions of the] R[oyal] H[istorical] S[ociety] 5th ser xxiii (1973), 19; A. Cameron, 'The Giving of Livery and Retaining in Henry VII's Reign', *Renaissance and Modern Studies* xviii (1974), 20.

[12] Dunham, *Hastings*, 119; M.A. Hicks, 'The Career of George Plantagenet, Duke of Clarence, 1449-1478' (Oxford D.Phil thesis 1974), 128, 144, 354-5; S.M. Wright, *The Derbyshire Gentry in the Fifteenth Century* (Derbyshire Record Society viii, 1983), 75.

[13] I. Rowney, 'Resources and Retaining in Yorkist England: William, Lord Hastings and the Honour of Tutbury', P[roperty] and P[olitics: Essays in Later Medieval English History], ed. A.J. Pollard (Gloucester 1984), 139-55; idem, 'The Hastings' Affinity in Staffordshire and the Honour of Tutbury', B[ulletin of the] I[nstitute of] H[istorical] R[esearch] lvii (1984), 35-45; Wright, *Derbyshire*, passim; M.C. Carpenter, 'The Duke of Clarence and the Midlands: A Study of the Interplay of Local and National Politics', *Midland History* xi (1986), 35-6.

or that of the king, but:

> On occasions, Hastings' influence in an appointment cannot be doubted . . .
> Hastings was also certainly behind the advancement of his own family. His
> brother, Richard, Lord Wells, became bailiff of Melbourne and the hundred of
> Gresley in Tamworth, while kinsmen among the Ferrers family of Tamworth
> also received preferment.

Whilst he promised only good lordship, this received concrete expression
from his distribution of:

> the plethora of offices and perquisites available to him as steward . . . In the
> Hastings contracts it was not that something new had replaced something old,
> merely that something of the old had been dispensed with. Hastings
> substituted patronage from the honour (something he would have had to give
> them anyway) for cash annuities from his own pocket . . . [Tutbury] was the
> base from which Hastings developed and financed an affinity to give viable
> and practical expression to his dominance . . .

He was thus able to finance his retinue at the crown's expense and indeed
made a considerable income himself from the offices and leases that he
accrued. He took over an existing kinship network based on the honour –
'he "bought" a clan rather than constructed an affinity' – whereas 'he
would have needed other inducements to win support elsewhere'.
Combined with other offices and wardships, it made him 'the most
powerful "local" magnate'. His retainers were so obviously eligible for
office in their own right that Rowney, like Dunham before him, found it
difficult to demonstrate Hastings' influence on local officeholding, which
was highlighted only when a particular appointment broke a traditional
pattern. Such problems, however, do not mean that Hastings lacked
influence or support from the J.P.s.

> it merely downgrades the significance of the indentured contract *in this instance*,
> and certainly destroys any notion of "haves" and "have-nots" based on
> evidence of retention alone. Surely we are not to believe that Edward IV's
> right-hand man would suffer this region of special interest to be governed by
> men hostile to him?

So too with sheriffs and knights of the shire. He employed his authority
sparingly, seeking to harness local aspirations rather than install his own
men as M.P.s or county officials. His affinity was a model of mutual
advantage, 'moulded to the contours of gentry society, which represented
and fostered stability rather than factional rivalry or social unrest'. He did
not try to do too much, to direct county affairs, recognizing that the
stewardship gave him only limited and impermanent authority and
resources that must not be overstrained. Given that their 'loyalty to him

personally was not to be relied upon', he did very well, and particularly well compared with Clarence:

> Hastings was a more skilled operator. He understood the parameters within which he had to work – what to interfere with and what to leave alone, who had to be worked with and who might be passed over. An appreciation of such niceties was the keystone of a quiet and successful 'rule' in a district. Perhaps much of the negative evidence concerning the relationship between office-holding and Hastings' retainers speaks not of any lack of influence, but of his appreciation of the finer points of good lordship.[14]

Rowney quotes his supervisor Dr Richmond, for whom Hastings in 1471 was a nobleman who managed to deliver his retainers, whereas others, notably Northumberland, could not. 'What Percy had failed to do Hastings succeeded in doing: the one was thus rendered powerless, the other powerful'. It was not Hastings so much as the retainers who decided the issue and they not Hastings who recovered Edward his throne. Similarly Richmond borrowed from Rowney the idea that they rather than Hastings ran Tutbury honour, admittedly on Hastings' behalf, and used Rowney's delicate lord-retainer relationship as a model of much wider application. Far from Dunham's picture of Hastings' fall being designed to prevent him bringing his local resources into play, it may have been motivated in part by the Duke of Buckingham's desire to supplant Hastings' dominance in his home shire.[15]

Dr Carpenter's analysis of the implications for Warwickshire resembles Rowney's picture for Staffordshire, even though no part of Tutbury honour was so far south. Many of Hastings' men actually lived in Warwickshire or had lands there, so that the construction of a great new connection there was bound to affect the balance of power in Warwickshire:

> Hastings, as the king's representative, dominated the north midlands . . . By 1477, having played little part in Warwickshire affairs before, he was linked to a network of north Warwickshire families, and this part of the county had become part of Hastings' north midlands domain . . .

This was one of a number of developments that weakened Clarence's power as Earl of Warwick and exposed him fatally in 1477-8.[16]

Dr Wright demonstrates the importance of the affinity in Derbyshire

---

[14] Rowney, *BIHR* lvii. 34-45, esp. 36, 42-5; Rowney, *P & P*, 141, 144-5, 150-2.

[15] See above p.229; C. Richmond, 'After McFarlane', *History* lxviii (1983), 58-9; C. Richmond, '1485 and All That, or what was going on at the battle of Bosworth?' *Richard III: Loyalty, Lordship, and Law*, ed. P.W. Hammond (London 1986), 185-6, 196-7.

[16] Carpenter, *Midland History* xi 35-6.

but, unlike Rowney and Carpenter, she doubts its effectiveness. Hastings already had some retainers there in the 1460s and was implicated through them in feuding in 1467-8, yet he had few lands in the county and his retinue really dates from 1474. Tutbury honour was certainly vital to it and honorial patronage did indeed reinforce good lordship, but she sees this as insufficient by itself. Hence the indentures, which 'created a formal and identifiable following' and one approved by the king: 'A nationalised retinue', 'Edward's creation', and 'an integral part of Edward's scheme of territorial reorganisation', it relied on the gentry's reluctance 'to antagonise Hastings by declining his offers'. Intending initially to exclude Clarence and latterly Buckingham:

> Edward IV put into motion a thorough-going reordering of the north midlands which included the subsuming of all interests other than Hastings' and the quelling of dissident elements by careful manipulation of all forms of patronage at the crown's disposal.

By reinforcing Hastings' authority, in any case inseparable from his own, Edward strengthened his own position locally. Hastings aimed at 'comprehensive support from the county's aristocracy and traditional ruling group', yet it probably never evolved from 'this amorphous collection of individuals' into 'a coherent body'. She found rather more evidence of the promotion of its members than did Dunham or Rowney and felt like them that activity as J.P.s, even by the unindentured:

> implies Hastings's approval. In their case, repeated selection in effect broadened Hastings's affinity without indentures. Thus in a variety of ways Hastings, with Edward IV's explicit support, dominated the county until 1483.

Similarly, when account is taken that nine Hastings' men – five of them already indentured – became sheriffs, then:

> Hastings's overwhelming influence on the shrievalty is clear. As chamberlain, Hastings was in a position to influence both the compiling of the short list and the pricking of the sheriff. This was also apparently true of Warwickshire and Staffordshire . . . [The] inexperienced Derbyshire sheriffs evidently owed their appointment to Hastings . . .

The shrievalty was more important than the commission of the peace, hence the higher proportion of sheriffs retained by him, and Hastings' connection with Derbyshire explains the higher proportion of Derbyshire men who were sheriffs of Nottingham and Derby. Hastings' example, however, has no wider applications. It was a highly exceptional, 'artificial creation ... no "ordinary" magnates's following but a nationalised retinue'.[17]

These analyses all draw on much information not available to Dunham and gain immensely from their vastly superior knowledge of their respective local scenes. For the most part they agree with one another, with Morgan and with Dunham that Hastings' indentured retainers made him politically dominant in the North Midlands and that this had wider political implications. They agree on the centrality of Tutbury honour, about its value to Hastings as a source of patronage, and hence on the importance of Hastings' influence with the king in enabling him to draw on it. Wright, like Morgan, agrees on the importance of Edward's territorial re-ordering of 1473-4 for creating the affinity – indeed, she suggests that it is rather Edward's affinity than Hastings'; she, Carpenter and Rowney see it as supplanting Clarence; and she and Rowney appreciate Hastings' exceptional position as *merely* steward and consider some of the implications of the unusual terms of his indentures. Obviously, therefore, they share much common ground.

On the other hand, as already indicated, there are considerable differences in detail, perspective, and in interpretation, which must not be minimised. There are several reasons for these. Pride of place must be given to the various preconceptions that these historians bring to their studies, for several schools of thought are represented here with different notions of how bastard feudalism and society related. Dr Carpenter, for example, sees retaining as a tie that was binding, exclusive, and yet constantly shifting. To be retained a second time implied the termination of the earlier bond and, since changes were frequent, retinues and local politics were in a constant state of flux. Dr Richmond and Dr Rowney in contrast present the gentry as politically independent. Although gentry had many lords, they committed themselves to none, and their lords could not command their obedience. Lordship was quite ineffective as a social cement. Yet others, such as the present author, do not accept the instability that is the conclusion of Carpenter, Richmond, and Rowney alike.[18] A second cause for their disagreements lies in their restricted view of the affinity, as it relates to Staffordshire, Derbyshire, Warwickshire, or to Clarence, which certainly explains some of the conflicts that arise. Dunham's strength was that he started from the indentures, on which he was exceptionally well-informed, and tried to take an overview. Thirdly and finally, they all suffer because they cannot see the totality of Hastings' activities and interests. Even Dr Wright, who comes closest to the truth,

---

[17] Wright, *Derbyshire*, esp. 78-82, 88-9, 92, 105, 107, 111-12, 117. See also R.E. Horrox, *Richard III: A Study of Service* (Cambridge 1989), 46.

[18] This is discussed at length in my 'Bastard Feudalism: Society and Politics in the Fifteenth Century', above chapter 1.

does not bring together all those features that make Hastings' retinue so remarkable.

Hastings' elevation to the peerage, appointments, and grants of land identify him in 1461 as a leading York retainer but not one of the most important. Before 1471 he never enjoyed the sort of regional hegemony bestowed in Wales on William Herbert, Earl of Pembroke or in the West Country on Humphrey Stafford of Southwick, Earl of Devon. Perhaps, indeed, it was not so much his York connections that determined his advancement in the 1460s, important though these were, but those he had with Warwick. It was his marriage to Warwick's widowed sister Katherine that secured him many of his lands and even at Warwick's coup d'état in 1469 the earl evidently counted on Hastings' support, restoring him to offices in North Wales just transferred by Edward to Pembroke.[19] It may be that it was not until Edward's exile late in 1470 that Hastings firmly committed himself to the king and not until 1471 therefore that he was given a position of real power – the captaincy of Calais – in preference to the king's brother-in-law Earl Rivers.

During the 1460s and indeed subsequently Hastings' key position was as chamberlain of the royal household. This gave him constant access to the king and enabled him to control access to him. He could influence the king's decisions, he signed a considerable number of warrants for the privy seal, and perhaps decided some of them.[20] This closeness with the king meant that many people wanted him to exercise his influence on their behalf, including the queen, queen's mother, king's brother and other noblemen, and consequently granted him stewardships and annuities.[21] So too Catesby under Richard III and 'patronage secretaries' later.[22] Hastings was not the client, was not obliged in person to act (for example) as steward of Seagrave, but instead it was he who had good lordship that even the great needed and sued for. It was this good lordship that he promised Lord Grey of Codnor in 1465 and that he exercised in his favour in 1467-8 when he was in trouble for a murder in Derbyshire.[23] Hastings was a powerful courtier, perhaps *the* most powerful one, though he appears to have been repeatedly challenged by the king's in-laws the Wydevilles. His itinerary shows him frequently at court and after 1471 at Calais too, much less frequently in the provinces. Even as steward of Tutbury he would have wielded little local power had he not been so strong at the centre.

[19] *C[alendar of] P[atent] R[olls] 1461-7*, 104; *1467-77*, 154, 165.
[20] E.g. P[ublic Record] O[ffice] PSO1/64/41.
[21] Dunham, *Hastings*, 21.
[22] E.g. J.S. Roskell, 'William Catesby', *Parliaments and Politics in Late Medieval England* (3 vols 1981-3), 325-6; A.G.R. Smith, *Servant of the Cecils* (1977).
[23] Dunham, *Hastings*, 133; Wright, *Derbyshire*, 78.

Of course, he was also powerful in the provinces. In March 1471, so *The Arrivall* tells us:

> At Leycestar came to the Kynge ryght-a-fayre felawship of folks, to the nomber of iij^M men, well habyled for the wers, such as were veryly to be trustyd, as thos that wowld uttarly inparte with hym at beste and worste in his qwarell, withe all theyr force and myght to do hym theyr trew service. And in substaunce they were suche as were towards the Lorde Hastings, the Kyngs Chambarlayn, and, for that entent above sayd, came to hym, stiryd by his messages sent unto them, and by his servants, frinds, and lovars, suche as were in the contrie.[24]

Dunham identified among them Lord Grey of Codnor, retained by Hastings in 1465 and rewarded for good service after the campaign, and the rest of Hastings' indentured retainers.[25] This, however, cannot be so. Only six indentures antedated 1471, so it can certainly not be those *known* to have already indented with him who explain his military strength. Even if we adopt Dunham's suggestion that some may have been retained before their surviving indentures, Hastings had no connection with Tutbury honour at this date, no presence in Staffordshire, and even his Derbyshire indentures may have been cancelled by the 1468 statute of livery.[26] If Hastings took the men from Derbyshire and Staffordshire, where did Clarence find the 4,000 men with him?[27] Ironically it was the deplorable Clarence, not Hastings, who was the more successful in delivering his men in 1471. Hastings' men joined him, so *The Arrivall* tells us, partly because they supported *Edward's* cause and only partly because they were Hastings' men. They joined him not at Derby, nor at Stafford, still less at Warwick, but at Leicester, because it was in Leicestershire (and Lincolnshire, even further east) that Hastings' estates and those of his descendants were concentrated,[28] there that he built castles at Kirby Muxloe and Ashby-de-la-Zouche, and there, we may assume, that his retinue was concentrated. Little is known about them, for there are no surviving household or estate accounts, no list of fees, though Hastings certainly granted them,[29] and no surviving indentures. Such unfortunate gaps can be filled in part, witness the case of Thomas Kebell,[30] and a

---

[24] *Historie of the Arrivall of Edward IV*, ed. J. Bruce (Camden Soc. i, 1936), 8-9.

[25] Dunham, *Hastings*, 25.

[26] *Rotuli Parliamentorum*, ed. J. Strachey and others (6 vols Record Commission London 1767-77), v 633. This might explain why Nicholas Knyveton indented anew in 1474, Dunham, *Hastings*, 119.

[27] *The Arrivall*, 10-11. The well-known defection of Henry Vernon cannot have been representative as is too often supposed.

[28] Dunham, *Hastings*, 28; *CPR 1461-7*, 103-4, 352, 354; *1467-77*, 26-7; *Calendarium Inquisitionum sive Escaetarum* (4 vols Record Commission 1828), iv 413, 415-6.

[29] Dunham, *Hastings*, 123n.

[30] E.W. Ives, *The Common Lawyers of Pre-Reformation England: Thomas Kebell. A Case Study* (Cambridge 1983).

detailed study of *Leicestershire* like those for Derbyshire, Staffordshire, and Warwickshire, could be expected to turn up evidence of his local activity there.

It is known that Hastings possessed Leicestershire estates and estate officials and that he granted fees from those estates, yet there are no surviving indentures with Leicestershire men for the 1460s. Almost certainly this is because none were made. Hastings' first six indentures were made in 1461 with William Griffith of North Wales, where Hastings had office but no land; in 1465-6 he indented with Lord Grey of Codnor, William Basset, Nicholas Knyveton and Sir Thomas Stathum, all from Derbyshire, where he had little land; and in 1469 with Sir Simon Mountford from Warwickshire, where again he had little land and local importance.[31] They were all *extraordinary* contracts relating to areas where Hastings had few lands and was not politically active. In the Derbyshire case he was extending his authority by subsuming that of Grey, for not only was Grey retained, but so too were Grey's men Basset and Stathum, the latter explicitly reserving Grey's prior claim to his services and making this priority doubly clear in his will.[32] The good lordship they were all promised was as king's chamberlain or, in Griffith's case, as chamberlain of North Wales, not in the locality, and the fee Hastings paid Knyveton was payable from his *Leicestershire* lordship of Ashby-de-la-Zouche.[33] These indentures closely resembled those contracted after 1474, the first of which, to Maurice Berkeley, was also with an esquire far from Hastings' local sphere of influence. Were they also *extraordinary* contracts attaching men outside Hastings' normal ambit? *Leicestershire* men, we may deduce, were not normally bound in this way, nor were those who entered Hastings' household or became his estate officials. Indentures were used for contracts that were genuinely out of the ordinary.

The 1468 statute of livery was provoked by disturbances in Derbyshire and cancelled existing indentures of retainer. Hastings' contracts with Grey, Basset, Knyveton, and Stathum may no longer have been in force in 1471. Hastings was appointed steward of Tutbury by Clarence in February 1472 because the duke wanted his support in his dispute with his brother Gloucester over the Warwick inheritance.[34] He himself remained in control of the honour until 1473, when King Edward resumed it, and it was not until 1474 that Hastings treated it differently from any of his other sinecures. Certainly there is no evidence that he used it as a power-base for himself independently of Clarence, still less that he challenged the duke

---

[31] Dunham, *Hastings*, 119.

[32] Ibid 124.

[33] Ibid 123n.

[34] M.A. Hicks, 'Descent, Partition and Extinction: The "Warwick Inheritance"', below, 329.

over the shire elections in 1472.[35] 1472 is too early to be looking for any concrete evidence of his exercise of local power. That could only come, if it came at all, after Edward IV asserted his authority on Hastings' behalf in 1474.

The immediate background was the resumption of all Clarence's lands with effect from 21 December 1473. Most of them were restored in July 1474, when the partition of the Warwick inheritance that the duke had been resisting was completed, but the price of this was the loss of Tutbury honour and his other lands in Nottinghamshire and Derbyshire. Tutbury had been his principal seat, where he frequently resided, and his principal concentration of power before 1471. Clarence gave it up very reluctantly and nursed a deep resentment.[36] Edward IV's visit to the area was part of a judicial progress that took in Nottingham and Shrewsbury as well and it was also designed to enforce the transfer of property from Clarence, which he did. During his stay at Burton Abbey on 30 March to 2 April he made twenty-four appointments,[37] ostensibly a big clean-out of Clarence's men. Given, however, that there were at least fifty-six officers of the honour, less than half were changed, and the total looks even less impressive when studied in more detail. Regrettably there are few records for Clarence's tenure and in particular no accounts, but the identity of most of his estate officials can be deduced by comparing records of 1462-4, before he acquired the estate, with a receiver-general's account of 1473-4. This shows twenty-one officials holding rather more offices remained unchanged from 1464, but thirty-five officers were different. Of these, five appointed by the king (including Hastings himself) were definitely already in situ and many others may well have been, two others (Whitford and Stele) accounted in 1473-4 and may therefore have preceded Clarence's expulsion, three were definitely new and another three may have been. There was thus no massive turnover among officers and no wholesale introduction of royal/Hastings' clients. Unfortunately the many new annuities and leases cannot be checked in this way. It is not safe to assume that those identified as members of the household were new, for their appointment is often the first record of this connection, perhaps because Edward simultaneously enrolled them, and service in the royal household was not incompatible with service to Clarence, who was a royal prince and had drawn his first officers from the king's entourage less than ten years before. It is similarly dangerous to assume that such men were

---

[35] As implied by Rowney, *BIHR* lvii 38-9.

[36] M.A. Hicks, *False, Fleeting, Perjur'd Clarence* (Gloucester 1980), 125; *The Crowland Chronicle Continuations 1459-86*, ed. J. Cox and N. Pronay (1986), 143.

[37] Hicks, *Clarence*, 125; Rowney, *P & P*, 141, 145-6; for what follows, see Hicks, thesis, 349-50 and table XVIII, and sources there cited. Only Basset, Bonteyn and Rede definitely and Mortrich, Stanley, and Agard (in one capacity) probably were new appointments, PRO DL 37/43/4, 8, 11, 12, 19, 23.

non-resident, since there is no evidence, or that Hastings was responsible for the appointments of his brother Lord Wells or Henry Ferrers, both of whom held office in the honour throughout Clarence's tenure. What Edward IV took over in 1474 was a going concern staffed by former servants of Clarence.

Clarence continued to employ local gentry, some in his household until his death. They were now the king's tenants and officials once more and it was probably illegal for lords to retain them except within their households or estates, but this did not mean that such retainder would not take place, as it had in the past, and provoke factional strife. It was necessary therefore to reinforce ties to the king and exclude Clarence, Grey of Codnor,[38] and any other lord with such aspirations. Following the king's departure, Hastings remained, binding the first eleven gentry by indenture in 13-28 April.[39] It is not really possible to believe that this was without the king's consent and that the good lordship Hastings offered was not as Edward's chamberlain but rather as steward of Tutbury. Indeed, Edward's nomination of Hastings' deputies indicates that he did not expect him to be resident and wanted his own men in control.[40] These and subsequent indentures reinforced the authority of the king and broke the bonds of key gentry with other lords by tying them first to Hastings. Henceforth they could offer other lords service only insofar as it was compatible with Hastings' prior claims. After Clarence's death in 1478, the principal sufferer was the Duke of Buckingham, who apparently could not compete with Hastings' good lordship until the chamberlain's death, when his men – presumably *these* men – joined his service.[41] Hastings' role in preventing the retainder of the king's tenants and gentry had the same objectives as royal prohibitions on retaining for royal townsmen and tenants. One such prohibition by Richard III related to Tutbury honour.

Was there ever more to Hastings' affinity than this? Was it ever more than a means of restraining the gentry from contracting with other lords? Three questions arise here. Did Hastings ever visit his North Midlands affinity? What use did he make of the honour of Tutbury? What was his retinue's place in local politics?

The first question, whether Hastings ever or indeed regularly visited Staffordshire and Derbyshire, cannot be answered conclusively. There seems inadequate evidence either way. We do not know precisely where

---

[38] *Records of the Borough of Nottingham*, ed. W.H. Stevenson (Nottingham 1883) ii 384-7.

[39] Dunham, *Hastings*, 119.

[40] PRO DL 37/43/7.

[41] *Stonor Letters and Papers of the Fifteenth Century, 1290-1483*, ed. C.L. Kingsford (Camden Society, 3rd ser xxix, xxx, 1919), ii 161. This indicates that the bonds with Hastings were binding and exclusive as the indentures themselves state. For what follows, see Rowney, *BIHR* lvii 45.

the final eighty indentures of 1474-83 were sealed. The fact that they are grouped by date in batches may indicate that they were the product of visits to the locality but they could equally have been sealed at court. Some surely were, since it is hardly credible that Hastings was anywhere but Westminster during the planning and trial of Clarence in December 1477 to February 1478.[42] He cannot have been personally active in carrying out his duties as steward or in participating in local politics.

Both Dr Rowney and Dr Wright presume that Hastings as steward was able to dispense the offices and leases of Tutbury honour as rewards for his retainers. Some stewards on some estates actually did this. They presume that the good lordship he promised was to take this concrete form rather than favour at court. They may of course be right, but there is no direct evidence that they are. Insofar as offices were filled locally, as some accounting offices were, we cannot know who was responsible. Insofar as they were made centrally and entered on the duchy chancery rolls, they were authorised without further comment by the king under his signet or sign manual. Hastings may have influenced him, as indeed he may have influenced all other appointments emanating from him, but there is no certainty that he did. He obtained some grants and leases for himself. Certainly the king did not hand over all his patronage and revenues to Hastings, for he granted few annuities and exploited the revenues himself.[43] If Hastings did indeed control this patronage, it does not seem that he exercised it, as one might expect, to benefit his retainers from elsewhere. Appointments of members of the royal household are decidedly ambiguous.

So too with appointments to county offices. Dr Rowney and Dr Wright have certainly identified many more appointments of Hastings' indentured retainers to local office. The latter proves Hastings to have successfully recruited the most influential local gentry into his retinue. It may be a reason for supposing that he actually influenced these appointments, but it does not constitute proof or even evidence. There is not and cannot be any direct evidence at this date. Too often they are reduced to arguments based on the assumption that he *must* have done so. Dr Rowney finds it 'hardly credible that he would have let slip so obvious a perk'.[44] Other examples by Rowney and Wright are cited above. They really indicate that evidence is lacking. One must be careful not to assume none ever existed, for it is common enough for it to be lost, as in Clarence's Warwickshire, but is there actually any reason to suppose that it ever did exist in this case? Given that Hastings' affinity was so exceptional, as all

---

[42] Certainly he attended the council that planned the trial in November 1477, Hicks, *Clarence*, 146.

[43] Rowney, *P & P*, 147.

[44] Rowney, *BIHR* lvii 38; Rowney, *P & P*, 150.

now agree, should it be judged by the standards of the ordinary affinity that it so evidently was not, by its representation among county offices and knights of the shire? Rowney and Wright have searched the records so diligently for signs of Hastings' activity locally that they can have missed very little and the task need never be done again. Yet they cannot show him to have interested himself in these matters in the North Midlands, nor indeed have they shown unambiguous evidence of his direct role in regional society or politics. Very rarely, for example, was he a feoffee or arbiter. There is no evidence to justify the confidence of Dr Rowney and Dr Richmond in Hastings as a subtle and skilful manager or model good lord. Instead of striving to make something of nothing, is it not better to recognise that this is not a normal retinue and that Hastings did not use it to dominate the North Midlands? As Mr Cameron long ago pointed out, he merely prevented other lords competing over a power vacuum, *perhaps* thereby quelling factional discord and even (as Dr Carpenter suggests) promoting local order and peace.[46]

This approach makes even better sense when the totality of Hastings' interests is considered. He left his heirs the estate in Leicestershire and he married his son to a West Country heiress, Mary Hungerford. Those forfeited properties that he could not be sure of retaining, such as Belvoir Castle, he wasted.[47] In Tutbury honour he was merely steward for life and had nothing to pass to his heirs. There is no evidence that he made any effort to acquire estates or permanently strengthen his position there. He did indeed receive stewardships for life and he secured the wardship of the young Earl of Shrewsbury, who married his daughter, and the relatively few lands that were not granted out. The only evidence that distinguishes his position in the North Midlands is the existence of the indentures and these, as we have seen, were an exceptional type of contract that he did not use in his heartlands. The evidence for his use of his affinity is negative, as Dr Rowney says,[48] because it was negative. Hastings did not use it locally at all and it served the interests of his master rather than himself. If Edward IV indeed undertook a territorial re-ordering in 1473-4, then in Hastings' case it was with Mr Cameron's negative objective of removing the North Midlands from national politics. Really Lord Hastings' indentured retainers were Dr Wright's 'nationalised affinity' or Edward IV's own retinue.

But what precisely does this mean? Does it mean, for example, that these gentry were effectively retained by the king, that they saw themselves as his men and represented his interests locally, and that

---

[45] Instances are noted by Wright, *Derbyshire*, 125-6; Rowney, *P & P*, 151.

[46] Though this has been demonstrated, Carpenter, *Midland History* xi 36.

[47] H.N. Bell, *The Huntingdon Peerage* (1821), 20.

[48] See above .

Edward IV's local authority was thereby enhanced? Was there thus a 'positive' side to Hastings' indentures? Regrettably not. The indentures testify to Edward's weakness, not his strength. The king was indeed the greatest landholder in the region, but he was unable even to prevent poaching by his tenants and to secure prompt accounting by his officials. It was his incapacity to secure the exclusive loyalty of his tenants, to prevent their retainder by other lords, and to control them politically that prompted Lord Hastings to indent with them directly. Apparently this did stop competitive retaining, but it did so firstly by shutting out other lords, who were left only what service Hastings did not require, and, secondly, by *delegating* the king's authority to Hastings. If Hastings as king's deputy scarcely exercised any authority locally, what likelihood is there that the king did? Royal patronage for the locality, of course, was decided centrally, at least nominally at the king's behest, and many local gentry received offices in Tutbury honour or in the county administrations, as they always had. What cannot be shown is that the king forged significant personal ties with them, that they committed themselves in practice to the advancement of his ends, or that he rewarded them specifically for these services. Conflict apparently ceased, just as it did in the north and Wales where Gloucester and the Wydevilles were allowed to take control, but this occurred more because rival lords like Clarence and Buckingham were excluded than because new ties were forged between king and gentry that made Edward IV's immediate authority effective locally. The territorial re-ordering of 1473-4 restored local order not, as apparently originally intended, because King Edward brought the troublesome marches, Midlands, and north under his direct control. Order returned rather because, in different ways, competitors for local power were excluded: by the unintended hegemonies of Gloucester in the north and the Wydevilles in Wales,[49] and by Lord Hastings' exclusive indentures in the North Midlands. By any conventional criteria of lordship and service, Lord Hastings' indentured retainers belonged in practice neither to him, nor the king, nor indeed anyone else.

This essay has served to demonstrate that Hastings' retinue was unique not just in Derbyshire but throughout the country. Other noblemen like William de la Pole, Duke of Suffolk built local power on influence at court but no others constructed an affinity that was essentially the king's. Hastings' indentures were exceptionally numerous at a time when such documents were rare and perhaps illegal. King Edward certainly

---

[49] These are discussed in my 'Changing Role of the Wydevilles in Yorkist Politics to 1483', *Patronage, Pedigree and Power in Later Medieval England*, ed. C.D. Ross (Gloucester 1979), 60-86 above, chapter 11; 'Richard III as Duke of Gloucester and the North', *Richard III and the North*, ed R.E. Horrox (Hull 1986), 15-16.

sanctioned a breach in the law. The indentures are without parallel in their emphasis on good lordship rather than fees. They are highly unusual in that the retinue so constructed was not based on tenure of land, normally so essential,[50] but merely on the office of steward, though there are later parallels.[51] Its use foreshadowed later efforts to de-politicise royal lordships by keeping them in hand and preventing the retainder of royal tenants. Lord Hastings' retinue was thus too exceptional to allow generalisation about others or about bastard feudalism as a whole.[52]

It is particularly regrettable that Lord Hastings' indentured retainers have distorted the study of the North Midlands at a time when so much valuable research has been undertaken. To accommodate a diminished role for Hastings, some of this must be rejected and much more must be reinterpreted. The way has also been cleared for a thorough re-examination along more conventional lines of Lord Hastings' retinue, the use he made of it, and its local significance. That, in turn, may cause historians to reinterpret Hastings' national role and may influence future interpretations of the crises of 1469-71 and 1483.

[50] M.C. Carpenter, 'The Beauchamp Affinity: A Study of Bastard Feudalism at Work', *English Historical Review* xcv (1980), 517.

[51] E.g. Cameron, loc cit 24; P. Williams, *The Tudor Regime* (Oxford 1979), 4; see also Horrox, *Richard III*, 43 sqq, though her claim is debatable.

[52] This topic is treated in my 'The 1468 Statute of Livery', *Historical Research* lxiv (1991).

13

Richard III as Duke of Gloucester:
A Study in Character

Richard III's quincentenary celebrations in 1983–85 were marked by an extraordinary upsurge of enthusiasm for him, which contrasts with the general lack of interest shown in the 500th anniversary of the accession of the house of Tudor. 'Richard III has been the most persistently vilified of all English kings'.[1] Scholarly historical works still repeat and indeed amplify the charges of contemporaries that he was an usurper, a tyrant and a murderer of innocent children. For William Shakespeare, writing almost four centuries ago, there was no alternative interpretation available, but today Richard enjoys the support of the vast majority of those knowledgeable about and interested in his career. Founded in 1924, the Richard III Society now has 4,400 members committed to clearing Richard's name.

In the belief that many features of the traditional accounts of the character and career of Richard III are neither supported by sufficient evidence nor reasonably tenable, the Society aims to promote in every possible way research into the life and times of Richard III, and to secure a re-assessment of the material relating to this period, and of the role in English history of this monarch.[2]

For them, Richard was not just innocent of the crimes of which he was charged, not just the victim of Tudor propaganda. He was a good man,

Essential research for this paper was undertaken in 1984 as Visiting Research Fellow at the Borthwick Institute, University of York. An earlier version of this paper entitled 'Richard III as Duke of Gloucester: A Man with a Future?' was delivered at Teesside Polytechnic in 1984. Unless otherwise stated, all documents at the Public Record Office are cited by their P.R.O. call-numbers only.

1   C. D. Ross, *Richard III* (London 1981), p 226. For what follows, see A. J. Pollard, 'The Tyranny of Richard III', *Journal of Medieval History*, iii (1977), pp 147-65; L. Attreed, 'From *Pearl* Maiden to Tower Princes: towards a new history of medieval childhood', *ibid.* ix (1983), pp 33-5.

2   Objectives of Richard III Society listed on inside front cover of *The Ricardian* 93 (June 1985). For the membership, see *Ricardian Bulletin* (Dec. 1985). For the historiography of Richard III, see Ross, *Richard III*, pp xix-liii; A. R. Myers, 'Richard III and the Historical Tradition', *History*, liii (1968), pp 181-202.

a good husband, a good duke, and a good king, who has been grievously wronged by historians for over five hundred years. Between these two absolutes there can be no common ground and the debate often involves the exchange of assertions rather than the calm assessment of the evidence.

It is not that the evidence is copious or easy to interpret. Quite the reverse. Richard III ruled for only twenty-six months, the shortest reign of any adult king since the Norman Conquest. His reign was dominated by external military threats, which restricted his freedom of manoeuvre and obliged him to react to events rather than imposing his own stamp upon his reign. There was too little time for him to have many initiatives in policy or successes to his credit and in any case medieval government was largely a matter of routine rather than innovation. There was little scope for originality. Those elements of novelty once credited to Richard by his supporters, such as the legislation of his parliament, now appear less obviously novel or less certainly the consequence of his personal initiative than they once did.[3] Not only is vital evidence often lacking, but the violence of historical debate has sought to discredit hitherto accepted sources, not just the Tudor historians but now also Mancini's account of the usurpation, and has thus made a rounded view more difficult to achieve. Moreover it should not be overlooked that some of our problems of interpretation arise from enigmatic and secretive elements in Richard's personality. Whatever befell the 'Two Little Princes in the Tower', it is certain that Richard deliberately concealed their fate. If we do not know precisely when Richard decided to take the throne, this is because he masked his real intentions so admirably in the weeks immediately preceding his usurpation that even with hindsight certainty and unanimity cannot be achieved. If we remain uncertain about his character, it is in part at least because his public statements are not easy to accept at face value. Richard did not wish everything to be known. In short, if Richard's character is difficult to divine, it is at least in part his fault. As Professor Ross suggested, our difficulties arise 'not from what we know about him, but from what we do not know . . .'[4]

All these problems serve only to stress the impossibility of accurately assessing the character of Richard as man and king solely from the evidence of his reign. But there is no need to do this. Whereas Richard reigned for only two short years, he lived to be 32 and was adult for twelve years before his accession. During these years he was of age, in control of his own affairs, politically independent, and free of those

---

3 P. M. Kendall, *Richard III* (London, 1955), pp 282-5. For a more balanced assessment, see C. D. Ross, *Richard III* (London, 1981), pp 184-9.
4 Ross, *Richard III*, p 229.

constraints on his freedom of action that emerged after his accession. It was at this time that he formed habits, patterns of conduct, attitudes and political policies that were unlikely to be changed by his promotion. Surely the study of his career before 1483 will reveal those facets of his character that endured beyond 1483? So, indeed, has been argued repeatedly in the last thirty years. To be sure, Richard's career as Duke of Gloucester has never been ignored, but it is only in recent years, principally as a result of the work of Professors Myers and Kendall,[5] that this evidence has been integrated with that of his reign to produce a fully rounded picture. The influence of this approach is most obvious in Professor Ross' standard biography, a quarter of which treats Richard's career before his accession. So far this technique has been used mainly by Richard's supporters, anxious to stress the positive side of Richard and to reveal an estimable individual surely incompatible with the wickedness alleged of him as king, but the conclusion need not be so favourable. The evidence is strictly neutral, waiting to be interpreted by the historian, and may, when fully analysed, support either interpretation. In spite of the value of this approach and the considerable work done on different facets of Richard's ducal career, nobody has attempted to examine it as a whole in isolation from his reign, as this paper sets out to do. By placing Richard's career as Duke of Gloucester on a sound footing, it is hoped ultimately to cast light on Richard as king. One area specifically excluded from this paper is Richard's religion, which I hope to discuss elsewhere.

This study makes certain assumptions about the material that is studied. First of all, it assumes that Richard cannot have *expected* to usurp the throne before 1483. King Edward was still relatively young and had two sons and until 1478 the claims of a middle brother, George, Duke of Clarence took priority over those of Richard. Richard's *decision* to take the throne was therefore made very late, certainly after Edward IV's death on 9 April 1483. The usurpation cannot have been expected — could not have succeeded had it been anticipated — and Richard may well have left his options open even after the execution of Lord Hastings on 13 June 1483. I should add here that I find particularly convincing evidence that Richard was not seeking the throne earlier in his carelessness about the validity of his marriage. Apparently married in 1472, Richard still had no dispensation in 1475 and there is no evidence

5 A. R. Myers, 'Character of Richard III' *History Today*, iv (1954), pp 513–14; *English Historical Documents, iv 1327–1485*, ed. A. R. Myers (London 1969), pp 314–17; Myers, 'Richard and Tradition', pp 181–202; Kendall, *Richard III*, pp 27–150. For the next sentence, see Ross, *Richard III*, chs. 1–3.

that one was ever secured.[6] As this failure to secure a dispensation bastardised his children and future kings, surely Richard would have been careful over such technicalities had he expected to usurp the throne? If one accepts that Richard did not expect to usurp, it follows that he was not trying to clear away intervening barriers in 1471 and 1478 as was afterwards alleged. The evidence for Richard's complicity in the deaths of Henry VI, Prince Edward and Clarence is anyway very scanty, as Professor Myers showed long ago.[7] It is too far-fetched to suppose that Richard was plotting over the longterm, from 1471 and 1478, to usurp the throne and that his career before 1483 was conditioned by such aims. On the contrary, there is every reason to suppose that his preoccupations became less national and more local in their orientation as Edward IV's reign proceeded.

Nothing is inevitable until it happens and nothing is more unhistorical than to interpret a period in the light of later events. If we accept that Richard was not aiming at the throne before 1483, then his career before 1483 should have a consistency and a purpose about it. It should be orientated towards a desired future and should make sense. This, however, brings me to a central problem or paradox, which this paper seeks to demonstrate. Richard's career before 1483 does not make sense, at least not if one is thinking of material motivation, self-advancement, and the establishment for himself and his heirs of an enduring noble dynasty, which the great aristocracy (so we are told) were always anxious to achieve. If, as Professor Stone reports, the nobility were preoccupied by 'the preservation, increase and transmission through inheritance and marriage of the property and status of the lineage',[8] then Richard was quite untypical.

II

An important guide to Richard's intentions during the 1470s and

---

6   *R[otuli] P[arliamentorum]*, (Record Commission), vi, p 101. There is no evidence that any dispensation was ever obtained: Mr C. A. J. Armstrong undertook a specific search at the Vatican archives and failed to find it. The absence of a dispensation would explain why it was thought that there were 'quite sufficient grounds' for a divorce of Richard and Anne, *Ingulph's Chronicle of the Abbey of Croyland*, ed. H. T. Riley (London, 1893), p 499.

7   Myers, 'Richard and Tradition', pp 182-3.

8   L. Stone, *Family, Sex and Marriage in England 1500-1800* (London 1977), p 85. Unless otherwise stated, the next twelve paras. are based on B[ritish] L[ibrary] MS. Cotton Julius BXII.

early 1480s is British Library Manuscript Cotton Julius BXII. This book binds together three separate volumes drawn up at different times, the third of which (ink foliation 111-315v) is a collection of grants, deeds and other memoranda relating to Richard, Duke of Gloucester. It is this third volume that concerns us here. Written throughout in 15th-century hands, mainly by one scribe, it formed a separate volume until at least the Elizabethan period, when blank spaces were filled with genealogical data. In or after 1611 it was bound up with the other volumes on behalf of Sir Robert Cotton, who repaginated the whole and compiled the index. The oldest pagination from 2-227v precedes this rebinding, comes after the loss of several leaves of text, and demonstrates that by then the items in the volume were already in their present order. Everything in the volume relates to Richard or his interests and nothing in it is later than February 1483. The two marginal annotators, the earlier one identifying the properties, the latter noting down Richard's legal title, were concerned with matters that were of interest only during Richard's lifetime. The volume is thus a register compiled by Richard, Duke of Gloucester's staff for his use for reference in the period before his accession to the throne.

Gloucester's part of Cotton Julius BXII has long been known and used by historians, but it has not been highly valued because few of the documents that it contains are not known from other sources and none of these are of major importance. It is however a unique survival from Gloucester's secretarial archive and can be made to shed light on the organisation of that archive, on the work of Gloucester's secretary, and on the ducal policies to which the secretary contributed. It is important to stress, however, what the volume is not. It is not a register of Gloucester's correspondence, his finances, the work of his council, or of his relations with his retainers, any of which historians would dearly love to have. It is not a cartulary, in that it does not systematically list all the title deeds to all his estates, neither is it a comprehensive collection of royal grants. What it appears to be is a reference volume concerned with his rights to land and office. It falls into two parts: firstly, a select collection of grants, leases and indentures conferring title to land and office before 1474 and, secondly, a collection of selected grants and precedents relating to his estate compiled thereafter.

The opening 28 folios are written in a single hand and the documents run on without a gap in no particular order or theme. All but the last three items comprise royal grants, leases or indentures conferring land or offices on Gloucester in the years 1462-72. The final item, the unfinished 1474 indenture of partition of the Warwick inheritance, could be a later addition, as indeed could the preceding two items, which are included as precedents: these are the 1446 charter of liberties for Richmondshire and the 1461 indenture for the wardenship of the West March. The other documents are set down in no particular order of date or theme and may be merely copies of those title deeds still in Gloucester's archive. This hypothesis gains some support from the presence in the volume of copies of grants since superseded by others and by the absence of the duke's 1464 exemption from payment of fees on royal letters which was later admitted to be lost.[9] This explanation of the contents, however, is unlikely to be correct. The documents included are selected by subject matter: royal commissions, grants of estate office, licences to enter lands, grants of presentations to ecclesiastical livings and of custody of minors are deliberately omitted. More striking yet is the inclusion in the list of at least two grants, those of the Hungerford lands in 1462 and of the Great Chamberlainship of England in 1471, that had already been cancelled and for which the surrendered originals survive in the chancery files for cancelled letters patent.[10] These two entries are therefore based on copies, which were probably taken deliberately from the enrolments on the patent roll. This section of the volume, in short, contains Richard's title to properties that he had held or still held. The most likely date of this portion is 1472, as it omits other documents of January 1473 of similar character, but it could be as late as July 1474. It may be significant that the latest item, the indenture of partition of that date, was left unfinished.

A major omission from this part of the volume is Richard's charter of creation as Duke of Gloucester in 1461, but otherwise all the main grants are included. For the period of his minority there are patents of Richmond honour, the forfeited lands of Lord Hungerford, the Beaufort Dukes of Somerset, the De Vere Earls of Oxford, and of various Duchy of Lancaster properties. These grants, however, were impermanent: Edward IV transferred Richmond honour to his other brother Clarence in 1462; the Beauforts and De Veres were all restored in blood and recovered their possessions; and Margaret, Lady Hungerford convinced the king that her grandson had never held the family estates and so could not have forfeited them. As the first monarch of a fragile new dynasty, Edward was anxious to come to terms with as many of his erstwhile opponents as he could and most attainders were ultimately reversed. That Gloucester, as recipient of such grants, was a minor who had not taken seisin and who was unable to object obviously made the king's decisions to restore these estates

9   C[alendar of] P[atent] R[olls] 1461-67, p 387; 1476-85, p 166.
10 CPR 1461-7, p 197; 1467-77, p 262; C 266/63/24, 34.

very much easier to make.[11] The result was that Gloucester had few lands to enter when declared of age sometime in 1468. Although still only sixteen years of age, the duke — or possibly his advisers — took immediate action to assert his rights. Following the second attainder of Henry Beaufort, Duke of Somerset, Gloucester was again entitled both to his possessions and to those of the dowager-duchess on her death in 1467. Further treasons in 1468 strengthened Richard's claim to the Hungerford estates. New patents of October/November 1468, copied into Cotton Julius BXII, identified more precisely the properties that had been granted to the duke. Not so easily fobbed off by Lady Hungerford as his royal brother, Gloucester concluded an agreement with her on 14 May 1469 that gave him immediate possession of Farleigh Hungerford Castle and the reversion of much else on her death.[12] To this Edward IV added the lordship of Sudeley in Gloucestershire and the duchy of Lancaster honours of Halton and Clitheroe in Lancashire and Cheshire. Taken together, these would have made Gloucester a major landowner in the north-west, on the Welsh borders, and in the West Country, where his three principal seats were the castles of Sudeley (Gloucs.), Corfe (Dorset) and Farleigh Hungerford. This pattern of scattered possessions was not dissimilar from the accrued inheritances of the greatest noble houses.

The political crises of 1470-1, however, gave Gloucester yet more importance as a royal agent: he was despatched in late 1469 to Wales, where he became Chief Justice of the northern and southern principality, and then in 1470 was appointed warden of the West March towards Scotland. These offices testified rather to Richard's potential value than to any considered long-term planning by Edward. The duke's exile with King Edward in 1470 and his return at the head of the victorious army in 1471 gave him new claims on his royal brother's generosity and indeed he secured the bulk of the forfeitures then available. Thereafter, as is well known, the duke concentrated his attention on northern England and made himself, in Professor Kendall's words, 'The Lord of the North'.[13] Any southern ambitions were secondary. He gave way in Wales to the Wydevilles and in

11 *CPR 1461-7* pp 197, 212-3, 228, 287, 292, 298; M. A. Hicks, 'Edward IV, the Duke of Somerset and Lancastrian Loyalism in the North', *Northern History* xx (1984), above, 153; 'Piety and Lineage in the Wars of the Roses: The Hungerford Experience', *Kings and Nobles 1377-1529*, ed. R. A. Griffiths and J. W. Sherborne (1986), above, 170-1; J. R. Lander, *Crown and Nobility 1450-1509* (London, 1976), p 133. The judgement in the next sentence corrects Ross, *Richard III*, p 10.

12 *CPR 1467-77*, pp 139, 179; also see above, chapter 9, 175-6. For what follows, see C[alendar of] C[lose] R[olls] 1468-76, nos. 198, 409; R. Somerville, *History of the Duchy of Lancaster*, i (London, 1953), p 257n.

13 Ross, *Richard III*, ch.3; Kendall, *Richard III*, title of ch.3.

north-west England to the Stanleys as part of the regional division of power that characterised Edward IV's second reign. After 1471, in short, the slate was wiped clean. Those earlier grants that remained effective became of purely marginal significance.

This orthodox interpretation is contradicted by the inclusion of early superseded grants in Cotton Julius BXII some time in or after 1472. Why were these obsolete, if still formally uncancelled, patents included? Why did Gloucester take the trouble to secure copies of patents that had been surrendered and cancelled? Either he still held these properties or had lost them to other people with better titles. It seems most likely that Richard remembered his former rights and hoped one day to make them effective. Richard recovered most of the forfeited estates that he was granted in the 1460s, those of the Hungerfords, De Veres and Beauforts, but not until long after the event: he had to wait for the De Vere estates until 1471, nine years after the original grant, and it was not for sixteen years, until 1478, that his 1462 grant of the Hungerford estates was made good. The two grants that were formerly surrendered and cancelled, those of the Hungerford lands in 1462 and the Great Chamberlainship of England in 1471, both became his property eventually. Richmond honour and the Great Chamberlainship were secured only in 1478 on the death of his brother Clarence, at his own request and as the result of a bargain struck with the king.[14] As regards Richmond, it is noteworthy that before Clarence's death, probably before 1474, he had a copy of the charter of liberty of the honour issued by Richard, Earl of Salisbury copied into Cotton Julius BXII. More striking evidence yet relates to his appointment as Chief Justice of South and North Wales in 1469-70, the former during the minority of the Earl of Pembroke, the latter for life. On his return in 1471, when Pembroke was two years older and there was a newborn Prince of Wales, the king had other plans in mind for the government of Wales in which Richard played no part. Nevertheless, claiming that both his original patents were lost, Richard secured exemplifications of both of them on 26 August 1471, only three days before the reappointment of the Earl of Pembroke and seventeen days before the nomination of the Earl of Shrewsbury as Chief Justice of North Wales. He must have known their grants were in the pipeline. His new patent for South Wales was actually cancelled by the king, but both appear in Cotton Julius BXII, whereas his appointment to the council of the Prince of Wales does not.[15] It appears therefore that

14 *CPR 1476-85,* pp 67, 90; M. A. Hicks, *False, Fleeting, Perjur'd Clarence: George, Duke of Clarence 1449-78* (Gloucester, 1980), pp 150-1; *Idem,* 'The Middle Brother: "False, Fleeting, Perjur'd Clarence",' *The Ricardian,* 72(1981), p 309.

15 *CPR 1467-77,* pp 179, 185, 275, 277, 366.

Richard included all these items in the hope, perhaps the expectation, of eventually making them good and did not give up hope just because they were granted to someone else. Richard, of course, had never actually held Richmond honour or the De Vere and Beaufort estates of which he was nominal recipient in 1462. He was too young and his nominal title was surely too brief for him to have become attached to them or to feel resentment at losing them. That said, he nevertheless seems to have remembered these grants or, at least, learnt of his previous title and seen in these old grants residual claims that might one day be made good. All magnates, of course, needed to have a long memory for their rights, real and potential, and for possible rivals to them, but Richard appears exceptional in retaining interest in royal grants that had been superseded or cancelled. Clearcut royal decisions, such as those transferring property to his brother and rearranging the rule of Wales, did not deter him. He was also surprisingly singleminded in pursuit of these claims, was prepared to wait for a long time to make them good, and was highly successful in achieving his aims.

The rest of Cotton Julius BXII, post-1472 and perhaps post-1474 as well, consists of miscellaneous items entered at different times in different ink in the empty spaces left in between: an arrangement which makes precise dating of most entries impossible. The contents seem to have been selected because they offered the opportunity for defending and extending the duke's rights or possessions. As lord of the Beaufort lands, it was natural that the duke should keep a copy of the inquisitions post mortem of the last Duke of Somerset, which recorded what he had held, what he had forfeited, and thus what Gloucester had acquired. Similarly, as lord of Helmsley in Yorkshire from 1478, it is understandable that he saw a use for an extent for 1353. As warden of the West March and constable of England, it was appropriate that Gloucester should have copies of the patent of the last constable, Earl Rivers, and of the 1461 indenture as warden of the Earl of Warwick. With such information, the duke could ensure that his rights were fully exercised and did not lapse through oversight. But there is more to it than that. By identifying rights due in 1353, the Helmsley inquisition set a standard against which to measure the current situation, to identify any that had lapsed, and thus constituted a basis for recovering them. The duke could therefore make more of his rights than his predecessors had done. Documents relating to Richmond and Gloucester honours reveal a particular interest in the appurtenant knights fees, militarily obsolete and generally neglected, though whether the duke was interested primarily in the potential income from feudal incidents or in rights of lordship is unclear. Another group of documents about forests could have referred to Gloucester's office of Keeper of Forests North of the River Trent, but that they are included in this volume and relate solely to the Forests of Inglewood (Cumbs.), Nidderdale and Galtres

(Yorks.) suggests that his concern was personal rather than the result of his official duties. The Inglewood documents, in particular, identified the boundaries of the forest, which he did not hold, and the enclosures within them, which he did, and may have justified the actions that rendered the forest treeless and gameless by 1487.[16] As coheir of the Warwick inheritance and its Beauchamp, Despenser, Neville, Montagu and Holland components, it was logical for him to record documents establishing his rights to an exchequer annuity, to the Warwick chamberlainship of the exchequer, and to the office of weigher of Southampton. The identity, extent, title, and appurtenances of the Neville estates were revealed by three sets of inquisitions and a further document listed knights fees held of the lordship of Sheriff Hutton (Yorks.). Together these provided information useful both in defending Gloucester's tenure and for identifying and asserting rights of lordship over his military tenants. It was logical that the duke should record both the act of 1461 reversing the forfeiture of John Montagu, Earl of Salisbury (d.1400) and the original grant of 1337 endowing the earldom. This latter patent included lands since lost, notably Trowbridge and Sherborne. Did Gloucester, like his wife's grandmother, contemplate recovering these properties under the pretext that they were included in the earlier forfeiture? Why did he include details of the process of 1397, whereby an Earl of Warwick lost the marcher lordship of Gower, if he did not regard it as something that might one day be recovered? The lordship of Gower, like that of Ogmore which he did acquire,[17] would have conveniently complemented his own lordship of Glamorgan.

Examination of these later folios of Cotton Julius BXII thus documents how Gloucester developed the long memory that was identified above. Considerable administrative effort was directed from the centre, almost certainly by the duke himself, to make the most of his rights. Historical research was commissioned into the rights and titles of his estates and offices. The results could have been useful in defence against his rivals, but his objectives seem more positive than negative. Most of the documents justified action, mainly to make the most of particular properties or offices by recovering lapsed rights. There was considerable attention to detail, even in minor estates, and a consciousness of the potential of neglected rights, such as those over knights fees. There was also a hint of aggression against military tenants and rival lords. What would the king, as lord of Trowbridge, or the

---

16   M. A. Hicks, 'Richard III as Duke of Gloucester and the North', *Richard III and the North,* ed. R. E. Horrox (Hull, 1986), p 15.

17   *History of the County of Glamorgan,* iii, *The Middle Ages,* ed. T. B. Pugh (Cardiff, 1965).

Earl of Pembroke, as lord of Gower, have thought if they had known
their titles were under review by potential rivals? But, so far as we
know, Gloucester did not actually pursue the latter two possibilities
before his accession, perhaps because the appropriate opportunities did
not arise. These later pages of Cotton Julius BXII offer the basis for
future action, some of which was taken before 1483, some not. All this
may appear speculative, since in most cases there is no evidence — and
we cannot expect to find any — to confirm my interpretation. But in
certain cases documented in Cotton Julius BXII it can be demonstrated
that Gloucester aggressively asserted and extended his rights. These are
the three disputes over the Warwick inheritance, and the Oxford and
Hungerford lands.

The best known, without a doubt, relates to the estates of Richard
Neville, Earl of Warwick and Salisbury (Warwick the Kingmaker).
Following Warwick's death in 1471, his Neville lands held in tail male
were considered forfeit, and those in Yorkshire and Cumberland were
granted to the Duke of Gloucester. A fortnight after the first patent,
Gloucester had his grant amended to cover lands held by the earl in tail
male of royal grant. Although these were in the process of being given
to others, such a patent offered the prospect, if the cirsumstances were
right, of securing them in due course as well. More immediately
important, Gloucester coveted those lands held by the late earl in tail
general both in these counties and elsewhere, which were held by his
brother George, Duke of Clarence in right of his wife Isobel,
Warwick's eldest daughter, even though much rightly belonged to her
mother Anne, Warwick's widow and the Beauchamp and Despenser
heiress. To obtain a half-share of these lands as well, Gloucester
proposed marrying Warwick's other daughter Anne and sought the
division of the estates in her favour. Edward IV was induced to agree to
a division in February 1472, although one involving the whole of
Warwick's estates, not merely a partition of the tail general lands that
would have left the northern Neville lordships out of consideration and
in Gloucester's hands. With the king's support Gloucester exerted
pressure, including the cynical manipulation of the Countess of
Warwick, to force Clarence to compromise. An indenture of partition,
partly recorded in Cotton Julius BXII, was sealed in July 1474, the
principles underlying it were confirmed by parliament in 1474-5, and
the late Earl of Warwick was therefore omitted from the 1475 act of
attainder. These measures enabled both dukes to enjoy the lands by
inheritance by a complex series of legal measures, which cut out the
legitimate rights of the politically impotent countess and of a minor,
George Neville, Duke of Bedford. Beneficial though the arrangement
was to Gloucester, it did not satisfy him, and he took advantage of
Clarence's execution in 1478 to secure the king's consent to some
revisions in his favour and at the expense of his infant nephew Edward,

Earl of Warwick. Certain lands in Rutland and Lincolnshire coveted by Gloucester, however, could not be secured by agreement, so he seized them by force, clinging onto them in defiance of the royal exchequer until, as king, he could silence it. Finally, he initiated litigation in chancery to secure an eighth share of the lands of the Beauchamp trust, which were probably excluded from the original partition in 1474-5.[18]

There are considerable parallels in the case of the Oxford estates. Like Warwick the Kingmaker, the Earl of Oxford was in the defeated Lancastrian army at Barnet, but, unlike Warwick, survived to continue resistance. His lands were also considered forfeit, although he was not attainted until 1475, and they were granted to Gloucester on 4 December 1471. In 1475 a second patent was issued, which added the lands of Anne Cobham, widow of the earl's elder brother.[19] Gloucester apparently encountered no difficulty in making good his title to the earl's paternal estates, but he also took the opportunity to build on what he was given by the king by securing those lands held in her own right by the earl's mother Elizabeth, Dowager-Countess of Oxford. Gloucester had a reversionary interest in these *only* if they descended to her son, but this was unlikely to happen, since they were enfeoffed to her use and she could direct by will how they descended after her death. Gloucester had no claim to them during her life, but he was granted custody of her and her lands on account of her son's treason and persuaded her and her feoffees to convey her lands to him by deeds copied into Cotton Julius BXII. The written agreement between duke and countess, if one existed, does not survive. At best, he secured her estates from the admittedly aged and frail countess in return for concessions which were extremely light and in no way a fair price, especially in view of her almost immediate demise. At worst, he terrorised her into giving up her birthright and disinheriting her heirs by threatening and maltreating her. Richard himself asserted the former, but there is considerable circumstantial evidence for the latter. There can be no doubt that the chancellor, Bishop Stillington, and most of the countess's feoffees strongly disapproved of these transactions and indeed Richard had to sue the latter in chancery before they would release their rights to him. Edward IV is reported to have disapproved as well. Another observer, William Tunstall, felt that it was

18 M. A. Hicks, 'Descent, Partition and Extinction: The "Warwick Inheritance",' B[ulletin of the] I[nstitute of] H[istorical] R[esearch] lii(1979), p 124; 'The Beauchamp Trust 1439-87', *ibid*, liv(1981), pp 141, 145; *Clarence*, pp 150-1; *CPR 1467-77*, pp 260, 266. See below, 331, 343-4.

19 *CPR 1467-77*, pp 197, 560. For what follows, see *CCR 1468-76*, nos. 1214-15; C 263/2/1/6. My interpretation agrees with Ross, *Richard III*, p 31. I hope to demonstrate the reliability of the depositions elsewhere. The next paragraph is based on Hicks, 'Piety and Lineage', above, 170-80.

incompatible with Gloucester's honour as a knight and king's brother
to take advantage of her, ironically drawing the wrong conclusion that
the countess would not be molested!

The same capacity to make the most of what he had emerges in
Richard's dealings with Margaret, Lady Hungerford. His original 1462
grant of the Hungerford lands of Lord Moleyns was of little immediate
value, because they had been enfeoffed by Moleyns' father Lord
Hungerford to their creditors and were controlled by the Dowager-
Lady Margaret. On his majority, however, Richard concentrated on
the ultimate devolution of the lands on the expiry of the mortgage and
death of Lady Hungerford and exploited her anxiety about the future to
secure concessions. On 14 May 1469 they agreed that she would hold
the bulk of the estates for life and dispose of some by will in return for
immediate possession of three properties and the reversion of more on
her death. This binding agreement, which converted his vestigial
claims into solid reality, was not the end of the matter, as in 1474 he was
granted immediate possession of further Hungerford estates. Some
were due to revert to him under the 1469 agreement, but others were
not. This grant took account of two inquisitions post mortem of 1470
and 1473. One found that Lord Hungerford could not have legitimately
enfeoffed certain estates that he held as life- or joint-tenant, the other
that certain properties never had been so enfeoffed. The former finding
was correct, the latter fraudulent. In both cases, the lands concerned
were subject to Moleyns' attainder and hence to royal grant, the 1469
agreement being ignored. It is impossible to *prove* who was responsible
for supplying the juries with this information and thus for procuring
the inquisitions, but Gloucester as beneficiary is the most likely
candidate. The inquisitions feature in Cotton Julius BXII together with
copies of Moleyns' quitclaims to his father's feoffees and to his mother,
which demonstrates that the duke was responsible for some research
into the title of the estates. It may be, moreover, that Richard never
intended to be bound by the 1469 agreement and merely saw it as a basis
for further gains. The absence from it of Edward IV's sign manual,
stated in the text to be appended as evidence of royal approval, is
suggestive.[20] Had Edward indeed signed it, would he have been willing
to overthrow its terms five years later? Moreover Richard did not, as
agreed, secure mortmain licences within a year, perhaps because he did
not try. However that may be, the duke's gains proceeded by stages, in
1469, 1474 and in 1478, when further lands reverted to him. Lady

20   The original is Huntington Library HAP 3466. I am indebted to Miss Mary
     Robertson for supplying a photocopy of this document and for confirming that
     Edward IV's sign manual is absent and to the Trustees of the Huntington Library for
     allowing me to quote from it.

Hungerford's inquisitions post mortem are also included in Cotton Julius BXII. Had Richard designs also on the remainder?

That Richard was acquisitive needs no emphasis and no justification. He had to be, if he was to achieve the level of resources, newly inflated for his brother of Clarence from 2000 marks to £4500, considered appropriate for a royal duke and to endow a ducal dynasty. In each of these three cases his starting point was a petition, which resulted in a royal patent. No doubt the contents of the petition itself resulted from some research, but once in possession more investigation followed, which identified other opportunities. Further patents were normally obtained, correcting errors of names and locations in the original, omitting properties wrongly included, but also adding lands initially overlooked — like those of Anne Cobham — and rephrasing the terms to allow for other possibilities, such as Warwick's tail male lands of royal grant. These display great foresight, a remarkable capacity to predict future eventualities, which we have already seen in the later entries in Cotton Julius BXII. In other instances, notably in Cumberland, the duke steadily extended what the king granted him and whittled down the rent due for it.[21] Gloucester's relations with his rivals show a similar step by step, carefully researched approach. He made the most of his strengths, whether they were merely his reversionary rights and potential for nuisance in the instance of the two dowagers, his access to royal favour, or his physical custody of the Countess of Oxford, which he had surely requested. He was extremely flexible in the means used. He was prepared to abandon rights under royal grant in return for a compromise, exchanging immediate gains for his reversionary rights and other concessions. Whether he ever intended honouring his promises is doubtful and certainly in neither the Hungerford nor the Warwick cases did the dispute end with the agreement, which became the basis of further action. If this was always his intention, he concealed it well and his opponents were not prepared for his subsequent conduct. His tactics were highly flexible. Sometimes he rigidly enforced a royal grant, sometimes struck a compromise, and once even exploited his hand in marriage. If appropriate, he used the courts of law and proper procedures, resorting to chancery on several occasions and obtaining new inquisitions on others. He himself had a good knowledge of the law and was able to argue his case most ingeniously before the royal council in 1472.[22] He was capable of pursuing alternative lines of argument, those about the Warwick inheritance being mutually contradictory, and it was probably he who was responsible for devising the legal fictions that enabled him to

21   Hicks, 'Richard III and the North', p 15; below, p.
22   *Ingulph's Chronicle*, p 470.

inherit by excluding the real heirs. Where research failed to expose weakness and legitimate channels were not enough, he employed fraud and presumably maintenance to secure favourable inquisitions. Where law and royal influence alike did not serve his ends, he used force, certainly seizing some land and probably terrorising the Countess Elizabeth. He exploited his opponents' weaknesses, whether they were political eclipse, extreme age or youth, or personal frailty, and showed no compunction in driving his advantage home. Yet he was prepared to wait and prepare his ground until the opportunity arose, as we have already seen with reference to Cotton Julius BXII, and did not confine his attention to one avenue of advantage. This combination of careful preparation, opportunism, flexibility in tactics, and utter unscrupulousness and ruthlessness in execution go a long way towards explaining why the duke was so uniquely successful in achieving his ends. Obviously Richard must have been well-served by researchers and lawyers — he could afford the services of the best — but their activities needed direction, which surely came from himself. It was he, surely, who identified the objectives and selected the means. It was he in person who is reported to have threatened the Countess of Oxford,[23] it was certainly he who put his case in royal council, and it can only have been he personally who exploited his access to and influence with his brother the king.

III

Gloucester, it has been said, was the creation of his brother the king. He owed his lands and income to the king's grants, exploited royal favour on behalf of himself and his retainers. Mr Morgan, Professor Ross, and Dr Horrox in turn have seen 'in the steady consolidation of Gloucester's power in the north over more than a decade the working of a conscious policy by Edward IV'. For them Richard's power was the expression and his activities the extension of the king's will.[24] This was true in the literal sense that his power derived from the king, but he was never content with what Edward gave him, always sought to build on it, and was reluctant to accept the limits that the king tried to place upon his freedom of action. He did not allow his obligations or sense of

23 C 263/2/1/6.
24 D. A. L. Morgan, 'The King's Affinity in the Polity of Yorkist England', *Transactions of the Royal Historical Society*, 5th series, xxiii(1973), pp 17-18; Ross, *Richard III*, pp 24, 26; R. E. Horrox, 'Introduction' to *Richard III and the North*, p 12.

loyalty to his brother to deprive him of his political independence. Richard is believed to have opposed the treaty of Picquigny in 1475 and in 1478 he co-operated in Clarence's fall only in return for the satisfaction of a shopping list of desirable ends.[25] Nor did he necessarily conform to the plans that the king had for him. When in 1471, as in 1469, Edward IV reassessed his patronage and distribution of responsibility, he revised his plans for Gloucester. The duke could now be provided for from forfeitures without dismembering the Duchy of Lancaster, so Halton and Clitheroe were resumed and the Stanleys recovered their former dominance of Lancashire and Cheshire. That Gloucester did not willingly resign anything emerges both from his inclusion of his grants of Halton, Clitheroe and the two Chief Justiceships in Cotton Julius BXII and in his exemplification of the latter patents in 1471 just before the offices were bestowed elsewhere. Evidently he still hoped to recover them. He expanded his Welsh holdings by securing the marcher lordships as part of his share of the Warwick inheritance and sought to develop them, while in the north-west he continued to back the Harringtons in their feud with the Stanleys. However, he gratefully accepted the new opportunities offered him. He enlarged his share of the Warwick inheritance at the expense of his brother Clarence and he extended his power in the north by recruiting the retainers of the other marcher warden, the Earl of Northumberland, and challenged his sway in his own country in the same way as he rivalled the Stanleys across the Pennines. His combative approach threatened public peace in the north-west, where the Stanley-Harrington feud dragged on; in the north-east, where the royal council intervened on Northumberland's behalf in May 1473; and in the midlands, where his quarrel with Clarence embroiled Lord Hastings and the Wydevilles and almost came to blows.[26] Although he exploited King Edward's influence, steadily extending what was granted him, he was not unduly concerned about his good opinion. Not that Edward was supine in his relations with his brother. In 1473 he sought to restrain Gloucester in the north, in 1474 Gloucester secured less than he wanted from the partition of the Warwick inheritance, and in 1475 the king deleted five manors from an ampler petition for the Oxford estates. Even such measures did not check Richard, who established his dominance of northern England in spite of royal wishes, just as the Wydevilles simultaneously exploited their control of Prince Edward to

---

25   Kendall, *Richard III*, p 118; Ross, *Richard III*, pp 34–5; Hicks, *Clarence*, pp 150–1.
26   Hicks, *Clarence*, p 121–2; *idem*, 'Dynastic Change and Northern Society: The Career of the Fourth Earl of Northumberland 1470–1489', *Northern History*,   below , 370–1; M. K. Jones, 'Richard III and the Stanleys' in *Richard III and the North*, pp 36–40.

establish their hegemony in Wales. Once Richard had built up his regional authority, Edward found it useful and came to regard the duke as his main representative in the north. Richard's power there had developed, however, in spite of royal wishes rather than as their expression.

While Gloucester was consolidating himself in the north, so the queen's family, the Wydevilles, and the Stanleys were strengthening their hold on Wales and the north-west. It was perhaps for this reason that the duke became less assertive in those areas, but a more important factor was the rationing of royal favour. After 1471 King Edward evidently felt that he had given Gloucester enough. Thereafter the duke secured new patents that enlarged the potential of what he held, but no more unconditional grants of land. Those admittedly substantial estates he obtained from King Edward were in exchange for other properties elsewhere or on leases for rent. Henceforth the two brothers bargained together to their mutual advantage. That Gloucester's interests remained very wide is clear from the list of favours requested in 1478, but he was obliged to decide what his priorities were, what he wanted to develop, what he was prepared to give up and what, just as vital, the king was prepared to accept in exchange. To obtain the castles and lordships of Scarborough, Richmond, Skipton and Helmsley, Richard had to abandon his lordship of Chirk in the Welsh marches to the Stanleys and his town of Chesterfield, his West Country castles of Sudeley, Corfe and Farleigh Hungerford, and two Hertfordshire manors to the king. As Edward IV also deleted five Essex manors from a new patent of the Oxford estates in 1475, he helped reduce Gloucester's holdings in the West Country and Home Counties and focus his attention on the north.[27] Probably Edward was motivated as much by his search for endowments for St George's Chapel Windsor as by any desire to make Gloucester primarily a northern magnate, but by 1475 that result had been achieved.

Edward's actions merely accelerated a process that Gloucester had already begun. The duke's interests were wide and the possibilities that he foresaw almost endless, but he was not universally acquisitive and aggressive, rather he was selective about what to develop and what to let go and initiated the rationalisation of his estates almost as soon as he was granted them. This emerges most obviously in the case of the forfeitures he was granted in 1471, which comprised not just the De Vere and Neville estates, but those of other traitors such as Sir Thomas

---

27 Hicks, 'Dynastic Charge', below, 370; 'The Warwick Inheritance', 329-30. C81/1511/1. For what follows, see M. A. Hicks, 'The Changing Role of the Wydevilles in Yorkist Politics to 1483', *Patronage, Pedigree and Power in Later Medieval England,* ed. C. D. Ross (Gloucester, 1979), above, 220-4.

Dymmock, Sir Thomas Delalaunde, Lewis Fitzjohn, Robert Harleston, John Truthale and John Darcy. Only Harleston, Dymmock and Delalaunde were attainted in 1475, the others escaping this fate, and only Delalaunde's lands were included in Richard's 1475 patent. A factor here may have been the title by which the lands were held, since Alice Harleston and Katherine Delalaunde recovered their jointures, the former presumably in response to her surviving petition to the duke. Gloucester also permitted Darcy to recover his lands, helped save Sir John Marny from forfeiture, and subsequently petitioned for and secured the custody of Marny's heir. Did a similar deal lie behind the decision to allow Dymmock's son to inherit in 1472?[28] It seems that some if not all of these escaped attainder because Gloucester preferred to compromise with the original owners, probably accepting cash instead, a secure title to part of the estates, or the wardship of the heir in lieu. Some even of the De Vere possessions were excluded from Gloucester's 1475 petition, but were given by the king to Lords Howard and Ferrers of Chartley, the king's feoffees, and Sir Thomas Grey in 1475-6, probably by prior agreement with the duke rather than resumption by the king. Such alienations did not stop in 1475, as he sold southern estates piecemeal thereafter.[29] His holdings in the south were increasingly peripheral to his main concerns, although he never totally abandoned his interest there and continued to employ southerners — notably the Suffolk knight Sir James Tyrell — in key positions.

There was nothing involuntary about Gloucester's advancement of himself in the north. Starting off with his Neville lordships, his wardenship, his chief forestership, and his chief stewardship of the north parts of the Duchy of Lancaster, he steadily accrued further lands and offices by purchase, exchange and by lease. Nothing illustrates his determination to consolidate his position more than the way he outbid others for leases, perhaps paying more than the true value because his concern was not financial but political. He displayed the same aggression towards the other northern magnates, intruding himself into their spheres of influence and adding conflicts with the Stanleys and Percies to his hereditary feud with the Neville Earls of Westmorland. Could he be content with nothing less than supremacy? Dominance was what he achieved, not by force but by compromises that made him pre-eminent throughout the region while leaving his rivals free of interference in their own countries. Details of Richard's indenture with Northumberland are well-known and were apparently

28 *CPR 1467-77*, pp 297, 336-7, 560; *RP* v. pp 130-1; C 81/1504/13; British Library Additional Charter 67545.
29 *CPR 1467-77*, pp 538, 543, 545, 560, 563, 567, 569; *CCR 1476-85*, no. 735; F. Devon, *Issues of the Exchequer* (London 1837), pp 499, 501.

observed; we know of his reconciliation with the Nevilles of Raby, but not the terms; and a formal agreement with the Stanleys can only be suspected. At the end the duke had a free hand in Cumberland, and north and west Yorkshire, and his authority was felt indirectly through the Percies, Nevilles and Stanleys in Northumberland, Durham and Lancashire.[30] What is most obviously missing here and what must have played an essential part is the diplomacy that persuaded his rivals to accept his assessment of mutual advantage rather than resorting to violent resistance and which, in the case of Northumberland at least, brought warmth and willing co-operation to the relationship. Similarly it was not Gloucester the aggressor who built up his retinue, but Gloucester the reconciler. The duke let bygones be bygones, welcoming former rebels to his brother into his service; he was a generous patron — an extravagant granter of fees — and an arbiter whose lordship was valued and could be trusted. His intra-personal skills, his capacity to get on with people, inspire them, manipulate them, and win their enduring loyalty and nostalgic memory, can only be deduced. Such techniques reinforced the existing ties of kinship, neighbourhood and lordship and brought not only the gentry but the lesser nobility into his service.[31] Thus, in only twelve years, he forged a connection that dominated Yorkshire and the four northern counties. Initially a disturbing influence, he became a source of peace and social cohesion.

At the centre of this regional hegemony was the duke's status as heir by marriage of Warwick the Kingmaker and thus of three centuries of Neville tradition. Hereditary right conferred greater security of tenure than a royal grant. He represented continuity, not a break with the past, and could draw on traditional ties of service and loyalty. He consciously fostered this image, developing the unity of his connection by residing on his estates, building up his retinue, reinforcing the ties of kinship and neighbourhood, building extensively at Middleham and Barnard Castle, founding a fair at Middleham, patronising local religious houses, and establishing two colleges.[32] It was prestigious to be the patron of religious houses and such houses could advance their patron's prestige if they identified with him. Their estates and their patronage could become an extension of his own. To found one's own college conferred these advantages with a personal tie and offered opportunities to advance clerics in one's service. But there was more to Gloucester's foundations than that. Gloucester's predecessors at Middleham and his

---

30 See below, chapter 21, pp. 371-5; Attreed, 'An Indenture between Richard Duke of Gloucester and the Scrope Family of Masham and Upsall', *Speculum* lviii(1983), pp 1018-25.

32 Hicks, 'Richard III and the North', p 18.

near rivals the Neville Earls of Westmorland had their spiritual centre in Durham cathedral and at their college at Staindrop in the same county. His immediate predecessor, Warwick the Kingmaker, inherited three such mausolea, that of the Beauchamp Earls of Warwick at Warwick College, that of the Despensers at Tewkesbury Abbey, and that of the Montagu Earls of Salisbury at Bisham Abbey. Warwick had wanted to rest at Warwick, but was buried instead at Bisham, like his father before him.[33] For Gloucester; Bisham was not enough, perhaps because it was too distant and also because it was Clarence, not himself, who was Earl of Salisbury. To build on his wife's Neville tradition and create a spiritual focus for his connection, to equal and indeed surpass his near-neighbours the Nevilles, he needed a substantial foundation of his own, at Middleham or Barnard Castle. To found one made him the equal of the Earls of Westmorland; to found two — and on such a scale — made him one of the oustanding founders of the later middle ages, ahead of those like the Nevilles, the Beauchamps, or the house of York, each of whom had only one such college.

Behind the obvious material uses of religion, Gloucester was a genuinely pious man, whose strange blend of practical materialism and spirituality was shared by many of his contemporaries. The duke differed, however, in the scale with which it was expressed. Rising costs meant that in the later middle ages new foundations were few and relatively small by the standard of earlier generations. Men with large incomes and no heirs, like bishops, could found them from income during their lives, but even the richest laymen, without near heirs to provide for, did not bear all the costs in their lifetimes and left much to their executors. Richard Beauchamp, Earl of Warwick, perhaps the second richest magnate of his age, left the Beauchamp chapels at Warwick and Guyscliff, which cost £3634, to be built and endowed after his death at the expense of his heirs by a trust with revenues of £328 that lasted almost fifty years. The second Hungerford chapel at Salisbury, which cost £823 to build and equip, was financed by borrowing secured by a similar long term trust. Gloucester's building projects were larger than this, yet work certainly began at Middleham. The scale of the proposed endowment, 200 marks for Middleham and

33   *Rous Roll* (Gloucester, 1980), no. 57.

400 marks for Barnard Castle, was also exceptional.[34] The endowments may have represented a tenth of Gloucester's income and a capital value of £8000. Many such schemes, like Lord Botreaux's North Cadbury College, failed because the founder could not afford to part with the land, but Gloucester, whose ambitions were even larger, could and did. An act passed in the 1478 parliament allowed him to alienate six of his wife's advowsons to the two colleges and in 1480 he actually did alienate six manors late of the Countess of Oxford to Middleham College. Other alienations can also be regarded as an extension of his northern connection: Seaham rectory, bought for £150, was appropriated in 1476 to Coverham Abbey and lands in Sutton in Derwent were given to Wilberfoss priory. Other alienations cannot be explained in these terms. Three of the Countess Elizabeth's manors and the Warwick advowson of Olney (Bucks.) were granted to St George's Chapel, Windsor and another manor, Foulmer, was given to Queens' College, Cambridge. St George's Chapel was the foundation most favoured by King Edward, who selected the chapel as his burial place, rebuilt and re-endowed it, and his consort Elizabeth Wydeville was recognized as second founder at Queens'. As a benefactor of these colleges, Richard was self-consciously identifying himself as a prince of the royal house.

The Yorkist period inflated the importance of the royal family and set them apart from the non-royal nobility. In the 1460s even the husbands of the queen's sisters were ennobled. The level of income thought appropriate for a royal duke in 1467 was seven times the 1000 marks thought suitable for Edward III's sons and Henry VI's half-brothers and three times the minimum qualification for a dukedom. In 1483 a sumptuary act set the royal family apart from the ordinary nobility:

> no maner person, of what estate, degre or conditon he be, were any clothe of golde, or silke of purpylle colour, but oonly the Kyng, the Quene, my Lady the Kynges Moder, the Kynges Childer, his Brother and Susters, upon payne to forfeite for every defaute twenty poundes.[35]

---

34 M. A. Hicks, 'Counting the Cost of War: The Moleyns Ransom and the Hungerford Land Sales 1453-87', see above, chap. 10; Hicks, 'The Beauchamp Trust', below, chap. 19, 337f; *CPR 1476-85*, p 67. For North Cadbury, see W. Dugdale, *Monasticon Anglicanum*, ed. J. Caley and others (Record Commission, London, 1846), vi(3), p 1423; *CPR 1422-29*, pp 189-90; *1446-52*, p 230. For what follows, see *RP* vi p 172; C. Sharp, *Rising in the North: The 1569 Rebellion*, ed. C. Wood (Shotton, 1975), p 369; Durham, Dean and Chapter Muniments, Register IV, ff.174v-5, 185v; North Yorkshire Record Office, Middleham College Documents, ZRC 17503; R. E. Horrox, 'Richard III and the East Riding', *Richard III and the North*, p 102 n.11; *CPR 1476-85*, pp 34, 255, 266. The fate of 10 other manors of the countess is unknown: were these granted to Barnard Castle College, whose records are lost?

35 *RP* vi pp 220-1. I am indebted to my colleague Dr T. B. James for this reference.

That Gloucester shared this heightened estimation of himself is suggested by his accumulation of great offices, whose value was primarily honourable and honorific. Already constable and admiral of England, he added the great chamberlainship in 1478.[36] It was his status as a royal prince that enabled him to create bannerets in 1481-2, when earls and barons could only dub knights. Lavish display was appropriate to his rank: we have treated his building operations, his large retinue, and his lavish religious foundations. The finishing touch, which recognized his distinction as a royal duke, was the grant of the Cumberland palatinate in 1483.[37] This gave him regal powers within the county of Cumberland rivalled among late medieval laymen only by the Dukes of Lancaster. In his own day he was unique.

The act of 1483 creating the Cumberland palatinate purports to confirm the demands of the duke and reads like a petition. It was a reward to the duke for his good service against the Scots and apparently reflects his desires. As we have seen, the palatinate fits his high opinion of himself. It is also consistent with his normal step by step approach. A succession of grants had given Gloucester everything that the king had to give in Cumberland except the forest of Inglewood: the wardenship of the West March, the shrievalty, the enclosures in Inglewood, and two Duchy of Lancaster manors. These were not held in fee simple or tail, but temporarily, for years, life or lease. Rents of £106 13s. 4d. were due for the sheriff's farm and the Duchy leases.[38] The duke's logical next step was to secure the freehold and cancel the rent, which the creation of the palatinate achieved. Obviously there was more potential for increasing revenue for a lord on the spot than for a distant king — more people would attend a local court than one at Westminster — and the palatinate would reinforce his authority over the other local magnates. The inducement for King Edward to give up his regalian rights, his rents, and indeed a lump sum of 10,000 marks was the prospect of permanent savings in the warden's salary, running at 1200 marks in peacetime and £1000 in war. Edward was certainly seeking to reduce the cost,[39] which was difficult to achieve in wartime, particularly as Gloucester's existing indenture still had seven years to run. As the duke's salary had not been regularly paid, the loss of income was initially more impressive in theory than in practice, especially as the lump sum itself was certainly not paid immediately. In the longer term, the duke lost income that was highly unlikely to be fully made up by more intensive administration. It might however be forthcoming from

36 *CPR 1461-67*, p 214; *1467-7*, p 178; *1476-85*, p 67. For the next sentence, see Hicks, 'Dynastic Change', below 391.

37 *RP* vi 204-5. This is the source of the next paragraph.

38 *CPR 1467-77* p 556; DL 37/55/29.

39 E 404/77/1/28; Hicks, 'Dynastic Change', below, 381.

any conquests in Scotland, which the act granted to Richard in fee simple. Historians have tended to play down this provision and certainly it was a high risk strategy. Yet, as we have seen, Gloucester often saw potential in unpromising circumstances and frequently sought to broaden the scope of royal grants in his favour at no extra cost to the king. As warden of the West March since 1470, sheriff since 1474, he knew what resources were available in the county. His recent campaign in Scotland had indicated what military resources were necessary, he could count on assembling the same manpower from his retinue for his own purposes as he had for the king, and he had raised 10000 marks towards the costs by capitalising his wardenship. The ruthless exploiter of weakness in his English disputes, he may well have seen a favourable opportunity in Scotland in its weak king and factional divisions. It had been these that had prevented any effective opposition to his 1482 campaign. The war was continuing and Gloucester could count on the hostility of the Duke of Albany to the government and on persistent fighting in the East March. In fact, as we know, factional strife was to persist until James III's death in 1488 and into the minority of his son. Perhaps therefore he was right to see a wonderful opportunity for his aggression, which had been so successful in England, to be applied towards constructing a semi-independent principality for himself in Scotland. The obvious parallels are those Norman warlords, who carved out territory for themselves in Wales and Ireland. It was a substitute for the throne that younger brothers of kings in England, France and Scotland so hankered after at this time. That he did not was because the throne of England proved a more attractive prospect.

IV

The Cumberland palatinate can thus be seen as the consummation of Gloucester's policy throughout the 1470s and set the finishing touches to his creation of a northern dynasty more concentrated, more powerful and more permanent than that of the Nevilles which preceded it. The stakes were very high, of course. Gloucester risked taking on forces too powerful for him to cope with by himself with financial resources that demanded quick and easy victory. Such a perilous course had to be pursued, however, if Gloucester was to retain the power that he had already constructed, which was threatened with imminent collapse in 1483.

The enhanced status of the Yorkist royal family implied higher expenditure for royal dukes. Accordingly Edward IV treated his brothers exceptionally generously. His grants were intended to endow their new ducal houses in perpetuity. The recipients were expected to retain the lands and live off the income. Clarence, indeed, did so, but Gloucester was different. Evidently he regarded the retention of his lands and their role as a source of income as subsidiary to his political and religious priorities. His lordship of Middleham[40] and no doubt all his northern lands were burdened with fees and can have yielded him little disposable income. We are ill-informed about Gloucester's ordinary expenditure — the cost of his household and his style of dress — but can recognize his building and land-purchases to be exceptional. The wardenship of the marches probably cost him more than the salary, particularly as he was irregularly paid. Rents were due from leasehold estates to the king. In his bargains with Lady Hungerford, Lady Latimer and the Countess of Oxford he agreed to pay annuities, debts and other expenses on their behalf.[41] Taken together, there is reason to suppose that the duke was spending above his income and may therefore have been running into debt. There is no direct evidence of this, however, and it should not perhaps be expected: in the absence of Gloucester's accounts, any evidence must necessarily be random and nothing can safely be deduced from its absence. The inadequacy of his ordinary income to meet his expenses may be why Gloucester sought other sources of revenue: mines, wardships,[42] and recovery of lost rights. He may also have administered his estates more efficiently, though this last remains to be demonstrated. He also sold lands. As we have already seen, Gloucester actually secured less lands than he was granted, sometimes because he compounded with the former owners, in other cases because he sold out to third parties. By such transactions he may have realised the capital value of these estates, occasionally investing the proceeds in other properties,[43] more commonly meeting immediate expenses. When account is taken of those properties

40 G. Coles, 'The Lordship of Middleham, especially in Yorkist and Early Tudor Times' (unpublished Liverpool University M.A. thesis, 1961), appendix B.
41 See above, chap. 9, p. 176; *Calendars of Proceedings in Chancery in the Reign of Queen Elizabeth,* (Record Commission, London, 1827), i, p.xc; see below.
42 *CPR 1467-77,* pp 329, 464; *1476-85,* pp 48, 226; C[alendar of] F[ine] R[olls] 1471-85, nos. 422, 491, 677; C 81/839/3468; C 81/1638/73; see above.
43 He sold Wivenhoe (Essex) for 1100 marks, Hutton Pagnell for £500, South Welles in Romsey and other lands in Hampshire for £200, and the FitzLewis lands in Essex worth 1,100 marks (£733 6s. 8d.) a year, and wanted to sell the Countess of Oxford's London house. He bought the FitzLewis lands, Seaham advowson for £100, Carlton in Craven (Yorks.) for £430 6s. 8d., South Wells and appurtenances in Hampshire, the manor of Utley, the advowson of Bulmer, and lands in Burton in Dustysdale (Yorks.)., *RP* vi p 127; *CCR 1468-76,* nos. 1428, 1432; *1476-85,* nos. 602, 735, 995; Devon, *Issues,* pp 499, 501; CP 40/853 m.350; CP 25(1)/281/165/4, 7, 9, 14; E 159/262 Rec.Hill.1 Hen.VII m.23.

resumed by the king, others lost for unrecorded reasons, and the large number alienated in mortmain, it is clear that the duke lost far more than he bought and that both the number of his estates and his income from them must have been declining. Instead of retaining his lands as a source of income, as an endowment as Edward IV had intended, he was spending his capital on current expenses. Instead of accumulating more lands than his brother Clarence, as Professor Ross suggested, he seems more likely to have ended up with less.

In the longer term, therefore, Richard was faced with two alternatives. To balance his books, he needed either to reduce his expenditure or to increase his income. The grant of the Cumberland palatinate in 1483 implied increased, rather than reduced, expenditure and thus indicates that he had rejected retrenchment as an option. To increase his income substantially was difficult: he had no hereditary expectations and was ineligible to marry another heiress. The king, the obvious source of bounty, was not prepared to give him anything more at his own expense. Their exchange arrangements were bargains of mutual advantage: it is not obvious that they were *financially* advantageous to the duke, who was concerned primarily with political considerations, and they involved the surrender of other lands for those acquired. The duke's chosen solution to his dilemma in 1483, it appears, was to carve out a new endowment for himself in Scotland. If he was successful, he would thus reconcile his high expenditure and falling income. The increased military expenditure required could be offset, at least in the short-term, by the 10,000 marks provided by the king. Failure, of course, would have exacerbated Gloucester's difficulties by imposing extra obligations on a reduced income.

The Cumberland palatinate was thus the gamble of a desperate or, more probably, a supremely confident man. Within four months, however, one premise on which it was based had changed and Gloucester's chances of success had dwindled disastrously, for reasons that were foreseen nine years beforehand. The duke's power on the borders, like that of Warwick and Salisbury before him, rested less on his authority and salary as warden than on his retinue and revenue as a great northern magnate. These, in turn, derived from his northern estates: Penrith in Cumberland, Barnard Castle on the Tees, Middleham and Sheriff Hutton in Yorkshire, all formerly held by Warwick and Salisbury, plus those other lordships — Helmsley, Richmond, Skipton, and Scarborough — acquired since. Gloucester, again like Warwick and Salisbury, used Middleham[44] and probably the others to support many feed retainers and consequently depended for

44 A. J. Pollard, 'The Northern Retainers of Richard Nevill, Earl of Salisbury', *Northern History* xi (1976), pp 52-69, esp. 57, 64-5; M. A. Hicks, 'The Neville Earldom of Salisbury 1429-71', *Wiltshire Archaeological Magazine* 72/73 (1980), p 144.

his income primarily on estates situated elsewhere. Warwick's
possessions elsewhere were certainly more extensive than Gloucester's,
particularly as Gloucester's exchanges and alienations reduced his
southern holdings and hence his capacity to support his northern
expenditure. Gloucester's lands in the north were thus essential to his
role as warden. Among these lands, the vital ingredient was his Neville
lordships of Penrith, Middleham and Sheriff Hutton, but his tenure of
these was fatally weakened on 4 May 1483 by the death of George
Neville, formerly Duke of Bedford, the son of John Neville, Marquis
Montagu (d.1471) and male heir of Warwick himself.[45]

These lands were settled in tail male jointly on Ralph Neville (d.1425)
and Joan Beaufort (d.1441), Earl and Countess of Westmorland (to the
disinheritance of subsequent earls of Westmorland) and descended on
Joan's death to their son Richard Neville, Earl of Salisbury (d.1460) and
to the latter's son Richard Neville, Earl of Warwick and Salisbury
(d.1471). As Warwick had no son, the line of succession led successively
to his brother John, Marquis Montagu and his male heirs, to Warwick's
third brother the celibate Archbishop Neville (d.1476), to the male line
of Salisbury's brother George, Lord Latimer, and thence to other
branches of the Neville family that need not concern us here. The
natural course of inheritance was interrupted by the death as traitors of
Warwick and Montagu in 1471. Initially Edward IV's declared
intention was to attaint them and he granted their Neville inheritance in
the north in tail male to Gloucester. In 1475 this arrangement was
revised by act of parliament, which gave them to the duke by right of
inheritance of his duchess, Anne Neville. The act barred the rights of
Montagu's son George Neville, bestowing the lordships on the duke
and duchess

> also long as there be any heire male begoten of the body of the seid
> Marquys . . . Savyng to all the Kings liege people and ther heires not
> atteynted, other than the heires male of the body of the said late
> Marquys begoten and Isabell late his wyf . . . such right, title and
> interesse as they had or shuld have had if this Acte had never been
> made.

The right heirs, defined as the heirs of Richard, Earl of Salisbury, the
feoffees of Richard Beauchamp, Earl of Warwick, their heirs and
assigns, could not be penalised as they had committed no offence to
justify forfeiture. Moreover,

> if the said issue male of the body of the said John Nevill knyght
> begoten and comyng dye withoute issue mayl of their bodies
> comyng, lyfyng the said Duke; that then the said Duke to have and

45   The next two paras. are based on my article; 'What Might Have Been. George
     Neville, Duke of Bedford — His Identity and Significance', below, chapter 15.

enjoie all the premisses for term of his lyfe.

However, if Richard and Anne's marriage was declared null — they were related within the prohibited degrees and had no dispensation — Richard would lose the lands if he remarried during Anne's lifetime. In 1475 George Neville, Duke of Bedford, aged 10, was the only male heir of the Marquis Montagu. One life only stood between Gloucester's tenure and the eventual succession of Richard Neville, Lord Latimer, who was also a young child born only in 1469. One may wonder what caused Gloucester to agree to such terms. Presumably, as Professor Lander suggested, it was the only way he could secure a share of Warwick's tail general estates.[46] He may also have felt that he could reinforce his position later.

Gloucester was certainly well-aware of the weaknesses in his title. He secured a quitclaim of the properties disputed with the Nevilles of Raby from the heir apparent Ralph Lord Neville in 1478.[47] Regarding George Neville, it was obviously important to Gloucester both that he should survive, marry and have sons and that he should not ally himself by marriage to anyone powerful enough to secure the reversal of the 1475 act and his restoration to his rightful inheritance. Remote though that possibility doubtless was during Gloucester's lifetime, it was a very real threat should he die. Initially there was very little that Gloucester could do about it, as George Neville was in the custody of his mother Isobel, Marchioness Montagu and her second husband. She, however, had no power to marry him. On her death in 1476, the opportunity arose for Gloucester to secure his custody and marriage. The grant was made formally in 1480, but an informal grant may have been made somewhat earlier.[48] An important interim stage, which can have benefitted nobody but Gloucester, was the act of parliament of 1478 that degraded George from the peerage. It was there argued that he lacked the means to support his estate, which was true of his dukedom but not of his father's barony. His demotion may have reduced his attractions on the marriage market, but the main purpose was evidently to prevent him from arguing his case for restoration in parliament when of age. Once the duke had secured the boy's custody, he had to keep him alive and marry him off. It was probably he who arranged the marriages of

---

46 *RP* vi pp 100–1; Lander, *Crown and Nobility*, pp 138–9.
47 Hicks, 'The "Warwick Inheritance",' below, 331.
48 The probability would be increased if Gloucester had indeed arranged the marriage on Montagu's daughter Elizabeth Scrope, as suggested in Attreed, *Speculum* 83(1983),.102n, but the marriage contract was made in 1468 by Montagu himself and Scrope's father, B.L.Add.Ch.73901. Scrope and Stonor were certainly married by 1483, when two (not three) daughters remained in wardship, *Stonor Letters and Papers of the Fifteenth Century*, ed. C. L. Kingsford (Camden Society, 3rd series, xxix, xxx, 1919), i, p.xxxiii; ii.158. FitzWilliam may have been married by 1484, *CPR 1476-85*, p 487. For what follows, see *CFR 1485-1509*, no. 131.

George's sisters to Sir William Stonor (1481), Thomas Lord Scope of Masham, Sir Thomas FitzWilliam and William Huddleston (both by 1487), but George himself was still unmarried at his death.

Perhaps Gloucester did not try to marry George off, but trusted instead on buying out the reversionary rights of Lord Latimer, who could inherit only on the deaths of George Neville and the duke and might have been willing to concede his rights for more solid benefits, providing of course that they remained shadowy and reversionary. Three obstacles stood in the way. Richard, Lord Latimer was also a minor, who was not scheduled to come of age until 1490, and could not therefore release his rights until then. As Lord Latimer and Beauchamp coheir, he was already an important nobleman and could not be removed from parliament like his cousin George. Thirdly, he was outside the duke's control. Following the deaths of his father and grandfather in 1469, the custody of Latimer and his lands and his marriage were granted in 1471 to his great-uncle Thomas Bourchier, Cardinal Archbishop of Canterbury (d.1486), who retained possession in 1480.[49] That Gloucester feared Latimer's rights emerges from the quitclaims of Middleham, Sheriff Hutton and Penrith that he obtained both from Latimer's aunt Katherine Dudley (née Neville) in 1477 and from his grandmother Elizabeth Lady Latimer (née Beauchamp) in 1480,[50] even though their rights to estates held in tail male were vestigial in the extreme! Their goodwill, however, was worth having and that Gloucester enjoyed it of Lady Latimer emerges from her involvment with him in litigation over the Beauchamp trust, from her will of 1481 that named him as supervisor, from her quitclaim to him, and from their indenture of 20 March 1480. This agreement revealed that the cardinal's custody of Latimer estates included her dower and jointure for which he paid an annuity in lieu. Should this annuity cease to be paid by the cardinal, she would be reimbursed by the duke. Why the cardinal should default is not specifically stated, but it was 'for accomplishing of the desire and pleasure of the said duke'. This could relate to the Beauchamp trust, but most probably concerns her quitclaim of the Neville lands to the duke the previous month, which Gloucester valued sufficiently to have registered on the close roll. Gloucester also undertook to pay the 300 mark annuity to her if 'he or eny other to his use have any tyme hereafter as well the warde and custodie of the body of the next heire of George Nevyll knight late lord latimer' or of the lands. Evidently Gloucester wanted custody of Latimer's person and

---

49 *CFR 1471-85,* no. 65; *CPR 1467-77,* pp 295-6. For what follows, see *CCR 1476-85,* nos. 650, 754; see below, chap. 19, p. 340; Burghley House, indenture of Gloucester and Lady Latimer. I am indebted to Dr M. K. Jones for a transcript of this document.

50 *CFR 1471-85,* no. 677; C 140/77/2/6.

lands and enjoyed Elizabeth's support in this project. Whether he was successful in obtaining it is less certain. In 1482 he leased the manors of Snape and Welle in Yorkshire, but these were part of the dowager's dower and jointure which came to Edward's hands on her death in 1481. The lease does not mean that Bourchier lost the custody of Richard, Lord Latimer, still less that Gloucester secured it.

What is clear from these transactions, therefore, is that Gloucester realised the fragility of his title, appreciated the significance of both Neville minors, wanted control of them both, but was unable to achieve anything concrete in either case before George's death. Precisely what the duke had in mind is obscure. George's death reduced Richard's tenure at a stroke from a hereditary to a life estate: his heirs could not inherit. Even his tenure, however, could not remain the same. When Latimer grew up, a reversionary interest would develop. Richard's grants would no longer be in perpetuity and his retainers would want their patents confirmed by his successor, Lord Latimer. His authority in his principal northern estates would decline and without them his heirs would be left only with Barnard Castle and his lesser properties, a more scattered, less valuable and less impressive collection. His estate even in these was uncertain, since certainly the Clifford and probably Roos heirs were living peacefully in England as heirs of their mothers.[51] No doubt Gloucester himself could keep what he had, but could his heirs? The duke was thus threatened not just with the loss of the resources necessary to make his Scottish principality a reality, but also with the loss to his heirs of his principal northern estates and regional hegemony.

There were three obvious ways forward for Gloucester to recover. Firstly, he could have had his marriage declared null, and remarried. This would have bastardised his son, deprived the duke of the Neville lands immediately, and would have required an heiress of equivalent resources as bride in compensation. The obstacles were much greater than in 1484, when his son was dead and the Neville inheritance ranked less highly among his resources. Secondly, he could have the partition of the Warwick inheritance revised to give him a larger share of the tail general estates that had been allocated principally to his brother Clarence. It would probably not have been difficult to persuade Edward IV to undertake such a division during the minority of Clarence's son Edward, Earl of Warwick. A revision would have reduced, rather than totally nullified, Richard's loss. Such lands, of course, would not have been in the north — he had already received all those and they would not therefore have enabled him to retrieve his position in that region. Thirdly, the duke could have petitioned the king to make up his losses by further grants, which Edward, as we have

---

51   Lander, *Crown and Nobility,* p 141; Hicks, 'The Beauchamp Trust', below, 343.

already seen, was reluctant to do.

On 4 May 1483, however, these possibilities were remote. Gloucester's brother King Edward had died one month before and had been succeeded by his young son Edward V. No major alienations of royal property to the disinheritance of the crown were likely during the king's minority, even though the duke himself became Protector on 10 May. His Protectorate was anyway temporary and was due to expire on Edward V's coronation on 22 June.[52] Thereafter the twelve-year-old king would be guided by a council on which Gloucester would sit but which he would be unlikely to dominate. The other principal faction, the queen-dowager's family the Wydevilles, had good reason since the arrest of Earl Rivers and Lord Richard Grey to regard Richard as their enemy and to oppose patronage to him. One of them, the Marquis of Dorset, had the custody and marriage of Clarence's son Warwick and thus had every reason to oppose the repartition of the Warwick inheritance to the young earl's loss. Political circumstances, in short, were unpropitious for Gloucester to repair his prospects in the immediate future. Apart from the unpalatable option of a sharp reduction in commitments and expenditure, Gloucester's best hope for the future now lay in the usurpation of the crown. Like the Scottish venture, usurpation was a gamble involving great benefits and risks, but was to be preferred because circumstances had made the former objective impossible to achieve. That he should have left himself so exposed to a single perfectly predictable misfortune is why his career to 1483 does not make sense.

V

By concentrating on Richard's political and territorial career and by deliberately omitting his piety, this detailed examination of his career as Duke of Gloucester has undoubtedly neglected those less material and more gentle aspects of his personality which he definitely possessed. That he was knowledgeable about the liturgy, the common law and the law of arms, able to discriminate between them in practice and to argue an ingenious legal case, points to considerable intelligence and eloquence that one could anyway deduce from other evidence. He was more than conventionally pious and had his own distinct and reasoned religious preferences. Affection as well as sensual lust may well have coloured both his liasions and his marriage, although the immediate

52   Ross, *Richard III*, p 74. When did Richard learn of George Neville's death?

motive for his wedding was territorial self-advancement.[53] His relations with his brothers appear emotional, if not necessarily warm. We know that he contracted abiding friendships and was loyal to the memory of those who died in his service[54] and that he was capable of inspiring loyalty and trust in others. He was generous, even extravagant, in his rewards, though sometimes at the expense of others. While well-acquainted with the laws and practice of arms, he does not seem to have placed a high value on keeping his word and was decidedly unchivalrous, in the modern sense, in his treatment of women like the Countess of Oxford who barred his path. That so many gentler traits can be qualified in this way indicates not only the complexity of his character,[55] but also the prominence of material motivation in his make-up.

On the evidence so far considered, Gloucester was proud, ambitious, aggressive, acquisitive and courageous. Not surprisingly, he was independent rather than subservient in politics. He examined his rights and possessions objectively, coolly identified his essential interests in the light of long-term aims and acted on them with singleminded determination. He possessed great foresight, took infinite pains, was prepared to wait for years for an appropriate opportunity and was then ruthless in its pursuit. Presented thus, he was almost a caricature of the "wicked baron", sharing the characteristics of many different individuals of his order, but these were mitigated by the flexibility, pragmatism, diplomacy, and capacity for compromise that he also displayed. No wonder he was so uniquely successful in gaining his objectives and advancing himself. This survey has also revealed other ways in which he was unconventional and unusual. He was surely unique in his reorganisation and dispersal of his estates. His religious foundations were more numerous than any other later medieval magnate, numbering more than those of any individual Hungerford, and his alienations in mortmain were also unusually extensive. He was also distinctive in his sense of dynasty. It is the latter that contains the key to his personality, to which all other facets relate, and it is to this that I now wish to turn.

Everybody "possessed his own kinship network, distinguished by a unique set of relationships with himself, within which his interests were paramount".[56] As a member of the house of York, Richard was related

---

53 Hicks, 'Clarence and Richard', *The Ricardian*, 76(1982), p 20.
54 C. D. Ross, 'Some "Servants and Lovers" of Richard III in his youth', *The Ricardian*, 4(1976), pp 2–4. I am indebted to Mrs Carolyn Hammond for a photocopy of this article.
55 I do not agree that Richard 'does not appear to have been a complex man', Ross, *Richard III*, p 229.
56 See above, 167.

to most English noble houses as well as to the king and queen. He identified himself with the house of York at the re-interment of his father at Fotheringhay in 1476, in his benefactions to the family colleges at Windsor and Cambridge, in his claim to be Protector as uncle of Edward V in May 1483, and of course in his claim to the throne by hereditary right six weeks later. He acknowledged other kin through his wife. He also had his own nuclear family, of which he was head — his wife and legitimate sons, only one of whom survived at his accession — and at least two illegitimate offspring whom he acknowledged and advanced while king. According to Professor Stone, great noblemen wished always to preserve the family inheritance intact, to add to it as far as they were able, and to ensure the succession by fathering as many sons as possible.[57] Richard had at least two sons: it was not his fault that they died prematurely. He does not conform to the rest of the pattern in that he did not seek to keep his estates intact.

To approach the topic from another direction, Richard was a younger son without hereditary expectations. Other than his wife's inheritance, everything he held had been granted to him in person, admittedly in tail male. Contemporaries generally acknowledged an obligation to keep intact for their heirs what they themselves had inherited, but felt free to alienate what they had acquired themselves. Richard thus found himself exceptionally free from moral restraints and indeed also from the entails that so often tied the hands of other tenants-for-life. Unlike others similarly placed, such as his brother Clarence, Richard exploited his position to buy, sell, alienate, exchange and generally reshape his estate to an extent quite without parallel in the later middle ages. His deliberate alienations in the south and concentration of lands in the north was unique for his time. Nor was this confined to his own lands, for he also alienated lands of his wife's inheritance, no doubt with her consent, both before and after his accession.[58] All this involved the disinheritance of heirs and suggests that he had an imperfect sense of dynasty. The 1474–5 settlement of the Warwick inheritance distinguished between the rights of himself on the one hand and his wife and issue on the other. If his marriage was declared null, he would retain the lands for life, but his children would inherit nothing. That no dispensation was secured by 1475 is surprising. That none was ever obtained denotes either an extraordinary carelessness inconceivable in a man of such remarkable foresight or indifference to the fate of his heirs when his life-estate terminated on his death. Like his contemporaries, Richard was well-

57 Stone, *Family, Sex and Marriage*, pp 85–9.
58 See below, 331–2.

aware of his *rights* as heir. Unlike them, he apparently lacked a sense of obligation to his own heirs, whose interests were subordinated to an unusual extent to his own.

Richard's selfishness denotes both exceptional egotism and individualism. Whereas other magnates thought in the long-term, seeking to maintain the family estates and to foster the interests of future generations of their dynasty, Richard gave priority to his own good, his immediate political needs and the eventual salvation of his soul. He was concerned only secondarily with the long-term interests of his heirs, whom he disinherited by his alienations in mortmain and otherwise. If Richard's career as Duke of Gloucester fails to make sense, it is because his aims were different from those of other magnates. Both as duke and king, Richard appreciated that heirs strengthened his own position by giving permanence to his tenure, but he did not acknowledge any obligation to give priority to their interests over his own. One wonders whether his sentimental attachments to the houses of York and Neville were sincere or were merely further expressions of Richard's self-interest. Certainly his seizure of the crown sacrificed the interests of his wider kindred to himself and led ultimately to the destruction of the royal house to which they all belonged.

While it is probable that Richard's character remained unchanged as king, it is not the purpose of this paper to demonstrate the point. It is an open question whether the same qualities were required of kings and magnates in late medieval England, but certainly much of what Richard did as king seems compatible with his conduct as Duke of Gloucester. Whatever one's verdict on Richard as king, this paper has revealed him beyond doubt as a remarkably successful and far from conventional member of the late medieval nobility.

14

The Cartulary of Richard III as Duke of Gloucester in British Library Manuscript Cotton Julius BXII

Richard III is now perhaps the most popular and most studied of English kings. Historical novels, popular histories, and plays galore are devoted to him, all of which are assured of immediate success. There are four issues each year of *The Ricardian*, the journal of the Richard III Society, and there is a constant flow of scholarly articles published elsewhere that treat some aspect of his career. Yet Richard lived to be only thirty-two and reigned for only two years, so the relevant material is not inexhaustible. What exists has probably been trawled more thoroughly than for any other late medieval English king. Much attention has been attracted by his admittedly unique signet letter book, the recently edited British Library Harleian MS 433, and a whole sequence of articles in *The Ricardian* has treated the considerable remains of his library.[1] Strangely, however, little attention has been paid to the cartulary in Cotton Julius BXII, the principal survivor from his archive before his accession, although its existence and a summary of its contents has been available in print since 1696.[2] Historians like the present writer have hitherto dipped into it rather than exploited it to the full. It is this cartulary which is examined here. This essay analyses MS Cotton Julius BXII as a whole, investigates the provenance and composition of the cartulary, describes its contents, and ends with some comments on how it was used.

In its present form Cotton MS Julius BXII is a composite volume created by Sir Robert Cotton. It comprises 319 folios of 28.5 cm by 23 cm. There are two foliations throughout. The pencil one is modern, probably dating from the rebinding in 1870. It is this which will be used for reference in this essay. An ink foliation is in the same hand as the index at the front, which can be dated to 1621 or soon after. The evidence for this is Sir Robert Cotton's catalogue in Harleian MS 6018, which was headed 1621 some time after it was begun. This contains two entries for Cotton Julius BXII:

---

[1] By P. Hammond, A.F. Sutton, and L. Visser-Fuchs in *The Ricardian* 94-5, 97-9, 101-3, 105, 107-11 (1986-90).

[2] T. Smith, *Catalogue of the Cottonian Library* (1696), 4-5.

the first, no. 351, on folio 130-v, summarises only a few of the items in the volume, the result of a cursory glance at the contents; the second, much fuller entry (no. 393 on f. 139) corresponds exactly with the index at the front of the volume and with the headings to documents in the volume itself,[3] which must therefore also be of this date. The catalogue and index together enable us to see that the volume was already in its present state in 1621 or very soon after.

The two continuous foliations give the volume a quite misleading unity, for it contains five distinct elements:

1 Ff 1-2v. Sir Robert Cotton's seventeenth-century index. Paper.
2 Ff 2v-66. A heraldic manuscript beginning with a pedigree and list of those who landed with the Conqueror. This was completed in the same late fifteenth-century hand that began a sequence of heraldic material relating to the early years of Henry VII. The last item is the christening of Margaret Tudor and at least some entries were made before the death of Prince Arthur in 1501.[4] There are several different handwritings and inks and some headings and rubrication have been inserted later. Paper.
3 Ff 67-82. An account of the trial of the Templars. Parchment, fourteenth century, after 1309. The folios are not now in the correct sequence.[5]
4 Ff 88-103. A heraldic account of the creation of the future Henry VIII as Duke of York in 1494. Paper.[6]
5 Ff 108-316v. Richard III's cartulary. Paper.

The greater age of the Templar manuscript and its use of parchment set it apart. There are two reasons for regarding items 2 and 4, the two heraldic manuscripts, as distinct rather than merely displaced. In each case a faint earlier foliation is visible on the top right-hand corner. That on item 2 runs from folios 10 to 81, indicating that at one time this item began 9 folios earlier. As that on item 4 runs from folio 2 to folio 17, it overlaps with 2, and must therefore once have been part of another volume. Secondly, almost all the heraldic material on folios 8v to 66 was printed by Thomas Hearne in the early eighteenth century in his edition of the

---

[3] Ironically Sir Robert supposed the documents related to Richard Duke of *York*, an impression which only the most cursory glance could have permitted, and this was not corrected until 1696.

[4] 'Dieu par sa grace deint bonne vie et long au treshault puissant et excellent prince Arthur par la grace de dieu ainsne fils du Roy prince dengleterre duc de Cornewall conte de Chestre and asmoche in Inglishe', f 19v. Ff 8-66 were printed in J. Leland, *Collectanea de rebus britannicis*, ed T. Hearne (Oxford 1715), iv 185-257. This deliberately omits the Norman pedigree and the mode of funeral of an earl.

[5] Partly printed from Bodleian Library MS Bodley F484 in J. Wilkins, *Concilia*, ii 335-57, 366-7.

[6] Printed in *Letters and Papers illustrative of Richard III and Henry VII*, ed J. Gairdner (2 vols Rolls Series 1861-3), i 338-404.

Collectanea of the Tudor antiquary John Leland.[7] That Hearne did not
include the very similar material in item 4, which was published instead
by James Gairdner in 1861,[8] suggests that it was not part of the same
volume when Leland saw it. This argument, however, is less than
conclusive, for the material in question does not survive among Leland's
manuscript collections in the Bodleian Library and may therefore have
been among the supplementary material added by Hearne, who noted
that it came from the Cottonian Library in his printed edition.[9] If so, it
was Hearne who inadvertently left out a lengthy passage on the Yorkshire
Rebellion of 1489 from the material he printed and overlooked or
deliberately omitted the item on 1494.[10] However that may be, the
binding together in a single volume of both sets of heraldic material was
evidently the decision of Sir Robert Cotton. The evidence for the
separateness of Richard III's cartulary is considered below.

We have seen that the whole volume was in its present form about 1621.
One element in it, the Templar material, has been identified as part of the
library of Henry Savile of Banke (d. 1617). It occurs in his two catalogues
of *c.* 1607-12, when it was bound up with a St Albans chronicle in the hand
of Matthew Paris, which is now Cotton MS Nero DV.[11] The much smaller
page size of Julius BXII is because Cotton trimmed the pages of the
Templar manuscript: the effects of trimming are also obvious on Richard
III's cartulary. As Savile disposed of some manuscripts in his own
lifetime,[12] Sir Robert Cotton *could* have acquired the Templar manuscript
in 1607/12-17, but it is far more likely that he bought it with many others
when the collection was sold after Savile's death. He ultimately acquired
about eighty manuscripts from this single source. This would mean that
Cotton split up Savile's volume and bound up Cotton Julius BXII in its
present form between 1617 and 1621. Where he obtained the other items
now comprising Cotton Julius BXII is less certain, but it is at least
possible that one or more also came from Savile, although neither they
(nor, indeed, the Templar material) contain Savile's cipher or show any
other of his distinctive marks. They cannot be identified in his catalogues,
but that is not conclusive, since these are not exhaustive and date only
from 1607: Savile could have relinquished them before 1607 or acquired
them afterwards, though neither is particularly likely.

Richard III's cartulary was obviously once a separate volume. It has its

---

[7] Bodleian MS Top Gen. c.1-4 [3117-20].

[8] Gairdner, loc cit.

[9] Leland, *Collectanea*, iv 185.

[10] M. Bennett, 'Henry VII and the Northern Rising of 1489', *E[nglish] H[istorical] R[eview]*cv (1990), esp 37, 56-9. Dr Bennett informs me that he did not consult Leland's manuscript collections.

[11] A.G. Watson, *The Manuscripts of Henry Savile of Banke* (1969), 21.

[12] Ibid.

own late-fifteenth-century ink foliation, which it shares with none of items 1-4, and which demonstrates that nothing preceded the cartulary when the foliation was made. On its first surviving folio (f. 108) it is signed by Sir Robert Cotton Baronet, which shows that it was still a separate entity at his creation in 1611 and suggests that he acquired it some time between then and 1621. Thirdly, it contains numerous notes of mid-sixteenth-century date on blank folios on genealogical and antiquarian topics that are not to be found anywhere else in the volume. It is clear, therefore, that it was Cotton who first combined it with the rest of MS Julius BXII. It was also he who trimmed the pages.

In the absence of other evidence of ownership, the genealogical notes provide the best clue to the volume's provenance and to Cotton's acquisition of it. They display, as the various catalogues long ago observed, a considerable interest in the FitzWilliams of Sprotborough. The main line of this family had expired in 1494, but there was a cadet branch, the FitzWilliams of Haltisley, whose last representative Hugh FitzWilliam, an antiquary, died in 1577. It was he who made these genealogical notes and signed them on folio 221v in 1562. From Hugh the cartulary could have descended to his cousin Henry Savile the elder, also an antiquary, the father of the Henry Savile of Banke, whose library was sold in 1617, and thus to Sir Robert Cotton. The objections to this, however, are formidable. First of all, the FitzWilliam of Sprotborough estates were the subject of litigation between Hugh FitzWilliam, as heir male, and the heirs general, represented by the Copleys and Saviles.[13] This cartulary indeed contains copies of Hugh's case, evidently drafts for the family history that still survives, and copies of writs etc relating to it. Hugh was hardly likely to pass such useful material – or indeed anything – to a cousin with whom he was litigating. Indeed, in his will of 1560 he bequeathed such evidences to his distant relative Sir William FitzWilliam of Milton and it is among their papers that his family history is now to be found.[14] Some evidences, admittedly, were in the custody of 'Swayle my lady Savells butler' in 1560 and might have remained with the Saviles at Hugh's death seventeen years later,[15] but they can hardly have included this cartulary, since Hugh himself was making notes in it until at least 1568. Even though not included in the younger Henry's library catalogue in 1607, this still seems the most likely route for the cartulary to have reached Sir Robert Cotton. However, no other manuscript either of FitzWilliam (or indeed Richard III) is known to have descended in this way.

---

[13] G.E.C. *Complete Peerage of England etc* (13 vols 1910-59), v 519-20; J. Hunter, *South Yorkshire* (2 vols London 1828-31), i 338-41.

[14] There are extensive notes from this volume by Revd Joseph Hunter in BL Add MS 24473, which show its close relationship to the material in Cotton Julius BXII.

[15] PRO PROB 11/60 (PCC 3 Langley). Note that apparently no other British Library MS contains any notes by Hugh FitzWilliam.

It is not difficult to explain how Richard III's cartulary reached Hugh FitzWilliam, although we cannot be sure which hypothesis is correct. At Richard III's death, it might have been taken from Middleham (or wherever it was stored) by Sir William FitzWilliam of Sprotborough himself. He was one of Richard's retainers as Duke of Gloucester. Either he or his father, also William (d. 1474), was summoned by Duke Richard to attend him from Doncaster to London on 19 October [1472-7] and he was in the duke's retinue in Scotland in 1481, when Richard knighted him. The cartulary, like Richard's letter,[16] could have passed with the rest of the family archive to Hugh. Secondly, Hugh claimed that his own great-grandfather, John FitzWilliam of Haltisley, was a captain with Duke Richard at the siege of Berwick in 1482-3,[17] a claim which cannot now be confirmed. As a ducal retainer, he too might have been in a position to acquire the volume. The third – and most probable route – was through Hugh's grandmother, Margery Clervaux. Her grandfather, Richard Clervaux of Croft, was a retainer of Duke Richard and used part of an account roll of 1457-60 of his lordship of Middleham to bind his own Clervaux Cartulary. This could have been acquired in 1460-1, as Dr Pollard suggested in 1976,[18] but more probably was obtained in or after 1485, since the Clervaux Cartulary was probably not bound until after 1490.[19] Since Clervaux took one document, he could well have taken Richard's cartulary too. Of course the title deeds to Croft itself, the Clervaux Cartulary, descended with the estate to the male heir, Marmaduke Clervaux. Richard III's cartulary, however, could logically have passed to Clervaux's heir general, Margery the daughter of his deceased elder son John, who was married to John FitzWilliam, and could hence have descended to Hugh FitzWilliam. At least with this explanation we need postulate only one member of Hugh FitzWilliam's family helping himself to Richard III's personal effects!

Richard III's cartulary is a paper volume of 208 folios, running from folio 108 to 316v (pencil) of MS Cotton Julius BXII. The folios have been trimmed to a standard size, so the volume was once generously spaced; it was never rubricated. The fifteenth-century foliation of the cartulary shows one folio only to be missing at the beginning and seventeen (folios 140-37; pencil 244-5) in the middle, which had already disappeared by

---

[16] Sheffield Public Library, MS WWM/D98; M.A. Hicks, 'Dynastic Change and Northern Society: The Career of the Fourth Earl of Northumberland, 1470-89', below, 392.

[17] BL MS Cotton Julius BXII f 307v.

[18] A.J. Pollard, 'The Northern Retainers of Richard Nevill Earl of Salisbury', *Northern History* xi (1976), 57.

[19] A.J. Pollard, 'Richard Clervaux of Croft: A North Riding Squire in the Fifteenth Century', *Yorkshire Archaeological Journal* 1 (1978), 152, 160.

1621 and probably by Hugh FitzWilliam's day too, since he inserts material on folio 139. The gap ends with the second half of a grant of Skipton-on-Craven to Sir William Stanley in 1464, the first part of which could have filled much of the missing space. The last folio of the cartulary is torn and part is missing, so some pages at least may have been lost there. Alternatively, the damage may indicate that the damaged folio was at the end. We cannot tell what, if anything, is missing.

The volume consists mainly of Richard III's title deeds as Duke of Gloucester to his estates and titles of honour (e.g. constable of England), together with some documentation of former holders. A few late entries are more miscellaneous in character. A long list may be made of the documents that did or do now exist which were not included, presumably quite deliberately: title deeds to lands that Richard held only briefly; commissions; appointments to office; household and estate accounts; in and out letters; documents relating to religious foundations; presentations to livings; indentures of retainer and material relating to the defence of the northern marches; conciliar memoranda; and grants made by the duke himself. Some record of at least some of these were kept and was perhaps entered in other volumes, now lost. The cartulary confined itself to the title of his permanent estate. It reveals nothing of his day to day affairs. The completed volume can thus appropriately be categorised as a cartulary, a description dismissed unduly hastily by the present author in 1986,[20] rather than as a commonplace book.[21]

Such contents could have been of interest only to Richard Duke of Gloucester himself. He was the first of his line, the younger son of Richard Duke of York, and thus inherited nothing from his ancestors. The estates recorded in the cartulary were either granted to him personally, for the most part the forfeited estates of former Lancastrians, or were of his wife's inheritance. Had he founded a ducal dynasty, the cartulary would have been the essential codification of the family's landed title, to be referred to and supplemented, like the Troponell or indeed Clervaux cartularies, but of course he did not. Indeed, the cartulary became irrelevant as soon as he became king. When Richard fell, he was attainted, his lands were forfeit, and anyway he left no legitimate heir, who could have been interested in compiling such a volume as evidence of his *own* hereditary title or claims or in retaining it. Most, indeed, of the properties listed were returned in 1485 to their former owners, the Hungerfords and De Veres, who were restored in blood.

Nothing in the cartulary suggests that it was compiled after Richard's death or even 1483. The latest entry is dated February 1483. No entry or

[20] M.A. Hicks, *Richard III as Duke of Gloucester: A Study in Character* (Borthwick Paper 70, 1986), above, 251.

[21] M.A. Hicks, 'The Last Days of Elizabeth, Countess of Oxford', below, 302.

marginal comment refers to Richard's accession or subsequent fall. One of the marginal commentators, whose notes occur throughout, identified not just the lands covered in each document, but also the title – tail male, tail general, for life or years: such matters could only be relevant during the duke's lifetime and indeed by his accession. Similarly the commentator's dating by regnal year – 'anno nono', 'anno undecimo' – indicates that at the time of writing Edward IV was still on the throne. It seems, therefore, that the volume was already complete, bound, foliated and marginally annotated before Richard's accession in 1483. The absence of subsequent comments or additions, despite the large number of blank spaces later exploited by Hugh FitzWilliam, suggests that it was no longer accessible to Richard's secretariat. Thus it could well have been left behind in Yorkshire, at Middleham or Sheriff Hutton, to be taken by Richard Clervaux or one of the FitzWilliams on Richard's fall. It was fortunate initially to avoid the fate of the Earl of Salisbury's Middleham receiver's account, which became scrap-paper, and to survive long enough to become of antiquarian interest and value.

The cartulary was probably compiled from 1472 and then bound up as it is today.[22] The consistent size of the written area – remembering that the pages have been trimmed – and the frequent occurrence of a single watermark might suggest composition at a single sitting, but this is contradicted by the variety of hands and inks, the blank spaces, and the obvious insertions of later documents in existing spaces. The first twenty-seven folios do indeed seem to have been composed at a sitting – there is no obvious break in the sequence of documents or handwriting – but the remainder seem to have been written subsequently in a sequence and at times that cannot now be recaptured. Since, however, the earlier folios cannot have been written sooner than 1472 and omit documents later that same year that are added later,[23] the whole cartulary can be dated quite precisely to the years 1472-83, after the duke's return from exile and at a time when he was endeavouring to establish himself as a great magnate during his brother Edward IV's second reign.

Richard Duke of Gloucester was a great public figure, who owed most of his possessions to the generosity of his brother Edward IV and who later became king himself. Most of his title deeds, his extracts from parliamentary acts, and his chancery bills are thus matters of public record and their repetition in his cartulary adds nothing to our knowledge. Even private documents, such as his transactions with Lady Oxford and Lady Hungerford, are enrolled in chancery, survive in original, and/or

---

[22] See above, 251.
[23] See above, 252.

have been calendared in print.[24] Relatively few documents are not to be
found elsewhere and these are not of great importance: the petition of
Anne Countess of Warwick and the preamble to his partition of her
inheritance with his brother Clarence are obvious exceptions. Many of the
most interesting of his private documents are preserved in repositories
elsewhere. If the survival of the cartulary is of importance for Ricardian
scholarship, it is not primarily because of the novelty of its contents, but
because of what its compilation tells us about Richard's private
administration and intentions.

The creation of a cartulary was not a passive or automatic process. It
implied the existence of an orderly and forward-looking individual or
administration, even if the finished result in this case is not as beautiful or
systematic as many ecclesiastical examples. The traditional function of a
cartulary was to record titles in a permanent and convenient form, thus
assisting the preservation and defence of the property. The presence of
many of these documents included here, such as royal grants, acts of
parliament, conveyances and inquisitions post mortem, are to be
explained in these terms. As the first holder under a royal grant, Richard
seldom had to prove descent, but obviously he wished to enjoy the full
extent of the property and all the appurtenant rights. Hence the many
precedents such as a charter of the honour of Richmond, a copy of an
earlier indenture of a warden of the march, and earlier patents, like that of
Richard Earl Rivers as constable of England. The lands of his duchess,
Anne Neville, had descended to her from her ancestors and a number of
documents relating to the earlier Nevilles, Beauchamps, and Despensers
illuminated her title or listed her rights. Presumably these items were
sought out and copied as and when they seemed important and relevant,
in other words according to need. Yet other, later items, such as the patent
appointing his attorney to the exchequer, are strays that should not really
have been included.

Not all entries can be so simply and innocently explained: not, for
example, Edward III's grant of Sherborne to Richard's duchess's
ancestor William Earl of Salisbury (d. 1344) and subsequently lost. The
inclusion of some such documents indicates an interest in making good
claims to property in other hands. These elements are present from the
start, for the first batch of documents includes not only properties that
Richard held, for which the documents were readily available in
Richard's hands, but also ones that he had lost and for which the patents
had been surrendered and cancelled.[25] The inclusion of these required the
compiler to search out the entry on the patent roll. That he took the

---

[24] E.g. Huntington Library California MS HAD 3466; R.C. Hoare, *A History of Modern
Wiltshire* (6 vols 1822-40), i ii 107; Wiltshire Record Office 490/1470 ff 193-4; cf BL MS
Cotton Julius BXII ff 123-5, 233-5.
[25] See above, 251-2.

trouble indicates that the matter was not considered closed and that the property concerned had not been given up as permanently lost. This should not surprise us, for a great prince like Richard had no difficulty in defending his estates, as his brother Edward IV observed,[26] and could concentrate on extending them immune from many of the restraints on lesser men. Richard III's cartulary is thus evidence not just of what was held but also of what was claimed and of his aspirations.

This argument has been made elsewhere,[27] and others have suggested that it goes beyond the evidence: such entries, if interpreted correctly, could be the work of his staff. It must certainly be they who undertook the searches and copying. But there are three obvious objections to this argument. First and weakest, such work was arduous, time-consuming and expensive, and would hardly be undertaken to no purpose. Secondly, whoever undertook the task was remarkably well-informed about Richard's intentions or alternatively was something of a prophet. He omitted lands that Richard did not intend keeping, like the advowson of Seaham (Dur.) and the manor of South Wells in Romsey (Hants.), and included others that he intended retaining. Why did he not mention forfeitures of Thomas Delalande and others, granted in 1471 and not retained, and yet include Hungerford and De Vere properties granted at the same time that he secured only later and kept? The third, perhaps most convincing argument, is that Richard took a personal lead in all his property disputes, as the history of the Hungerford, De Vere, and Warwick inheritances clearly shows.[28] It was his intentions, not those of his secretary, that determined what the cartulary contained and the contents of the cartulary indicate not what title deeds were in his archive, but what was found necessary for the preservation, defence, and *expansion* of his estate during his own lifetime.

All cartularies are of value to the historian and that of Richard III clearly has a wider interest than many. If it is disappointing at first sight, since it contains so little that is not to be found elsewhere, it can be made to yield data not only on Richard's actions but on his intentions, which give it a much more general significance. To make the most of it, however, it has to be recognised for what it is and to be understood, which this essay has aimed to elucidate. Certainly Cotton Manuscript Julius BXII has not yet yielded all its secrets and it deserves to receive much more study in the future.

---

[26] See below, 309.
[27] See above, 253-9.
[28] See chapters 9, 16, and 18.

15

What Might Have Been: George Neville, Duke of Bedford 1465-83: His Identity and Significance

George Neville, Duke of Bedford was a major figure in Yorkist England and bulked especially large in the career of his cousin Richard, Duke of Gloucester, yet he has been sadly neglected and has attracted no biographer. This is hardly surprising, since he died under age. His three known actions – birth, betrothal and death – are not the stuff of which biography is made. George was a pawn in the schemes of others and never devised his own. What qualified him even to be a pawn was his pedigree, which was a potent fact of politics. It was who he was, not what he did, that mattered. An earlier essay considered him from the angle of Richard, Duke of Gloucester.[1] This essay focuses on him personally and establishes his identity and significance.

George Neville was born on the feast of St Peter's Chair, 22 February 1465,[2] the only son among the six children of John Neville and his wife Isobel Ingoldsthorpe. John Neville was the second son of Richard Neville (d. 1460) and Alice Montagu (d. 1462), Earl and Countess of Salisbury, the brother of Richard, Earl of Warwick and Salisbury (d. 1471) – Warwick the Kingmaker – and George, Archbishop of York (d. 1476). Created Lord Montagu in 1461, John Neville was Earl of Northumberland at George's birth. Isobel was the daughter of Sir Edmund Ingoldsthorpe and Joan Tiptoft, one of the three sisters of John Tiptoft, Earl of Worcester (d. 1470). In 1469, as part of Edward IV's strategy to control Warwick and Clarence, George was betrothed to the king's eldest daughter, the three-year-old Elizabeth of York, heiress presumptive to the throne and later Henry VII's Queen. George was created Duke of Bedford and his father Marquis Montagu.[3] The latter defected to Henry VI in 1470 and was killed in 1471. No more was heard

---

[1] M.A. Hicks, 'Descent, Partition and Extinction: The "Warwick Inheritance"', *Bulletin of the Institute of Historical Research* lii , see below, 325-32; 'The Warwick Inheritance – Springboard to the Throne', *The Ricardian* lxxxi (1983), esp 177-80. Unless otherwise stated, genealogical information is taken from G.E.C. *Complete Peerage etc*, ed H.V. Gibbs and others (13 vols 1910-59) esp xii(1) 748-9; xii(2) 845, 846n, and valuations of lands are taken from inquisitions post mortem and are probably underestimated.

[2] *C[alendar of] I[nquisitions] p[ost] m[ortem Henry VII]*, i 210.

[3] M.A. Hicks, *False, Fleeting, Perjur'd Clarence* (Gloucester 1980), 58-60.

of George's royal marriage. From 1472 he was in the custody of his mother Isobel, who remarried to Sir William Norris, bore him three more daughters, and died in 1476. In 1478 parliament deprived George not only of his dukedom but also of his peerage altogether, in 1480 his wardship and marriage was granted to Richard, Duke of Gloucester, and on 4 May 1483 he died, still unmarried, leaving his sisters as coheiresses.

When George was degraded from the peerage in 1478, the justification offered was that he lacked the resources to support the dignity. He may not have had the income usually required of a duke, but he certainly had sufficient for a baron. Apart from his £40 annuity as Duke of Bedford, he was then heir to his father's estates, to the lands held jointly by his parents, and to his mother's Ingoldsthorpe inheritance. Had he lived until 1484, he would then have become coheir to his cousin Edward Tiptoft, second Earl of Worcester through his grandmother Joan Ingoldsthorpe, sister to the first earl. Finally, but for his father's political miscalculations, he would have inherited those Neville lands of Warwick the Kingmaker that were entailed in the male line – Middleham, Sheriff Hutton and Penrith – that were so vital to Richard III as Duke and King. None of this was accidental, as George's birth was the intended culmination of a series of deliberate dynastic marriages. Even in 1478 George had sufficient estates to support a peerage: had all gone to plan, he might have been the greatest heir of his time. That such prospects never materialised was due *primarily* (but not solely) to his death, still under age, in 1483.

Because George's prospects did not materialise and because he achieved nothing, he has not been considered worthy of study by modern historians. Contemporaries did not know what was going to hapen. They lacked our advantage of hindsight. They expected George to survive. They had indeed to assume that he would and planned accordingly. While history is about what happened rather than what did not, we must allow for prospects that were never fulfilled – what might have been – if we are fully to understand what did occur. George did not have to do anything: he merely had to exist and his existence was a political reality that could not be ignored.

George's father, John Neville, was a younger son with no expectations of inheriting anything from his parents the Earl and Countess of Salisbury. They, however, sought to provide for all their children and were prepared to make generous settlements for them. In 1458, on John's marriage to Isobel Ingoldsthorpe, they settled seven outlying manors in southern England jointly on the young couple, with remainder to their heirs. These were valued at £30 13s 4d in 1486.[4] This jointure may have

---

[4] These were Goathill (Dors), Knowle (Soms), Roughdercote (Gloucs), Shenley (Herts), Oakford (Devon), Eastney and Efford (Hants), P[ublic] R[ecord] O[ffice] CP 25(1)/293/73/426; *CIPM* i nos. 217, 219, 222, 241, 246; *Feet of Fines, Henry IV to Henry VI* (Somerset Record Society xx, 1906), 205.

been the inducement that secured the marriage for John in the first place.

For Isobel Ingoldsthorpe was a considerable heiress. She was the sole daughter and heiress of Sir Edmund Ingoldsthorpe and his wife Joan Tiptoft. At his death in 1457 Sir Edmund held an annuity of 500 marks (£33 13s 4d) from the Exchequer and twenty-four manors in eight counties, including ten in Norfolk, four in Cambridgeshire and six in Gloucestershire. These were valued – or surely considerably undervalued? – at only £73 in his inquisition post mortem.[5] Even so, the income yielded was at least £406, quite sufficient to support the dignity of a baron, but at least a third was held in dower by Sir Edmund's widow throughout the lives of her daughter Isobel and grandson George. Even taken together, therefore, Isobel's inheritance and their jointure did not make John Neville a great magnate, but they were ample justification for his elevation to the peerage as Lord Montagu in 1461.

John Neville was a relatively minor member of the faction that made Edward IV King and thus received relatively minor rewards in the early years of the new regime. At first he received nine forfeited manors to be held in tail male. One, Hellow, had belonged to Lord Welles, but the other eight, situated in Norfolk, Suffolk, Nottinghamshire and Leicestershire, had belonged to Viscount Beaumont.[6] Together they added substantially to John's resources without totally transforming them. Two manors soon escaped from his grasp, Hellow being restored to Lord Welles and another to Lady Beaumont, but these were counteracted by the spectacular rewards John received for his military achievements in the north, notably his victories at Hedgeley Moor and Hexham in 1464. He was promoted Earl of Northumberland, granted lands in Northumberland worth perhaps as much as £1,000 a year, plus the reversion of others on the death of the Countess Eleanor.[7] That John saw his future as being in the north is suggested by those properties that he acquired by purchase or force during these years: miscellaneous small-holdings in Yorkshire and nine manors including Seaton Delaval in Northumberland, together valued at £71 in 1483.[8]

From the moment of his birth George Neville was assured of an earldom and property worth about £1,500 a year on the deaths of his parents and his grandmother Joan Ingoldsthorpe. But this was not all. Unless his paternal uncle Warwick remarried and had a son, George would succeed as heir male to the Earl's Neville inheritance, which comprised the lordships of Middleham and Sheriff Hutton in Yorkshire and Penrith in Cumberland and their appurtenances, which may have been worth £1,500-£2,000 a year. Nor was this all. Unless his cousin the

---

[5] PRO C 139/165/2; *CIPM* i 212.
[6] *CPR, 1461-7*, 195.
[7] *CPR, 1461-7*, 341, 484; *1467-77*, 91.
[8] PRO C 140/83/11/1-2, /12/1; *Calendar of Fine Rolls, 1485-1509*, nos. 135, 137.

Earl of Worcester married for a third time and bore a son – which appeared improbable, as he had been a widower since 1452 – George would become entitled to a third share of the Tiptoft inheritance on his death and those of his grandmother Joan Ingoldsthorpe (*née* Tiptoft) and his own mother. The Tiptoft estates had been valued at 1,100 marks (£733 6s 8d) in 1436.[9] In short, George appeared destined to inherit estates worth over £4,000 a year, a sum that would have made him one of the greatest of noblemen. The king's own brother George, Duke of Clarence, was worth only £4,500 in 1467. While these lands were distributed all over England and on the marches of Wales, they were concentrated in the north, where he would be an even greater landholder than Warwick himself. No wonder that almost as soon as he was born his marriage was proposed to the Duchess of Exeter's daughter Anne. Her inheritance would have lifted George into a class of his own, the greatest nobleman of his generation, had the king not induced the duchess with 4,000 marks to see more immediate advantages in a match with his stepson Thomas Grey. Warwick is reported to have been enraged by her decision,[10] a sure sign that he regarded George as his ultimate heir, but there was ample time to find a suitable heiress for the infant George.

Following his remarriage in 1467, a son was born to the Earl of Worcester in 1469, who cut George out of his Tiptoft inheritance. More important, as part of King Edward's reconstruction of his support, George was betrothed in November 1469 to Elizabeth of York, a match that *could* have led to his accession as her consort had Edward IV died without a son, which he had no intention of doing and made sure did not happen. More permanent was George's creation as Duke of Bedford – the highest rank of the peerage, that eluded his great uncle Warwick the Kingmaker – and the grant to him of an annuity of £40 a year. Next spring George's father, John Neville, was induced to surrender his earldom and his Percy estates in Northumberland for a 'pies nest' – the prestigious title of Marquis Montagu and Courtenay lands in Devon possibly equal in value to those surrendered, but not what he wanted. John Neville's rebellion in 1470 did not recover him his Percy estates: instead he lost his Courtenay lands to the restored Earl of Devon and was confirmed only in his tenure of Wressle.[11] Young George could then expect only to inherit his parents' jointure, his maternal inheritance, the limited property held by his father in his own right, and Warwick's Neville estates. The chances of a share in the Tiptoft inheritance brightened somewhat in 1470 when the execution of the Earl of Worcester left only one life, that of his one-

[9] J.S. Roskell, *Parliament and Politics*, iii (1983), 114.

[10] 'Annales rerum anglicarum', in *Letters and Papers illustrative of the Wars of the English in France*, ed. J. Stevenson (2 vols Rolls Series, London 1861-4), ii (2), 786.

[11] Hicks, *Clarence*, 100; *CPR, 1467-77*, 239.

year-old son Edward, standing between inheritance and partition. George was still assured of about £3,000 a year, ample for a duke certainly, but less than had seemed likely five years before.

The two Neville brothers Warwick and Montagu died fighting Edward IV in 1471 in an unavailing effort to keep him from his throne. Montagu was thus a traitor, the blood of himself and his heirs was corrupted, his possessions were forfeit and could not be inherited by his descendants. Accordingly King Edward gave away Montagu's Beaumont lands, seized his own trifling possessions, and gave the Neville inheritance, which he also considered confiscated, to his own brother Richard, Duke of Gloucester.[12] This disaster did not, however, touch George's rights to inherit his parents' jointure, his mother's property, or indeed anything else that he could inherit from her Ingoldsthorpe or Tiptoft ancestors. Nor did it affect his dukedom and £40 annuity, which had been given to him personally. He was still assured of a considerable inheritance, about £400 a year, but one more appropriate for a baron than for a duke.

Warwick and Montagu were indicted of treason by a commission of oyer and terminer in 1472 and it was probably intended to confirm their attainder by a special act of parliament against them. This, however, was never done, so George's title to his father's lands and to his uncle's Neville patrimony was left open. It was explicitly barred by an act of parliament in 1475 that gave the Neville lands to the king's brothers the Dukes of Clarence and Gloucester as long as there were heirs male of the Marquis Montagu living – George and his as yet unborn sons.[13] The royal dukes thus had a parliamentary title to the Neville lands, but acts of parliament could always be reversed. In particular, it was normal for acts of attainder to be revoked. Clarence and Gloucester, of course, were secure so long as George was a minor, but in due course he would come of age. Would they be able to resist pressure for his restoration to the Neville inheritance? He was, after all, a duke like themselves and related by marriage to most of the nobility. His maternal inheritance alone placed him among the leading aristocracy. He remained an attractive catch on the marriage market and, if he married wisely, to the daughter of someone powerful at court, he might be able to insist on his rights. There were fathers-in-law who speculated on these kinds of matches for their daughters. Even if he failed initially, how could the king's two brothers ensure that George Neville's rights were not made good at the expense of their heirs? By 1478 it must have seemed most unlikely that George Neville's inheritance was forever lost to him.

It is here that George's dukedom and annuity become important, as it was these that made him a royal ward. In 1472 the king gave him into the

[12] *CPR, 1467-77*, 422, 511; PRO C 140/83/11/2, 12/1; Hicks, *The Ricardian* lxxxi 177.
[13] Hicks, *The Ricardian* lxxxi 178.

custody of his mother and granted her 200 marks a year for his upkeep from the royal purse. But Edward did not give her the right to marry him off.[14] Had he done so, she could have wed her son to the daughter of someone able to protect him against his demotion from the peerage in 1478. Instead she died in 1476, leaving George – still a minor, still unmarried – as a royal ward. It was the Duke of Gloucester who became his guardian on the strength of his maternal inheritance, formally in 1480, informally perhaps somewhat earlier.

George was degraded from the peerage by parliament in 1478 on account of his lack of means. Actually, as we have seen, he had substantial possessions, if no longer sufficient to place him in the front rank. His demotion meant that, when he came of age, he could not put his own case in the Upper House. It marginally reduced his prospects on the marriage market. That was the other problem. If Gloucester was to retain his Neville lands, he had to ensure that George married and had a son, but he also had to ensure that he did not marry into a family powerful enough to make good his claims. For Gloucester the best way to achieve his end was to arrange the marriage himself and the first step towards this conclusion was Gloucester's acquisition of George's custody. He had not, however, married George off before he died on 4 May 1483 – an event disastrous both to George himself and to Gloucester. With George's death, there were no longer heirs male of the Marquis Montagu living. Under the 1475 act, this meant that Gloucester became only life-tenant of the Neville inheritance. On his death, the heir would no longer be his son Edward, Earl of Salisbury, but Richard, Lord Latimer. For reasons beyond the scope of this essay, Latimer's good fortune also failed to materialise.[15] Gloucester's son Edward could not succeed as 'Lord of the North'. Duke Richard had wasted the twelve years 1471-83 and needed now to build his power and wealth anew.

Next year George's cousin Edward Tiptoft, Earl of Worcester died childless and his possessions were partitioned among his aunts, one of whom was Joan Ingoldsthorpe, who died in 1494. Had George been living, he would have grossed her share. Instead it was eventually divided into relatively small parcels among his five sisters, three half-sisters, and their heirs. George Neville was dead and soon forgotten, his prospects never materialised, yet they played an essential part in the machinations of contemporary politicians. If his recorded actions – his birth, death and betrothal – were strictly involuntary, they were also major political events that shaped the power and career of, among others, the future of Richard III.

---

[14] *CPR, 1467-77*, 313, 335.
[15] See below, 332.

16

The Last Days of Elizabeth, Countess of Oxford

THE twelfth Earl of Oxford and his eldest son were executed for treason in 1462, but his second son, John de Vere, was allowed to succeed as thirteenth earl. He supported the restoration of Henry VI in 1470, shared in his defeat in 1471, and continued his resistance to Edward IV thereafter, landing in 1473 successively in Essex and at St Michael's Mount in Cornwall, where he was captured next year. Although formally attainted only in 1475, his lands were considered forfeit from 1471 and were granted to the king's brother Richard, Duke of Gloucester. By a series of conveyances in 1473-4 the duke also acquired all the extensive lands of the earl's mother, Elizabeth Howard, Dowager-Countess of Oxford.[1] Gloucester acceded as King Richard III in 1483 and was killed in 1485 at Bosworth, when Oxford was in the opposing army. At the Parliament of 1485, which recognized Henry VII as king and attainted Richard III, Oxford secured the reversal of the attainders of himself, his brothers and three retainers killed at Barnet in the service of Henry VI, who was seen as Henry VII's last legitimate predecessor. He thus recovered all the lands he himself had forfeited, but his mother's property, which represented 'grete part of his inheritance', had not been confiscated but had been alienated perfectly legally. Oxford, however, alleged that it had been extracted from her under duress. The Countess Elizabeth, for the service she

> owed and did to the foresaid most blessed Prince King Herrie, was so manassed, put in feare of her Lyfe, and ymprisoned by Richard the IIId, late in dede and not of right King of England, whilst hee was Duke of Glouc', in such tyme that the same John Veer was not att his Libertee, but in Prisone, for that drede, and by meane of the same, the same Countess, in Salvacion of her Lyfe, was compelled to do and make, and cause her Feoffees to do and make, such State, Releases, and Confirmacions, and other thynges, to the seid late Duke of Glouc' and other to hyse use, of divers Lordshipps, Mannors, Lands, Tennements and Hereditaments of inheretaunce, as by the same late Duke and his Councell was advised, as hit is notoriously and openly knowne, ayenst all reason and good conscience.

Parliament therefore annulled the countess's releases and the earl was allowed to inherit the lands.

1. G.E.C., *Complete Peerage of England*, ed. H. A. Gibbs and others (13 vols. 1910–59), x. 236–43; C. L. Scofield, 'The Early Life of John de Vere, 13th Earl of Oxford', *ante*, xxix (1914), 228–45; C[alendar of] P[atent] R[olls] 1467–77, p. 297; C[alendar of] C[lose] R[olls] 1468–76, nos. 1214–15. Oxford was indicted of treason in 1472 and therefore strictly attainted from then, P[ublic] R[ecord] o[ffice], King's Bench, Ancient Indictments, KB 9/41/38. I am grateful to Dr R. Virgoe, Miss M. Condon and Dr C. Rawcliffe for advice about this article.

In the circumstances of Henry VII's victory and Richard III's deposition in 1485, it was sufficient for Oxford to claim that the facts were 'notoriously and openly knowne'.[1] Ten years later, however, the 'dyuers wurshipfull and credibill persones priuie' to the circumstances were 'of grette age' and the earl feared that, if they died without their testimony being recorded, he and his heirs would be unable to prove that his mother had been coerced and that they therefore might be deprived of their lands under the terms of her conveyances. Accordingly he petitioned Cardinal Morton, Chancellor of England, to take depositions of six named individuals: Sir John Risley, Sir James Tyrell, and the four esquires William Tunstall, Henry Robson, William Paston, and John Power. Writs of subpoena were issued on 29 November 1495 and the depositions were taken on 2, 3 and 5 December following. Neither the petition nor the depositions survive in the original, but on 7 December Oxford secured an exemplification of the whole proceedings. The petition and depositions printed below are taken from this inspeximus.[2]

These documents cast a flood of light on the circumstances surrounding the countess's conveyances, but their significance is not limited to this minor historical episode. They also illuminate the characters of both Edward IV and Richard III, the politics of the 1470s and early 1480s, and the treatment of women in the Wars of the Roses. Supporters of Richard III have attempted to counter the traditional charges of villainy by pointing to his estimable character as Duke of Gloucester and have argued that his supposed crimes as king were therefore out of character. These depositions reveal Gloucester to have been just as acquisitive, unscrupulous and ruthless before 1483 as afterwards. The man who maltreated the frail old Countess of Oxford was potentially *capable* of murdering the Princes in the Tower. His actions offended contemporary standards of conduct, notably those of his own retainer William Tunstall and his brother Edward IV,[3] who – contrary to the claims of Ricardians – did not wholeheartedly approve of his brother's actions. Edward disapproved of the coercion of the countess but avoided trouble by refusing to intervene, surely an abdication of the responsibilities of kingship.[4] In contrast, Edward's Chancellor, Robert Stillington, Bishop of Bath, took a strong line with the duke in the interests of justice to the countess, whereas his successor Lawrence Bothe, Bishop of Durham, a closer associate of the duke,[5] was

---

1. *Rot[uli] Parl[iamentorum]*, ed. J. Strachey and others (Record Commission, 6 vols., London 1767–76), vi. 281–2.

2. PRO Chancery, Exemplifications, C 263/2/1/6.

3. See below, pp. 309, 311.

4. For a parallel, see *Paston L[etters] and P[apers] of the Fifteenth Century]*, ed. N. Davis (2 vols. Oxford, 1971–6), i. 544–5.

5. For an alternative view, see A. J. Pollard, 'St Cuthbert and the Hog: Richard III and the Palatinate of Durham', in *Kings and Nobles 1377–1529: A Tribute to Charles Ross*, ed. R. A. Griffiths and J. W. Sherborne (Gloucester, 1986), pp. 111, 115.

more partial. The depositions further substantiate the close relations of the duke with his cousin George Neville, Archbishop of York (d. 1476), who was again engaged in treason in March 1472.[1] They indicate that the duke was already on good terms with John, Lord Howard, who as Duke of Norfolk was to be a principal supporter to him as king, and with Sir Thomas Vaughan, whom he executed as a Wydeville supporter in 1483. Finally, the treatment of the countess goes far to refute the belief that aristocratic ladies came to no harm in the Wars of the Roses. Historians too easily assume from the examples of the two dowager-countesses of Northumberland that ladies lost only their dowers and retained their liberty, jointures and inheritances.[2] Actually it was commonplace for wives and mothers of traitors still at large to be placed in custody to deny the traitors access to their assets.[3] Though her case is particularly well-documented, the Countess Elizabeth is not the only lady to be deprived under this pretext of her own estates, but these depositions alone illustrate the brutality with which ladies in custody could be treated. When the history of women during the Wars of the Roses comes to be written, this case will need to be set against those justifying a more optimistic interpretation.

If these documents are so valuable, why have they not been used more? It is not because they are little known, for they are cited by the *Complete Peerage*[4] and have been used several times with reference to Richard III, most recently by Professor Ross. They have not been employed for the other purposes indicated and have not taken the prominent place they evidently deserve even in accounts of King Richard. The reason for this is that they cannot easily be accepted as statements of fact. In Professor Ross's words, they are 'both *ex parte* and *ex post facto*'.[5] The depositions are not contemporary, but date from twenty years after the event in vastly changed political circumstances. In 1485 Parliament made no attempt to verify the story, and the climate of opinion then and indeed in 1495 was strongly hostile to Richard III. All the documents concerned – the act of 1485, Oxford's

1. Durham, Dean and Chapter Muniments, Registrum Parvum iii, fos. 158, 161, 162v; *Paston L & P* i. 472; PRO KB 9/41/41. Master Edmund Chadderton, treasurer of the archbishop's household and treasurer of Richard III's chamber, is one of several archiepiscopal servants who later joined Richard: PRO KB 9/41/41; A. R. Myers, *The Household of Edward IV: The Black Book and the Ordinance of 1478* (Manchester, 1959), p. 211; A. F. Sutton, "'A Curious Searcher for our Weal Public'": Richard III, Piety, Chivalry, and the Concept of the "Good Prince"', in *Richard III: Loyalty, Lordship and Law*, ed. P. W. Hammond (London, 1986), pp. 68–69. For what follows, see also *Richard III: Crown and People*, ed. J. Petre (London, 1986), p. 93.

2. E.g. J. R. Lander, *Crown and Nobility 1450–1509* (London, 1976), pp. 150–1; R. Archer, 'Rich Old Ladies: The Problem of Late Medieval Dowagers', in *Property and Politics: Essays in Later Medieval English History*, ed. A. J. Pollard (Gloucester, 1984), p. 20.

3. See below, p. 304.

4. *Complete Peerage*, x. 238n.

5. C. D. Ross, *Richard III* (London, 1981), p. 31.

petition to Morton, the depositions, and the inspeximus – emanate from the same partial source, the Earl of Oxford himself. We do not know what inducements may have been offered to the various deponents, some still in Oxford's service, to testify as they did. They were obviously handpicked to support the earl's case, they may have been coached about what they were to say, and obviously those who had supported Gloucester felt differently about the events recounted at the time.

Moreover the earl's motive is crystal clear. His title to his mother's lands depended on his claim that she had been coerced. If that could not be substantiated, his mother's releases were valid and could be used to dispossess him. Not only would the title of Gloucester and his feoffees be good, but so too would be the estates of their assigns: Middleham College; St George's Chapel, Windsor; Queens' College, Cambridge; Sir Robert Percy (controller of Richard's household) and his wife; and John Lord Howard, from 1483 Duke of 'Norfolk, who bought Wivenhoe (Essex) for 1,100 marks (£733 6s. 8d.) in 1480 and was granted Woodham Ferrers (Essex) in 1483.[1] But for the cancellation of Elizabeth's conveyances, those lands held by Richard and Norfolk, both attainted in 1485, and Percy, attainted in 1487,[2] would have passed not to Oxford but to King Henry VII, the rights of the religious corporations remaining undisturbed. While the Windsor and Cambridge colleges may have become more influential as Henry VII's reign progressed, it was most probably the political recovery of Norfolk's son Thomas Howard, Earl of Surrey, that prompted Oxford to secure his title in 1495. Attainted with his father in 1485, Surrey was gradually restored to the lands of his wife, his father and other ancestors by four acts of Parliament between 1489 and 1495. The second of these in 1489 restored his father's Howard lands, which presumably included Wivenhoe. That of 1492 covered Woodham Ferrers. This act and overt royal pressure caused recipients of Norfolk's Mowbray lands to return them to Surrey, Oxford himself giving up Framlingham and other properties by 1494 in return for a substantial annuity. Surrey's restoration to favour was sealed by the marriage of his heir Thomas Howard to the queen's sister Anne on 4 February 1495 and the settlement on them of an annuity from the king and jointure from the earl, the latter dated 20 October 1495, all of which were confirmed by Parliament later the same year. A further act of 1495, which reversed another of 1485 to restore eight manors to Surrey and refute the charge that

1. *CPR 1476–85*, p. 34; *CCR 1476–85*, nos. 735, 1168, 1445; *British Library Harleian Manuscript 433*, ed. P. W. Hammond and R. E. Horrox (4 vols. Gloucester, 1979–83), i. 134–5, 169, 266; iii. 143, 152; North Yorkshire Record Office, Middleham Parish Documents, ZRC/17503; Windsor, Dean and Chapter Muniments, XI.P.11. For Percy as controller of the household, see Myers, *Household of Edward IV*, pp. 289–90.

2. *Rot. Parl.* vi. 275–8, 397–400.

an earlier release had been made under duress,[1] represented exactly what Oxford may have feared could befall his mother's lands. These three acts were all passed in a parliamentary session lasting from 14 October to 22 December 1495 that coincided with Oxford's petitions and depositions: did it prompt them? The loss of Wivenhoe and Woodham Ferrers would have been significant rather than vital to Oxford, but such a misfortune would have encouraged the claims of Percy, now restored in blood, the three colleges, and, most formidable of all, King Henry himself. Perhaps Oxford himself was powerful enough to resist the pressure of Surrey (though not the king), but his heir might not be so fortunate. Probably he was secure so long as he could produce eye-witnesses to support his case, but, as he alleged in his petition, these were gradually dying off. Of his mother's feoffees, six were already dead: Baxter in 1476, Grey in 1478, Debenham in 1481, Timperley in 1491, Townshend in 1493, and Montgomery in 1495; another, William Paston, was to die next year. We cannot know whether it was because of the depositions that Oxford was able to retain his mother's estates, although it is striking that the testimony of the witnesses that the countess was coerced was added to the parliament roll. What is clear is that Oxford's title to his mother's lands depended on his capacity to prove duress, that the depositions were intended to provide that proof, and therefore that they cannot be accepted without question as true.

It is such considerations that have deterred historians from relying on the depositions as they might have liked, although some have accepted the general outlines of the account. Nobody has atempted to substantiate the story and thus rehabilitate the depositions as reliable evidence. Inevitably much of the detail cannot be confirmed – if it could be, the depositions themselves would not be necessary as evidence – but it is the contention of this article that so much can be verified that the remainder should also be credited. If the outlines of the story were correct, it was hardly in the interests of the deponents to perjure themselves – for the depositions were made on oath – on circumstantial details. Moreover at least two of them, Sir John Risley and Sir James Tyrell, respectively royal councillor and feoffee for the king's will in 1495,[2] were too high in Henry VII's favour to require patronage from the Earl of Oxford. No new evidence will be brought into play, but more can certainly be made of the countess's conveyances and

1. *Rot. Parl.* vi. 410–11, 426–8, 448–9, 474, 478–80; Lander, *Crown and Nobility*, pp. 145–7; R. Virgoe, 'The Recovery of the Howards in East Anglia, 1485–1529', in *Wealth and Power in Tudor England: Essays presented to S. T. Bindoff*, ed. E. W. Ives, R. J. Knecht and J. J. Scarisbrick (London, 1978), pp. 12–13; see also how another royal patentee of Howard lands, Lord Delawarr, surrendered his grant in 1494 'ad requisicionem dicti domini Regis', PRO Exchequer, King's Remembrancer, Memoranda Roll, E 159/274, *commissiones*, Easter, 13 Henry VII.

2. J. C. Wedgwood, *History of Parliament 1439–1509*, ii, *Biographies of Members of the Commons House 1439–1509*, (London, 1938), p. 890; R. Virgoe, 'Sir John Risley (1443–1512) Courtier and Councillor', *Norfolk Archaeology*, xxxviii. ii (1982), 144–5.

Gloucester's chancery suit with her feoffees. Fortunately both are recorded not only in the public records, but also with other vital evidence in the duke's own commonplace book, British Library Manuscript Cotton Julius BXII.

The Countess Elizabeth was a considerable heiress in her own right. Born about 1410 and therefore in her sixties at her death, she was the daughter and heiress of Sir John Howard by Joan, sister and heiress of Sir Richard Walton, son and heir of John Walton. From the Howards she inherited the manors of Great and Little Oakley, Mose, Great Bentley and Bentfieldbury in Essex; Fowlmere in Cambridgeshire; Brooke, Mileham, Narborough, Wiggenhall, South Clench, and Garboldisham in Norfolk, and various rents and advowsons. From the Waltons she inherited Oldhall in East Bergholt and Overhall in Stratford in Suffolk, the manor of Batayles in Stapleford, lands in Woodham Ferrers, and probably also Wivenhoe in Essex.[1] These were hers by right and would normally have passed on her death to her eldest surviving son John, Earl of Oxford. Following his forfeiture in 1471, they would pass on her death not to him but to Gloucester, the royal patentee, unless something was done to prevent this outcome. It was probably for this reason that in or after 1471 Elizabeth enfeoffed all her estates to use, which meant that she could devise them by will.[2] It is likely that she intended, at the very least, to order in her will that the income should be used to defray her debts and pay for her bequests. Providing the trust did not benefit any attainted person, immediate forfeiture could be averted, and Elizabeth could also direct her feoffees to convey the lands on fulfilment of the trust to a third party as ultimate beneficiary. As her three elder sons were attainted, it is difficult to see who this could be. One deponent said that she still regarded Oxford as her heir.[3]

What actually happened is that Elizabeth and her feoffees under three enfeoffments released their rights in her estates to Gloucester, his heirs and assigns in three deeds dated 9 January 1473, that Gloucester's attornies took physical seisin of the lands and received the attornment of the tenants on 22 February following, that the feoffees alone confirmed the duke's title on 9 February 1474, by which time Elizabeth was dead, and that they acknowledged the enrolled deeds in chancery on 25 June following.[4] There is no dispute about any of this. What is open to doubt is why Elizabeth gave up her inheritance. One explanation is presented in the depositions. Oxford's six chosen witnesses fall

1. *Complete Peerage*, x. 238; *Calendarium Inquisitionum post Mortem sive Escaetarum* (Record Commission, 4 vols., London, 1806–28), iii. 322; *CCR 1422–9*, p. 172.

2. That Elizabeth enfeoffed her lands after the battle of Barnet, at which the de Veres were heavily engaged, is suggested (a) by the absence of any of her sons among her feoffees; (b) by the absence of any noted Lancastrians; (c) by the fact that none of the feoffees had yet died.

3. See below, p. 313.

4. *CCR 1468–76*, nos. 1214–15; B[ritish] L[ibrary] MS Cotton Julius BXII fos. 227–9, 315–16v.

into three main categories: former servants of Gloucester – this accounts for Sir James Tyrell and William Tunstall;[1] three associates of the countess, comprising two feoffees, the lawyer Henry Robson and William Paston, and an annuitant, John Power;[2] and Sir John Risley, a bystander. Their depositions record that at Christmas 1471 or 1472 the countess was living in the nunnery at Stratford le Bow (Essex), where she was visited by the Duke of Gloucester. He informed her that he had been granted the custody of herself and her possessions. Tyrell testifies to her tearful response to this unwelcome news and to Sir John Pilkington's seizure of her coffers on Gloucester's behalf. The duke removed her to his lodgings in Sir Thomas Vaughan's house at Stepney. Tyrell, Tunstall, Robson and Paston report how distressed she was there, where William Tunstall somewhat unrealistically reassured her by saying that Gloucester was a knight and the king's brother and would therefore do her no harm! Robson and Power both recall how fearful she was that she would be sent to the north of England. Robson at first hand, Power at second hand, and Tyrell and Tunstall from rumour state that this threat was designed to make her surrender her lands, which of course she did. Once she had conceded that point, the duke let her move to more congenial surroundings at Walbroke, and sought the compliance of the feoffees. Tyrell said he had heard Lord Howard threaten Master Piers Baxter, Elizabeth's confessor and one of the feoffees, Robson explained that his own fears prompted him to comply, and both Robson and Paston told how the latter tried to avoid releasing his interest in the estates. Paston recalled two court hearings, one in which Chancellor Stillington took the countess's part and another when Bothe, his successor as chancellor, forced him to release to the duke. Robson reported the countess's subsequent remorse at the disinheritance of her heirs and his own reassurance that this would not be permanent, as her lands were entailed. Finally, Sir John Risley testified that several years later King Edward IV advised him against buying Elizabeth's London house from Gloucester, because the duke had secured it by duress.

There is nothing inherently improbable about what the depositions record. The events recounted evidently belong to Christmas 1472. Elizabeth's conveyance is dated 9 January 1473 but she was still in control of her affairs on 20 September 1472, when James Arblaster and Sir John Paston (William's nephew) unsuccessfully sought to influence the parliamentary election at Maldon (Essex) on her behalf.[3] It was probably Oxford's continued treason that prompted her arrest: although his naval activity at Dieppe is only recorded from April

---

1. Tyrell was in Gloucester's service by 1473 and Tunstall by 1479, *Paston L & P* i. 464; *Calendar of Close Rolls, 1476–85*, no. 650. Tyrell's connections with the duke were particularly close and both remained in his service as king.

2. PRO Duchy of Lancaster, Ministers' Accounts, DL 29/295/4848 m. 2d.

3. *Paston L & P* i. 580–1.

1473,[1] just a month before his landing at St Osyth (Essex), his prepar-
ations must have begun earlier. Elizabeth, like other Lancastrian ladies,
may have been confined to a nunnery by royal command and, again
perfectly normally, may have been placed in custody, as indeed she
had been a decade before, although (as usual) there is no surviving
royal record of this.[2] Some other details seem plausible. Sir John
Pilkington was such a prominent ducal retainer[3] that he may well
have been Gloucester's chamberlain. Baxter and Arblaster were indeed
feoffees of the countess. The duke had no London house before he
acquired Elizabeth's at London wall and in 1476 he leased a house
called the Tower in the parish of St Thomas the Apostle in the City
formerly occupied by John Beaufort, Duke of Somerset (d. 1444).[4]
This latter lease suggests that he did not appreciate the countess's house
and may well have wished to sell it, just as he sold Wivenhoe and
alienated other manors in mortmain.[5] None of this is conclusive.
Anyone in the service of duke or countess may have known about
the individuals concerned and so the precise detail of their testimony
need not mean that their stories are true. If we had more independent
information, we might be able to identify more discrepancies. Tyrell
and Tunstall were involved as witnesses in Gloucester's later estate
transactions with the De Vere lands, Power continued to receive his
annuity from Elizabeth's former estates during Gloucester's tenure,
and from 1475 Risley was bailiff of the De Vere manor of Lavenham.[6]
All, therefore, knew more than they revealed in their depositions, which
could be justification for doubting their veracity. The consistency of
their testimony, somewhat exaggerated in my summary, does not however seem to arise from careful coaching. Greater precision over dates
could then have been expected and there are many ways in which
Oxford's case could have been strengthened, for example if the pressure
brought on Elizabeth had been presented as physical violence rather
than purely psychological. Taken together, 'they read more like the
reminiscences of twenty years before rather than deliberate fabrications,
but that is a subjective impression.

1. *Ibid.*, i. 460, 464. Cf. *Calendar of State Papers and Manuscripts, Milan*, i, ed. A. B. Hinds
(London 1902), 174–5.

2. For parallels for confinement in nunneries, see R. C. Hoare, *A History of Modern Wiltshire*
(6 vols. London 1822–40), i (2), 101–2; BL MS Cotton Julius BXII fos. 314–15. For instances
of custody, see *CPR 1461–7*, pp. 181, 184; Hoare, i (2), 102; Scofield, loc. cit. 229; PRO Exchequer,
Treasury of Receipt, Council and Privy Seal, E 28/89/9. It seems that such matters were normally
transacted under the signet, sign manual and privy seal, not the great seal, whose records have
survived much better. I hope to discuss this topic more fully elsewhere.

3. *Testamenta Eboracensia*, iii (Surtees Society, xlv, 1864), 239–41; PRO Exchequer, King's
Remembrancer, Memoranda Rolls, E 159/254 Recorda Easter 17 Edward IV m. 3; Exchequer,
Treasury of Receipt, E 405/55 m. 1.

4. PRO Chancery, Warrants for the Great Seal, Treasurer's Bills, C 81/1638/61.

5. See above, p. 300.

6. *CPR 1467–77*, 534; North Yorkshire RO, ZRC/17503; *CCR 1476–85*, no. 1168; PRO DL
29/295/4848 m. 2d.

The most substantial reason for doubting their testimony is that Gloucester himself presented a quite different – and strictly contemporary – account of his acquisition of the countess's estates. This was in his chancery suit against Elizabeth's feoffees. Here he states that it was 'atte desire of the said countesse, and by thadvice of hir counsel bitwene hir and the said duc' that her lands should be released to him in return for an annuity of 500 marks to her for life, the payment of debts totalling £240, the promotion to

> competent benefices of a son of hirs beyng at studye in Cambrigge, proposing to be a prest, with other dyvers benefaites, costes, and charges, by the said duk promysed to be doon for the said countesse and hir children and children's children at hir speciall request and desire.[1]

It cannot be confirmed that such an agreement ever existed, as none is included in Gloucester's commonplace book, where the duke carefully recorded other transactions relating to his acquisition of this and other estates. Supposing that one was made, however, there seems to have been nothing in Gloucester's concessions to tempt Elizabeth to give up her inheritance. The annuity may have been no more than the normal issues of her lands. Payment of her relatively small debts and of her bequests, provision for her children, and even the ecclesiastical advancement of her son could easily have been managed by her feoffees from the resources of her enfeoffed estates.[2] The annuity, moreover, was payable only for the duration of the life of the countess, who was old and infirm and who died within a year. There is no evidence that Gloucester paid any of Elizabeth's bequests, provided for her children or grandchildren, or promoted any of her sons to benefices. Master Richard de Vere, at Cambridge in 1469–70, is not known to have secured any benefice thereafter.[3] The duke did continue to pay some of the countess's annuities,[4] perhaps because he valued the services of the recipients just as much as she had done. Even had all the terms of the supposed agreement been observed, Gloucester paid far less than the capital value for Elizabeth's estates, which at twenty years purchase ran to thousands if not tens of thousands of pounds. If such an uneven agreement was ever contracted, it is highly unlikely that the countess entered into it of her own free will, still less that her council recommended it to her.

Actually Elizabeth's council did not support her releases to Gloucester or, at least, did not do so unanimously. The chancery suit itself

---

1. *Calendars of Proceedings in Chancery in the Reign of Queen Elizabeth* (Record Commission, 3 vols. London 1827–32), p. xc.

2. E.g. M. A. Hicks, 'The Beauchamp Trust, 1439–87', *Bulletin of the Institute of Historical Research* liv (1981), below, chapter 19, pp. 337-51.

3. A. B. Emden, *Biographical Register of the University of Cambridge to AD 1500* (Cambridge 1963), p. 608. George Vere, there in 1459, remained a layman and was knighted, *ibid.*, p. 608; *Rot. Parl.* vi. 144–6.

4. PRO DL 29/295/4848 mm. 2, 2d.

indicates disagreement. The duke's care to record his receipt of seisin of the lands as well as his registration of the various conveyances in chancery may also be seen as evidence that he anticipated trouble. His petition to Chancellor Stillington sometime after Elizabeth's conveyance of 9 January 1473 reveals that only six feoffees had actually sealed the deed by then, the other seven refusing.[1] These seven included two royal councillors in Sir Thomas Montgomery and the king's kinsman William Grey, Bishop of Ely, a future serjeant at law in Roger Townshend, Grey's client Master John Warkworth, Master of Peterhouse, Cambridge, William Paston, who was Elizabeth's councillor, and James Arblaster, who probably was.[2] They were certainly more substantial figures than the two Mowbray retainers (Gilbert Debenham and John Timperley),[3] Elizabeth's confessor Master Piers Baxter, and the three relative nonentities (John Coke, Henry Robson, and Henry Wilcox) who *had* sealed the release. The hearing was fixed for 11 February 1474, being presumably advanced somewhat, but it was nevertheless not until Hilary term 1474 that Chancellor Bothe heard the case and decreed that the recalcitrant feoffees should convey their rights to the duke.[4] Only then can they have sealed the deeds dated 9 January 1473, which they confirmed on 9 February and acknowledged in June. Thus the regularity and legality presented by the deeds and the unanimity claimed by Gloucester's petition is quite misleading. Some of Elizabeth's feoffees and councillors refused to seal the original deed, the duke's seisin and the attornment of tenants to him were therefore invalid, and the recalcitrant seven did not actually comply until after Elizabeth was dead and her personal wishes could no longer be ascertained.

Why did they not comply with Gloucester's wishes? Their response to Gloucester's bill survives as an original and as a copy in his commonplace book,[5] but is unfortunately somewhat opaque in its content. The feoffees refer to an earlier, otherwise unrecorded, hearing 'in this Courte' before the king's justices and Chancellor Stillington before his dismissal on 18 June 1473, at which session Elizabeth had been received 'atte their instaunce'. Presumably this was the meeting before the king that she was bound to attend daily at Easter 1473 on pain

1. *Chancery Proceedings*, i, p. xc.
2. PRO DL 29/295/4848 m. 2d; *Paston L & P* i. 580–1. Arblaster was a longstanding De Vere servant, who was a receiver in 1466–8 and auditor general and surveyor, temp. Henry VII, and who was warmly attached to his employers. In his will of 1492 Arblaster appointed Oxford as supervisor in return for the 'love and service' he had shown the earl and his parents since childhood. He asked to be buried at the foot of the tomb built for the earl's parents and paid for the remains of the Countess Elizabeth to be transported to Colne to be put in the tomb, so that he might be near her in death. PRO Prerogative Court of Canterbury, Probate Registers, PROB 11/16; Essex Record Office, D/DPr 128, 129. I am indebted to Dr Rawcliffe for this information.
3. Wedgwood, *biographies*, ii. 265, 857.
4. *Chancery Proceedings*, i. xci.
5. BL. MS Cotton Julius BXII fo. 315; P.R.O. Chancery, Answers, C4/2/51. I am indebted to Miss Condon for this reference.

of her own recognizance of £3,000 and sureties of £8,000, from which she was discharged on fulfilment on 9 July following.[1] The seven feoffees also declared that the countess was dead and that she was believed to have made a will of which her confessor Baxter was executor, but the content of which they did not know.

> And what couenaunt was made be twene the seid Duk and Countesse or what was the seyd confession of the same Countesse vpon her seyd examinacion or what was her last wyll nor what thei aught of right to doo Wherefore for their trought and declaracion thei prayen that such persones examinacions and matieres as be necissarie in this behalfe may be heard and examynyd . . .[2]

It is hard for us to make much of such comments addressed to those possessed of information we lack, but it appears that the feoffees felt that the events of the previous hearing justified their recalcitrance and that as Elizabeth's trustees they considered themselves bound to obey her directions in her will rather than implement the earlier deeds. One could deduce from this that they considered the earlier deeds to be invalid, that the countess later regretted them, and perhaps also that the duke suppressed Elizabeth's will, which certainly does not survive. Apparently they expected all these conclusions to emerge from the depositions they suggested, which, so far as we know, were never taken.

Such strained deductions from the contemporary evidence are not necessary, however, since they conform precisely to the story in the depositions, which throw a flood of light on the course of events. Paston's deposition records that there was indeed an earlier hearing afforced by the judges and royal councillors, at which Chancellor Stillington asked Elizabeth whether she had acted freely and she declared that she had not. No wonder the seven feoffees felt this sufficient justification for their recalcitrance! Paston adds that the reason for his refusal to comply, which he declared in court to Chancellor Bothe, was that he doubted whether it was Elizabeth's wish to alienate her estates, an explanation perfectly compatible with the weight that the seven attached to her last will. He appealed as witnesses to Arblaster, who was still alive in 1495, and to Cardinal Morton himself, who had been present as Master of the Rolls at the second hearing. Moreover, the depositions also state that some even of those who had sealed before the chancery suit, Baxter and Robson, did so from fear, having been menaced by the duke and Lord Howard.[3] Chancellor Bothe, on their evidence, was a highly partial judge and one certainly cannot accept his decree without question as just. Indeed, as we have already seen, it was generally assumed to be unjust from at least 1485.

1. Dated 21 March 1473, *CCR 1468–76*, no. 1103.
2. PRO C4/2/51.
3. See below, 310, 313-14.

To accept Gloucester's version of events, one has to believe that Elizabeth gave away her estates of her own free will for quite trivial payment and this story, as we have seen, was not believed at the time. At least some of Elizabeth's councillors and the majority and the most eminent of her feoffees can be shown from strictly contemporary evidence to have doubted her free will. They only released their rights after protracted resistance and considerable pressure from the duke. The claim of duress is thus contemporary and was not fabricated by Oxford in 1485. The account of events drawn from such evidence conforms well with that presented in the depositions, which cannot be faulted at any significant point. In spite of the partial purpose they were intended to serve, the depositions appear to be a reliable guide to events in 1472–4 and may therefore be used in all the ways indicated at the beginning of this essay. There is no more vivid record of the villainy of Richard III as Duke of Gloucester, of power-politics in the early 1470s, or of the miserable last days of Elizabeth, Countess of Oxford.

Public Record Office, Chancery, Exemplifications, C 263/2/1/6.
Crown-copyright material in the Public Record Office is reproduced by permission of the Controller of Her Majesty's Stationery Office.

1. *Petition of John, Earl of Oxford.*
To the most reverent Fader in god and gracious lord/the lord Cardinall Archebisshop of Caunterbury and Chaunceller of England. Bisechith your goode and gracious lordship John Erle of Oxenford that where Elizabeth late Countesse of Oxenford his moder whose heier he is for the true and feithfull aligeaunce and seruice that she owid and did to the most blessid and cristen prince kyng Henry the Sixt was/in the tyme of the reigne of Kyng Edward the iiijth by imprisonament and for drede of her distruccion compellid by cohercion ayenst her will to departe with her lyuelod to Richard late callyng hym selff kyng Richard the thirde thenne Duke of Gloucestre your seid suppliaunt thenne being atteyntid of high treason for his true seruice don to the seid most/Cristen prince and therfor durst not ne myght be at his libertie in this londe. Of the which imprisonament cohercion and maner of departyng of her seid lyuelod there were dyuers wurshipfull and credibill persones priuie and had perfitte knowlege therof of whom dyuers be of grette age. And if they shuld dissese their witeness in that behalfe not had ne entred of record the knowlege of the seid imprisonament and (coher)cion mygh renne oute of mynde and therof myght ensewe wrongfull vexacion and trouble to the seid Erle and his heiers of and for the enheritaunce of his seid moder. Wherfor in escheuing therof hit may please your noble grace to directe seuerall writtis of

sub pena to Sir James Tyrell knight Sir John Risley knyght/William
Tunstall esquier William Paston ... Henry Robson and John Power
esquier the which weere privie and had perfite knowlege of the maner
of departyng of the seid Countes frome her seid lyvelod/comaunding
them to appere by fore the kyng in his Chauncery atte a certeyn day
there to depose and witteness alle that they knowe touchyng imprisonament and/cohercion the which was putt to the seid Countes in that
behalfe and all other thyngis concernyng the departyng of her seid
lyuelod to the seid late Duke. And that there deposicions and wittenes
maibe there entred and remayne of recorde to thentente aforseid. And
the seid erle shall pray to God for your prosperous estate long to
contynewe and to his plesure.

2. *Deposition of Sir John Risley.*

John Rysle of Totenham in the Counte of Middlesex knyght of thage
of lij yeres and more sworn and examynyd the seconde day of Decembre
in the xjth yere of the reigne of our soueraigne lord kyng Henry the
vijth seith and deposith vppon (his) othe that vppon iiij yeres or theruppon afore the dissese of kyng Edward the iiijth to his remembrance
this deponent comme to the seid kyng Edward thenne ridyng in hun-
tyng in Waltam Forest bitwene Walwoorde and langfordes place. And
thenne and there this deponent shewed/to the same kyng Edward that
he entendid havyng the favoure of h(...) purchace of the dewke of
Glocestre a place beside london Wall callid the Erle of Oxenfordes
place besechyng his grace to geve hym his goode councell whether
he myght so sewrely do ye or nay. And thenne and there the seid
kyng Edward askid of this deponent by what/right and title the same
place comme to the hondes of his brother of Gl(ouc)estre. And this
deponent answerid to the same kyng Edward that the seid dewke of
Gloucestre come vnto hit by a release made by the lady of Oxenford
moder to my lord of Oxenford nowe beyng and thenne and there
the same kyng Edward seid to this deponent Risley me(ddl)e/notte
ye with the biyng of the seid place for though the titill of the ...
place be goode in my broder of Gloucestres handes or in an other
mannys hondes of lyke myght hit wol be daungerous to the to by
hit and also to kepe hit and defende hit sayng thenne also to this deponent that the seid lady was compellid and constreynyd by the seid
dewke of/Gloucestre to release and forsake her ryght in the seid place.
For which cause this deponent surceacid and made no further labour
in the seid matter att which communicacion were present no mo persones and heryng the same communicacion but they too forasmoche
as they thenne were rydyng by the wey but by what meanes the seid
lady was so compellid to/release her ryght as is aforeseid he cannot
sey but he hath herde sey of diuers persons whose names he remembir
nott that the seid lady was vnder the streight kepyng of the seid dewke
in london but in what place he cannot sey and more he knowth nott.

3. *Deposition of Sir James Tyrell.*

James Tirell of Gippyng in the Counte of Suffolk of thage of xl yeres sworn and examynyd the seconde day of Decembre in the xjth yere of the reigne/of oure souerayne lord kyng Henry the vijth seith and deposith vppon his othe that he knewe well my lady of Oxenford moder to my lord of Oxenford nowe beyng by sight. Also he seith that in the xjth or xijth yere of kyng Edward the iiijth as he supposeth abowte Cristemasse as he remembrith this deponent thenne beyng seruaunt with the dewke of Gloucestre/thenne beyng wente with the same dewke frome Stepeneth vnto Stratford where the seid lady thenne lay and thenne and there this deponent within the Abbey there herd the seid dewke reporte and sey to the seid lady that the kyng his brother had gevyn vnto the seid dewke the kepyng and rewle of the seid lady and of her londes./Whereuppon this deponent thenne sawe the seid lady wepe and make grette lamentacion but what answere she thenne gaue vnto the seid duke this deponent herd not. And thenne and there this deponent herd Sir John Pilkyngton thenne Chamberleyn to the seid duke desire to haue her keies of suche Cofers as she had which this deponent/thenne sawe her delyver to hym thenne present dyvers seruauntis of the seid duke whos names he remembir nott. Also this deponent seith that within shortt space after what dayes he remembir not this deponent sawe the seid lady at Stepeneth beside London atte logyng of the seid duke and ther he sawe her contynewe by the space of iij or iiij daies/by the which space he sawe the same lady wepe and make grete lamentacion dyuers tymes but for what cause he cannot certenly sey. But he seith that a communicacion and a talkyng was thenne amongest the housold of the seid duke that her wepyng was for as moche as she was desirid and entretid by the seid duke to make a state/to hym of certeyn of her londes which were of her enheritaunce but of what londes this deponent cannot sey. Also this deponent seith that he hath herd reportid that the seid lady made a state of her londes to the seid duke but of whatt/londes or by whome the seid reporte was made this deponent cannot perfitely sey but/whether the same a state were made by compulcion and cohercion he cannot precisely sey but he seith that he herd the lord howard at that tyme beyng geue great wordes of manasse in the place of the Archbisshop of Yorke beside Westminster to on Maistre Baxtre thenne beyng on of the feoffes of the seid lady in her seid landes callyng/hym fals preeste and ypocrite by cause he wold not graunte to the seid state and release thenne present Sir John Pilkyngton knyght and other. And he seith that he demeth only in his conscience that the seid a state and release was by cohercion by reason of the seid woordes of manasses so made to the seid Baxter, which Master/Baxter after the seid mannasses moued the seid lady and causid her to make the seid astate as this deponent hath herd reported. And more he cannot sey in this matter.

4. *Deposition of William Tunstall esquire.*

William Tunstall of Scardeburgh in the Counte of York Squyer of thage of lx yeres and more sworn and examynyd the seconde day of December in the xjth yere of our souerayne lord kyng Henry/the vijth seyth and deposith vppon his othe that he knewe my lady of Oxenford moder to my lord of Oxonford nowe beyng. And he seith furthermore that in Cristemas season aboute the xijth yere of kyng Edward the iiijth a seruaunt of the duke of Gloucestre whos name he remembir not come thenne to this deponent to Stepeneth beside london and/seid to this deponent that the mynde of the seid duke was that this deponent and other seruauntis of the seid duke should goo in to a Towne callid Stratford beyng aboute iij myle owte of london and fett the seid lady from the seid Stratford and bryng her vnto Stepeneth aforesaid where the seid duke att that tyme kepid his housold. And/this deponent thought in his mynde that hit was not for the profite of the seid lady to be brought to the seid place. And therfore he absentid hym selffe and medeled no further therin. Furthermore this deponent seyth that within ij or iij daies after dyvers seruauntis of the seid duke whos names he remembir nott to the nowmber of xvj persones/or theraboutes went vnto Stratford aforseid in pesibill wise and fette the seid lady fro Stratford aforseid and brought her vnto Stepeneth aforseid. And thenne and there this deponent sawe the seid lady wepe wherfor he thenne comforted her seiyng to her that the seid duke was a knyght and a kyngis brother and trusted that he/wolle do her no wrong. And the seid lady thankid this deponent for his goode comforte thenne beyng present on Master Baxter thenne confessour to the seid lady and dyvers other persones whos names he remembir nott. Also this deponent seith that the same day that the seid lady was brought from Stepeneth aforeseid by the comaunde/ment of the seid duke with dyvers of his seruauntis this deponent at her desire wettyng vppon her was sent upon her feete to a place of the seid dukes at Walbroke in London and thenne and there the seid lady gaue to this deponent a purs and thankid hym and so this deponent departid levyng the seid lady in a Chambir/within the seid place at Walbroke with dyvers other persones whos names he remembir nott nor whos seruauntis the seid persones were this deponent cannot sey but howe the seid lady was entretid in the seid place by the seid duke or by his seruauntis this deponent cannot sey. Also this deponent seith that he knowth/not if eny astate or release made by the seid lady or by eny other persone for her to the seid duke of eny of her londes nor of eny compulcion or cohercion made by the seid duke or any of his seruantis to the seid lady. But hit was thenne commened and reported amonges the seruauntis of the seid duke and other persones/there that the seid lady was sent for to thentente that she shulde be compellid to make an a state to the seid duke of certeyn of her londes but of whatt londes this deponent

cannot sey nor whether she was so compellid or not butt by the said
reporte and more he knowth nott.

5. *Deposition of Henry Robson esquire.*

Harry Robson of lincolns ynne in London Gentilman of thage of xlvij
yere and more sworn and examynyd the second day of Decembre in
the xj yere of the reigne of oure soueraigne lord kyng henry the vijth
seith and deposith by his othe that aboute Cristemas in the xij yere
of kyng Edward the iiijth in/the moneth of Januarij as he remembrith
what day he remembrith not my lady Elizabeth thenne Countes of
Oxenford and moder to my lord of Oxonford that nowe is thenne
beyng at Stepeneth beside London in the kepyng of the Duke of Gloucestre sent for this deponent to come to speke with her yf he durste
she/thenne beyng at Stepeneth aforeseid logid over the porter logyng
in a place there thenne callid Sir Thomas Vaughan place wherin the
seid duke thenne kepid his housold att whiche desire this deponent
wentto the seid Countes to the seid place and Chambir. At whoos
commyng the seid Countes thankid hym for his commyng and seid/
these woords: I thank god hertely besechyng hym to haue mercy on
my frendes sowles by whome I haue these londes which nowe shall
save my lyfe. And then she shewde and reported to this deponent
that withoute she wolde make a state to the seid duke of all suche
londes as she thenne had and cause her feoffes to release/their right
and titill to hym therof that he wolde send her to Middelham there
to be kept. Wherfor the seid lady consideryng her greate age the greate
iourney and the grett colde which thenne was of Frost and snowe
thought that she cowde not endeure to be conueid theder withoute
greate iopardie of her lyf and also sore feryng/how she shuld be there
entretid requyrid and desirid this deponent forasmoche as he with other
were enfeffid in parcell of her londes that if eny writyng or dede vnder
her seale comme to hym to be sealid that he shuld enseale hit in lyke
wise as he loved her and her lyff thenne present diuers seruauntis to
the seid lady bothe Master/Piers Baxter her confessour Thomas Barton
thenne her Steward and other nowe disseasid. Also this deponent seith
that within ij daies after this deponent came ayen to the seid lady to
Stepeneth aforseid in the seid Chamber where she was afore and thenne
and there the same lady shewd to this deponent that she/had fulfillid
the mynde and entent of the seid duke as touchyng hir seid londes
vnto which tyme she remaynid still in the seid Chamber wherfor he
supposeth verely in his conscience that the seid lady ensealed dyuers
dedes of her seid londes vnto the seid duke by cohercion and compulsion
and fere as is aforeseid and as she hath/shewd and reported often tymes
to this deponent after which seconde beying of this deponent with
the seid lady for asmoche as she had fulfillid the mynde of the same
dewke she was conveid the same nyght from the same dukes place

vnto a place of on Chadworth in Stepeneth aforseid and so from thens
in to Walbroke/to a place of the seid duke and within was v or vj
deyes after that the seid duke sent on Watkyn Chaundeler his seruaunt
for this deponent to come to speke with the seid duke at Seynt Jones
beside Smythfelde. And so he did at whos commyng the same duke
thenne seyd to this deponent that the seid lady had ensealed to hym
a dede feoffament of suche londes as she had and that the seid Master
Baxter her cofeoffe thenne beyng present had also ensealed the same
dede and there the seid duke causid the same dede there to be redde
which dede was thenne redde but by whome he nowe remembir nott.
And whanne the Reder therof came to the/name of William Paston
which was on of the feffes of the seid lady the same duke demaunded
of this deponent yf he knewe hym or loved hym seyyng that he vnder-
stode that the same Paston repungned ayenst the same feoffament wherfor the same duke commaunded this deponent to sey to the same Paston
that/withoute he wolde enseale the said dede hit shuld cost hym that
he loved best thenne present Sir John Pilkyngton the seid Master Baxter
and mony other persones whos names he remembir nott. After which
commaundement so made the seid Reder of the same dede rad the
name of this deponent in the seid dede and thanne/the same duke
incontinent after the redyng of the name of this deponent demaunded
of this deponent yf he wolde enseale the same dede which deponent
feryng the same duke wolde haue seid or doon to hym in lyke wise
as he seid of the same Paston seid that he wolde enseale hit and so
thenne did thenne present the seid Master Baxter the seid Pilkyngton
and other how be hit he durst not otherwise doo. Also this deponent
seith that he herd the seid lady often tymys sithen the seid tymes reporte
and sey that she was sory that she for savyng her lyff had disheritt
her heiers. Which deponent comforted her seiyng that in so moche
as moste/parte of her londes were entaillid and be matter of record
and also that she had don ayenst her wyll he trusted that her heiers
shuld not be disherited therby notwithstondyng the seid duke had
caried awey all her evidencis and more he cannot sey.

6. *Deposition of William Paston esquire.*

William Paston of London Sqwier/of thage of lx yeres and theruppon
sworn and examynyd the thirde day of decembre the xj yere of the
reign of our souerayne lorde kynge henry the vijth seith and deposith
vppon his othe that apon a xxvij yere past or thervppon by his estima-
cion he was thenne of goode knowlege and in fauour with Elizabeth
thenne Countes of Oxenford/Moder to John nowe Erle of Oxonford
and was of counsell and of fe thenne wyth the seid Countes. Ferther-
more thes deponent seith that apon a xxiij yere past or theruppon
as he remembrith he herd/by the report of James Arblaster thenne
seruaunt ... Countess and also on Harry Robson and other whos
names he remembir not/thenne shewd to this deponent beyng in london

that Richard thenne Duke of Gloucester had been at Stratford of the
bowe with the seid Countes there beyng within the place of the Non-
nery and that the same duke had there shewed and reported . . . Edward
his brother had geven to the same duke the rewl and gidyng/of the
same Countes and of her maners londes and goodes and the seid James
seid also that the seid duke had causid the seid Countes by dredefull
manasses ayenst her will to be brought from Stratford aforseid vnto
a place in Stepeneth thenne pertaining to Sir Thomas Vaughan and
there was kept in a Chambir vnto suche/season that by the meanes
of the seid duke she was compelled to agree that all such feffes as were
enfeffid in her seid maners and londes to her vse should make a state
and release the right and titill of the seid maners and landes to the
seid duke. Furthermore this deponent seith that in the tyme of Doctour
Stilington/Bisshop of Bathe and thenne Chaunceller of Englond the
same Chaunceller a litill afore he was dischargid of the office of the
Chauncellership but what yere which moneth or day he remembir
nott the seid Chaunceller beyng then in the Chekir Chambir in Westminster heryng of the myso entretyng of the seid Countes by the seid
duke on/the premisses callid the seid Countes thenne and there afore
hym and thenne this deponent herd the seid Chaunceller thenne sey
vnto the seid Countes thees woordes. Shew ye me the trouth of the
dealyng of the Duke of Gloucestre with you and fere no person to
sey the trouth. Which Countes there shewd that she was compellid
by grette fere/and drede to make the bargain which she made with
the seid duke concernyng her seid maners and landes and no thyng
of fre will thenne and there present dyuers and mony Juges and other
of the kyngis Councill. Whos names this deponent perfitely remembir
nott. Furthermore this deponent seith that aboute the seid season but
what yere/moneth or day this deponent remembir nott the seid duke
dyuers and mony tymes sent vnto this deponent by the seid Robson
and be dyvers others of the Councell of the seid duke by grett thretenyn-
gis and manassingis and vppon payn of deth that this deponent shuld
release to the seid duke all suche right and titill as he had of and/in
the maners and londes belongyng to the seid Countes which to do
this deponent vtterly refused. Wherfor the seid deponent in eschewyng
of inconveniens that myght growe to hym by reason of the premissis
conveid his plate and goodes in to the Custodie of the lord Ormonde
nowe lyvyng to thentente to withdrewe his own person/secretly and
so did. Which not withstondyng the seid duke havyng vndirstondyng
where this deponent was causid a sub pena to be delyueryd to hym
to appere afore the kyng in his Chauncery at a certeyn day vppon
a grette payn att which day this deponent there apperid afore the lord
laurens Bothe thenne Bisshop/of Durram and Chaunceller of England
thenne settyng in the kyngis Chauncery at Westminster by whom theire
satte the seid duke mi lord Chaunceller nowe beyng and thenne Mayster
of the Rollis with dyvers of the masters of the seid Chauncery the

seid duke thenne seiyng these Woordes vnto this deponent: William/ Paston I haue sent to you many tymys to seale a relesse accordyng to the bargayn had bytwene me and the seid Countes. Why will yo not seal it as your Cofeoffes hath don. Which deponent this answerid I neuer knewe that hit was the fre wil of the seid Countes that I shulde release. Thenne the seid Chaunceller/thenne beyng William Paston herkyn what my lord of Gloucestre seith to you that ye shall release and ye shall not chose but relese. William Paston what sey ye therto. Which William thenne seid I most do as the Courte woll awarde but whether this deponent relesid in dede or not he perfitly remember nott/and referrith hym to suche recordes as thenne were recordid in the same Courte concernyng the seid release thenne and there present Sir Thomas Montgomery Maister Piers Baxter stondyng within the seid Courte and mony other persones whos names he remembir nott. And more he knoweth nott.

7. *Deposition of John Power esquire.*

John Power seriaunt of the larder/vnto our souerayne lord kyng Henry the vijth sqwyer of thage of lxvj yeres or theruppon sworn and examynyd the v day of Decembre in the xj yere of our seid souer- ayne lorde seith and deposith vppon his othe that he knew well dame Elizabeth Countes of Oxenford Moder vnto John nowe Erle of Oxon- ford for he was dyvers and/mony tymys with her and consisaunt and also was her fede (seru)aunt. Furthermore this deponent seith that aboute the xiij yere of kyng Edward the iiijth but what day or moneth this deponent remembir not he was in london whan the seid Countes was fett from Stratford of the Bowe by dyverse of the seruauntis of Richard/thenne Duke of Gloucestre and brother to the seid kyng Edward and this he knowith for as he was goyng to the seid Countes to Stratford aforseid he mette on Thomas Barton thenne Steward to the seid Countes and many other of her seruauntis which shewd these woordes to this deponent. By Ware go ye not to my/lady to Stratford for there is mony of the seruauntis of the seid dukes that hath serchid my ladies place where she ley and also her cofers and woll convey my lady away. But whether thenne she shuld be conveid this deponent knewe nott. Furthermore this deponent seith that soone after but what day or moneth this/deponent remembir not the seid Countess was had by the seruauntis of the seid duke vnto a place of on Thomas Vaughans and incontinent theruppon this deponent went to the seid place to se the seid Countes as his dutie was where he fonde the same Countes. The Countes thenne seyng this deponent seide theese woordes: I mervell gretly that ye durst come se me remembryng the troubill that I am yn. Wherevppon the seid deponent seid to the same Countes: How is it with you Madame? Which Countes thenne answerid and seyd: sore troubled./Neuetheless I know well ye haue loued me and all my blode wherfore I trust you and pray you to shewe vnto

my sonne John Erle of Oxenford yf euer ye speke with hym as I trust
in god ye shall that all such estates and relesis as I most make of my
maners and londes to the Duke of Gloucestre I do for gret/fere and
for the sauacion of my lyff for yf I make not the seid astates and releses
I am thretened to be had in to the North Cuntre where I am sewre
I shuld not lyve long and for the lengthyng of my lyff this I doo.
Furthermore this deponent seith that apon Seynt Thomas Eves Eve
afore Cristmas/afore the discease of the seid Countes but what yere
this deponent remembir nott this deponent was atte Stratford aforseid
within the Place in the Nonery there where the seid Countes thenne
was in her Chaumber by her bedside and thenne and there the seid
Countes shewde to this deponent/that she was seeke and grevously
disesid wherfor she thowght sche cowde not longe lyve and thenne
and there the same Countes remembrid the woordes and shewyng what
she had shewid to the deponent in the seid place of Vaughans which
woordes the same Countes there rehersid to this/deponent and praid
hym in eny wyse that he wold kepe in mynde the same woordes what
so euer became of her and so shewe hit vnto her son whann he spake
with hym and also to sey that she sent hym goddis blessyng and hers
which Countes died within eight daies after. Also this deponent seith
that the seid/Countes within ij daies next after as he remembrith was
buryed in the Church of freres Augustines in London afore the high
auter there at which buryng this deponent was thenne and there present
also the seid duke the lord Howard and other. Furthermore this deponent seith that he herde dyvers and/mony tymes by reporte of Arblaster
and Paston which stode feoffes in the seid maners and londes to thuse
of the seid Countese that they were dyvers tymes tretenyd by the
seid duke and his seruantes to lease there lyvis by cause they woll
not release all suche right and title as they had in the same maners
and/londes to the vse of the seid duke but whether they releasid or
not this deponent cannot sey and more he knowth nott.

17

Richard III and Romsey[1]

The adult career of Richard III falls into two distincts parts: a brief two years as King Richard III (1483-5) and a much longer period (1469-83) as Duke of Gloucester. Although few of his archives as duke have survived, many of his activities are recorded elsewhere. They relate mainly to his acquisition and litigation over land. Several of his transactions are sufficiently well documented to cast light on his intentions and character and are thus deserving of further exploration. One such instance explored below concerns the Hampshire manor of South Wells in Romsey.

Whether as duke or king, Richard III does not ring an immediate bell as a Hampshire worthy. Following a Welsh childhood, he spent his adolescence and manhood predominantly in the north, ultimately becoming the most northern of medieval English kings. His Hampshire properties, a feefarm rent from Andover and the office of weigher of Southampton, were inadvertent inheritances of his wife. Richard himself seems to have regarded his southern possessions as expendable, to be alienated for cash, for masses for his souls, or in exchange for lands in the north, where his priorities evidently lay.

Why, then, in or immediately before 1480, did he purchase the manor of South Wells in Romsey? The seller, Thomas Greenfield, had been known to him since at least 1474, when he was in the duke's service on the Scottish borders.[2] He was thus well-placed to draw Richard's attention to the availability of his manor of South Wells, but Richard's desire to do a servant a good turn is hardly sufficient motive for the purchase. Probably the price was highly favourable: no doubt partly because of the financial difficulties that caused Greenfield to become an almsknight at Windsor in 1482;[3] partly, with hindsight, because of the poor title that Greenfield had to sell. South Wells was actually held by feoffees to use, his own trustees so

---

[1] This essay revises my two earlier articles: 'Romsey and Richard III', *Hampshire Field Club Local History Newsletter* 7 (1983), 151-3; 'Further Comments on Richard III and Romsey', *Hampshire Field Club Section Newletters* new series 8 (1987), 5.

[2] *Rotuli Scotiae* (Record Commission), ii 451.

[3] *C[alendar of] P[atent] R[olls], 1476-85*, 306.

Greenfield said, but when Duke Richard asked them to convey the manor to him, they declined. Standing no nonsense, the 'full high and mighty prince' subpoenaed all parties in the court of chancery.

South Wells in Romsey had been held by the Greenfield family for at least three generations. John the elder, in occupation in 1442,[4] died a very old man in 1448, when he was succeeded by his namesake John Greenfield the younger of Winchester. The younger John, clerk to the counting-house of Henry VI, was MP for Melcombe Regis in 1455-6, steward of Odiham and constable of Winchester, and held lands in Romsey, Nursling, and many other places in Hampshire.[5] His Winchester connections explain the marriage of his daughter Agnes to the lawyer John Hammond, recorder of Winchester from 1467, several times MP, and from 1465-70 JP for Hampshire;[6] his other daughter Christine married the relative obscure Simon Crouchman; and his heir, our Thomas, made little impact on the records. The family was not an important element in Hampshire society, although John the elder appointed two county magnates as his trustees, Sir Maurice Berkeley and Sir Thomas Uvedale.

Thomas Greenfield first leased South Wells – and doubtless other properties too – to his brother-in-law, John Hammond,[7] and then, on 16 April 1472, he agreed to surrender his lands to his sisters. In return he received annuities of £19 for life and 19 marks (£12 13s 4d) for his wife Isabel after his death. His sisters thus anticipated their inheritances. Maybe Greenfield already realised that his marriage would be barren, but this circumstance and the annuities alone were insufficient incentive to sell up: probably both sisters paid him lump sums, Christine perhaps as much as 85 marks (£56 13s 4d). Christine's share, scattered throughout Hampshire, falls outside the scope of this essay; it was the Hammonds who received South Wells and other lands in Romsey, Nursling and Sholing, which they had bought subject to the payment of the aforesaid annuities. Even in 1472 there was little love between the parties, who promised to eschew fraud and swore on the Bible to observe their agreement. Some time later, no doubt finding it difficult to live on £19 a year, Greenfield created trouble and screwed a further £20 from John Hammond, the sum awarded by Bishop Waynflete as arbiter.[8]

Greenfield had promised to instruct his trustees to convey South Wells to Hammond, but instead – probably at Hammond's request – they settled them on John Eastby and Hammond's brother William. Later Eastby surrendered his rights to William Hammond, who – definitely at

[4] Windsor [Dean and Chapter] MS IX M 2 f 56v.
[5] J.C. Wedgwood, *History of Parliament, 1439-1509* (2 vols. London 1936-8), ii 394.
[6] Ibid ii 412-13.
[7] C 1/52/145. For what follows, see Windsor MS XV 41 50.
[8] C 1/52/142.

John Hammond's instigation – passed South Wells on to a third panel of trustees, including John Baker, Warden of Winchester College, Master Davy Husband, Thomas Well, and John Tichborne.[9] By 1474 South Wells was held by this third panel, John Hammond's trustees, and in 1479 the manorial court of South Wells was held in Hammond's name.[10] This was the situation when Thomas Greenfield, again needing money, sold South Wells to Gloucester.

In his bill to the chancellor, Gloucester recited the various settlements (but not the 1472 convenant) and alleged that Eastby, William Hammond, and the third set of trustees held South Wells in trust for Greenfield.[11] John and Agnes Hammond quickly disabused him, asserting that they had bought South Wells from Greenfield and that all the trustees were theirs. Unfortunately the trustees let them down: Tichborne pleaded ignorance and was willing to accept the court's decision; Well and Husband denied that they had ever taken seisin, so the conveyance was invalid; and Eastby appeared for Greenfield.[12]

Eastby, understandably praised by Gloucester as 'a trew man and thryfty' of Romsey,[13] was illiterate and forgetful. He remembered being enfeoffed at Greenfield's direction and, perhaps not unreasonably, thought that he was Greenfield's trustee. He remembered being approached by John Hammond to seal a conveyance of the manor, but could not recall the nature of the transaction: 'the said John Estbie remembreth nat sertainly for so moche as he is nat lerned'. However that may be, Eastby refused to seal the deed without Greenfield's consent. Hammond, justifiably irritated, threatened him with a subpoena and would not allow him time to consult Greenfield. Eastby, by now much alarmed, anxious about Greenfield's right but fearful for himself, sealed his release to William Hammond before witnesses, to whom he declared it conditional on 'the wille and agreement of the said Thomas Greenfield'. No wonder Hammond wanted to keep the condition secret,[14] since it offered a loophole in his title for Greenfield to exploit further.

It was a godsend to Gloucester, who asserted in his replication that Hammond had dishonestly played on Eastby's illiteracy to make him seal the deed, who contrasted Hammond's deceit and Eastby's honesty, and who argued that the release was void since it had not received Greenfield's consent. Furthermore, as a second line of argument, Gloucester argued that South Wells had been leased, not sold, to Hammond, who held it

[9] C 1/52/139-45.
[10] Windsor MS XI M 2 f 54v.
[11] C 1/52/139.
[12] C 1/52/140, 142-3; Windsor MS XV 24 85.
[13] C 1/52/141.
[14] Windsor MS XV 24 85.

subject to annuities to Greenfield and his mother Felicia, which had not been paid.[15] In his rejoinder Hammond cited the 1472 covenant,[16] thus ruling out the lease, but may have been unable to show that all instalments of the annuities had been paid. This, however, was of secondary importance, for the Hammond's case was lost when their trustees failed to back them up.

The verdict does not survive, but there are two grounds for supposing that Richard won. First of all, only victory can explain his continued favour to the disreputable Greenfield, now Sir Thomas Greenfield.[17] Had the case been lost, Richard could hardly have relied on him again. Secondly, the issue roll of the exchequer for Michaelmas term 1480 records that the king paid £200 to Gloucester for the purchase of the manors of South Wells and Roke and various other lands in Odiham and Crondall in Hampshire late of John Greenfield, father of our Thomas.[18] This strongly suggests that Richard won the lawsuit and, having made his speculative title good and having no particular interest in Hampshire, he realised his capital for redeployment elsewhere. There are many other examples of him engaged in the speculative purchase and disposal of the property and also of him selling land in the south to finance purchases in the north of England. However, an alternative interpretation which cannot be ruled out is that Richard sold up before the lawsuit was concluded, although in that case Edward IV paid a high price for an unstable title.

Either interpretation is compatible with a second piece of evidence, a final concord relating to the same lands in Easter term 1483 – very shortly before the king's death on 9 April 1483. The suitors were William Lord Hastings, the king's chamberlain, Thomas Danet clerk, dean of St George's College at Windsor, and Richard Pigot serjeant-at-law, who were presumably King Edward's trustees. The defendants were Thomas Greenfield, his two sisters Agnes and Christine and their husbands Hammond and Crouchman. The conclusion, so obviously arranged in advance, was that the defendants recognised the rights of Dean Danet to the lands.[19] Evidently it was the king who wanted to give them to St George's Chapel, of which he was almost a second founder and the builder of the surviving chapel, where he lies buried. Clearly he wanted the college's chapel as secure as possible and therefore bought out the claims of the previous owners. The fact that Greenfield was associated with his sisters and their husbands suggests that it was their residual rights that

[15] C 1/52/141.
[16] C 1/52/145.
[17] *CPR, 1476-85*, 306; *Calendar of Close Rolls, 1468-76*, no 941.
[18] F. Devon, *Issues of the Exchequer* (London 1837), 501.
[19] CP 25(1)/206/34/30.

were being brought rather than their agreement to drop the lawsuit –
Greenfield had already sold his title – but this is a detail that remains
unclear and does not really affect our understanding of the story. St
George's Chapel did indeed secure the lands by 1488 and retained control
until selling in 1860 to the then Prime Minister Viscount Palmerston,
already owner of the Broadlands estate in Romsey.[20]

The basic outlines of the story seem clear. What Richard acquired from
Greenfield was a highly dubious title, as he must have been aware. He
must also have realised how fortunate he was to make it good and how
unjust his victory was for the Hammonds and Crouchmans. Whilst his
support for Greenfield has connotations of good lordship, it is clear that
Richard's main interest was financial: he had no need or use for the lands
themselves and merely wanted to make a profit from his dubious
investment. It was clearly Edward IV, not Richard, who was the
benefactor of St George's Chapel.

[20] Windsor MX XV 60 62 [acquittance 16 Dec 1488]; *VCH Hants* iv 459.

Descent, Partition and Extinction:
The Warwick Inheritance[1]

THE LATE Professor Galbraith argued that the relations between medieval magnates were as important as they are prominent in chronicles. They were not merely the background to politics but the essence of politics itself.[2] If his criterion is applied to the years 1471–5, it is apparent that the quarrel between the dukes of Clarence and Gloucester was of exceptional significance. To informed official opinion, it was the burning political issue of the day,[3] outweighing treason at home and abroad. The main protagonists were the two brothers of King Edward IV and their disagreement ruptured the newly established family unity that had just enabled Edward to recover his precarious throne. Historians have generally blamed it on the greed of Clarence but this is an oversimplification. At issue was the fate of the Warwick inheritance, which was already subject to conflicting claims and political considerations. This article will examine in turn these preliminaries to the quarrel, the dispute itself and its repercussions, showing the interaction between each.

The Warwick inheritance was well worth fighting for. One of the largest medieval estates, it had been the foundation of the power of Richard Neville, earl of Warwick and Salisbury, the outstanding nobleman of the preceding decade. Like other great inheritances, it comprised the fortunes of several families combined in the same hands.[4] From his father and namesake, the earl of Salisbury, had come Warwick's north-country patrimony. His Montagu possessions descended from his mother Alice, heiress of the last Montagu earl of Salisbury. In right of his wife, Anne Beauchamp, Warwick held the estates of her father Richard Beauchamp, earl of Warwick and her mother Isabel *suo jure* Lady Despenser.

What these inheritances had in common was antiquity and size. All four families can be traced to the thirteenth century, when three inherited older fortunes. As few noble houses survived in the male line for more than a few generations, so each of these families accumulated sufficient possessions from defunct dynasties to qualify for the estate of earl. They survived the usual threats to continued existence until the fifteenth century, when all passed to the junior branch of the Nevilles.

This broke the just course of descent, for Warwick's title to each was debatable. The lordships of Raby (co. Dur.), Sheriff Hutton and Middleham

---

[1] The work for this article was supervised by Mr. C. A. J. Armstrong. I am indebted to Mr. T. B. Pugh and Professor C. D. Ross, who read and criticized it. Unless otherwise stated, genealogical details are from the *The Complete Peerage*, comp. G. E. Cokayne and others (13 vols., 1910–59). Lands granted by Edward IV are deliberately excluded.

[2] V. H. Galbraith, 'A new life of Richard II', *History*, xxvi (1941–2), 223–39, esp. 229–30.

[3] *Rerum Anglicarum Scriptorum Veterum*, i, ed. W. Fulman (Oxford, 1684), p. 557.

[4] For the next 4 paragraphs, see M. A. Hicks, 'The career of George Plantagenet, duke of Clarence, 1449–78' (unpublished University of Oxford D. Phil. thesis, 1975), ch. vi, and sources there cited. The inheritance was encumbered by two dowagers, Eleanor Neville, countess of Northumberland (d. 1474) as Lady Despenser, and Alice Chaucer, duchess of Suffolk (d. 1475) as countess of Salisbury.

(Yorks.) would have passed with the Neville barony until 1569 had not the first earl of Westmorland conveyed them to Richard (later earl of Salisbury), his eldest son by his second wife Joan Beaufort. She was a daughter of John of Gaunt and close relative to the Lancastrian kings: hence her husband's promotion. Thus the junior branch was endowed, quite legally but at the expense of the second earl of Westmorland. Finding himself dispossessed and without a case at law, the latter resorted to force, but by exploiting royal favour Salisbury was able to restrain him until his own title was recognized in return for the Durham lands. Royal support, however, was lacking in 1449, when the death of her niece made Anne Beauchamp's claim to the Beauchamp and Despenser inheritances a practical issue. According to a well-known common law principle, her claim to the Beauchamp estates as whole sister of her brother Henry was superior to that of their three half sisters, but it could not be made good, since one of them was married to the duke of Somerset, who was paramount at court. Only in 1454 was a favourable verdict obtained, at a moment of temporary ascendancy for the Nevilles and eclipse for Somerset, and Warwick implemented it by force. The exclusion of the half-blood was inapplicable to the Despenser inheritance, which was divided between Anne and her young nephew George Neville, son of her half-sister Elizabeth and Lord Abergavenny. As this arrangement did not meet with Warwick's approval, he obtained custody of the other share during the minority, gained possession by force and retained it even after George came of age, ignoring commands to desist. Finally, in 1461, it was on the strength of a fraudulent title that the Nevilles recovered certain Salisbury lands which had escheated in 1429 and to which they had no legitimate title.

Political factors were crucial in each case: the exploitation of royal favour when forthcoming, an opportunist sense of timing and a readiness to use force when it was not, and a ruthless disregard for intimate family ties. Such single-minded pursuit of personal ambition undoubtedly affected the Nevilles' political stance. It is an improbable coincidence that it was only when royal support was denied that they gravitated to the opposition, exploiting its victories to secure the Beauchamp and Salisbury lands. The incidental alienation of certain kinsmen helps explain the disunited conduct of the seven Neville peers in the civil war. Once secured, the retention of the inheritance became a prime consideration. Warwick's possession was only provisional, since it depended on his capacity to prevent his rivals from receiving a fair hearing, which in turn pre-supposed that he and his heirs would always be dominant at court—an improbable contingency. Should this advantage be lost, his vengeful enemies would mercilessly expose the rickety basis of his power: thus George Neville of Abergavenny temporarily recovered his share of the Despenser inheritance following Warwick's exile in 1470.[5] Awareness of his weakness affected Warwick's action in three ways: in 1466 he made territorial concessions to reach a settlement with the Beauchamp coheirs; it was one of the factors that impelled him to desperate measures to recover his lost influence at court; and he sought for his daughters husbands powerful enough to keep hold of their estates.

Hardly were these inheritances gathered in than it became apparent that their union would last only for the lives of the earl and countess. They had no son. Their daughters Isabel and Anne were coheiresses of the Beauchamp, Despenser and Salisbury inheritances as heirs general, but not of the Neville patrimony. The heir to this was Warwick's brother John, Lord Montagu, from 1464 earl of Northumberland and from 1470 marquess Montagu, and his son George, from 1470 duke of Bedford. There were contingent remainders to the younger sons of

[5] Public Record Office, PSO 1/34/1784, 1786; see also P.R.O., *35th Annual Rept.* (1874), p. 97.

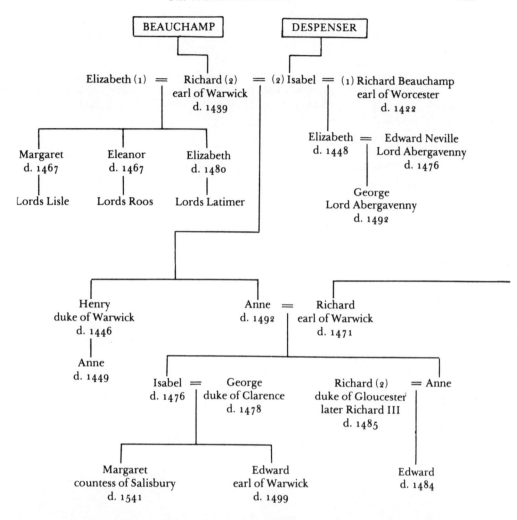

the first earl of Westmorland's second marriage and their issue. This is what should have happened but it did not because of the collapse of Warwick's political schemes.

Warwick wanted advantageous marriages for his daughters and his nephew George,[6] a future head of the family. As great heirs, they would normally have attracted suitable spouses, but unfortunately Edward IV's intervention on the marriage market for his Wydeville in-laws had exhausted the supply. Certainly Warwick was aiming high, for he married his wealthy ward Lord Lovell to a niece rather than a daughter. This lends credence to the otherwise unsupported statement of the chronicler Waurin that Warwick wanted to marry both his daughters to Edward IV's brothers.[7]

[6] See his anger at the rupture of George's betrothal to the duke of Exeter's heiress, *Letters and Papers illustrative of the Wars of the English in France*, ed. J. Stevenson (2 vols., Rolls Ser., 1861–4), II. ii. 786.

[7] *Complete Peerage*, viii. 223n, 225; J. de Waurin, *Recueil des Croniques et Anchiennes Istories de la Grant Bretaigne*, ed. W. and E.L.C.P. Hardy (5 vols., Rolls Ser., 1864–91), v. 458–9.

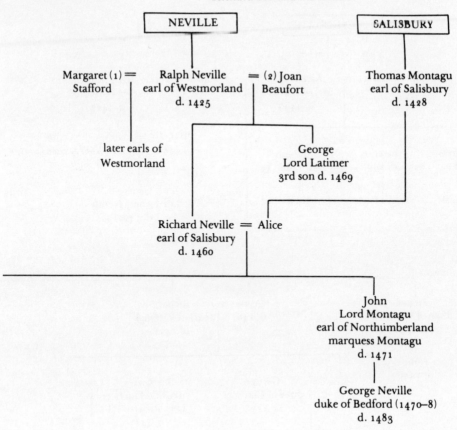

In spite of Edward's disapproval, Warwick concluded a marriage between Isabel and the duke of Clarence. Her prospective purparty was large but Clarence can have had little hope of speedy admission. Should the countess of Warwick die first, her husband would enjoy her estates for life by law of England. If he died first, their daughters could have shared only that portion of the Montagu inheritance unencumbered by the jointure and dower of Alice, dowager-duchess of Suffolk. In the event the countess of Warwick lived until 1492, twenty-one years longer than her husband, sixteen more than Isabel and seven more than Anne. In the short run, far from receiving a half share of the countess's estates,[8] Clarence received at most a few manors of trivial value in Rutland and Northamptonshire.[9]

On their exile in 1470 Edward IV seized Warwick's and Clarence's estates[10] but

---

[8] As stated in *Hall's Chronicle*, ed. H. Ellis (1809), p. 271.

[9] He held Easton Neston (Northants.) but can have had held very little else, Kent Archives Office, Maidstone, De Lisle MSS. U1475/M201 m.1d, M226–7; P.R.O., SC 11/825.

[10] B. P. Wolffe, *The Crown Lands, 1461–1536* (1970), pp. 103–4; *Calendar of Patent Rolls 1467–77*, pp. 208–9; P.R.O., SC 2/177/25 m.3.

Warwick resumed possession at the readeption of Henry VI.[11] Immediately following Warwick's death in 1471 Clarence took control as earl of Warwick and Salisbury and Lord Despenser.[12] Evidently he claimed all the lands that his wife could have inherited, disregarding in the process the rights of the countess of Warwick and Anne Neville, the younger coheiress.

Both Warwick and Montagu were killed at the battle of Barnet. By bearing arms against the king when his banner was displayed, they incurred the penalties of treason, for which they were posthumously indicted.[13] Their estates were thereby forfeit. Forfeitures were normally confirmed by act of attainder in parliament but this was not essential for them to take effect. In this case Edward could not rigorously exact his legal rights. In consideration of Clarence's assistance in recovering his throne, he could not deprive him of his wife's inheritance,[14] so he granted him all those lands to which the duchess had hereditary expectations. As one of two daughters, she received more than her deserts. She had no claim to the Neville patrimony, entailed in the male line, so Edward granted it and the other tail male lands to his youngest brother Richard, duke of Gloucester.[15] At this stage Clarence had no grounds for dissatisfaction.

The titles of each duke depended on royal grant not on inheritance. Only thus could the rights of the countess of Warwick be set aside. Even then her husband's forfeiture should have affected only her dower in the Neville and Salisbury estates, not her own heritage nor her jointure, unless she were herself guilty of treason. Of this she was never accused. From sanctuary at Beaulieu abbey she pursued her claims with petitions to those about the king.[16] Had her rights been recognized, her daughters would have lost possession, but without her husband she lacked influence and was ignored.

The other daughter Anne must have known Gloucester during his sojourn in her father's household during the fourteen-sixties.[17] At Michaelmas 1471 Anne was a widow aged fifteen, in the custody of the duke of Clarence, who had strong reasons for preventing her remarriage. Only the duke of Gloucester was powerful enough to rescue her and recover her inheritance for her, so it was probably with her co-operation that he abducted her. He intended to marry her. It was not her person but her claims to property that attracted him. He hoped for a half share of the tail general estates as well as those in tail male that he already held.

What Gloucester desired was impossible as the law stood. Anne could inherit the Salisbury estates only if Warwick did not suffer forfeiture. In that event not only would they be encumbered by the dower and jointure of her mother but the tail male lands would pass to George Neville. This could be prevented by attainting George's father, the marquess Montagu, but he was less guilty than Warwick.[18] Anne could inherit part of her mother's estates on her death, not

[11] P.R.O., SC 2/194/108 m.1; Worcestershire Records Office, Reg. Carpenter II, BA 2648/6 (iii) fo. 34.

[12] Birmingham Reference Library, MSS. 347914, 347865; P.R.O., SC 2/194/108 m.2; *ibid.*, SC 2/177/25 m.4; Oxfordshire County Record Office, Dil. X/a/II; *Cartae et alia munimenta quae ad dominium de Glamorgancia pertinent*, ed. G. T. Clark (6 vols., Cardiff, 1910), v. 1695–6.

[13] J. G. Bellamy, *The Law of Treason in England in the Later Middle Ages* (Cambridge, 1970), p. 201; P.R.O., KB 9/41/38.

[14] The grant does not survive either on the rolls or among the warrants of chancery, perhaps because it was originally oral, but see *Cal. Pat. Rolls 1467–77*, p. 330; P.R.O., C 81/1504/5.

[15] *Cal. Pat. Rolls 1467–77*, pp. 260, 266.

[16] British Library, Cotton MS. Julius B. xii fo. 314r–v.

[17] He was in Warwick's custody by Michaelmas 1465; *Issues of the Exchequer . . . Henry III to Henry VI*, ed. F. Devon (1837), p. 490.

[18] J. R. Lander, *Crown and Nobility, 1450–1509* (1976), p. 139.

before, yet Gloucester wanted them at once. He could not have it all his own way. Moreover, to enjoy Anne's inheritance he had to marry her but they were related several times within the prohibited degrees, so this might not be possible. Clarence was cousin of Isabel Neville, who was his mother's godchild: it had not been easy to obtain a dispensation for them. In Gloucester's case the marriage of his brother and Anne's sister was an additional impediment. A dispensation might be unobtainable: the settlement reached in 1474 provided for the voidance of the marriage.[19] This would have illegitimated any offspring.

Clarence's anger is understandable. He had been given lands for services rendered, had entered and enjoyed them, and would lose heavily if Gloucester's claim were met. If his own title derived from royal grant, no hereditary title was valid. In any case until Gloucester contracted a legal marriage he had no legitimate interest in Anne's inheritance. This attitude was quite logical and the conflicting elements in Gloucester's case could be reconciled only with the king's assistance. Edward could make Clarence disgorge by cancelling the letter patent, either by persuading him to surrender it or by act of resumption. Gloucester turned to him and Edward reacted favourably. His gift to Clarence had undoubtedly been influenced by the duchess's hereditary expectations, so it was not difficult for him to take those of Anne into account. The partition of the estates would enable him to provide for Gloucester at no cost to himself.

On 16 February 1472 Clarence, while prepared to accept the marriage of Gloucester and Anne, remained adamant that he would not divide the tail general estates.[20] This was on the eve of a conference held at Sheen to thrash out their differences. Clarence gave way. Partition was agreed and in return for surrendering certain possessions Clarence's title was strengthened in others.[21] On 25 March he was created earl of Warwick and Salisbury[22] and on the same day, by a warrant not enrolled in chancery, he was granted four manors, two parks and a messuage in London.[23] Taken together these documents reveal that the whole inheritance was to be divided, leaving Clarence with lands in the West Country and west Midlands. The tail male estates granted to Gloucester were included in the new settlement,[24] which indicates that Gloucester's case was not accepted unreservedly.

Clarence capitulated to political pressure. A warrant of 18 March, which guaranteed compensation to him and his heirs in the event of future losses of land, refers specifically to the Courtenay estates and to acts of resumption:[25] an indication that he was threatened with the resumption of his other estates, which posed a choice between rebellion or submission. This ultimatum by the king, who signed all the warrants, was made with powerful backing. Queen Elizabeth attended the conference. On 21 February she renewed a grant to Gloucester of a stewardship that carried a fee of £100,[26] a sign that he enjoyed her support. The Wydevilles' hostility to Clarence as their political enemy probably persisted in spite of formal reconciliation in 1471.[27] An indication that the meeting convinced Clarence of the urgent necessity for strengthening his influence with

[19] *Rotuli Parliamentorum*, vi. 101. There is no direct evidence that a dispensation was ever granted.
[20] *Paston Letters and Papers of the 15th Century*, i, ed. N. Davis (Oxford, 1971), p. 447.
[21] P.R.O., C 81/1504/5; *Cal. Pat. Rolls 1467–77*, p. 330.
[22] *Calendar of Charter Rolls 1427–1516*, pp. 239–40.
[23] P.R.O., C 81/1504/7.
[24] *Ibid.*
[25] *Ibid.*, C 81/1504/5; *Cal. Pat. Rolls 1467–77*, p. 330.
[26] Brit. Libr., Cott. MS. Jul. B. xii fos. 121v, 126v–127.
[27] See e.g. P.R.O., KB 27/848, Rex, m.8d.

the king is his appointment on 20 March to key offices on his estates of the king's chamberlain Lord Hastings,[28] who had opposed him in politics and with whom he did not agree on local affairs.[29]

The marriage of Gloucester and Anne Neville, already decided on 18 March, was probably concluded soon after,[30] although no dispensation was to arrive for at least two years. Only the principle of division was decided, not the detailed partition, and it had probably not been resolved how to make it valid in law. Certain lands were surrendered by Gloucester to Clarence,[31] who apparently did not reciprocate. He had good reason to delay: should Gloucester not obtain a dispensation, he might not have to surrender anything. Such Fabian tactics had soured the dukes' relations again by early June 1473, when Gloucester removed the countess of Warwick from sanctuary to his protection. This understandably annoyed Clarence,[32] as it endangered the 1472 settlement and threatened to dispossess him of his wife's estates in Gloucester's favour. It was rumoured that the countess was to be restored so that she could surrender her possessions to Gloucester.[33] Two correspondents agree that Edward supported Gloucester. In 1471–2 her inheritance was held mainly by Clarence, so it appears that he retained lands provisionally allocated to his brother. This is supported by the resemblance of the ultimate partition to that projected in 1472 and Clarence's later surrender of lands to Gloucester.[34]

The removal from sanctuary of the countess of Warwick did not reduce the tension. Instead Clarence was said to be preparing to 'dele wyth' Gloucester in November, while Edward tried to restrain them.[35] Edward had probably expected the release of the countess to bring Clarence to heel. When it failed, he did not implement the threat: perhaps her co-operation could not be relied on, as Gloucester and her daughter might yet be divorced. Had Edward restored her, the result would have been quite different from that planned in 1472. Instead he denied Clarence a proviso of exemption to the act of resumption of December 1473.[36] This deprived him of all his estates, not merely his wife's inheritance, as all of them had been granted by letters patent. By withholding the proviso Edward dispossessed Clarence entirely, forcing him once again to choose between rebellion or submission. As he did not rebel, subsequent events are the fruit of his submission.

A partition was effected on 20 July 1474,[37] by which date the necessary transfers of land had probably taken place.[38] On 18 July Clarence was restored to most of his own estates, although the king retained property in the north Midlands worth £1,200 a year.[39] The principles of the agreement were laid down

[28] Historical Manuscripts Commission, *Hastings MSS.*, i. 302.
[29] *Wars of the English in France*, II. ii. 789.
[30] See *Glamorgan County History*, iii, ed. T. B. Pugh (Cardiff, 1971), p. 200 n.233. The marriage could not however have been concluded in Lent: P. Heath, *The English Parish Clergy on the Eve of the Reformation* (1969), pp. 7–8; *Provinciale seu Constitutiones Angliae*, ed. W. Lyndwood (Oxford, 1679), iii. 16. 1 note e (p. 185).
[31] P.R.O., C 81/1504/7.
[32] *Paston Letters and Papers*, i. 464.
[33] Hist. MSS. Comm., *11th Rept.*, app. pt. vii, p. 95.
[34] P.R.O., SC 2/177/25 mm. 8–9.
[35] *Paston Letters and Papers*, i. 468. The hypothesis that Clarence was also involved in treason is fully discussed in Hicks, pp. 131–8.
[36] First observed by J. Gairdner, *History of the Life and Reign of Richard III* (Cambridge, 1898), p. 30.
[37] Brit. Libr., Cott. MS. Jul. B. xii fos. 136v–137v.
[38] P.R.O., SC 2/177/25 mm. 8–9.
[39] For details, see Hicks, pp. 143–6, 284.

by acts of parliament of July 1474 and February 1475.[40] The intention was to enable the earl of Warwick's daughters to inherit by barring the rights of others. The lands in tail male were to be enjoyed by them so long as there was a male heir of the marquess Montagu living and, in the event of their extinction, by the two dukes for their lives. The countess of Warwick's estates, whether held in dower, jointure or inheritance, were to be enjoyed by her daughters as if she were naturally dead. Each duke would hold the lands of his consort after her death by courtesy. Since Gloucester's marriage was still of doubtful validity, it was provided that even if divorced he should still enjoy a life estate, so long as he did not remarry. It was agreed that neither duke could make any alienation or settlement that would exclude the rights of inheritance of the other. As the earl of Warwick was not attainted, his daughters entered the Salisbury inheritance without further provisions.

The act governing the tail male lands lists those assigned to each duke. Gloucester was to have everything except le Erber in London and Clavering (Essex), which were assigned to Clarence. So uneven was the division that the inheritance must have been partitioned as a whole, although there is no direct evidence of this. The division of lands under the 1474 act was enshrined in indentures of partition, of which only Clarence's half survives.[41] Its extreme brevity and imprecision explains the omission of some items; others may have been excluded because Clarence and his duchess held them in jointure or by separate grant. At first sight this suggests that Clarence secured an unduly large share but this is at variance with his unexpectedly low income from it. The partition was on geographic lines, reflecting the interests of the two dukes. All the lands north of the Trent and in Wales passed to Gloucester, while those in East Anglia, the east Midlands and south-east England were divided. No provision is mentioned for the reversion of lands held for life by the two dowagers, for the support of the countess of Warwick, or for satisfying rival claims like that of George Neville of Abergavenny.

As an instrument to end discord, the schedule is strangely imprecise. So much was omitted and so vaguely were items defined that ample fuel was left for differing interpretations and future lawsuits. Perhaps both dukes hoped for loopholes—certainly Gloucester acted rapidly on Clarence's fall[42]—but it was probably considered adequate for a temporary settlement. On the death of the countess of Warwick, which was not expected to be eighteen years away, normal rules of inheritance would apply. The 1474 act forbade actions designed to bar either coheir's rights of inheritance in the other's share. The 1475 act, designed to be permanent, was more precise. However temporary and restricted in scope, Edward had achieved a notable triumph by imposing the agreement. Quite different from the results had the laws of treason or inheritance taken their course, it was moulded by short-term political needs. As such, as the earlier descent of the components had revealed, it was liable to be amended with changing conditions. Within a decade all the beneficiaries were dead and the political climate was profoundly different.

Neither duke liked the 1474–5 arrangements. Clarence accepted them under duress in preference to total ruin. Instead of obtaining all he sought, Gloucester also had to compromise. He had reservations about the details and principles of

---

[40] *Rot. Parl.*, vi. 100–1, 124–5, the source for the rest of this paragraph.

[41] The preamble survives in Brit. Libr., Cott. MS. Jul. B. xii fos. 135–136v; the indenture is P.R.O., DL 26/69. These can be supplemented from other sources. A complete list of Clarence's share is in Hicks, table XVI.

[42] See below p. 124.

the agreement. His opportunity to adjust it in his own favour occurred in 1478, when his rival coheir was Clarence's two-year-old son Edward, earl of Warwick, a royal ward. The duchess of Clarence had died in 1476, the duke in 1478, having been arrested in the previous year and later condemned for treason.

No act had been necessary to settle the Salisbury inheritance but its partition had been combined with that of the other tail general estates. Gloucester objected to the assignment of Essendine and Shillingthorpe (Rut.) to his brother. In 1477–8 he seized them by force, received the issues, and ignored a process by the royal exchequer against him until he became king in 1483. The process was then stopped and the lands were alienated.[43] In 1478 Gloucester's son Edward was granted the earldom of Salisbury, bestowed on Clarence in 1472.[44]

Under the 1474 act, the Beauchamp and Despenser inheritances were to be kept intact during the lifetime of the countess of Warwick. The intention was that, should the issue of either coheir fail, the other would inherit its purparty as sole heir on the countess's death, as would have occurred had there been no act. Gloucester did not draw the line at disinheriting his nephew. At the 1478 parliament an act authorized him to alienate certain specific estates and it was under this provision that in 1481 he gave Olney rectory to St. George's Chapel, Windsor.[45]

Another act of this parliament degraded George Neville, duke of Bedford from the peerage as unable to support any estate,[46] though this was untrue. Miss Scofield thought that he was degraded because Edward IV wanted the title for his third son,[47] but Gloucester was probably responsible: he had been assigned most of the Neville estates, he had founded his power on them and was anxious to keep them. In 1478 he obtained a quitclaim from Ralph, Lord Neville, heir to the earldom of Westmorland and later 3rd earl, of any vestigial claims of the senior branch of the Nevilles.[48] Gloucester's title depended on the 1475 act, but for which George would have inherited. In a climate where acts of attainder were frequently reversed for heirs, the danger of George's restoration increased as he grew older, and Gloucester wished to prevent this. It was in his interest to remove him from where his voice could be heard, as a peer in parliament. Later, in 1480, he also obtained a grant of his custody and marriage.[49] The duke's position was delicate, for, while he had security for life, his heirs' title (in accordance with the acts of 1474–5) would last only so long as there were male heirs of the marquess Montagu living. For them to retain the inheritance the marquess's only son George had to marry and produce a son, yet his restoration had to be prevented. It was a sensible precaution to acquire the claims of the beneficiary should George Neville die without male issue. This was Richard, Lord Latimer, grandson and heir of George, Lord Latimer (d. 1469), third son of the 1st earl of Westmorland's second marriage. He was a minor. In 1480 Gloucester troubled to obtain a release from his aunt Katherine.[50] When Richard came of age in 1489 Gloucester presumably hoped to acquire his rights, which might have appeared slender as George was only about four years older. Had

[43] P.R.O., DL 29/640/10388 m.5d; DL 29/639/10386 m.1d; E 159/259, Rec. Trin. 22 Edw. IV m. 14(2).
[44] *Cal. Pat. Rolls 1476–85*, pp. 67–8.
[45] *Rot. Parl.*, vi. 172–3; P.R.O., C 81/1521/19.
[46] *Rot. Parl.*, vi. 173; for the next phrase see *Calendar of Inquisitions Post Mortem, Henry VII*, i, nos. 210–22, esp. no. 212.
[47] C. L. Scofield, *The Life and Reign of Edward IV* (2 vols., 1923), ii. 214–15.
[48] P.R.O., CP 25(1)/281/164/32.
[49] *Cal. Pat. Rolls 1476–85*, p. 192; Brit. Libr., Cott. MS. Jul. B. xii fo. 166r–v.
[50] P.R.O., CP 25(1)/281/165/23. Her second husband was James Ratcliffe.

Gloucester succeeded, his descendants would have enjoyed the estates so long as
there survived male heirs of Lord Latimer or the marquess Montagu. How he
could control George from his majority until Richard came of age is unclear. No
marriage had been concluded for George before his death on 4 May 1483,
shortly before Gloucester's accession as Richard III. On George's death the title
of Gloucester and Clarence's heirs was extinguished, the reversion on the
former's death belonging to Lord Latimer. As Gloucester's heirs lost most, this
could ultimately have resulted in the revision of the partition.

As the earl of Warwick was a minor, Richard III acquired the custody of his
half of the inheritance and could have altered the partition to his own
satisfaction. He did not, perhaps because the expectations of his heir had been so
enhanced by his accession. He was no more respectful as king to the alienation
clause of the 1474 act: he allowed Queen Anne to give lands (extended at £329)
to Queens' College, Cambridge in 1484; he granted the Despenser manor of
Haverhill to Lord Grey of Codnor; and on the incorporation of the college of
heralds he licensed it to purchase the Neville messuage of le Erber in London.[51]
His reduced interest in the fate of the inheritance is revealed by his licence to
Lord Abergavenny to enter two manors in Suffolk, as 'parcel of his [Despenser]
inheritance'.[52] Even so, as king, Richard depended on the retainers feed from his
wife's northern estates: they overawed London at his usurpation and were the
main beneficiaries of his patronage and his local agents. In 1484 he was suspected
of plotting the death or divorce of Queen Anne so he could marry his niece,
Elizabeth of York: two key supporters, William Catesby and Sir Richard
Ratcliffe, both owing loyalty primarily to the queen, told him publicly:

all the people of the north, in whom he placed the greatest reliance, would rise in
rebellion against him and impute to him the death of the queen, the daughter and one of
the heirs of the earl of Warwick, through which he had first gained his present high
position.

According to the *Croyland Continuator* this and the impossibility of a dispensation
made him give way.[53] He was caught in a political impasse.

Had Richard reigned for much longer his nephew, the young earl of Warwick,
would have had little to inherit. Richard's life estate terminated with his death at
Bosworth in 1485, when the reversion of the tail male estates belonged to Lord
Latimer, of the tail general estates to Warwick. As both were minors, their
inheritances were in the king's hands and they could not prosecute their claims.
So that he could attaint his opponents of treason, Henry pretended to have
succeeded before Bosworth, thus making traitors of members of Richard's
army;[54] under this pretext he attainted Richard III and in his forfeiture included
the Neville lands, to the disinheritance of Lord Latimer, even though Richard
had held them only for life. At first Henry regarded Edward, earl of Warwick as
heir of the Despenser, Beauchamp and Montagu inheritances,[55] but the weakness
of his title was exposed by petitions for restoration and the reversal of the 1474

[51] *Cal. Pat. Rolls 1476–85*, pp. 423, 477; Brit. Libr., Harley MS. 433 fos. 39v, 45, 283v, 289v.

[52] Brit. Libr., Harl. MS. 433 fo. 160v. It may have been then that he acquired Ashley, Mapledurwell
(Hants), Speenhamland (Berks.), and Rotherfield (Suss.), *Victoria History of Berkshire*, iv. 101; *V.C.H.
Hants*, iv. 151, 441 & n; *Cal. Inq. Post Mortem Hen. VII*, i, no. 103; P.R.O., SC 11/825. For Mereworth
(Kent), see *Calendar of Inquisitions Post Mortem*, iv. 378; D. Rowland, *An Historical and Genealogical Account
of the Noble Family of Nevill* (1830), p. 137.

[53] *Ingulph's Chronicle of the Abbey of Croyland*, ed. H. T. Riley (1854), p. 499, trans. from *Rerum
Anglicarum Scriptorum Veterum*, i. 572.

[54] *Rot. Parl.*, vi. 275–8.

[55] P.R.O., DL 29/640/10392: SC 6/Hen.VII/1364.

act from the countess of Warwick.[56] Provision made for her in 1486 was augmented in 1490,[57] in return for which she broke the entail and remitted her rights to the king.[58] As she had been left destitute on Richard III's death, she can hardly be blamed for her action, which disinherited her grandson Warwick. Still heir to the Montagu estates, he was executed in 1499, but his estates were granted in 1513 to his sister Margaret, countess of Salisbury,[59] who enjoyed them until her execution in 1541. In 1547 the earldom of Warwick, endowed with some of its former estates, was revived for John Dudley, Lord Lisle, heir of the eldest daughter of Richard Beauchamp, earl of Warwick (d. 1439).[60] The other lands remained in royal hands.

To the medieval magnate his estates were an everyday reality that could not be ignored. To the modern historian they possess two invaluable qualities: even where their own administrative records are lost, a concrete impression is left on those of the Crown, and in their devolution they obey fixed rules, in the light of which the evidence may be interpreted. The future course of descent can be foretold and should any subsequent deviation from this occur, the effect is readily apparent and the motive behind it may often be deduced. One can thus achieve a precision that owes relatively little to the historian's personal judgement, so important (and so debatable) in calculating the relative weight of kinship, lordship, friendship and other imponderables. Certainly land did not always play such a prominent part as in this case and there were few who played for such high stakes, but it exercised a constant restraint on freedom of action. To understand a magnate's conduct, it is desirable to discover what was to his advantage or provided the clue to his ambitions, grievances and potential sources of disagreement with others. Magnates would not willingly, and could not safely, depart from these guidelines, as their friends and foes were aware. On certain points there could be no compromise: one of these was tenure of their estates, key to their power and wealth.

Without the Warwick inheritance none of these magnates could have filled their historical role. Salisbury's power derived directly from his northern lordships, later so vital to Warwick and Gloucester, and it was on the strength of their Beauchamp–Despenser possessions that Warwick and Clarence dominated the west Midlands. From his wife's property Clarence drew about £2,200 of a total disposable income of about £4,600,[61] rivalled perhaps by Gloucester and no other immediate contemporary. It was no accident that Warwick was most powerful when in possession of the whole inheritance. To each of them it was vital to win and hold it and, if the two Richard Nevilles would occasionally compromise on details, the two royal dukes would not. By concentrating on this theme one can illumine one aspect of their conduct. These lands gave successive generations the same interests, ambitions and constraints and forced on them common attitudes and actions, which sometimes impinged directly on national politics. In this sense it is possible to speak of hereditary interests, hereditary policies and hereditary enemies. Far from merely supplying the resources for

[56] The Red Paper Book of Colchester, ed. W. G. Benham (Colchester, 1902), p. 62; P.R.O., C 1/77/30.

[57] Materials for a History of the Reign of Henry VII, ed. W. Campbell (2 vols., Rolls Ser., 1873–7), ii. 66, 84; Cal. Pat. Rolls 1485–94, p. 298.

[58] Rot. Parl., vi. 391–2; Materials for the Reign of Henry VII, ii. 211–12; Warwickshire Feet of Fines, iii (Dugdale Soc., xviii, 1943), no. 2729; Calendar of Close Rolls 1485–1500, no. 474.

[59] Complete Peerage, xi. 400. This grant, after most of the estates had been in royal hands for 35 years and the rest for 28, was virtually a new creation.

[60] V.C.H. Warwicks., viii. 453.

[61] Hicks, pp. 341–2.

political activities, the inheritance and its descent was itself a strand in politics: on occasion it developed into a burning national issue which embroiled other magnates and even the Crown.

The descent of the inheritance is also a measure of the growing strength of the monarchy from Henry VI to Henry VII, which is accentuated by the weakness of Henry VI compared with his predecessors. The four constituent estates followed (with intermissions) their natural course of descent until his reign. While one cannot be sure that none of his acts mirrors his own desires, it appears that those with access to him could extract what they wanted. It was the fluctuating dominance of rival groups that accounts for his apparent vacillations. Key decisions were usually favourable to the Nevilles but, if not, force yielded dividends: at first because Henry could not enforce his will and afterwards because the Nevilles' rivals were beaten in the field. Early in his reign Edward IV was reluctant to challenge important magnates[62] but later he asserted himself: the settlement imposed on his brothers in 1472–5 was a notable victory. In his actions there was an element of self-interest and calculation lacking in Henry VI but present in earlier kings. Like them Edward was primarily an arbiter or 'styfflere'[63] between opposing parties. In contrast Henry VII, at least in this case, was less interested in reconciling contenders than in exploiting the situation to his own benefit. Even less respectful than Richard III of the rights of others, Henry VII treated all participants equally badly. Although his acts were legalized by parliament, they were unjust. They were conceived so that no redress was possible except by rebellion, a remedy that Lords Abergavenny and Latimer preferred not to take. His approach recalls the arbitrariness of Edward I[64] and earlier kings. He foreshadowed the greater authoritarianism of Henry VIII. Although these estates were valuable and were retained in his hands, Henry VII was probably motivated less by fiscal factors than the desire to destroy one of the most formidable magnate inheritances.

In this he was entirely successful. One should not belittle his achievement. The four main components were each among the relatively few estates to support an earl: still divided in two during the fourteen-fifties, they placed the earls of Salisbury and Warwick among the half-dozen leading magnates; united in the fourteen-sixties, they made their lord unrivalled in power; and divided again in the fourteen-seventies, each was the major part of one of the four leading estates, the others belonging to the dukes of Buckingham and Norfolk. It is true that Warwick would have had to live to be over seventy to remarry and have a son and that his chances of preventing partition were small, but even in two or three parts this inheritance would have stood out. There were heirs to each segment and in destroying their expectations Henry VII dashed the hopes not only of Warwick and Latimer but also of Lords Abergavenny, the Despenser coheir, and Roos and Lisle, two of the Beauchamp claimants.[65] These estates stood out not only because of their size, but on account of their long descent in the same families, their traditions and formidable retinues.[66]

It is a historic commonplace that the medieval nobility were destroyed in the Wars of the Roses. First challenged in 1872 by T. K. Oliphant, it was dismissed as

---

[62] *Glamorgan County History*, iii. 198; *Paston Letters and Papers*, i. 544–5. Edward was still apprehensive of the duke of Norfolk in 1475, *ibid.*, i. 595.

[63] *Paston Letters and Papers*, i. 468.

[64] For which see K. B. McFarlane, *The Nobility of Later Medieval England* (Oxford, 1973), pp. 248–67.

[65] The Beauchamp heirs still entertained hopes, P.R.O., C 1/77/30.

[66] For the Neville and Beauchamp retainers see A. J. Pollard, 'The Northern retainers of Richard Nevill, earl of Salisbury', *Northern Hist.*, xi (1975), 52–69; Hicks, pp. 360–8.

a myth by K. B. McFarlane in 1964.[67] Yet here is one instance where an estate was destroyed which could have survived but for the dynastic struggle. During the fourteen-fifties Warwick had been one of the three leading magnates and his father was certainly among the next half-dozen. Both were extinguished, not because there were no heirs, but by the arbitrary acts of a king. For the sheer size of the estates concerned and the permanence of the result there is no parallel in late medieval England.

[67] For which see K. B. McFarlane, 'The Wars of the Roses', *Proc. Brit. Acad.*, l (1964), 115–17.

19

The Beauchamp Trust, 1439-87

ENFEOFFMENTS TO uses or trusts are a common but rather obscure feature of late medieval English landholding. Hitherto historians have either regarded them as a device to evade feudal incidents or alternatively have viewed them through chancery petitions accusing feoffees of dereliction of duty. Some pertinent remarks about the administration of uses have been made by Dr. Bean[1] but the scope of his observations was restricted by the formal character of the records he employed.

The limitations of the source material are a serious deterrent to research. Generally what survives is either formal or else lively and detailed but virtually impossible to substantiate: thus deeds of enfeoffment, ministers' accounts and inquisitions *post mortem* often reveal the existence of a use, but seldom significantly more; many wills contain directions to feoffees, but one cannot check whether they were obeyed; chancery petitions present disputes from one side only and the verdict is usually lacking. It is rare for all these sources to survive for a single trust and, even when they do, they give an incomplete record of its operation. For a full picture one needs records of how the trust was administered, ideally itemizing not only income but also expenditure. Details about receipts are readily available in many ministers' accounts, but information about payments is rarer and less systematic. Only with such materials can a use be adequately studied.

It is therefore important that all these sources exist for the Beauchamp trust, which was governed by the will of Richard Beauchamp, earl of Warwick (d. 1439). In this instance the operation of the trust can be studied both with reference to the directions in the will and to charges made subsequently in chancery litigation. This particular trust is also important because of its exceptional duration and because it financed the building of the Beauchamp chapel at Warwick, one of the most lavish architectural works of fifteenth-century England.

In spite of these unusual features, the Beauchamp trust casts light on the operation and purpose of trusts in general and on the framework of law

---

[1] J. M. W. Bean, *The Decline of English Feudalism, 1215–1540* (Manchester, 1968), esp. pp. 205ff. I am indebted for advice and criticism to Mr. T. B. Pugh and Professor C. D. Ross. Unless otherwise stated, this article is based on *The Complete Peerage of England*, comp. G. E. Cokayne and others (13 vols., 1910–59); *Victoria History of Warwickshire*, viii. 452–3; A. Goodman, *The Loyal Conspiracy: the Lords Appellant under Richard II* (1971), pp. 135–52; C. D. Ross, *The Estates and Finances of Richard Beauchamp, Earl of Warwick* (Dugdale Soc., Occasional Papers, xii, 1956); K. B. McFarlane, *The Nobility of Later Medieval England* (Oxford, 1973), pp. 187–201; R. L. Storey, *The End of the House of Lancaster* (1966), pp. 231–41; M. A. Hicks, 'Descent, partition and extinction: the "Warwick inheritance"', above, chapter 18.

The Descendants of Richard Beauchamp

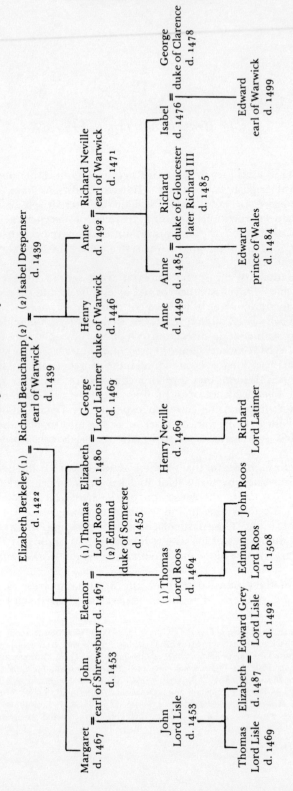

surrounding them. Enfeoffment to use was the conveyance of land by the holder (the feoffor) to a third party (the feoffee), who held it in trust for him, and thus involved the transfer of seisin of an estate, not of the legal title. By themselves such transactions were sometimes advantageous to feoffors, but they were more often components in a wider plan. Frequently the aim was to provide money for the execution of the feoffor's will: this purpose could be extended to permit capital expenditure, religious foundations, security for debts and provision for younger children, all after the feoffor's death. The Beauchamp trust illustrates the use as a flexible device extending the current tenant's control at the expense of the heir. The price paid was entry into an ill-defined field of law, where there were few remedies against dishonest feoffees. Light is cast on the opportunities open to the feoffee, the courses of action open to the heir and the role of the Crown.

The aim of this article is to narrate the history of the trust, to analyse its administration and draw certain conclusions. For a complete understanding of its history, however, some knowledge is needed of the descent of the main Beauchamp estate. This has not been adequately charted elsewhere, and will be outlined first.

In 1268 the earldom of Warwick was inherited by William Beauchamp of Elmley castle (Worcs.), whose descendants held the title until 1499. Although the Beauchamps held land all over England, their principal estates were in Warwickshire and Worcestershire, where they were the dominant family. During their long tenure they inherited the lands of defunct families such as the Bassets of Drayton, the De Toenis and the Beauchamps of Abergavenny; they also purchased other property in the west Midlands.[2] In 1397 an income of £2,900 placed Earl Thomas II (d. 1401) among the half-dozen richest magnates and in 1432–3 Earl Richard's revenues of £5,471 were equalled only by those of the duke of York.

Earl Richard's income was inflated by the inheritances of his two wives, which could not pass to the same heirs. His first wife Elizabeth was daughter and heir general of Thomas, Lord Berkeley (d. 1417) by the Lisle heiress. Elizabeth bore Earl Richard three daughters: Margaret (d. 1467), later countess of Shrewsbury; Eleanor (d. 1467), later Lady Roos and duchess of Somerset; and Elizabeth (d. 1480), later Lady Latimer. They were coheiresses of their mother's lands and also (until 1425) of the Beauchamp patrimony. By entailing his estates on his male descendants, Earl Thomas I (d. 1369) had averted their division between the daughters of his eldest son, but by 1422 only a single male line survived, represented by Earl Richard. On his death the entail would fail and his daughters would divide his estates.

Earl Richard, like Earl Thomas I, was proud of his lineage: in 1423 he founded a chantry at Guy's Cliffe by Warwick 'that God wold send him Eyres male'.[3] This was on his remarriage to the widowed countess of Worcester, Isabel Despenser. She bore him a son Henry (d. 1446) and a daughter Anne (d. 1492). Henry was heir to both his parents. Had he predeceased his father or died a minor, Earl Richard's four daughters would have partitioned the inheritance.

---

[2] For Wolverton and Baginton (Warwicks.), see below; for Grovebury (Beds.), see *V.C.H. Bedfordshire*, iii. 403; for Erdington (Warwicks.), see *Ministers' Accounts of the Warwickshire Estates of the Duke of Clarence, 1479–80*, ed. R. H. Hilton (Dugdale Soc., xxi, 1952), pp. x–xi.

[3] J. Rows, *Rol*, ed. W. H. Courthope (1845), no. 50. The legal guidelines of the paragraph are from *Littleton's Tenures in English*, ed. E. Wambaugh (1903), pp. 4–5.

Henry had livery of it before his death, when he left an infant daughter as heir under the entail. She died in 1449, still under age. As Henry had taken seisin, his sole heir was his whole sister Anne, to the exclusion of their three half-sisters, on the principle that possession by the brother makes his sister heir. The inquisitions of 1449 are unanimous that Anne was heir.[4]

This eventuality was not foreseen by Earl Richard, who on his remarriage settled twenty-two manors on his male issue, with remainder to his right heirs. He clearly expected his daughters to inherit, if he had no son. In 1437 he regarded all four daughters as heirs in default of a son.[5] Finding their expectations dashed, it is hardly surprising that Margaret, Eleanor and Elizabeth disputed Anne's title. Surviving schedules of the lost Beauchamp deeds confirm her right: there were no entails rendering the exclusion of the half-blood inapplicable for certain estates; neither Earl Richard nor Duke Henry made other remainders of the lands. The strength of Anne's title did not dissuade her elder sisters from trying to recover 'the lyuelode of the Erldome of Warrewyk the which we the said Countesse [Margaret] claymen to be departed as our enheritaunces'.[6] Fortunately Anne's husband, Richard Neville, heir to the earldom of Salisbury, was an astute politician with powerful friends.

At first the elder sisters sought royal approval. They persuaded Henry VI to keep the lands in custody pending a final decision which, however, confirmed Anne's title. Henceforth Richard Neville was earl of Warwick in her right. This verdict was pronounced on 15 February 1454, during the protectorate of Warwick's friend, the duke of York, and was not reversed when York was ousted. Margaret at least did not abandon hope. By 1456 she had seized Drayton Bassett (Staffs.), retaining control subsequently in spite of Edward IV's confirmation of Anne's title. Her sisters may have acted likewise, as the three died seized of nine Beauchamp manors.[7] The Staffordshire inquisition reveals that Margaret held Drayton jointly with her sisters as right heir of her father and, without further detail, says that it was assigned to her. Presumably this refers to the agreement of 15 November 1466, between the elder sisters and Anne, by which the inheritance was settled on Anne's issue.[8] In default it would remain to Earl Richard Beauchamp's right heirs: Warwick and certain neighbouring estates would then fall to Margaret as eldest daughter.

This agreement ended the dispute over the main Beauchamp estate, but certain properties held to uses were excluded. It ensured an undisputed succession for Anne's own daughters but, after Warwick's death in 1471, she was deprived of her inheritance by act of parliament. It was then divided between her daughters Anne and Isabel, wives of King Edward's brothers the dukes of Clarence and Gloucester. The bulk of the Beauchamp inheritance, including the manors in the west Midlands, were assigned to Isabel, duchess of Clarence.

[4] Public Record Office, C 139/135/5/2, C 139/135/5/6, C 139/135/5/16.

[5] P.R.O., CP 25(1)/291/65/15; see below pp. 139, 144.

[6] Devon County Record Office, Exeter Diocesan Records, Misc. Bk. 722 fos. 3–50v, esp. fo. 38; P.R.O., SC 11/947; *Sir Christopher Hatton's Book of Seals*, ed. L. C. Loyd and D. M. Stenton (Northants Record Soc., xv, 1950), pp. 165–6.

[7] *Hatton's Book of Seals*, pp. 165–6; Lichfield Joint Record Office, Reg. Hales, B/A/1/12 fos. 40, 41, 42r–v, 44–5. The 9 manors were as follows: Elizabeth had Beoley, Great Cumberton, Wadborough (Worcs.) and Noke (Oxon.); Eleanor had Fritwell (Oxon.), Walthamstow Tony (Essex) and Grafton Flyford (Worcs.); Margaret had Drayton Bassett (Staffs.) and Ribbesford (Worcs.) (*Calendar of Inquisitions Post Mortem, Henry VII*, iii, no. 117; P.R.O., C 140/24/4/13 and 17; C 140/26/3/4 and 14; C 140/77/2/8 and 10).

[8] *Descriptive Catalogue of the Charters and Muniments ... at Berkeley Castle*, ed. I. H. Jeayes (1892), nos. 615–16; *Warwickshire Feet of Fines*, ed. E. Stokes, F. C. Wellstood and L. Drucker (Dugdale Soc., xi, xv, xviii, 1932–43), iii, no. 2683.

Although anxious to perpetuate his line, Earl Richard Beauchamp also wanted to provide for his other children. His elder daughters, heiresses in their own right, needed no support, but it was possible that in addition to a son and heir his second wife might bear other children without hereditary expectations. The provision he could make was restricted by entails, but it may have been partly with this in mind that in 1425 he conveyed fifteen manors and the reversion of eight others to feoffees.[9] These included Baginton (Warwicks.), which he bought and could dispose of freely, and the eight manors of Snitterfield (Warwicks.), Chaddesley Corbett, Hervington in Chaddesley, Sheriff's Lench, Naunton Beauchamp, Pirton Power (Worcs.), Kemerton (Glos.) and Spelsbury (Oxon.), which he regarded in the same light. These comprised the 400 marks' worth of lands settled by his father on his uncle William, Lord Abergavenny (d. 1411) and his wife Joan and their male issue. The reversion fell in on Joan's death in 1435, when the reeve of Spelsbury discussed the transfer of control with John Throckmorton, a feoffee.[10] Wolverton (Warwicks.), also bought by the earl, Langley (Oxon.), and the reversion of Grovebury (Beds.), held by other feoffees, were in the same category. Only temporarily could the earl vary the descent of the thirteen entailed manors. These properties were the nucleus of the estate of the Beauchamp trust.

In 1437, in his last will,[11] Earl Richard specified the objects of the trust. Only after fulfilling the instructions in his will could the lands pass to his heirs. No reference was made to lands over which he had no permanent control, but he wanted Baginton, Grovebury and the eight Abergavenny manors to pass to his younger son, should he have one. Failing this, Duke Henry and his heirs were to enjoy them, with remainder to the earl's daughters. Henry was to have Langley to himself and his issue, with remainder to other sons and ultimately to Anne. No provision was made for the earl's daughters except in remainders: all had married peers by 1437.

Before the manors descended to the heirs, Earl Richard's will had to be performed. The first call on the revenues—he stressed its primary importance—concerned the good of his soul. His debts were to be paid and 5,000 masses said. A new chapel was to be erected at St. Mary's collegiate church at Warwick to receive his body. Before going to France in 1437 the earl had obtained royal consent to endow the college[12] and the will fixes the amount to be alienated at forty pounds yearly. Twenty marks income was to be amortized to Elmley castle chantry to augment the stipends of existing chaplains and to endow another; an obit was to be provided at Tewkesbury abbey; and the revenues of Guy's Cliffe chantry were to be legally secured. The money to meet these charges was to come from the issues of the estates.

The Abergavenny lands passed to the feoffees in 1435 and Shenstone (Staffs.) presumably reverted in 1449, on the death of the life-tenant Lord Strange.[13] As laid down in the will, all lands in trust were conveyed to the executors by John Throckmorton's death in 1445.[14] Two Despenser manors in Suffolk, formerly held for life by Margaret, duchess of Clarence (d. 1439), had been conveyed to

[9] *Warwickshire Feet of Fines*, iii, no. 2539. For what follows see W. Dugdale, *History and Antiquities of Warwickshire*, ed. W. Thomas (2 vols., 1730), i. 232.

[10] Oxfordshire County Record Office, Dil. II/b/1 m. 2. The next sentence is based on Dugdale, ii. 665; see below p. 140.

[11] The will is edited in *Historia Vitae et Regni Ricardi Secundi*, ed. T. Hearne (1729), pp. 244–6. This is the source of all later references to it.

[12] Dugdale, i. 409.

[13] P.R.O., SC 11/947.

[14] By 12 Apr. 1445 (*Calendar of Fine Rolls 1437–45*, p. 301).

them by 1446.[15] Other lands were bequeathed by Nicholas Rody (d. 1458). At probate, administration was granted to Rody, Throckmorton and Thomas Hugford (d. 1469). They were associated with William Berkeswell, once chaplain at Guy's Cliffe, later treasurer and from 1454 dean of Warwick college. From 1447 he was an active executor. They held the lands in survivorship until 1485, when John Hugford died. He had succeeded his father Thomas, the longest liver, as sole trustee.

The first call on their revenues were the masses and the payment of the earl's debts: fortunately the king, potentially the greatest creditor, waived his rights.[16] The total extent of the earl's liabilities is not known and there is no inventory of his goods, which were considerable. They included a statuette of the Virgin and Child, made of gold and garnished with a ruby, pearls and a green stone, which stood 20½ inches high and contained 95¾ ounces troy. Worth £190 in metal alone, it was the earl's mortuary[17] and was not available to meet his debts. Nor was the plate that he left to his wife. As late as 1447 the executors were unable to produce a complete account of the earl's goods: the commissary-general demanded an inventory, which was presumably produced later in the year, when probate was granted. As the earl died abroad, moveables other than deeds may have been difficult to collect.

The executors may have been hampered by shortage of money after the commencement in 1442 of the building programme required by the will. It can have left little for other purposes. Between 1442 and 1463 £3,634 or an average of £173 yearly was spent on the building alone.[18] The Beauchamp chapel at Warwick college, under construction in the years 1442–57, cost over £200 per annum in 1442–6, with a peak of £332 in the second year. Little less was spent in the next two years, but from then on costs were lower, permitting work to start on the earl's tomb. When finished in 1459 it had cost £715. As the chapel intruded on the smaller college cemetery, complicated conveyances were required to make up for this and to provide extra space, mainly for the enlarged deanery and college needed for the four extra priests that the earl had desired. These arrangements were confirmed in 1455 by Earl Richard Neville, who gave some of the land. Work on the college and deanery continued until at least 1463. At Guy's Cliffe the building begun in 1449 concerned only the chapel: by 1460 it had cost £184. It was virtually finished in 1454, when the two altars were consecrated.

After erecting the buildings, the executors had only to secure the endowments for Warwick, Elmley and Guy's Cliffe to complete the business of the trust. The manor of Ashorne and lands in Wellesbourne and Whitnash (Warwicks.), held by the chantry of Guy's Cliffe at its dissolution, were alienated under a licence obtained by Earl Richard Beauchamp in 1429, but still unexecuted at his death:[19] probably the necessary conveyance was made *c.* 1454. At Warwick the chapel and tomb were ready by 1459, but the conveyance of the lands may have been delayed until the completion of the other works, in or after 1463. The £67 10s paid in fines for licences to alienate forty pounds' worth of land to Warwick college, twenty marks' worth to Elmley college and twelve marks' worth to

[15] P.R.O., CP 25(1)/224/115/24, CP 25(1)/224/116/5, C 139/123/2/37. For the next phrase, see *Catalogue of Ancient Deeds*, iii, no. A. 4653.

[16] Dugdale, i. 409.

[17] P.R.O., E 154/1/46 m. 5. The valuation is based on McFarlane, p. 98.

[18] This paragraph is based on P. B. Chatwin, 'Documents of "Warwick the Kingmaker" in possession of St. Mary's church, Warwick', *Trans. Birmingham Archaeol. Soc.*, lix (1935), 2–8; J. G. Nichols, *Description of the Church of St. Mary, Warwick* (1838), pp. 33–6.

[19] *Calendar of Patent Rolls 1429–36*, p. 100; *V.C.H. Warwicks.*, viii. 534.

Tewkesbury abbey[20] were presumably met from the issues of these estates. So too were the vestments, ornaments and plate (worth forty-one pounds in metal alone) that was handed over to the sexton for the Beauchamp chapel on 31 March 1468. Although the licences were obtained in 1463, it was only on 29 September 1468 that Hugford and Berkeswell conveyed Wolverton, Baginton and Preston Capes (Northants.) to the earl and countess of Warwick, on condition that they remitted them by fine to Warwick college. Reciting this condition, they granted them to the college and appointed attornies on 16 December, the same day as the college named its attornies. The transaction was cemented by final concord early in 1469.

With the chapel built, endowed and furnished, the scene was set for the translation of Earl Richard Beauchamp's body. Relatives, including a grandchild, had been buried in the chapel in 1469 and Earl Richard Beauchamp had wished to lie there, but it was only on the initiative of the duke of Clarence that the chapel was consecrated: on 2 December 1475 the bishop of Worcester licenced the bishop of Lichfield to consecrate it for the final interment of Earl Richard Beauchamp.[21] A similar delay occurred in the endowment of Elmley college with Naunton Beauchamp manor and advowson, conveyed to it by Clarence in 1472. As for Tewkesbury abbey, Hugford was not licensed to alienate Pirton Power, Dodes (unidentified) and Batsford (Glos.) until 1482, and the grant was never implemented. Such tardiness is extraordinary. The deaths of the elder Hugford and Berkeswell in 1469 and Earl Richard Neville in 1471, the latter's political pre-occupations in 1469–71, and the inheritance dispute of 1471–5 are some explanation, but do they suffice? One suspects that the delays were deliberate. Until the religious provisions of the trust were complete, it could not be wound up and the estates could not devolve on the heirs. Obviously this was against the interests of the heirs. Had anybody anything to gain from prolonging the trust and deferring its termination?

One clue is to be found in three petitions to the chancellor. They disclose the impatience of two of the late earl's daughters and the heirs of the other two to enter these estates. The petitions are as follows:[22]

(1) Dating between 1478 and 1480, presented on behalf of Edward and Elizabeth Grey, Lord and Lady Lisle, as heirs of Margaret, eldest daughter; Elizabeth, Lady Latimer, the third daughter; and Richard and Anne, duke and duchess of Gloucester and Edward Plantagenet, earl of Warwick, coheirs of Anne, the fourth daughter.

(2) 1484–5, for Lord and Lady Lisle; John Roos, son of Eleanor, the second daughter; Lord Latimer, grandson of Elizabeth, third daughter; and Anne, countess of Warwick, fourth daughter.

(3) 1485–6, for Lord and Lady Lisle; Edmund, Lord Roos, heir to Eleanor, the second daughter; Lord Latimer; and the countess of Warwick.

Each petition states that Earl Richard Beauchamp, who held these lands in fee simple, settled them on trustees, who held them at his death. All four daughters were declared to be his heirs and hence entitled to the estates. They had

---

[20] *Cal. Pat. Rolls 1461–7*, pp. 295–6; *Cal. Pat. Rolls 1467–77*, p. 153. For the rest of the paragraph, see P.R.O., E 154/1/46; *Catalogue of Ancient Deeds*, ii, no. B.2957; *Warwickshire Feet of Fines*, iii, no. 2694; P.R.O., E 326/B6461 and B4461; Bodleian Library, MS. Dugdale 15 p. 73.

[21] Rows, no. 58; *Testamenta Vetusta,* ed. N. H. Nicolas (2 vols., 1826), i. 358; Worcestershire Record Office, Reg. Carpenter ii, BA 2648/6(iii), p. 162. For what follows, see P.R.O., C 142/80/107; *Cal. Pat. Rolls 1476–85*, p. 318; P.R.O., C 143/455/12.

[22] P.R.O., C 1/66/376, C 1/58/156, C 1/77/30. These are the source for later references.

frequently required John Hugford to hand them over, but he had always refused. The plaintiffs could have pleaded that, following the execution of the ecclesiastical provisions of the trust, they should receive the rights of inheritance set down in the will, but they chose not to do so. Instead they claimed all the enfeoffed lands, without distinguishing between the various titles by which the feoffor had held them, the various enfeoffments by which they had passed to Hugford, and between those he still held and those that had been alienated. The earl's heirs had no legal remedy against the recipient of land conveyed by the feoffees, but they could have based a case on the literal reading of the will: although ordering the alienation of land in mortmain, the earl had not specifically authorized the application of any of the enfeoffed lands for this purpose and had indeed given quite contrary instructions regarding Baginton and Pirton Power. Evidently his heirs wanted all the lands regardless of title, which suggests that the chancery suits represent the continuation for these properties of the dispute settled for those in fee in 1466. This in turn indicates that the trust was being prolonged by Anne, countess of Warwick and her heirs and that it was the elder sisters who wanted it wound up, who were trying to recover their inheritance. One objection to this interpretation is that the heirs of the three elder coheirs feature in the petitions on the same side as their opponents on that occasion, the countess Anne, her son-in-law Gloucester and her grandson Warwick. Each petition states Hugford personally to be at fault.

Some assessment of how the feoffees, particularly Hugford, executed their trust can be derived from the surviving records.[23] The building accounts of 1442–63 and a *valor* of 1481–2 cast light on expenditure. These documents show that the feoffees made allowances, respited or forgave sums due, placed rents among 'decays', allowed ordinary and extraordinary reprises, drew up rentals, granted annuities, and nominated to offices and benefices. Each collected money from local ministers, usually giving indented receipts, many of them still appended to the account rolls. The accounts bear the marks of careful perusal by auditors, who demanded warrants, examined rentals and vouchers, and noted deliveries of money, for which the recipient was answerable. Such notes occur not only in instances involving the receiver, John Hethe, but also those concerning a feoffee. Berkeswell apparently had to produce detailed building accounts, which were audited and summarized, just as the local ministers' accounts were consolidated into *valors*. The feoffees, not the auditors, had the final word, each presumably holding his colleagues to account for their actions.

This system applied when there were three feoffees. There was some change after 1469, when John Hugford became sole feoffee, with the final say in his own conduct. Certain of his expenses would not normally have been allowed—for example, 6s 8d paid from Chaddesley in 1480–1 to repair a banner at Wotton church commemorating him and his ancestors. Later accounts reveal that he made numerous allowances. Arrears were growing: in 1480–1 they exceeded forty pounds at both Shenstone and Budbrooke (Warwicks.), twenty pounds at Snitterfield, Spelsbury and Chaddesley Takeball, and in some cases were larger than the potential annual receipts. Frequently the accountant had been permitted to run up arrears over a period of years. Rents were continually

---

[23] The main sources are: a series of court rolls and 2 ministers' accounts for Chaddesley Corbett with Hervington (Worcs.); 2 series of ministers' accounts for Spelsbury (Oxon.) and Pipehall in Erdington (Warwicks.); accounts for Warwick and Whitnash (Warwicks.), 1480–5; a partial set of ministers' accounts for 1480–1; part of a *valor* for 1481–2: P.R.O., DL 29/643/10439, DL 29/645/10464; Oxfordshire C.R.O., Dil.II/b/3–16, Dil.II/w/135/1; Birmingham Reference Library, 347930–43; Stratford-on-Avon, Shakespeare Birthplace Trust, DR 5/2741–76. These are the source of the next three paragraphs.

respited instead of being recognized as decayed. Confusion makes ordinary and extraordinary expenditure hard to disentangle. Such slackness and neglect partly explain the small percentage of potential revenue that was delivered to the receiver. Yet although Hugford's administration was evidently lax, it does not seem to have been corrupt. Sums received by him in 1481–2 were wholly accounted for and he admitted a balance of £136. He was not peculating the issues, still less treating the estate as he would his own, as charged in the chancery petitions, but was holding it to uses. This does not mean that he failed to appreciate the local eminence and fund of patronage derived from his position as sole feoffee.

To whose use then was the estate held? Clearly Earl Richard Beauchamp retained control during his lifetime, in spite of the enfeoffment, for which he had not yet declared the trust. The estates feature in the *valor* of his estates of 1430–1. Probably because he was receiving the issues himself, he left the endowment of Guy's Cliffe to his executors, even though he himself had obtained a licence. After his death one has to deduce the identity of the 'cestui que use' from odd references in the records. His son Duke Henry was his undoubted heir and was treated as such by the feoffees. They conveyed Kemerton and the reversion of Grovebury to him: as his title to the latter was uncertain, Henry wisely exchanged it for the reversion of the Channel Isles.[24] In 1445–6, at his request, a fee was granted from Snitterfield and in 1446, at his special desire, another was conceded from Spelsbury. In a signet letter of 10 July 1445 Henry, calling himself 'duke of Warrewyk and Prime Count of Englond', ordered John Hethe, 'oen of our Receiuours in Englond', to pay £8 15s 9½d to Richard Laventon. It was paid and the auditors accepted the letter as sufficient warrant. On Henry's death, the estates were included in his inquisitions *post mortem*.[25]

After the death of the duke and his daughter, there was a dispute over the main Beauchamp estate, which was resolved in favour of Earl Richard Neville. It is clear that Hugford, Rody and Berkeswell also accepted him as heir to the enfeoffed estate, turning to him for help in 1455, 1463 and 1468–9. Their relationship is illustrated by two letters he sent to them as feoffees, one nominating the steward of Saham Toney (Norf.), the other suggesting a rector for Kibworth Beauchamp (Leics.). Each letter ends with the recognition that his nominee might not be acceptable: 'And of your disposicion in this bihalf we pray you to certify vs'.[26] Probably it was at Warwick's instance that the outlying manor of Farndon (Northants.) was exchanged for land in Warwick.[27]

It is indicative of how close Earl Richard Neville's relations were with the feoffees that in 1471, following his death, his son-in-law Clarence held a court at Pipehall in Erdington (Warwicks.), at which tenants acknowledged his lordship, before he realized his mistake! Neither he nor the tenants doubted that he was the heir. Later Clarence participated in the consecration of the Beauchamp chapel and the alienation of Naunton Beauchamp. On his instructions payments, later respited, were made from Shenstone. In 1475 he appointed John Digby as bailiff of Barrowden (Rut.), a grant that was allowed to stand. Although these lands do not feature in his inquisitions *post mortem*, the royal exchequer regarded them as held to his use. The other coheir of the main Beauchamp estate, the duke of Gloucester, is not mentioned in these accounts, but from 1473

[24] *Cal. Pat. Rolls 1441–6*, pp. 400–1; Throckmorton of Coughton MSS. Box 59 (consulted at Warwick C.R.O.).
[25] P.R.O., C 139/123/2.
[26] Chatwin, p. 3; J. H. Bloom, 'Two Warwickshire muniment rooms', *Trans. Birmingham Archaeol. Soc.*, xxx (1904), 26–7.
[27] P.R.O., SC 11/825; *Ministers' Accounts of the Warwickshire Estates*, p. 13.

he held Blaxhall and Burwash, in Witnesham (Suff.).[28] These were Despenser lands, to which the elder Beauchamp sisters had no claim, yet they also occur in the chancery petitions.

It is therefore clear that the feoffees held the estates to the use of Earl Richard Beauchamp's successive heirs. Consequently they took account of the wishes of these heirs when appointing local ministers, presenting to benefices and granting annuities. The lands of the feoffees, where intermingled with the main estate, consolidated the influence of the heirs; elsewhere they extended it. The ministers on the enfeoffed manors testified to their belief that the lands were held to the heirs' use by paying occasional bills. All this need be evidence of no more than an informal relationship, supplementary to the main purpose of the trust. On the other hand there is a clear possibility that the interests of an heir took priority over the fulfilment of the trust and were sufficiently advantageous to the heirs to justify the trust's prolongation. Did any heirs collect any surplus revenue from the enfeoffed lands or otherwise treat them as their own? A tentative answer to these questions can be reached by examining the surviving accounts.

In 1482 the enfeoffed lands were valued at £323 over reprises, of which Hugford actually received £208. After deducting twenty-six pounds in running costs, there was a balance of £182. At this date he no longer held Kemerton, worth £12 10s 9d in 1479–80; lands alienated in mortmain, extended at £68 13s 4d; or Blaxhall and Burwash, which yielded liveries of about six pounds in 1476–7.[29] By adding all these sums together, one arrives at a disposable surplus of about £270 for the whole estate. This represents the approximate value in 1468–82; one can only speculate about any change in revenues since 1439. £270 may, however, be an underestimate: in 1482, £125 was spent locally, a very large amount; accounts of the previous year for only part of the estate include forty-nine pounds, which constituted extraordinary expenditure rather than administrative overheads. To arrive at the true value such items should be discounted, but this is not very realistic: they were a normal feature from at least 1436 and were never available to the feoffees in cash. The actual liveries were nearer to £270, a sum several times exceeded by building expenses. If allowance is made for administrative and other expenses, there can have been little margin in 1442–63. After 1463 something may have been available for the late earl's heirs; after 1469, when the conveyances and furnishing of the Beauchamp chapel were completed, this would have been a very substantial sum. There is a strong presumption that it was passed on to Earl Richard Neville and Clarence, although there is no direct evidence on this point. In 1481–2 the king took it.

By regarding Anne and later Clarence as heirs, the feoffees set aside Earl Richard Beauchamp's will. As neither Duke Henry nor his daughter had seisin of these estates, it was as if they had predeceased Earl Richard: in such circumstances he had wanted his four daughters to share the Abergavenny lands, just as they divided those in tail male. The feoffees apparently applied the verdict on the main inheritance to the property in trust. This was a subtle legal problem, especially as it was doubtful whether Duke Henry enjoyed them. To John Hugford, who had never served Earl Richard Beauchamp, a strong argument was available: not all four daughters were heiresses to the earl but only Anne and her issue, who enjoyed the principal estates and carldom. Was not the heir of the earl of Warwick the present earl? We cannot tell whether he replied in such terms, but the similarities of successive chancery petitions suggest that the detailed titles were never discussed. The heirs of the elder sisters could not afford

[28] P.R.O., SC 2/204/24 m. 1, DL 29/637/10360A, DL 29/295/4848 m. 1r–d.
[29] P.R.O., DL 29/638/10371 m. 9r–d, DL 29/637/10360A m. 1; see above.

to admit that Hugford held to uses other than their own. Their litigation may also have been impaired by the deaths of Lady Latimer in 1480 and Lady Lisle in 1487. In short it seems that Hugford was prolonging the trust in the interests of the heirs of Anne, the fourth daughter.

An examination of the plaintiffs in the chancery petitions shows a process of development compatible with this interpretation. In the first petition Eleanor was not represented and Edward Plantagenet, born only in 1475, cannot have been actively engaged. Gloucester's participation indicates that he could gain from even half of a quarter share: his action corresponds to his other attempts to adjust his 1474-5 settlement with Clarence after the latter's death. Lady Latimer was also active: in her will in 1480 she instructed John Hugford, her father's feoffee, to provide 100 marks' income to support her widowed daughter, Katherine Dudley.[30] Lord Lisle was probably also interested, as by Michaelmas 1484 he had seised Kibworth Beauchamp and Chaddesley Corbett and the manorial records of the latter. With these he had acquired a copy of the 1425 fine, by which some of the lands were enfeoffed, and of the 1482 *valor*. It was presumably for him that the *valor* was endorsed with the names of all enfeoffed manors, including some already alienated. This may account for the greater precision of the second petition. The case was probably weakened by the minority of Lord Latimer, by the legal death of the countess of Warwick, and by the fact that John Roos was not Eleanor's heir. In 1485-6 not only Lord Lisle but the countess of Warwick was active: simultaneously she petitioned parliament for the return of her ˙inheritance.[31] Chancery had to respond this time, since John Hugford had died on 20 November 1485, leaving as heirs his teenaged daughters Anne and Alice and his infant grandson John Beaufo, son of his deceased daughter Joan; Shenstone was stated in his inquisition *post mortem* to have been seised by Lord Strange.[32]

The only remedy open to the elder daughters and their heirs against Hugford was appeal to the king. In any case kings paid close attention to enfeoffments, which were a means whereby their rights as feudal overlords might be avoided, particularly their claim to wardship of tenants-in-chief who were under age. Such occurrences were not purely accidental, for lands were frequently settled on feoffees with this objective in view: such enfeoffments, when designed solely to defraud kings of their legitimate rights, were collusive and illegal. It was natural that kings should scrutinize particularly closely enfeoffments of valuable estates, such as those of the Beauchamp trust, and that such trusts should be carefully administered to avoid being condemned as collusive. An obvious pointer to collusion was if the feoffor had prescribed no other use except the enfeoffment of his heir when of age. The Beauchamp trust was intended primarily to fulfil the will of the feoffor and the feoffees could produce concrete evidence that they were fulfilling it: thus royal custody was avoided during the minorities of Duke Henry and his daughter.[33]

Another mark of collusion which justified royal intervention was where the lands of a trust were administered jointly with those in fee, since this suggested that a proper estate had never been made by the feoffor to the feoffees—that in practice the lands had never left his possession. Thus separate administration of an enfeoffed estate was an important rule. It was carefully observed in this case.

---

[30] *Testamenta Vetusta*, i. 261; for what follows, see Shakespeare Birthplace Trust, DR 5/2870, 5/2874, 5/2876, 5/2883; P.R.O., SC 6/908/18.

[31] *The Red Paper Book of Colchester*, ed. W. G. Benham (Colchester, 1902), p. 62.

[32] *Cal. Inq. Post Mortem, Henry VII*, i, no. 200.

[33] Bean, pp. 205–12; *Cal. Pat. Rolls 1441–6*, pp. 433–4; *Cal. Pat. Rolls 1476–85*, p. 136.

After Earl Richard Neville's purchase of Erdington, it was not united with the feoffees' adjacent manor of Pipehall, as Professor Hilton believed.[34] Similarly accounts of the bailiff of Budbrooke and the approver of Grove Park in Budbrooke contain no reference to one another.[35] The earl's ministers attended audits of their accounts at Warwick, those of the feoffees at Guy's Cliffe. Thus the feoffees scrupulously guarded themselves against charges of collusion and legitimate royal interference.

Nevertheless there were close informal ties between the two estates. The feoffees themselves served successive earls and the overlap of personnel in the two estates reflects the earls' influence over appointments. Action on the enfeoffed estate was frequently initiated 'be the Wylle and commawndement of Mayster Thomas Hygford' during the fourteen-fifties, when he was supervisor of Earl Richard Neville's west Midlands estate.[36] John Hugford was initially feed from Snitterfield at Duke Henry's request: it was probably because Clarence was satisfied with his services that the estate was not conveyed to other feoffees. Successive bailiffs of Pipehall were also bailiffs of Sutton Coldfield (Warwicks.): even Nicholas Rody, one of the feoffees, failed to distinguish their functions when receiving their liveries.[37] Sir Walter Scull was simultaneously steward of Chaddesley and Salwarpe (Worcs.). Robert Fitzwarren was collector of rents in Warwick for both estates and was bailiff of Snitterfield as well.

Although theoretically separate for so long, the estate accounts contain evidence of activity by Earl Richard Beauchamp's heirs, including Clarence. The 1480–1 accounts, probably filed immediately with those of the estates in fee, reveal this to the most cursory scrutiny. Such direct intervention was only possible for the 'cestui que use', the beneficiary of the trust. The trust was allowed to continue but the exchequer took the issues, which suggests that the estate was considered to be in trust for Clarence's son Edward, the king's ward.[38] Perhaps, in defending himself against the claims of the elder sisters in chancery, Hugford had been unable to deny that he held to Edward's use. In any case he probably welcomed royal support, especially as the king appointed him chief officer in the Warwickshire estates. In 1484 Queen Anne, formerly duchess of Gloucester, alienated the enfeoffed East Anglian manors to Queens' college, Cambridge: the gift was later cancelled, but she is remembered as a benefactor. Henry VII, like Edward IV, may have initially regarded Edward, earl of Warwick as 'cestui que use', but if so he soon changed his mind. Issues due at Michaelmas 1486 were paid by royal command to Anne, countess of Warwick, who next year surrendered the enfeoffed lands with those in fee to the king.[39] This was the end of the Beauchamp trust. Her grandson Edward never had any estate in them and neither had the heirs of her sisters, except the Lords Lisle, who clung on to Kibworth Beauchamp and Chaddesley Corbett. Much later, when John Dudley was created earl of Warwick in 1547, he remembered that he was heir to

[34] Prof. Hilton attributes certain changes in accounts between 1461 and 1480 to the amalgamation of Erdington with Pipehall in Erdington. However, there is an account of 1480–1 for Pipehall alone. His 1460–1 account refers to Pipehall and his 1479–80 account to Erdington (*Ministers' Accounts of the Warwickshire Estates*, p. xix n. 3; P.R.O., DL 29/645/10464 m.7d; Birmingham Ref. Libr., 347943).

[35] *Ministers' Accounts of the Warwickshire Estates*, pp. 28–30; P.R.O., DL 29/645/10464 m. 7r–d.

[36] Bodleian Libr., MS. Dugdale 13 p. 434; Birmingham Ref. Libr., 347940 (attached bill).

[37] Birmingham Ref. Libr., 347936 (attached bill). For the next two sentences, see P.R.O., DL 29/645/10461 m. 6, DL 29/645/10464 mm. 6d, 7d; *Ministers' Accounts of the Warwickshire Estates*, p. 1.

[38] Shakespeare Birthplace Trust, DR 5/2870.

[39] P.R.O., E 315/41/259; *Cal. Pat. Rolls 1476–85*, pp. 423, 477; British Library, Harley MS. 433 fos. 68v, 289v.

Margaret, Earl Richard Beauchamp's eldest daughter, and 'oon of the doughters and heyres of the right and nat defyled lyne'.[40]

The persistent disputes over these manors reflect little credit on the feoffor's heirs. His elder daughters and their issue wanted livery of the estates and were not unduly concerned about their strict entitlements. By denying the feoffees' right to alienate, they were questioning grants made in mortmain for the soul of the earl.[41] Anne and her issue struggled to retain control and exclude their rivals, even at the price of delaying the execution of the will. On the other hand the earl's executors gave up to thirty years of their lives to executing the will, a thankless task presumably motivated by a sense of personal loyalty.

The trust lasted for forty-eight years from the testator's death. Most of the manors had been held in trust for sixty-two years from the 1425 fine. Much longer enfeoffments are known of ecclesiastical estates, at first apparently accidental but later deliberately intended to be perpetual.[42] A cheap alternative to alienation in mortmain, such ecclesiastical enfeoffments were quite different from the Beauchamp trust, which combined temporary religious functions with continued tenure by the testator's heirs. However, there was no theoretical limit even to such secular trusts, providing that the arrangements remained convenient to the 'cestui que use'.

By dint of such trusts a feoffor or testator could control the devolution of his lands after his death, even including those held in tail to which he was only life-tenant. He was no longer limited in his bequests and benefactions to a third of his moveable estate, but could finance them from revenues due after his death. Hitherto his creditors had no claims against the heirs of his lands, so he had been restricted in the scale of borrowing to the value of his moveable goods and their estimate of the value of his life-interest in his estates (which involved an assessment of his life-expectancy). Now a debtor like the 3rd earl of Northumberland could guarantee future repayment after his death from the income of entailed lands held in trust:[43] this increased his credit-worthiness substantially. Such trusts resembled the true mortgage devised a century later, since security for the creditor was combined with continued tenure for the debtor. Uses were thus a highly flexible device to extend the influence of landholders beyond their natural lives.

This was important for more than purely financial reasons. Earl Richard Beauchamp, as we have seen, prescribed how certain enfeoffed lands should devolve after his death. The same effect could have been achieved by entailing them, but the entail was a more rigid mechanism. Once he had settled his manors, the donor's hands were tied and he could not alter the provisions to meet changed circumstances. In contrast any directions in a will could be modified in a codicil or superseded completely in a later will.[44] Earl Richard Beauchamp was able to provide in his will for children yet unborn and made other arrangements dependent on them. Entails lacked this flexible and conditional character.

[40] H. Miller, 'Henry VIII's unwritten will', *Wealth and Power in Tudor England*, ed. E. W. Ives, R. J. Knecht and J. J. Scarisbrick (1978), p. 101.

[41] Mr. Barton points out that 'if the heir re-entered he got back his ancestor's fee simple, free of the claims of all the beneficiaries' (J. L. Barton, 'The medieval use', *Law Quarterly Rev.*, lxxxi (1965), 566).

[42] *Ibid.*, p. 565. Alienation in mortmain by way of uses was prohibited in 1391, but continued as a means of settling chantry and charity estates (e.g. *V.C.H. Middlesex*, vi. 97–8).

[43] J. M. W. Bean, *The Estates of the Percy Family, 1416–1537* (1958), pp. 100–4; see also Barton, pp. 572–3.

[44] Barton, pp. 570–2.

Trusts also conferred some control over entailed estates, important less in scope than because of the growing extent of entailed land. By 1437 the unbreakable entail, which had originally given power to the donor over his children and their descendants, had spread so widely that the great had few lands at their unfettered disposal. It was no longer easy to settle outlying properties on younger sons: instead they had to be endowed with lands bought out of income, if at all. But trusts of this type, which deferred the inheritance of the main line, offered an alternative form of provision. Annuities from lands in fee were subject to cancellation by the heir, but feoffees could be directed to pay them: thus the 4th earl of Northumberland required the continued payment of fees to his retainers[45] and, as we have seen, Lady Latimer wanted the trust to pay her daughter an annuity. A testator could order the purchase of lands for his younger son: the feoffees probably bought Batsford and Dodes and they certainly alienated other estates. Trusts offered limited opportunities to provide for younger children.

The principal beneficiary in these cases was the feoffor, who diverted future income from the heir, if of age, or the king, if not. Both had an interest in invalidating the trust, but at least in this case the feoffees' title was too strong for either. One can hardly exaggerate the loss to the heirs: the income of the Beauchamp trust was twice the capital value of the land and several manors were permanently alienated. No wonder Earl Richard Beauchamp and others preferred to leave the prohibitively high expense of building and endowment until after their deaths. Such uses deprived the king of income, but this was not the primary aim: the bulk of the Beauchamp inheritance was taken into custody and successive kings enjoyed the wardship of the heir in 1439, in 1446 and again in 1478. Waste and disparagement remained undesirable attributes of wardship, sufficient justification for continued collusion, but evasion of feudal incidents was clearly not the only, nor perhaps even the prime, purpose of trusts. Richard III's act against fraudulent enfeoffments in 1484 explicitly recognized the performance of wills as a proper function of trusts.

Trusts were attractive as means of financing bequests and benefactions, settling estates and providing for younger children, but they had one clear disadvantage: the feoffor or testator could not be sure that his directions would be obeyed. The Beauchamp trust graphically illustrates the difficulty of holding feoffees to account and the danger that the estates would be lost to the family of the feoffee. There seems little doubt that long before 1485 Earl Richard Beauchamp's will had been performed, yet John Hugford was able to prolong the trust, in spite of pressure from powerful heirs. Even if he himself was honest, the coinciding minorities of the young earl and Hugford's daughters and grandson might have resulted in annexation of the estates by his descendants, Lord Strange and others. This eventuality was forestalled by royal intervention, admittedly self-interested, but not necessarily to the disadvantage of heirs. On this evidence royal oversight as feudal overlord offered more effective protection for the heirs than the court of chancery.

[45] *Testamenta Eboracensia*, ed. J. Raine and J. W. Clay (Surtees Soc., iv, xxx, xlv, liii, lxxix, cvi, 1836–1902), iii. 306.

APPENDIX

List of Enfeoffed Lands constituting the Beauchamp Trust

Unless otherwise indicated, all these manors were held continuously by the Beauchamp feoffees from 1425 to 1487. Abergavenny manors acquired in 1435 are marked (A) and Despenser manors acquired and held between 1439 and 1473 are marked (D). The sources are cited in the preceding pages except where shown.

Bedfordshire
  Grovebury[46]

Essex
  Walthamstow Franceys

Gloucestershire
  Batsford and Dodes[47]
  Kemerton (A)[48]

Leicestershire
  Kibworth Beauchamp[49]

Norfolk
  Little Cressingham
  Necton
  Panxworth
  Saham Toney

Northamptonshire
  Farndon[50]
  Preston Capes[51]

Oxfordshire
  Langley
  Spelsbury (A)

Rutland
  Barrowden
  Gretton

Staffordshire
  Shenstone[52]

Suffolk
  Blaxhall (D)
  Burwash (D)

Warwickshire
  Ashorne
  Baginton[53]
  Budbrooke
  Haseley
  Pipehall
  Snitterfield (A)
  Wolverton[54]

Worcestershire
  Chaddesley Corbett (A)[55]
  Hervington (A)
  Naunton Beauchamp (A)[56]
  Pirton Power (A)
  Sheriff's Lench (A)

[46] The reversion of Grovebury was held by the feoffees from 1429 and was conveyed to Duke Henry by 1446.

[47] They occur in the 1480–2 accounts under Worcestershire (P.R.O., C 143/455/12, DL 29/645/10464; *Cal. Pat. Rolls 1476–85*, p. 318). Batsford was presumably the Gloucestershire manor; Dodes, farmed for only £1, is unidentified.

[48] Conveyed to Duke Henry by 1446.

[49] Seized by Lord Lisle by 1484 (P.R.O., SC 6/908/18).

[50] Exchanged by 1479 (*Ministers' Accounts of the Warwickshire Estates*, p. 13).

[51] Alienated in 1469.

[52] Held 1449–85 (P.R.O., SC 11/947; *Cal. Inq. Post Mortem, Henry VII*, i, no. 200).

[53] Alienated in 1469.

[54] Alienated in 1469.

[55] Seized by Lord Lisle by 1484.

[56] Alienated in 1472 (P.R.O., C 142/80/107).

20

The Neville Earldom of Salisbury, 1429-71

Edward III stands out among late medieval English kings as a creator of earls. In 1335 he recognised the title of Hugh Courtenay of Okehampton (Devon) as heir of the Redvers family to the earldom of Devon,[1] and in 1337 he created six new earls: William Clinton as earl of Huntingdon, William Bohun earl of Northampton, William Montagu earl of Salisbury, Robert Ufford earl of Suffolk, Hugh Audley earl of Gloucester, and Henry of Grosmont as earl of Derby. To support his new estate Henry of Grosmont was granted an annuity of 1,000 marks during the lifetime of his father, the earl of Lancaster. The other five shared a novel characteristic absent in earlier creations. Although their comital titles were granted to them and the heirs of their bodies, the endowments they received specifically to support these titles were granted in tail male, to them and their masculine issue. This endowment was calculated in Gloucester's case at £100, in Northampton's at £1,000 and for the other three at 1,000 marks above the third penny (£20) that each enjoyed from the county from which their title was taken. This casts light on what Edward III thought the suitable income for an earl. It follows, as the editors of the *Complete Peerage* observed, that the king cannot have meant to separate the title from the income intended to support it: evidently he expected the title to escheat with the estates in default of male issue.

The best indicator of Edward's intentions ought to be the fate of the earldoms, as the family of each earl had failed in the male line by 1429.[2] In practice not all devolved the same way and there has been much dispute over the lessons to be derived from each case. The first failure occurred in 1347 on the death of Hugh Audley, earl of Gloucester, who left a daughter Margaret (d. 1348). His title was evidently chosen because he had married one of the three coheiresses of the Clare earls of Gloucester. By itself her purparty was endowment enough for an earl, which presumably

---

[1] *5th Rep from the Lords Committee . . . touching the Dignity of a Peer of the Realm*, 26-7. For rest of para see ibid 27-34; *Calendar of Patent Rolls, 1334-8*, 400, 414-16; G.E. Cokayne, *Complete Peerage*, ed H.V. Gibbs and others, x, appendix K, 123.

[2] This para is based upon *Complete Peerage*, x, appendix K.

was why Edward felt no need to give Audley more than £100 income to support it. Her inheritance descended to their daughter, whose husband Ralph, Lord Stafford (d. 1372) was created earl of Stafford in 1351. In spite of these circumstances, the earldom of Gloucester and the endowment reverted to the crown.[3] As Edward III was still king, this probably best expresses his original intentions. He was not yet dead in 1373 when the male line of the earldom of Northampton failed, the 2nd earl leaving only two daughters. Under the terms of the original grant, half of the original £1,000 was to revert to the crown should the earl or his heirs inherit the earldoms of Essex and Hereford from the senior line of the Bohun family: this apparently took effect in 1361.[4] The other half escheated in 1373, but the third penny of the county descended first to one coparcener, later to the other, each using the title intermittently from 1399. Certainly each daughter, as coheiress of the other Bohun earldoms, could support the dignity, just as Margaret Audley could have done. Edward's attitude may have changed because the beneficiaries were his youngest son Thomas of Woodstock, ultimately duke of Gloucester, and his grandson Henry of Bolingbroke, later Henry IV, as husbands to the two heiresses. Such close kinship to the king was absent in the heirs of William Ufford, earl of Suffolk. When he died in 1382 the king was a minor. The estates and earldom escheated. He left his coheirs, his four sisters or their heirs, very little to divide between them,[5] certainly too little to justify the revival of the earldom. Neither of the other fourteenth-century failures is relevant: William Clinton, earl of Huntingdon (d. 1354) left no issue, male or female, and in 1337 Henry of Grosmont, earl of Derby had been exceptional. On his father's death in 1345 his annuity of 1,000 marks reverted to the crown,[6] but he retained the earldom and third penny of Derbyshire until his death without male issue in 1361. Title and third penny descended to his sole surviving daughter Blanche, whose husband John of Gaunt styled himself earl of Derby until his death and whose heirs enjoyed the third penny in the fifteenth century. The endowment of the former Ferrers earls of Derby was held by the earls and dukes of Lancaster throughout the fourteenth century. The grant of 1337 was akin to a 'courtesy' title and a similar grant was made in 1377 to Henry of Bolingbroke, the heir apparent.

There were thus conflicting precedents in 1428 when Thomas Montagu, earl of Salisbury died. He left a daughter Alice and a male heir

[3] *Cal Pat, 1334-8*, 415, 522; *1338-40*, 441-2, 458; *Calendar of Inquisitions post mortem*, ix 60.

[4] *Cal Pat, 1334-8*, 416-17; cf *Cal Inq pm* x, no. 639; xiii, no. 167, esp London and Berkshire; *Complete Peerage*, vi 476n, 477.

[5] *Cal Inq pm* xv, nos. 599-626, esp 604, 610-11.

[6] *Cal Pat, 1343-5*, 552; R. Somerville, *Hist of Duchy of Lancaster*, i 67n, 340; *Calendar of Close Rolls, 1374-7*, 48.

in his uncle Sir Richard Montagu: the latter received the endowment of 1337. Not he but Alice's husband Richard Neville took the title of earl, although his claim was not unchallenged. On 7 May 1429 it was considered in council, the king being a minor: the royal judges decided that he should be accepted as earl in right of his wife; the magnates accepted him as such with the same precedence as previous earls of Salisbury.[7] The fact that the council discussed the matter and that he was not permitted merely to assume the title shows that the exceptional nature of the problem was realised. Subsequently the earldom passed among Earl Thomas's descendants until the execution of Margaret Plantagenet in 1541.

The issue was raised again in 1442, when Richard and Alice were granted the third penny of Wiltshire, which they claimed that they lacked.[8] They explained this by stating that in 1400 Earl John had suffered forfeiture, his sentence being confirmed by parliaments until 1421, when lands in tail were restored to his son Earl Thomas. This, they implied, had not included the third penny, so Earl Richard had nothing with which to support his dignity. There is no reason to doubt their statement that they were not receiving the third penny but the reason that they alleged was incorrect. It is true that the restoration in 1421 concerned only lands in tail, not those in fee simple. But Earl Thomas had livery of the third penny in 1409, when the entailed annuity clearly fell within the act of restoration. Earl Thomas held it at his death: Alice and Richard could not have been ignorant of this. It is uncertain why it did not descend to Earl Thomas's heirs but, as there is no evidence of default by the sheriffs, it was presumably because they were not entitled to it by the 1429 council decision. In 1442 they may have fabricated this explanation because they did not want any further investigation of their right to the earldom itself. It is likely that in 1429, as in 1409, the third penny was considered to be in tail male and consequently escheated.

As the third penny and title were granted by the same charter, it is difficult to believe that the royal judges preferred to interpret it literally. Certainly in accepting Richard as one of themselves, the magnates were influenced by who he was. He was the eldest son of Ralph Neville, 1st earl of Westmorland by his second wife Joan (d. 1440), daughter of John of Gaunt by Katherine Swynford. Joan was half-sister of Henry IV, aunt of Henry V, great-aunt of Henry VI and whole sister of Cardinal Beaufort (d. 1447). Her marriage enhanced the Nevilles' importance. Grants were made by the Lancastrian kings to her and her husband jointly, which

---

[7] *Proceedings and Ordinances of the Privy Council of England* (Rec Com), iii 324-5.

[8] *Cal Pat, 1441-6*, 111; Public Record Office, C 81/734/6465. For rest of para, see *Rotuli Parliamentorum* (Rec Com), iii 459; iv 17-19, 35-6, 141-2; *Cal Close, 1405-9*, 447; PRO C 137/75/1/17; C 139/41/1/35.

eventually passed to their son Richard, who was also the beneficiary of his
father's conveyance of most of the Neville patrimony away from the issue
of his first marriage. At the culmination of Richard's career, as a vital
supporter of the duke of York in the 1450s, his wife's lands may have
provided about a third of his income. It is doubtful whether in 1428 it
sufficed to support the estate of an earl.

The oldest element of the inheritance in 1428 consisted of lands granted by
Edward I to Simon, 1st Lord Montagu, to Simon's son William and the
latter's heirs.[9] Simon, William, and William's son William served the
crown well. For his assistance in overthrowing Isabella and Mortimer, the
younger William received among other lands estates in Hampshire,
including the castle of Christchurch Twynham, caput of the later
earldom. Created earl in 1337, William received 1,000 marks endowment,
to be exchanged for lands of equivalent value: this process was never
completed. The 2nd earl failed to establish his title to some of those
assigned, others were lost, and, in spite of inheriting possessions of the
Monthermer family, income from the 3rd earl's estate in 1398-1400 was
only £725.[10] He was executed in 1400, but his possessions in tail were
restored to his son Thomas, who at his death in 1428 held the Salisbury
inheritance in tail male, the Montagu and Monthermer lands in tail
general, and the lands of his first wife by courtesy of England. She had
been Eleanor Holland, mother of his daughter and coheiress of Edmund
Holland, earl of Kent (d. 1408). Without her purparty Thomas could
hardly have maintained the estate expected of an earl, for his *total* income
was only £725 on inquisition valuations.

As second wife Earl Thomas had married Alice Chaucer, a young
widow, on whom he had settled eight manors in jointure. As he had no
licence for this transaction, his daughter objected, and the differences
between her and the dowager were arbitrated by Cardinal Beaufort, who
was kinsman of both parties. On 1 December 1428 Beaufort directed
Richard and Alice to confirm the countess's title in the three manors of
Chedzoy (Soms), Stokenham, and Yealmpton (Devon) for life. In return
she was to pay them £16 rent and renounce all rights of jointure and dower
in other estates to which they were heirs. These provisions were duly
carried out.[11] Alice Chaucer, who remarried to William de la Pole, earl
and ultimately duke of Suffolk, held Chedzoy, Stokenham, and
Yealmpton until her death in 1475, when they reverted to Isabel, Duchess
of Clarence, granddaughter of Richard and Alice.

[9] PRO C 139/41/1/24, /34. For next para, see G.A. Holmes, *Estates of the Higher Nobility
in Fourteenth-Century Eng*, 27-9.

[10] PRO SC 6/1122/2. This and next four paras are based on PRO C 139/41/1; E 357/30.

[11] Northants. R.O. Fitzwilliam (Milton) MS 2046; *Cal Pat, 1429-36*, 36; PRO CP 25(1)/
292/66/95. For what follows see PRO C 140/51/17/2; E 149/30/9.

Alice and Richard immediately entered Earl Thomas's Holland estates in 1428. Not all of these had fallen in at the death of his first wife Eleanor. There were already three dowager-countesses of Kent in 1408 when a fourth, Lucy Visconti, was added. She was assigned dower before Earl Edmund's sisters were admitted to their purparties. In 1411 the sisters also divided the dower of Elizabeth of Juliers, the long-lived widow of John, earl of Kent (d. 1352). This had originally consisted of property, mainly feefarms, worth £910 a year.[12] In 1428 Eleanor's share was extended at £280. At her death two dowers and the purparty of a childless sister were yet to be divided: in 1425 Alice received a fifth of Lucy's dower; in 1434 a quarter of the purparty of Joan, dowager-duchess of York; and in 1442 a quarter of the jointure of the Countess Joan. Two partitions show how fragmented were the estates after several divisions. In 1434 Alice's share may have been worth £450, the value attributed to that of the duchess of York, on whose death it should have grown to *c*. £560. With lands extended at £114 assigned in 1442,[13] her share of the Holland inheritance would have been worth £675. Such calculations based on inquisition valuations are hypothetical and probably serious underestimates: the share of another sister Elizabeth Neville (d. 1423) was worth at least £618 as early as 1422-3.[14] They do however suggest that the Holland lands were worth more than all the rest put together.

As the fee simple estates were held to Earl Thomas's use, they were exempt from dower at his death. Since they were extended at £215, Alice's estates were valued at *c*. £665 above reprises in 1428, not quite enough to support the earldom. Probably Richard also had northern estates held jointly with Alice: they are implied by his appointment in 1431 of a receiver of the South Parts, defined as the estates south of the Trent plus two Holland manors in Yorkshire.[15] These properties presumably account for some of the surplus of £463 over the extended value of Alice's possessions in Richard's income tax assessment of £1,238 in 1436. Her estates should have yielded *c*. £880 by 1442, a figure surprisingly close to the £851 and £817 received from the South Parts in 1445-6 and 1455-6.[16] The earlier account records considerable expenditure by the earl,

---

[12] *Cal Close, 1349-54*, 530-1; *Cal Fine Rolls, 1405-13*, 211-12; PRO SC 12/41/3. I am grateful to Mr T.B. Pugh for these references.

[13] T.B. Pugh and C.D. Ross, 'The English Baronage and the Income Tax of 1436', *Bull Inst Historical Research*, xxvi 17n; PRO C 47/9/35 m 1.

[14] These figures come from a valor of enfeoffed lands (£503) and inquisition values of fee simple lands in Devon: Westminster Abbey MS 9192 (ref supplied by Mr Pugh); PRO C 139/6/2/18, cf *Cal Inq p.m* xvi, nos. 725-50; *Cal Inq p.m* (Rec Com), iii 200, 324. The feoffment was made 13 December 1422: PRO C 139/6/2/12.

[15] PRO E 159/207, recorda, Trin 9 Hen VI, m 1.

[16] H.L. Gray, 'The Income Tax of 1436', *Eng Hist Review*, xlix 615; PRO SC 6/1122/3, /4.

countess and their family in the north and at London, but they did not
visit their southern estates. The level of extraordinary fees was very low.
This indicates, as one would expect, that Richard, who was primarily a
northern magnate, had little time for them. He even alienated parts to
provide for a younger son. These estates probably provided one-third of
his income, delivering it in cash, an important consideration for a
magnate whose northern income was probably appropriated largely in
annuities.[17] After 1455-6 the shape of Alice's estate altered and it was
reorganised into two receiverships.[18]

By 1428 the Salisbury endowment had dwindled to a third of its
original value. Extended at £230 in all, the largest part was an annuity of
200 marks from the stannaries that had not been exchanged for lands.
Altogether it yielded a third of the income of one of the poorest earls. Alice
could inherit only two-thirds, her great-uncle Sir Richard Montagu only
one-third, neither sufficient for an earl. As the tail male properties were in
chief, the dower-countess was assigned dower and Sir Richard had livery
only of two-thirds of five manors, two hundreds, and of annuities of £160,
with the reversion of the remainder on her death. On his death without
male heir in 1429, the male heirs of Earl William I became extinct and the
lands escheated. The annuities were permanently lost; some lands were
demised for terms of years, most were alienated. In 1433 Sir Richard's
two-third's share of five manors was granted to the duke of Bedford in tail
male, together with the reversion of the thirds of the dowager. On his
death without issue in 1435, some were assigned in dower to his duchess
Jacquetta of Luxembourg (d. 1472), who held them in 1438-9.[19] The rest
again escheated.

On 25 May 1439, for 13,350 marks paid by Cardinal Beaufort, trustees
including himself were granted among other lands the manor of
Henstridge (Soms), two-thirds of the manor of Amesbury (Wilts), certain
parcels of land in Charlton Camville (Soms), the reversion of the countess
of Salisbury's dower in Amesbury, Winterbourne Earls (Wilts), and
Canford (Dorset), the reversion of the duchess of Bedford's dower in
Charlton Camville, and the reversion of the remaining two-thirds of
Canford, held by the cardinal for life. In 1440-1 he bought both dowagers
out of the lands to which he held the reversions and on 2 March 1443 was
licensed to convey them at will to whoever he chose. His intention was to
expand vastly the hospital of St Cross at Winchester, for which these

----

[17] A.J. Pollard, 'The Northern Retainers of Richard Neville, Earl of Salisbury', *Northern
History*, ii, 52-69.
[18] PRO SC 6/831/3; /765/12; /1122/5, but see also *Original Letters illustrative of Eng
History*, ed H. Ellis, ii (2), (1827), 117.
[19] *Cal Pat. 1429-36*, 297-8; PRO SC 6/1116/13. For next para see *Cal Pat, 1436-41*, 311,
479; *1441-6*, 47, 174; *1452-61*, 233-4.

estates were to be the endowment. Having been licensed to alienate lands worth £500 a year in mortmain, he granted Henstridge, Charlton Camville, Winterbourne Earls and Amesbury to the master and brethren by charter dated 1 February 1446. This was the year before his death, when nothing had been done towards the physical expansion of the hospital. Only on 8 April 1455 was the cardinal's nephew Edmund Beaufort, duke of Somerset, authorised to proceed. Following his death on 22 April delays persisted.

In 1486 William Waynflete, Beaufort's successor as Bishop of Winchester, observed that the hospital's endowment was lost 'and occupied by the power of noble persons'.[20] The antiquary John Rous mentions that the earl of Warwick and Salisbury proposed improvements to the chantry of Guyscliff.[21] Among them he:

> wold have a certen of pore gentylmen found ther as were at seynt Cros of Wynchestre by the fundacon of maistre herre Beauford cardynal and bishop of Wynchestre . . . wich place was endowed with forfet lyvelode of the Earl of Salisbury slayn at Cisseter . . . and thys lord had by auctorite of parlement recouerd hit a geyn.

As the entailed lands had been restored in 1421, the reversal of Earl John's condemnation in 1461 should have affected only lands in fee simple. The inquisition on his death and on that of his predecessor in 1397 are incomplete and reveal nothing, if anything, in fee simple that he could have lost. Nothing held in fee simple is known to have passed to the St Cross hospital. By the reversal of Earl John's attainder his granddaughter Alice recovered lands that had been lost after 1400 and which had never been held in fee simple. These included Henstridge, Charlton Camville, Winterbourne Earls and Amesbury, with which the cardinal had endowed the hospital. Canford, perhaps intended for the same fate, remained to his feoffees at his death.[22] In 1455 it was held by the duke of Somerset, in 1457 by his duchess, but by 1462-3 it was in the hands of the countess of Salisbury. This version is confirmed by the account of the sheriff of Somerset and Dorset in 1470-1. He reveals that the earl of Warwick and Salisbury died seised of Henstridge, which he had inherited from his mother. She had recovered it from St Cross Hospital on the reversal of the forfeiture of Earl John.[23] It had not been confiscated in 1400

---

[20] L.H. Humbert, *Memorials of Hospital of Holy Cross and Alms House of Noble Poverty* (1868), 33.

[21] For this and ensuing quotations see J. Rows, *Rol*, ed W.H. Courthope (1845), no. 57.

[22] Although in 1444 it was rumoured that he planned to sell it: K.B. McFarlane, *Nobility of Later Medieval England*, 56. For next sentence see B.P. Wolffe, *Royal Demesne in Eng History*, 281; PRO E 326/12383; SC 6/831/3.

[23] PRO E 199/62/1/15 m 1d.

but escheated in 1429, as Alice must have remembered.

This distortion of history enabled her to recover lands to which she was not entitled. As in the case of the Percies in 1470, the reversal of an attainder confused the differing titles governing lands. The exploitation of Earl John's sentence was the same tactic as that used by Richard and Alice in 1442 to recover the third penny of the county of Wiltshire. This suggests that the effects were deliberate and that a technique previously successful was deliberately repeated. It indicates that it was Alice's idea, as Warwick had been a minor in 1442, but it was he who secured an exemplification of the act and a writ to the Upper Exchequer.[24] In 1461 Edward IV, first king of a new dynasty, was anxious to legitimise his title and therefore reversed the sentence of his own grandfather the earl of Cambridge, executed in 1415 for supporting the Mortimer title. Others involved then and earlier in plots against the Lancastrian kings were ignored, but the Nevilles obtained the reversal of the sentences of their ancestors Thomas, Lord Despenser and John, earl of Salisbury, of whom they were heirs. In the political circumstances nobody could object to such reversals and probably few foresaw the dangers,[25] least of all the hospital or its protectors. They knew it held no fee simple lands of Earl John. With his brother George Neville, bishop of Exeter, as chancellor, it cannot have been difficult for Warwick to obtain writs to local royal officials. The hospital's patrons, the Beauforts, were attainted and Bishop Waynflete was under a political cloud. For such opponents Edward would not offend indispensable supporters.

This was not the end of the story. In 1492 the heir of Alice and Warwick was Edward Plantagenet, earl of Warwick, a royal ward and too dangerous a pretender to the crown ever to be allowed his liberty; the heir of Cardinal Beaufort was Margaret Beaufort, countess of Richmond and Derby, mother of King Henry VII. It was the cardinal's heir who now carried greater political weight. A bill was submitted to parliament which recited accurately how the manors of Amesbury, Winterbourne Earls, Henstridge, and South Charlton had escheated and how they had been recovered by the act of 1461 reversing the sentence of Earl John, even though his only title was in tail male 'as pleynly appereth by the Letteres Patentes thereof made by King Edwarde the thirde' and in spite of the purchase by Cardinal Beaufort. Clearly the 1461 act should not have altered the descent of these lands and it was accordingly asked that it should not affect them. The aim was that they should be restored, not to the hospital, but to Margaret Beaufort as heir of the cardinal. She disregarded both the rights of the hospital and her great-uncle's pious

---

[24] PRO E 159/239, recorda, Trin 2 Edw IV, m 13-d.
[25] *Rot Parl* v 484-5. But Geo Neville secured a proviso for his Despenser inheritance: PRO C 49/52/8/11; E 159/239, recorda, Trin 2 Edw IV, m 13-d.

wishes, of which she must have been aware from the documents on which her bill was based. The bill was duly passed into law.[26] She apparently held them until *c.* 1506, when they were recovered by Henry VII, perhaps in part exchange for Canford which he granted to his mother for life in 1506. Subsequently Henry VIII included Winterbourne Earls, Amesbury and South Charlton in the grant of the earldom of Salisbury to Margaret Plantagenet (d. 1541), sister of the late earl of Warwick, in 1513. Canford was not included and she tried continuously to recover it as parcel of the earldom of Salisbury; Henry VIII considered it part of the duchy of Somerset. Although not successful, her heirs were able ultimately to make their title good.

Although historians should avoid moral judgement, one should consider more closely what Alice and her son had done. They seized manors to which they had no right from the legal owner. They had taken land held in mortmain, dedicated to God's service and charitable purposes. They had done this in defiance of the donor's intentions, although he was both a cardinal and a kinsman with whom they had enjoyed close relations. Their action was ungrateful, shocking, even sacrilegious. The project of the earl of Warwick and Salisbury to transfer the lands to Guyscliff for a similar purpose may reveal a guilty conscience. It need not be taken seriously: little that Rous alleged that Warwick planned was achieved or even begun and it would not have undone the damage done to Beaufort's foundation.

One should also set this fraud in its context. The Nevilles have a bad reputation. All four inheritances on which Warwick's power was based in the 1460s were acquired by dubious means. The Neville lands were conveyed from the legitimate heirs; the whole Despenser inheritance was seized, although the countess of Warwick was entitled to only half;[27] the Beauchamp inheritance was disputed with her three half-sisters; and both in 1442 and 1461 fraud enlarged the Salisbury estates. Each time the Nevilles displayed political shrewdness. By offering service abroad, Richard earl of Salisbury obtained royal protection against the earl of Westmorland. By obtaining the custody of the other Despenser purparty, although the heir's family was still alive, Warwick was able to retain it on his majority and ignored successive grants of livery. The final decision on the Beauchamp dispute was made during the protectorate of the duke of

---

[26] Rot Parl vi 446-8. For rest of para see *Cal Pat, 1494-1509*, 450, 526; PRO SC 6/Hen VII/1330, m 11; /Hen VII/1234, m 24; /Hen VIII/3822-41; *Letters and Papers of Hen VIII*, iv (2), no. 4828; vi, no. 299 iii; vii, no. 923 xxxviii; xi, no. 1217; xiii (2), no. 819; C. Cross, *Puritan Earl*, 87-92.

[27] This para is based on R.L. Storey, *End of the House of Lancaster*, 231-41; *Cal Close, 1435-41*, 56-7; PRO E 159/244, brevia, Mich 7 Edw IV, m 12-d; E 159/245, brevia, East 8 Edw IV, m 9.

York, when his rival Edmund Beaufort, duke of Somerset was *hors de
combat*. The seizure of the tail male Salisbury lands was a piece of
opportunism: it had been impossible in the 1450s and the hospital had
powerful patrons as well as a secure title. The Nevilles' power was
founded on such dubious expedients. There was a constant danger that in
unfavourable circumstances they might suffer crippling losses. To prevent
this they had always to be vigilant. They needed to retain power at almost
any price to stop their rivals from receiving a fair hearing. This necessity
may have determined their political alignment: in the 1450s Warwick
joined the duke of York when his rival the duke of Somerset was supreme
at court; the following decade, when his power was failing, the threat to his
estates may have influenced his retreat into opposition.

To accumulate these inheritances the Nevilles were ruthless to their
rivals, each a close relative. They thereby made enemies of natural
friends. In most instances their rivals behaved as badly: Westmorland,
Abergavenny, and the dowager-countess of Shrewsbury all resorted to
force. Perhaps they had no hope of fair consideration for their claims. The
Nevilles were exceptional in the extent of their self-help and their
willingness to act with calculated and cynical dishonesty. They were
outstanding in exploiting Henry VI's and, at first, Edward IV's weakness.
Perhaps as much as any other family they gave Henry VI's reign its
reputation for lawlessness.

What should be made of the conduct of Margaret Beaufort, who
deserves equal censure for her cynical pursuit of personal gain? After all
she too was a close kinswoman of the cardinal, she too was aware of his
pious intentions yet thwarted them, and her own charitable foundations
do not excuse the destruction of those that he had planned. Perhaps she
should not be remembered as 'Lady Margaret', the munificent benefactor
of education, but as the shrewd conspirator of 1483, as depicted by
Polydore Vergil?[28] As such machinations were still possible under Henry
VII, had his accession only altered the individuals who could benefit from
the illicit exercise of royal power? Or was its use now confined to royal
advantage, direct or indirect? In 1492 and later the king was Margaret
Beaufort's heir.

Finally, what does this investigation of the earldom of Salisbury suggest
about the creation of earls in 1337? Even when created, the six earls were
treated individually rather than as a group: they were endowed in at least
four different ways. It is apparent that as applied the entails governing
their endowment varied from case to case, even among the four earls who
died in the lifetime of Edward III. As donor he knew, if anyone did, what
he had originally intended. The reason for this, it is not surprising to learn,

---

[28] *Three Books of Polydore Vergil's English History*, ed H. Ellis (Camden Soc xxix, 1844), 191
sqq.

was that he and his successors were influenced on each occasion by the political balance of the moment. Short-term considerations were paramount.

21

Dynastic Change and Northern Society:
The Fourth Earl of Northumberland, 1470-89[1]

ON 28 APRIL 1489 HENRY PERCY, fourth Earl of Northumberland, was
murdered at South Kilvington near Thirsk (Yorks.). His death was an
incident in a rising that is normally dismissed as a protest against excessive taxation and which was quickly suppressed. This interpretation
derives from the near contemporary account of Polydore Vergil.[2] In 1964
it was challenged by Mr M. E. James, who argued instead that the Earl's
death was incited by Henry VII himself.[3]

Mr James did not consult the record of the oyer and terminer commission appointed to try the rebels.[4] This amply confirms the contemporary
view that the insurgents were 'naked men', 'a mayny of rude villayns'.[5]
Altogether sixty-six Yorkshiremen were indicted, sixty-two of whom
were yeomen and husbandmen from the countryside or artisans and
tradesmen from the towns. More noteworthy were Eli Casse and Thomas
Bullock, two of the four governors of Beverley, Thomas Wrangwish, an
alderman of York, and the knight John Egremont, but none of these had
rebelled by the Earl's death. Some contemporaries speculated whether a
great man or enemy of Henry VII was behind the rebellion.[6] Probably
they suspected that it was another in the chain of risings by Richard III's
northern supporters, but only five of those indicted can be connected

[1] This article is based on my 1971 Southampton Univ. M.A. thesis, 'The Career of Henry
Percy, 4th Earl of Northumberland (c. 1448–89)'. For advice and criticism at various stages I
am indebted to Mr T. B. Pugh and Dr R. A. Griffiths.
[2] *The Anglica Historica of Polydore Vergil*, ed. D. Hay (Camden Society, 3rd series,
LXXIV, 1955), p. 38.
[3] M. E. James, 'The Murder at Cocklodge', *Durham University Journal*, LVII (1964–5),
pp. 80–7.
[4] P(ublic) R(ecord) O(ffice), King's Bench, Ancient Indictments, K.B.9/381. This file is
the basis of this paragraph.
[5] *Paston Letters and Papers of the Fifteenth Century*, ed. N. Davis, 2 vols (Oxford, 1971–6),
II, p. 460; *The Reign of Henry VII from Contemporary Sources*, ed. A. F. Pollard (1913), I,
p. 74.
[6] *Calendar of State Papers . . . Venice*, ed. R. Brown (1864), I, p. 181; Vergil, *Anglica
Historica*, pp. 38–9.

with Richard[7] and of these three rebelled after 28 April and a fourth was acquitted. There seems no doubt that the Earl was murdered by men who were otherwise obscure.

Mr James presumed that Henry VII wanted a free hand in the North but had first to rid himself of the Earl. An earlier attempt in 1485 to manage without him by employing Lords Strange and FitzHugh had apparently been a failure and therefore a deterrent to further attempts. In 1489 the king had no ready-made agent among the northern magnates. He did not trust the Earl of Westmorland, formerly Lord Neville, or the Lords Scrope; Lord Roos was unfit for responsibility and Lords Dacre and Clifford had provoked riots;[8] Lords Strange, Ogle and Lumley were of purely local, rather than regional, importance; the Duke of Buckingham and Earl of Shrewsbury, respectively lords of Holderness and Sheffield, and Lord FitzHugh were minors; and Lord Latimer, who was potentially the outstanding northern magnate as heir to the Neville lordships of Penrith (Cumb.), Middleham and Sheriff Hutton (Yorks.), was ruled out by Henry's decision to keep them himself.[9] Henry therefore had to gamble and the man he chose, the Earl of Surrey, had only just emerged from the Tower and lacked northern connections. The omens were not good for his success. Moreover Mr James's argument presupposes that the Earl's death was predictable but in fact it was an immense surprise. When Northumberland confronted the rebels he did so in overwhelming force. No king could afford to provoke a rebellion, least of all Henry VII in the hostile North whence had come the army that nearly defeated him at Stoke in 1487.

The commons needed no prompting to kill the Earl, who had aroused their hostility by coercing them to pay taxes. The Earl had been forewarned of the danger of confrontation and was accompanied by his retinue, which was well-armed, probably outnumbered the rebels, and included barons, knights and gentlemen, some in his household and others in receipt of

---

[7] For Wrangwish, Egremont and Thomas Wade of Knaresborough, see *York Civic Records*, ed. A. Raine, 2 vols (Y(orkshire) A(rchaeological) S(ociety) R(ecord) S(eries), XCVIII, CIII, for 1939, 1941), I, p. 68; C(alendar of) P(atent) R(olls), 1476–85, pp. 198, 206, 428; *Rot(uli) Parl(iamentorum)*, VI, p. 545. Two others were from Sowerby and Thirkleby, where Richard had lands before his accession.

[8] R. L. Storey, *The Reign of Henry VII* (1968), p. 67; *C.P.R.* 1485–94, pp. 190, 216, 238, 273; G. E. C(okayne), *Complete Peerage of England etc.*, ed. H. V. Gibbs and others (12 vols, 2nd edn, 1910–59), XI, p. 106; *Select Cases in the Council of Henry VII*, ed. C. G. Bayne and W. H. Dunham (Selden Society, vol. LXXV, for 1956), p. 20.

[9] R. H. C. FitzHerbert, 'Original Pedigree of Tailboys and Neville', *The Genealogist*, new series, III (1886), p. 110; *Rot. Parl.*, VI, pp. 124–5, 275–8. I hope to discuss this more fully elsewhere.

fees.[10] He would have been safe in their company had they not deserted him. The poet John Skelton suspected that 'what kindeled the wild fyr that made al this smoke' was that the Earl's men 'were lynked with a double chaine, And held with the comones vnder a cloke'.[11] He implies that they were hostile to Henry VII, on whose behalf the Earl was acting, and that with sufficient backing they would also have rebelled. However none did join the commons, and Sir Robert Plumpton at least helped to suppress the rebellion.[12] Evidently the retainers' motives for deserting the Earl differed from the commons's reason for killing him. The contemporary author of the *Great Chronicle of London* bluntly remarked that Northumberland died because the commons bore him 'dedly malyce ffor the dysapoyntyng of kyng Rychard at Bosworth ffeeld'.[13] This was not, in fact, a strong motive in the rebellion but it may have influenced the Percy retainers. It may also be that the rift between the Earl and his retainers was connected with that between him and Sir John Egremont *alias* Percy, who was his closest adult male relative and whom he was in the process of disinheriting.[14] Such speculation indicates that the death of the Earl, but not the rebellion itself, was intimately linked with the relations of the Earl, other northerners and his retainers with Richard III, with Henry VII's policies towards the region and the Earl's role in formulating and executing them, and with the effect of these factors on his retinue. This article will examine each in turn.

I

In the mid-fifteenth century the leading northern families were the Percies and the junior line of the Nevilles. The latter had inherited the family's Yorkshire lands at the expense of their rivals, the earls of Westmorland of the senior line, who retained only those in Durham.[15] The two families were powerful both in Yorkshire and on the Borders. The Percies were supreme in the East and Middle Marches and in the

---

[10] *Plumpton Correspondence*, ed. T. Stapleton (Camden Society, IV, 1839), p. 61; Pollard, *Henry VII*, I, p. 75.

[11] Ibid.

[12] *Plumpton Corr.*, pp. 61, 62n.

[13] *The Great Chronicle of London*, ed. A. H. Thomas and I. D. Thornley (1938), p. 242.

[14] This is based on *Calendar of Inquisitions post mortem, Henry VII*, I, no. 741; P.R.O., King's Bench, Controlment Rolls, K.B. 29/94, Easter m. 24d; *Plumpton Corr.*, p. 74. For his doubtful legitimacy, see *Collins' Peerage of England*, ed. E. Brydges (1812), II, p. 281; C. H. Hartshorne, *Memoirs illustrative of the History and Antiquities of Northumberland* (1858), II, p. clvi; *Feet of Fines for Yorkshire for the Tudor Period*, I (Y.A.S.R.S., II, 1887), p. 4.

[15] R. L. Storey, *The End of the House of Lancaster* (1966), pp. 112–14.

West March the Nevilles were usually wardens. After their rebellions, defeats and forfeiture of 1403–8 the Percies had been restored but had still not fully recovered by 1461. In their rivalry the two families resorted to force. The Nevilles won, first, the private war in Yorkshire and Cumberland in 1452–5[16] and, later, the civil war of 1459–61. Most northern magnates were killed in the Lancastrian defeat at Towton and suffered forfeiture, among them the third Earl of Northumberland.

The Nevilles were granted most of the forfeitures, the Earl of Warwick receiving Percy and Clifford lands in Cumberland and Craven and his brother John the Percy estates in Northumberland with the title of earl.[17] They monopolised regional power and patronage. Some Percy retainers became their committed supporters[18] but others continued to resist them. Yorkshiremen's memories of the death-toll at Towton were still bitter in 1471,[19] when both Neville brothers were killed fighting against Edward IV.

In 1470, to counteract the effects of Warwick's coup the previous summer, King Edward restored the estates and earldom to the son of the last Percy Earl of Northumberland. Next year his own brother Richard, Duke of Gloucester was granted Warwick's northern estates, and his marriage soon after to Warwick's daughter strengthened his title[20] and placed him at the head of the Neville retainers. The Percy connection had been decimated in 1461, and in the following years it had been denied its traditional lordship and there had been no recruitment. Warwick's retainers had gained a Pyrrhic victory at Edgecote in 1469 and may have suffered further losses in 1470–1. Each, therefore, needed rebuilding and the Duke of Gloucester and restored Earl of Northumberland now sought new recruits. Northumberland retained Christopher Curwen of Workington and John Pennington of Muncaster (Cumb.) in 1470 and by Michaelmas 1470 had burdened his Northumberland estates with fees.[21]

[16] R. A. Griffiths, 'Local Rivalries and National Politics: The Percies, the Nevilles and the Duke of Exeter, 1452–5', *Speculum*, XLIII (1968), pp. 589–632.

[17] *C.P.R.*, 1461–7, pp. 186, 189, 332, 340–1, 434–5.

[18] Notably Sir John Mauleverer, W. C. Metcalfe, *Book of Knights Banneret, Knights of the Bath and Knights Bachelor* (1885), p. 2; *Calendar of Documents relating to Scotland, 1357–1509*, ed. J. Bain (Edinburgh, 1888), p. 408.

[19] C. D. Ross, *The Wars of the Roses* (1976), p. 77; *Historie of the Arrivall of Edward IV*, ed. J. Bruce (Camden Society, I, 1838), pp. 6–7.

[20] G.E.C. *Complete Peerage*, V, p. 741; *C.P.R.* 1467–77, pp. 260, 266; *Glamorgan County History*, III, ed. T. B. Pugh (Cardiff, 1971), p. 200.

[21] Carlisle County R.O., D/Lons. WO8, wrongly dated 1469 in F. W. Ragg, 'De Culwen', *Transactions of the Cumberland and Westmorland Antiquarian and Archaeological Society*, new series, XIV (1914), pp. 422–3; H(istorical) M(anuscripts) C(ommission), *10th Report*, IV, p. 228; *Percy Bailiffs' Rolls of the Fifteenth Century*, ed. J. C. Hodgson (Surtees Society, CXXXIV, for 1921), passim.

From his North Riding lordship of Middleham, Gloucester granted ten fees in 1471 and eighteen, altogether worth 210 marks, by Michaelmas 1474.[22] Even so, neither retinue changed in character. Many of those enlisted by the Earl were from families that had traditionally served his own, such as Curwen and Pennington, John Cartington, son of a retainer of the same name, and John Ilderton, whose kinsman Sir Thomas had fought beside the 3rd earl in 1460–1.[23] Among former retainers who renewed their bonds were Robert Thomlinson of Healaugh Park (Yorks.) and Gawen Lampleugh of Warkworth (Northum.), whose attainders of 1461–4 were still unreversed. Similarly, Gloucester's men bore names familiar among Neville retainers like Conyers and Metcalfe. In spite of their rebellions in 1469–71, those feed at Middleham in 1474 differed little from those feed there eight years earlier.[24] What concerned both magnates was loyalty to themselves, not the Crown, as this continuity of service shows.

Not all of those granted fees had longstanding ties with their new lords, for some had served proscribed noble houses and now Gloucester and Northumberland competed for their service. The Earl attracted Sir Lancelot Threlkeld, the son of a Neville retainer and second husband of Lady Clifford and de Vessy,[25] and William Rilston, executor of Lord de Vessy.[26] These may be isolated instances, for it is clear from his indenture with Gloucester in 1474 that he was on the defensive.[27] The last clause, which

---

[22] G. M. Coles, 'The Lordship of Middleham, especially in the Yorkist and Early Tudor period' (unpub. M.A. thesis, Liverpool Univ. 1961), appendix B, pp. 17–18b; C. S. Perceval, 'Notes on . . . Documents . . . of Sir John Lawson . . . Baronet', *Archaeologia*, XLVII (1882), p. 195.

[23] J. M. W. Bean, *The Estates of the Percy Family 1416–1537* (1958), p. 97; Hodgson, *Percy Bailiffs' Rolls*, pp. 6, 93; Metcalfe, *Book of Knights*, p. 2; *The Priory of Hexham*, ed. J. Raine, I (Surtees Society, XLIV, for 1863), p. ciii. For the next sentence, see *Rot. Parl.*, V, pp. 477–9, 511–12; Alnwick (Castle) MS. CVI/2c, p. 27; Petworth (House) MS. MD 9/7, rot. 7, m.1.

[24] Coles, thesis, appendix B, pp. 12–13, 17–18b.

[25] Cockermouth (Castle) MS. D/Lec. 29/8, m.8; G.E.C. *Complete Peerage*, III, p. 294; F. W. Ragg, 'An Indenture in English of 1431 between Richard Earl of Salisbury and Sir Henry Threlkeld', *C.W.2*, IX (1909), pp. 282–6. In 1472–3 he promised to move the late Lord Clifford's children to be 'lovyng and tendre' to William Rilston, T. D. Whittaker, *The History and Antiquities of the Deanery of Craven* (1805), pp. 322–3.

[26] Petworth MS. MD 9/8, i, f.19.

[27] W. H. Dunham, *Lord Hastings' Indentured Retainers 1461–83* (Transactions of the Connecticut Academy of Arts and Sciences, XXXIX, 1955), p. 140. This is the source of the next two paragraphs. Dunham's date of 1474 for the Nottingham meeting is unlikely as Northumberland was at Warkworth on 11 May 1474, Alnwick MS. CIII/4a, m.4d; see also CVI/2b, m.3d. It was probably in 1473, as in H.M.C. *6th Report*, I, pp. 223–4; E. B. De Fonblanque, *Annals of the House of Percy* (1887), I, p. 549.

was not reciprocal, provided that with one exception the Duke would retain none of his men. It is an indication of how Gloucester was influencing even Northumberland's principal retainers that this exception was John Widdrington of Chipchase (Northum.), already the Earl's master forester of Alnwick and shortly to be his undersheriff of Northumberland. In 1482 he served under the command of the Duke rather than the Earl.[28]

The indenture, dated 28 July 1474, is in three parts:

1. The Earl 'promits and grants unto the said duke to be his faithful servant . . . to do service unto the said duke at all times lawful and convenient when he thereunto by the said duke shall be lawfully required', saving his allegiance.
2. The Duke 'promits and grants unto the said earl to be his good and faithful lord at all times; and to sustain him in his right afore all other persons' . . .
3. The Duke promises 'that he shall not ask, challenge, nor claim any office or offices or fee that the said earl hath of the king's grant, or of any other person or persons, at the making of these presents . . . And also the said duke shall not accept nor retain into his service any servant or servants that was or at any time sith hath been, with the said earl retained of fee, clothing, or promise, according to the appointment taken betwixt the said duke and earl by the king's highness and the lords of his council at Nottingham the xiith day of May' in the 13th year (1473).

The royal council had tried to impose a settlement on the two lords. This had proved inadequate and the indenture represents a subsequent change. As the first two clauses are reciprocal and the mention of the Nottingham meeting follows the third clause in the same sentence, it seems that only the third clause survives from the council's award. It was in the royal interest to keep at peace those on whom local government and defence depended. The award was an attempt to safeguard this peace and protect the Earl against the Duke's encroachments. This attitude to his brother may seem strange in Edward IV and his council, but the Earl had powerful friends as the protegé of the Wydevilles, kinsfolk of the Queen. In 1468 he was ward of William, Lord Herbert, later 1st earl of Pembroke, the ally and in-law of the Wydevilles, and in 1469–70 representatives of both the Herberts and the Wydevilles stood surety for Northumberland with the King.[29] By Michaelmas 1472 Northumberland

---

[28] *List of Sheriffs* (P.R.O. Lists and Indexes, IX, 1963 edn), p. 98; Hodgson, *Percy Bailiffs' Rolls*, p. 6; see below, appendix.

[29] P.R.O. Special Collections, Ministers' Accounts, S.C. 6/1236/11, m.1; *Calendar of Close Rolls*, 1468–76, nos. 403–4. For the next sentence, see Hodgson, *Percy Bailiffs' Rolls*, pp. 59, 114.

had married Maud Herbert, sister of the 2nd earl of Pembroke, whose countess was the Queen's sister. That he was *persona grata* at court is shown by his election as a knight of the Garter in April 1474.

The first two clauses placed the Earl in a dependent position. Evidently he gave up his independence in return for the perpetuation of traditional Percy power, and Gloucester gave guarantees in return for the addition of the Earl and his retinue to his own affinity. The Duke received a massive augmentation of power. The Earl ended the erosion of his support and warded off the financial ruin likely to result from competition with one of greater resources and whose service offered greater access to royal patronage.

The agreement lacked detail and rested on the mutual interest of both parties. To P. M. Kendall, Gloucester, chief authority in the North, allowed the Earl a role in northern government out of his benevolent desire for harmony.[30] But he had no authority that would override the Earl's commission in the Marches, and he explicitly renounced any direct link with those who regarded the Earl as lord. This was the condominium detected by Miss Reid and Dr Brooks, who believed that the two magnates had separate spheres of influence.[31] Was the agreement observed, as Miss Reid supposed? If so, did it merely fix spheres of influence or could the Earl rely on the Duke as 'good lord' and the Duke on the Earl for military support? It is necessary first to discover whether they had different spheres of influence.

The Earl of Northumberland was unchallenged in Northumberland, where he continued to retain the leading gentry,[32] who deputised for him as warden, sheriff and constable of royal castles.[33] They dominated the county commissions of the peace[34] and, from 1478, those of north

[30] P. M. Kendall, *Richard III* (1955), pp. 130–1.

[31] R. R. Reid, *The King's Council in the North* (1921), pp. 43–4; F. W. Brooks, *York and the Council of the North* (Borthwick Papers, no. 5, 1954), p. 4. In what follows, for sheriffs see *List of Sheriffs*, passim; for M.P.s, *History of Parliament, 1439–1509*, ed. J. C. Wedgwood (2 vols, 1936–8); for J.P.s, *C.P.R.* 1467–77, pp. 610, 624, 634–5, 636–8.

[32] Cf. Hodgson, *Percy Bailiffs' Rolls*; Alnwick MSS. CVI/2c, CIII/4a.

[33] *York Memorandum Book 1388–1493*, ed. M. Sellers, II (Surtees Society, cxxv, for 1914), pp. 199–200; *C.P.R.* 1467–77, p. 258; R. Somerville, *History of the Duchy of Lancaster*, I (1953), pp. 524, 538.

[34] John Lilburne (see Hodgson, *Percy Bailiffs' Rolls*, p. 81), John Widdrington and John Cartington. John Haggerston probably shared the Percy allegiance of Thomas and Richard Haggerston, ibid., pp. 68, 93; Alnwick MS. CVI/2c, p. 45.

Durham too.[35] Three of the knights elected for the shire in 1472 and 1478 were his men.[36] With the recovery of Berwick and his appointment as captain in 1483,[37] the Earl acquired another key office which carried with it substantial wages and the gift of 600 paid places in the garrison. Gloucester intruded north of the Tyne only in the disputed liberty of Tynemouth.[38]

In the West March almost a whole generation of Percy retainers passed away in 1454–79 and only three out of forty-three ministers and a mere two annuitants survived. Offices were filled, but the number of annuities fell to seven. Of these, two were granted by 1454, two in 1470 and at most three in 1471–9.[39] The Earl could afford more but he granted them only in 1470 and from 1483. The absence of new fees was a deliberate act of restraint presumably connected with the 1474 indenture. The West March was to be Gloucester's preserve. If Gloucester's estate accounts had survived, one would have expected to find that most of his retainers had served his Neville predecessors. As warden of the West March and sheriff of Cumberland, Gloucester monopolised royal offices. He employed as his lieutenant-wardens Humphrey, Lord Dacre of Gilsland and Sir William Parre,[40] himself sheriff of Westmorland: each carried weight locally. At least four of the ten known knights of the shire for Cumberland and Westmorland in 1472–83 were his men;[41] none served the Earl. In 1483 the elevation of Cumberland into a palatinate for the Duke[42] threatened to subordinate the Percies to his heirs for ever.

However, it was on his lordships in north Yorkshire and south Durham that Gloucester's power was based. Here the Earl was no rival. In 1476 the Duchess of Gloucester was admitted to the 'sisterhood' of Durham

[35] *35th Report of the Deputy Keeper of the Public Record Office* (1874), pp. 97, 143. Roger Heron, sheriff, escheator, steward and constable until 1481–2, was a Percy retainer, ibid., pp. 100, 141; Hodgson, *Percy Bailiffs' Rolls*, p. 86.

[36] Robert Collingwood (see Hodgson, *Percy Bailiffs' Rolls*, pp. 85–6), Ralph Hotham (see *York Memorandum Book*, II, pp. 199–200) and John Cartington.

[37] *Grants of King Edward the Fifth*, ed. J. G. Nichols (Camden Society, LX, 1854), pp. 20–3.

[38] *A History of Northumberland*, ed. E. Bateson and others (15 vols, Newcastle, 1893–1940), VIII, pp. 105–6.

[39] Cf. Cockermouth MSS. D/Lec. 29/3,/4,/5,/6. For 1470 see above, for 1483 see below.

[40] *Rotuli Scotiae* (1819), II, p. 452; *York Memorandum Book*, II, p. 217; P.R.O. Exchequer, Warrants for Issue, E.404/75/3/63, /76/1/86.

[41] James Moresby, Sir William Parre and Sir William Redmayne, P.R.O. Exchequer, Issue Rolls, E.401/930, m.11; *Extracts from the Municipal Records of the City of York*, ed. R. Davies (1843), pp. 62–3. John Parre and Edward Redmayne probably shared their brothers' allegiance.

[42] *Rot. Parl.*, VI, pp. 204–5.

cathedral priory and in 1475–6 the prior sued for the Duke's intercession. It was needed outside the county,[43] not within, for, as the prior assured Bishop Dudley in 1476, by

cherishyng and kepyng in of the love of my lordes Westmerland & [his heir] Nevyll, & such as belongith theim, your lordship hath doe, and doth full notably & full worshipfully . . . for and your lordship and thei stand as one, ye may reule & guyde all othre that inhabits the cuntre.

Except in the episcopate of Bishop Robert Neville (d. 1457), the senior Neville line dominated the county.[44] After a decade of self-effacement, Westmorland and his nephew Lord Neville feature on commissions from 1470 onwards and in 1476 the latter became the bishop's steward.[45] As heir of the senior line, Neville was reconciled with Gloucester, the heir of the junior line, by 1477 and entered his service.[46] The Duke also retained Sir George Lumley, heir of the other leading Durham magnate Lord Lumley, and from 1470 sheriff of the county. Gloucester and his retainers Miles and Thomas Metcalfe and John Vavasour were added to commissions after Bishop Dudley's appointment in 1476.[47] It is a sign of the Duke's growing power that in 1477 Gerard Salvin petitioned him not only for a fee but for redress of grievances.[48]

Miss Reid believed that similar spheres in Yorkshire emerge in the composition of commissions, which the Duke and Earl certainly could influence.[49] Neither had as much land in the West Riding as the duchy of

---

[43] *Historiae Dunelmensis Scriptores Tres*, ed. J. Raine (Surtees Society, ix, for 1839), pp. cclvi–ix. For what follows see ibid., p. ccclix.

[44] This is not brought out in M. Reiss, 'A Power in the North? The Percies in the Fifteenth Century', *Historical Journal*, xix (1976), p. 504. Bishop Neville, Lords Salisbury, Warwick, Fauconberg, Latimer, Abergavenny, Montagu and Sir Thomas Neville were of the cadet branch, John, Lord Neville of the senior line, see R. L. Storey, 'The north of England', *Fifteenth-century England, 1399–1509: Studies in politics and society*, ed. S. B. Chrimes, C. D. Ross and R. A. Griffiths (Manchester, 1972), pp. 138–9.

[45] P.R.O. Durham, Cursitors' Records, DURH 3/49/84.

[46] P.R.O. Common Pleas, Feet of Fines, C.P.25(1)/281/164/32; *The Paston Letters, 1422–1509*, ed. J. Gairdner (1904), vi, pp. 71–2.

[47] *35th Deputy Keeper's Report*, pp. 101, 138; Wedgwood, *Hist. Parlt. Biographies*, p. 562; Raine, *Hist. Dunelm.*, p. ccclx; Somerville, *Duchy*, i, pp. 422, 426; Coles, thesis, appendix B, p. 18.

[48] R. Surtees, *History and Antiquities of the County Palatine of Durham* (1840), iv, pp. 114–15.

[49] *Plumpton Corr.*, p. 33. As Miss Reid wrongly believed that the Earl did not sit in the West Riding or the Duke in the East Riding (Reid, *Council*, pp. 43–4), the following analysis is based on commissions of the peace for 1475.

Lancaster and neither dominated the bench.[50] The Earl had most land in the East Riding, where most justices were his men,[51] and most of those in the North Riding served Gloucester,[52] who held most land there. He was also steward of Ripon and a retainer was understeward of Pickering honour.[53] That commissions reflect the actual balance of power need not, by itself, indicate co-operation. Some dependants of each magnate sat on every commission and the Riding boundaries were no bar to the recruitment of gentry, at least by the Earl. In 1471–9 annuities on eight of his scattered Yorkshire manors increased in number from three to twenty-six,[54] several of the recipients being heads of county families. That the 1474 agreement had not broken down but was being flexibly observed emerges from the shire elections of 1477, at which a retainer of each was returned.[55] This must have been an agreed arrangement, for the Duke was maximising his parliamentary representation in 1477 but nevertheless allowed his town of Scarborough to return two Percy retainers.[56] A similar compromise may explain why, of nine sheriffs pricked in 1474–83, three served the Earl, four the Duke, and two of the Earl's men were pricked as late as 1480 and 1482.[57] York, focus of Percy-Neville rivalry in

[50] Lord Greystoke, Sir John Pilkington, Sir James Harrington and William Hopton served the Duke, Davies, *York Recs.*, p. 41; *Test(amenta) Ebor(acensia)*, iii (Surtees Society, xlv, for 1864), pp. 239–41; Reid, *Council*, p. 58n; P.R.O. Chancery, Warrants for the Great Seal, C.81/1639/20. Sir William Plumpton, Sir William Gascoigne and Guy Fairfax were Percy retainers, *Plumpton Corr.*, pp. 32–4; *Test. Ebor.*, iii, p. 306. The lawyer Thomas Middleton served both, Petworth MS. MD 9/8, ii, f. 29; P.R.O. C.P.25(1)/281/164/32.

[51] e.g. Henry Thwaites, Sir Robert Constable and William Eland, Bean, *Estates*, pp. 100–1, 134n; *Cal. Inq. p.m. Henry VII*, i, no. 542; Petworth MS. MD 9/8, i, f.10v. John Vavasour served Gloucester.

[52] e.g. Sir John Conyers, Sir Edmund Hastings, Richard Pigot, Miles Metcalfe, Coles, thesis, appx. B, p. 18b; Davies, *York Recs.*, p. 41; Somerville, *Duchy*, i, p. 426. Sir William Eure and Sir John Pickering were Northumberland's councillors, Petworth MS. MD 9/9, m.1; Alnwick MS. CVI/2c, pp. 44, 157; Davies, *York Recs.*, pp. 62–3.

[53] P.R.O. C.81/840/3511; Somerville, *Duchy*, i, p. 534.

[54] Cf. Petworth MSS. MD 9/7, /8.

[55] Sir John Pilkington served the Duke and Sir Robert Constable the Earl. In 1472 Pilkington was elected with Sir Hugh Hastings, probably at that date Gloucester's man.

[56] M. A. Hicks, 'The Career of George Plantagenet, Duke of Clarence (1449–78)' (unpub. D.Phil. thesis, Oxford Univ., 1974), pp. 178–81, 186–7, table IX(iv); the M.P.s were Edmund Thwaites (see *Test. Ebor.*, iii, p. 308) and Ralph Hotham.

[57] Sir John Conyers, Sir James Harrington and Sir Edmund Hastings (twice) served the Duke, Sir William Eure, Sir Robert Constable and the latter's son Marmaduke served the Earl. In contrast a ducal retainer, Sir Ralph Ashton, was sheriff in 1471–3, P.R.O. C.81/1314/9.

the fourteen-fifties, was a potential source of friction, but the city council was able to look to Gloucester as 'good lord' while maintaining friendly relations with Northumberland,[58] who studiously avoided involvement there. Their relations were not visibly affected by the Duke's accumulation of further lordships. Their intercourse was more subtle than the commissions imply and was marked by give and take on both sides.

In their own 'countries' each was self-sufficient, raiding independently into Scotland from their wardenries: it was only in 1480 that Gloucester had overall authority as king's lieutenant.[59] Where they were rivals, the Earl gave way, but the two men co-operated on certain issues, such as fishgarths.[60] The Duke seems to have kept his promise to retain no Percy retainers and the numerous opportunities for friction seem to have been avoided. There was a particular danger that Duke and Earl might be drawn into disputes between their retainers by appeals to their 'good lordship'. To avoid this they encouraged arbitration, a common means for settling differences *within* retinues, and co-operated personally in making awards.[61] No riots between their retainers were uncovered by the Yorkshire oyer and terminer commission of 1478.[62]

The will to overcome such practical obstacles was essential. Although Professor Kendall alleged that Gloucester 'never touched Henry Percy's heart', their joint exploitation of certain mines points to amicable relations and, as Kendall himself observed, they worked in 'apparent harmony' in the Scottish war of 1480–83.[63] A truer guide to their relationship is the Earl's part in Gloucester's usurpation of the throne in 1483. Northumberland was the commander of the northern army that overawed London and he presided over the trial and execution of Earl Ryvers, Sir Richard Grey and Thomas Vaughan,[64] an act which committed him to Richard against Edward V's maternal relations. Surely he would not have dared undertake such a role had he not been aware of, and committed to, Gloucester's impending usurpation? It was not without risk that Richard gave him command of his northern followers[65] but his confidence was

---

[58] e.g. Davies, *York Recs.*, pp. 39, 73; *York Civic Recs.*, I, pp. 28–31. The Earl's supporters there included Guy Fairfax, recorder, and Alderman John Marshall, ibid., I, pp. 12, 28.

[59] *Northumberland County Hist.*, V, p. 50; *Accounts of the Lord High Treasurer of Scotland*, I, ed. T. Dickson (Edinburgh, 1877), p. 49; *C.P.R.* 1476–85, p. 205; *Rot. Scot.*, II, p. 458.

[60] Davies, *York Recs.*, pp. 61–2; *C.P.R.* 1467–77, p. 572.

[61] *Plumpton Corr.*, p. lxxxix; *Calendar of Close Rolls* 1468–76, no. 1317.

[62] P.R.O. King's Bench, Ancient Indictments, K.B.9/349.

[63] Kendall, *Richard III*, pp. 130, 138; *C.P.R.* 1467–77, pp. 464, 505–6, 513.

[64] J. Rossus, *Historia regum angliae*, ed. T. Hearne (Oxford, 1716), p. 213.

[65] *York Civic Recs.*, I, p. 74; Gairdner, *Paston Letters*, VI, pp. 71–2.

rewarded by Northumberland's faithfulness. Their indenture enshrined a living and lasting tie rather than a purely formal one.

By 1483 the Duke's retinue included not only Northumberland but also Lords Neville, Greystoke, Dacre of Gilsland, probably Scrope of Masham and, indirectly, Scrope of Bolton.[66] Through them Yorkshire and the four most northern counties followed him and, as Richard III, he relied on northerners to quell rebellion and administer distant parts of the realm on his behalf. In return, he distributed the forfeited possessions of his foes to individuals[67] among them and bestowed unprecedented privileges on local corporations: Hull, Beverley, York and Newcastle received financial concessions, Scarborough became a county and Pontefract a borough.[68] The Earl of Northumberland himself benefited greatly but nevertheless failed to support Richard at Bosworth.[69] This was rightly regarded by contemporaries as a betrayal.

II

The Earl of Northumberland may have made a private arrangement with Henry VII. Polydore Vergil records that Henry considered marrying a sister of William (not Walter) Herbert, Earl of Huntingdon and sought the aid of Northumberland, the latter's brother-in-law.[70] Percy and Tudor were together in the Herbert household at Raglan in the fourteen-sixties,[71] and the former married the latter's intended bride. Northumberland was still friendly with the Herberts in January 1485.[72] The relations of Northumberland with the Herberts were not soured by his execution of Ryvers and Grey, who had become enemies of the Herberts by 1479 when

[66] For Scrope of Masham, see H.M.C. *9th Report*, I, p. 411. Lord Scrope of Bolton and his son Henry, who had married Elizabeth Percy, were the Earl's feed men, Petworth MS. MD 9/8, i, f.2v; *Test. Ebor.*, III, p. 308.

[67] *Rerum Anglicarum Scriptorum Veterum*, I, ed. W. Fulman (Oxford, 1684), p. 572. This is confirmed from record sources by Kendall, *Richard III*, p. 317; A. J. Pollard, 'The tyranny of Richard III', *Journal of Medieval History*, III (1977), pp. 147–66.

[68] *York Civic Recs.*, I, pp. 101 sqq; *Calendar of Charter Rolls*, 1427–1516, pp. 262–5; *C.P.R.* 1476–85, pp. 415, 455, 484, 509; Somerville, *Duchy*, I, p. 149n; *The History of Scarborough*, ed. A. Rowntree (1931), p. 134.

[69] Fulman, op. cit., I, p. 574; *Rot. Scot.*, II, pp. 463–4; *C.P.R.* 1476–85, pp. 367, 409; Bean, *Estates*, p. 122; *Rot. Parl.*, VI, pp. 252–4.

[70] *Three Books of Polydore Vergil's English History*, ed. H. Ellis (Camden Society, XXIX, 1844), p. 215. There was an unmarried sister Catherine, later countess of Kent.

[71] P.R.O. S.C. 6/1236/11, m.1; Westminster Abbey MS. 5472, ff. 8v, 38, 41v sqq.

[72] When Cecily Herbert and Sir John Greystoke were licensed to be married in the Earl's chapel at Wressle by the Earl's chaplain William Rowkshaw or someone else deputed by him, *Test. Ebor.*, III, p. 349.

the Prince of Wales's council, which they dominated, received the lordship of Pembroke which William Herbert was forced to exchange for lands elsewhere.[73] By then the Countess Mary Wydeville may already have been dead: she had certainly died by 1484, when her erstwhile husband agreed to marry Richard III's illegitimate daughter Katherine. The Herbert-Percy friendship need not have favoured Henry, who contemplated a Herbert match only when it seemed that Richard would marry Elizabeth of York, a scheme scotched in 1484.[74] Admittedly Jean Molinet thought that the Earl 'avoit entendement aveuc le comte de Ricemont' and a confused foreigner thought that he intervened directly on Henry's side,[75] but neither seems likely, as the Earl was arrested after Bosworth. Huntingdon supported Richard[76] and his satellite, Lord Ferrers of Chartley, was killed fighting against Henry at Bosworth.

Another reason must therefore be sought for Northumberland's treachery. Had he quarrelled with Richard, in public or private, it would surely have been known and Richard would not have trusted him. It is certain that the Earl expected to benefit from Richard's defeat. How had their interests come into conflict?

It is unlikely that Northumberland was grateful to Richard for his grants. While prestigious, the great chamberlainship of England[77] was an empty title, and the Earl may have regarded livery of his de Brian inheritance as no more than his due. That he cared little for the lordship of Holderness emerges from his failure to add it to the comital estates; instead, it was entailed to a younger son and the latter's male heirs.[78] Richard's accession involved little practical change in the North, where the balance of the Yorkshire commissions was unaffected, and the Earl's authority still applied only to the East and Middle Marches, in spite of his grander title of warden-general.[79] In the West March, Lord Dacre as lieutenant possessed the authority of warden, Richard's favourite Sir Richard Ratcliffe was sheriff of Westmorland and not one of the five great

---

[73] T. B. Pugh, 'The magnates, knights and gentry', Chrimes, *15th-cent. Eng.*, p. 111. It was then that the earldom of Pembroke was exchanged for Huntingdon. For the next sentence see C. A. Halsted, *Richard III as Duke of Gloucester and King of England* (1844), II, pp. 569–70.

[74] Fulman, op. cit., I, p. 572; Vergil, *English History*, p. 215.

[75] J. Molinet, *Chroniques 1476–1506*, ed. G. Douttrepont and O. Jadogne (Brussels, 1935), I, p. 435; A. Goodman and A. Mackay, 'A Castilian Report on English Affairs, 1486', *English Historical Review*, LXXXVIII (1973), pp. 92–9.

[76] Vergil, *English History*, ed. Ellis, pp. 216–17.

[77] *C.P.R.* 1476–85, p. 367.

[78] Ibid., p. 409.

[79] Ibid., pp. 578–80; *Rot. Scot.*, II, 463–4.

commissioners was a Percy retainer.[80] Richard kept up his retinue throughout his former 'country', and instead of succeeding to his domin- ance the Earl was still restricted to the East Riding and Eastern Marches.

Richard's accession to the throne made the 1474 indenture out of date. Edward IV had seldom intervened in the North, delegating responsibility to successive wardens; Richard, on the other hand, was well informed and concerned. The council[81] that he established in Yorkshire around his sons and nephews, the Earls of Warwick and Lincoln, exercised equitable jurisdiction previously performed by himself as duke. Like the king's council itself, it had power of *subpoena*, and all Yorkshiremen were expected to be attendant upon it. Its working in practice is obscure but in 1484, after a riot, the city of York ignored Northumberland and applied instead to Lincoln and the council.[82] The council represented Richard, and Richard ruled through his retinue. In 1484, for instance, the conser- vators of the Scottish treaty came from all over the North and numbered most of the regional nobility: four were Percy adherents and the majority of the remaining fifteen had been Richard's men when he was Duke of Gloucester.[83] As king, Richard could intervene throughout the North and not just in the sphere assigned him as Duke of Gloucester. As warden, the Earl executed policies of which, in at least one instance, he cannot have approved: Dunbar was excluded from the Scottish treaty and the Earl himself remained responsible for its defence until its capture by the Scots.[84]

The indenture of 1474 no longer restrained Richard from recruiting Percy retainers. Kings employed whomever they chose. In theory all subjects owed them exclusive service, but in practice this rarely clashed with the claims of magnates. Richard could still offer effective lordship in the North and he placed a high value on the service of northerners. Five of those Percy retainers knighted in 1481–2 received grants from the King and they included some of those closest to the Earl: his brother-in-law, Sir William Gascoigne was feed; one cousin was granted lands in Devon and

[80] Reid, *Council*, p. 60; *List of Sheriffs*, p. 151; *Foedera, Conventiones et cujuscunque Acta Publica*, ed. T. Rymer (20 vols, 1727–35), xii, p. 247.

[81] For this paragraph see *Letters and Papers illustrative of the reigns of Richard III and Henry VII*, ed. J. Gairdner, i (Rolls Series, 1861), pp. 56–9; Reid, *Council*, pp. 59–70.

[82] *York Civic Recs.*, i, 103–4.

[83] Rymer, *Foedera*, xii, p. 241. The Percy men were the Earl, Lord Scrope of Bolton, Eure and Constable.

[84] Rymer, *Foedera*, xii, pp. 236–40. It fell within the East March. The Earl's servant Thomas Elrington was responsible for supplying it, B.L.Harl. MS. 433, ff. 156v, 182v; Hodgson, *Percy Bailiffs' Rolls*, p. 90.

another an annuity.[85] A king's normal patronage exceeded that of any subject and, in addition, Richard had forfeitures at his disposal. He was lavish with his gifts and concentrated them on northerners, many of whom benefited substantially. Such grants were not sinecures, for Richard demanded service. Many Percy clients were among those employed in distant parts of England. Sir Christopher Ward, who became master of the hart hounds, was steward of Whitley and Worplesdon (Surr.), sheriff of Surrey and Sussex, and commissioner in Surrey and Hampshire.[86] Sir Marmaduke Constable evidently acted as steward of Tonbridge in Kent and may even have become a royal councillor. In such cases, service was practical and genuine. At first, Northumberland may have welcomed the advancement of his retainers as a guarantee of his own future interest and a sign of his good lordship, but later he may have wondered where their primary lordship lay. He could not offer comparable rewards and was threatened therefore with an erosion of loyalty.

It is unlikely that Richard consciously attacked the Earl or was aware of the latter's unease. Probably he felt that he was continuing their previous arrangement, but he and his northern council represented immediate authority even in the Earl's country which, because institutionalized, might have become permanent. Such factors help explain why the Earl deserted King Richard and dared contemplate dynastic change even without personal guarantees.

Northumberland was not attainted in 1485 but he was imprisoned and was neither summoned to parliament nor required to swear allegiance.[87] His release under surety by 6 December and subsequent restoration to many offices[88] immediately preceded his departure northwards, where his services were needed. Whatever their former relations, the Earl had little influence with Henry Tudor and at court he lacked political allies. Apart from breaking with the Wydevilles in 1483, he had helped suppress a rising of their supporters[89] known as Buckingham's rebellion. It was these rebels and former Lancastrians, with whom he no longer had any ties, who dominated the Tudor court. Two of these were Thomas Butler, Earl of Ormond, the queen's chamberlain, and Sir Edward Poynings,

---

[85] See appendix below; B.L.Harl. MS. 433, ff. 67v, 71v, 174.

[86] Ibid., ff. 40v, 49v; *C.P.R.* 1476–85, pp. 397, 399; see appendix below. For the next sentence, see B. P. Wolffe, *The Crown Lands 1461–1536* (1970), p. 126; *Bishop Percy's Folio MS.*, ed. J. W. Hales and F. J. Furnivall (1868), III, p. 246.

[87] Wedgwood, *Hist. Parlt. Register*, p. 501n; Pollard, *Henry VII*, I, pp. 26–8.

[88] *Materials for a History of Henry VII*, ed. W. Campbell, I (Rolls Series, 1873), p. 199; Somerville, *Duchy*, I, p. 524; *Rot. Scot.*, II, pp. 470–1; *C.P.R.* 1485–94, pp. 120, 138, 201.

[89] He was with Richard III 19 Oct.–26 Nov. 1483, Rymer, *Foedera*, XII, p. 203.

from 1494 deputy of Ireland. They had rival claims to the de Brian inheritance, which the Earl had entered as rightful heir in 1484–5. On Henry's accession the issue was reopened and in October 1488, under a new settlement, Northumberland retained only a quarter, equal shares passing to Ormond, Poynings and a fourth claimant.[90] To those at court the result was predictable: John Cheyne took Ormond's side against Northumberland, risking thereby a fee which he clearly expected Ormond to compensate.[91] Since Cheyne was created K.G. in 1486 and a baron in 1487, his action indicates the relative influence of the two earls. Northumberland was not even a royal councillor and seems to have visited London only twice, in November 1487 and in the winter of 1488–9.[92] An awareness of his political impotence probably explains his grant of fees to Lord Daubeney, the king's chamberlain, in 1489, to Sir Reginald Bray in 1487 and to the earl of Arundel, a king's councillor, in 1488–9.[93]

Initially Henry ruled the North without the Earl, but he found few men prominent locally on whom he could rely. One such was his mother's stepson, George, Lord Strange, whom he made warden of the Marches and commander against the Scots.[94] In Yorkshire, Nottinghamshire, and the Border counties, there were sixteen commissioners of array, among them former supporters of Richard III whose oaths of allegiance the new steward of Middleham, Lord FitzHugh, was authorized to receive.[95] Strange and FitzHugh were opposed by English rebels and, at the latters' invitation, by the King of Scots, who besieged Berwick.[96] Although the town was relieved, resistance continued west of the Pennines. Neither FitzHugh nor Strange were Border magnates or outstanding landowners in Yorkshire. It was this local frailty that prompted the recall of Northumberland.

The Earl became warden of the East and Middle Marches, but the youthful Thomas, Lord Dacre succeeded his father as lieutenant in the

---

[90] Bean, *Estates*, pp. 118, 122.

[91] P.R.O. Special Collections, Ancient Correspondence, S.C. 1/51/148.

[92] J. Leland, *De rebus britannicis collectanea*, ed. T. Hearne (Oxford, 1774), IV, p. 229; *Northumberland County Hist.*, V, p. 51; Davis, *Paston Letters*, I, p. 668. Even his indentures as warden were sent to him for sealing, P.R.O. Warrants for the Privy Seal, Series 2, P.S.O. 2/2 (memo. 24 Nov. 1486).

[93] Bean, *Estates*, pp. 131n, 132n; *Cal. Inq. p.m. Henry VII*, I, no. 548.

[94] *C.P.R.* 1485–94, p. 40; he also became constable of Knaresborough, P.R.O. Duchy of Lancaster, Coucher Books, D.L. 42/21, f. 63.

[95] *C.P.R.* 1485–94, pp. 39–40.

[96] P.R.O. Duchy of Lancaster, Chancery Rolls, D.L. 37/62, m. 1; Davis, *Paston Letters*, II, pp. 445–6; H.M.C. 12 *Rutland*, I, p. 8.

west.[97] While employing experience from previous reigns, Henry devised his own policy towards the Borders. To each warden was customarily delegated custody of the Marches for long terms at wages sufficient to finance standing forces, together with command of a fortified town, Carlisle in the west and (from 1483) Berwick in the east. This gave the King only indirect control and was expensive. Henry VI had experimented with 'cut price wardens' and Edward IV had reduced peacetime emoluments: those of the eastern warden fell in stages from £3,000 (1463) to £1,000 (1477), which was still more than the normal peacetime expenses of office.[98] The cost of garrisons was harder to reduce but even so expenditure at Carlisle fell from 1,000 marks in 1471 to 300 marks by 1488, when two-thirds was assigned from the lordship of Penrith. From 1488 Berwick, too, was financed exclusively from northern estates.[99] In an effort to make the West March self-supporting, Edward IV had resigned Cumberland, his revenues there and the office of warden to Gloucester, but Henry characteristically wanted greater control. In 1488 Berwick was removed from the Earl's custody and given a separate governor on the pattern of Carlisle.[100] Henry also followed Richard's practice of appointing warden and lieutenant annually.[101] These measures reduced the warden's rôle and, although Henry may not have realized it, were steps towards rule of the Marches by royal officials rather than local magnates. The intractable problems of the Marches persisted, however, and lesser men lacked the military might that made the great such attractive wardens. They could not, by themselves, resist Scottish incursions and their indentures provided for speedy reinforcement. In practice, this could not be achieved without local support, and so Henry arranged with the Earl of Northumberland and Bishop of Durham that on the outbreak of war they would put 200 and 300 men respectively into Berwick. This compared with 1,000 required of the Earl as captain in

[97] *Rot. Scot.* II, p. 471. Unless otherwise stated, for this paragraph see R. L. Storey, 'The Wardens of the Marches of England towards Scotland, 1377–1489', *E.H.R.*, LXXII (1957), pp. 593–615.

[98] *C.P.R.* 1476–85, p. 38; *Cal. Docs. Scotl.*, 1357–1509, p. 281. Cf. P.R.O. Exchequer, Warrants for Issue, E.404/80/4 Hen. VII/145.

[99] Campbell, *Materials*, II (1877), p. 390; E.404/80/4 Hen. VII/145; D.L.37/47A/42; *Rot. Parl.*, VI, p. 394.

[100] *Rot. Parl.*, VI, p. 394; *Rot. Scot.*, II, pp. 483–4. Carlisle had a separate constable by 1485, P.R.O. E.404/79/I/12.

[101] *Rot. Scot.*, II, pp. 470–2, 479, 484–6.

1483.[102] One cannot tell whether Henry planned to dispense with the Percies, as he later did,[103] but Northumberland cannot have felt secure.

In 1486, 1487 and 1489[104] the Earl proved the King's most valuable northern agent at moments of crisis, and at other times too his authority was greater, if the records of York are a reliable guide. Whenever there was trouble, the city turned to him, and in response he arranged arbitration between it and the cathedral chapter or a private citizen. Once he charged the mayor 'on the King our soverain lords behalf . . . and on myne', but it was the King, not the Earl, who had the final say. Henry employed other agents, such as his councillor Sir Richard Tunstall, steward of Pontefract. Although without local rivals, the Earl is unlikely to have swayed royal policy. Because its recorder was too intimately connected with Richard III, the city of York was compelled to replace him. Henry nominated Richard Green, who enjoyed the Earl's favour, but then preferred Thomas Middleton, enabling the city to play one off against the other and appoint John Vavasour. Each was suitable, but King and Earl were at cross purposes. On encountering resistance to a tax in 1489, the Earl 'informed the king in writing that the people refused to pay the stipulated sum'.[105] This suggests that he was against extreme measures, but Henry directed him to use whatever means were necessary. Northumberland was implementing a policy that he did not support.

This was a matter of significance because the North suffered under Henry's early policy. To a certain extent, it was inevitable as he swept away the legacy of Richard III. Richard's patronage had mainly benefited northerners, who now lost their grants,[106] and the northern towns, which lost their concessions and charters.[107] Many northerners had been attainted for supporting the *de facto* king in 1485 and others suffered in 1487.[108] Richard's attainder was made the pretext to seize the Neville inheritance, the largest estate in Yorkshire, to the loss of the heir. Such grievances were fuel for opposition and demonstrations of support for Richard's heir. Henry's policies towards sanctuaries and taxation were of general

[102] *Select Cases in the Council of Henry VII*, p. 16; Nichols, *Grants of Edward V*, p. 22.
[103] M. E. James, *The Tudor Magnate and the Tudor State* (Borthwick Papers, no. 30, 1966).
[104] Fulman, op. cit., I, p. 582; *York Civic Recs.*, II, pp. 22–3; Vergil, *Anglica Historica*, p. 38. For what follows see *York Civic Recs.*, I, II, passim.
[105] Vergil, *Anglica Historica*, p. 38. The version in the footnote is much stronger.
[106] e.g. only four of twenty-eight local ministers of Knaresborough honour in 1484 remained in 1485–6, P.R.O. Duchy of Lancaster, Ministers' Accounts, D.L.29/482/7778, /7780.
[107] e.g. Somerville, *Duchy*, I, p. 41n; Rowntree, *Scarborough*, p. 134.
[108] *Rot. Parl.*, VI, pp. 275–8, 397–400.

application, but were felt most keenly north of Trent,[109] where he would brook no opposition. He could be moderate and lenient, granting general pardons to such rebels as submitted,[110] but this was not common. In 1485 it was on his personal insistence that the act of attainder was passed and in 1486, before his progress northwards, it was said that 'he purposes to doe execution quickly ther on such as have offended agaynst him'.[111] Such an attitude was bound to stiffen resistance. As royal policies appeared so hostile, Northumberland intensified his own unpopularity as Richard's betrayer by implementing them. He was murdered in the King's quarrel because the people saw him as 'author of their wrongs'.[112]

III

Richard's northern retainers were responsible for the disorder of the late fourteen-eighties. Their loyalty was due first to Richard's queen as Warwick's heir.[113] After her death in 1485 Richard had only a life interest in the Neville estates but by then he had inspired in them a devotion transcending the 'bastard feudal' bond. Not only did they fight for him, but many seem to have wanted the accession of his heir, who was normally considered to be the Earl of Lincoln. Of course, many of his former intimates accepted Henry VII, but others resisted, sought foreign help and repeatedly rebelled. Resistance was most marked on Richard's northern estates in Cumberland and around Middleham, but was not confined there. York accepted Henry, but was disobedient and divided in allegiance in 1489.[114] It was in an inn there bearing Richard's cognisance that conspirators gathered in 1487. They thought, correctly, that Lincoln 'had many good frendes in this cuntree' and that 'right good gentelmen shall take my Lordes parte'.[115] In 1485 rebels were associated with Robin of Redesdale, the figurehead of Warwick's rebellions in 1469, who re-appeared in Viscount Lovell's insurrection around Ripon and Middleham in 1486.[116] Richard's retainer Sir Thomas Mauleverer was not involved, but in November he was pardoned with others associated with Middle-

---

[109] See above; Davis, *Paston Letters*, I, p. 659.
[110] Campbell, *Materials*, I, pp. 512–13, 540–1.
[111] *Plumpton Corr.*, pp. 49, 50.
[112] Vergil, *Anglica Historica*, p. 39.
[113] Fulman, op. cit., I, p. 572.
[114] P.R.O. K.B. 9/381; *York Civic Recs.*, II, pp. 43, 47.
[115] Ibid., II, p. 4.
[116] H.M.C. 12 *Rutland*, I, p. 8; C. D. Ross, *Edward IV* (1974), pp. 119–20, 126 sqq; *York Civic Recs.*, II, p. 3.

ham, and early next year he was plotting with Lincoln.[117] During Lambert Simnel's invasion, which ended at Stoke on 16 June 1487, Lincoln was joined by several of Richard's retainers.[118] On 8 June he was at Masham, and five days later Lords Scrope of Bolton and Masham attacked York, thereby distracting Northumberland from his march southwards.[119] West of the Pennines such gentry as Sir Thomas Broughton, James and Thomas Harrington, and Sir John Huddleston remained at arms; some joined Lincoln after his landing at Furness (Lancs.).[120] After the battle of Stoke, where Lincoln was killed, full-scale rebellion ceased, although there were numerous instances of treason and disaffection. In 1536 the tenants of Middleham still wanted a resident lord.[121]

During the Scottish truce of 1486–9, Richard's seditious affinity fully occupied Henry's northern agents, notably Northumberland. The Earl's retainer of gentry in areas formerly dominated by Richard illustrates his desire to augment his power there and hence, indirectly, throughout the North. In his attempt to win the loyalty of Richard's former retainers, he would logically wish to overcome antipathy towards himself as Richard's betrayer by reconciling them to the new regime and smoothing their relations with it. At least as regards poorer Yorkshiremen in 1489 he tried to do this.[122] He would also wish to avoid any clash with their political inclinations, which may be presumed to have favoured Henry's opponents. It is worth remarking that in 1471, when the Earl's policies differed from those of his pro-Lancastrian retainers, he could not make them support Edward IV but kept them neutral.[123] Again, in 1485 it may have been his inability to commit his retainers against Richard and their inclinations that made him stand aside. Similarly, it is remarkable how easily he let himself be diverted northwards by the diversionary attack on York in

[117] Leland, *Collectanea*, IV, p. 186; *C.P.R.* 1485–94, p. 39; Coles, thesis, appx. B, p. 18 (for Thomas Otter); *York Civic Recs.*, II, pp. 3–4. He was pardoned and his forfeiture remitted in 1488, Campbell, *Materials*, II, p. 320; see also *Plumpton Corr.*, p. 85.
[118] e.g. Edward Franke, Richard Knaresborough, Thomas Metcalfe, Richard Bank, Richard Middleton, *Rot. Parl.,* VI, pp. 397–400; *Plumpton Corr.*, p. 55; *Rot. Scot.*, II, p. 440; Coles, thesis, appx. B, p. 18; *Test. Ebor.*, III, p. 344.
[119] *York Civic Recs.*, II, pp. 22–3. He was at Richmond on 23 June, *Plumpton Corr.*, p. 55.
[120] P.R.O. Chancery, Warrants for the Great Seal, Series 2, C.82/2/395; Chrimes, *Henry VII*, p. 71n; *Rot. Parl.*, VI, p. 397; Pollard, *Henry VII*, I, p. 74.
[121] M. H. and R. Dodds, *The Pilgrimage of Grace 1536–7 and the Exeter Conspiracy 1538* (1915), I, p. 208.
[122] Vergil, *Anglica Historica*, p. 38; Skelton says he 'holp them oft at nede; He was their bulwark, their paues, and their wall', Pollard, *Henry VII*, I, p. 74.
[123] *The Arrivall*, pp. 6–7.

1487, thus avoiding the battle of Stoke. A magnate whose attitudes were as ambivalent as this, who kept not only the enemy but his own followers in the dark about his intentions, had to guard his own counsel. Edward IV had appreciated his difficulties in 1471 and credited him with 'right gode and notable service';[124] but in 1485 Henry had imprisoned him. Uninterested in the Earl's own power base, the King required complete commitment to his policies whilst conceding nothing in return. As Henry demanded the repression of the rebels, so Northumberland was forced to act in a manner contrary to that needed to win the trust of Richard's former followers.

The Earl's resources were insufficient for the payment of fees to all Gloucester's former retainers. Nevertheless, Dr Bean found that in 1489 ordinary and extraordinary fees absorbed the surprising total of 42.26 per cent of all his rents and farms, of which annuities represented 27.11 per cent. This discovery prompted his observation that the 'valor of 1489 shows clearly that the burden of fees on the Percy estates . . . had not lightened during the period of the fourth earl'.[125] Since the level of fees in Cumberland and possibly in Yorkshire had been voluntarily restrained during the fourteen-seventies, this suggests that they had increased substantially in the last years of the Earl's life.

His continued recruitment of gentry is best shown by Northumberland, where new fees were being granted until shortly before his death.[126] There Gloucester had been no rival, but the situation differed in the West March, where Richard's accession removed the restraint of the 1474 indenture on the Earl's enlisting of retainers. Two of the seven annuitants of 1479 were dead by Michaelmas 1483, but there were five replacements, who may have been granted their fees after Richard's accession. By Michaelmas 1484 the number had doubled, from ten to twenty, and annuities were being granted until at least Michaelmas 1488. Some of the 'new men' had longstanding family connections with the Percies, such as those of the Curwens, the Heighmores and Lancelot Threlkeld; others had not. Among those latter were Thomas Ratcliffe of Derwentwater (whose second son Richard was Richard III's councillor), Ralph Dacre, and two members of the Skelton family. Sir Thomas Broughton became lieutenant of Cockermouth castle, Sir John Huddleston was a local

[124] Ibid., p. 6.
[125] Bean, *Estates*, pp. 130, 133.
[126] J. Hodgson, *A History of Northumberland* (Newcastle, 1840), II(iii), p. 129n.

minister,[127] and perhaps other retainers of Richard might be identified if his records as duke had survived.

The same expansion of the retinue occurred in Yorkshire, although it cannot be quantified in the absence of estate accounts. Among individual instances are Sir Gervase Clifton, retained by Lord Hastings (d. 1483) in 1478, and Edward Redmayne, brother and heir of Richard's retainer Sir William (d. 1482), who joined the Earl's service by 1485.[128] Sir Edmund Hastings had served Gloucester and his brother Sir Hugh served in a retinue other than the Earl's in 1482; yet Sir Hugh joined Northumberland by 1485, his son John by 1489 and the third brother Roger by 1484.[129] Such examples could be multiplied, but a more general picture can be obtained by examining a readily identified group: the knights and bannerets created by Gloucester and Northumberland in Scotland in 1481–2. These may be divided into two categories: those in Northumberland's retinue in peace and war, and those who were not. Of the latter an unknown proportion served Gloucester. Of sixty-three knighted and made bannerets by Gloucester who may have been his own men, fifty-six outlived him and at least nine of these, a sixth of the total, became Percy retainers. They were nearly half as numerous as the twenty-one surviving Percy retainers created knights and bannerets in the Earl's retinue. If non-Yorkshiremen are excluded, thirteen had belonged to the Percy retinue in 1481–2 and eight had not: the new element was nearly two-fifths of the Yorkshire total. Among the armed feed men that accompanied the Earl to York in 1486, there were thirty-three knights, twenty-five of them known by name: seventeen were in his service in 1481–2[130] and eight had joined since; the newcomers were nearly a third of the total. On another occasion, the Earl summoned eleven retainers, of whom not less than six were new to his service.[131] Impressive though these figures are, they probably understate the case by ignoring the military command of bannerets over knights bachelor. After 1485, seventeen of the bannerets created in 1481–2 were in the Earl's service; eleven of them were already his retainers and six were not. The proportion of new men increased from over a third to almost two-fifths following the deaths of Sir Henry Percy

[127] Cf. Cockermouth MSS. D/Lec. 29/5, /6, /8; box 302. For the next paragraph, see appendix below.
[128] Dunham, *Lord Hastings' Indentured Retainers*, p. 130; *Test. Ebor.*, III, p. 309; *York Civic Recs.*, I, p. 177; Davies, *York Recs.*, pp. 62–3.
[129] *Test. Ebor.*, III, pp. 309, 348; *Plumpton Corr.*, p. 53.
[130] Cf. Leland, *Collectanea*, IV, p. 186; appendix, below; Petworth MS. MD 9/7, rott. 4, 7; 9/8, i, ff. 2, 9v, 10v; 9/8, ii, f. 31v; 9/9, f. 1; *C.P.R.* 1467–77, p. 526.
[131] *Plumpton Corr.*, p. 53; see appendix below.

(1486) and Sir William Gascoigne (1487). There were eleven bannerets in the retinue of war in 1486, when the five in the Earl's service by 1481–2 were actually outnumbered by the six new recruits. Nor was their growing importance confined to the battlefield. Not all the knights belonged to the inner circle of the Earl's councillors, which in August 1485 was probably the same as the Earl's executors, overseers and men whose service was to be retained at all costs. Among the twenty-three names, two — Thomas Ratcliffe and Hugh Hastings — were newcomers. With the deaths of councillors like Percy, Gascoigne and Sir Robert Constable (1488), some of the new men entered the inner circle: three of them were among the eight councillors who conducted the Earl's relations with York after 1485.[132]

Evidently the traditional element was diminishing in the Percy retinue, not in total but in proportion. Many of the new recruits had served Richard III and some actually conspired or rebelled against Henry VII, among them Sir Thomas Broughton, Sir Thomas Mauleverer, Sir John Huddleston and Clement Skelton.[133] Others, like Thomas Ratcliffe, had close ties with someone killed on behalf of Richard or his heirs, and yet others, like the kinsmen of Sir Edmund Hastings, with someone who had suffered forfeiture.[134] Altogether, there is reason to suspect them of sympathy with the rebels of 1486, 1487, and, as Skelton believed,[135] of 1489, and of opposition to Henry's policy in the North as executed by the Earl of Northumberland. The Earl had done nothing to make them raise a finger to save him and they were quite numerous and influential enough to undermine the military effectiveness of his retinue. Their attitudes may have rubbed off on the traditional retainers, many of whom had served (albeit indirectly) in Gloucester's connection before 1483, had shared his patronage as king and lost it at his fall, and more recently had observed the new king's hostility towards the North. The deaths of close kinsmen may have given greater importance to the Earl's quarrel with his cousin Sir John Egremont, whose disinheritance he was completing in his last months. Although Egremont was never a retainer and played no part in the initial stages of the 1489 rebellion, this quarrel may have divided the traditional retainers, rendering it particularly unfortunate that the Earl should have to appeal for protection. By failing to exercise good lordship, the Earl had given them little cause to keep him alive.

---

[132] *Test. Ebor.*, III, pp. 306–9; *York Civic Recs.*, I, p. 177; II, pp. 2, 43.
[133] *Rot. Parl.*, VI, p. 397; Cockermouth MSS. D/Lec. 29/8, mm. 6, 8; box 302, f. 12.
[134] Campbell, *Materials,* II, p. 191; see also ibid., II, p. 218.
[135] Pollard, *Henry VII*, I, p. 75.

IV

This study reveals how, even in the distant North, local politics were affected by royal action. The easy-going Edward IV intervened twice, in 1470 and 1473, to maintain a favourable political balance. In peacetime royal administration, as expressed in taxation, the filling of local offices, concern to economize and in the inability of royal courts to settle disputes, was the constant pre-occupation of northern magnates. In time of war, internal or external, kings were more active locally and interfered in a wider range of activities. A magnate's local position, in so far as it rested on royal office and delegated royal authority, always depended on influence at court and was vulnerable to enemies there. Although each king had different emphases, an orderly succession affected such factors relatively little. In 1470–89 there were five kings and four usurpations, and with different kings came changes in policy, sometimes diametrically opposed to one another, which magnates had not only to obey but, as royal officers, execute. Coupled with closer oversight by insecure kings, the unquestioning service required made it hard to avoid harming their own interests or to exercise self-interest within the framework of royal policy.

What emerges clearly in Northumberland's case is the degree to which his actions depended on the conduct of his feed men, the 'officers' of his retinue of war. As a 'good lord', it was his duty to advance their interests and remove conflicts with his own policies to their satisfaction. By upsetting existing relationships, dynastic change complicated the reconciliation of royal, personal and retainers' demands. In attempting to balance the first two, the Earl failed as a 'good lord'. Ultimately, any magnate who consistently acted against his retainers' wishes would erode the most ingrained of allegiances. Only in 1483 had Earl and retainers agreed. His career illustrates how 'difficult it was for any member of his class to remain aloof'.[136]

Mr Reiss[137] rightly discounts 'the golden era' under the 4th Earl to which Mr James, writing of the early sixteenth century, looked back. It is patently untrue that the Earl was 'the most powerful nobleman in England', that he could at will 'have renewed the Wars of the Roses', or that under him the North knew no other lord.[138] He deferred to another magnate until 1483 and from then on to a royal control more stringent than any

---

[136] K. B. McFarlane, 'The Wars of the Roses', *Proceedings of the British Academy*, L (1964), p. 102.

[137] Reiss, *Historical Journal*, XIX, pp. 505–6, 509.

[138] James, *Durham Univ. Journal*, LVII, pp. 80–1.

since Henry IV. His career has the appearance of a constant struggle against odds that nevertheless should not be overstressed. His military resources were impressive. With a baron and a few bannerets, he led 6,700 men in the Scottish campaign of 1482, and with several other companies, none more than 600 strong, he commanded 6,000 men in Yorkshire in 1487. On the Picquigny campaign his retinue surpassed the companies of the Dukes of Norfolk and Suffolk and of the courtiers Earl Ryvers and Lord Stanley, and it was only smaller than those of the two royal dukes.[139] He always dominated the East Riding and Northumberland. By surviving the violent death-throes of Richard's partisans, beside which the rising of 1489 was a minor affair, he was well-placed to benefit from the break-up of the Neville affinity. Existing retainers still drew their fees and survived to serve the 5th Earl but the decade of the minority prevented Percy competition for former Neville retainers and may have assisted the establishment in different districts of the Stanleys, Cliffords, Dacres and Talbots, which was to be the feature of the ensuing century. No longer was the whole region to be dominated by one or two families. It was the Earl's death that first forced Henry VII to introduce 'direct rule' to the North. If, however, he and his son won the prime loyalty of the gentry by exercising the vast patronage of the crown, as their predecessors had failed to do, it remains for Mr James to demonstrate it. Such 'immediacy' called for attention more constant than Henry VIII is likely to have provided.

Perhaps for the first time, the demise of the Neville affinity left a body of important gentry whom no single magnate or all magnates together could afford to fee. The troubles of the fourteen-eighties stemmed from the disintegration of an ancient affinity which took longer to complete than can be explained by the personal tie that K. B. McFarlane thought lay at the root of bastard feudalism.[140] With the many forfeitures after 1461 such instability may have been a feature in many counties until new connections developed. The restoration of old lords, as in the North in 1485, threw into doubt the compromises of the intervening generations. The resultant conflicts in loyalty may have prompted some gentry to

---

[139] *Hall's Chronicle*, ed. H. Ellis (1809), p. 231; *York Civic Recs.*, II, p. 22; *Foedera*, XI, pp. 84–7; F. P. Barnard, *Edward IV's French Expedition of 1475* (Oxford, 1925), pp. 15–16. 1v–2v.

[140] K. B. McFarlane, 'Bastard Feudalism', *Bulletin of the Institute of Historical Research*, XX (1943–5), pp. 163–80.

avoid commitment and opt for political independence, which became feasible with the reduction in retainer.

APPENDIX

There are several extant lists of knights and bannerets created by magnates in the Scottish war of 1480–3. They have a potential value as lists of magnates' retainers.

Four lists survive for 1481. Only Harleian MS. 5,177 distinguishes between the knights and bannerets created by Gloucester, and only Alnwick Castle MS. 467 between those made banneret and those made both knight and banneret.[141] For 1482 there is also a Plumpton list,[142] which differs in its details. The list of De Fonblanque appears wholly wrong.[143] All these lists have been collated and tested against record evidence to establish that those named were living and whether they were knights and bannerets after their supposed creation but not before. No cases have been found to disprove the veracity of the list in the table below.

In 1481 Northumberland and Gloucester campaigned independently, each dubbing knights, and Gloucester also made bannerets. There is no reason to doubt that these men were actually under their respective commands, although some of Gloucester's creations may have been serving the lesser magnates in his retinue. In Northumberland's case, ten of the eighteen named can be shown to have been already in his retinue; six others certainly were later. One exception was Sir John Salvan, who died in the next year and whose father was a long-standing Percy retainer.[144] At least five of Gloucester's creations were his men.

In 1482 Duke and Earl were two of those who dubbed knights, the others being Lord Stanley and the Duke of Albany. All three dubbed by the Earl were his

[141] B.L. MS. Cotton Claudius, CIII, ff. 61–7, printed in Metcalfe, *Book of Knights*, pp. 5–7; B.L. Harleian MS. 5177, ff. 105–6; Harleian MS. 293, ff. 208–v; Alnwick MS. 467, ff. 41a–44a, of which a copy was kindly supplied to me by Mr D. P. Graham.
[142] 'Gentlemen knighted at Hutton Field in Scotland, 1482', *Northern Genealogist*, II (1896), pp. 83–4.
[143] De Fonblanque, *Annals*, I, p. 294n. For another unreliable version, see B. L. Harleian Roll E2.
[144] Bean, *Estates*, p. 92n.

men. There is a strong presumption that this was also true of the other magnates. The Plumpton list adds several names, only one obviously incorrect,[145] particularly among the knights. Six of these were made bannerets by Gloucester and Stanley without already being knights, so these additions are probably correct. Gloucester also made bannerets, including twelve Percy retainers knighted by the Earl in 1481 and others who had just been dubbed by Stanley. Whereas all peers could dub knights, it seems that only army commanders or princes like Gloucester could make bannerets.[146] This is supported by the Plumpton list, which divides bannerets into three groups, distinguishing those in the vanguard and 'of lord Stanley'. Of the thirteen in the vanguard, which was led by the Earl but did not consist exclusively of his men, eleven were retainers of the Earl but the other four are not known to have been. Of the six bannerets of Lord Stanley, four had just been knighted by him and Sir John Savage and Sir Alexander Houghton haled from his 'country', being from Lancashire and Cheshire and hence under his command on the right wing. The remainder were presumably from the middle ward, under Gloucester's command but not composed exclusively of his men. Among them were the treasurer of war, Sir John Elrington, Sir Robert Greystoke and Sir Edward Wydeville,[147] each of whom had separate companies, and the heir of Lord Grey of Wilton. Only in this category have retainers of Gloucester been identified.

To sum up, it seems that the knights dubbed by the Earl were his own men, that those made by Gloucester were not those of any other magnate present, and that bannerets created by Gloucester in 1481 and of the middle ward in 1482 were not retainers of the Earl, Stanley or Albany. There is a strong presumption that the last two categories represented Gloucester's own retainers.

In the table below, the retinues of Stanley and Albany have been excluded. The columns indicate who of those knighted in 1481–2 were made bannerets in 1482; which gentry had served in the Percy[148] or Gloucester's retinues[149] before 26 June 1483; whether they benefited from Richard III's patronage;[150] and

[145] Sir Robert Middleton, made banneret in 1481.

[146] See the remarks in N. H. Nicolas, *History of the Orders of Knighthood of the British Empire* (1841), I, pp. ix–xii, xxxv sqq. For the rest of the paragraph, see *Hall's Chronicle*, p. 331.

[147] *The Coventry Leet Book*, II, ed. M. D. Harris (Early English Text Society, original series, cxxxv, 1913), p. 505.

[148] Source: G. Poulson, *The History and Antiquities of the Seigniory of Holderness* (Kingston-upon-Hull, 1840), I, p. 227; Hodgson, *Percy Bailiffs' Rolls, Plumpton Corr., List of Sheriffs*, passim; Petworth MSS. MD 9/7–9; Alnwick MSS. CVI/2c, pp. 21, 23, 139; CVI/2b, m. 25d; Cockermouth MS. D/Lec. 29/6, ff. 7v, 48v.

[149] Source: Coles, thesis, appx. B, pp. 17–18b; A. Hanham, *Richard III and his early historians 1483–1535* (Oxford, 1975), p. 167; B.L. MS. Harleian 433, passim; see above.

[150] Source: B.L. MS. Harleian 433, *C.P.R.* 1476–85, Somerville, op. cit., I, passim. Appointments as commissioners only are excluded.

whether they were in the Percy retinue in 1483–9.[151] None of these lists can be exclusive.

The categories in which the names are arranged are:

A: Bannerets made by Gloucester at Hutton field by Berwick, 22 August 1481.
B: Those knighted and made banneret there and then by Gloucester.
C: Knights dubbed then and there by Gloucester.
D: Knights dubbed by Northumberland at the main of Sefford at the same time.
E: Bannerets made by Gloucester then and there.
F: Knights made by Gloucester then and there.
G: Bannerets made by Gloucester then and there from the vanguard.
H: Knights made by Northumberland then and there.

TABLE 1

	Banneret 1482	Retinue by 1483 Percy	Retinue by 1483 Gloucester	Patronized by Richard III	Percy retainer 1483–89
A					
George Lumley			×		
Thomas Pilkington				×	
Robert Rither				×	
B					
William Darcy					×
John Melton*					
John Saville				×	
Ralph Bulmer					
Ralph Bigod*				×	
Ralph Bowes					
John Constable			×	×	
C					
Lord Lovell				×	
Lord FitzHugh				×	
Lord Scrope of Masham			×	×	
Robert Greystoke*	×				
James Strangways	×			×	×
Robert Middleton				×	
William FitzWilliam					
Thomas FitzWilliam				×	

[151] *Test. Ebor.*, III, pp. 306–9; Leland, *Collectanea*, IV, pp. 186–9; *Plumpton Corr.*, p. 53; Cockermouth MSS. D/Lec. 29/8, f. 6; box 302; Alnwick MS. CVI/4a, ff. 23, 26, 27.

TABLE 1—*continued*

	Banneret 1482	Retinue by 1483		Patronized by Richard III	Percy retainer 1483–89
		Percy	Gloucester		
Thomas Wortley				×	
James Danby	×			×	
Thomas Mauleverer	×			×	×
Ralph FitzRandall					
Charles Pilkington			×	×	
Robert Waterton*					
John Neville				×	
Richard Conyers			×		×
William Beckwith				×	×
D					
Marmaduke Constable		×		×	
Christopher Ward	×	×		×	×
Roger Heron*		×			
Thomas Grey of Wark.	×	×		×	×
William Malory					×
Piers Middleton	×	×			×
Stephen Hamerton	×				×
Robert Hilliard					×
Ralph Widdrington	×				×
Ralph Harbottle		×			×
John Everingham	×	×		×	
John Aske	×				×
Ralph Babthorpe					×
Roger Thornton*	×	×			
Christopher Curwen		×			×
John Salvan*					
Thomas Grey of Horton		×		×	×
Thomas Tempest	×				×
E					
Edward Wydeville					
Walter Herbert				×	
John Elrington*				×	
Edmund Hastings			×	×	
James Tyrell			×	×	
Ralph Ashton			×		
William Redmayne*			×		
Richard Ratcliffe			×	×	
Brian Stapleton				×	

TABLE 1—*continued*

	Banneret 1482	Retinue by 1483 Percy	Gloucester	Patronized by Richard III	Percy retainer 1483–89
F					
Henry Percy		×		×	×
Thomas Broughton				×	×
William Gascoigne		×		×	×
Hugh Hastings				×	×
William Eure		×		×	×
Robert Harrington			×	×	
Lionel Percy					
G					
William Neville*					
Richard Haute					
John Widdrington		×	×	×	
William Ingleby				×	×
Thomas Gower			×	×	
Randall Pigot					×
John Darell					
William Houghton				×	
William Parker				×	
Roger Cotton					
Thomas Bowles |Bridges				×	
Alexander Baynham				×	
Alexander Jardine				×	
Richard Huddleston	×			×	
Edward Stanley	×			×	
John Grey of Wilton	×			×	
Richard Howton					
H					
Robert Plumpton		×			×
Martin of the See		×			×
John Pennington		×			×

*denotes death before 23 August 1485

22

The Yorkshire Rebellion of 1489 Reconsidered

HISTORIANS NOW RECOGNIZE REBELLIONS, riots, and popular protest in general as exceptional opportunities to study the attitudes and aspirations of those lower orders normally only visible, if at all, through the eyes of their social superiors. It is generally accepted that the classic popular uprising arose from a sense of injustice among the rebels, who regarded their cause as legitimate, and was characterized by a respect for order and property, by the absence of casual crime or violence, and by organization and self-discipline. Such risings aimed not to overthrow the established order, but to relieve grievances by self-help or by extracting concessions from authority, and have been viewed as merely the final — reluctant — expedient after other forms of redress had failed. Such 'loyal rebellions' were led by respectable propertied men, the leaders of their local communities below the gentry.[1]

This model has been applied mainly to early modern England, but is also relevant to the Middle Ages. In 1381 and in 1450 insurgents sought a negotiated settlement and peasants also displayed a profound respect for the law in disputes with their manorial lords.[2] While the decline in demesne farming and villeinage reduced the scope for such conflict and the value of court rolls for studying it, there can be little doubt that popular insubordination and insurrections persisted. Apart from those incidents of which we know nothing, there are many of which we know little,[3] and yet others are disguised by the involvement of other elements. The problem of distinguishing between popular rebellions with aristocratic elements and aristocratic rebellions with popular elements is well illustrated by the controversy about the Pilgrimage of Grace. Other

[1] Rebellion, Popular Protest and the Social Order in Early Modern England, ed. P. Slack (Cambridge, 1984), pp. 1–15. Professor R. A. Griffiths and Mr T. B. Pugh kindly advised on earlier drafts of this work and the University of York assisted by electing me Borthwick Visiting Research Fellow in 1984. I gratefully acknowledge the influence of the written work of Mr M. E. James and of Dr I. Arthurson's unpublished paper 'The Cornish of 1497: A Revolt of the Peasantry?', which is the source of comparison with that rebellion.

[2] E. B. Fryde, The Great Revolt of 1381 (1981); R. A. Griffiths, Reign of Henry VI (1981), pp. 610–49; T. G. Watts, 'Peasant Revolts on the Manors of the Abbot of Titchfield 1345–1420', Proceedings of the Hampshire Field Club and Archaeological Society, xxxix (1983), 121–34, esp. 132–34.

[3] For example, the Ackworth Rebellion of 1492, Plumpton Correspondence, ed. T. Stapleton, Camden Society, iv (1839), 96–97.

northern examples include the rebellions in Holderness, Richmondshire, and Lincolnshire in 1469–70, about which we know (or think we know) the names and aims of the aristocratic figureheads but little else.[4] The Yorkshire rebellion of 1489 also has popular, urban, and aristocratic strands. Smaller in scale then those of 1381, 1450, 1497, 1536–37 and 1549, it may have had more in common with those rural riots about which we know so little at this date. As few medieval risings are susceptible to analysis, it is of interest for its own sake — inevitably it included its own intriguing and distinctive elements — and raises issues of wider significance.

I

In April 1489 Henry VII, the first king of a new dynasty, had reigned for less than four years. His infant regime faced formidable challenges at home and abroad. Although Richard III himself was dead, many of his former supporters, particularly in the North, supported other Yorkist princes and rebelled in 1486 and 1487. Lambert Simnel's revolt in 1487 had enjoyed Irish and Continental support and, although defeated at Stoke, it had exposed the unreliability of Henry's own army and left significant royalists to plot in the North. Not surprisingly Henry viewed all northern disturbances with alarm. Moreover events abroad forced the King to intervene in Brittany in 1488 against the King of France, the most powerful ruler in northern Europe, whose support had been crucial in Henry's own accession. It was at this time of international and domestic tension that the Yorkshiremen once again rebelled.

The rising in 1489 apparently originated in a treasonable conventicle at Ayton in Cleveland on 20 April. The next known event, which greatly impressed contemporaries and so generated the sources for this study, was the murder of Henry Percy, Earl of Northumberland, at South Kilvington by Thirsk on 28 April by rioters led by the yeoman Robert Chamber of Ayton. The Earl was the leading magnate and principal royal agent throughout Yorkshire and northern England. More insurgents were recruited in both the East Riding (under Sir John Egremont) and in North Yorkshire. These groups met at Sheriff Hutton and advanced as far

---

[4] K. R. Dockray, 'The Yorkshire Rebellions of 1469', *The Ricardian*, 83 (1983), 246–57; A. J. Pollard, 'Lord FitzHugh's Rising in 1470', *Bulletin of the Institute of Historical Research*, LII (1979), 170–75; 'Chronicle of the Lincolnshire Rebellion', ed. J. Bruce, *Camden Miscellany*, I (1836), 6–10; cf. Arthurson, pp. 1–14. A good recent study, which remains somewhat ambiguous, is C. F. Richmond, 'Fauconberg's Kentish Rising of May 1471', *English Historical Review*, LXXXV (1970), 687–92.

south as Doncaster (13 May), before doubling back on 15 May to seize York with the aid of traitors within the city. The largest town and unofficial capital of the North, York had successfully resisted the much more dangerous invasion of Lambert Simnel two years previously. Understandably alarmed by this further threat to his fragile regime, Henry VII raised a powerful army and marched north. The advance guard, led by the Earl of Surrey, was alone sufficient to disperse the rebels and entered York on 20 May. A commission of oyer and terminer sat at York to try the offenders, executing *inter alios* Robert Chamber. Other leaders, most notably Alderman Wrangwish and Sir John Egremont, eventually submitted and were pardoned. The only longterm effect, in retrospect, was Surrey's appointment as king's lieutenant, a decisive stage in averting Percy domination of the North.[5]

The murder of the Earl and capture of York were unexpected victories in a generally unsuccessful and unimportant rebellion. It rates only half a paragraph in Professor Palliser's *Tudor York*, but has nevertheless attracted considerable attention from historians. All modern accounts derive ultimately from the near-contemporary narrative of Polydore Vergil, an Italian moving in official circles, who presented it as an isolated demonstration against excessive taxation, which got out of hand. Superficially it thus resembles those other 'loyal rebellions' discussed above. In 1965, however, Mr M. E. James argued ingeniously that it was Henry VII's deliberate provocation that drove the rioters to violence and prompted the Earl's retainers to abandon him. Writing in 1978 the present author separated the rebellion from the desertion of the Earl's followers, attributing the latters' disaffection to the interplay of dynastic changes on northern power politics. The King did not deliberately provoke the rebellion.[6] While the standard view of the uprising has thus been undermined, much new evidence has been uncovered, which has made this reassessment much easier.

---

[5] M. A. Hicks, 'Dynastic Change and Northern Society: The Career of the Fourth Earl of Northumberland 1470–1489', *Northern History*, XIV above, 366–8; P(ublic) R(ecord) O(ffice), King's Bench, Ancient Indictments, KB9/381.

[6] D. M. Palliser, *Tudor York* (Oxford, 1979), p. 44; *The Anglica Historica of Polydore Vergil*, ed. D. Hay, Camden Society, 3rd ser. LXXIV (1955), 38–39; M. E. James, 'The Murder at Cocklodge', *Durham University Journal*, LVII (1964–65), 80–87; Hicks, *NH*, XIV, 78–103. Professor Scattergood has recently interpreted Skelton's account of the desertion of the Earl's retainers as literary convention, saying 'none of the surviving records even hints at it', 'Skelton and the Elegy', *Proceedings of the Irish Academy*, LXXXIV (1984), 333–47, esp. 340–41 (I am indebted to Dr G. W. Bernard for this reference). This conflicts with the fact that the Earl alone was killed. Evidently Skelton adopted the elegiac form as particularly appropriate for the events of 1489.

To date no historian has fully exploited what must be the fundamental source, the returns of the royal commission of oyer and terminer that tried the defeated rebels.[7] Without these, one cannot trace the progress of the rebellion or identify the principal ringleaders. The returns comprise forty-two items, mainly indictments, but also including the commissions, writs to empanel juries, lists of jurors, and the record of the trial of those in custody. While the information is somewhat meagre, there is no reason to suppose that the returns are incomplete. Little is added by the relevant controlment roll.

Altogether sixty-six people were indicted, only forty-four for rebellion. Some other criminals were uncovered, who *perhaps* committed their offences under cover of the general disorders: for example the bastard William Aldeburgh, who on 13 May expelled Sir Robert Plumpton and Ralph Neville from various lands in the West Riding. Most offenders were indicted of treasonable offences, typically with levying war against the King intending 'the final destruction of King Henry VII and the subversion and annihilation of the realm of England and the good government of the same'. This count of treason enabled Chief Justice Husy to hear charges arising not just from the county and the city of York, as in the King's commissions, but from the liberties: juries were empanelled from the Archbishop of York's liberty of Beverley and from the Durham liberties of Howden and Allerton, though not from the palatinate of Durham itself. The jurors chosen were generally men of substance: thus the York alderman Thomas Wrangwish was indicted by a jury including a knight and four fellow aldermen; the thirteen jurors from Dickering wapentake included seven members of the gentry. Such men may have been judged unsympathetic to low-born rebels and also unlikely to be intimidated by anybody of higher rank. However that may be, there can be little doubt that the authoritative commission of thirteen peers and six judges sitting in state in the York Guildhall and the close supervision of the King in person speeded the proceedings and facilitated the conviction and execution of the defendants.

This need not mean that the accused were denied a fair trial. For one thing, the King was merciful, pardoning at least seven during 1489 —

---

[7] PRO, KB 9/381. This is the file of the records of the oyer and terminer commission that sat at York Guildhall to try the rebels on 27 May–1 June 1489 and was subsequently returned to the court of King's Bench. Unless otherwise stated, this article is based on this source; Vergil, pp. 38–39; and 'The Yorkshire Rebellion in 1489', *Gentleman's Magazine*, cxxiv(2) (1851), 459–68 (an anonymous account of the rebellion, probably by Robert Davies, from the records of the city of York).

including Alderman Wrangwish, who was sentenced to hang — and others thereafter. *The Great Chronicle of London* records that many of the poor commons, fearing severe punishment, approached Henry clad only in their shirts and with halters about their necks to obtain clemency, which he conceded. Only five were condemned to death, at most only four were hanged. Moreover the surviving records do not permit the assumption that indictments were rubber stamped by cowed jurors: the charges against John Slingsby, for example, were modified in two particulars by a jury and Henry Middlewood was actually acquitted. As only forty-four out of several thousand rebels were charged, it may be that the jurors were not anxious to indict. This is also suggested by the small number from each place — fourteen places are named — and by the predominance of those from York (14) and its liberty (3), where the King and his commissioners could exercise their authority most effectively. It is also significant that only six of those charged were in custody — even those from York itself were missing. Nineteen outlaws never made their peace with the Crown — surely an admission of guilt? It would appear that only the most blatant offenders were indicted by the jurors and that their evidence can be safely used to illuminate the rebellion. There is now a chronological framework to which to relate the literary evidence.

II

Opposition to taxation can be traced back into early 1488, but the judicial record commences only on 20 April 1489 with a treasonable conventicle at Ayton in Cleveland attended by the yeoman Robert Chamber of Ayton, the first leader, a chaplain, two yeomen and presumably others from the locality. It may be significant that this district was not normally dominated by any magnate, least of all the Percies, but had been overseen most recently by Richard III as Duke of Gloucester and lord of Scarborough. It was probably at this meeting that the rebels resolved to march towards Thirsk, a decision which had come to the ears of the Earl of Northumberland four days later. After leaving parliament about 14 February, he had been (apparently for the only time in his career) at his manor of Seamer by Scarborough from at least 23 March, probably executing a commission to repair Scarborough Castle. He was still there on 24 April, when he summoned Sir Robert Plumpton, his company and other retainers from the Knaresborough area to meet him three days later at Thirsk, obviously with the intention of intercepting the rebels. He may have hoped to persuade them to disperse, but certainly he was prepared to use moderate force, since Plumpton was instructed to attend 'having bowes and arrowes and pryvy harnest'.[8] Northumberland duly met Chamber and 700 rebels at South Kilvington on 28 April, but, for reasons explained elsewhere, the Percy retainers declined to protect him and the Earl was slain — the only person to be killed in the entire rebellion. Apparently spontaneous and certainly counterproductive, the murder caused Skelton, with some justice, to denounce the rioters as 'stark mad', with 'frantyk frensy . . . in your brayne', and to compare them with the irrational 'bestis'.

Before Northumberland's death the rebels' plan was apparently to press their grievances on him as representative of the King and thus persuade Henry VII to make concessions. By killing the Earl, they removed the only person in the county able to speak for the King or to negotiate with them. Moreover, since he had been acting 'in the king's quarrel', the rebels had 'levied war against the crown and dignity of the said lord king' — a treasonable offence. It was no longer possible to disperse and escape punishment. In the meantime they had killed the only Yorkshire magnate powerful enough to restrain them and had thus secured time in which to recruit and organize themselves.[9] Indecision about what to do next may partly explain why they lingered nearby until at least 5 May, perhaps staying there until 9 May. 5 May was the date when new recruits were summoned by proclamation to join them at Allerton Moor in the east and Gatherley Moor in Gilling, five miles north of Richmond, in the west. At Sheriff Hutton Moor they were joined by at least 200 rebels from the East Riding.

These more southerly disturbances began after the Earl's restraining hand was removed. The commissioners recorded an initial meeting on 1 May at Bridlington between three yeomen from Kilham and Burton Agnes, a husbandman from Haysthorp, and a wright from North Burton. They proceeded to Brandsburton (3 May), Borow by Cowlam (5 May), and Beverley, probably joining forces on the way with Sir John Egremont, who had been recruiting 'in Holderness' (whose lord the Duke of Buckingham was an absentee and a minor) and had certainly secured one

---

[8] *Paston Letters and Papers in the Fifteenth Century*, ed. N. Davis, (2 vols Oxford, 1971–76), I 668; PRO, Duchy of Lancaster, Chancery Rolls, DL 37/62 m.5d; Alnwick Castle MS. CIII/ 4a m.13; *Plumpton Corr.* p. 61. While Northumberland's men were clearly not fully armed, they were not 'withoute eny harneys' as Oxford alleged, *Paston L.&P.*II, 460. For what follows, see J. Skelton, *Complete English Poems*, ed. V. J, Scattergood (1983), p. 31.

[9] *Paston L.&P.* I, 659. For a parallel in 1450, see Griffiths, *Henry VI*, p. 612: 'Had it not been for this disaster (Stafford's defeat), the rebels might well have dispersed relatively peacefully to their homes' . . .

adherent from Hedon. At the archbishop's town of Beverley, normally under the eye of the Percy household at Leconfield, two of the twelve governors, the dyers Eli Cass and Thomas Bullock, were sympathetic to the rebels. They caused 'le belman' of Beverley — the civic bell-ringer — to revoke the King's proclamation against the rebels, corresponded with Egremont, and permitted men of Beverley to join them. Altogether, only 200 accompanied Egremont northwards from Beverley via Manyhous and Malton to Sheriff Hutton to join those from north Yorkshire.

At this point, a fortnight after the Earl's death, Sir John Egremont seems to have taken control and the rebels' movements become more urgent. Vergil reports that 'the mob . . . openly proclaimed that it would march to attack Henry'. Gathering recruits on the way, the combined force marched to Doncaster (13 May) via Bramham Moor and Ferry-bridge, but instead of continuing southwards it turned towards York. A York fletcher, Hugh Bunting, supplied the rebels with arrows and Thomas Wrangwish, the York alderman, suborned three men from Acomb with promises of wage . The rebel army was joined at Dring-houses by disaffected citizens on 14 May and on the next day 5,000 insurgents stormed the city through Walmgate and Fishergate, which were Wrangwish's responsibility and which were alleged to have been inadequately defended, through his negligence. Egremont communi-cated with the mayor, but did not remain long in York. On 17 May he was about to depart for Richmondshire.[10] As for the remainder,

'when it came to fighting, flying in all directions as a cowardly crowd usually does, the conspiracy dissolved, and . . . all . . . sought their own safety. For as soon as the king heard of the rising he went at once to York; at his approach the terrified rebels all took to their heels'.

The Earl of Surrey took the credit, but the absence of prisoners suggests that the rebels dispersed before he actually arrived. Indeed, his life-story inscribed on his tomb made no reference to any battle.[11]

Understandably alarmed and obviously fearing another aristocratic uprising, Henry determined initially to go north himself equipped for a full-scale campaign. The clerk of the ordnance was directed to supply twelve brass falcons, two serpentines of brass, a last of gunpowder, 1,300 bowstrings and bows, 2,600 sheaves of arrows, 1,000 bills, and 2,000 brigandines for yeomen.[12] The King's proclamation of 10 May somewhat hysterically denounced all those, who

[10] *Y(ork) C(ivic) R(ecords)*, ed. A. Raine, II, Yorkshire Archaeological Society, Record Series, CIII, (1941), 48.
[11] *Reign of Henry VII from Contemporary Sources*, ed. A. F. Pollard (London, 1913), I, 81.
[12] PRO, Exchequer, Warrants for Issue, E 404/80/4Hen.VII/68.

in mayntenaunce of ther treason and murdre intende not only the distruccion of
the kynges most noble person and of alle the nobles and lordis of this realme, but
also of the subduersioun of the politique wele of the same, and to robbe, dispoyle,
and distroye all the southe parties of this his realme, and to subdue and brynge to
captiuite all the people of the same . . .

It appealed to traditional southern prejudices, recently reinforced by
Richard III's so-called northern tyranny,[13] rather than accurately reflecting the rebels' aims. As more information flowed in, much of it from York
itself, the King became less alarmed. On learning of the small numbers of
the rebels, the Earl of Oxford became less insistent in his demands and
ultimately took less men than he could have arrayed. Although probably
in the advance guard, he left Cambridge only on 12 May and the King did
not leave Hertford until 22 May, after the rising was over. Even so, he
took with him a 'grete Hoste' including the four Earls of Surrey, Oxford,
Derby, and Shrewsbury and nine other peers[14] — more than turned out
for the battle of Stoke in 1487. The sessions of the judicial commission in
the York Guildhall and the hangings of the three yeomen Robert
Chamber, Christopher Atkinson of Ayton, James Binks of Sowerby and
the York cobbler William Lister demonstrated the completeness of his
victory.

That Henry was content that his commission should sit only at York
and that so few people should be indicted or executed, indicates how little
threat with hindsight he considered the rebellion to have posed. In
contrast, the more numerous Cornish insurgents of 1497 were much more
dangerous: they rose twice, marched to London, and made common
cause with his dynastic rival Perkin Warbeck, and consequently Henry
pursued them relentlessly, so that even the humble were fined.[15] In view
of the fears of the 'many-headed monster' so well documented by Dr Hill
and Mr James, it is striking that Henry was relieved that the rebellion was
purely popular in character and was satisfied with the dispersal of the
rebels and some token executions. Did government alter their perceptions of the relative importance of aristocratic and popular risings during

[13] *Materials for a History of Henry VII*, ed. W. Campbell, Rolls Series (2 vols 1873–77), II,
447–48; A. J. Pollard, 'North, South and Richard III', *The Ricardian*, 74 (1981), 384–90.
[14] Pollard, *Henry VII*, I, 81; *C(alendar of) S(tate) P(apers) Venetian*, I, 181; *Paston L.&P.*
II, 658–59; *De rebus britannicis collectanea*, ed. T. Hearne (Oxford, 1770), IV, 24.
[15] Arthurson, p. 10. For what follows, see C. Hill, 'The Many-Headed Monster', in *Change
and Continuity in Seventeenth-Century England* (1974), pp. 181–204; J. Walter, 'Grain riots
and popular attitudes to the law: Maldon and the crisis of 1629', in *An Ungovernable People*,
ed. J. Brewer & J. Styles (1980), p. 50; J. Walter, 'A "Rising of the People?" The
Oxfordshire Rising of 1596', *Past and Present*, 107 (1985), 90–143, esp. 94, 102, 127–29, 138.

the Tudor period? Obviously popular insurrections came to bulk larger as the sixteenth century progressed and aristocratic sedition declined, but it appears that Tudor governments came to attach more weight *absolutely* as well as *relatively* to the popular variety — no doubt understandably as growing poverty, unemployment, and vagrancy increased the potential grievances and recruits. If this assessment is correct, did the later Tudors feel the need to take more account of popular opinion than Henry VII had done? Did the greater perceived threat of popular rebellion cause them to tailor their rule to the interests of the lower orders as well as the 'political nation' and thus admit the former to a say, however tacit and indirect, in the operation of government? And did this take the form not just of the relief of potential grievances, as with the enclosure commissions or in the well-attested reactions of the Privy Council to dearth, but also in avoiding courses of action unpalatable to the lower orders? And was Henry VII's attitude representative of his immediate predecessors or did his fear of aristocratic opponents cause him to underrate popular rebellion until the alarming events of 1497 disabused him?

The legal records demonstrate not only that the rebellion was confined to Yorkshire, but that it was restricted to the north-east and south-east of the county, with no recruits further west than Ripon. To some extent, no doubt, this was because no juries were empanelled from the western wapentakes, but the commission's decision not to empanel any there presumed that few rebels were to be found. Evidently recruitment at Gatherley Moor and in Richmondshire failed. There is no direct evidence confirming Vergil's claim that the insurrection spread into the bishopric of Durham, though the Durham liberties in Yorkshire were affected. As only 200 of the 5,000 came from the East Riding and almost none of these are recorded from the march south, it seems that the bulk of the rebels came from Cleveland and Allertonshire or were citizens of York itself. The rebellion was thus extremely localized within Yorkshire and the numbers do not compare with the 20,000+ rebels of 1469.

Contemporary reporters were agreed that this was a popular uprising —a rebellion of the 'commons' to York city council, of 'naked men' to the Earl of Oxford, and of 'a mayny of rude villayns' to Skelton. If a document among the *Paston Letters* accurately paraphrases their proclamation, the rebels sought support for the 'Kynge and the Comowns of Engelond . . . in the name of Mayster Hobbe Hyrste',[16] a fictitious name that appealed to the rural poor. At first sight, as the present author

---

[16] See above, 365; *Paston L. & P.* I. 659.

supposed in 1978,[17] this impression is confirmed by the indictments, which include among the sixty-six names only one gentlemen — Egremont himself. The total is made up of chaplains, yeomen, husband-men, labourers, and craftsmen from York, Beverley, and the market towns — dyers, weavers, shoemakers, a pedlar, a wright, a fletcher, a fisherman, a panierman, a baker, a draper, and tailors. Such occupations do not, however, encompass the lowest ranks of Yorkshire society. At York, where Wrangwish and Bunting alone were of the freedom,[18] only two of those indicted were labourers, the others all being identified by a trade. At Beverley three of those implicated were dyers, two already and one yet to be a governor of the town.[19] Most of the countrymen were yeomen and husbandmen, although the occupation of the three men of Acomb is not reported. As with other popular rebellions, known rebels appear to be men of some property, men of fixed address, probably householders with some standing in their local communities and with much to lose by rebellion. If such men were representative of the insurgents, which we cannot be sure, they were certainly not the 'robbers, theves and ill-dysposed persones' denounced by the King.

Before accepting this conclusion, we need to remember that we possess the names of only a tiny fraction of the rebels — less than 1 per cent of the total — and that York, with fifteen names, is disproportionately repre-sented. We know the names of at most eight of those at Northumber-land's murder and only eleven of those from the East Riding. The Crown normally concentrated its attention on ringleaders and juries found it easier to identify householders of higher social status, as opposed to the humble or young. Much more extensive prosecution was necessary to uncover the rank and file. In 1497, when spies were systematically employed to uncover offenders, most of those *attainted* were gentlemen and yeomen, but there is no record of the rank and occupation of 4,000 of those who were fined,[20] presumably because they were socially of little account. It may well be that those indicted in 1489 are unrepresentative of the rebels as a whole.

In so far as the term rebellion carries connotations of violence, it is quite misleading. In spite of assertions to the contrary by the chronicler

[17] Hicks, *NH*, XIV, 78–79.
[18] *Freemen of York*, ed. F. Collins, I, Surtees Society, XCVI (1896), 248. For the reliability of this register, see R. B. Dobson, 'Admissions to the Freedom of the City of York in the Later Middle Ages', *Economic History Review*, 2nd ser. XXVI (1973), 1–21.
[19] Humberside Record Office, Beverley Borough Records, BC/II/3, fol. 73 (Great Guild Book). Edward Johnson was also a governor in 1498, ibid. fol. 26.
[20] Arthurson, p. 10.

Edward Hall,[21] the only recorded casualty was Northumberland himself, whose death would have been averted had his retainers done their duty. Although people were urged to join the uprising on pain of death, the threat was not implemented. Judging from the indictments, which should surely record them, the rebels committed no other crimes on their advance south or in York itself. The crimes in the indictments were not committed by known rebels. Their armed assault on York, in which Fishergate was burnt, apparently (and amazingly) resulted in no loss of life. The city was not looted — indeed it was fear lest Egremont 'and his people wold rob the Cite' that prompted the city council to send men with Egremont to Richmondshire.[22] The council continued to meet and manage affairs and the Mayor was at church as usual, when Egremont wished to communicate with him. The seizure of the city passes unremarked in the surviving accounts of the Minster and vicars-choral. While the council feared for the safety of Archbishop Rotherham, a former royal chancellor, and guaranteed his security, it is surely remarkable that he remained apparently unmolested at Cawood, just outside the city, throughout the disturbances.[23] This absence of violence and crime also features in other studies of popular protest and is generally considered indicative of a high degree of order and self-discipline among respectable rebels respectful to property. Too much should not be read into the absence of thefts of food, which taken at face value would however suggest that starvation was not the principal motivation for rebellion.

III

Why did the rebellion occur? Was it indeed a protest against taxation, as most historians have supposed? Were the rebels activated by other popular grievances? Was it just another political rising, like the northern rebellions of 1486 and 1487? Or was it a mixture of all three?

---

[21] The judicial records do not substantiate Hall's claim that 'diuers of his household seruantes (were) furiously and shamefully murthered' (*Hall's Chronicle*, ed. H. Ellis (1809), p. 443) and would certainly have done so if the report was true.

[22] J. Leland, *Itinerary*, ed. L. Toulmin-Smith (6 vols, 1964), I, 54; *Y.C.R.* II, 48. For what follows, see ibid. The college of vicars-choral did entertain Sir Richard Tunstall and paid his servants' travel expenses to London, York Minster Library, VC 6/1/10.

[23] *Y.C.R.* II, 48; *Register of Archbishop Rotherham*, ed. E. Green, I, Canterbury & York Society, LXIX, (1976), passim. This is in striking contrast to 1381, when the palaces of the notorious Archbishop Neville were attacked, R. B. Dobson, 'The Risings in York, Beverley and Scarborough 1380–81', in *The English Rising of 1381*, ed. R. H. Hilton & T. H. Aston (Cambridge, 1984), p. 125n.

The rebellion occurred at a time of unusually heavy taxation on a population that had grown unaccustomed to it. Although war with Scotland had been almost continuous in the years 1480–84, there had been only one general tax — in 1483 — and only one benevolence levied since 1475, although the North had played a disproportionate role in supplying men and equipment for military operations on the Borders. In November 1487, however, parliament voted two whole tenths and fifteenths, payable in two years. The city of York reluctantly collected the first instalment of the first fifteenth, the second instalment (due 10 November 1488) being four months overdue. In rural Yorkshire, collection of the first instalment had not begun at midsummer 1488 in the hope that the King would 'remit and fully pardon' the liability, which he did not. Consequently the second instalment was also overdue. Ultimately much was paid, for on 20 August 1489 allowance was made for payments totalling £561 from lay taxes in the hands of the abbot of St Mary, York. Had it been paid punctually, this tax would not have overlapped so much with the collection of a further grant of £75,000 made in January 1489, of which the first instalment was due on 1 May 1489. Together these grants amounted to almost five fifteenths due in three years, an exceptional and unfamiliar level of taxation, even if it had been levied to time. This second subsidy employed a novel assessment and omitted the allowances customary in a fifteenth, exemption being made for the Border counties but not for Yorkshire.[24] It was the attempt to collect the new tax that apparently provoked the rebellion.

Certainly the earliest account of the Earl's death, written two days later on 30 April 1489 by the Earl of Oxford, attributes it to hostility to taxation:

And for asmoche as it is certeinly vnto the Kynges grace (shewed) that my lord of Northumberland, havyng the auctorité to se the Kynges money levied in the north parties, had knowleche that certeyne persones of comvnes wer assembled at Topclif and at a nother lordship of his nygh to the same, sayng they wolde pay no money, my seid lord of Northumberland heryng thereof . . . addressed hym-self towardes theym . . . trustyng to haue appeased theym. Howe be it as hit is seid that he is distressed . . .[25]

This agrees with the versions written later not only by Polydore Vergil but also by Skelton:

---

[24] *Rot(uli) Parl(iamentorum)*, vi, 400–01, 422; 'The Yorkshire Rebellion in 1489', *Gentleman's Magazine*, cxxiv(2), 459–63; PRO, Privy Seal Office, Warrants for the Privy Seal, Series i, PSO 1/52/2685; E404/80/4Hen.vii/118; S. B. Chrimes, *Henry VII* (1972), pp. 196–97. The 1489 tax was considered an unaccustomed levy, *CSP Venetian*, i, 181.
[25] *Paston L.&P.* i, 460.

The grounde of his quarel was for his sovereyn lord,
The welle concernyng of all the hole lande,
Demaundyng soche duties as nedis most acord,
To the ryght of his prince, Which shold not be withstand.[26]

This alludes to the subject's obligation to support the King financially in his necessity, for example to finance foreign war: these taxes were required for Henry VII's intervention in Brittany. When the King sought taxes in his necessity, subjects were not entitled to refuse his demands and, if they did, the King was allowed to take what he required. Nevertheless the rioters refused to pay — in Skelton's words, 'They saide they forsede not, nor carede not to dy' — and, when Northumberland insisted on payment, they killed him.[27] The sources are unanimous: the rebellion *originated* in the taxation and Northumberland was no more than a royal agent.

Perhaps Yorkshiremen were exceptionally sensitive about taxation. Hostility to the poll-tax is the most obvious factor unifying town and country in 1381. The right of St Leonard's Hospital, York to petercorn — a thrave of corn from each ploughland throughout Lancashire, Westmorland, Cumberland, and Yorkshire — was most resented in the East Riding and was the principal cause of the rising in Holderness in 1469. In the same year taxation was one of the grievances of the Richmondshire rebels.[28] By 1487, when two fifteenths were granted, Yorkshiremen were used to recognition of their poverty by the Crown in the form of tax allowances and remittances of fee farms. They had come to regard these not as concessions but as rights, 'which we trust his grace wolbe inclined as to do unto us, in consideration of the said poverte, ruyne, and decae, as unto eny other his sugettes in these parties'. This letter of 23 June 1488 reveals not only the York oligarchy's confidence in its case — the economic decline of the city is well-attested — but their expectation that rural Yorkshire would also be relieved. Indeed, the 'common opynyon' in the county was that such allowances would be made, so collection was delayed in the hope that it could be avoided and £30 of the first instalment was actually withheld, though full payment was eventually required.

Petercorn and fifteenths, however unwelcome and highly assessed, were traditional levies, but the 1489 subsidy was novel and ungraduated: no allowances were made for Yorkshire, which consequently paid a

---

[26] Skelton, p. 31.
[27] G. L. Harriss, 'Aids, Loans and Benevolences', *Historical Journal*, VI (1963), 1–19; Skelton, p. 31.
[28] Dockray, *Ricardian*, 83, 246–57, esp. pp. 250, 252. For what follows, see *Gentleman's Magazine*, CXXIV(2), 459–63.

higher rate than usual. There may well have been a heavier burden for the relatively poor. It was seen as unaccustomed and contributed to the heightened sense of legitimacy characteristic of such risings. To remit its tax the city of York employed its recorder, John Vavasour, and Archbishop Rotherham as intermediaries with Lord Dynham, the royal Treasurer, and with the King himself. Even after Dynham's refusal in October, Alderman Sir Richard York was sent to the King's council and in January the city's M.P.s were instructed to intercede with the King's ministers. Simultaneously the 'country people' were lobbying the King, also without success, though we do not know through what channels. Certainly every effort was made to secure redress before resorting to violence.

Perhaps Northumberland too was sympathetic and interceded with the King, since Skelton writes:

> Unkindly thai slew hym that help them oft at nede:
> He was ther bulwarke, ther paves, and ther wall,
> Yet shamfully thei slew hym . . .
> He was your chyfteyne, your shelde, your chef defens,
> Redy to assyst you in every time of nede.[29]

The Earl may have stood between the commons and the King, representing their grievances to him, acting as good lord to them, just as he did to his noble retainers. Everything was done to persuade the King to remit the tax, but Henry VII remaining adamant, the city, despite its sense of grievance, 'as fereful for his greit displeasour as eny other his sugettes within this his realme',[30] paid up. Presumably most rural taxpayers did likewise. In the north-east of the county, however, they remained defiant, refused to pay and proceeded to the last resort — an armed demonstration. Informed of this by the tax-collectors, Northumberland, so Vergil reports, 'informed the king in writing that the people refused to pay the stipulated sum'. The implication, indicated by Mr James, is that the Earl favoured alleviating grievances by tax-allowances,[31] thus fulfilling his proper role as regional good lord. When Henry remained unyielding, it was Northumberland's duty — as the King's agent — to inform the rioters that they must pay. To this, the rebels responded 'as though he were author of their wrongs' by killing him. Thus far the sequence of events conforms precisely to the pattern of the 'loyal rebellion' outlined above.

[29] Skelton, p. 30.
[30] *Gentleman's Magazine*, cxxiv(2), 461.
[31] James, *Durham Univ. Journal*, lvii, 82.

If there was thus a widely shared sense of grievance and oppression, why was it that only in certain areas did it result in rebellion? Compared with France, taxation in England was relatively light — even in 1489 — and was seldom enough to provoke a crisis of subsistence: a multi-sided crisis, involving dearth and high food prices, was normally necessary for that. The 1488 harvest was not bad: the prices of wheat, barley, and rye, the main bread crop of the northern poor, were not significantly above average. We have seen that most of Yorkshire remained quiet and how few rebelled in the East Riding. It is impossible, of course, to assess the severity of the tax on individuals, but it was clearly insufficient to reduce taxpayers to starvation or to drive Yorkshiremen as a whole to desperation, however outraged they were at the level and form of taxation.[32] Taxpayers suffered from relative deprivation — they merely *felt* worse off than they had been. One area, however, was different, no doubt for sound economic reasons: the north Yorkshire agricultural region of Blackamore. Blackamore was predominantly high ground incorporating the North Yorkshire Moors: good sheep country, with some arable. 'Wheat could be grown only in the most favoured parts, and oats and rye were the chief crops.' 1488 was a good year for all grains except oats, for which prices were unusually high in 1489.[33] Possibly — but not probably — in this corner of the county taxation bore more heavily on a population suffering from a shortage of food and/or fodder and the inhabitants of Blackamore were driven to a desperation that other Yorkshiremen were spared. Only taxpayers could be directly affected: the poorest were exempt from taxation, if not from dearth. Even in Blackamore, however, only 700 men had joined Chamber on his march from Ayton when he reached South Kilvington.

Taxation, however, played little part in what follows, perhaps because collection was interrupted, more probably because opposition to taxes even in 1489 had limited social and geographical appeal as a rallying cry for rebellion once the rebels had left Blackamore. Certainly the rebels' so-called proclamation, obviously designed to broaden support, makes no mention of taxation. Instead its declared aim was:

---

[32] C. J. Harrison, 'Grain Price Analysis and Harvest Qualities 1465–1634', *Agricultural History Review*, xix(1971), 139–42, 148; *Agrarian History of England and Wales*, iv, *1500–1640*, ed. J. Thirsk (1967), 816; C. S. L. Davies, 'The Pilgrimage of Grace Reconsidered', in Slack, *Rebellion*, pp. 30–31.

[33] E. Kerridge, *The Agricultural Revolution* (1967), p. 167; Harrison, *AgHR*, xix, 139–42; Thirsk, p. 816.

to geynsstonde suche persons as is abowtwarde for to dystroy owre suffereyn lorde the Kynge and the Comowns of Engelond for such vnlawfull poyntys as Seynt Thomas of Caunterbery dyed for.[34]

The word 'vnlawfull' makes nonsense of the rest and must surely be William Paston's hostile gloss on the original: certainly the surviving copy anticipates accurately enough the events that were to follow and is thus probably based on an authentic original. But to what precisely does it refer? St Thomas, of course, was identified with the privileges of the Church, most obviously with benefit of clergy for criminous clerks. This might well be regarded as unlawful in the circumstances of 1489, since an 'Act to take awaye the benefytt of Clargye from certayne persons' had been passed by Parliament earlier the same year. This, however, was a limited first measure, which specified that 'every persone not being within orders', who had once been admitted to benefit (by demonstrating his capacity to read) for a serious crime, would not be allowed it again. There were two chaplains among the early conspirators, John Whitwell of Ayton and John Smith of Thirsk, and it may be, as Dr Davies suggests for 1536–37, that benefit was purely a sectional interest of the clergy. Certainly, if the 1489 act was understood, it possessed limited popular appeal. No clerks, criminous or otherwise, are known to have joined the insurrection afterwards and the clergy do not seem to have played as important a role in recruiting as in the 1470 and 1536 Lincolnshire uprisings. More credibly, perhaps the rebel proclamation does not refer to benefit of clergy, but to another urgent matter.[35]

Another clerical privilege, a distinctive feature of the North, was sanctuary. St Thomas's murder was itself an infringement of sanctuary, and Henry VII steadily encroached on it, although its abolition had to wait until 1536. Traitors took refuge in the extensive northern franchises in both the fourteen-sixties and after 1485. Their immunity was respected until 1486, when Sir Humphrey Stafford was removed from the chapel of St Paul, Culham (Oxon.), tried and executed. This high-handed act was justified by a literal interpretation of Culham's charter, which did not *specifically* mention traitors, and was the model for future action in the North. On 13 June 1486 the King's council ordered the removal from the palatinate of Durham of the traitor Robin of Redesdale, who had been

---

[34] *Paston L.&P.* I, 659.

[35] *Statutes of the Realm*, II, 538; J. G. Bellamy, *Criminal Law and Society in Late Medieval England* (Gloucester, 1984), pp. 131–32; Davies, in Slack, *Rebellion*, pp. 30–31; M. E. James, 'Obedience and Dissent in Henrician England: The Lincolnshire Rebellion 1536', *Past and Present*, 48 (1970), 18; M. A. Hicks, *False, Fleeting, Perjur'd Clarence* (Gloucester, 1980), p. 68.

involved in Viscount Lovell's rising, 'the priviledg of St Cuthbert to be seene in the meane tyme'. Robin's fate is unknown, but the scrutiny of the charter cannot have been wholly favourable, as in 1491 the extradition of Sir Robert Chamberlain was so arranged that the episcopal franchise *appeared* undamaged and in 1495 the sheriff of Durham surrendered two further traitors. Similarly on 20 August 1487 the King assured Archbishop Rotherham that he had not infringed the privileges of the archiepiscopal liberty of Hexhamshire and would not do so in future, if he removed the convicted traitors Thomas and Herbert Redshaw, adding that any such sanctuarymen 'shalbe (ar)raigned uppon the same high treason and not uppon no petite treason ne felonye'.[36] In cases of treason, therefore, Henry had largely overcome the obstacle of sanctuary by 1489, when indeed his commissioners heard cases arising from the liberties of Allerton, Howden, and Beverley and required the franchise jurors to make their presentments at York. Given our limited knowledge of the franchises and traitors active in the North after 1485, it may well be that every liberty was affected by these encroachments. The natural protectors of the franchises, Archbishop Rotherham and Bishop Sherwood, apparently acquiesced in the infringement of local liberties in the national interest. We cannot know the response to these encroachments by the sanctuarymen or those northerners sympathetic to the traitors. Perhaps the infringement of sanctuary became a general grievance. Otherwise law-abiding northerners, in the words of Edward Hall, may have rebelled 'only for the tuicion and defence of their common liberties and freedom, where he would plucke and by his extreme power taken from them'. Hall, of course, was writing after the abolition of such franchises and after their re-assertion by the rebels during the Pilgrimage of Grace.[37] The danger may have been less obvious in 1489, but Hall's comment gains support from recruitment of rebels from Allertonshire and Beverley and by disturbances reported in the Durham palatinate. This in turn strongly suggests (but does not prove) that sanctuary was one unlawful point to which Northumberland's killers turned to broaden their appeal.

[36] I. D. Thornley, 'The Destruction of Sanctuary', in *Tudor Studies*, ed. R. W. Seton-Watson (1924), pp. 199–200; Chrimes, *Henry VII*, pp. 71, 161; *Y.C.R.* II, 3; *Select Cases in the Council of Henry VII*, ed. C. G. Bayne & W. H. Dunham, Selden Society, LXXV (1956), 8; *Letters and Papers illustrative of the Reigns of Richard III and Henry VII*, ed. J. Gairdner, Rolls Series (2 vols, 1861–63), I, 98–100; G. T. Lapsley, *County Palatine of Durham* (1924), p. 229n; *A History of Northumberland*, ed. A. B. Hinds and others (15 vols, Newcastle, 1893–1940), III, 41; *Reg. Rotherham*, I, 220; J. C. Cox, *Sanctuaries and Sanctuary-Seekers in Medieval England* (1911), pp. 136 sqq, 144 sqq.
[37] *Hall's Chronicle*, p. 443; A. J. Fletcher, *Tudor Rebellions* (1968), p. 129.

Not all liberties were ecclesiastical. The city of York was itself a county. Its full records tempt historians to ascribe undue importance to it, and in 1489 its citizens bulk larger in the record than they probably did in the rising as a whole simply because the commission sat at York. Certainly the citizens of this decaying provincial capital shared the hostility to taxation shown by the rural rebels, perhaps particularly because of the especially favourable treatment on financial matters they had received from Richard III.[38] York was acutely jealous of its rights and clashed, sometimes violently, with other jurisdictions, such as the Minster, St Mary's Abbey, and the sheriff of Yorkshire. Themselves committed to the defence of the city against the rebels, the city council somewhat officiously urged the Abbey, Minster, four orders of friars, and St Leonard's Hospital — all with liberties within the city — to prepare 'defensable array for keping of this Cite as they woll answer to the King'. They allowed the sheriff of Yorkshire and nine retainers to enter York castle and also agreed to admit Lord Clifford and a hundred retainers subject to the consent of the townspeople. The latter were even more jealous of the city's liberties than their social superiors: they

denied the entrie of the Lords Clifford and othre, that in nowise noon othre gentilman of what degre or condicon he be of be suffred to enter this the Kyngs Chaumbre and so all to be excludet and noon to have reule bot the Maiour, Aldermen and the Shireffs.

On 11 May Sir Marmaduke Constable, sheriff of Yorkshire, sought to garrison York with the gentry of the county, but was refused admittance[39] — a decision perhaps influenced by traitors within, already in contact with the rebels without, and certainly one that facilitated the fall of the city. It is ironic that it was the defences subject to the corporation and not those of the liberties that proved unequal to the challenge.

Citizens of York felt strongly about taxation, but it is unlikely that this lies at the root of Wrangwish's treachery. The corporation was quite unable to control the populace and may indeed have been divided by faction. Certainly the annual mayoral elections on St Blaise's day (3 February) were hotly contested — this office, at least, was much sought after — and were frequently accompanied by disturbances. A riot during the 1489 elections, at which the commons petitioned about the city's finances, was anxiously reported to Northumberland by the city council, 'to the intent that if privily any misreport were made to him, he might be

[38] See above, p. 376 ; L. Attreed, 'The King's Interest: York's fee farm and the central government, 1482–92', *NH*, xvii (1981), 30–31.
[39] *Y.C.R.* ii, 46–48.

ascertained of the truth'. Unfortunately the King intervened, determined to punish the offenders, and on 10 April 1489 appointed a commission to inquire into 'all trespasses, embraceries, maintenances, assemblies and other offences . . . and to commit the offenders to prison to await trial'. The King intended that 'the offenders should be punished according to his lawes'.[40] Alderman Wrangwish may well have been among the offenders: a leading alderman and twice mayor, he was probably ambitious to serve again and was formerly Richard III's most committed supporter in the city. There may have been others like John Brampton, formerly imprisoned for insubordination, and the fletcher Hugh Bunting. As in 1381[41] the proposed commission was itself regarded as a breach of the civic franchises, to be resisted if possible. The motive of Wrangwish and the humbler rebels may have been to secure the city against the King and to avoid punishment for their involvement in the election riot, presumably either by negotiation or military victory. Acquiescence with the rebels, if not outright support, characterized the attitude of the citizens. The city council was isolated in its obedience to the King and its opposition to the commons, but its loyal stance alone may have prevented the suspension of the city's privileges. The council blamed the disputed elections for the trouble, proposing as a remedy less democratic electoral procedures. King Henry agreed with both diagnosis and remedy, duly issuing a new charter,[42] and dropped the inquiry into the 1489 riots. Nevertheless the cure did not work and riots persisted at election time, because the root causes — the ambition of individual aldermen and the issues associated with them — remained. Indeed, they were much like those of the thirteen-eighties.

Taxation, sanctuary, and local faction, though undoubtedly live issues in York and Yorkshire, lured too few into insurrection seriously to threaten Henry VII or the existing social and political order. The rebel proclamation denounced not the King, but 'such persons' — the

[40] *Gentleman's Magazine*, cxxiv(2), 463; *Calendar of Patent Rolls*, 1485–94, p. 283. For Wrangwish and factions in York, see D. M. Palliser, 'Richard III and York', *Richard III and the North*, ed. R. E. Horrox (Hull, 1986), pp. 64–67. Compare the situation in 1381 described by Professor Dobson in Hilton & Aston, *English Rising*, pp. 119–20. For attitudes to office-holding, see R. B. Dobson, 'Urban Decline in Late Medieval England', *Transactions of the Royal Historical Society*, 5th ser. xxvii (1977), 13–14; J. I. Kermode, 'Urban Decline? The Flight from Office in Late Medieval York', *Economic History Review*, 2nd ser. xxxv (1982), 179–98. I hope to discuss the election of mayors of York elsewhere.

[41] Dobson, in Hilton & Aston, *English Rising*, pp. 119, 122–23. For what follows, see Hicks, *Clarence*, p. 68: 'the king was comming downe wt grete power into Lincolneshire, where the Kinges jugges shuld sitte and hang & draw grete noumbr' of the commons'.

[42] *Y.C.R.* ii, 49.

perennial evil councillors? — directly responsible. Without such 'evil councillors', however fictional, the demonstration could not be legitimate and there could be little hope of redress.[43] Few were prepared to face the King in battle — even in Yorkshire the *de facto* King commanded allegiance — and hence perhaps Sir John Egremont's premature departure from York to Richmondshire in search of recruits of sterner stuff. This was precisely what Henry VII feared — an aristocratic uprising designed to supplant him with a Yorkist successor of Richard III — and this was also what past experience had revealed unrest in Yorkshire to involve. Henry's proclamation and indictments alike accused the insurgents of treason and a case can be made out that this was an aim of the 1489 rebellion. Two of the original five plotters were natives of Thirkelby and Sowerby, Richard's manors as Duke of Gloucester, and one later recruit, Thomas Wady, had rebelled in 1487. Both Wrangwish and Egremont had served Richard. The rebel proclamation attempted to widen the scope of the rebellion, appealing to the whole North, seeking the adherence of the gentry and yeomen. The Gatherley Moor rendezvous was clearly chosen to attract Richard's Middleham affinity and Egremont's visits to Sheriff Hutton and Richmondshire were meant to recruit former Ricardians. The name in the proclamation — Hobbe Hyrste — had a suspicious sound, since northern rebels with pseudonyms traditionally led risings with political and dynastic objectives. Several sources suspected that the commons were being directed on behalf of a third party.[44] In fact the rising falls chronologically between the careers of the pretenders Lambert Simnel and Perkin Warbeck, and between the death of the Earl of Lincoln and majority of the Earl of Warwick, both genuine Yorkist princes, so (as in 1536) there was no credible claimant to support. In contrast to other rebellions, when they claimed to be coerced, local gentry and clergy had no apparent difficulty in resisting summonses on pain of death. On the lookout for wider ramifications and an evil genius in the background, Henry's justices found nothing. They could not connect the various disturbances before 28 April and failed to implicate either Wrangwish or Egremont in Northumberland's murder or other events before that date. The native of Thirkelby was acquitted, Wady occurs no sooner than 13 May, and nobody was recruited from either Richmondshire or Sheriff Hutton. That King Henry was content with these findings and accepted the submission of the rebels shows that he appreciated the limited nature of the insurrection.

[43] *Paston L.&P.* I, 659. The conventional phrase was quite wrong in this case.
[44] Skelton, p. 31; *Great Chronicle of London*, ed. A. H. Thomas & I. D. Thornley (1938), p. 242; see above, 365.

The tempo of the rebellion was very slow. No doubt the insurgents were mainly illiterate pedestrians, recruited by word of mouth. It is significant that the *written* proclamation was addressed to the gentry and yeomen, more commonly literate than the craftsmen, husbandmen, and labourers, who made up most of the rebels. By employing the official Beverley bell-ringer the rebels were drawing on the established local channel of communication, used for example to summon townsmen to funerals and obits.[45] The relative immobility of the rebels, who travelled only thirty miles in three weeks, is reminiscent of the Lincolnshire Rebellion of 1470, Kett's Rebellion of 1549, and the Pilgrimage of Grace of 1536–37, although the words 'inkennell' and 'camp' were not yet used.[46] Since they sought redress of grievances, not revolution, their forces existed only to compel the authorities to make concessions. Having killed Northumberland, these rebels had to wait for someone to arrive to treat with them and had also to attract enough recruits to preclude a military solution and force the King to negotiate. Only the numbers of Cade's rebels in 1450 persuaded Henry VI's government to treat rather than use force. By 17 May Egremont at least realized that the number and calibre of the insurgents was insufficient to deter a royal attack. Even in those popular risings where recruitment was successful, such inertia surrendered the initiative to the authorities and enabled them to choose their tactics. Time always favoured the government, and negotiated agreements, when reached, were seldom honoured. Indeed, it was irrational to suppose that they would be respected and to rely on the word of those who regarded the insurgents as traitors. Small-scale riots, which represented only a limited threat, stood a better chance of success and were less likely to end in the punishment of those involved.

In contrast to both popular riots and rebellions, aristocratic risings were characterized by speed and urgency. Lambert Simnel's campaign in 1487 took only a fortnight from his landing at Furness to the battle at Stoke by Newark. Generally mounted and familiar with arms, aristocratic rebels aimed to wrest the initiative from the Crown by penetrating deeply into the heart of the kingdom, thereby denying the King time to

[45] Compare the use of the municipal bell-ringer at Doncaster in 1536, the pulpit in Lincolnshire in 1470, and 'Markets, fairs, kin and service' in Oxfordshire in 1596, G. W. Bernard, *Power of the Early Tudor Nobility: A Study of the Fourth and Fifth Earls of Shrewsbury* (Brighton, 1985), p. 38; Hicks, *Clarence*, p. 68; Walter, *P&P*, 107, pp. 104–06.
[46] *Camden Misc.* I, 6–10; D. MacCulloch, 'Kett's Rebellion in Context', in Slack, *Rebellion*, pp. 39–67, esp. pp. 47–49; A. J. Fletcher, *Tudor Rebellions* (2nd edn, 1973), pp. 24–32. In 1596 the Oxfordshire rebels saw such camps as ends in themselves, Walter, *P&P*, 107, p. 92.

make good his natural superiority in men and resources and forcing on him the pitched battle that offered them the best hope of victory. In 1487 opportunities to recruit were sacrificed for speed. Kings orchestrated their counter-measures equally rapidly. In contrast, the Lincolnshire rebels of 1470 and the Yorkshire ones of 1489 showed urgency only when pressed by Sir Robert Welles and Sir John Egremont, two aristocratic leaders who knew what must be done. No wonder then and on subsequent occasions Yorkshire rebels respected their social superiors and sought their leadership. Certainly there was no class element in the 1489 rising.

If popular rebellions required such long periods for recruitment, should they not normally have been scotched at birth by the local magistracy, as at Ackworth in 1492?[47] Even aristocratic risings took time to take off, like that of Robin of Redesdale in 1469 and Buckingham's rebellion in 1483.[48] Invading pretenders needed substantial escorts if they were to survive long enough ashore to start recruiting.[49] Had not Northumberland succumbed to unrelated divisions in his retinue, the 1489 rebellion would have ended at South Kilvington. That the insurgents were already 700 strong may be because Blackamore had no powerful resident lord. Thereafter the vacuum left by the Earl's death permitted sufficient recruitment to deter attack by any other local magnate, but the rebels were nevertheless opposed by such notables as Lord Clifford, Abbot Senhouse, and the sheriff. Like Northumberland in 1471,[50] the natural leaders of 1489 *may* have sought to restrain their inferiors from pursuing their natural inclinations and thus forced recruitment to fail at Gatherley Moor, in west and south Yorkshire, and to limit its success in the Percy country of the East Riding. Could rebellions attain serious proportions only if the local rulers were absent or sympathetic? Such a conclusion can be supported with reference to power vacuums not just in Yorkshire in 1489, but in the West Country in 1496, in two risings in 1549, and with reference to aristocratic sympathy for popular rebels in Kent in 1471 and perhaps in 1450, in Lincolnshire in 1470, in the Furness peninsular in 1487, and in the south-west in 1497.[51] If such favourable

[47] *Plumpton Corr.* pp. 94–97.
[48] Compare Dockray, *Ricardian*, 83, 248–49; C. D. Ross, *Richard III* (1981), pp. 115–17.
[49] For example, Edward IV in 1470, *Historie of the Arrivall of Edward IV*, ed. J. O. Halliwell, Camden Society, I, (1838), 2–6.
[50] *The Arrivall*, p. 6. Compare the restraining influence of the 4th Earl of Shrewsbury in 1536, Bernard, *Tudor Nobility*, ch. 2.
[51] Slack, *Rebellion*, p. 7; Griffiths, *Henry VI*, pp. 620–23; Hicks, *Clarence*, pp. 62–69; Arthurson, pp. 3–7; Richmond, *EHR*, LXXV, 687–92; Hicks, *NH*, XIV, 97.

conditions were essential for popular risings to progress, may not Tudor kings have been right in suspecting that local aristocrats were involved in major revolts in 1497 and 1536?

IV

The Yorkshire Rebellion is thus a classic example of the 'loyal rebellion'. Respectable, non-violent, and confident of their own rightness, the rebels turned first to the magnates for intercession with the King, which was apparently forthcoming. Aristocratic sympathy, however, was not synonymous with aristocratic commitment. The rebels were not the county community in action—to say the entire country was involved is nonsense[52] — but a coalition of numerically weak sectional interests.

The capacity of monarchs, competent or not, to reject good advice is graphically illustrated by this rising. If it was Henry's own refusal to make tax concessions that initially precipitated the rebellion, its defeat did not cause him to change his mind. His insistence on obedience, his refusal (in stark contrast to Edward IV)[53] to temporize with former rebels, and his disregard of advice reduced Northumberland's capacity to satisfy those he ruled, diminishing his contribution to social peace and his capacity to quiet unrest. In contrast, following his victory at Ackworth in 1492, Surrey 'sued the Kynges Hyghnes for ther Pardones, whiche he obteyned, and *wan therby the favour of the Countrey*'.[54] Local rulers preferred to avert rebellion rather than suppress it and to prevent the rancour and insubordination that might otherwise colour local relations for years to come.

On the evidence of 1489, Henry rated his financial needs and authority above popular consent. He could have reduced the offensive taxation without endangering his authority in the North or driving the disaffected into rebellion. Instead the revolt destroyed the Earl, the King's intermediary, and launched Henry into a risky experiment in regional government. On other occasions, too, Henry's well-known preference for rigour over conciliation may have promoted rather than dispelled unrest. Perhaps, as Mr James remarked,[55] the rising was forced on the rebels by a King more familiar with French absolutism than the mixed constitution and the compromises of medieval England on which governors and governed normally relied.

[52] James, *Durham Univ. Journal*, LVII, 80–87. But such a comment *is* appropriate for 1497, Arthurson, p. 6.
[53] *Camden Misc.* I, 12–16.
[54] Pollard, *Henry VII*, I, 81.
[55] James, *Durham Univ. Journal*, LVII, 82–83.

Such compromises, it must be admitted, sacrificed certain objectives, such as tax-revenue, in return for peace, order, and unity. Most monarchs opted for such *political* benefits and preferred government by consent to arbitrary rule. Yet we should not forget that in 1489 Henry achieved his objective, making no allowances and apparently securing payment in full from Yorkshire. He did likewise on other occasions[56] and moreover overawed the aristocracy, quelled risings of all types, and secured an unusual degree of obedience among his officers and subjects. However unattractive, however difficult to apply, an uncompromising rigour was apparently a genuine alternative to conciliation when employed with his consistency. Was Henry VII unique, or will research reveal other instances of this alternative strategy to set against the conciliatory response so fully documented by Dr Walter and others?[57]

[56] 'Henry VII was evidently very successful in obtaining, usually with expedition and efficiency, the most that could be got out of the traditional subsidy of fifteenths and tenths', Chrimes, *Henry VII*, p. 197. For what follows, see J. R. Lander, *Crown and Nobility 1450–1509* (1976), ch. 11.

[57] J. Walter & K. Wrightson, 'Dearth and the Social Order in Early Modern England', in Slack, *Rebellion*, pp. 108–28; Walter in *An Ungovernable People*, pp. 47–84; Walter, *P&P*, 107, 90–143.

23

The Case of Sir Thomas Cook, 1468

IN mid-June 1468 agents of Edward IV arrested a tailor at the Kentish port of Queenborough. His name was John Cornelius and he was a servant of Sir Robert Whittingham,[1] an irreconcilable Lancastrian. After his own attainder in 1461, Whittingham had continued to support the deposed King Henry VI. In 1463 he escorted Queen Margaret to Burgundy and, on the defeat of the northern Lancastrians, he accompanied her to St Michel in Bar, her next refuge. In the summer of 1468 he was among the garrison of Harlech Castle,[2] the last Lancastrian possession on the British mainland. Cornelius had been employed by Margaret as emissary to her partisans in England and at the time of his capture he was probably returning to France. Under examination he named those for whom he had brought letters.[3] They were a hitherto unknown circle based on London. Among them was a John Hawkins, a servant of Lord Wenlock, who made accusations against Sir Thomas Cook.[4]

Cook was a draper of uncertain origin who rose to be mayor of London.[5] In 1468 drapery remained his main business interest,[6] but he also traded in other commodities,[7] farmed royal estates[8] and acted as customer of Southampton.[9] He was a leading creditor of Edward IV[10] and enjoyed the favour of Princess Margaret.[11] As his

1. 'Annales rerum anglicarum', *Letters and Papers Illustrative of the Wars of the English in France*, ed. J. Stevenson (Rolls Ser., 1864), ii. ii. 789, later cited as *Annales*. I wish to acknowledge the assistance of Mr C. A. J. Armstrong and Miss M. M. Condon, both of whom read and criticized this article. Miss Ann Sutton kindly allowed me to read the draft of her article, 'Sir Thomas Cook and his "Troubles": An Investigation', *Guildhall Studies in London History*, iii (1978).
2. C. L. Scofield, *Life and Reign of Edward the Fourth* (London, 1923), i. 180, 220, 301, 368, 459.
3. *Annales*, p. 790.
4. *Ibid.*
5. For biographies see B. Brogden Orridge, 'Some particulars of Alderman Philip Malpas and Alderman Sir Thomas Cooke, K.B.', *Illustrations of Jack Cade's Rebellion* (London, 1869), pp. 1–22; *Dictionary of National Biography*; J. C. Wedgwood, *History of Parliament, 1439–1509, Biographies* (London, 1938), pp. 217–18; S. L. Thrupp, *The Merchant Class of Medieval London* (Univ. of Michigan, 1948), p. 333.
6. See the quantity of cloth in his possession, *Issues of the Exchequer (10 Henry III to 39 Henry VI)*, ed. F. Devon (London, 1837), 491; P.R.O. E 405/48 m. 1.
7. E.g. salt fish, P.R.O. E 122/128/10 m. 5d.
8. *Cal. Fine Rolls, 1461–71*, 18; A. R. Myers, 'The Household of Queen Elizabeth Woodville, 1466–7', B[ulletin of the] J[ohn] R[ylands] L[ibrary] l (1967–8), 221.
9. *The Great Chronicle of London*, ed. A. H. Thomas and I. D. Thornley (London, 1938), p. 205, henceforth cited as *G.C.*
10. Scofield, *Edward IV*, i. 453.
11. *Ibid.* i. 455. For evidence of their continued relations see B[ritish] L[ibrary] Add. MS 48031, fo. 187ᵛ; P.R.O. DL 29/41/800 m. 1.

wealth grew, he became prominent in London, being elected alderman in 1456, sheriff in 1453–4 and mayor in 1462–3,[1] and marrying
a daughter of Philip Malpas, draper and alderman, whose other
daughter married another draper, Ralph Josseline, mayor in 1464–5.[2]
Cook spent his wealth in conspicuous personal luxury. At his house
in the parish of St Christopher Stocks, ward of Breadstreet, he
had an elaborate set of tapestries depicting the Last Judgement
and Passion, Alexander and Nebuchadnezzar, which were con-
servatively valued at £984[3] and were coveted by the duchess of
Bedford.[4] His plate was worth £397.[5] Like other successful businessmen, Cook had a country residence at Gidea Park in Essex, which
he embellished and improved.[6] He operated extensively in the land
market, his name being one of the most frequent to occur among
the Essex feet of fines.[7] His wealth was known to be great. His
arrest was a sensation.

It was not that he was the only public figure to be implicated,
nor even the leading Londoner to be involved. But Cook was the
only member of either category whom Edward was able to arrest
and was consequently the only one to stand trial. To judge from the
London chronicles, he overshadowed his humbler co-defendants.
Other important Londoners who escaped are mentioned in passing[8]
but the lesser men who were convicted, sentenced and hanged are
ignored.

In parliament in 1470, according to Robert Fabyan, Cook campaigned boldly for the reversal of his sentence and for compensation
from those whom he held responsible.[9] Although he pleaded not
guilty in 1468, one cannot tell if he spoke so plainly as there is
no description of his trial.

It is uncertain who wrote the *Annales* formerly attributed to
William Worcester[10] which contains material not found elsewhere.
It has been used to supplement the city chronicles even though the
compiler was not obsessed with Cook but was interested in all the
accused. He believed that there was a plot and does not state that
Cook was innocent.[11]

1. Wedgwood, *Hist. Parl. Biogs.* p. 217.
2. Brogden Orridge, *Illus. of Cade's Rebellion*, p. 7.
3. P.R.O. E 405/48 m. 1; see below p. 96, n. 7.
4. *G.C.* 208, which states that it depicted the siege of Jerusalem.
5. P.R.O. E 405/48 m, 1.   6. Wedgwood, *Hist. Parl. Biogs.* p. 217 n.
7. *Feet of Fines for Essex*, iv (*1423–1547*), ed. P. H. Reaney and M. Fitch (Colchester, 1964).
8. 'Gregory's Chronicle' in *Historical Collections of a Citizen of London*, ed. J. Gairdner, Camden Soc. n.s. xvii (1876), 236–7; 'A Brief Latin Chronicle' in *Three Fifteenth-Century Chronicles*, ed. J. Gairdner, Camden Soc. n.s. xviii (1880), 182.
9. R. Fabyan, *New Chronicles of England and France*, ed. H. Ellis (London, 1811), p. 660.
10. For its authorship see K. B. McFarlane, 'William Worcester: a Preliminary Survey', *Studies presented to Sir Hilary Jenkinson*, ed. J. Conway-Davies (Oxford, 1957), pp. 206–7, 207 n. It is generally hostile to Edward IV; C. D. Ross, *Edward IV* (London, 1974), p. 432.   11. *Annales*, p. 789.

The fullest London narratives, Fabyan's Chronicle and the *Great Chronicle of London*, both depend on the lost 'Main City Chronicle' up to 1496 and are therefore later.[1] Robert Fabyan's authorship has been argued for both[2] but this conflicts with a statement in *G.C.* regarding the Cook affair that the author was Cook's apprentice,[3] which Fabyan was not.[4] This passage at least can hardly be by Fabyan, but the two resemble each other more closely than any other city chronicle. The shorter account of the Cook affair in Fabyan's chronicle seems to paraphrase *G.C.* which, for 1468, was probably its source.[5]

Written after 1478, John Warkworth's brief account is generally unfavourable to Edward IV[6] and is the first source to give prominence to Cook's innocence. If the 'Main City Chronicle' is faithfully represented by the scanty Vitellius AXVI,[7] it is improbable that Cook's innocence was accepted until well into the Tudor period. It can hardly have been common knowledge in May 1483, where it appears in a later work of Sir Thomas More.[8]

To Fabyan and the author of *G.C.*, Cook had been framed by his enemies. They thought him falsely accused on charges under torture and that he was denied a fair trial. *G.C.* alleges that Chief Justice Markham directed a jury to acquit Cook of treason, for which he was relieved of his office, and on being convicted only of misprision, Cook was fined 8,000 marks. On payment he was dismissed from his aldermanry and a further 800 marks was demanded in queen's gold. According to them, both Cook and his wife were imprisoned for long periods, which enabled the queen's father to ransack their houses in London and Essex.[9] This stress on financial loss reflects their belief that the case was concocted for financial motives and that Cook was hounded for his wealth. To them the true villain was not Edward IV but the Wydevilles.[10]

Fabyan's chronicle was printed in 1516 but *G.C.* was lost for several centuries, although certain details were included in John Stow's *Annales of England*.[11] Their interpretation has been accepted by modern historians, notably Miss Scofield. Like pseudo-Worcester but unlike these city chronicles, she believed that there was a

1. *G.C.* lxxii.
2. This is mainly because surviving manuscripts are in the same hand, *ibid.* xliii–lxix.
3. *Ibid.* 205.
4. *Ibid.* xl, xliv, 430.
5. The editors of *G.C.* did not rule out a common scribe rather than common authorship, *ibid.* xliv.
6. J. Warkworth, *Chronicle of the First Thirteen Years of the Reign of King Edward the Fourth*, ed. J. O. Halliwell, Camden Soc. vi (1839), 5.
7. *G.C.* lxxiv.
8. Written *c.* 1514–18, this may draw on Fabyan's chronicle, T. More, *History of King Richard III*, ed. R. S. Sylvester (*Complete Works*, Yale edn. ii, 1963), 70.
9. *G.C.* 205–7; see below p. 94.
10. *Fabyan's Chronicle*, p. 660.
11. J. Stow, *Annales or a Generall Chronicle of England* (London, 1631), p. 420.

Lancastrian conspiracy[1] but she thought that Cook was not involved. She knew that it was the king who benefited from Cook's misfortunes and was also aware of his financial straits. All his resources scarcely sufficed to pay for his sister's marriage to the duke of Burgundy, the wedding being twice postponed on these grounds alone. Miss Scofield thought that initially Edward believed in Cook's guilt, but later persecuted him because he wanted his possessions. To her 'the truth of the whole ugly story seems to be that Earl Rivers and his wife, who for some reason wanted to get rid of Cook, played on the cupidity of the king . . . in order to accomplish their purpose', a view closely akin to that of Fabyan and in *G.C.* The latest modern commentator, Dr C. D. Ross, reached similar conclusions after studying sources not available to Miss Scofield.[2]

Miss Scofield's book was published before *G.C.*, which contains much more than Stow included in his *Annales* and gives the fullest account of Cook's case. She was also unable to use the record of the commission that tried Cook. This is incomplete, as it consists only of the returns of the London sessions,[3] but it confirms that Cook was tried for treason, acquitted of this but convicted of misprision.

Together with pseudo-Worcester, these new sources offer the means of reconstructing what happened, but neither can be accepted without question. To compare the biased *G.C.* with the apparently dispassionate record, one is bound to share Professor Bellamy's conclusion that all was done by orderly legal process and hence to discount reports of miscarriage of justice.[4] The formal record always appears orderly however irregular the trial, but it comprises the indictments framed by the prosecution. It is natural to point to inconsistencies in the indictments if they are approached only for material supporting the narrative accounts,[5] but this is unfair to the commission. The justices presided over permutations of four juries of presentment, four trial juries, about ten indictments, and eighteen defendants.[6] Cook was only one of these. All were tried on treason charges, fabricated or otherwise, and, rightly or wrongly, several were convicted of treason or misprision, including Cook himself. One cannot afford to neglect the other defendants.

There is no doubt that Edward made a profit from the affair,

1. For what follows see Scofield, *Edward IV*, i. 450, 454, 459–62.
2. C. D. Ross, 'The reign of Edward IV', *Fifteenth-century England, 1399–1509*, eds. S. B. Chrimes, C. D. Ross and R. A. Griffiths (Manchester, 1972), p. 51; idem, *Edward IV*, pp. 100–1.
3. P.R.O. KB 9/319. There were others in Middlesex for which one indictment survives, P.R.O. KB 9/321/109. At least one man, William Britte, was indicted for whom there is no record, P.R.O. E 218/11/Edw. IV [unnumbered p.s. writ, 30 July 1468].
4. J. G. Bellamy, 'Justice under the Yorkist kings', *American Journal of Legal History* ix (1965), 143–5.
5. Ross, *Fifteenth-century Eng.* p. 51 n. 11.   6. P.R.O. KB 9/319.

although not to the extent suggested by John Warkworth.[1] Of the eight known to have been fined,[2] three were aldermen but one was so obscure as to be almost unidentifiable. The fines were not the sentences imposed in court. The justices of king's bench were exonerated from sentencing Cook, whose fine was assessed by the royal council.[3] He was fined at the king's pleasure, the penalty for his offence,[4] but he is exceptional because he was convicted first. Others agreed fines out of court before the verdict[5] or even without being tried.[6] If Edward wanted to make money, he would have benefited more had they been condemned for treason and forfeited their lands. These fines were the defendants' compositions in lieu of the penalties for their offences and were presumably less damaging than the sentence itself. They were the price of immunity for the accused, by which they were protected from their due sentences and from complete exposure, from the physical discomfort of prison or sanctuary, from the neglect or wasting of their effects. They were also Edward's means of reaching those who could not be convicted, either because he lacked the necessary proof or because they failed to appear in court. Judicial proceedings depended on the appearance of the accused. Defaulters could be outlawed and their chattels seized but their estates were not forfeit.

These fines were intended by the king to be a real penalty and also had a gratifying effect on royal finance. Yet they had to be acceptable to the payer. If royal demands were inordinate, the defendant was better off as an outlaw. He could not be fined to his utter ruin. As a result of his massive fine, Sir Thomas Cook had to give up some of his luxurious fittings[7] and even sell some tenements on unfavourable terms,[8] yet he was able to retain his main estates and was back in business in 1469.[9] These fines were based on bargains reflecting the balance of advantage of the two parties. They should have been adjusted to the accused's circumstances.

It is possible that the whole case was fabricated to obtain fines. Did Edward use prosecution and imprisonment to bully victims into buying pardons? This might apply to the three aldermen, but not in every case. Most of the accused, although prosperous, lacked resources significant in terms of royal finance. In practice Edward could not insist on payment in cash, as their wealth was in stock. Cook paid his fine by 24 November,[10] which would have been

1. *Warkworth's Chron.* p. 5.
2. Scofield, *Edward IV*, i. 460 n., citing P.R.O. E 404/74/1/54.
3. *G.C.* 207; P.R.O. KB 27/829, *Rex*, m. 92d.;/830, *Rex*, m. 188d.
4. *G.C.* 207. 5. *E.g.* Hugh Pakenham, P.R.O. E 404/74/1/54; see below, p. 92.
6. *E.g.* Sir John Plummer, see below, p. 92-4.
7. *G.C.* 207-8; P.R.O. E 405/48 m. 1.
8. P.R.O. C 1/93/53.
9. *G.C.* 208; P.R.O. E 122/128/10 m. 5d.
10. P.R.O. E 159/245, Rec. Mich. 8 Edw. IV m. 31d.

impossible had he been required to convert his moveables into coin. Edward had to wait months or even years[1] for full satisfaction. Sir John Plummer's fine may have been partly paid from the moveables that he recovered from the escheator of Buckinghamshire.[2] The fines had so little impact on the treasury that they were used for assignments.[3] If Edward's motive was to secure a rapid influx of cash, he was disappointed. These fines made no contribution to the expense of his sister's wedding.

Only a few of the accused were former Lancastrians. Sir Gervase Clifton was suspected of treason in 1465 and Hugh Mulle's elder brother was attainted.[4] He had as clear a grievance against Edward IV as had Hugh Pakenham, who had lost the benefit of offices at Odiham (Hants.) that he had acquired before Edward's accession.[5]

Pakenham was servant to William Waynflete, bishop of Winchester,[6] chancellor and confessor of Henry VI.[7] It was probably by his influence that Pakenham attracted the favour of Henry VI and Queen Margaret, which earned him the keepership of the park of Freemantle (Hants.) in 1459.[8] At Queen Margaret's instigation, he was appointed customer of Southampton in 1458.[9] Pakenham replaced Thomas Cook, whom she had also nominated,[10] and who had held office almost continuously from 1448.[11]

G.C. adds that Cook was 'wardrober' to Queen Margaret.[12] If this means that he was keeper of her great wardrobe or treasurer of her chamber, the chronicler probably erred.[13] It is, however, possible, that as a draper Cook supplied her with cloth just as she was provided with jewels by Humphrey Hayford,[14] another of those accused of treason in 1468.

---

1. If payment was accompanied by a pardon: Plummer was not pardoned until Nov. 1468 or Husy until Feb. 1470, P.R.O. C 67/46 m. 22; C 237/46 [loose].

2. P.R.O. E 13/154, Hill. 8 Edw. IV mm. 5, 18.

3. P.R.O. E 405/48 m. 1.

4. Wedgwood, *Hist. Parl. Biogs.* pp. 195, 594.

5. *Cal. Pat. Rolls, 1452–61,* pp. 363–4; *Cal. Close Rolls, 1454–61,* pp. 215, 217–18; P.R.O. SC 6/1094/5 m. 5.

6. *Cal. Close Rolls, 1454–61,* p. 147; see below p. 88.

7. P.R.O. E 101/410/14, fo. 7.   8. *Cal. Pat. Rolls, 1452–61,* p. 505.

9. *Cal. Fine Rolls, 1452–61,* pp. 215–17. She was entitled to nominate a customer to ensure prompt payment of £1,000 annually, one of her more regular sources of income, A. R. Myers, 'The Household of Queen Margaret of Anjou, 1452–3', *B.J.R.L.* xl (1957–8), 83–84, 110, 111.   10. *G.C.* 205.

11. *Cal. Fine Rolls, 1445–52,* pp. 98–99, 134–6 ff. Even so Cook dishonoured some of her tallies, P.R.O. E 122/64/182.

12. *G.C.* 205.

13. John Norreys, 1446–58, and Sir Robert Whittingham, 1458–61, were successive keepers of her wardrobe; Norreys was treasurer of her chamber until succeeded by Edward Ellesmere in 1452, Myers, *B.J.R.L.* xl. 427 n.; P.R.O. DL 29/58/1106 m. 3d; Wedgwood, *Hist. Parl. Biogs.* p. 994.

14. Myers, 'The Jewels of Queen Margaret of Anjou', *B.J.R.L.* xlii (1959–60), 118; *Cal. Close Rolls, 1446–52,* p. 529. In 1446–7 he repaired her crown, P.R.O. E 101/409/17 m. 3. She wrote a letter on his behalf, *Letters of Queen Margaret of Anjou,* ed. C. Monro, Camden Soc. lxxxvi (1863), 124.

Service to Margaret probably introduced Cook to members of her household, such as her chamberlain Lord Wenlock, and he certainly knew her financial officers: Robert Tanfield, her receiver-general, with whom he conducted private business,[1] and John Norreys I,[2] father of one of the plotters of 1468. Cook and Norreys were associated in the conveyance of the former's land in Havering (Essex) in 1452.[3] It was probably they who were executors of William Aiscough, bishop of Salisbury in 1449.[4] Cook, Pakenham and Bishop Waynflete were associated in a charter in 1460.[5] Cook was clearly at home among Queen Margaret's servants.

It is possible but unlikely that this case was carefully contrived to extract money and round up Lancastrians. If the names extracted from Cornelius and Hawkins were false, then surely they were suggested by the government? The accused could then be expected to be either very rich or prominent former Lancastrians. In fact the majority had neither served Henry VI nor were wealthy; most were at best well-to-do and lacking in political weight rather than obvious targets of royal policy. Many more important ex-Lancastrians were in England against whom the crown could have proceeded. If Edward picked his victims, would he not have ensured their arrest by watching over them carefully? Would not they, if innocent, have been unaware of the danger and easy to apprehend? It was not like this at all. Only six of the accused were captured[6] and none of the remainder appeared in court. Several took sanctuary.[7] One of these, Sir John Plummer, was deprived of his aldermanry by his fellows as soon as he defaulted.[8] Is not one entitled to assume with the corporation of London that the fugitives were guilty? As outlaws they forfeited their chattels, as sanctuarymen their freedom of movement, so they must have anticipated even worse penalties if they stood trial.

The verdicts of the juries should be conclusive evidence. They are not because of allegations that the trial was rigged. According to *G.C.*, 'many enqyries were made ffor to fynde hym [Cook] gylty, and evyr he was quytt, tyll oon Jury by the meanys of sir John Fogg & other endighthid hym of treason'. Later he was tried at the Guildhall, where he was acquitted.[9] *G.C.* adds that the chief justice, Sir John Markham, was removed from office because, at his prompting, 'It was determynyd somewhat agayn the kyngys

1. P.R.O. E 122/140/71 m. 1; *Cal. Close Rolls, 1454–61*, p. 50.
2. Myers, *B.J.R.L.* xl. 392.
3. *Cal. Pat. Rolls, 1446–52*, p. 517.
4. P.R.O. E 159/231, Rec. East. 33 Hen. VI m. 27.
5. *Cal. Close Rolls, 1454–61*, pp. 433–4.
6. P.R.O. KB 9/319.
7. P.R.O. E 159/245, Rec. Trin. 8 Edw. IV m. 16; Corp. of London R.O. Journal 7, fo. 175.
8. On 4 July, Corp. of Lond. R.O. Journal 7, fo. 175.
9. *G.C.* 205–6.

pleasure & myend, that the offences doon by hym [Cook] were noo Treason but myspricion'.[1] When this occurred is uncertain.[2] At the trial proper no treasonable charge was redefined as misprision.[3] Of the two charges that were laid against Cook, the one of misprision was recognized as such before it was referred for trial,[4] so if there was ever any doubt about the status of the offence, Markham must have defined it at the presentment stage. No other reason is known for his replacement, which occurred by 23 January 1469.[5] G.C. also refers to the labouring of presenting juries, in support of which Dr Ross cites the dismissal of a jury and undue delays,[6] which imply that the whole process, not merely Cook's case, was rigged.

There were twenty-two members of the commission of oyer and terminer, headed by the duke of Clarence, which included four earls and eleven judges. It could act in numbers as small as two, of whom one had to be a judge or the mayor of London.[7] The commissioners probably availed themselves of this clause and operated in several committees so that business could be transacted more rapidly. The committees' composition is not known but they were probably three in number as three juries functioned at once. The names of the jurors in each case are recorded on the dorse of each indictment. From 4/6 July nine cases were heard by the jury headed by William Envelt,[8] henceforth called Jury A. The juries of Thomas Hill and Nicholas Plomme, B and C, were empanelled under a writ of 1 July.[9] Respectively they listened to three cases on 4/5 July[10] and eight on 4/6 July.[11] Jury D, led by William Bacon, was authorized on 5 July and empanelled next day,[12] when it heard three cases.[13]

Different juries made similar amendments of date and place to identical indictments,[14] an indication that the corrections of the first jury were not incorporated in the charge submitted to the others. This suggests that several copies were prepared in advance and that each of the original juries was meant to hear every case. This was not unusual.[15] The case against a defendant was apparently considered to be stronger if similar indictments had been approved by

1. *Ibid.* 207.
2. It occurs in the chronicle long after 18 July, but must be earlier, P.R.O. KB 9/319/1. It relates not to Edward's obstinacy but to the trial.
3. P.R.O. KB 27/830, *Rex*, m. 188d.
4. P.R.O. KB 9/319/10.
5. *Cal. Pat. Rolls, 1467-77*, p. 120. His successor had certainly taken over by then. Precisely when Markham ceased to be chief justice is not clear but he was acting as such on 28 Nov. 1468, P.R.O. KB 9/322/37, /47, /57, /67.
6. Ross, *Fifteenth-century Eng.* p. 51 n. 11; *Edward IV*, pp. 100-1.
7. P.R.O. KB 9/319/45.
8. *Ibid.* /26-30, /36-37, /40-41.
9. *Ibid.* /46-48.
10. *Ibid.* /24-25, /39.
11. *Ibid.* /31-35, /42-44.
12. *Ibid.* /20-21.
13. *Ibid.* /17-19.
14. *Ibid.* /39, /41, /42.
15. E.g. *ibid.* /41/38, /42.

different juries.[1] If one remembers that they not only heard evidence
but were expected to have special knowledge themselves, it is
comprehensible that the combined testimony of several presenting
juries could influence the panel at the trial. There was nothing
suspicious in the case being heard successively by several juries,
but it did not always happen: for example when charges against
defendants were rejected outright.[2]

The dates of indictments and amendments to them assist one in
tracing the progress of each case. Jury C, for instance, seems normally to have heard cases after Jury A.[3] Jury B appears under-
worked. It was apparently released on 5 July, perhaps because its
justices were required for the trial proper. This jury did not resist
the king's will: that was done by Jury A, which threw out indictments[4] and yet was retained. Jury B's release and the selection of
Jury D may not have been connected.

It is unreasonable to stress the slowness of the process. Admittedly
the first arrests occurred on or before 18 June, the commission
was not issued until 20 June, the empanelling of juries was ordered
only on 1 July and the trial did not commence until 4 July. Yet there
is little more than a fortnight between the discovery of the conspiracy and the start of the trial, less than in many later or modern
cases. Over the three days of 4/6 July twenty-four indictments were
heard and trials proper commenced on 5 July, when four defendants,
each indicted for the last time that day, were brought from the
Tower to Guildhall. One admitted guilt, another produced a
pardon, and the rest pleaded not guilty, necessitating trial by jury.
These juries were empanelled on 7 July, when their duties were
performed.[5] All those in custody had been tried on 8 July,[6] although
further charges were to be brought against two of them. On 14 July
the king granted a general pardon.[7] Far from being unduly slow, the
trial progressed at breakneck speed.

Lapse of time might stem from efforts at labouring recalcitrant
jurors to obtain a favourable verdict. Juries A, B and C started
work as soon as empanelled and achieved such an impressive turnover of cases that royal officers had little opportunity to pressurize
them. If they tried, they were unsuccessful. The juries freely amended
both the detail and substance of the indictment.[8] Three defendants
were acquitted outright. In several cases each jury indicted certain

---

1. E.g. *ibid.* /319/39, /41–42, /50.
2. They were Robert Knolles, William Belknap, and John Shuckburgh, *ibid.* /25–27, 39.
3. *Ibid.* /40, /42–43; see below pp. 91–2.
4. P.R.O. KB 9/319/26–27, /29. Dr Ross confused these two juries, *Edward IV*, pp. 100–1.
5. P.R.O. KB 9/319/49d.–50.   6. *Ibid.* /49d.–51d.
7. P.R.O. C 67/46 m. 38.
8. P.R.O. KB 9/319/18, /39, /41–42. Usually they amended the place and sometimes the date of the indictment.

defendants and acquitted the rest,[1] or they rejected certain charges while accepting others in the same indictment.[2] This is the essence of independence and discrimination.

In nominating the commission, Edward accepted Thomas Oulgreve, mayor of London, as *ex officio* chairman. Described as a 'replete and lumpish' man, Oulgreve slept in court[3] and was clearly not intimidating juries to obtain convictions. Jurors were empanelled by the sheriffs of London, one of whom was himself shortly to be indicted[4]: reason enough to suspect that they did not try to pick panels favourable to the crown, even were this possible when such panels were 86 strong.[5] Yet each juror indicted his near neighbour. Not only is it untrue that they would not 'accept charges of treason against prominent and respectable London citizens', but each jury did.[6] In three apparently politically sensitive cases where juries A, B and C returned only verdicts of misprision, this was the only charge under consideration when writs were issued to empanell trial juries.[7] Up to this stage there is no evidence of effective royal control.

Subsequently Jury D was empanelled to hear only the three cases of misprision and in each returned a true bill to the original treason charge.[8] These verdicts, which contradict what went before, must stem from political pressure, presumably exercised by labouring jurors who had not been involved hitherto. If Edward's influence could achieve such results, it is clear that it had not been fully exerted previously. This is consistent with *G.C.*'s statement that after being tried by several juries Cook was indicted by another that was laboured.[9] Yet Edward's authority failed to sustain these charges at the trial.

One of these cases concerned Sir Thomas Cook. It was originally alleged that on 20 October 1466 he was approached by Hugh Mulle and John Hawkins, who told him of Queen Margaret's invasion plans and that Cook offered them monetary support and conspired with them to destroy the king. Jury A acquitted Cook but indicted the other two,[10] implying that the meeting took place but that Cook did not concur. Amended charges were submitted to Jury C. One, designed to catch Mulle and Hawkins, said that they excited and procured Cook and others to send money to Margaret to assist her invasion, thereby adhering to her against the king.[11] The other, intended to ensnare Cook, stated that he concealed and laboured men known to be traitors.[12] A true bill was returned to each. Mulle

1. *Ibid.* /25–26, /32.
2. *Ibid.* /34–37.   3. *G.C.* 206.
4. Humphrey Hayford, P.R.O. KB 9/321/109.
5. *Ibid.* /319/47, of whom 28 served.
6. Ross, *Edward IV*, p. 101; P.R.O. KB 9/319/39, /41–42.
7. P.R.O. KB 9/319/40.   8. P.R.O. KB 9/319/17–19.
9. *G.C.* 205–6.   10. P.R.O. KB 9/319/40.
11. *Ibid.* /43.   12. *Ibid.* /44.

pleaded a pardon at his trial and Hawkins, who pleaded not guilty, was convicted and hanged.[1] Jury D approved the original charge of treason against Cook,[2] but at his trial, facing both counts, he was convicted only of misprision.[3] This was a just conclusion: even *G.C.* admits that he failed to expose Hawkins and Mulle, though denying that he offered them what they asked.[4]

Two other cases followed the same course. On 20 October 1466 Hugh Pakenham was approached by Piers Alfrey, told of Margaret's plans and asked for money, which he is alleged to have given. Jury A crossed out the bill and made no charges.[5] Jury C found Alfrey guilty, rejected the counts against Pakenham but added that he had concealed Alfrey's treason:[6] this jury, in other words, accepted that the meeting in the indictment took place. Jury D, to which the original charge was submitted, indicted both Alfrey and Pakenham.[7] Likewise Thomas Porthaleyn, who appears in several bills, was supposedly approached by Mulle and agreed to his requests. This was repudiated by juries A and C, the latter finding Porthaleyn guilty of misprision, and accepted in full by Jury D.[8] As Mulle and Alfrey were successfully prosecuted on other counts, neither was tried on these charges. At Pakenham and Porthaleyn's trials, only the indictment of Jury D was heard. Each was acquitted but the prosecution revived the charges of misprision against them and juries were summoned to hear them.[9] Like Cook they would probably have been convicted: there seems no doubt that the meetings took place. Rather than face the charges, Porthaleyn and Pakenham agreed fines with the king.

They and Cook stand out because they were tried. Only six stood trial of the fifteen indicted and each seems guilty to some extent. Two were convicted of treason, another of misprision, and Mulle who pleaded a pardon can hardly have been less guilty than his accomplices who were condemned[10]: he was excluded from the general pardon.[11] In confessing one count Piers Alfrey admitted the guilt of Sir John Plummer, his accomplice,[12] who was indicted in another county and took sanctuary.[13] Dare one assume that Alfrey – and his co-defendants – were guilty in other charges for which they were not tried? John Cornelius, although indicted, was not tried in king's bench: caught redhanded, he may have been summarily dealt with by the constable. Probably each at least concealed treason. Imperfect though the machinery of justice was, nine defendants defaulted, surely a sign of the accuracy of the charges.

1. *Ibid.* /49d.
2. *Ibid.* /17.
3. P.R.O. KB 27/830, *Rex*, mm. 188–d.
4. *G.C.* 205.
5. P.R.O. KB 9/319/36.
6. *Ibid.* /35.
7. *Ibid.* /18.
8. *Ibid.* /19, /34, /37.
9. *Ibid.* /2–5, /50–51d.; *Annales*, p. 790.
10. P.R.O. KB 9/319/49d., /52.
11. P.R.O. C 67/46 m. 38.
12. P.R.O. KB 9/319/50.
13. *Ibid.* /321/109; see above p. 88.

Contemporaries lacked the benefit of hindsight, which illustrates later Lancastrian links of the plotters. Sir Gervase Clifton died in Margaret's army at Tewkesbury[1]; Sir John Plummer was to be keeper of the great wardrobe at the Readeption[2]; William Tyler served Henry VI as clerk of the market and Henry VII as captain of Berwick and clerk of works[3]; and even William Britte supplied munitions for the expeditionary force of 1485.[4] None is more noteworthy than Sir Thomas Cook, who was restored to his aldermanry, acted as lieutenant mayor and was conspicuous in parliament at the Readeption and fled on Edward's return.[5] However strong his motives for changing sides and whatever his propaganda value, could Henry VI's government have risked him in a key position if he was really innocent of the crimes imputed against him and a fervent adherent of Edward IV? There are grounds for suspecting him guilty of more than could be proved.

By capturing Cornelius, Edward learnt of the guilt of the accused. As treason was a most heinous crime, he rightly tried to seize them before they could escape. He was justified in remanding them in the Tower until their trials less than three weeks later. Far from acting precipitately or blindly crediting the charges, he did not prosecute them all and was forced to reconsider by Princess Margaret's intercession in Cook's own case. After her departure Cook was arrested.[6] As he was certainly involved, the princess's support is not proof of innocence but of his skill in using his connections. He was apprehended on 23 June, a fortnight before his trial. His wife was placed in custody which was normal for the wives of those liable for forfeiture.[7]

Escheators acted only on death or forfeiture, usually in response to a royal writ. Escheators' accounts or files survive only for Buckinghamshire and London among the relevant counties and record the chattels of Plummer, Britte and Alfrey.[8] Detailed inventories were compiled, which were accepted as accurate even by the accused,[9] and receipts were given on delivery of chattels to ensure allowance to the escheators at their account. This slow process could enable goods to disappear,[10] so the king often seized the lands and chattels of those accused.[11] This was usually done by royal command and in this case earl Ryvers, as treasurer of the exchequer,

1. C. L. Kingsford, *English Historical Literature in the Fifteenth Century* (Oxford, 1913), p. 378.

2. *Cal. Pat. Rolls, 1467–77*, p. 228.   3. Wedgwood, *Hist. Parl. Biogs.* p. 889.

4. P.R.O. E 404/79/1/102.   5. Wedgwood, *Hist. Parl. Biogs.* p. 217.

6. *Fabyan's Chronicle*, p. 656.

7. *E.g.* Lady Hungerford, *Cal. Pat. Rolls, 1461–7*, p. 181, and Cecily duchess of York in 1460, Scofield, *Edward IV*, i. 37.   8. P.R.O. E 153/1080/2; /520/2.

9. P.R.O. E 13/153, Hill. 8 Edw. IV m. xv.

10. *E.g.* those of Sir John Fastolf.

11. *E.g.* those of the duke of Clarence at Mich. 1477, B. P. Wolffe, *The Royal Demesne in English History* (London, 1972), p. 172 n. 94.

was responsible. The identity of his provincial agents is unknown, but at London he co-operated with his kinsman Sir John Fogge, treasurer of the royal household.[1] Their task entailed searching the houses of the accused and recovering property concealed at the houses of friends, to which G.C. and Fabyan took exception.[2] Although all cases are not documented, the goods of each defendant were probably seized by one of these methods. If they were later acquitted or pardoned, the crown would (in theory at least) relinquish possessions to which it had no title. As Edward had no right of forfeiture to Cook's goods, earl Ryvers' agents were ordered to return their seizures on his instructions.[3] After his pardon, Sir John Plummer sued the Buckinghamshire escheator to recover his chattels.[4] There was nothing wrong or unusual in principle in these seizures.

In practice it may have been different. G.C. claims that there was private pillage and waste of Cook's property.[5] In the event of conviction, such activity harmed the king who entered property of diminished value. It was in his interests to prevent it. Nevertheless it often did occur.[6] If it happened in any case it was deplorable but it is hard to believe that Cook suffered more than anyone else subjected to the tender mercies of royal officials. He certainly received some exceptionally favourable treatment. Not only was he permitted to pay his fine in kind and set it against the goods previously seized, but these were appraised by an independent tribunal of merchants.[7] These privileges probably reduced his losses. They were certainly much less than his exaggerated claim of £14,666,[8] which was probably more than his whole fortune.

Sentences accompany convictions, so John Hawkins was hanged and Sir Thomas Cook was fined. When considering the justice of the fine, one should avoid regarding misprision as a trivial offence. It was not. Cook had not exposed traitors or their plots against the king, as he was bound on his allegiance to do. In harbouring them, he showed sympathy for their cause. There were no mitigating factors as they were neither his kindred, servants or friends. A tough businessman, Cook must have been aware of his offence: he made use of his connections as far as possible and concealed what goods he could. While intended to severely punish a rich man, the fine was determined in a way that prevented his ruin. This case apart, one is struck more by Edward's generosity than his harshness. Only the

1. G.C. 204–5.　　　　　　　2. *Ibid.* 206; *Fabyan's Chronicle*, 656.
3. B.L. Add. MS 48031, fo. 42v.　　4. See above p. 87.
5. G.C. 206.
6. See *e.g.* the condition of the estates of the 3rd duke of Buckingham, a minor 1483–98, in *Marcher Lordships of South Wales, 1422–1536*, ed. T. B. Pugh (Cardiff, 1963), pp. 239–61.
7. G.C. 207. As the arras said to have cost £800 was valued at £984, Cook can have lost little by this process, *ibid.* 208; P.R.O. E 405/48 m. 1,
8. *Fabyan's Chronicle*, 660.

habitual traitor Sir Gervase Clifton was not pardoned[1] and only one individual was executed. Piers Alfrey, on the scaffold, and Hugh Mulle, who was on trial for his life, were saved by pardons[2] and so were others who had defaulted. Pardoned on 29 July, Sir John Plummer returned next day for the insertion of a clause protecting his goods.[3] By 27 July Edward was budgeting for fines from eight of the accused.[4] As on other occasions, he preferred to hang people by their purses rather than their necks,[5] a policy which ensured the survival of enemies to plague him.

On 18 July 1468 Sir Thomas Cook found sureties[6] and was immediately moved from the Marshalsea prison to the keeper's house, where he could buy privileges.[7] On 26 July he was pardoned[8] but it was not until 29 November that to terminate the process against him he produced his patent at king's bench together with a letter to the justices which stated that the fine had been paid in full and ordered his exoneration.[9] On 24 November the tellers of the receipt certified the exchequer of account that payment had been completed.[10] Until then it is possible that Cook, a convict, remained in prison.

These events follow his dismissal as alderman on 21 November at Edward's instructions.[11] The corporation had previously removed Sir John Plummer and suspended Humphrey Hayford, who 'lost hys cloke' on 9 December.[12] Their involvement in treason makes it understandable that Edward wanted them removed from positions of trust and influence.

On 1 December the queen sued Cook for 800 marks in queen's gold, which was thought by *G.C.* to be a malicious act.[13] By the late fifteenth century this ancient due was derived from 10 per cent of fines of over 10 marks offered at the courts of common law and in chancery. Convictions of misprision did not automatically result in such levies.[14] The largest source was the fines in chancery for favours such as the custody of wards, the exemplification of charters or licences to alienate in mortmain. Normally the chief baron of the exchequer, acting on information enrolled on the *Originalia* roll in chancery and the rolls of fines in the courts, proceeded by writ against those involved. These writs were enrolled on the L.T.R.

1. P.R.O. C 67/48 m. 38.

2. P.R.O. KB 9/319/49d.–50; *Annales*, p. 790.

3. P.R.O. C 81/1499/4, /5.

4. Scofield, *Edward IV*, i. 460 n.

5. *G.C.* 220–1.

6. P.R.O. KB 9/319/1.

7. *G.C.* 206.

8. P.R.O. C 81/1500/1. A clause in the patent specifically excluded proceedings in the courts.

9. P.R.O. KB 27/830, *Rex*, m. 188d.; B.L. Add. MS 48031, fo. 42. On 22 Nov. the court had rejected the pardon as insufficient by itself to terminate his case.

10. P.R.O. E 159/245, Rec. Mich. 8 Edw. IV m. 31d.

11. Corp. of Lond. R.O. Journal 7, fo. 182.

12. *Ibid.* fo. 184; *Gregory's Chronicle*, 237.

13. *G.C.* 208.

14. This and the following sentences are based on P.R.O. E 163/8/27.

Memoranda Roll. Other fines, such as that of Cook, were not recorded on the *Originalia* roll and hence not pursued for queen's gold. The exceptional nature of Elizabeth's demand is shown by the abnormal procedure: she sued Cook at the exchequer of pleas.[1] The case was never decided in court, perhaps because it was unprecedented. *G.C.* states that 'by the ffavour of oon mastyr page then solycytour unto the Quene he hadd his ende' but gives no details.[2] This need not mean that Cook paid 800 marks but it implies that a compromise was reached reflecting his anxiety to free himself from pressure and Elizabeth's dubious case at law.

What was the role of the Wydevilles? Cook's conviction shows that their greed does not explain his misfortunes. If they really engineered the dismissal of the chief justice, it shows that they wanted the conviction of the accused including Cook, whom Elizabeth removed from office in her lordship of Havering.[3] No frivolous reason is likely for their antipathy, for in 1465 earl Ryvers and Lord Scales became Cook's feoffees.[4] As the councillor most intimately concerned in the case, earl Ryvers had exceptional information. It is unlikely that the Wydevilles were any less conscious than in 1478 and 1483 that treason threatened the queen and her offspring,[5] the basis of their power. These were strong reasons for opposing leniency but Edward pardoned those involved. The queen's gold suit may be an attempt to punish Cook twice for the same offence but it coincides with other treason trials,[6] in which he could have been implicated. His pardon made him untouchable, so the suit was probably an attempt to harrass him for other offences. It coincides with his dismissal as alderman by Edward's direct order in a signet letter[7]: the king and the Wydevilles were still at one.

Edward emerges quite well from the affair. If there was any danger that by acting firmly he might alienate London it did not materialize. He had good reason to believe the accused guilty and was genuinely alarmed on learning of the plot: this partly excuses any pressure on the juries and justices. It did not affect the result. His limited authority contrasts with that of his later years[8] and of the Tudors. He acted with discrimination and generosity, even to Cook. If anything he was too lenient, enabling traitors to escape to fight another day. The affair was not badly handled and he does not deserve that it should be a blot on his reputation.

---

1. P.R.O. E 13/154, Hill. 8 Edw. IV m. 12.
2. *G.C.* 208.   3. P.R.O. DL 29/41/800 mm. 5, 6, 7, 7d.
4. P.R.O. C 140/68/5/2. John Forster, receiver-general of the queen, was probably Cook's son-in-law, Myers, *B.J.R.L.* l. 221 n.
5. D. Mancini, *The Usurpation of Richard III*, ed. C. A. J. Armstrong (Oxford, 1969), pp. 62, 70–71.   6. *E.g.* P.R.O. KB 9/329.
7. Corp. of Lond. R.O. Journal 7, fo. 182.
8. *Rerum Anglicarum Scriptorum Veterum*, ed. W. Fulman (Oxford, 1684), i. 562.

Index

Richard III and his Rivals